Lecture Notes in Computer Science 14684

The series Lecture Notes in Computer Science (LNCS), including its subseries Lecture Notes in Artificial Intelligence (LNAI) and Lecture Notes in Bioinformatics (LNBI), has established itself as a medium for the publication of new developments in computer science and information technology research, teaching, and education.

LNCS enjoys close cooperation with the computer science R & D community, the series counts many renowned academics among its volume editors and paper authors, and collaborates with prestigious societies. Its mission is to serve this international community by providing an invaluable service, mainly focused on the publication of conference and workshop proceedings and postproceedings. LNCS commenced publication in 1973.

Masaaki Kurosu · Ayako Hashizume
Editors

Human-Computer Interaction

Thematic Area, HCI 2024
Held as Part of the 26th HCI International Conference, HCII 2024
Washington, DC, USA, June 29 – July 4, 2024
Proceedings, Part I

Editors
Masaaki Kurosu
The Open University of Japan
Chiba, Japan

Ayako Hashizume
Hosei University
Tokyo, Japan

ISSN 0302-9743 ISSN 1611-3349 (electronic)
Lecture Notes in Computer Science
ISBN 978-3-031-60404-1 ISBN 978-3-031-60405-8 (eBook)
https://doi.org/10.1007/978-3-031-60405-8

This Springer imprint is published by the registered company Springer Nature Switzerland AG
The registered company address is: Gewerbestrasse 11, 6330 Cham, Switzerland

If disposing of this product, please recycle the paper.

Foreword

This year we celebrate 40 years since the establishment of the HCI International (HCII) Conference, which has been a hub for presenting groundbreaking research and novel ideas and collaboration for people from all over the world.

The HCII conference was founded in 1984 by Prof. Gavriel Salvendy (Purdue University, USA, Tsinghua University, P.R. China, and University of Central Florida, USA) and the first event of the series, "1st USA-Japan Conference on Human-Computer Interaction", was held in Honolulu, Hawaii, USA, 18–20 August. Since then, HCI International is held jointly with several Thematic Areas and Affiliated Conferences, with each one under the auspices of a distinguished international Program Board and under one management and one registration. Twenty-six HCI International Conferences have been organized so far (every two years until 2013, and annually thereafter).

Over the years, this conference has served as a platform for scholars, researchers, industry experts and students to exchange ideas, connect, and address challenges in the ever-evolving HCI field. Throughout these 40 years, the conference has evolved itself, adapting to new technologies and emerging trends, while staying committed to its core mission of advancing knowledge and driving change.

As we celebrate this milestone anniversary, we reflect on the contributions of its founding members and appreciate the commitment of its current and past Affiliated Conference Program Board Chairs and members. We are also thankful to all past conference attendees who have shaped this community into what it is today.

The 26th International Conference on Human-Computer Interaction, HCI International 2024 (HCII 2024), was held as a 'hybrid' event at the Washington Hilton Hotel, Washington, DC, USA, during 29 June – 4 July 2024. It incorporated the 21 thematic areas and affiliated conferences listed below.

A total of 5108 individuals from academia, research institutes, industry, and government agencies from 85 countries submitted contributions, and 1271 papers and 309 posters were included in the volumes of the proceedings that were published just before the start of the conference, these are listed below. The contributions thoroughly cover the entire field of human-computer interaction, addressing major advances in knowledge and effective use of computers in a variety of application areas. These papers provide academics, researchers, engineers, scientists, practitioners and students with state-of-the-art information on the most recent advances in HCI.

The HCI International (HCII) conference also offers the option of presenting 'Late Breaking Work', and this applies both for papers and posters, with corresponding volumes of proceedings that will be published after the conference. Full papers will be included in the 'HCII 2024 - Late Breaking Papers' volumes of the proceedings to be published in the Springer LNCS series, while 'Poster Extended Abstracts' will be included as short research papers in the 'HCII 2024 - Late Breaking Posters' volumes to be published in the Springer CCIS series.

I would like to thank the Program Board Chairs and the members of the Program Boards of all thematic areas and affiliated conferences for their contribution towards the high scientific quality and overall success of the HCI International 2024 conference. Their manifold support in terms of paper reviewing (single-blind review process, with a minimum of two reviews per submission), session organization and their willingness to act as goodwill ambassadors for the conference is most highly appreciated.

This conference would not have been possible without the continuous and unwavering support and advice of Gavriel Salvendy, founder, General Chair Emeritus, and Scientific Advisor. For his outstanding efforts, I would like to express my sincere appreciation to Abbas Moallem, Communications Chair and Editor of HCI International News.

July 2024   Constantine Stephanidis

HCI International 2024 Thematic Areas
and Affiliated Conferences

- HCI: Human-Computer Interaction Thematic Area
- HIMI: Human Interface and the Management of Information Thematic Area
- EPCE: 21st International Conference on Engineering Psychology and Cognitive Ergonomics
- AC: 18th International Conference on Augmented Cognition
- UAHCI: 18th International Conference on Universal Access in Human-Computer Interaction
- CCD: 16th International Conference on Cross-Cultural Design
- SCSM: 16th International Conference on Social Computing and Social Media
- VAMR: 16th International Conference on Virtual, Augmented and Mixed Reality
- DHM: 15th International Conference on Digital Human Modeling & Applications in Health, Safety, Ergonomics & Risk Management
- DUXU: 13th International Conference on Design, User Experience and Usability
- C&C: 12th International Conference on Culture and Computing
- DAPI: 12th International Conference on Distributed, Ambient and Pervasive Interactions
- HCIBGO: 11th International Conference on HCI in Business, Government and Organizations
- LCT: 11th International Conference on Learning and Collaboration Technologies
- ITAP: 10th International Conference on Human Aspects of IT for the Aged Population
- AIS: 6th International Conference on Adaptive Instructional Systems
- HCI-CPT: 6th International Conference on HCI for Cybersecurity, Privacy and Trust
- HCI-Games: 6th International Conference on HCI in Games
- MobiTAS: 6th International Conference on HCI in Mobility, Transport and Automotive Systems
- AI-HCI: 5th International Conference on Artificial Intelligence in HCI
- MOBILE: 5th International Conference on Human-Centered Design, Operation and Evaluation of Mobile Communications

List of Conference Proceedings Volumes Appearing
Before the Conference

1. LNCS 14684, Human-Computer Interaction: Part I, edited by Masaaki Kurosu and Ayako Hashizume
2. LNCS 14685, Human-Computer Interaction: Part II, edited by Masaaki Kurosu and Ayako Hashizume
3. LNCS 14686, Human-Computer Interaction: Part III, edited by Masaaki Kurosu and Ayako Hashizume
4. LNCS 14687, Human-Computer Interaction: Part IV, edited by Masaaki Kurosu and Ayako Hashizume
5. LNCS 14688, Human-Computer Interaction: Part V, edited by Masaaki Kurosu and Ayako Hashizume
6. LNCS 14689, Human Interface and the Management of Information: Part I, edited by Hirohiko Mori and Yumi Asahi
7. LNCS 14690, Human Interface and the Management of Information: Part II, edited by Hirohiko Mori and Yumi Asahi
8. LNCS 14691, Human Interface and the Management of Information: Part III, edited by Hirohiko Mori and Yumi Asahi
9. LNAI 14692, Engineering Psychology and Cognitive Ergonomics: Part I, edited by Don Harris and Wen-Chin Li
10. LNAI 14693, Engineering Psychology and Cognitive Ergonomics: Part II, edited by Don Harris and Wen-Chin Li
11. LNAI 14694, Augmented Cognition, Part I, edited by Dylan D. Schmorrow and Cali M. Fidopiastis
12. LNAI 14695, Augmented Cognition, Part II, edited by Dylan D. Schmorrow and Cali M. Fidopiastis
13. LNCS 14696, Universal Access in Human-Computer Interaction: Part I, edited by Margherita Antona and Constantine Stephanidis
14. LNCS 14697, Universal Access in Human-Computer Interaction: Part II, edited by Margherita Antona and Constantine Stephanidis
15. LNCS 14698, Universal Access in Human-Computer Interaction: Part III, edited by Margherita Antona and Constantine Stephanidis
16. LNCS 14699, Cross-Cultural Design: Part I, edited by Pei-Luen Patrick Rau
17. LNCS 14700, Cross-Cultural Design: Part II, edited by Pei-Luen Patrick Rau
18. LNCS 14701, Cross-Cultural Design: Part III, edited by Pei-Luen Patrick Rau
19. LNCS 14702, Cross-Cultural Design: Part IV, edited by Pei-Luen Patrick Rau
20. LNCS 14703, Social Computing and Social Media: Part I, edited by Adela Coman and Simona Vasilache
21. LNCS 14704, Social Computing and Social Media: Part II, edited by Adela Coman and Simona Vasilache
22. LNCS 14705, Social Computing and Social Media: Part III, edited by Adela Coman and Simona Vasilache

https://2024.hci.international/proceedings

Preface

Human-Computer Interaction is a Thematic Area of the International Conference on Human-Computer Interaction (HCII). The HCI field is today undergoing a wave of significant innovation and breakthroughs towards radically new future forms of interaction. The HCI Thematic Area constitutes a forum for scientific research and innovation in human-computer interaction, addressing challenging and innovative topics in human-computer interaction theory, methodology, and practice, including, for example, novel theoretical approaches to interaction, novel user interface concepts and technologies, novel interaction devices, UI development methods, environments and tools, multimodal user interfaces, human-robot interaction, emotions in HCI, aesthetic issues, HCI and children, evaluation methods and tools, and many others.

The HCI Thematic Area covers four major dimensions, namely theory and methodology, technology, human beings, and societal impact. The following five volumes of the HCII 2024 proceedings reflect these dimensions:

- Human-Computer Interaction - Part I, addressing topics related to HCI Theory and Design and Evaluation Methods and Tools, and Emotions in HCI;
- Human-Computer Interaction - Part II, addressing topics related to Human-Robot Interaction and Child-Computer Interaction;
- Human-Computer Interaction - Part III, addressing topics related to HCI for Mental Health and Psychological Wellbeing, and HCI in Healthcare;
- Human-Computer Interaction - Part IV, addressing topics related to HCI, Environment and Sustainability, and Design and User Experience Evaluation Case Studies;
- Human-Computer Interaction - Part V, addressing topics related to Multimodality and Natural User Interfaces, and HCI, AI, Creativity, Art and Culture.

The papers in these volumes were accepted for publication after a minimum of two single-blind reviews from the members of the HCI Program Board or, in some cases, from members of the Program Boards of other affiliated conferences. We would like to thank all of them for their invaluable contribution, support, and efforts.

July 2024

Masaaki Kurosu
Ayako Hashizume

Human-Computer Interaction Thematic Area (HCI 2024)

Program Board Chairs: **Masaaki Kurosu,** *The Open University of Japan, Japan* and **Ayako Hashizume,** *Hosei University, Japan*

- Salah Uddin Ahmed, *University of South-Eastern Norway, India*
- Jessica Barfield, *University of Tennessee, USA*
- Valdecir Becker, *Federal University of Paraiba, Brazil*
- Nimish Biloria, *University of Technology Sydney, Australia*
- Zhigang Chen, *Shanghai University, P.R. China*
- Hong Chen, *Daiichi Institute of Technology, Japan*
- Emilia Duarte, *Universidade Europeia, Portugal*
- Yu-Hsiu Hung, *National Cheng Kung University, Taiwan*
- Jun Iio, *Chuo University, Japan*
- Yi Ji, *Guangdong University of Technology, Australia*
- Hiroshi Noborio, *Osaka Electro-Communication University, Japan*
- Katsuhiko Onishi, *Osaka Electro-Communication University, Japan*
- Julio Cesar Reis, *University of Campinas, Brazil*
- Mohammad Shidujaman, *Independent University Bangladesh (IUB), Bangladesh*

The full list with the Program Board Chairs and the members of the Program Boards of all thematic areas and affiliated conferences of HCII 2024 is available online at:

http://www.hci.international/board-members-2024.php

HCI International 2025 Conference

The 27th International Conference on Human-Computer Interaction, HCI International 2025, will be held jointly with the affiliated conferences at the Swedish Exhibition & Congress Centre and Gothia Towers Hotel, Gothenburg, Sweden, June 22–27, 2025. It will cover a broad spectrum of themes related to Human-Computer Interaction, including theoretical issues, methods, tools, processes, and case studies in HCI design, as well as novel interaction techniques, interfaces, and applications. The proceedings will be published by Springer. More information will become available on the conference website: https://2025.hci.international/.

General Chair
Prof. Constantine Stephanidis
University of Crete and ICS-FORTH
Heraklion, Crete, Greece
Email: general_chair@2025.hci.international

https://2025.hci.international/

Contents – Part I

Emotions in HCI

HCI Theory and Design and Evaluation Methods and Tools

Through the Waves: An Auto-ethnographic Perspective on HCI Design and Research

Ali Arya[✉]

Carleton University, Ottawa, Canada
`arya@carleton.ca`

Abstract. This paper is an auto-ethnographic review of HCI research and design waves, or paradigms, as seen from the perspective of the author's personal experience. Through reflection on a series of research projects spanning more than twenty years, the paper explores the answers to questions such as how methodologies are chosen based on worldviews, how they affect findings and conclusions, and what are possible directions for upcoming paradigm shifts in HCI.

Keywords: Human-Computer Interaction · Wave · Paradigm · Reflection

1 Introduction

The field of human-computer interaction has experienced multiple overlapping yet distinct waves or paradigms [1]:

- The first wave was mainly positivistic, based on HCI's engineering roots, focused on human factors, and giving clear answers to specific problems using experimental and mostly quantitative methods.
- The second wave considered users in a more situated way, allowing for social, cultural, ethnic, and gender influences and some qualitative methods.
- The third wave was influenced by social constructivism, emphasizing the role of the researcher's opinions, and also cultural and social values, and encouraging pluralism for design, with common reliance on qualitative methods.
- A fourth wave is suggested by various researchers with alternatives such as transdisciplinary design [2], entanglement [3], and critical realism-based views [4].

In its early years, prior to the widespread use of personal computers, HCI was primarily focused on human factors in computerized workspaces. It was in the late 1980s and early 1990s that the notion of human "actors" started what was later called the second wave of HCI [5]. What mainly distinguished these two waves was the shifting focus from individuals in well-controlled special work environments to groups of different users, working on various applications, and with different situations, that required more user-centred and participatory design approaches [1, 5, 6]. The methodology observed a shift from traditional engineering approaches to social ones, and introduced some qualitative methods. The third wave happened when computers became widespread in non-work

M. Kurosu and A. Hashizume (Eds.): HCII 2024, LNCS 14684, pp. 3–15, 2024.
https://doi.org/10.1007/978-3-031-60405-8_1

situations and used by a variety of people from different socio-cultural backgrounds [6]. As for methodology, we see a stronger shift towards qualitative methods, understanding relativity and pluralism, and paying more attention and giving more value to the designer and researcher's opinions and biases. The key difference between the second and third waves is this attention to pluralism [6], which is both using methodologies that support multiple points of view and also using multiple methodologies. It shows itself in different ways such as using mixed or multiple research methods and also personalization and customization in the design of HCI solutions. There are various alternatives suggested for the basis of a fourth HCI wave [2–4], which is still a topic of discussion and I will propose my own thoughts on it.

While HCI publications show active engagement of researchers in three established HCI paradigms and a lively discussion on the possible fourth, the number of HCI researchers pursuing research under the third and fourth paradigms is fairly small. The majority of HCI studies are still following a positivistic worldview represented by traditional user studies that assume a "better" solution exists and can be found through the comparison of limited quantitative metrics.

As an HCI researcher with an engineering background, I have worked on different research projects in the past twenty-plus years. These projects cover three established HCI paradigms and have started to move towards possible fourth ones. In this paper, I focus particularly on my personal experience in six research projects (some consisting of sub-projects). Based on personal notes and email communications related to these projects and revisiting the data that was collected and our published papers, I contextualize the experiences with auto-ethnographic recollections and systematically [7] reflect on my growth as a researcher. My recollections highlight the significant aspects of my experiences and are presented as a short narrative or vignette [8, 9]. Reflecting on these narratives and in the context of existing HCI theories, I discuss what I have learned from my experience in HCI research and how my perspective has changed from a positivistic one that is looking for the right answer to a more holistic one that recognizes the possibility of different rights and wrongs, and tries to bring together various perspectives from individual to groups of users, and possibly other entities with agency, such as intelligent machines.

Following this auto-ethnographic methodology, I discuss some reflective insights related to the following research questions:

1. How did I choose a research approach (and epistemology) for a particular project and how was that choice influenced by my worldview (and ontology) at that time?
2. How did my research approach (and so, my worldview) influence my findings and conclusions?
3. How did my research approach change over time?
4. What are the barriers to (or reasons against) moving onto further waves?
5. What are some of my research elements that go beyond the 3rd wave, and suggest new aspects for the 4th wave?

2 Research Approach

Auto-ethnography, i.e., research through self-observation and reflection, and other first-person approaches have recently drawn the attention of the HCI community [10, 11]. This attention is in line with the third wave of HCI. Focusing on the researcher's first-hand experience, auto-ethnographic HCI research admits the subjective nature of research and aims to use reflection on personal experience to gain insight on various topics. Contrasting typical ethnographic work that is based on the researcher's observation in a particular site over time, multi-sited auto-ethnography uses the researcher's reflections on their own experience in various related experiences [9].

In this paper, I briefly review some of my research projects as the experiences for the multi-sited auth-ethnography. They are presented in almost chronological order, although there are overlaps, and each may encapsulate multiple projects, related to each other under six themes:

- **Animated agents**. The project started my HCI journey by recognizing the importance of user perceptions, aiming to measure how users perceive the personality and emotions of animated agents.
- **Gesture-based and multimodal interaction**. With the advances in motion tracking back in the 2000s, this project investigated the effectiveness of gesture-based input compared to mouse and keyboard.
- **Augmented and virtual reality-based learning**. The availability of augmented and virtual reality devices in the 2010s encouraged me and many others to study their effectiveness in providing learning experiences. The user experience in these projects started to be more situated and embodied, as in the 2nd wave of HCI.
- **Game-based learning**. Various forms of game-related activities, such as game jams and co-design workshops, have been the subject of my research, where I started to (1) use qualitative methods and (2) consider social and cultural issues that influence the user experience.
- **Community-based design**. Working with different communities, such as Indigenous Peoples, I stepped into the 3rd wave of HCI and started to appreciate the pluralism while facing the new artificial intelligence trend that promotes a single truth. It also introduced the notion of user empowerment, which goes beyond adopting and using technology and includes owning and managing it, something that I believe should be essential in the 4th wave.
- **Transformative learning**. My current umbrella project aims to understand how technology can help learners with reflection, empathy, and perspective change.

The experiences are presented through short descriptions, a.k.a. *vignettes,* that are based on my field notes, emails, and publications. These descriptions act as the archive on which reflections and discussions are based [9]. *Vignettes* are written in *italics* and, to the best of my ability, represent facts, or the explicit story (i.e., recollection of what happened). They are accompanied by a short explanation and contextualization, which is aimed at showing how that experience is related to what was going on in the research world, and also my thoughts and feelings about these experiences, or the implicit story (i.e., my subjective reflections). This reflective process provides answers to research questions 1, 2, and 3. A discussion of generated insights will then attempt to offer possible answers to research questions 3 and 4, which go beyond the actual experiences.

3 Reflection on Experiences

Before discussing the experiences, it is helpful to get an idea of how I positioned myself for these research projects.

I studied electrical engineering and worked as a computer engineer (both hardware and software) for about 10 years before coming back to school to get my PhD. My engineering background got me into many research and design tasks where the output was evaluated against clear specifications, such as precision when controlling a robotic arm or the ability to enter and show text bilingually when localizing a computer terminal's firmware. While almost all projects that I worked on had the notion of user in them, none of my experiences prior to my doctoral studies involved any user study, and my understanding of human-computer interaction was limited to the notions of text-based console vs. graphical user interface. This applied to both my work in Iran, where I was born and trained, and in Canada, where I worked for two years before pursuing a PhD. In Canada, both at work and during my university application process, my training and background as a computer engineer were considered strong and up to the relevant standards. After finishing my PhD at the University of British Columbia, I did two years of post-doctoral work at Simon Fraser University, and then joined Carleton University's School of Information Technology. While I did my doctoral studies in a typical Electrical and Computer Engineering department, my academic units both at Simon Fraser and Carleton were focused on Interactive Multimedia with a more interdisciplinary and human-oriented nature.

Looking back at my education and work experience, I find it noteworthy that user-centred design was not considered an important part of the training for an engineer, even computer engineer and software programmer. Human-computer interaction, for example, was a course in computer science degrees relevant mostly to those who would work on interface design. Interdisciplinarity and human focus were unusual among many university programs I had seen and made my post-doc and new faculty position rather different compared to mainstream (at least, back in early 2000s).

3.1 Contextualizing the Experiences

Animated Agents. During my doctoral and post-doctoral studies, and the first couple of years as a faculty member, I worked on facial animation. This group of projects started my HCI journey by recognizing the importance of user perceptions, aiming to measure how users perceive the personality and emotions of animated agents. The first project used transformations on a photograph to create various facial states, and was evaluated using a variety of input images and some objective measures. Inspired by traditional animation and the concept of "believable character" [12], I soon realized that facial animation cannot be evaluated objectively, and its quality depends, primarily, on viewers' perception. As such, the second and third projects used facial actions to cause certain perceptions of personality and emotion in viewers. They were evaluated by users through Likert scale quantitative data (for example, the effect of head-nod as an action on the perception of dominance as a personality dimension). The projects enjoyed the collaboration of researchers from psychology who not only could advise on matters such as perception, personality, and mood, but also on running user studies.

The majority of computer graphics and animation research papers in the 20th century and early 2000s used either objective measures such as image-based metrics or presented a variety of examples to show the system's ability to generate a diverse set of outputs. The notion of perceptual validity was rather novel at that time but became more common as we moved towards the 2nd wave.

Gesture-Based and Multimodal Interaction. With the advances in motion tracking and 3D cameras like Microsoft Kinect back in the 2000s, my gesture-based interaction project investigated the effectiveness of body gestures, tracked using computer vision, as input device compared to mouse and keyboard. Simple games were developed by my research team, and the users were asked to perform game tasks such as selecting an object or hitting/catching a virtual ball, using body motion tracked by camera and traditional mouse and keyboard. The evaluation was hypothesis verification and quantitative. But we supported both objective measures (such as the number of errors) and subjective ones (such as ease of use). The participants were asked to provide any qualitative comments they might have, although these were not analyzed or used in hypothesis verification, and only considered for future revision of our experience design or general ideas on vision-based input. This research resulted in ideas on a more holistic approach to multimodal interaction where different modalities can seamlessly combine [13].

Similar to user perception, body gestures were a motivation for the move towards the 2nd wave. Using a mouse and keyboard has clear embodied/ergonomic aspects and can cause fatigue and other physical impacts. However, full body or arm gestures more clearly originate from how we interact with our environment holistically. They suggest that the interaction with computers also needs to be holistic and multimodal.

Augmented and Virtual Reality-Based Learning. The availability of augmented and virtual reality devices in the 2010s encouraged me and many others to study their effectiveness in providing learning experiences. The user experience in these projects started to be more situated and embodied, as in the 2nd wave of HCI. The studies commonly used quantitative measures (both objective and subjective) to evaluate the learning activities using AR/VR compared to control groups that used traditional methods such as lecture notes and slides. Later studies in this group (in the early 2020s) analyzed some qualitative data collected through short written comments and observations, particularly to investigate topics such as inclusion and engagement. We tried to do a thematic analysis, but there was no rigorous approach to data collection and coding, mainly due to limited ability to interact with participants, lack of proper planning in advance, and general unfamiliarity with qualitative research and its nuances.

In the fields of educational technology or HCI, comparing the effectiveness of a method to a control group (more traditional and established method) is common. In reality, though, instructors use a variety of modalities and methods. One may argue that observing how people use a method and seeing what they think and feel can be much more useful when it comes to incorporating that method into actual educational scenarios. 2nd and 3rd waves of HCI included a growing number of studies that replaced research questions such as "Is A better than B?" with those such as "How is A useful compared to B?", which resulted in more qualitative research approaches.

Game-Based Learning. In the 2010s and 2020s, various forms of game-related activities, such as game jams and co-design workshops, have been the subject of my research, where we started to (1) use qualitative methods and (2) consider social and cultural issues that influence the user experience. Our research methods started with surveys with quantitative metrics and short interviews. Later, we also collected notes based on our workshop observations. However, the workshop experience was short, so we had limited observations, and it became evident that interviewing is an important skill that significantly affects the usefulness and validity of findings. The inclusion of special considerations for the target group (children, in this case) was another important aspect of this study, in line with the second wave of HCI research.

Despite a significant amount of research on game-based learning and gamification, there are still many contradictory claims about their effectiveness. Similar to the previous group of projects, a common problem is the way research questions are structured that aimed at finding metrics showing the success or failure of a method. The alternative way of presenting a research question (in the form of how something happens) is more in line with the 2nd and 3rd waves of HCI as they allow pluralism and avoid binary single-view perspectives.

Community-Based Design. Working with different communities, such as Indigenous Peoples, we stepped into the 3rd wave of HCI and started to appreciate the pluralism. The main point of our community-based research was that communities are more than a group of individuals and, as such, have their own holistic protocols, traditions, and knowledge that need to be taken into account for research and design [14]. In addition to exploring models for involving communities in research, this group of projects introduced the notion of user empowerment, which goes beyond adopting and using technology and includes the ability to create, own, and manage technology products, something that requires proper training and I believe should be essential in the 4th wave of HCI. Our methodology in this research was mainly qualitative, as notions such as engagement and inclusion are subjective and hard to quantify.

There is a growing body of research on working with communities with an emphasis on direct involvement and the community's ability to own and manage technology [14]. In particular, Indigenous communities in North America, Africa, Australia, and New Zealand have been the subject of a few community-based research and development projects. Despite these efforts, more needs to be done to develop proper models for designing and using emerging technologies such as AI and VR, as they have their own specific characteristics. The 3rd and 4th waves of HCI are particularly important here, as there is no unique "right way" when it comes to different communities. Denying a single truth for product and interaction design is in line with what is sometimes called ontological design [15] which moves away from the modernist one-world ontology to a pluralistic approach with multiple community-based worldviews and designs based on them.

Transformative Learning. *Earlier projects on personalized exercise games and recommender systems introduced my research to the idea of understanding users individually, rather than as members of different categories (personalization vs. categorization). Together with the community-based approach presented earlier, I started to see a more holistic view that locates an individual within a community. Following the idea of using VR in education, my current umbrella project aims to understand how technology (especially VR) can help learners with reflection, empathy, and perspective change, and ultimately, help them become better members of their society. The notions of inclusion, emotional engagement, and critical thinking are essential in these studies. Relying on 2nd wave notions such as situated and embodied learning in VR, we also incorporate 3rd wave ideas, such as socio-cultural concerns and personalization, to understand how VR can help with reflection, followed by perspective and behaviour change.*

Transformative learning is considered a natural step after transactional and experiential learning [16]. It relies on the hands-on and situated aspects of experiential learning and extends its reflective nature to a more critical state that can transform the learner by fostering changes in opinions, attitudes, and behaviours. These notions offer potential characteristics for HCI research and design that can go beyond the 3rd wave and suggest transformation as a new essential feature in the 4th wave. They also encourage a more holistic approach to research and design, which can bring various notions together, such as transformation [16], empowerment [14], and multimodalities [13].

3.2 How Did I Choose a Research Approach (and Epistemology) for a Particular Project and How was that Choice Influenced by My Worldview (and Ontology) at that Time?

Cartesian mind-body dualism (followed by other dualisms such as truth-false and good-evil) is the foundation of many western schools of thought. This worldview tends to believe in an objective truth that is out there, independent of the subjective mind of the observers. Such ontological approaches further promote positivism and related empirical epistemologies that aim at observing, measuring, and theorizing that objective truth through scientific method. Despite the well-established notion of uncertainty in science (managed by probability and possibility theories), even postpositivist critiques of positivism still believe that there is an objective truth, even though they admit that the observer's biases can affect how we measure and understand the truth, so try to control and limit that bias and uncertainty through various methods. Social constructivist epistemologies, on the other hand, embrace uncertainty and bias by questioning the notion of an objective truth. Most researchers and practitioners in natural sciences and engineering, and many in social sciences, follow the positivist/postpositivist schools as seen in the 1st and 2nd waves of HCI.

My earlier projects clearly followed such an approach. In the case of facial animation, for example, there was an implied assumption that there is an association between facial actions and the perception of an emotion or personality type. Despite the understanding that such an association is varied and changes from one person to another (no single truth, in that case), the project aimed at establishing another form of objective truth, in the form of statistical averages. By experimenting over a range of viewers, we defined a "typical association" when a single individual one was not possible. In other terms, as a researcher from the positivist/postpositivist camp, I acknowledged the fact that people are different but was still looking to find one "typical/average" truth that could be used for practical purposes such as creating an animation that is likely to be perceived as expected.

Similarly, using limited quantitative measures (such as success in a sample task) to compare two educational methods was based on the assumption that one method can be "overall" or "on average" better than the other. So, the research question becomes, "is this (VR-based, AR-based, etc.) methods better than the control group?" which assumes a single Yes/No truth. As educators, we know that various methods are tools, each with its own advantages and drawbacks. A more appropriate question would have been, "How and where can this method be more effective than the control group?" This question is based on a more pluralistic worldview in which there is no right or wrong method, and we try to understand how and where to use them. It should be noted that the lack of statistical significance in results doesn't offer a third option (besides Yes and No), but only says that we can't answer.

As I moved forward with my projects, the idea of pluralistic worldviews and ontologies became clearer, and resulted in epistemological decisions in research design, demonstrated by more in-depth interviews and observations, as opposed to aggregated numbers, allowing us to develop different insights based on the information from different users.

3.3   How Did My Research Approach (and so, My Worldview) Influence My Findings and Conclusions?

The notion of an objective and measurable truth has been questioned even within the boundary of natural sciences (for example, by Heisenberg's Uncertainty Principle). Still, such a notion can have its value in many areas of natural sciences and engineering, especially if we consider a scientific theory as a mathematical (or otherwise formal) representation of a practical model that tries to, within certain limits, explain and predict a phenomenon as opposed to a presentation of the objective truth. But the introduction of human (and social) elements drastically changes the way we work with phenomena, as quantitative measurements become less effective in presenting a meaning than the subjective (and different) ideas of individuals or societies.

There are two different ways in which a positivist (or postpositivist) approach can limit the research or even cause invalid or deceiving results: (1) quantitative data can cause the impression of precision while they may have been collected for highly controlled and oversimplified experiments, (2) aggregated/averaged quantitative data encourage ignoring nuances and individual differences even if we consider statistical features like variance, (3) collecting quantitative data requires knowing in advance what parameters are important so we collect their data. In many research projects, the researcher may not be able to identify the important parameters (for example, what is important to users when working with a new technology). Open-ended and qualitative data collection methods such as observation and interviews can be much more effective in such cases. Using the inappropriate research method will then result in unreliable data, which may look precise due to its numeric nature. Contradictory experimental results on new technologies are examples of how unreliable such methods can be.

Back to the example of facial animation, a single association between facial actions and personal characteristics simply propagates stereotypes and promotes ignoring variations (in line with the dualism that I mentioned earlier). My results on the effectiveness of vision-based gestures as an input method or VR as an educational tool had a similar limited and possibly deceptive nature. Performance in one or two simplified and isolated tasks during a lab experiment is far from the actual real-world usage, where we deal with various elements and possibly combine different methods, in ways that are person-dependent. A more insightful approach would have been observing how people use a particular tool, having in-depth conversations, and trying to see what patterns of knowledge emerge, which can then be used to enhance technology design. Later on, a more qualitative and open-ended approach helped us explore user requirements such as inclusion and engagement when working with multi-platform VR and develop models of how the VR design process needs to be inclusive both for users and the developers. We did not even consider these topics at the start of the research, so we could not collect quantitative data for them.

Earlier examples of community-based work assumed certain well-known criteria as the important factors. In line with the 1st and 2nd waves of HCI, these criteria were mostly quantitative and included objectives ones such as the number of engaged users and subjective ones such as ease of use and learnability. While valuable, these "standard" criteria were not enough to understand, for example, the use of VR by Indigenous communities. They were more concerned about authenticity, following protocols, embedding community knowledge and tradition, and ownership. Ethnographic observation of community members and how they worked with technical developers for a VR prototype resulted in novel insights into managerial and educational needs in a community-based project and a new model of technology empowerment. The combination of socio-cultural considerations and qualitative methods are typical of the 3rd wave and move away from positivist approaches to enable a more pluralistic, socially constructed, understanding of the subject matter.

3.4 How Did My Research Approach Change Over Time?

At the time when the literature on three waves of HCI research started (2000s), I was not particularly familiar with them. I considered myself more of a computer graphics and games researcher than an HCI one. And the boundaries between these felt stricter to me. Despite that, by the time I became familiar with the concept of three (and four) waves of HCI, I found that despite working on games, animation, VR, and educational technology, I was indeed an HCI researcher and was following those waves in my own work. Human-computer interaction was the thread that connected my various projects and by the late 2010s, I had experienced the first three waves and was starting to, subconsciously, consider the fourth one.

As I mentioned earlier, starting my career as an engineer, my worldview was highly affected by the typical engineering training I had. This meant a positivist approach to knowledge and reliance on objectivity and measurement. Working in multidisciplinary project teams and getting involved with different user groups influenced my work and worldviews, which resulted in moving in a direction that I later found matched that of the HCI waves. Two points are worth mentioning here, though: (1) An engineering education does not have to be positivist. Engineers and natural scientists need to be trained in human aspects of their work, and in many cases, they do get that training now. The stereotypical idea of engineers vs. social scientists is part of the incorrect dualism that is the source of many problems. (2) There is value and place for all research methods, and they are complementary, not contradictory. Even practitioners of 3rd and 4th HCI waves can benefit from quantitative and positivist approaches in some cases, and that is what mixed methods promote.

4 Discussion

4.1 What are the Barriers to (or Reasons Against) Moving onto Further Waves?

Despite the growth of qualitative and situated, embodied, and socio-culturally sensitive research motivated by the 2nd and 3rd waves of HCI, a large body (if not majority) of HCI research is still in the 1st and 2nd waves and relies on positivist notions. Based on my personal experience and observing colleagues, this is due to multiple reasons that form barriers for moving to further waves of research.

The primary reason (or barrier) for not using a more qualitative approach that takes into account social and individual differences is the lack of familiarity with the associated theories and methodologies. Looking back, in the first decade of my research career, starting with doctoral studies, I had no training in any form of evaluation and research design other than quantitative and positivist ones. Coming from natural science and engineering, it was common to design, develop, and then evaluate using clear test cases that are repeatable and measurable. It is expected, with such a background, to apply the same methodology in other research projects. New efforts in training courses and workshops on qualitative research in HCI and engineering schools and conferences is a step towards overcoming this barrier and allowing the researchers and practitioners to choose the most appropriate methods.

The second reason is the assumption that a quantitative and measurable method is necessarily more precise than a qualitative method, and so can prove, support, or at least demonstrate something meaningful. As such, qualitative approaches are, at best, initial investigations to generate starting ideas. While this may be true for cases such as testing the energy efficiency of an engine or lossless image compression by a software algorithm, it is not as helpful when dealing with a notion such as technology adoption that depends on many socio-cultural factors. An experiment can involve so many simplifications and assumptions that make it no more reliable than participants' opinions and the researcher's interpretation of them. The examples from my facial animation and educational technology research projects demonstrate this lack of reliability in positivist approaches. The increased attention to 2nd and 3rd wave methodologies in the HCI community, as shown by the increased number of qualitative research in the ACM CHI conference, for example, and also recent special issues in prestigious journals on such methodologies are encouraging the community to accept the validity and rigor of these methodologies and question the universalities of positivist and postpositivist approaches.

Last but not least, the emphasis on quantitative measures, avoiding subjective (especially first-person) opinions, and avoiding sources of bias and uncertainty instead of trying to incorporate them into the research method, originate from the dualist notions such as mind-body and true-false that aim at finding a single truth. Such a notion costs HCI research the ability to see the world in its pluralistic form and be inclusive to many different cultures, groups, and styles.

4.2 What are Some of My Research Elements that Go Beyond the 3rd Wave, and Suggest New Aspects for the 4th Wave?

As mentioned earlier, while the first three waves of HCI are mostly agreed upon, there are multiple suggestions for what constitutes the fourth wave. Frauenberger [3] discusses a group of theories, that he refers to as entanglement, to propose a paradigm shift in HCI where users/humans are no longer central and the computer/objects have an equal role and agency. This extends the notion of ontological design, in emphasizing the ability of design to shape us, just like we shape our design [15]. Extending the notion of mixed methods, critical realist HCI has also been suggested as a way to avoid extreme relativism observed by some social constructivist methods and yet manage to not fall into pure positivism. Researchers [2] have also suggested that the 4th wave of HCI is going towards a trans-disciplinary nature, where a holistic new discipline/approach is created.

While I find all of these suggestions valuable, and believe they can be the basis for some paradigm shifts, my personal experience allows me to propose some other ideas. These proposals are neither well-formed nor contradictory to the existing ones. They are thoughts that can help define a more holistic approach.

Two notions of personalization and community-based design became essential in my research over the last decade. A proper balance between these two seems to be essential in HCI research and design. Avoiding design decisions that are based on "average" findings and moving towards individualization through understanding and modeling users is one aspect of this balance, while incorporating the community concerns (knowledge, protocols, etc.) not as average of individual users but as a gestalt whole entity, is the other aspect. Such a balance gives a new dimension to holistic design, which I previously considered as a seamless combination of modalities. Holistic, in this case, means bringing modalities, user groups, and possibly other dimensions, together.

User empowerment and transformation are two other elements of HCI research and design that should be considered as foundations of a 4th wave. We cannot design HCI systems without putting the user in the driver's seat and empowering them to take charge. Nor should we think of an HCI system as something separate from its application or purpose, which should be social impact and transforming the user (and the society) for the better (however we define that).

4.3 Limitations of this Study

My investigation is limited and preliminary, as it very briefly reviews some of the projects I have worked on. There is also a lack of a theoretical framework and contextualizing the reflection within various theories that may be helpful in explaining the reflective questions. For example, considering the effect of my methods on my findings can benefit from a more ontological and epistemological discussion and how the existing theories see such effects. Similarly, choosing (or not choosing) particular methodologies can have more fundamental socio-cultural reasons. One may even argue that a critical theory-based approach can explain some of the contexts for the choice of specific research methodologies. A genealogical approach [9], that tries to understand the present (and challenge our understanding of it) in light of a critical analysis of the past, can be a helpful approach, in this regard. Last but not least, researchers have discussed mixed (qualitative and quantitative) methods and their advantages and drawbacks [17, 18]. A study of HCI waves needs to contextualize the HCI developments within the general area of research methods.

5   Conclusion

Reflecting on my personal experiences shows the effect of my worldviews on the chosen methodologies and, in turn, on the findings and conclusions. As a researcher, I have learned the value of different methods and their appropriate combination and application. The observed progression suggests moving toward what I can call Holistic HCI, which brings together quantitative and qualitative methods [13, 14], individual and community-based approaches and builds on the notions of understanding and empowering users to build, own, and manage emerging technologies, and not just using them.

Acknowledgments. I am grateful to all co-authors, collaborators, and research assistants who participated in different projects mentioned here. There are too many to name individually, but they all have offered invaluable help in achieving research goals and evolving research ideas and approaches.

References

1. Harrison, S., Tatar, D., Sengers, P.: The three paradigms of HCI. In: Alt. CHI. Session at the SIGCHI Conference on Human Factors in Computing Systems (2007)
2. Lopes, A.G.: HCI four waves within different interaction design examples. In: IFIP Work-ing Conference on Human Work Interaction Design. Springer (2021)
3. Frauenberger, C.: Entanglement HCI the next wave? ACM Trans. Comput.-Hum. Interact. (TOCHI) 27(1) (2019)
4. Frauenberger, C.: Critical realist HCI. In: Proceedings of the 2016 CHI Conference Extend-ed Abstracts on Human Factors in Computing Systems (2016)
5. Bannon, L.: From human factors to human actors: the role of psychology and human-computer interaction studies in system design. In: Greenbaum, J., Kyng, M. (eds.) Design at work: cooperative design of computer systems table of contents, Erlbaum, pp. 25–44 (1991)
6. Bødker, S.: When second wave HCI meets third wave challenges. In: Proceedings of the 4th Nordic Conference on Human-Computer Interaction: Changing roles (2006)
7. Poulos, C.N.: Essentials of autoethnography. American Psychological Association (2021)
8. Agar, M.: Literary journalism as ethnography: Exploring the excluded middle. Representation in ethnography (1995)
9. Mahadevan, J.: An auto-ethnographic narrative of corporate intercultural training: In-sights from the genealogical reordering of the material. Organization 30(5), 1004–1023 (2023)
10. Rapp, A.: Autoethnography in human-computer interaction: theory and practice. In: New Directions in Third Wave Human-Computer Interaction: Volume 2-Methodologies, pp. 25–42 (2018)

11. Desjardins, A., et al.: Introduction to the special issue on first-person methods in HCI. ACM Trans. Comput.-Hum. Interact. (TOCHI) **28**(6) (2021)
12. Johnston, O., Thomas, F.: Disney Animation: The Illusion of Life (1995)
13. Chan, E., Chan, E., Kroma, A., Arya, A.: Holistic multimodal interaction and design. In: International Conference on Human-Computer Interaction, pp. 18–33. Springer (2022)
14. Yong, A., Arya, A., Mantch, M.: Indigenous technology empowerment model: a community-based design framework. In: 2023 IEEE International Conference on Engineering, Technology and Innovation (ICE/ITMC), pp. 1–9 (2023)
15. Escobar, A.: Designs for the Pluriverse: Radical Interdependence, Autonomy, and the Making of Worlds. Duke University Press (2018)
16. Mezirow, J.: Transformative learning theory. In Contemporary theories of learning, pp. 114–128. Routledge (2018)
17. Steckler, A., et al.: Toward integrating qualitative and quantitative methods: an introduction. Health Educ. Q. **19**(1), 1–8 (1992)
18. Bazeley, P.: Issues in mixing qualitative and quantitative approaches to research. Applying Qualitative Methods Marketing Management Research **141**, 156 (2014)

A Study of the Impact of Different Teaching Methods on Students' Learning in Design Thinking Courses in Taiwan

Ching-Ya Chen[1], Hsi-Jen Chen[1]([⊠]), and Chia-Han Yang[2]([⊠])

[1] Department of Industrial Design, National Cheng Kung University, Tainan, Taiwan
p36111117@gs.ncku.edu.tw
[2] Institute of Creative Industrial Design, National Cheng Kung University, Tainan, Taiwan
chyang@ncku.edu.tw

Abstract. This study explores the landscape of design thinking courses in Taiwan, focusing on 50 relevant courses and identifying four primary teaching methods: Experiential Learning, Active Learning, Learning by Teaching, and traditional lecturing. Experiential Learning, ranking highest, involves guiding students through the design thinking process, while Learning by Teaching requires students to teach their peers in a simple manner. Active Learning emphasizes student engagement in the learning process. Google Trends analysis indicates a close relationship between design thinking and these methods. The study delves into three courses—"Thematic Design Thinking Workshop", "Design Thinking Practice and Promotion", and "Bootcamp"—conducting interviews to gain insights into post-course experiences. The research evaluates participants' perceptions of teaching methods and self-assessed learning abilities. Teaching methods encompass visualized teaching materials, feedback and guidance, teaching strategies, and a safe and inclusive classroom atmosphere. Each method develops specific abilities in students, such as change desire, experimentation, adjustment after failure, conceptualization, and teamwork. Self-assessment results using a design thinking cognitive scale reveal high scores in maintaining an open mindset across all methods, aligning with design thinking's core philosophy. The research underscores the importance of tailoring courses to instructors' capabilities and classroom needs, optimizing the effectiveness of design thinking education and fostering diverse abilities in students.

Keywords: Design Thinking Course · Acquired Competency · Experiential Learning · Learning by Teaching · Active Learning

1 Introduction

As society rapidly changing, courses related to design thinking are becoming increasingly popular in many fields. These courses apply a variety of teaching methods aimed at fostering students' problem-solving abilities. Currently, there is a diversity of design thinking courses, with intensive workshops being the most common format. In these workshops, participants tackle complex and challenging problems, exploring user needs and issues through interdisciplinary collaboration and human-centered approaches. For example, a group of American art teachers combined design thinking with community issues to offer a summer course that encouraged students to engage in critical thinking, teamwork, and interdisciplinary learning [1]. These diverse teaching methods pique our curiosity about the specific skills developed in each course. Therefore, the purpose of this study is to gain in-depth insights into students' learning outcomes after participating in different design thinking courses through interviews and to further categorize the characteristics of each course for reference in the design of future related courses.

This study identifies four teaching methods among 50 relevant design thinking courses in Taiwan, including experiential learning, Learning by Teaching, Active Learning, and traditional lecturing. Experiential learning is the most prevalent, followed by Active Learning, with Learning by Teaching and traditional lecturing tied for third place. As a result, this study focuses on three commonly used teaching methods applied to courses offered by National Cheng Kung University.

1.1 Experiential Learning - Thematic Design Thinking Workshop

According to David A. Kolb's Experiential Learning Cycle theory proposed in 1984 [2], a curriculum should encompass four main components: Concrete Experience, Reflection, Abstract Conceptualization, and Active Experimentation. In the context of a design thinking workshop, instructors guide students through the design thinking process, allowing them to engage in the Concrete Experience phase. Subsequently, students are encouraged to engage in Reflection, during which they can learn more and discover the strengths of their team members through observation and contemplation. Through this process of Reflection and observation, students move on to Abstract Conceptualization, contemplating how to apply design thinking tools. Finally, they transition into the Active Experimentation phase, where they apply what they've learned to real-world scenarios and assess problems and challenges.

1.2 Learning by Teaching - Design Thinking Practice and Promotion

Learning by Teaching known as "Lernen durch Lehren," proposed by the German professor Jean-Pol Martin in 2017 [3], is also known as the Feynman Technique. Its core idea is that students should take on the role of the teacher and impart the knowledge they have learned to others in a simple and understandable way. In Taiwan, this method is applied in design thinking practice and promotion courses. This course emphasizes that students play a primary role, while the teacher provides assistance and guides students in transforming design thinking concepts into easily comprehensible formats. Students also design entertaining lesson plans to promote design thinking to elementary school students. Before officially engaging in teaching at the elementary school level, teachers provide instruction on design thinking concepts and allow students to practice teaching. After teaching the courses in practice, students can ask questions, learn from one another, and review their lessons to improve their teaching plans.

1.3 Active Learning - Boot Camp

According to the four engagement modes within the Interactive-Constructive-Active-Passive (ICAP) framework proposed by Chi and Wylie in 2014 [4], the study suggests that the interactive mode has the most significant impact on learning outcomes, followed by the constructive, active, and passive modes. In the context of Boot Camp, a proactive learning approach is employed. Firstly, students are encouraged to actively apply design thinking tools, engaging in practical learning, which falls under the active engagement mode. Moreover, through group discussions and post-workshop assignments, students are required to reflect on and consider what constitutes an excellent design thinking workshop, which is considered a constructive mode of engagement. Lastly, students must independently select the topic for the design thinking workshop and take on the role of a coach during the class, providing practical guidance to other students and continually addressing their questions, thus encompassing the interactive engagement mode.

In summary, each teaching method has its advantages and disadvantages. Furthermore, when we look at Google Trends data, it is evident that the trends in design thinking and the three teaching methods mentioned earlier have followed similar patterns in recent years. They all decreased in 2021 and then experienced simultaneous increases in 2022. This suggests a close and interconnected relationship between them, which warrants further investigation (Fig. 1).

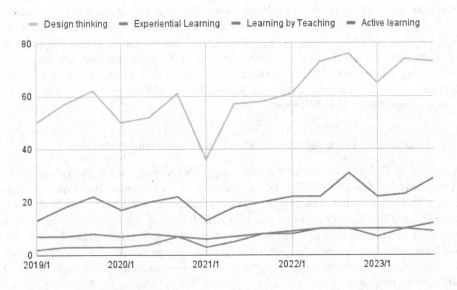

Fig. 1. Trend of design thinking and three kinds of teaching methods

2 Method

2.1 Target Courses and Participants

Three courses offered at National Cheng Kung University in Taiwan that apply the teaching methods described previously are selected as target courses. These courses include a "Thematic Design Thinking Workshop" using the experiential learning approach, a "Design Thinking Practice and Promotion" course implementing Learning by Teaching, and a "Boot Camp" utilizing the Active Learning. A total of nine participants (three from each course) are recruited for one-on-one qualitative interviews. The interviews are recorded in their entirety, and the average interview duration is approximately 1.5 h. The participants range from sophomores to doctoral candidates, all of whom are female. Among the participants from the three teaching methods, one has no prior experience with design thinking, while the other two each have more than six months of course experience in this domain.

2.2 Research Design

Firstly, a focus group consisting of five individuals with more than four years of design thinking learning experience collaboratively develops the interview framework. The qualitative interviews will encompass two main areas of inquiry: the participants' perceptions of the teaching methods and a self-assessment of acquired competencies. In the segment concerning the perceptions of teaching methods, the interviewees will be questioned about their views and experiences related to the courses and teaching methods. This will be based on research regarding instructional methods in architectural design courses [5], with adjustments made to suit this study's interview structure. Questions may include their understanding of design thinking, feelings and impacts after completing the courses, their level of interest in such courses, their most profound impressions, what they have learned, the most significant challenges faced, the advantages and disadvantages of the courses, and their overall preferences for the courses. Secondly, for the self-assessment of acquired competencies, the Design Thinking Mindset Measurement [6] will be utilized. This scale comprises 19 thinking dimensions, incorporating 71 subquestions. During the interview, the participants will be directly asked whether they have acquired these thinking dimensions in their respective courses. They will then rate their level of acquisition as "Very Much," "Much," "Moderate," "Little," or "Very Little." For the "Very Much" and "Much" items, the participants will be further prompted to elaborate on the aspects in which they have learned these thinking dimensions in the course. Participants will receive the interview outline before the interview commences and will be informed that they only need to answer questions based on their own experiences without feeling pressured. They will also be encouraged to raise any questions they may have during the interview process.

2.3 Data Analysis

In this study, the audio recordings of the first part of the interviews, concerning the participants' perceptions of the teaching methods, will be transcribed verbatim. The transcribed text will undergo an initial extraction of meaning units through the focus group and will be further classified, grouped, and named using the KJ method.

For the second part, which involves the self-assessment of acquired competencies, the responses from the participants related to the Design Thinking Mindset Measurement will be transformed into numerical values. A rating scale will be used, with 5 indicating "Very Much," 4 for "Much," 3 for "Moderate," 2 for "Little," and 1 for "Very Little." The responses within the same thinking dimension will be summed and then averaged to determine the mean score.

3 Results

The results of this study are divided into two parts: participants' perceptions of the teaching methods and a self-assessment of acquired competencies.

3.1 Perceptions of Teaching Methods

Based on the interviews, it was observed that the Design Thinking courses encompassed four distinct aspects, namely "Substantial Course Arrangement and Visualized Teaching Materials," "Teacher Feedback and Guidance," "Teaching Strategies Through Hands-on Learning," and "Comfortable and Inclusive Classroom Atmosphere." These four aspects contributed to the development of different competencies in students. Below, each aspect is discussed in detail:

Substantial Course Arrangement and Visualized Teaching Materials: Both Experiential Learning and Active Learning methods allowed students to be aware of the stages they were in. Experiential Learning made students more conscious of any gaps in their understanding, while Learning by Teaching enabled students to learn from their peers.

Teacher Feedback and Guidance: In this aspect, all three methods were found effective in evoking empathy among students through appropriate examples. Active Learning, in particular, made students more conscious of their shortcomings. In Experiential Learning, students were able to learn the desire for change, the willingness to experiment, the ability to adjust after failure, the concretization of concepts, and the establishment of new knowledge, all of which were crucial competencies.

Teaching Strategies Through Hands-on Learning: Both Learning by Teaching and Active Learning methods helped students develop the desire for change, the willingness to experiment, the ability to adjust after failure, and the concretization of concepts, and the establishment of new knowledge, among other competencies. Learning by Teaching also offered students the opportunity to realize the smoothness of the process, understand different perspectives, learn effective communication methods (including self-expression and active listening), be conscious of their shortcomings, and gain the courage to face the unknown, which included a total of six competencies.

Comfortable and Inclusive Classroom Atmosphere: Experiential Learning and Active Learning methods jointly fostered teamwork, mutual support among group members, learning from peers, understanding different ideas, learning to accept feedback from others, and the courage to face the unknown, contributing to six competencies. Experiential Learning, additionally, encouraged students to try new things and ideas, without considering feasibility, and think outside the box, which added two more competencies. Active Learning emphasized learning communication methods, including self-expression, listening to others, and enhancing the ability to structure and integrate information, covering two competencies. However, redefining tasks and fostering collaborative teamwork was common to Experiential Learning and Learning by Teaching. Lastly, value creation was a competency nurtured by all three teaching methods.

Table 1. Self-Assessment of Acquired Competencies

	Experiential Learning - Thematic Design Thinking Workshop	Learning by Teaching - Design Thinking Practice and Promotion	Active Learning - Boot Camp
Desire for change	○	□	□
Try, adjust after failure	○	□	□
Conceptualization	○	□	□
Building new knowledge	○	□	□
Learning from peers	☆	△	☆
Understanding different ideas	☆	□	☆
Appropriate examples that resonate with students	○	○	○
Use of knowledge	□	□	□
Creating value	☆	☆	☆
Redefine	☆	☆	
Team co-creation	☆	☆	
Awareness of Current Stage	△		△
Encouraging student teamwork	☆		☆
Mutual support among team members	☆		☆
Learning to accept feedback	☆		☆
Awareness of flow smoothness		□	□

(continued)

Table 1. (*continued*)

	Experiential Learning - Thematic Design Thinking Workshop	Learning by Teaching - Design Thinking Practice and Promotion	Active Learning - Boot Camp
communication skills, including self-expression and listening		□	☆
Awareness of personal weakness		□	○
Awareness of lack	△		
Courage of facing the unknown	☆	□	☆
Unconstrained style	☆		
Willingness to try new things	☆		
Transforming between roles of designer and user			□
Capability of integration and construction			☆

Icon Presentation:
△:Substantial Course Arrangement and Visualized Teaching Materials ○:Teacher Feedback and Guidance
□:Teaching Strategies Through Hands-on Learning ☆:Comfortable and Inclusive Classroom Atmosphere

3.2   A Self-assessment of Acquired Competencies

The Design Thinking Mindset Measurement questionnaire [6] was analyzed and found to comprise a total of 19 cognitive dimensions, as shown in the table below.

In this study, participants were asked with the Design Thinking Mindset Measurement questionnaire [6], the average scores for each dimension of design thinking mindset were calculated based on the responses of three students within the same teaching method (blue for Experiential Learning, green for Active Learning, and red for Interactive Learning). The results were presented in a radar chart. From the radar chart, it is evident that students in the Active Learning method generally had higher scores across various dimensions, with the highest scores achieved by "J. Open to different perspectives /diversity", followed by "R. Desire to make a difference", "D. Empathy/Empathic", "G. Problem reframing", "K. Learning oriented". On average, students in the Experiential Learning method had the second-highest scores, with "J. Open to different perspectives/diversity", achieving the highest scores, followed by "C. Human centeredness", "H. Team Working", "I. Multi-/inter-/cross-disciplinary collaborative teams", "D. Empathy

Table 2. Design Thinking Mindset [6]

A. Tolerance for - Being comfortable with Ambiguity - Uncertainty	B. Embracing Risk	C. Human centeredness
D. Empathy/Empathic	E. Mindfulness and awareness of process	F. Holistic view/consider the problem as a whole
G. Problem reframing	H. Team Working	I. Multi-inter-cross-disciplinary collaborative teams
J. Open to different perspectives/diversity	K. Learning oriented	L. Experimentation or learn from mistake or from failure
M. Experiential intelligence/Bias toward action	N. Critical Questioning ("beginners mind", curiosity)	O. Abductive Thinking
P. Envisioning new things	Q. Creative confidence	R. Desire to make a difference
S. Optimism to have an impact		

/ Empathic". Finally, the Interactive Learning method had lower average scores, but within this method, "J. Open to different perspectives/diversity", also had the highest scores, followed by "E. Mindfulness and awareness of process", "R. Desire to make a difference", "S. Optimism to have an impact", "Q. Creative confidence" (Fig. 2).

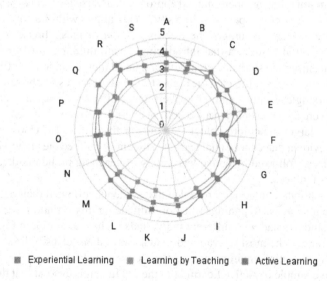

Fig. 2. Radar Chart of Design Thinking Mindset (Letter code in Table 2)

4   Discussion

In each teaching method, aside from the observed cognitive abilities aligning with existing literature, some new discoveries were made. Let's first explain each teaching method individually and then provide a comparative analysis of both participants' perceptions of the teaching methods and a self-assessment of acquired competencies.

For example, the literature mentions that experiential learning helps students cultivate essential skills required for future careers, such as communication, interaction, empathy, and teamwork, providing an effective teaching model [7]. According to the results presented earlier, students not only develop the skills mentioned in the literature but also acquire the ability to recognize gaps, a willingness to experiment with new ideas, and engage in imaginative thinking.

Regarding the use of Learning by Teaching in chemistry education to develop 21st-century competencies [8], the findings indicate that this approach enhances self-confidence, communication skills, teamwork, and other advantages. Furthermore, this study discovered that this teaching method also helps students identify their own shortcomings in the design thinking process.

In the study involving Active Learning mechanisms integrated into pharmaceutical interactive learning materials [9], it was found that this approach not only reduces students' cognitive load but also enhances learning efficiency. It more effectively aids nursing students in acquiring pharmaceutical knowledge, and it was observed in this study that students could shift roles and develop skills in synthesizing and structuring information.

As for the self-assessment of cognitive abilities, all three teaching methods scored the highest in maintaining an open-minded approach to diverse perspectives, represented by "J. Open to different perspectives/diversity". This aligns with the core principle of design thinking, which encourages the free expression of ideas, breaking traditional constraints. Carroll also suggest that introducing design thinking in secondary school classrooms can stimulate students' creativity and build their confidence [10].

In addition, this study subtracted the highest and lowest scores for the same cognitive ability within a single teaching method, converting the difference into a magnitude value. These values were then presented in a stacked bar chart. Each color represents a cognitive ability, and the larger the colored block, the greater the difference. Upon stacking the blocks, it was evident that experiential learning students exhibited the highest differences in their responses, followed by active learning, with teaching in the middle, indicating the smallest differences.

First, the qualitative interviews revealed that students attributed their acquired abilities to different sources. A significant factor influencing this variation was the diverse relationships students had with different individuals in the classroom, in Fig. 4. Within the learning context, the most relevant individuals were themselves, followed by peers, teachers, and the learning environment, as depicted in the chart.

Taking the example of Active Learning in the red line, it is evident that this teaching method emphasizes the individual student. Consequently, the learning outcomes can vary due to personal feelings and experiences. When cross-referencing the interview results, it becomes apparent that students mentioned many abilities related to their personal skills,

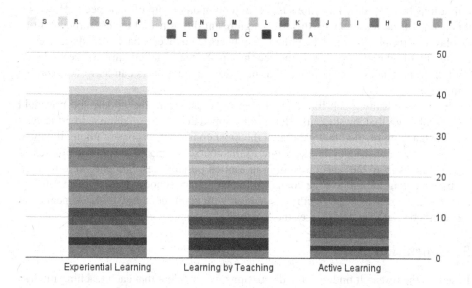

Fig. 3. Stacked Chart of Design Thinking Mindset (Letter code in Table 2)

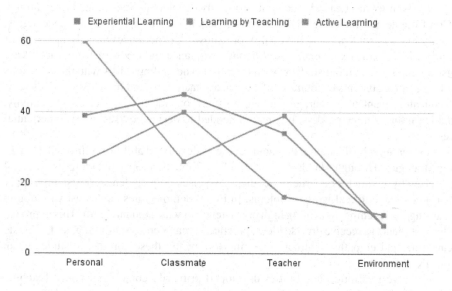

Fig. 4. Relevant of Learning

such as their capacity for integrating structures and the role shift between the designer and user.

In the case of Experiential Learning represented by the blue line, peers play a significant role. Students are more courageous in trying new things and breaking free from their limitations because they have the support and companionship of their peers. However, this is one of the reasons why there is a significant difference in the cognitive abilities displayed in the assessment. The influence of peers from diverse backgrounds, as well as the quality of relationships within the peer group and team, directly affects the students' learning experiences. Any conflicts that may arise among peers can leave unfavorable impressions.

Even though the green line of Learning by Teaching in the middle did not yield specific abilities that the students felt they developed during the qualitative interviews, it was the teaching method that generated the most consistent responses among the three methods. This consistency is likely due to the course having clear and specific learning objectives from the outset, resulting in limited possibilities. Students were focused on transforming the knowledge content into elementary school teaching materials and reaching a consensus through communication with team members. It also appears that this method relatively emphasizes the feasibility of design.

5   Conclusion

Based on the research findings and discussions, it is evident that each teaching method has its advantages and disadvantages, and different design thinking courses come with associated implementation limitations and characteristics. Therefore, the following summarizes each of these three teaching methods separately.

For Experiential Learning, students primarily develop abilities related to creating a "Comfortable and Inclusive Classroom Atmosphere" in Table 1. Peer influence significantly impacts students, and the quality of teamwork experiences directly affects their learning and overall experiences. Additionally, guidance and feedback from teachers are instrumental in providing students with direction. The findings align with the variations in Fig. 3 since students encounter different peers each time, and these experiences vary. If educators want to encourage students to think outside the box, employ creativity, and learn through the process, it is recommended to design courses using Experiential Learning.

For Learning by Teaching, the main source of developed abilities is through "Teaching Strategies Through Hands-on Learning" in Table 1. Proper planning of practical exercises by instructors is crucial, as these exercises help students consistently apply their knowledge to real-world problems. In Fig. 3 demonstrates the lowest variation in Learning by Teaching, indicating high consistency in what students learn. This approach allows students to receive diverse ideas, practice human-centered thinking, and cultivate teamwork and empathy. Instructors aiming to develop these abilities in students can consider using this method.

In Active Learning, the abilities developed primarily come from both "Teaching Strategies Through Hands-on Learning" and "Comfortable and Inclusive Classroom Atmosphere" in Table 1. These results confirm that Active Learning emphasizes students' active participation in the course, and what they learn varies based on their level of involvement and personal experiences. The variations in the assessment data indicate that Active Learning ranks second in Fig. 3. It is recommended for instructors aiming to foster students' skills in synthesis, structured thinking, empathy, or control over design thinking progress.

In the future, it is hoped that comprehensive research and analysis will provide guidelines for educators to choose the appropriate teaching method in specific contexts when focusing on developing specific skills in students. This will aid in shaping the direction of future design thinking courses.

References

1. Vande Zande, R.: Design education as community outreach and interdisciplinary study. J. Learn. Through Arts **3** (2007). https://doi.org/10.21977/D93110053
2. Kolb, D.: Experiential learning: experience as the source of learning and development (1984)
3. Lernen durch Lehren: Konzeptualisierung als Glücksquelle (2017, 9, 7). https://jeanpol.wordpress.com/2017/09/07/lernen-durch-lehren-konzeptualisierung-als-gluecksquelle/
4. Chi, M.T.H., Wylie, R.: The ICAP framework: linking cognitive engagement to active learning outcomes. Educ. Psychol. **49**(4), 219–243 (2014). https://doi.org/10.1080/00461520.2014.965823
5. TSAI, SHIUAN-YU. (n.d.): The Relationship between the Design Studio Applied by Multi-teaching Methods and Learning Willingness—A Case Study on the Department of Architecture at Southen Taiwan [Nanhua University]. https://hdl.handle.net/11296/esj557 (中文)
6. Dosi, C., Rosati, F., Vignoli, M.: Measuring Design Thinking Mindset. 1991–2002 (2018). https://doi.org/10.21278/idc.2018.0493
7. Lee, W.E., Perdana, A.: Effects of experiential service learning in improving community engagement perception, sustainability awareness, and data analytics competency. J. Account. Educ. **62**, 100830 (2023). https://doi.org/10.1016/j.jaccedu.2023.100830
8. Temel Aslan, S.: Is Learning by Teaching Effective in Gaining 21st Century Skills? The Views of Pre-Service Science Teachers. Educational Sciences: Theory and Practice 15 (2015). https://doi.org/10.12738/estp.2016.1.0019
9. Yiin, S.-J., Chern, C.-L.: The effects of an active learning mechanism on cognitive load and learning achievement: a new approach for pharmacology teaching to Taiwanese nursing students. Nurse Educ. Today **124**, 105756 (2023). https://doi.org/10.1016/j.nedt.2023.105756
10. Carroll, M., Goldman, S., Britos, L., Koh, J., Royalty, A., Hornstein, M.: Destination, imagination and the fires within: design thinking in a middle school classroom. Int. J. Art Des. Educ. **29**(1), 37–53 (2010). https://doi.org/10.1111/j.1476-8070.2010.01632.x

Designing Artificial Serendipity

Xuanning Chen[✉], Angela Lin, and Sheila Webber

Information School, University of Sheffield, Sheffield S10 2SJ, UK
xchen158@sheffield.ac.uk

Abstract. Designing for serendipity in online platforms has drawn considerable attention and debate over the last decade. To shed light on the debate and seek effective strategies for designing serendipity, a narrative inquiry was conducted with 32 Chinese online consumers. By learning from their experience of the designed serendipity (i.e. artificial serendipity) from real-life stories told via diary and interview, the findings revealed that artificial serendipity is a unique type of serendipity that provides platform users with constant surprises that can lead to both beneficial and harmful outcomes. Further, users appreciate artificial serendipity when it incorporates elements such as personalisation, controllability, and moderate propagation. These findings provide insights for research by expanding the current understanding of serendipity as an interplay between individual and random contexts, revealing that serendipity can also stem from a conscious designed context. For practice, these findings underscore that the design of artificial serendipity should focus more on platform users' ideas while refining existing online platform designs.

Keywords: Serendipity · information system · human–computer interaction

1 Introduction

In the last decade, designing for serendipity (i.e. a valuable surprise) in the digital environment has drawn considerable attention [1, 2]. Online giants, such as Amazon, Google, Netflix, and eBay, have all invested in curating serendipity in their platforms to enhance user engagement and satisfaction [3, 4]. Such a design trend gives rise to artificial serendipity, namely, serendipity that is rooted in conscious design involving human (and non-human) actors [5, 6]. There has been an ongoing debate about whether artificial serendipity can genuinely bring surprise and value to platform users.

Critics argue that the pre-curated nature of artificial serendipity makes its occurrences expected, and when the occurrence of an event becomes expected, it ceases to be a surprise [7, 8]. Further, the potential conflicting interests between platform designers and users may deteriorate the value of artificial serendipity. Designers may use artificial serendipity to manipulate users, creating an illusion of value while laying commercial traps [1, 9].

The core reason why artificial serendipity's surprise and pleasure levels are questioned is that the design strategies are mostly proposed through laboratory experiments.

© The Author(s), under exclusive license to Springer Nature Switzerland AG 2024
M. Kurosu and A. Hashizume (Eds.): HCII 2024, LNCS 14684, pp. 28–45, 2024.
https://doi.org/10.1007/978-3-031-60405-8_3

There is a lack of empirical evidence demonstrating their effectiveness in real-world applications [10, 11]. Serendipity, however, is a subjective phenomenon; its value and surprises are best understood by those who experience it directly (i.e. the serendipitists) [7, 12]. To assess the effectiveness of current strategies in designing surprising and valuable serendipity, gathering feedback from platform users is essential. However, studies probing users' feedback about artificial serendipity and corresponding serendipity-oriented designs are scarce.

This study seeks to bridge this gap by directly seeking insights from serendipitists' real-life experiences of artificial serendipity. Specifically, it aims to address two research questions:

1. How do platform users feel about artificial serendipity?
2. What features make artificial serendipity beneficial from users' perspectives?

This study reveals that platform users feel that artificial serendipity is a special type of serendipity. It can bring genuine surprise to platform users, but experiencing surprise can sometimes harm them. The harm stems from current serendipity-prone designs overlooking three key elements deemed necessary for making a beneficial artificial serendipity: personalisation, controllability, and moderate propagation.

This article is structured into six sections to elaborate on these findings and discuss their implications for both research and practice. Following this introduction, the following section offers a literature review of serendipity and its design. The methodology section comes next, detailing the research approach. Section 4 then presents the research findings. Section 5 details the theoretical contributions and practical implications of this research. The article concludes with Sect. 6, which summarises the study's key points and implications.

2 Literature Review

In this literature review, the nature of serendipity, the ways of designing artificial serendipity, and the debates around artificial serendipity are illustrated.

2.1 The Nature of Serendipity

Serendipity was first introduced by Horace Walpole, who described it as a beneficial discovery rooted in chance and sagacity [13]. Expanding upon Walpole's original concept and his assertion that serendipity is best comprehended through the deviation rather than a fixed definition [2, 13], serendipity can be identified by three essential conditions: unexpectedness, sagacity, and valuableness.

The unexpectedness of serendipity refers to its emergence without prior awareness or intentional pursuit [16]. For serendipitists, serendipity often appears as a fortunate and accidental surprise rooted in contextual randomness [5, 15]. By leveraging sagacity that roots back to past experience and domain expertise, serendipitists effectively capture and explore the surprise and translate it into a valuable opportunity [16]. The value derived from serendipity can be intangible, such as bringing emotional pleasure or evoking fond memories [17, 18], or tangible, such as fostering cognitive innovation, indicating promising directions for development, offering solutions to longstanding problems, or even enhancing the social democracy level [1, 19]. Overall, serendipity is a product of the interplay between individuals and random occurrences.

2.2 Artificial Serendipity

Artificial serendipity, also known as serendipity by design, demonstrates characteristics distinct from those of the naturally occurring serendipity. Specifically, artificial serendipity often finds the right serendipitists at the right time [1], making it deliberate and expected [5]. However, despite the lack of random and unexpected occurrences of traditional serendipity [5], artificial serendipity can still surprise serendipitists by bringing novel and unexpected content. Specifically, novel content can surprise serendipitists with unfamiliar elements, while unexpected content surprises by defying serendipitists' anticipation of information acquisition [10, 11]. These artificial surprises, crafted based on predictive analysis of serendipitists' online footprints [21], are also relevant to serendipitists' preferences and needs. Therefore, serendipitists can still value them and experience their benefits [10, 11]. Thus, artificial serendipity results from human–platform interaction, as individuals interact with platform-generated content.

2.3 Strategies for Designing Artificial Serendipity

The conscious design strategies that give rise to artificial serendipity cover three main areas: the design of serendipity-prone recommendation systems (RSs) that generate delightful artificial surprises [20, 22]; the design of interfaces that facilitate platform users' discovery of the artificial surprise [23, 24]; and the propagation of artificial serendipity that enhances platform users' embracing of the designed surprise [15].

In practice, the design of serendipity-prone recommendation systems (RSs) often involves adding more novel and unexpected items to the accuracy-oriented personalised recommendation lists [10, 22]. Specifically, novel items are often with contents that are unfamiliar or even unknown to the RSs' users [10, 22], bringing a sense of freshness and surprise. Unexpected items contain content that users might not have discovered independently [10], creating a sense of delight and surprise. To integrate these two types of items, the accuracy-oriented recommendation lists are adjusted either by re-ranking their results [10] or altering their underlying algorithms [10, 25].

In designing interfaces that facilitate the discovery of artificial serendipity on online platforms, three main groups of techniques are employed: (1) optimising the presentation structure in to better engage the users with the information offered by the platform [26, 27]; (2) highlighting the designed surprises to ensure the users can quickly notice a potential serendipitous opportunity [23, 28]; (3) providing supportive tools (e.g. social tools and visualisation tools) to aid users in quickly recognising and exploring the value of the artificial serendipity [29].

In the propagation of artificial serendipity and in stimulating platform users to engage with it, two main groups of techniques are commonly employed – the use of incomplete introduction and the use of multimedia elements [11, 14]. Both techniques leverages the natural human inclination towards exploring attractive knowns information, thereby driving more profound engagement with the designed surprises.

Although these design strategies have seen some successes, as showcased by [15] and [29], they do not provide complete insight into the problem. Nearly all of these strategies have been proposed directly by platform designers and researchers, and their effectiveness has primarily been tested through laboratory studies or structured surveys. The perspectives of platform users, who are the actual experiencers of the designed artificial serendipity, have been largely overlooked.

Given the subjective nature of surprise and value [12], disregarding platform users' viewpoints could create serendipitous experiences that are neither surprising nor valuable. Due to this concern, a debate has emerged over whether artificially created serendipity can still be classified as genuine serendipity.

2.4 Debates on Artificial Serendipity

Regarding whether artificial serendipity can be considered true serendipity, there are two conflicting viewpoints. Critics argue that artificial serendipity does not qualify as genuine serendipity because it inherently lacks authentic surprise and value. According to these critiques, the neglect of actual serendipitists' viewpoints in the design process renders artificial serendipity incapable of delivering genuine value to platform users [9, 21]. This perspective emphasises that what designers consider delightful surprises may not resonate with serendipitists. A key example cited is the public library system, where even an altruistic design of serendipity causes seek–encounter tensions in users [3, 9]. Instead of enhancing the user experience, artificial serendipity in such contexts can deteriorate the pleasure of using library systems. The situation is deemed even more problematic with commercial players. In a landscape where profit is the main driver behind design decisions, designers may regard artificial serendipity as a way of manipulating users [30]. Consequently, these designed serendipitous experiences could be reduced to mere marketing tactics, losing the essence of genuine serendipity.

Critics also argue that artificial serendipity deprives platform users of encountering genuine surprises. Genuine surprises arise from spontaneous and unregulated events, characterised by their elusive and continuously refreshing nature [18, 30]. By contrast, artificial serendipity, shaped by conscious designs, often remains confined within the boundaries of serendipitists' digital footprints [9, 21]. Although these designed surprises may initially seem novel, their allure is likely to be transient [21]. As users become familiar with their patterns over time, the surprises become predictable, diminishing their refreshing and novel appeal [9]. Essentially, such designed surprises offer only an illusion of genuine unexpectedness [21].

Despite the critics, there are proponents who suggest that artificial serendipity is indeed a form of serendipity. They argue that with the assistance of advanced computational technologies, such as artificial intelligence (AI), online platforms can transcend time and spatial limitations to ensure uninterrupted connectivity and offer serendipitists an array of choices [14]. Within these choices, there are often unknowns that users would not be able to discover independently [6]. Further, as the design of artificial serendipity is considered a competitive advantage, designers frequently choose not to reveal the technical details of their algorithms [31]. This intentional secrecy makes it challenging for platform users to predict when artificial serendipity might occur, thereby retaining its element of surprise.

To address the debate surrounding artificial serendipity, it is crucial to directly engage with platform users active in today's online environment. Indeed, the most profound understanding of any subjective experience comes from those who directly encounter it [17]. Despite its importance, there is a notable lack of research exploring platform users' perspectives on this matter, leaving a significant research gap. To fill this gap, this study adopted a serendipitist-centric approach, focusing on authentic stories shared by consumers within the online marketplace, a context in which the design for artificial serendipity is especially pronounced.

3 Methodology

To fully understand platform users' perceptions of artificial serendipity, this study was structured as a narrative inquiry. Insights were gleaned directly from the stories told by the participants. Figure 1 illustrates the overall research design, whose feasibility was validated through a pilot study.

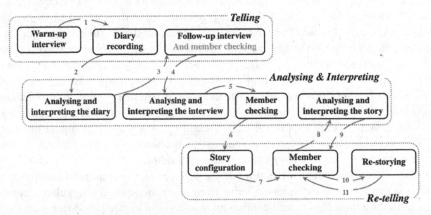

Fig. 1. The research design and process.

3.1 Narrative as the Research Strategy

Narrative inquiry, a research strategy that grounds the research in participants' stories [32], was adopted to guide this study. The core reason for adopting a narrative strategy is that stories can offer a more intricate and nuanced portrayal of participants' perceived realities [33]. Storytelling is a communication and sense-making technique that individuals naturally possess and refine in their daily lives [34]. Thus, participants can conduct storytelling with minimal researcher interference [35], guaranteeing their autonomy in faithfully revealing what they have experienced and thought [34].

In this study, stories were collected from 32 Chinese consumers aged between 18 and 34 years. The reasons for selecting this group as the targeted participants were threefold:

1. Choice of online consumers: Online marketplaces are notable for implementing artificial serendipity in their design [6, 36], with major platforms such as Amazon and eBay integrating artificial serendipity. These marketplaces provide a rich context for exploring users' experiences with artificial serendipity.
2. Choice of Chinese participants: This selection was influenced by the shared cultural background between the participants and the main researcher. A shared cultural context is believed to facilitate clearer understanding and communication between researchers and participants [37], ensuring accurate interpretation of participants' stories with minimal distortion [33].
3. Choice of consumers aged 18 to 34: This specific age range was chosen, considering that these consumers represent a significant portion of online consumption power globally [38]. Thus, consumers from this age group are likely to have richer online shopping experiences and potentially more encounters with artificial serendipity, contributing to more detailed and diverse stories.

Ethical approval for this research was obtained from the researchers' institution before approaching and recruiting participants. All participants were informed about the research objectives and the intended use of their stories. They provided their informed consent before the commencement of data collection. To gain a nuanced understanding of participants' feelings about artificial serendipity, they were further divided into four distinct age groups (18–19, 20–24, 25–29, and 30–34), aligning with the indicators specified by the population census standards in China [39]. However, this study revealed that participants across these various age groups exhibited a fundamentally consistent view of artificial serendipity and an effective serendipity-prone design. This consistency indicates that the insights gained from this study may be transferable to other populations.

Indeed, despite the transferable potential of this study, its focus solely on Chinese online consumers is a limitation. Given the inherent subjectivity and context sensitivity of serendipity, platform users from various cultural backgrounds and online contexts might perceive and interact with artificial serendipity differently. Therefore, to enrich this study, it would be beneficial to conduct further research involving empirical investigations of artificial serendipity from the perspectives of serendipitists from other national backgrounds.

3.2 Data Collection

In this study, the data collection session (i.e. the telling session in Fig. 1) was conducted via the adoption of self-administrated diaries and follow-up interviews.

The adoption of self-administered diaries ensured the faithful collection of detailed stories. The diaries allowed the participants to record their experiences as soon as they encountered artificial serendipity, mitigating the fallibility of memory and capturing more details [40]. Previous studies have highlighted the effectiveness of diaries in capturing detailed serendipitous experiences [e.g. 41, 42, 43]. Diary writing also permitted the participants to reflect on their experiences with minimal researcher interference, promoting an authentic representation of their views on artificial serendipity.

Interviews were conducted as intimate in-person conversations, allowing the capturing of experiential nuances, such as emotions, that might be missed in written form [44].

Additionally, the interviews served as a method of triangulation with diaries, enhancing the reliability of the study. Each interview was specifically tailored to the stories documented in the diaries.

The data collection session was conducted from early April to late October 2021, amid the COVID-19 pandemic. Thus, all communications with participants were conducted through real-time chat over WeChat, a platform whose suitability for a serendipity-based study was validated in both the pilot study and in research by [43].

3.3 Data Analysis

Since the narrative inquiry is interpretative at every stage [34], data analysis was woven throughout this research, with insights gained from early analysis informing and refining the direction of further data gathering.

Analysing and interpreting. The objective of the analysis and interpretation session was to empathise with the participants, facilitating an in-depth understanding of their viewpoints. This session was structured into three stages:

1. Analysing and interpreting diaries: This stage involved identifying ambiguities in the diary entries by examining the timelines within each story [46]. Graphic notes were used for visualising the timelines. The identified ambiguities were subsequently addressed with the participants in follow-up interviews.
2. Analysing and interpreting interviews: This stage identified the actions, emotions, and agency that made up the participants' experiences, leading to an in-depth understanding of participants' perceived realities.
3. Analysing and interpreting stories: Focusing on understanding the plot (i.e. the consequential structure) of the stories, this stage illuminated how participants experienced artificial serendipity. The stories were broken down line by line [33, 46] to clarify their structure. The analysis and interpretation were then carried out from the denouement, considering that the full scope of human experiences often becomes apparent when the outcomes are clear [33, 34].

Re-telling. The re-telling session aimed to translate the stories told by the participants into explicitly understandable forms [45], allowing a broader audience to empathise with the participants' perceived realities. Two tasks made up this session:

1. Story configuration: The goal was to assemble comprehensive and detailed stories by synthesising information from both interviews and corresponding diary entries. To achieve this, the ambiguities identified in the diaries were clarified and integrated at appropriate junctures within the stories. Additionally, novel ideas from the interviews were compiled into a separate document. Participants were then given the opportunity to select relevant content from this compilation to include in their diary narratives. Any content that was not incorporated into the diaries was stored in a background file, providing the researchers with additional insights into the participants' viewpoints.
2. Re-storying: This task involved initially summarising each story based on its identified plot. These summaries were then used for a cross-story comparison to identify common serendipitous patterns across the participants' experiences. By focusing on these recurrent patterns, prevalent actions, emotions, scenes, and agencies within the stories

were reconnected and interlinked. The outcome was a comprehensive framework that effectively depicted the artificial serendipity experienced by the participants.

To ensure the fidelity of the participants' viewpoints, member checking was conducted after each data analysis stage [33, 45]. This approach ensured the authenticity of the interpretations derived from the data.

4 Findings

4.1 On Artificial Serendipity: A Genuine yet Harmful Surprise

For the participants, the implementation of conscious design in online platforms did not signify the end of serendipitous experiences. Instead, artificial serendipity was viewed as a distinct and welcome type of serendipity. This positive reception was highlighted by the fact that over half of the participants visited online marketplaces without any particular needs; yet, their visits were motivated by the enjoyment of experiencing serendipity that was 'served by AI' (P4-2[1]) or 'guided by big data analysis' (P3-8).

More concretely, being supported by 'intelligent technologies' (P3-10) with 'powerful mining and analytical abilities' (P2-1) of these 'intelligent technologies' (P3-10), artificial serendipity can nudge them to embrace more surprises—namely, findings beyond their routines and expressed plans and preferences.

Further, given that the designers of artificial serendipity—typically e-commerce practitioners—possess 'superb market insights' (P3-8), the serendipitous findings they curated are likely to be superior to the participants' regular selections. One such example comes from P2-1. With Taobao's assistance, P2-1 discovered a high-quality beauty blender—one that was different from the makeup brush she intended to find. However, this surprising finding was a more suitable choice for her needs. The beauty blender offered' a quicker and more seamless makeup application' (P2-1) compared to the brush she had initially sought. By embracing these 'insightful surprises' (P2-1), the participants benefitted from: (1) an emotional pleasure, (2) a satisfying purchase, and (3) a slight gain in knowledge.

- **P4–2 S1** – Watching the recommendation made me feel as though I was playing with the toy myself. For me, this experience was enjoyable and memorable.
- **P2–9 S4** – I was quite satisfied with encountering this experience and the purchase it triggered […] I spent a certain amount of money and received items.
- **P2–10 S2** – This comprehensive exploration gave me a well-rounded understanding of the gift-giving culture.

Nonetheless, not all instances of artificial serendipity resulted in valuable outcomes as those mentioned above. In some cases, artificial serendipity can harm participants for two primary reasons:

---

[1] P4–2 refers to the second participant from the fourth age group; subsequent participant references adhere to this naming convention.

1. E-commerce practitioners' pursuit of commercial interest. Given that the core motive behind e-commerce practitioners' design for serendipity often 'revolves around satisfying their own commercial interests' (P3-9), some artificial serendipitous experiences may essentially be commercial traps. This kind of artificial serendipity may 'benefit the [e-commerce practitioners] by sacrificing [participants'] benefits' (P3-2).
2. The e-commerce practitioners' over-providing of novel findings. As noted by P1–2, e-commerce practitioners tend to design serendipity under 'an excessively strong intent for novelty'. This approach may lead users towards choices that are entirely unknown to them. The uncertainty and unfamiliarity associated with such unknown options can naturally evoke 'a sense of harmful and risky' (P4-6), discomforting the users.

In more detail, the potential harm brought about by artificial serendipity clusters into three categories:

1. A waste of time and energy. For example, P1–1 was disappointed to realise that the promotional event she encountered on Pinduoduo[2] was just 'fake news' (P1-1). The waste of time and energy can lead to participants feeling frustrated and angry. Sometimes, negative emotions could lead to a decrease in trust or even 'great disgust' (P2-9) towards the designers who curated the artificial serendipity. For instance, when P1–2 realised that she had been duped by an incredible discount that she could never get, she uninstalled Pinduoduo immediately and did not use it again. In this case, the artificial serendipity brought a 'loss-loss situation' (P2-9) to both the participants and the e-commerce practitioners.
2. A regretful purchase. An example was P4–6, who brought a box of 'bad-tasting' crayfish due to a serendipitous recommendation offered by Douyin[3]. Similar to the reaction to a wasted time and energy, the realisation of a regrettable purchase was also followed by participants' temporary avoidance of a given e-commerce practitioner, leading to a 'reduced consumer traffic to [that platform]' (P4-6).
3. A loss of selection autonomy. In this case, participants may be manipulated to overtrust the AI system, relying on the system to conduct all information searches. This reliance, in turn, limited the participants' 'purchase alternatives in a limited range' (P2-8).

Notably, the outcomes of artificial serendipity may take time to be fully revealed. Some initially perceived beneficial serendipity might shift into harmful ones later on after the 'influence of [AI systems] gradually diminished' (P3-4).

4.2 Features of Beneficial Artificial Serendipity

Through in-depth discussions with participants about the factors contributing to both beneficial and harmful instances of artificial serendipity, three designed features that

---

[2] Pinduoduo (拼多多) is a major Chinese e-commerce platform renowned for its low-price strategy. However, it has been criticised for its poor handling of false information and failure to deliver high-quality products.

[3] Douyin (抖音), internationally known as TikTok, is a popular short-video social media platform originating in China. As it has evolved, it has become a significant social commerce platform on which vendors market their products.

made up a beneficial artificial serendipity emerged: personalisation, controllability, and moderate propagation.

Personalisation. For the participants, a beneficial artificial serendipity was often a personalised one that 'closely aligned with' (P2-1) their expressed preferences and needs. By contrast, artificial serendipity that lacked personalisation was seen in a less favourable light, being regarded as a 'source for uncertainty and potential ambiguity' (P4-6).

Two reasons led to the participants' preference for personalised recommendations. First, shopping, as an 'everyday practicality' (P3-5), did not always derive its value and attractiveness from discovering novel items. Instead, the joy of shopping predominantly came from encountering familiar content that could be immediately useful in participants' everyday lives.

- **P2-3 I3** – Shopping is not conducting scientific research; I do not need a lot of shopping-related innovativeness. I just need findings based on my shopping history and search history. [...] I do not have a use for extremely novel products, so if you introduce them to me, it is just a waste of both your and my time.

Further, novel surprises may not only be less immediately useful but may also be contrary to their existing preferences and interests, potentially leading to 'discomfort' (P2-3). For instance, P2-3 mentioned that while horror comics are 'definitely a novel and unknown area' for her (P2-3), she would never buy and read them due to her 'fear of ghosts and terror' (P2-3).

Second, because of the arrival of the 'information era' (P3-3), the participants were already 'overwhelmed with novel and unknown findings' (P3-3). Continual exposure to novelty could lead to a state of 'overload' (P2-7), impairing participants' ability to make rational decisions to address their needs. For instance, P3-6 experienced difficulty choosing products due to an excess of unfamiliar brands recommended by Taobao during shopping. This difficulty in choice eventually led her to 'a regretful' (P3-6) abandonment of the purchase. Under this circumstance, the participants felt that they did not lack novelty and 'no longer have the capacity' (P3-10) to absorb additional novelty; instead, they lacked a personalised filtering that could help them 'accurately identify relevance from the chaotic' (P3-10).

Controllability. Another key aspect that constitutes a beneficial artificial serendipity, according to the participants, is 'controllability' (P2-9). That is, the participants valued artificial serendipity that they could influence and whose development they could anticipate, even if the anticipation and influence were more of an 'intangible perception rather than tangible reality' (P3-4).

- **P3-4 I3** – If I have no say in the entire experience and cannot influence its development, then I feel that the experience would be difficult to be enjoyable [...] For an [artificial serendipity] experience to be enjoyable, at the very least, its development should be able to be influenced by me.

This perceived controllability reassured the participants that they were not solely serving the interests of e-commerce practitioners to their detriment; this, in turn, instilled 'confidence and willingness' (P2-5) in participants to engage with and enjoy the artificial serendipity.

The participants' need for controllability, albeit intangible, was rooted in two main reasons. The first reason was their 'distrust' (P2-10) of e-commerce practitioners. Since e-commerce practitioners and consumers have contrasting interests, the participants were sceptical that practitioners would design serendipity altruistically to meet their shopping needs. Instead, they worry that these designs might just be 'tactics [employed by practitioners] to enhance in-store sales or traffic' (P2-10). Due to this awareness, there is some degree of control to safeguard against practitioners' potential manipulations in the experience of artificial serendipity.

The second reason was related to the participants' concerns about the 'deceptive effect' (P3-1) caused by intelligent technologies. With their 'superb data tracking and analytical power' (P3-4), technologies such as AI can understand participants' preferences and needs more 'timely and clearly' (P3-4), thereby crafting a 'virtual fairyland' (P3-9) for participants. In this fairyland, the participants were deceived to trust emotions over logic, leading to irrational decisions. Therefore, to avoid falling into deceptive traps created by intelligent technologies, the participants tended to prefer engaging with artificial serendipity, whose development route they could anticipate.

According to the participants, the perceived controllability of artificial serendipity came from the following:

1. A clear indication of the reasons behind its occurrence. This assured the participants that e-commerce practitioners were 'ethically collecting and using their online footprints' (P2-9). As a result, the participants could worry less about 'being surveillance and manipulated by [e-commerce practitioners]' (P2-9) during their artificial serendipity experience.
2. Avoidance of interruptions during the serendipitous process. This means that during the experience of artificial serendipity, the participants' decision-making processes were not disrupted by 'sudden pop-ups' (P4-2) or similar interruptions. This assured the participants that they could 'make independent decisions in an undisturbed way' (P4-2) while experiencing artificial serendipity, making the participants feel that the outcome of serendipity was controllable.

Moderate Propagation. Apart from the aforementioned features, the participants also highlighted that a beneficial artificial serendipity was one that moderately propagated itself. It used 'limited multimedia elements to offer detailed explanations about its value' (P4-2) rather than explaining itself and value via excessive multimedia and incomplete information.

Three reasons made the artificial serendipity with moderate propagation more beneficial. First, moderate propagation allowed the participants to effectively recognise the value of the serendipitous opportunity, ensuring that they did not miss valuable surprises. The restrained use of multimedia elements ensured that the participants 'did not have to wait long for information to load' (P4-2), providing a 'quick acquisition' (P4-2) to the introduction of the serendipity. Meanwhile, with complete information about the 'captivating snippets' (P3-5) of the serendipity, the participants could 'swiftly understand'

(P4-2) how the finding might be useful in their daily lives from the acquired introductions. The understanding, in turn, alerted the participants to embrace the serendipity.

Second, moderate propagation ensured that the participants set reasonable and rational expectations about the potential value of artificial serendipity. Sometimes, regret about an artificial serendipity was not due to its actual low value but because participants had unrealistic value expectations at the start, influenced by excessive promotion of it. P4–7's experience illustrates this. In his story, P4–7 expected to find an adaptor small than the size of his palm because the vendor propagated it as one that 'extremely smaller than other similar products' (P4-7). This expectation led to regret when P4–7 found that the received product was just 'a little bit smaller than other similar products' (P4-7).

Third, the moderate propagation of artificial serendipity signified the trustworthiness of the e-commerce practitioners who designed it. This perceived reliability encouraged the participants to engage with and enjoy the serendipity 'without reservation' (P3-5). By contrast, excessive marketing tactics often amplified the participants' concerns, making them view the suggested serendipity as simply a commercial ploy. As a result, they tended to avoid these surprises and felt 'more uncertain' (P3-5) when engaging with serendipity. This corresponds to the viewpoints of P3–8:

- **P3–8 I3** – Whenever a recommendation includes overly exaggerated language, such as 'lose ten pounds in three days' or 'biggest discount ever', I tend to view the product or the marketing campaign negatively. These words give me the impression that they are trying too hard to mask some undisclosed flaws or issues with the product or campaign. As the saying goes, 'The more insecure you are, the more you tend to overcompensate.'

5 Discussion

5.1 Artificial Serendipity Through Platform Users' Eyes

The participants' stories illuminate how platform users perceive artificial serendipity. For platform users, conscious design does not eliminate serendipity in the online context; instead, it introduces attractive surprises—the very core of serendipity [5]. Artificial serendipity that incorporates conscious designs, however, does not ensure consistent benefits for users; sometimes, artificial serendipity may harm users. As experienced by platform users, the surprising yet potentially harmful nature of artificial serendipity arises from multiple roots.

The multidimensionality and neutrality of surprises. Surprises are not just about the emergence of novel content; they can also stem from the unexpected presentation of familiar content [18, 44]. This study, along with previous research on serendipity, demonstrates that surprises often arise from unusual arrangements of known knowledge [e.g. 44, 47]. Therefore, it is an oversimplification to equate genuine surprise and serendipity solely with novel content.

Further, compared to novel surprises, familiar surprises often attract more user attention. At its core, a surprise is essentially a neutral event [48]. Its classification as attractive or disruptive is subject to individuals' personal interpretations [48]. Given that human beings are inherently path-dependent [49], platform users naturally consider the known issues to be more reliable and valuable and, thus, would devote more attention to these familiars. Conversely, those who significantly diverge from or radically innovate upon these experiences are often perceived as disruptive and are likely to be disregarded. Notably, the preference of individuals for surprises that echo their past experiences has also been acknowledged in several other studies. These studies emphasise that past experiences are pivotal to fostering enjoyable serendipity [e.g. 50, 51].

The Benefits can Differ for Every User. Specifically, the perception of benefits or value is inherently subjective. Due to this subjectivity, what designers consider beneficial may be perceived as harmful by platform users. To create artificial serendipity that is beneficial for platform users, design strategies should incorporate certain features that are different from the designers' ideas:

1. Personalisation. Whereas designers often see personalisation as a barrier to serendipity [10], users consider it a key feature leading to 'highly beneficial' (P4-2) artificial serendipity. After all, personalised findings are often of immediate use to users. Notably, the link between personalisation and the benefits of artificial serendipity extends beyond this study. Studies with business professionals and academic researchers [e.g. 52, 53], who are generally keen on innovation, also suggest that the most fulfilling serendipitous experiences are those pertinent to their pre-existing knowledge and spheres of interest.
2. User control. The 'most satisfying' (P3-2) serendipitous experience, as per users, are those where they have the autonomy to decide its development. However, the assistance offered by designers, intended to support the noticing and exploration of the surprise, is often seen as intrusive by users. Ultimately, for users, exercising their sagacity without interference is crucial to benefitting from serendipity. This preference is supported by findings from [55] and [10]. External support, especially when it is 'too prompt' (P3-2), can make users feel like their every move is under surveillance. This can intensify their uncertainty during the serendipitous experience [55].
3. Moderate propagation. To effectively convey the value of artificial serendipity, a complete and straightforward introduction to the designed surprise suffices rather than an eye-catching advertisement replete with marketing tactics. The former approach, by avoiding excessive promotion, prevents users from developing overly high expectations for the serendipitous discovery [2]. Consequently, users can more openly accept the outcome of the serendipity without deeming a potentially good artificial serendipity as unfavourable due to a gap between their expectations and reality [31].

5.2 Guidelines and Strategies for Designing Artificial Serendipity

By exploring the platform users' perceived artificial serendipity, two guidelines for designing artificial serendipity were identified.

First, respecting platform users' voices leads to effective serendipity-prone designs. Given the subjective nature of value and surprise, platform users are often best positioned to define what constitutes a satisfying serendipitous experience for them. By aligning with these insights, designers can create positive artificial serendipity experiences that resonate with their customers. These experiences can boost users' satisfaction and trust, leading to higher return rates and long-term loyalty to the online platforms [31]. By contrast, disregarding users' voices can result in ineffective design strategies that destroy user–platform relationships. Thus, ineffective serendipity-prone designs can lead to harmful artificial serendipity for platform users, resulting in a loss of satisfaction and trust in the practitioner. Dissatisfaction not only affects immediate sales but can also negatively impact user loyalty and the platform's reputation. This study witnessed instances in which platform users, after experiencing harmful artificial serendipity, chose to uninstall an e-commerce platform altogether.

Second, designing for serendipity does not require a complete overhaul of existing online platform strategies. Instead, certain existing design elements can facilitate beneficial artificial serendipity for users. In particular, users generally favour personalisation, a need that existing accurate and relevance-focused recommendation systems can meet. Furthermore, users value maintaining control over their choices. This, in turn, reduces the need to introduce overly intelligent supportive tools in online platforms. Moreover, users prefer to have realistic expectations at the outset of an experience, which suggests that practitioners do not need to invest heavily in elaborate marketing campaigns.

Based upon these two guidelines, three strategies for designing artificial serendipity are further proposed: prioritising personalisation, guaranteeing users' control, and employing modest promotion.

1. Prioritising personalisation. When designing artificial serendipity online, personalisation should still be prioritised over other serendipity-related design concepts of unexpectedness and novelty. To achieve better personalisation, designers need to pay closer attention to platform users' recent online footprints, as individuals' preferences and needs often change fast. Also, designers could consider uncovering and prioritising offerings on the periphery of users' profiles. Although related to consumers' stated preferences and needs, these offerings are often overlooked, providing a mix of personalisation and novelty.

2. Guaranteeing users control. To enhance users' control over artificial serendipity, designers can leverage two strategies: providing clear explanations for each recommended surprise and reducing the offering of supportive tools. The first strategy fosters a more transparent online experience, diminishing users' perceived uncertainty regarding the encountered surprises [31]. The second strategy ensures an undisturbed online visit, providing users with an independent decision-making environment for exploring the encountered surprises.

3. Employing modest propagation. When promoting the designed surprise, a detailed and accessible explanation of the full features is advisable rather than solely accentuating the positives. This approach not only makes users feel that the designers are transparent, thereby strengthening their trust in the designers and the surprises offered, but also helps users form realistic expectations and fully appreciate the charm of the artificial serendipity experience.

6 Conclusion

This study addresses a topic of growing importance but with considerable debate: the design for artificial serendipity in online platforms. By focusing on platform users, who actually experience artificial serendipity, this study reveals key features of artificial serendipity and effective approaches for its design.

According to platform users, artificial serendipity is a unique form of serendipity, bringing them constant surprises that turn out to be either beneficial or harmful. The occasional harm of artificial serendipity stems from the misalignment between users' requirements and designers' design intents. Users appreciate artificial serendipity when it incorporates elements such as personalisation, controllability, and moderate propagation. However, designers frequently neglect these aspects; sometimes, they even actively work against them. Designers attempt to eliminate personalisation by introducing more novel and unexpected content, weaken users' control over their experiences through the provision of supportive tools, and try to entice users towards artificial serendipity with excessive marketing. Consequently, artificial serendipity sometimes fails to align with users' value pursuits, leading to harmful outcomes.

The findings regarding the features of artificial serendipity and its design can contribute to its benefits and have implications for research and practice. As for research, the findings shed light on the ongoing debate over whether artificial serendipity can be classified as genuine serendipity, suggesting new factors for future serendipity-related studies:

1. The currently widely accepted three characteristics (i.e. unexpectedness, sagacity, and value) warrant reconsideration. With the arrival of artificial serendipity, serendipity does not only consist of grasping chances from a given serendipitously passive context. It evolves into a synergistic interplay between users' recognition of a serendipitous encounter and the more serendipitously proactive environment in which it occurs, converging in a mutual voyage of discovery. Notably, this dynamic has gained prominence in our digital age, where most everyday life and working activities are realised via the intermediation of intelligent technologies.
2. The everyday context and users' voices warrant greater emphasis. Everyday life is rich with serendipitous opportunities that frequently remain unexplored. Delving deeper into these moments, especially the artificially created ones, necessitates hearing directly from those who encounter them. After all, the intricacies of a subjective experience might be imperceptible to outsiders.

In practice, it is recommended that designs for serendipity should be personalised to users' needs and preferences. While novel and unexpected recommendations can indeed capture users' attention, they also risk triggering scepticism and distrust, as users might perceive these as commercial tactics. Additionally, it is important for users to have control over why they encounter designed surprises, enabling them to independently explore these moments. Although this independent exploration may require more effort, it allows users to interpret surprises from their own perspective, ensuring they derive value from the experience. Lastly, the promotion of designed serendipity should be balanced and not overly sensational, to avoid disappointment from unfulfilled expectations.

This study contributes to both the theoretical and practical aspects of serendipity. Theoretically, it identifies artificial serendipity as a distinct type of serendipity, thereby broadening the current understanding and urging researchers to consider contemporary societal developments in their serendipity studies. On the design front, it highlights the shortcomings in existing strategies, emphasising that successful serendipity design requires not just designers' insights but also crucial input from platform users. These contributions, whether theoretical or design-related, are instrumental in fostering a more user-friendly online environment.

Acknowledgments. Sincere thanks to Professor Nigel Ford for his insightful feedback on this paper.

Disclosure of Interests. The authors have no competing interests to declare that are relevant to the content of this article.

References

1. Reviglio, U.: Towards a taxonomy for designing serendipity in personalized news feeds. Inf. Res. **24**(4) (2019)
2. Smets, A.: Designing for serendipity: a means or an end? J. Documentation **79**(3), 589–607 (2023)
3. Reviglio, U.: Serendipity as an emerging design principle of the infosphere: challenges and opportunities. Ethics Inf. Technol. **21**(2), 151–166 (2019)
4. Yi, C., Jiang, Z., Benbasat, I.: Designing for diagnosticity and serendipity: an investigation of social product-search mechanisms. Inf. Syst. Res. **28**(2), 413–429 (2017)
5. de Melo, R.M.C.: On serendipity in the digital medium: Towards a framework for valuable unpredictability in interaction Design. Doctoral thesis. Universidade do Porto, Portugal (2018)
6. Reviglio, U.: Cultivating serendipity in personalization systems: theoretical distinctions. In: Serendipity Science. New Methodologies for Studying Serendipity: Tracing an Emerging Field. Springer Nature (2023)
7. Andel, P.V.: Anatomy of the unsought finding. serendipity: orgin, history, domains, traditions, appearances, patterns and programmability. British J. Philosophy Sci. **45**(2), 631–648 (1994)
8. Carr, P.L.: Serendipity in the stacks: Libraries, information architecture, and the problems of accidental discovery. Coll. Res. Libr. **76**(6), 831–842 (2015)
9. Erdelez, S., Jahnke, I.: Personalised systems and illusion of serendipity: a sociotechnical lens. In: Workshop of WEPIR 2018 (2018)
10. Kotkov, D., Wang, S., Veijalainen, J.: A survey of serendipity in recommender systems. Knowl.-Based Syst. **111**, 180–192 (2016)
11. Smets, A., Vannieuwenhuyze, J., Ballon, P.: Serendipity in the city: user evaluations of urban recommender systems. J. Am. Soc. Inf. Sci. **73**(1), 19–30 (2022)
12. Makri, S., Blandford, A.: Coming across information serendipitously – Part 2. J. Documentation **68**(5), 706–724 (2012)
13. Merton, R.K., Barber, E.: The travels and adventures of serendipity: A study in sociological semantics and the sociology of science. Princeton University Press (2011)
14. Makri, S., Blandford, A., Woods, M., Sharples, S., Maxwell, D.: "Making my own luck": serendipity strategies and how to support them in digital information environments. J. Am. Soc. Inf. Sci. **65**(11), 2179–2194 (2014)

15. Kim, A., Affonso, F.M., Lanran, J., Durante, K.M.: Serendipity: chance encounters in the marketplace enhance consumer satisfaction. J. Mark. **85**(4), 141–157 (2021)
16. Foster, A.E., Ellis, D.: Serendipity and its study. J. Documentation **70**(6), 1015–1038 (2014)
17. Erdelez, S.: Information encountering: It's more than just bumping into information. Bull. Am. Soc. Inf. Sci. Technol. **25**(3), 26–29 (1999)
18. McCay-Peet, L., Toms, E.G.: Researching serendipity in digital information environments. Synthesis Lectures Inf. Concepts Retrieval Serv. **9**(6), i–91 (2017)
19. Busch, C.: Towards a theory of serendipity: a systematic review and conceptualization. J. Manage. Stud. (2022)
20. Reviglio, U.: Serendipity by design? How to turn from diversity exposure to diversity experience to face filter bubbles in social media. In: Proceedings of International Conference on Internet Science, pp. 281–300. Springer International Publishing (2017)
21. Erdelez, S., Agarwal, N.K., Jahnke, I.: Serendipity and critical thinking: fighting disinformation in a socio-technical society. In: ASIS&T SIG Social Informatics Research Symposium, 82nd Annual Meeting of the Association for Information Science and Technology (2019)
22. Ziarani, R.J., Ravanmehr, R.: Serendipity in recommender systems: a systematic literature review. J. Comput. Sci. Technol.Comput. **36**(2), 375–396 (2021)
23. Björneborn, L.: Three key affordances for serendipity: toward a framework connecting environmental and personal factors in serendipitous encounters. J. Documentation **73**(5), 1053–1081 (2017)
24. Kefalidou, G., Sharples, S.: Encouraging serendipity in research: designing technologies to support connection-making. Int. J. Hum. Comput. Stud. **89**, 1–23 (2016)
25. Said, A.B., Fields, B., Albayrak, S.: User-centric evaluation of a k-furthest neighbor collaborative filtering recommender algorithm. In: Proceedings of the 2013 Conference on Computer Supported Cooperative Work, pp. 1399–1408. ACM (2013)
26. Jannach, D., Jesse, M., Jugovac, M., Trattner, C.: Exploring multi-list user interfaces for similar-item recommendations. In: Proceedings of the 29th ACM Conference on User Modeling, Adaptation and Personalization, pp. 224–228. ACM (2021)
27. Niu, W., Huang, L., Chen, M.: Spanning from diagnosticity to serendipity: an empirical investigation of consumer responses to product presentation. Int. J. Inf. Manage. **60**, 102362 (2021)
28. Afridi, A.H., Outay, F.: Triggers and connection-making for serendipity via user interface in recommender systems. Pers. Ubiquit. Comput. **25**(1), 77–92 (2021)
29. Grange, C., Benbasat, I., Burton-Jones, A.: With a little help from my friends: cultivating serendipity in online shopping environments. Inf. Manage. **56**(2), 225–235 (2019)
30. Schmidt, A.: The end of serendipity: Will artificial intelligence remove chance and choice in everyday life? In: CHItaly 2021: 14th Biannual Conference of the Italian SIGCHI Chapter, pp. 1–4. ACM (2021)
31. Kim, G.M., Mattila, S.A.: Does a surprise strategy need words? the effect of explanations for a surprise strategy on customer delight and expectations. J. Serv. Mark. **27**(5), 361–370 (2013)
32. Bates, J.A.: Use of narrative interviewing in everyday information behavior research. Libr. Inf. Sci. Res. **26**(1), 15–28 (2004)
33. Riessman, C.K.: Analysis of personal narratives. In Inside Interviewing: New lenses, New Concerns, pp. 331–346. Sage Publishing. (2003)
34. Jovchelovitch, S., Bauer, M.W.: Narrative interviewing. In: Qualitative researching with text, image and sound, pp. 57–74. Sage Publishing (2000)
35. Bronstein, J.: A transitional approach to the study of the information behavior of domestic migrant workers: a narrative inquiry. J. Documentation **75**(2), 314–333 (2019)

36. Oh, J., Sudarshan, S., Lee, J.A., Yu, N.: Serendipity enhances user engagement and sociality perception: the combinatory effect of serendipitous movie suggestions and user motivations. Behav. Inf. Technol. **41**(11), 2324–2341 (2022)
37. Du, J.: T: Understanding the information journeys of late-life migrants to inform support design: information seeking driven by a major life transition. Inf. Process. Manage. **60**(2), 103172 (2023)
38. Statista: Ecommerce worldwide. In Statista – The Statistics Portal. Retrieved July 22. https://www.statista.com/outlook/243/100/ecommerce/worldwide#market-age. Accessed 12 Jan 2023
39. National Bureau of Statistics of China: Tabulation on the 2020 Population Census of the People's Republic of China. https://www.stats.gov.cn/sj/pcsj/rkpc/6rp/lefte.htm. Accessed 12 Jan 2023
40. Ritchie, J., Lewis, J., Nicholls, C.M., Ormston, R.: Qualitative research practice: A guide for social science students and researchers. Sage Publishing (2023)
41. Jiang, T., Guo, Q., Xu, Y., Fu, S.: A diary study of information encountering triggered by visual stimuli on micro-blogging services. Inf. Process. Manage. **56**(1), 29–42 (2019)
42. Sun, X., Sharples, S., Makri, S.: A user-centred mobile diary study approach to understanding serendipity in information research. Inf. Res. **16**(3) (2011)
43. Zhou, X., Sun, X., Wang, Q., Sharples, S.: A context-based study of serendipity in information research among Chinese scholars. J. Documentation **74**(3), 526–551 (2018)
44. Foster, A.E., Ford, N.: Serendipity and information seeking: an empirical study. J. Documentation **59**(3), 321–340 (2003)
45. Fraser, H.: Doing narrative research: analysing personal stories line by line. Qual. Soc. Work. **3**(2), 179–201 (2004)
46. Shibly, S.A., Chatterjee, S.: Surprise rewards and brand evaluations: the role of intrinsic motivation and reward format. J. Bus. Res. **113**, 39–48 (2020)
47. Murayama, K., Nirei, M., Shimizu, H.: Management of science, serendipity, and research performance: evidence from a survey of scientists in Japan and the US. Res. Policy **44**(4), 862–873 (2015)
48. Heilman, C.M., Nakamoto, K., Rao, A.G.: Pleasant surprises: consumer response to unexpected in- store coupons. J. Mark. Res. **39**(2), 242–252 (2002)
49. Björneborn, L.: Adjacent possible. In: The Palgrave encyclopedia of the possible, pp. 16–28. Springer International Publishing (2023)
50. Erdelez, S.: Investigation of information encountering in the controlled research environment. Inf. Process. Manage. **40**(6), 1013–1025 (2004)
51. McBirnie, A.: Seeking serendipity: the paradox of control. ASLIB Proc. **60**(6), 600–618 (2008)
52. Maloney, A., Conrad, L.Y.: Expecting the unexpected: Serendipity, discovery, and the scholarly research process [White paper] (2016)
53. Pontis, S., et al.: Academics' responses to encountered information: context matters. J. Am. Soc. Inf. Sci. **67**(8), 1883–1903 (2016)
54. Cunha, M.P., Rego, A., Clegg, S., Lindsay, G.: The dialectics of serendipity. Eur. Manag. J. **33**(1), 9–18 (2015)
55. Cutright, K.M., Wu, E.C.: In and out of control: Personal control and consumer behavior. Consumer Psychol. Rev. **6**(1), 33–51 (2023)

Integrated DBR and ADDIE Model to Improve Pedagogical Practices in Mechatronic Design

Jui-Hung Cheng[✉]

Department of Mold and Die Engineering, National Kaohsiung University of Science and Technology, Kaohsiung, Taiwan
rick.cheng@nkust.edu.tw

Abstract. Nowadays, the industry is diversified and interdisciplinary technology integration, requiring high teamwork and interaction. This mechatronic Design course introduces industry-academia co-teaching and simulates the problems for senior mold engineering students about to enter the workplace. It integrated the DBR design-oriented method, ADDIE curriculum framework, and the P-TECH workplace soft skills training model. Students will build up their knowledge of mechatronic systems and start from scratch with IoT applications through ESP8266 and ESP32 control boards and extendable components, guided by the practical design needs of the industry. This innovative teaching model trains students to have professional hard and soft skills in the workplace. That can solve the gap between students and industry demands, enhancing students' problem-solving abilities and improving no learning motivation, direction, and other issues. The study results showed that students' learning confidence and outcomes met the predictions at the beginning of the semester and exceeded their set initial goals after learning.

Keywords: DBR · ADDIE · P-TECH · Mechatronic Design

1 Introduction

In previous implementations of Mechatronic Design practical courses, a systematic design framework was constructed by integrating Problem-Based Learning/Project-Based Learning (PBL/PjBL), STEAM education (Science, Technology, Engineering, the Arts, and Mathematics), Design-Based Research (DBR), and the ADDIE (Analyze, Design, Develop, Implement, and Evaluate) inquiry-Based model, resulting in significant student performance outcomes. However, recent years have witnessed a decline in students' learning attitudes and critical thinking abilities, particularly when faced with unfamiliar interdisciplinary domains. If students seek solutions directly from instructors without prior self-reflection, there is a risk of needing more proactive learning and problem-solving skills. Even students possessing specific technical expertise or creative ideas may lower their goals or abandon projects when encountering difficulties, which is unfortunate. Considering diverse student backgrounds and individual cognition and capabilities variations, some find tasks too simple, while others perceive them as overly challenging. The outcomes of practical project work, overall learning effectiveness, and teaching quality may significantly impact, placing a heavier burden on educators. In this study, with guided adaptive teaching designs, students can handle rushed and extensive learning when faced with extended challenges related to specialized projects, reducing efficiency. Therefore, through differentiated instructional activities and guided group work, fostering peer discussions, mutual assistance, and communication skills is crucial for students to develop the ability to adapt dynamically. The transformation of the traditional teacher's role from an authoritative, one-way instructor to an interactive coaching role, along with adaptive grouping guidance, is essential. This approach, complemented by relevant soft skills, industry practices, and technology tool applications, assists students in building future-ready capabilities through team communication and collaborative work. Efforts are also directed toward enhancing student engagement, reducing cognitive load, and maximizing the benefits of self-directed learning. A central focus is reinforcing students' overall participation and capabilities in engagement and active learning.

2 Literature Review

2.1 Problem-Based Learning/Project-Based Learning (PBL/PjBL)

In the past, students participating in Problem-Based Learning (PBL) and Project-Based Learning (PjBL) have acquired skills in problem definition, analysis, and project execution, including data collection, analysis, and synthesis. The purpose of PBL is not merely to solve predefined problems but rather to assist students in understanding problems, identifying learning needs, synthesizing relevant information, and applying it to the focused problem. Clear problem definition facilitates efficient learning interactions among group members and instructors. This type of focused problem-based learning effectively enhances professional competence and maintains the core ability for proactive learning in the face of rapid changes. PjBL, on the other hand, emphasizes understanding and exploring the structure of problems, and the resulting Knowledge Roadmap revolves around authentic problems, leading to solutions filled with various unknown possibilities. Mihardi and Bunawan [1] suggest that the PBL/PjBL model enhances students' design thinking and creativity while integrating feasibility assessments of relevant engineering technologies for commercial development. Although different, Chen et al. [2] propose that problem-oriented or project-oriented learning can complement and integrate into basic or advanced engineering education. Balram [3] argues that PBL or PjBL methods, being teacher-focused on specific student problems, benefit students who can independently solve problems. However, for relatively passive learners, there may be limitations in learning effectiveness. To encourage active learning, broaden knowledge content, and not solely rely on direct answers from instructors, considering the complex learning needs of modern students, traditional lecture-style learning and experiential learning alone may not be sufficiently compelling. Therefore, there is a need to incorporate more innovative teaching methods to enhance student learning, motivation, and engagement in a flexible learning process.

2.2 Design-Based Research (DBR) and ADDIE Inquiry-Based Teaching Model

Given that this course focuses on practical project work, it necessitates utilizing the Design Thinking (DT) framework to enhance student motivation and improve learning and teaching effectiveness. Zhang et al. [4] assert that the four stages of DBR, including Design, Testing, Evaluation, and Reflection, provide a hybrid research approach incorporating elements of Problem-Based Learning/Project-Based Learning (PBL/PjBL) and Inquiry-Based Learning (IBL). This method facilitates the development of learning theories and enhances educational practices. Students engage in practical exploration, propose solutions, and validate initial design concepts by establishing standard teaching processes and simulating real industrial scenarios in curriculum implementation. Regarding instructional course structures and planning, Spatioti et al. [5] highlight the ADDIE (Analysis, Design, Develop, Implement, Evaluate) inquiry-based teaching framework and process as a systematic approach for developing instructional methods and training course development models. The ADDIE model spans the entire process from analysis, design, development, and implementation to evaluation, integrating instructional methods, curriculum, and tool development for effective teaching practices and research methods with feedback. Baharuddin [6] applied the ADDIE model in teaching, utilizing surveys and test data analysis, revealing that students achieved a high level of practical skills (80%), a success rate of 90%, and an overall learning outcome average of 85 points. Almelhi [7] demonstrated significant improvement through the ADDIE model, employing pre-tests, post-tests, and comparative analysis between experimental and control groups. Therefore, incorporating DBR and the ADDIE inquiry-based teaching model can enhance learning outcomes and achieve preset objectives. Combining various inquiry-based teaching methods can improve traditional teacher-centered knowledge transmission, providing solutions to real-life problems and enabling the comprehensive application of acquired knowledge and skills. Meanwhile, it enhances students' attitudes and learning abilities [8–12].

3 Instructional Design and Planning

Due to the practical nature of the hands-on project-based course, an inquiry-based teaching model can be employed to guide students in exploring problems and developing solutions. Includes selecting project topics, assessing feasibility, setting design objectives, prototyping, testing functionality, and presenting outcomes. Therefore, the course adopts the Design-Based Research (DBR) method in practical education. It integrates the ADDIE inquiry-based teaching framework through a developmental and iterative process, encompassing the entire course delivery process from analysis, design, development, and implementation to evaluation. It involves rigorous data collection, reliability, supporting research results' objectivity, reliability, and validity, and integrating quantitative and qualitative aspects. The course involves practical exploration and employs a case study approach. Collaborative evaluation with industry experts is conducted to assess students' practical skills, providing timely guidance and converging design directions. The goal is to instill new, progressive, and industrially applicable values in students' work. The four-stage instructional design research process of the DBR method and the five-stage inquiry-based teaching framework of ADDIE is shown in Table 1.

This study ensures the structural, deep, and comprehensive nature of the course content and predictability of learning outcomes; the emphasis is not only on understanding whether students can do something but also on enhancing the effectiveness of teaching and learning through processes such as investigation, exploration, inquiry, questioning, research, seeking answers, and iterative scrutiny. During the preparation phase, teachers establish theoretical foundations, guide students in executing designs based on development strategies, and explore problem-solving effectiveness through practical exercises and design adjustments. This process validates the connection between theory and practice, culminating in disseminating outcomes—comparing before and after learning plans to assess the effectiveness of instructional design. At the course's beginning, students must contemplate their learning motivation and set learning goals, addressing questions such as: Why take this course? What do they hope to learn? Are they confident in achieving preset goals by the end of the semester? After completion, do you conduct to determine goal attainment? Moreover, do a self-analysis to explain unmet goals and propose methods for resolving future learning challenges.

The course is held at the Product Integration Design and Pilot Production Center of the Mold and Die Engineering Department, National Kaohsiung University of Science and Technology. The course focuses on design thinking, covering multi-model extension, multi-method guidance, and whole-approach integration. The 18-week course is divided into five phases for teaching adjustments:

1. Interdisciplinary Knowledge Exploration (Weeks 1–3): Analyzed students' knowledge in product design, creative engineering, mold design, and electromechanical integration through collaboration with industry experts. Initial surveys explore the impact of prior knowledge and self-learning experiences.
2. Project Planning and Execution Inquiry (Weeks 4–6): Design activities based on students' understanding, preferences, and goals. Students refine project topics, considering past outcomes. The investigation includes the impact on learning for students with different experience levels.
3. Communication and Coordination Skills Inquiry (Weeks 7–10): Adjusting based on weekly feedback and exploring industrial cases if there is a positive interaction. Inquiry involves understanding the impact of course content on learning and adjusting accordingly.
4. Implementation and Analysis Skills Inquiry (Weeks 11–14): Collaborative teaching aids project implementation. Students create prototypes, share suggestions, and conduct tests. The investigation includes the impact on learning through surveys and adjustments.
5. Self-Learning Mode Inquiry (Weeks 15–18): Conduct a comprehensive learning and teaching effectiveness analysis and seek confirmation of preset goal standards through relevant competitions. Students reflect on design principles, and teachers promote teaching effectiveness through industry-academia cooperation. The investigation includes assessing the impact on learning and achieving preset goals.

Table 1. Research Process and Implementation Emphasis of DBR Design-Based Research Method and ADDIE Inquiry-Based Teaching Framework

DBR Design-Based Research Method		ADDIE Inquiry-Based Teaching Framework
Phase 1: Design (Curriculum Planning and Design):	In the preparation stage, collaboration between teachers and industry experts initiates curriculum activity planning, focusing on practical industrial applications. Students are instructed to establish a theoretical foundation and prerequisite knowledge before guiding them to generate creative ideas based on real-world industrial problems	**Analyze (Problem Hypothesis and Analysis):** Conduct an initial pre-course survey to investigate students' relevant prerequisite knowledge, including experiences in project work and teamwork. Explore the impact of related prerequisite knowledge and self-learning experiences on learning
Phase 2: Testing (Execution and Testing):	In the execution stage, students engage in discussions based on selected practical project topics. They refer to past project outcomes and award-winning examples, leading to adjustments in project topics and execution scopes. Feasibility assessments are discussed	**Design (Activity Design):** Based on students' understanding of the course outline, learning preferences, and preset goals, design course activities. For those without a foundation or experience, establish basic skills and team-building, including project procedures and adaptive team roles. Investigate the impact of course content on students with and without a foundation or experience and how to adjust course content accordingly

(*continued*)

Table 1. (*continued*)

DBR Design-Based Research Method		ADDIE Inquiry-Based Teaching Framework
Phase 3: Evaluation (Assessment and Validation):	During the evaluation stage, collaborative teaching involving teachers, industry experts, teaching assistants, and peer interactions assists in project implementation and confirms improvement effectiveness	**Develop (Development of Interactive Teaching Practices):** Through course implementation and weekly student feedback, understand students' learning progress. Adjust interactive teaching practices based on student learning conditions. Investigate the impact of course content on different student groups and adjust accordingly
Phase 4: Reflection (Reflection and Expansion):	In the promotion stage, students reflect on design principles to enhance solution improvement. Teachers promote the effectiveness of practical project work teaching practices through industry-academia cooperation	**Implement (Pre- and Post-course Surveys and Rolling Teaching Adjustments):** Through course implementation and weekly student feedback, understand students' learning conditions. Conduct rolling teaching adjustments based on initial and midterm surveys. Investigate the impact of course content through pre- and post-course surveys and rolling teaching adjustments

4   Learning Assessment Tools and Methods

The assessment methods for learning are divided into quantitative and qualitative assessments. Quantitative assessment encompasses academic learning outcomes, proactive learning motivation, learning attitudes and interests, and problem-solving abilities. Pre- and post-tests are conducted to assess learning, followed by a comparative analysis. Qualitative assessment involves in-depth student interviews, serving as one of the indicators for measuring teaching effectiveness. This study alleviates the burden on teachers during assessments and enhances objectivity; this project adopts a 360-degree assessment model, including self-assessment, peer assessment, and industry expert co-assessment.; this project adopts a 360-degree assessment model, including self-assessment, peer assessment, and industry expert co-assessment. The learning outcome assessment tools employed consist of weekly individual and group reflections, team oral and outcome presentations, Google online surveys, and online/offline feedback interactions through the course Line group (pre-course notifications, post-course supplementary materials, course activity records). This approach allows for seamless integration of remote learning for confirmed cases in home isolation, running concurrently with physical classroom teaching, as illustrated in Fig. 1.

Pre-teaching and after-school supplemental materials

Learning logs for weekly program activities

Distance Learning and classroom Instruction

Fig. 1. Online and Offline Feedback Interaction

The research employed the Likert scale as a research tool and utilized Google online survey forms. The study focused on fourth-year students majoring in Mold Engineering at the National Kaohsiung University of Science and Technology. The class taught in the previous year served as the control group, while the class taught in the current academic year was designated as the experimental group. Assessments were conducted at the beginning, midterm, and end of the semester, along with comparing teaching and learning experiences before and after the intervention, aiming to validate this instructional study's objectivity, reliability, and validity. For example, students were required to contemplate their learning motivations and set learning objectives at the outset of the course, addressing questions such as: Why did they choose to enroll in this course? What do they hope to learn from this course? Do they have confidence in achieving the predetermined goals by the end of the semester? After the semester concludes, assessments are conducted to determine goal achievement. Students are then expected to conduct self-analysis, explaining the reasons for unmet goals and proposing how the methods learned can be applied to address future learning challenges.

Setting the scope of research objectives encompasses: 1. Problem hypotheses and analysis, 2. Course activity design, 3. Development of interactive teaching practices, 4. Pre-and-post-test questionnaire surveys with rolling teaching adjustments, 5. They are learning and teaching effectiveness checks, among others. The relevant research inquiries cover self-efficacy, learning attitudes, learning motivations and preferences, peer evaluations, problem-solving abilities, online and offline feedback, and the construction of a network-based assessment. Through this, a comparison of differences in pre- and post-learning assessments (at the beginning, midterm, and end) is conducted. It includes assessments of learning conditions (student self-assessment, peer assessment within the team, assessment by other groups), learning problem checks (weekly homework reports and teaching performance feedback), and other vital points. After considering assistant teachers' and industry mentors' co-assessment, the teacher integrates and comprehensively evaluates students' overall learning outcomes and then provides an objective assessment score.

Additionally, from the content of students' final project presentations, quantitative assessments of professional technical hard skills and qualitative assessments of workplace soft skills are conducted. Each group member must also reflect and self-evaluate throughout the learning process, providing mutual action recommendations through student self-assessment and peer assessment forms. In the peer evaluation process, effective mutual care is encouraged among group members. Group members propose reward suggestions for those who perform well, while those whose performance falls below expectations receive joint care and encouragement from group members and teachers. This approach enhances students' learning motivation, particularly after the distribution of work tasks within the group, leading to an increase in each student's self-perceived competence.

Through this 360-degree assessment method, teachers provide recommendations on the creativity and execution of learning outcomes for each group's proposed problem analysis and solutions, rather than solely relying on numerical scores. In addition to strengthening students' professional competence, this approach cultivates interdisciplinary professionals, aligns with relevant industries, and establishes interactive mechanisms. Furthermore, from the practical courses of this curriculum, adaptive development of students' expertise can be observed and identified, fostering students' abilities in logical thinking and hands-on learning. The emphasis is on diverse learning effectiveness assessments through hands-on implementation.

In terms of qualitative assessments, a radar chart diagnosis assists students in career exploration and evaluates learning process effectiveness. For quantitative assessments, end-of-term project presentation score data diagnoses provide students with references for pursuing either diversified (breadth) or focused (depth) learning, contributing to their future career development adaptability. This data can also serve as a basis for industry talent development and recruitment assessments. Collaborative teaching with industry partners allows for the adjustment of courses and learning content based on industry needs, addressing issues such as the gap between academia and industry. The grading breakdown is as follows: regular assignments and feedback account for 40%, midterm presentations account for 30%, and final presentations account for 30%.

5   Results and Discussion

This course conducts a three-stage analysis of learning outcomes: 1. Learning confidence and learning effectiveness, 2. Learning and interaction patterns, and 3. Learning objectives and evaluation. The previous year (2022), Academic Year 110, served as the control group with a class size of n = 46. The current year (2023), Academic Year 111, represents the experimental group with a class size of n = 41, as explained below:

1. Learning Confidence and Learning Effectiveness Comparative Analysis: As shown in Table 2, the analysis of learning confidence is presented first. Before the course, in response to whether they possessed the prerequisite knowledge for this course, the control group had 65.3% strongly agreeing or agreeing, which increased to 87.0% by the midterm and reached a high of 93.4% by the end of the term. The research experimental group had 54.9% strongly agreeing or agreeing initially, rising to 97.7% by the midterm, and all members fully agreed by the end of the term. Additionally, in the analysis of learning objectives, the control group had 97.8% of students who initially believed they could apply what they learned, slightly decreasing to 95.7% by midterm, and all fully agreed after rolling adjustments to the course content. The research experimental group, from the beginning to the midterm and the end of the term, unanimously agreed that they could apply what they learned. From the comparative analysis of learning confidence and effectiveness in these two-course offerings (Fig. 2), in the first offering, the control group consisted of fourth-year students in the academic year 110. Due to less experience in previous relevant course designs and the establishment of prerequisite knowledge, students needed more confidence in learning effectiveness. The research experimental group, composed of fourth-year students in the academic year 111, benefited from previous relevant course offerings and adjustments made by the teaching faculty in teaching methods and content. In the second offering, students with references from their seniors' works and experiences showed a higher level of learning confidence and motivation, with 95.3% strongly agreeing or agreeing compared to the previous academic year (93.4%). Furthermore, when comparing students' satisfaction with the learning outcomes regarding the applicability of their knowledge to future careers all students expressed high satisfaction.

2. Learning and Interaction Patterns Comparative Analysis: The learning patterns of students in the research experimental group for the current academic year are similar to those of the previous academic year. Students tend to emphasize hands-on practice and request instructors to use examples and provide supplementary reference materials. The teaching approach preferred by students involves using examples as the main method, supplemented by reference materials and hands-on practice. Initially, 95.4% favored this approach, slightly decreasing to 93.0% by midterm, and maintaining the same level by the end of the term. The PjBL & STEAM diversified interactive learning model, which students were initially unfamiliar with, gained popularity over time. By midterm, 83.7% of students liked this learning and teaching model and believed it enhanced their learning interest. By the end of the term, the satisfaction with this learning and teaching model, along with the perception that it enhances learning interest, increased to 93.0%. The remaining 7.0% found it acceptable and not affecting their learning interest, with all students expressing satisfaction with this teaching model. Although initially, 4.6% preferred traditional one-way textbook teaching, favored static learning, or preferred self-directed learning, as some students were not accustomed to the open-ended self-research learning model, 7% continued to use textbooks. In terms of interactive learning modes, initially, all students favored cooperative group work. However, by midterm, 83.7% were willing to collaborate

in a team, with 32.7% wanting to lead the team, and nearly half (46.5%) preferring to be team members without the desire to take the lead. While willing to engage in team activities, 16.3% still preferred independent work. Similar proportions were observed by the end of the term, mainly because many students lacked ideas and were not proactive, exhibiting a relatively passive approach.

3. Learning objectives and evaluation Comparative Analysis: Regarding learning objectives, in the previous academic year, the control group, at the beginning of the term, had 73.9% of students confident in achieving the preset goal of a grade B (81–90) or above. By midterm, the proportion of students confident and achieving the preset goal decreased to 69.6%. Other students believed that, even if they had not yet reached the standard, they were still confident they could do so by the end of the term. By the end of the term, 71.7% of students believed they could achieve the instructional preset goal (grade B) or thought they could achieve it in the future. The final actual grades of B or above were achieved by 76.4%, with a class average of 81.1 points. Comparatively, for the current academic year's research experimental group, at the beginning of the term, 86.0% of students were confident in achieving the preset goal of a grade B (81–90) or above. By midterm, the proportion of students confident and achieving the preset goal slightly decreased to 76.7%. Other students believed that, even if they had not yet reached the standard, they were still confident they could do so by the end of the term. By the end of the term, 79.0% of students believed they could achieve the instructional preset goal (grade B) or thought they could achieve it in the future. The final actual grades of B or above were achieved by 81.4%, with a class average of 86.0 points, surpassing the overall learning objectives of the previous year. In addition to aligning with students' grade predictions at the beginning of the term and exceeding their initially set goals, the course achieved the instructional practice goals set.

1. Learning Confidence 1 (LC1): Before taking this course, I believed that I possessed the foundational knowledge required for learning in this course.
2. Learning Confidence 2 (LC2): From the beginning to the midterm, the foundational knowledge I acquired has benefited my learning in this course.
3. Learning Confidence 3 (LC3): After a semester, I confirm that the foundational knowledge I previously acquired has helped me learn this course.
4. Learning Effectiveness 1 (LE1): Before taking this course, I knew that attending it would enable me to apply the knowledge gained in practical situations in the future.
5. Learning Effectiveness 2 (LE2): From the beginning to the middle of the semester, I learned that the content could be applied to future career planning.
6. Learning Effectiveness 3 (LE3): After one semester, I confirmed that the learning outcomes could apply to future career planning.

Table 2. Comparative Analysis of Learning Confidence and Learning Effectiveness before and after the Three Stages of Learning

		Beginning		Midterm		End	
		LC1	LE1	LC2	LE2	LC1	LE2
Control Group (n = 46)	Strongly Agree	28.3%	35.5%	43.5%	47.1%	54.3%	58.6%
	Agree	37.0%	61.3%	43.5%	50.0%	39.1%	41.4%
	Neutral	26.1%	3.2%	10.9%	2.9%	6.5%	
	Disagree	8.7%		2.2%			
	Strongly Disagree						
Experimental Group (n = 41)	Strongly Agree	20.9%	53.3%	62.8%	55.8%	58.1%	65.1%
	Agree	34.9%	34.9%	34.9%	39.5%	37.2%	34.9%
	Neutral	39.5%	9.3%	2.3%	4.7%	2.3%	
	Disagree	4.7%	2.3%			2.3%	
	Strongly Disagree						

In addition to the quantitative analysis mentioned above, qualitative analysis is primarily presented as word clouds. This qualitative analysis is derived from students' weekly assignments and feedback from three surveys, including aspects such as learning motivation and satisfaction (Fig. 2), desired future learning content (Fig. 3), strategies to overcome learning obstacles and achieve preset goals (Fig. 4), as well as related suggestions or reflections (Fig. 5).

Fig. 2. Learning Motivation and Satisfaction

我希望以後能不靠複製 個人認為像現在的教學模式就非常棒 在未來自動化業發展 就業後學以致用 因為自己家裡有田地 未來想更精進微機電的知識 步進馬達 但是成效不是很好 這些所學可以讓我有更多的幫助 幾年前有發自動灑水的系統 晶片有可能是感測器的問題 經過這一學期 對於未來進入機電程式相關行業時 目前所學大多都是plc與arduino的程式語言寫法 自動化 可以的話想學關於c語言相關的程式基本結構的學習 植物成長也會變好 這學期的課程操作大部分是把原由本的程式複製上去 在稍微配個線就能結束了 自己寫出一些好玩的東西 若是有機會自然也挺希望編寫程式碼也可以更加了解 但是有時過多的東西反而很難吸收 希望可以自己組合創作出新的作品等

Fig. 3. Desired Future Learning Content

雖說大多都是單個零件故障的問題 有些地方是沒有搞懂的 同學在討論的時候 浪費時間 同常檢查 遍後才開始更換零組件 Win 明明接線沒問題 還需要專研學習 我認為至少可以準備三副來備用 自行學習 未來遇到這些問題之前會好好確認一下程式與程式之間的相容性與學習更穩定的除錯 遇到電腦作業系統或是函數庫未安裝完全或版本不同等相容性問題 不要一次性同時裝太多函數庫與程式以免除錯困難花費更多時間找問題 要多加練習 這學期大部分遇到的問題都是感應不良或是配件原本就損壞 跟著老師進度走 不然每次都因為這樣搞很久 然後無法作動 學長 有些程式內容看不太懂 遇到問題最多的就是 程式老師的 導致在運行中不順利

Fig. 4. Strategies to Overcome Learning Obstacles and Achieve Preset Goals

尤其是人臉辨識的部分讓我蠻驚奇的 如沒問題再來添購教材與授課 因有發生不少與學生電腦之間的相容性問題或是程式版本不相容 下次關於新東西例如人臉辨識 謝謝 閱讀 但是 謝謝老師 原以為那是高科技 Ttgo等的操作版與程式 這個課程讓我收穫很多 居然能自己實做

Fig. 5. Related Suggestions or Reflections

6 Conclusion

After implementing the PjBL & STEAM teaching model, a survey explored its impact on student interest. Results show students highly appreciate this innovative approach, with adaptability starting at 86.0%, slightly decreasing to 83.7% at midterm, and increasing again to 93.0% by term-end. While 7.0% find it challenging, they can still accept the method without losing interest. In terms of interaction, students preferred real-time engagement with the teacher, but at midterm, 9.3% preferred privacy, rising to 14.0% by term-end, possibly due to information overload. Regarding assessment tools, 95.3% initially favored no exams, with 48.8% desiring diversified grading. By midterm, 62.8% sought flexibility due to ongoing group adjustments, slightly decreasing to 58.1% by term-end—some still preferred exams (4.7%). In self-assessment, students solve problems independently before seeking help from peers or teachers, a consistent approach.

The course, integrating PjBL, STEAM, and P-TECH with DBR and ADDIE methods, shows positive impacts. Findings, shareable with stakeholders, highlight improved industry-academia collaboration, addressing the learning-application gap and enhancing students' employability. The model proves feasible, significantly advancing students' technical and vocational skills.

References

1. Mihardi, S., Bunawan, W.: Analyze instrument for improved visualization creativity in learning physics with matlab software using PjBL and KWL. Adv. Soc. Sci. Res. J. **4**(17) (2017)
2. Chen, J., Gao, F., Kong, L., Cui, L.: Study on teaching methods of fundamental electrical courses in engineering education. In: 2018 5th International Conference on Industrial Engineering and Applications (ICIEA), pp. 515–519. IEEE, April 2018
3. Balram, S.: Teaching and learning pedagogies in higher education geographic information science. GIScience teaching and learning perspectives, pp. 1–8 (2019)
4. Zhang, X., Wang, Y., & Sharma, S. (2021). Design and analysis of flipped classroom experiment teaching based on DBR in information technology environment. International Journal of System Assurance Engineering and Management, 1–8
5. Spatioti, A.G., Kazanidis, I., Pange, J.: A comparative study of the ADDIE instructional design model in distance education. Information **13**(9), 402 (2022)
6. Baharuddin, B.: ADDIE model application promoting interactive multimedia. In: IOP Conference Series: Materials Science and Engineering, vol. 306, No. 1, p. 012020. IOP Publishing (2018)
7. Almelhi, A.M.: Effectiveness of the ADDIE model within an E-learning environment in developing creative writing in EFL students. Engl. Lang. Teach. **14**(2), 20–36 (2021)
8. Chen, C.H., Chen, C.Y.: Instructional approaches on science performance, attitude and inquiry ability in a computer-supported collaborative learning environment. Turkish Online J. Educ. Technol.-TOJET **11**(1), 113–122 (2012)
9. Spronken-Smith, R., Bullard, J.O., Ray, W., Roberts, C., Keiffer, A.: Where might sand dunes be on Mars? engaging students through inquiry-based learning in geography. In: Active Learning and Student Engagement, pp. 72–87. Routledge (2013)

10. Ishartono, N., Nurcahyo, A., Waluyo, M., Razak, R.A., Sufahani, S.F., Hanifah, M.: GeoGebra-based flipped learning model: an alternative panacea to improve students' learning independency in online mathematics learning. J. Res. Adv. Math. Educ. **7**(3), 178–195 (2022)
11. Bai, S., Hew, K.F., Gonda, D.E., Huang, B., Liang, X.: Incorporating fantasy into gamification promotes student learning and quality of online interaction. Int. J. Educ. Technol. High. Educ. **19**(1), 1–26 (2022)
12. Hanna, A., Conner, L., Sweeney, T.A.: Enhancing employability and e-business capacities for Arabic-speaking residents of Australia through START online training. Social Science Protocaols **3**, 1–18 (2020)

Spontaneous Theory of Mind
for Artificial Intelligence

Nikolos Gurney[1]($\boxtimes$)(iD), David V. Pynadath[1,2](iD), and Volkan Ustun[1](iD)

[1] Institute for Creative Technologies, University of Southern California,
Los Angeles 90094, USA
{gurney,pynadath,ustun}@ict.usc.edu
[2] Computer Science Department, University of Southern California,
Los Angeles 90007, USA
http://ict.usc.edu/

Abstract. Existing approaches to Theory of Mind (ToM) in Artificial
Intelligence (AI) overemphasize prompted, or cue-based, ToM, which
may limit our collective ability to develop Artificial Social Intelligence
(ASI). Drawing from research in computer science, cognitive science, and
related disciplines, we contrast prompted ToM with what we call spontaneous ToM—reasoning about others' mental states that is grounded in
unintentional, possibly uncontrollable cognitive functions. We argue for
a principled approach to studying and developing AI ToM and suggest
that a robust, or general, ASI will respond to prompts *and* spontaneously
engage in social reasoning.

Keywords: Theory of Mind · Artificial Social Intelligence · Human
Cognition · Human-AI Interaction

1 Introduction

The ability to represent the content and state of each other's minds, commonly
referred to as *Theory of Mind* (ToM) [39], underpins much of human social
cognition. It is theorized to take part in cognitive tasks as diverse as planning how
to cheer somebody up who got stuck in traffic [25] and complex financial decision
making [6] (see also [57] in which they suggest its lack may be instrumental in
contrasting behaviors, such as bullying). With much of human social cognition
hinging on ToM, it is unsurprising that AI researchers see it as a possible solution
to many hard problems in artificial social intelligence (ASI). Existing work in this
space focuses on deliberate (prompted) rather than spontaneous (unprompted)
ToM. In this theoretical contribution, we consider spontaneous ToM's role in
humans and how a similar ability for AI could revolutionize work in ASI.

The idea that people maintain internal representations of each other's minds
is by no means new. Ancient philosophies, such as Platonism [13] and Confu-
cianism [40], directly address social reasoning that matches modern definitions
of ToM. It appears later during the Renaissance when philosophers, such as

M. Kurosu and A. Hashizume (Eds.): HCII 2024, LNCS 14684, pp. 60–75, 2024.
https://doi.org/10.1007/978-3-031-60405-8_5

Descartes [46], considered the ability to represent other minds. And, of course, it has a place in contemporary research, much of which is founded on seminal work that examined primate ToM [39]. The accepted definition for ToM, the ability to ascribe mental states to others and use those ascriptions for behavior predictions [21], stems from this research. The term *theory of mind* comes from the idea that we develop an explicit theory as part of the underlying cognitive process for representing minds. This theory-theory is far from the only explanation. For example, other researchers have posited models that function based on simulations [16] and that rely on the presence of a specific module for social cognition [9] (which may or may not rely on the development of explicit social theories). AI researchers have adapted many of these models for agents of all types, from virtual agents to robots [20, 21].

Extensive experimentation supports the various models and theories, which, at a high level, can be bifurcated into two categories: those that prompt ToM and those that do not. The quintessential ToM study, the Sally-Anne Test or False Belief Task (FTB), relies on a prompt: Participants observe a short skit that portrays a character, Sally, hiding a marble and another character, Anne, moving it in her absence. The key question, which is also a prompt to the participants, that tests ToM is, "Where will Sally look for her marble?" [1, 67]. Many studies of ToM in human-computer interactions rely on the basic Sally-Anne test paradigm (e.g., [37]). However, not all human cognition studies rely on prompts of ToM reasoning. For example, instead of asking participants for a particular action or explanation, researchers observe behaviors, such as gaze duration, to study *spontaneous* ToM. A typical finding of these studies is that participants' gaze at a scenario is statistically longer when their beliefs differ from a character's (typically false) beliefs [36, 54].

Actual spontaneous and prompted instances of ToM differ considerably from the common experimental paradigms. For example, while standing in line to purchase some goods, a person may spontaneously construct a model of the person in front of them which explains the items they are buying, e.g., they just reached a significant career milestone and are celebrating by treating themselves. Similarly, the person may have a friend whisper a prompt in their ear that triggers an entirely different model, e.g., "That item is so indulgent, how wasteful!" Despite this prompt, the observer may still come to the same conclusion. They also may conclude something more cohesive with their friend's suggestion. We believe there is more than a nuanced difference between these scenarios *and* the difference matters to the development of artificial social intelligence capable of similar reasoning. The observer may not be another person but an AI-powered shopping assistant and the friend, the developer of the AI. In the former case, the shopping assistant might not say anything, but in the latter, it might chime in about budget constraints. The normative response hinges on the actual dynamics of the purchase event, but getting it wrong could sour a celebration or lead to an account overdraft.

Our interpretation of the AI literature suggests that most ToM-enabled agents rely on models of prompted rather than spontaneous ToM. That is, they need explicit, pre-identified cues to know when they should activate their ToM.

We remain agnostic about which approach is "best" or "optimal," however, the overreliance on prompted ToM reasoning may leave AI researchers unable to definitively state whether a system does or does not have ToM—just like psychologists assumed that people with autism spectrum disorder did not have rich ToM until they started testing for spontaneous ToM [54]. Indeed, evidence of this is already emerging in the study of the social reasoning abilities of large language models [26,62].

Based on our literature review, we lay out principles for studying ASI, take a stance on core features of robust (human-level) ASI, and highlight significant challenges to its realization. To better understand the current state-of-the-art in ASI, we need to start with a review of the psychological study of ToM.

2   Theory of Mind

The ability to ascribe mental states to others and use those ascriptions for predicting or understanding behavior, i.e., Theory of Mind, is a core function of human social cognition. ToM helps us predict others' intentions and may play a critical role in developing and maintaining other cognitive abilities, such as emotional intelligence [52]. Moreover, its role is so prominent in cognition that we seemingly cannot help engaging it: People routinely ascribe mental states to inanimate objects, including computational systems, even when they are well aware of the objects' inanimacy [7]. This reality makes it unsurprising that we want intelligent systems to mimic, if not engage directly in, the same level of ToM reasoning as we do, i.e., have ASI. Considerable effort has gone into realizing this potential; an understanding of the modern research into ToM abilities will enable us to both frame the state-of-the-art ASI and explain why some researchers argue that building machines capable of thinking like humans necessitates engineering in intuitive theory usage, such as ToM [28].

2.1   History

Premack and Woodruff's research into chimpanzee social intelligence [39] is commonly cited as the modern foundation of ToM research. They argue that the proper view of ToM is as a *theory* because it involves making predictions about mental states that are not directly observable. Such prediction-making, they posit, requires a model founded on assumptions about how minds work. Diving into Premack and Woodruff's research will lead a reader back to famous research by Heider and Simmel that examines interpretations of apparent social interactions in non-human agents, specifically geometric shapes [23]. Their experiment involved two-dimensional shapes that "moved" in and out of a rectangle, "collided" or "interacted" with each other, and, in so doing, displayed behavior that study participants interpreted as being social. Premack and Woodruff's research also has forward links to seminal work on the emergence of ToM in childhood development that gave us the prototype for empirical studies of ToM, the false belief test [1,67]. A cascade of research flowed from this early work, leading to a rich debate around the ToM cognitive process and how to study it.

2.2 Perspectives on the Theory of Mind Process

Carving up the ToM body of research into meaningful divisions is not an easy task. Researchers, ourselves included [20], typically divide the field based on distinct theoretical positions. A common starting point is to sort research into theory-theory and simulation-theory bins. Theory-theory states that people develop folk or naive theories to explain their social world through science-like experimentation that transpires during social interaction [53,67]. Simulation theory states that people accomplish ToM reasoning by simulating the cognitive state of others within their own mind [16]. Each theoretical bin contains more precise theories describing the emergence and function of ToM. For example, the child-scientists perspective argues that the scientific method is a blueprint of ToM development and function [14,15].

Theories within both camps (and some that do not fit nicely into either) have contributed to advancing AI ToM [20,21]. However, we believe another distinction between approaches to studying ToM is equally meaningful to the development of ASI: ToM as a spontaneous mental process versus a prompted mental process. As will become clear, we use the term spontaneous to highlight the uncontrollable, often inexplicable, nature of thoughts related to the mental states of others. We shied away from the term unprompted because, we believe, it overemphasizes the role of otherwise unrelated stimuli in the ToM reasoning process. This logic is also why we landed on prompted: other terms, such as intentional or deliberate, fail to capture the role of external stimuli in the process.

Spontaneous Reasoning. We define spontaneous reasoning as the set of unintentional mental processes that give rise to spontaneous thoughts. Spontaneous thoughts are those that happen seemingly uncontrollably and without reason [34]. Spontaneous reasoning, albeit under various guises, has a storied history of scientific inquiry. After a long run of prompting study participants to explain the higher-order mental processes that gave rise to particular cognitive states, researchers began to question whether people actually have access to internal mental states at all [35]. Even though psychologists have gone to considerable lengths to refine their methods for eliciting cognitive processes from people (e.g., [17,18]), it remains the case that there is no objective way to verify the veracity of reports on cognitive processes or know if a person is, in fact, accessing them [8]. This methodological gap means that, at least given the current state of cognitive science, there is not a well-founded method for uncovering the spontaneous reasoning that underpins a given thought—including those related to the belief states of others.

Viewing ToM as spontaneous, i.e., a mental process grounded in unintentional, possibly uncontrollable cognitive functions, forces a reconsideration of existing theories, models, and empirical approaches. Consider theory-theory explanations. Having direct access to one's thoughts is implicit in the idea that children function as scientists experimenting with models of cognition to explain the reasoning of others. This implication exists because a person needs to isolate projections of others' mental states from their own mental states. Although they may not view it in this fashion, ToM researchers have acknowledged this reality, at least in their empirical methods: Children with greater inhibitory control of their cognition perform better in classic ToM tasks [4]. This insight is an interpretation of an experimental phenomenon in which children report reality rather than what a person with a false belief believes. Given sufficient inhibitory control, a child can repress the urge to report on reality and provide the modal answer that indicates they "have" ToM. This observation does not give much insight into the cognitive functions underpinning the child's social intelligence. It just confirms that spontaneous reasoning can impact their social reasoning abilities. Moreover, it does not verify the emergence of ToM abilities, as they may have existed before inhibitory control was sufficient but hidden by the overwhelming impulse to report on reality.

Prompted Reasoning. Much like spontaneous reasoning, the psychology research community has long recognized the role of prompts, usually studied in the form of explicit questions or cues, in cognition. This recognition extends to the relatively small body of work committed to ToM, but it did go underappreciated for some time. Early work documenting the emergence of ToM capabilities noted how providing a mother with cues for reporting their child's speech abilities may have resulted in different responses. However, it did not consider how prompts to the children may impact utterances [3]. More significantly, prompts played a major role in research into the ToM abilities of autistic people. Much of this significant body of literature documents a high degree of correlation between deficits in ToM and autism spectrum disorder [1,10,22,38], however, this conclusion is increasingly doubted [12], in part due to its reliance on explicit prompts.

Referencing research from other domains of cognition can facilitate a better appreciation of prompts' possible impact on ToM. The role that prompts (and cues) can play in cognition is arguably understood thanks to research on memory. The long-established result in memory studies is that cues facilitate recall. For example, people are more likely to recall to-be-recalled words that are associated with cue words at the time of memory than to-be-recalled words without cue words or that were associated with the cue words after the initial memory event [61]. Endel Tulving later made the provocative argument that people do not actually forget some memories. Instead, the necessary triggering cue is lost [60]. This insight spawned troves of research studying how exactly prompts impact, even alter, memory. Most relevant to the study of ToM is the finding that prompts can create false memories [29,30]. Imagining an experience, such as a trip to Disney Land, can lead a person to believe that some part of the imagined scenario actually took place [2]. Another important insight is that the content of a cue can impact its effectiveness in generating the target memory [63].

It is reasonable to think of prompts as intentional, overt acts like giving a person a word to associate with a to-be-recalled word. In reality, prompts can lack intention and be covert. Asking a misbehaving child to consider how their actions may make another person act or feel is an example of an intentional, overt prompt intended to elicit a particular type of ToM reasoning. Overhearing two adults discuss the harm caused by another person's bad behavior may elicit the same ToM reasoning, but, in this case, the prompt was unintentional. In the case of ToM research, prompts that researchers unintentionally embedded in the experimental methods they used to study it, which we review below, contributed to them not accurately identifying when ToM emerges in childhood development. Once they recognized this oversight, researchers developed implicit ToM tasks to study spontaneous engagement in ToM reasoning.

2.3   Empirical Approaches to Studying Theory of Mind

Reviews of empirical approaches to studying ToM typically divide them into two categories: those with explicit and those with implicit requests for ToM reasoning, the latter of which researchers developed in response to criticisms about the former's ability to definitively detect the earliest examples of ToM in childhood [31]. The classic example of an explicit approach is the most well-known false belief test of ToM reasoning: the Sally-Anne test [1,67]. This test involves a small skit enacted by two dolls, Sally and Anne, followed by a simple question. Anne (and the child) see Sally hiding a marble in her basket and leaving the room. While Sally is away, Anne transfers the marble into her own box. Later, Sally returns to the room. A researcher then asks the child, "Where will Sally look for the marble?"

With the impact of prompts on cognition in mind, the fatal critique of the Sally-Anne test is obvious: Asking a child where Sally will look for the marble may prompt them to consider the wider context of the skit. Not only does the child need to realize that Sally *might* have a false belief (it may be the case Sally has a true belief because she knows Anne and predicted the stealing of the marble), but they need to recognize the demand of the researcher asking the question. Does the researcher expect a response demonstrating first-order beliefs (the modal response) or something richer?

In response to this and other criticisms, researchers developed implicit ToM tasks that do not require direct interaction with research. For example, eye-tracking and measures of gaze duration suggest that children as young as fifteen months are able to predict the belief states of others [36]. This and related experimentation build upon the violation-of-expectation method [11]. The prototypical violation-of-expectation design has a child watch a person repeatedly reaching for one of two toys (the target and decoy) that are always in the same locations, in theory teaching the child of a preference for the target, after which the locations of the toys are switched. The person then randomly reaches for the target in its new location or the decoy that is now in the target's former location, with the result being that children tend to gaze longer at instances of decoy reaches [68].

To elevate this design to a ToM test, Onishi and Baillargeon [36] had infants watch an actor hide a toy in one of two locations. Next, its location was changed. For some infants, the actor observed the change, thus maintaining a true belief. For other infants, the actor did not observe the change, thus developing a false belief. The critical result confirming ToM is longer gaze times when the actor held a false belief (they did). This design, however, has also come under intense scrutiny given its less-than-ideal replication performance [12,27].

A meta-criticism of ToM research, thanks to the success and reality of the various criticisms of ToM tests, is now common in the literature: Popular explicit and implicit tests of ToM abilities may only capture other, low-level social-cognitive processes [24,43]. To illustrate, consider the dot perspective task [47,48]. Participants see one of four scenes: two dots are in front of an avatar (alternatively, a rectangle or arrow) in a room, one on the forward wall and another on the side wall, or the dot on the side wall is behind their field of view (or the location of the rectangle or arrow). Critically, faster correct responses are recorded when the arrow or avatar's perspective matches the participants (both dots are in front) [48]. When there is a rectangle in place of the arrow or avatar, there is no difference in response times [47]. These combined results suggest that the dot perspective and related tasks are not studying Theory of Mind. Instead, they may only study other, low-level cognitive processes [24]. Summarily, there is not a widely accepted method for studying ToM, whether in children or adults, that lacks such fatal confounds.

3   Artificial Intelligence and Theory of Mind

Note that this review is not an exhaustive or systematic review of AI ToM research. It is a high-level treatment of important work related to developing artificial social intelligence capable of ToM. Knowing the current state of affairs in the psychological study of ToM allows us to frame the accomplishments of artificial intelligence research related to ToM. Unlike human psychology, where ToM is studied for its own sake, in AI spaces, it is typically studied in applied settings as a means of overcoming another computational challenge. Thus, it is most present in fields like human-computer interaction [20] and human-robot interaction [21], but not as a fundamental problem of computation (although cognitive scientists have approached it as a computational problem). In the computational spaces that do pursue ToM research, much of it is focused on the human components of interactions, asking questions such as do people perceive ToM capabilities in the computational agents (whether it is there or not) (e.g., [45] which documented similar neurological responses to human and computer opponents in the ultimatum game).

Rudimentary examples of systems capable of modeling mental states have existed for nearly five decades [33], but robust computational approaches to ToM only emerged early this century. Virtual agents that were increasingly human-like opened an opportunity for simulation work centered around predicting how people with differing perspectives and beliefs might interact with them. This research opportunity led to the development of PsychSim [32], a continually maintained platform that enables researchers to implement psychologically valid models of human behavior in virtual agents. The decision-theoretical capabilities of PsychSim allow it to model rich features of human cognition, including ToM

[42]. Researchers have used PsychSim to study topics in human-computer/robot interactions as varied as calibrating trust [66], disaster responses [41], and generating characters for interactive narratives that are capable of ToM [55,56].

Advances in machine learning (e.g., transformers [64]) and modern models of cognition (e.g., hierarchical Bayesian models [58]) have led to chatter about the possibility of developing human-level AI. Psychologists argue that in order to achieve this, computer scientists need to develop technologies beyond what is currently available [5,28]. In response, computer scientists have demonstrated just how close to higher-order human cognition machines can come. Researchers from Google's Deepmind and Brain, for example, developed a ToM neural network model capable of not only learning to model the behavior of other artificial agents but also of passing classic ToM tests (e.g., false belief tests) [44].

More recently, large language models have overtaken research in artificial intelligence and related fields. Our interests lie in whether they, or any other computational models, can represent the belief and belief-like states of others, i.e., can they achieve a theory of mind? If we only consider their ability to perform in standard false belief tests, then the answer may be yes. A large-scale, multimodal language model outperformed six-year-old humans, achieving 75% on 40 false belief tests [26]. Unfortunately for this model, trivial alterations to the tests undermine its performance [62], and it seems reasonable to assume that these alterations would not impact human performance. Additionally, even when they are able to arrive at the correct answer to a false belief test, large language models appear to lack an understanding of why it is the modal answer [59], meaning they lack a "theory" of mind beyond pure statistical associations. Researchers argue that this shortcoming may result from a lack of pragmatic representation, a feature for which state-of-the-art models still rely on explicit definitions [49].

Equally important to how researchers instantiate ToM in computational systems is how they test it—not unlike the case for humans. Most studies of computational ToM rely on some adaptation of a false belief test, and they are prompted studies—that is, the machines are explicitly asked to report on a hidden mental state. But, contingent on how one views training and validation, some approaches hint at spontaneous ToM.

Obviously, how we ask questions of and give cues to machine intelligence is markedly different from how we do the same with humans. In many ways, the prompts given to AI models of ToM are present in their design, training, and tasks. To illustrate a design impact on ToM, consider PsychSim [32,42]. PsychSim agents rely on behavioral policies for both their own actions and interpreting the actions of other agents. These policies are typically a bounded lookahead procedure that accounts for other agents' actions as well as environmental dynamics. By adjusting the parameterization of these models, researchers can capture different ToM abilities. In practice, adjusting a model's lookahead length is telling it how to execute its ToM reasoning about other agents. In a human setting, it is akin to telling people in a prisoner's dilemma how many rounds they will play, knowledge that will undoubtedly alter how they model each other's decision-making.

An alternative to endowing agents with predetermined models is allowing them to learn optimal parameterization from data [69], or more generally, what model best accounts for variance in behavioral data [44]. ToMnet [44], for example, posits an observer agent (which is a deep neural network) and policy-based agents. The latter execute their policies in simple grid-world environments, while the observer learns from their behavior. The observer has its own reward function which hinges on its ability to learn to represent multiple agents with differing policies, rewards, and parameterizations functioning in the grid-world. Critically, the observer agent has access during training and testing to the entire grid-world. This access allows it to embed end-to-end representations of behavior that it can later draw on when making ToM predictions. When considered in the context of the observer's reward function, this access is also explicitly prompting it about what to pay attention to. In effect, the observer only knows one type of question, so when presented with data, it answers that question (in this instance, what will a policy-based agent do next).

It is reasonable that computer scientists turn to psychology for ToM tasks. Human behavior, after all, is the source of our interest in ToM. Realizing human-level reasoning abilities in AI is the goal for many researchers, so naturally, they want to train, validate, and test their models just like psychologists test humans. Adopting test protocols from psychology, however, is a fraught practice. As noted, many of the tests are flawed. For example, the prototypical false belief test explicitly tells participants what behavior matters to the researcher and what answers are acceptable. In the case of humans, these details are implicitly negotiated through conversational norms, such as Gricean maxims [19], that dictate how we interact. In the case of AI, it is often the case that the systems must be engineered to perform a given task. In so doing, the prompts, along with any flawed reasoning, are inbuilt. This reality is excellently illustrated between the two large language model papers we cited above: Kosinski gave the model standard tests of ToM and concluded that the system either had ToM or the test was flawed [26]. Ullman perturbed the tests in minor ways, which he argues would not prove a challenge for children, and found that the model failed and concluded that it did not have ToM [62].

AI systems that are able to perform on classic ToM tests still tend to be relatively narrow intelligences. Most state-of-the-art systems still rely on human-defined models of social reasoning. This reliance limits their abilities: current models of ToM lack generalizability, particularly when considered from a computational resources perspective [20]. AI ToM models are also constrained by the data that they learned from. As Ullman pointed out, this challenge is surmountable to some extent by adding new training cases [62]. Ultimately, however, that does not appear to create intelligence with the same abilities for generalization as humans, just one that has 'seen' a lot of data, i.e., instances of a particular type of reasoning. Other domains, such as competitive video game models, more clearly illustrate this observation. Consider the state-of-the-art deep learning project AlphaStar, a model trained to excel in playing a particular game (Star-Craft II) [65]. Even though it is super-human in its abilities, humans who are able to generalize their strategies ultimately beat it. This illustration is analogous to the state of ToM and AI: although given enough data, models can perform at super-human levels, they remain brittle and are particularly prone to fail when confronted with tests that require generalization.

We believe a reasonable hypothesis is that the prompt and prompt-like archi-tectures researchers use when developing AI ToM models may inhibit general-ization. Moving away from prompt-based and towards spontaneous reasoning models might uncover new insights into AI and human ToM. Artificial social intelligence, just like human intelligence, should be capable of more than just prompted social reasoning. State-of-the-art research, however, exclusively studies instances of prompted ToM. Assuming that ASI is the goal of studying AI ToM, which appears to be the case for many research teams, then a more principled approach to its study is needed.

4   A Principled Approach to Studying Artificial Social Intelligence

Theory of Mind is just one component of a broader class of cognitive skills that help people navigate the social world. Reproducing our ability to (seemingly) read each others' minds in a machine is an alluring prospect. Unfortunately, not only does it appear that currently available computational resources are not sufficient, but the psychology is also incomplete. These hurdles, of course, do not mean AI ToM and ASI are not worth pursuing. However, a more principled approach could benefit our collective efforts, particularly since we cannot rely entirely on human psychology research to provide definitive answers about the phenomena we are working to replicate.

4.1   Consider How a Question Shapes the Answer

There is an art to asking questions, whether of other people or AI. Social psychol-ogists have long appreciated that how we ask a question can shape the answer we get from a respondent [51]. This appreciation stems from the observation that answering a question requires an understanding of the semantic meaning of the actual words *and* an appreciation of the intent of the questioner [50]. We believe the same general insight about asking questions applies to scientific research in that how a research question is asked can ultimately determine what answers are possible. For example, well-executed false belief tests can assess whether a child is capable of representing the belief state of another person, but does not directly answer the question of whether they have robust ToM and are capable of representing a rich set of mental states. The same is true of AI ToM. Research methods that rely on prompting for a response will generate answers that reflect the prompt(s), whereas research methods that rely on observation of sponta-neous ToM will generate answers that reflect the structure of the observation.

Both are valuable but can provide different answers about ToM. We believe that a foundational principle to any research is the consideration of how a question may shape the answer. Ullman has already demonstrated this in the LLM ToM space with his minor modifications to classic reasoning tasks that undermined the models' performance [62].

4.2   Focus on Definable Social Intelligence Skills

The research into human ToM is undoubtedly informative (else we would not have reviewed it here), but its prominent role in how we think about ASI may hinder success. Theory of Mind takes more than assessing whether somebody has a false belief—beliefs are just one of many mental states we predict about each other. Nevertheless, belief plays an outsized role in the study of ToM abilities. Similar to beliefs are the general class of mental phenomena, sometimes called propositional attitudes, that reflect how we view a given proposition. These belief-like states are arguably as important to our social cognition but spectacularly underrepresented in the ToM literature. To illustrate, consider the statement *student A is hoping for a good grade*, in which *hoping* is the propositional attitude. Like a belief, another person can represent this attitude and hold their own attitude about it, thus have ToM related to the mental state of hoping. A robust ASI will keep track of more than just beliefs; arguably, it will be able to maintain representations of the same mental phenomena as humans, including beliefs, hopes, desires, and more.

Theory of Mind eludes a consensus definition, possibly due to the related psychology research having a relatively narrow scope (i.e., focusing on beliefs rather than a more general ability). The lack of an accepted definition means that AI researchers are left to select, even invent, an operational definition of ToM that they can test their systems against. Formally defining the social intelligence skill in question is one principle we believe will yield quicker progress toward ASI. Formal definitions will facilitate such progress by improving our communication about the AI abilities we are working on and what we have accomplished. Formally defining the general ability to represent the mental states of others, i.e., ToM, and studying that definition in an AI fits with this principle. However, it may be more beneficial to define and study less nebulous abilities, for example, the ability to represent a belief, hope, or desire. This scope narrowing will naturally necessitate a change in how researchers talk about AI ToM, such as saying they are working on a specific ToM skill rather than ToM in general. The predicted benefit is that it may facilitate quicker, more effective development of ASI.

4.3   Establish Ground Truth of Social Intelligence

A valuable insight from existing tests of ToM, whether in psychology or computer science, is the need to rely on scenarios in which ground truth exists. Consider the Sally Anne test. Children likely view the prompt regarding the marble as genuine. That is, they do not think that the researchers are trying to deceive them or willfully withholding valuable information (e.g., Sally does not trust Anne based on prior marble-moving behavior). Meanwhile, adults might consider the prompt more cautiously. Although there is ground truth with respect to the marble, there is not necessarily ground truth available for Sally's belief state outside of what the researcher claims. This lack of ground truth is not problematic for naive agents. However, for sophisticated agents, it introduces another variable to consider. The agent, whether an adult or computational system, must consider other possibilities, such as the mental states of the person issuing the prompt and critical information about the characters they might not know. A wrong answer about where Sally will look for the marble may indicate robust ToM, just not in the expected fashion.

5   Robust Artificial Social Intelligence

A robust ASI is an artificial intelligence with social reasoning abilities on par with adult humans. This definition differs from other robust AI systems in which the robustness typically describes their inertness to perturbations or adversarial attacks. Like humans, ASI may not always know the normative response to a social query or quandary. However, robust ASI will be able to reason about the mental states of the agents it observes and make predictions based on that reasoning. This ability means a robust ASI can respond to prompts about social situations, such as where a person will look for an object that they previously hid but was moved by another agent, as well as spontaneously engage in reasoning about the mental states of others, such as recognizing when a person is searching for something and offering to help. Minimally, robust ASI will:

– **Respond to social prompts**: It will engage social intelligence to answer questions, react to cues, and respond to similar stimuli.
– **Spontaneously engage in social reasoning**: It will engage in reasoning about the mental states of others without explicit or deliberate prompts.

We think that the current models of Theory of Mind reasoning and associated empirical approaches to testing them do not fully consider both prompted and spontaneous reasoning. An over-emphasis on prompt-based tests of theories may falsely confirm their validity as models can learn the normative response to a prompt but not actually need to represent the mental state in question. Without an actual representation of the mental state, a model might fail to generalize its knowledge to trivially different social settings [26,62].

6   Conclusion

Our collective, likely unintentional, focus on prompted Theory of Mind for AI will almost certainly slow and possibly inhibit progress toward ASI. The brilliant experimental paradigms that allowed researchers to unlock core insights about how people reason about the mental states of others, such as the Sally-Anne test, appear to have created this exact effect in human psychology. Relying on prompted studies of ToM is already leading to erroneous conclusions in AI research, as we saw with the competing studies of a large language model's ToM abilities. A more principled approach to studying AI ToM that considers how questions shape answers, focuses on definable social intelligence skills, and seeks out the ground truth of social intelligence, we believe, will enable the research community to avoid unnecessary delays in developing robust ASI that can respond to social prompts *and* spontaneously engage in social reasoning. And, hopefully, such an approach will allow us to enjoy the help of an AI assistant that has enough social intelligence to not spoil the celebration of a small victory by reminding us of financial obligations.

Acknowledgments. The project or effort depicted was or is sponsored by the U.S. Government under contract number W911NF-14-D-0005. The content of the information does not necessarily reflect the position or the policy of the Government, and no official endorsement should be inferred

Disclosure of Interests. The authors have no competing interests to declare that are relevant to the content of this article.

References

1. Baron-Cohen, S., Leslie, A.M., Frith, U.: Does the autistic child have a "theory of mind"? Cognition **21**(1), 37–46 (1985)
2. Braun, K.A., Ellis, R., Loftus, E.F.: Make my memory: how advertising can change our memories of the past. Psychol. Mark. **19**(1), 1–23 (2002)
3. Bretherton, I., Beeghly, M.: Talking about internal states: the acquisition of an explicit theory of mind. Dev. Psychol. **18**(6), 906 (1982)
4. Carlson, S.M., Moses, L.J.: Individual differences in inhibitory control and children's theory of mind. Child Dev. **72**(4), 1032–1053 (2001)
5. Cuzzolin, F., Morelli, A., Cirstea, B., Sahakian, B.J.: Knowing me, knowing you: theory of mind in AI. Psychol. Med. **50**(7), 1057–1061 (2020)
6. De Martino, B., O'Doherty, J.P., Ray, D., Bossaerts, P., Camerer, C.: In the mind of the market: theory of mind biases value computation during financial bubbles. Neuron **79**(6), 1222–1231 (2013)
7. Epley, N.: A mind like mine: the exceptionally ordinary underpinnings of anthropomorphism. J. Assoc. Consum. Res. **3**(4), 591–598 (2018)
8. Ericsson, K.A.: Protocol analysis. A companion to cognitive science, pp. 425–432 (2017)
9. Fodor, J.A.: The Modularity of Mind. MIT Press, Cambridge (1983)
10. Frith, U., Happé, F.: Autism: beyond "theory of mind." Cognition **50**(1–3), 115–132 (1994)
11. Gergely, G., Nádasdy, Z., Csibra, G., Bíró, S.: Taking the intentional stance at 12 months of age. Cognition **56**(2), 165–193 (1995)
12. Gernsbacher, M.A., Yergeau, M.: Empirical failures of the claim that autistic people lack a theory of mind. Arch. Sci. Psychol. **7**(1), 102 (2019)
13. Gerson, L.P.: Knowing Persons: A Study in Plato. Clarendon Press, London (2003)
14. Gopnik, A., Meltzoff, A.N.: Minds, bodies, and persons: young children's understanding of the self and others as reflected in imitation and theory of mind research. (1994)

15. Gopnik, A., Meltzoff, A.N., Kuhl, P.K.: The Scientist in the Crib: Minds, Brains, and How Children Learn. William Morrow & Co., New York (1999)
16. Gordon, R.M.: Folk psychology as simulation. Mind Lang. **1**(2), 158–171 (1986)
17. Greenwald, A.G., Banaji, M.R.: Implicit social cognition: attitudes, self-esteem, and stereotypes. Psychol. Rev. **102**(1), 4 (1995)
18. Greenwald, A.G., Banaji, M.R.: The implicit revolution: reconceiving the relation between conscious and unconscious. Am. Psychol. **72**(9), 861 (2017)
19. Grice, H.P.: Logic and conversation. In: Speech Acts, pp. 41–58. Brill (1975)
20. Gurney, N., Marsella, S., Ustun, V., Pynadath, D.V.: Operationalizing theories of theory of mind: a survey. In: Gurney, N., Sukthankar, G. (eds.) AAAI-FSS 2021. LNCS, vol. 13775, pp. 3–20. Springer, Cham (2021). https://doi.org/10.1007/978-3-031-21671-8_1
21. Gurney, N., Pynadath, D.V.: Robots with theory of mind for humans: a survey. In: 2022 31st IEEE International Conference on Robot and Human Interactive Communication (RO-MAN), pp. 993–1000. IEEE (2022)
22. Happé, F.G.: An advanced test of theory of mind: understanding of story characters' thoughts and feelings by able autistic, mentally handicapped, and normal children and adults. J. Autism Dev. Disord. **24**(2), 129–154 (1994)
23. Heider, F., Simmel, M.: An experimental study of apparent behavior. Am. J. Psychol. **57**(2), 243–259 (1944)
24. Heyes, C.: Submentalizing: I am not really reading your mind. Perspect. Psychol. Sci. **9**(2), 131–143 (2014)
25. Ho, M.K., Saxe, R., Cushman, F.: Planning with theory of mind. Trends Cogn. Sci. **26**(11), 959–971 (2022)
26. Kosinski, M.: Theory of mind may have spontaneously emerged in large language models. arXiv preprint arXiv:2302.02083 (2023)
27. Kulke, L., von Duhn, B., Schneider, D., Rakoczy, H.: Is implicit theory of mind a real and robust phenomenon? Results from a systematic replication study. Psychol. Sci. **29**(6), 888–900 (2018)
28. Lake, B.M., Ullman, T.D., Tenenbaum, J.B., Gershman, S.J.: Building machines that learn and think like people. Behav. Brain Sci. **40**, e253 (2017)
29. Loftus, E.F.: Make-believe memories. Am. Psychol. **58**(11), 867 (2003)
30. Loftus, E.F.: Planting misinformation in the human mind: a 30-year investigation of the malleability of memory. Learn. Memory **12**(4), 361–366 (2005)
31. Low, J., Perner, J.: Implicit and explicit theory of mind: state of the art (2012)
32. Marsella, S.C., Pynadath, D.V., Read, S.J.: PsychSim: agent-based modeling of social interactions and influence. In: Proceedings of the International Conference on Cognitive Modeling, vol. 36, pp. 243–248 (2004)
33. Meehan, J.R.: Tale-spin, an interactive program that writes stories. In: Ijcai, vol. 77, pp. 91–98 (1977)
34. Morewedge, C.K., Giblin, C.E., Norton, M.I.: The (perceived) meaning of spontaneous thoughts. J. Exp. Psychol. Gen. **143**(4), 1742 (2014)
35. Nisbett, R.E., Wilson, T.D.: Telling more than we can know: verbal reports on mental processes. Psychol. Rev. **84**(3), 231 (1977)
36. Onishi, K.H., Baillargeon, R.: Do 15-month-old infants understand false beliefs? Science **308**(5719), 255–258 (2005)
37. Pantic, M., Rothkrantz, L.J.: Toward an affect-sensitive multimodal human-computer interaction. Proc. IEEE **91**(9), 1370–1390 (2003)
38. Perner, J., Frith, U., Leslie, A.M., Leekam, S.R.: Exploration of the autistic child's theory of mind: knowledge, belief, and communication. Child Dev. 689–700 (1989)

39. Premack, D., Woodruff, G.: Does the chimpanzee have a theory of mind? Behav. Brain Sci. **1**(4), 515–526 (1978)
40. Pu, P.: From confucius to mencius: the confucian theory of mind and nature in the guodian chu slips. Contemp. Chin. Thought **32**(2), 39–54 (2000)
41. Pynadath, D.V., et al.: Disaster world: decision-theoretic agents for simulating population responses to hurricanes. Comput. Math. Organ. Theory **29**(1), 84–117 (2023)
42. Pynadath, D.V., Marsella, S.C.: PsychSim: modeling theory of mind with decision-theoretic agents. In: IJCAI, vol. 5, pp. 1181–1186 (2005)
43. Quesque, F., Rossetti, Y.: What do theory-of-mind tasks actually measure? Theory and practice. Perspect. Psychol. Sci. **15**(2), 384–396 (2020)
44. Rabinowitz, N., Perbet, F., Song, F., Zhang, C., Eslami, S.A., Botvinick, M.: Machine theory of mind. In: International Conference on Machine Learning, pp. 4218–4227. PMLR (2018)
45. Rilling, J.K., Sanfey, A.G., Aronson, J.A., Nystrom, L.E., Cohen, J.D.: The neural correlates of theory of mind within interpersonal interactions. Neuroimage **22**(4), 1694–1703 (2004)
46. Rozemond, M.: Descartes's Dualism. Harvard University Press, Cambridge (2009)
47. Samson, D., Apperly, I.A., Braithwaite, J.J., Andrews, B.J., Bodley Scott, S.E.: Seeing it their way: evidence for rapid and involuntary computation of what other people see. J. Exp. Psychol. Hum. Percept. Perform. **36**(5), 1255 (2010)
48. Santiesteban, I., Catmur, C., Hopkins, S.C., Bird, G., Heyes, C.: Avatars and arrows: implicit mentalizing or domain-general processing? J. Exp. Psychol. Hum. Percept. Perform. **40**(3), 929 (2014)
49. Sap, M., LeBras, R., Fried, D., Choi, Y.: Neural theory-of-mind? On the limits of social intelligence in large LMS. arXiv preprint arXiv:2210.13312 (2022)
50. Schober, M.F.: Asking questions and influencing answers. In: Questions about Questions: Inquiries into the Cognitive Bases of Surveys, pp. 15–48. Russell Sage Foundation, New York (1992)
51. Schwarz, N.: Self-reports: how the questions shape the answers. Am. Psychol. **54**(2), 93 (1999)
52. Seidenfeld, A.M., Johnson, S.R., Cavadel, E.W., Izard, C.E.: Theory of mind predicts emotion knowledge development in head start children. Early Educ. Dev. **25**(7), 933–948 (2014)
53. Sellars, W., et al.: Empiricism and the philosophy of mind. Minn. Stud. Philos. Sci. **1**(19), 253–329 (1956)
54. Senju, A., Southgate, V., White, S., Frith, U.: Mindblind eyes: an absence of spontaneous theory of mind in asperger syndrome. Science **325**(5942), 883–885 (2009)
55. Si, M., Marsella, S.C.: Encoding theory of mind in character design for pedagogical interactive narrative. Adv. Hum.-Comput. Interact. **2014**, 10 (2014)
56. Si, M., Marsella, S.C., Pynadath, D.V.: Thespian: using multi-agent fitting to craft interactive drama. In: Proceedings of the Fourth International Joint Conference on Autonomous Agents and Multiagent Systems, pp. 21–28 (2005)
57. Sutton, J., Smith, P.K., Swettenham, J.: Bullying and 'theory of mind': a critique of the 'social skills deficit' view of anti-social behaviour. Soc. Dev. **8**(1), 117–127 (1999)
58. Tenenbaum, J.B., Kemp, C., Griffiths, T.L., Goodman, N.D.: How to grow a mind: statistics, structure, and abstraction. Science **331**(6022), 1279–1285 (2011)
59. Trott, S., Jones, C., Chang, T., Michaelov, J., Bergen, B.: Do large language models know what humans know? Cogn. Sci. **47**(7), e13309 (2023)

60. Tulving, E.: Cue-dependent forgetting: when we forget something we once knew, it does not necessarily mean that the memory trace has been lost; it may only be inaccessible. Am. Sci. **62**(1), 74–82 (1974)

61. Tulving, E., Osler, S.: Effectiveness of retrieval cues in memory for words. J. Exp. Psychol. **77**(4), 593 (1968)

62. Ullman, T.: Large language models fail on trivial alterations to theory-of-mind tasks. arXiv preprint arXiv:2302.08399 (2023)

63. Uzer, T., Brown, N.R.: The effect of cue content on retrieval from autobiographical memory. Acta Physiol. (Oxf) **172**, 84–91 (2017)

64. Vaswani, A., et al.: Attention is all you need. In: Advances in Neural Information Processing Systems, Vol. 30 (2017)

65. Vinyals, O., et al.: Grandmaster level in starcraft ii using multi-agent reinforcement learning. Nature **575**(7782), 350–354 (2019)

66. Wang, N., Pynadath, D.V., Hill, S.G.: Trust calibration within a human-robot team: comparing automatically generated explanations. In: 2016 11th ACM/IEEE International Conference on Human-Robot Interaction (HRI), pp. 109–116. IEEE (2016)

67. Wimmer, H., Perner, J.: Beliefs about beliefs: representation and constraining function of wrong beliefs in young children's understanding of deception. Cognition **13**(1), 103–128 (1983)

68. Woodward, A.L.: Infants selectively encode the goal object of an actor's reach. Cognition **69**(1), 1–34 (1998)

69. Wu, H., Sequeira, P., Pynadath, D.V.: Multiagent inverse reinforcement learning via theory of mind reasoning. arXiv preprint arXiv:2302.10238 (2023)

The Trends and Research Progress of Mental Models in Interaction Design: A Bibliometric Study

Yuqi Liu and Zhiyu Zhao[✉]

Beihang University, Beijing 100191, China
zhaozhiyu@buaa.edu.cn

Abstract. This study systematically summarizes the global characteristics of interaction design centricity model research in the international context, which grasps the current research progress and hotspots and explores the new trends of future development based on the current research hotspots. Using the literature on mental models of interaction design indexed in Web of Science as the data source, the authors use VOSviewer and CiteSpace to draw a scientific knowledge map by bibliometric method from the distribution of literature in terms of year and output, countries/regions, research institutions, authors, journals, and keyword clustering, etc., and carry out a visual analysis to sort out the research lineage. The results show an overall upward trend in the number of literatures within the search scope, particular in China and the United States which are at the forefront of research. The research hotspots mainly focus on the study of the theoretical concepts of mental models, the study of design strategies for matching user mental models, and the study of constructing effective user mental model measurement methods and evaluation systems. It also concentrates on the future research focuses on automation, affective computing, task analytics, deep learning, and human-robot interaction, etc. Furthermore, the trend of the research is to pay more and more attention to the development of intelligent applications as well as more scientific measurement methods and evaluation systems. The research institutions and organizations are working together to establish a scientific knowledge map. The establishment of evaluation system, research institutions and authors failed to cooperate closely. The current situation is that there are lack of many high-yield authors and lack of in-depth research results on users' micro-mind model. The authors believe that the evaluation method of interaction design based on the mind model is still to be further researched.

Keywords: Interaction design · Mental model · Bibliometrics · VOS viewer · CiteSpace

1 Introduction

Mental Model was first proposed by Scottish psychologist Kenneth Craik in 1943, referring to those many assumptions, stereotypes and impressions that are deeply rooted in people's minds and influence how they recognize the world, interpret the world, face the world, and how they act [1]. Subsequently, Philip Johnson Laird, an expert in the field of cognitive psychology, described the mental model as how people deal with problems through reasoning [2]. Donald Norman, a famous cognitive psychologist, summarized on the basis of applied theoretical research that the mental model has the characteristics of subjectivity, learning transfer, dynamics, functionality, and similarity, etc., In his representative work *Design Psychology*, he classified the mental models involved in human-computer interaction systems into three categories: designer models, user models, and representational models. He concluded that mental models are the summary of people's experience of the real or hypothetical world based on their previous life experience, which affects people's cognition of the world around them and their behavioral decision-making [3]. Indi Young defined the purpose of human beings, the thinking process, as well as the changes in emotions and thinking during actions. Indi Young defined the human purpose, thought process, and emotional and thinking changes in actions as mental models, and first started the application of user mental models in the field of interaction design in the book *Mental Models* [4].

In 1984, Bill Moggridge, an American designer, first proposed the concept of "Interaction Design" (IXD) at the International Design Conference, defining it as the design of the product's use behavior, task flow and information architecture [5]. With the development of Internet technology and the increase in the variety of digital products, the concept of interaction design has been applied to the design of various digital products. It is defined as the design of interactive digital products, environments, systems, and services, which is used to improve the interaction between the product and the user, which enhances the user experience. Interaction design focuses on the behavioral interactions between humans and machines. The design goal is to satisfy the usability, ease of use, and pleasantness of human-machine contact. However, due to the complexity of the internal design principles of the machine and the fact that they are failed to fully compatible with human cognition and psychology. It leads to a gap between the product and human psychological cognition, i.e., a mismatch of mental models. In order to help solve the cognitive obstacles of human-computer interaction, it is necessary to fully understand the user's mental model and use the mental model as a guide for interaction design. According to previous theories and practical experiences, in the field of interaction design, it is generally believed that the closer the product is to the user's mental model, the better interaction experience it can bring to the user. In recent years, the theory of mental model is becoming the theoretical basis for the research of interaction design of information technology products, which plays an important role in the fields of smart home, human-intelligence collaboration, automatic driving, medical and health care, and ageing-friendly design. For example, with the development of computer and intelligent technology, autonomous driving has become more common in automobile driving mode. However, human-computer conflicts often arise in practice. In addition, the root cause is the inconsistency of human-computer mental models. For example, in the design of aging-adapted smart home, the usage habits and thinking patterns of the elderly users will also greatly affect the usage experience and safety of the elderly users. Therefore, in-depth analysis and research on different mental models can further guarantee the working efficiency and system safety.

In recent years, many scholars have researched and explored the Mental Model in Interaction Design Research (hereafter referred to as MM-IDR) and produced a large number of literature outputs. However, the outputs of these literatures are complicated and diverse which have strong interdisciplinary attributes, involving knowledge from multiple disciplinary fields, including psychology, artificial intelligence, neuroscience, cognitive science, design, and philosophy. It is difficult to objectively analyze the changes and development trends of the research hotspots in this field by solely relying on traditional literature review methods. Therefore, this paper employs the method of bibliometrics and comprehensively applies VOSviewer and CiteSpace. The authors also draw the knowledge map from the year output of literature, research institutions, authors, and keyword clustering. Moreover, they carries out visual analysis to systematically sort out the application of mental models in interaction design, grasp the current research hotspots, and explore the future research trends in this field according to the current research hotspots, so as to provide certain information for the future scholars engaged in this field. This paper mainly focuses on the following five research questions. This paper mainly carries out MM-IDR research through the following five research questions:

1. what is the annual output trend of MM-IDR literature?
2. What are the main countries/regions and organizations that study MM-IDR?
3. what are the most influential authors as well as journals in MM-IDR?
4. What are the hot research topics and future cutting-edge trends in MM-IDR?
5. What are the shortcomings of current MM-IDR and the suggestions for future research?

2   Research Design

2.1   Research Methodology

This study adopts bibliometric analysis as the primary method for analyzing the literature related to driving user experience and usability, aiming to identify the most influential studies, define research areas, and provide insights into current research interests and future research directions.

Bibliometrics, first proposed by Pritchard in 1969, refers to the quantitative analysis of various types of literature to discover potential patterns and information in a large amount of literature data [6]. The advantages of bibliometrics have been confirmed by many studies. Firstly, compared with peer review and expert judgment, bibliometrics can ensure the objectivity of academic output by providing quantitative indicators through statistical analysis [7]. For example, ZG. Liu et al. used CiteSpace to study the structure and evolution of innovation systems research [8]. In addition, bibliometric analysis enables scholars to monitor and summarize the content and trends of research on a given topic, which can help young researchers to seek future research directions [9]. It involves a variety of analytical methods, including author citations, literature co-citation, history mapping, and co-word analysis. In this study, co-word networks and evolutionary footprints are used as research objects to explore mental models in interaction design.

Both VOSviewer and CiteSpace are visualization tools for citation metrics analysis, which can effectively establish mapping relationships between knowledge units in the literature, and clearly demonstrate the macrostructure of knowledge through visual information. VOSviewer has advanced graphical representation capabilities, which are suitable for large-scale data to locate the focus and hotspots of research topics, while CiteSpace can intuitively CiteSpace. On the other hand, it can intuitively display the development trend as well as the evolution process of a certain discipline or research topic in a specific period of time, which has been widely used in bibliometric analysis in recent years [10]. In order to obtain more rigorous and comprehensive data indicators, this study uses VOSviewer and CiteSpace software through bibliometric method and knowledge structure visualization to obtain more comprehensive data.

2.2 Data Collection

Since high-quality scientific literature is subject to rigorous peer review and strict scrutiny of published journals, its research results are more representative of the discipline [11]. In this paper, the authors chose the literature related to the Centerwise Model of Interaction Design included in the authoritative academic database WOS as the main data source for this study. SSCI, SCI, A&HCI were selected as the search sources in the WOS core collection. In order to collect all the relevant articles, the search time was set to the full year. The sources were not streamlined in order to avoid the loss of interdisciplinary literature. The search conditions were set as TS = (mental model) AND (interaction design) and the retrieved literature was exported to a txt file in the format of "full record and cited references". Moreover, the data such as deviation from the research topic, missing field information (e.g., time, keywords, authors, and other key information), duplicated data, and so on, were eliminated. The authors also eliminated the interfering articles such as deviation from the research topic, missing field information (e.g. time, keywords, authors, etc.), duplicate data, etc., and finally obtained a total of 489 valid articles for further quantitative analysis.

3   Results and Analysis

3.1 Publications Trend

The pattern of change in the output of academic literature over time is an important method to measure the development trend of research topics, which can effectively assess the research dynamics of the discipline. After cleaning and de-weighting, the retrieved data for field extraction, and arranging the number of publications in the field according to the year, the distribution of MM-IDR literature annual output can be obtained, as shown in Fig. 1. As seen from the WOS publications, the number of literature in this field was small before 2009, with no more than 10 publications per year, and the overall trend was slowly increasing. In 2010, there were 21 publications, which reached a small peak. 2010–2018 was the period of steady increase in the number of publications in this field, and the increase of publications in this period was larger than that in the past. After 2018, the number of publications showed a rapid increase phase, from 20 in 2018 to a rapid increase to 54 in 2022, reaching a peak in 2022. From the literature output, it can be seen that the research topic of MM-IDR is constantly developing and has been in a period of rapid rise in recent years, and the topic has been the focus of scholars' attention in the past five years.

$$y = 1.1718x - 2336.8$$
$$R^2 = 0.753$$

Fig. 1. Publicátions trend of MM-IDR

3.2 Top Contributing Countries/Regions and Institutions

The number of publications and the number of citations by country/region in the dataset depicts the high-producing countries/regions in the research field and their impact. In terms of country/region output, a total of 51 countries/regions around the world have contributed to this research field, and the ranking of the top 10 countries/regions in terms of publication volume is shown in Table 1. The top 10 countries/regions accounted for more than 77.05% of the total number of publications, and all of them have a production of more than 15 papers within the search, which is an important source of output of MM-IDR around the world. The United States is the most productive country/region in MM-IDR research, with a total of 165 papers (28.45% of the total number of publications), ranking 1st in the total number of publications, followed by China (57 papers, 9.82% of the total number of publications), and then followed by the United Kingdom (54), Germany (45), Norway (25), Canada (24), and Italy (24) in that order, Australia (23 articles), France (18 articles), and South Korea (15 articles). In terms of the number of articles published, the number of articles published in both China and the United States is more than 50. In addition, the average number of citations in China and the United States is also in the top rank, with more than 700 citations in both countries/regions. In the research cooperation network, China, the United States, the United Kingdom, Germany, Canada, Australia and many other countries/regions maintain cooperative relationships, but not close enough, as shown in Fig. 2.

A total of 696 research organizations around the world have conducted MM-IDR related research. Run VOSviewer, select Organizations to set the node threshold to 3, and get the institutional cooperation network with the number of nodes as 76, the number of cooperative relationships as 131, and the density as 0.0015, see Fig. 3. The node size of the institutions in the figure indicates the production of the articles, and the connecting line between the institutions represents the strength of the cooperation, and the closer the cooperation is, the wider the connecting line is between the institutions [12].

Table 1. Distribution of MM-IDR high-yield countries/regions

NO.	Country/Region	Documents	Citations	Avg. citations	Links	Total link strength
1	USA	165	5478	33.2	22	50
2	China	57	725	12.7193	9	28
3	England	54	1141	21.1296	19	32
4	Germany	45	924	20.5333	15	23
5	Netherlands	25	460	18.4	5	6
6	Canada	24	440	18.3333	8	16
7	Italy	24	268	11.1667	10	14
8	Australia	23	440	19.1304	9	15
9	France	18	380	21.1111	6	7
10	South Korea	15	100	6.6667	6	7

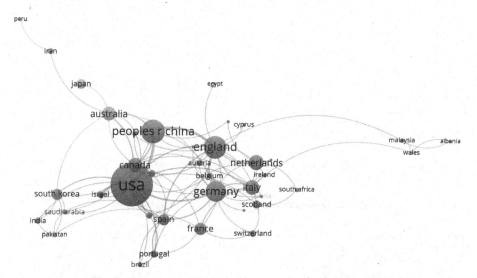

Fig. 2. Cooperative countries/regions co-occurrence network

From the distribution of the strength of cooperation relationship (number of times of cooperation) within each sub-network, the international cooperation of MM-IDR is not close, showing strong geographical characteristics, mainly focusing on the cooperation between institutions in their own countries/regions and regions. Institutional cooperation is "regionally concentrated and overall decentralized", with "Delft University of Technology", "Georgia Institute of Technology", "Chinese Academy of Sciences" as the main high-level institutions. Three large subgroups of high-impact research institutions were formed, mainly by "Delft University of Technology", "Georgia Institute of Technology" and "Chinese Academy of Sciences". Within the search scope, Delft University of Technology and Georgia Institute of Technology tied for the first place with 8 articles, followed by the Chinese Academy of Sciences (7 articles), the University of Illinois (7 articles) and the Massachusetts Institute of Technology (MIT) (7 articles), etc. The top 10 high-yield institutions are shown in Table 2.

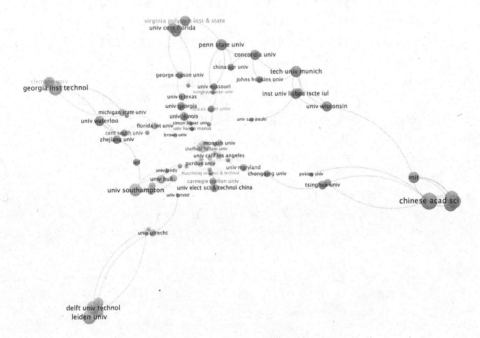

Fig. 3. Cooperative institutions co-occurrence network

Table 2. Distribution of MM-IDR high-yield institutions

NO.	Institution	Documents	Citations	Avg. citations	Links
1	Delft Univ. Technol.	8	121	15.125	4
2	Georgia Inst Technol.	8	663	82.875	6
3	Chinese Acad Sci	7	155	22.1429	7
4	MIT	7	223	31.8571	5
5	Univ. Illinois	7	718	102.5714	3
6	Clemson Univ.	5	33	6.6	2
7	Michigan State Univ.	5	469	93.8	2
8	Penn State Univ.	5	123	24.6	5
9	Tech. Univ. Chemnitz	5	40	8	0
10	Texas A&M Univ.	5	424	84.8	2

3.3 Most Influential Authors and Journals

Authors are the smallest unit of literature output and direct contributors to MM-IDR. By studying author co-citations, it is possible to identify the more active scholars in this field worldwide. Through the preliminary analysis of authors' names and co-citation analysis after disambiguation of authors, from 1703 authors and 102 pairs of collaborations, the distribution table of authors' outputs and collaborations of MM-IDR is extracted, as shown in Table 3. Highly productive authors are not found through the data statistics, among which Cynthia Breazeal from Massachusetts Institute of Technology has the highest number of publications and is ranked 1st with 3 publications within the search, followed by Raja Parasuraman, Bobbie D. Seppelt, Robert Larose, and Sanjay Chandrasekharan. The most frequently cited author is Michael T. Braun, with a total of 270 citations, who is considered to be a representative of MM-IDR; in addition, collaborative research among scholars is not close and is mostly sporadic.

Table 3. Top 10 contributing authors

NO.	Author	Documents	Citations	Avg. citations	Links
1	Cynthia Breazeal	3	244	81.3333	7
2	Raja Parasuraman	2	204	102	5
3	Bobbie D. Seppelt	2	118	59	17
4	Robert Larose	2	80	40	5
5	Sanjay Chandrasekharan	2	66	33	2
6	Alessandro Gardi	2	61	30.5	5
7	Yixiang Lim	2	61	30.5	5
8	Subramanian Ramasamy	2	61	30.5	5
9	Roberto Sabatini	2	61	30.5	5
10	Martin Baumann	2	56	28	4

The articles within the search originated from 235 journals, and this paper lists the top 10 high-yield journals in terms of publication volume, as well as their respective 5-year IF (Impact Factor), which accounted for 26.58% of the total number of articles published, as shown in Table 4. The 1st ranked journal in terms of publication volume is International Journal of Human-computer Interaction, with 35 articles, 210 citations, and an impact factor of 4.503; ranked 2nd is frontiers in psychology, with 17 articles, 116 citations, and an impact factor of 4.426; and ranked 3rd is human factors, with 16 articles, 586 citations, and an impact factor of 4.212. These journals reflect their significant influence in the field of MM-IDR research and are at the core of journals in this field.

Table 4. Top 10 contributing journals

NO.	Journal	Documents	Citations	Avg. citations	5 Year IF
1	International Journal of Human-computer Interaction	35	210	6	4.503
2	Frontiers in Psychology	17	116	6.8235	4.426
3	Human Factors	16	586	36.625	4.212
4	International Journal of Human-computer Studies	12	220	18.3333	4.435
5	Plos One	10	133	13.3	4.069
6	Ergonomics	9	221	24.5556	3.177
7	Interacting with Computers	9	138	15.3333	1.532
8	Human-computer Interaction	8	242	30.25	5.727
9	Journal of Medical Internet Research	7	257	36.7143	7.68
10	Computers in Human Behavior	7	236	33.7143	10.097

3.4 Research Hotspots of MM-IDR

The keywords of the literature are highly refined by the authors of their research, and the high-frequency co-occurring keywords reflect the research hotspots of MM-IDR for a long time. The 489 documents within the search scope contain a total of 2,683 keywords, and the keyword co-occurrence frequency is set to 3 by running VOSviewer, and the keyword co-occurrence clusters formed by merging and filtering the synonyms are obtained from 278 keywords, as shown in Fig. 4. The keywords with the same color in the figure are the same clusters, and a total of 4 main clusters are formed. From the analysis results, the hot research topics of MM-IDR can be divided into four major categories, which are #1 Theories and Methods, #2 Application Scenarios and Design Strategies, #3 Design Evaluation and Usability Research, and #4 Comprehensive Factors of Human-Computer Interaction for Intelligent Systems in the order of the research stages from the oldest to the newest, respectively, as shown in Fig. 4.

Cluster #1 (green) - Mental Models Theory and Methods contains 90 cluster members, mainly containing the keywords Mental Models, Knowledge, Information, Models, Cognition, Attention, Cognitive Load, Framework, Attention, Cognitive Load, Framework, Visualization and Perception. The research in this category focuses on the concepts, elements, classifications, and extensions of mental modeling theories to continuously add and improve them, making the theory of mind more comprehensive and diversified.

Cluster #2 (red) - Application Scenarios and Design Strategies of Mental Models contains 65 cluster members, mainly including Behavior, Impact, Stress, Technology, Time, health, reliability, and so on. Health, reliability, internet and depression. The main research content of this clustering is the research on the application scenarios of mental

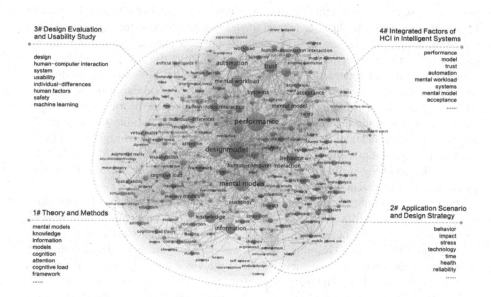

Fig. 4. Keywords co-occurrence clustering network

models and the research on the design strategies to match the users' mental models. In the research, scholars focus on how to choose appropriate design strategies to match and influence users' mental models, and how to effectively reduce users' mental workload and mental load. In this phase of research, scholars gradually began to introduce the concept of mental models into the specific product design process, research more accurate construction of the user's mental model method, put forward the corresponding design strategies and examples of application, through experiments to prove the importance of the research and application of the mental model in interaction design, and in different application scenarios to match the user's mental model design strategy to improve the user's experience in different application scenarios.

Cluster #3 (purple) - Design Evaluation and Usability Study contains 69 cluster members, mainly including Human-computer Interaction, Usability, Individual-differences, Human Factors, and Individual Differences. Human-computer Interaction, Usability, Individual-differences, Human Factors, Safety, Machine Learning, Management, and Task EEG. This type of research is the cutting-edge research in this field, which aims at constructing and perfecting the effective user mental model measurement method and evaluation system research in the field of interaction design. Through scientific and rigorous analysis, the user mental model of the interaction design before and after optimization is measured and evaluated, and the concluding data is used for comparison and verification, so as to confirm that the optimization is effective. In the field of interaction design, the evaluation of the user mental model is generally centered on the usability test of the interactive interface and the evaluation of user experience, which is mainly based on the theory of the user mental model to construct the evaluation system, and then evaluated for the interactive interface. The research at this stage can better verify whether the optimization of interaction design under the guidance of the research findings of the UMM is effective. Some scholars also take the disorientation test as a clue, and the lower the disorientation degree, the higher the validity of the study. In addition, the importance of mental model evaluation has also been highlighted in the study of user mental model and interface matching, for example, Jing Ma conducted a study on the matching of digital interface interaction patterns with user mental models by constructing an ensemble of mental model actions [13].

Early collection of user feedback information in this field was mostly qualitative research, and the acquisition route was mental acquisition, such as Davidson's systematic account of the general acquisition methods of user mental models in the article "User Mental Models and Usability", which was based on the user interview method, observation, questionnaires and surveys, out-of-the-voice thinking, focus groups, and card sorting methods [14]. There are more quantitative and empirical studies after that, such as Ping Zhengqiang, based on this study, summarized the methods of user mental information acquisition into the acquisition path of psychological information and the acquisition path of physiological information [15]. Among them, the psychological information acquisition path refers to the traditional method of acquiring mental information; the physiological information acquisition path is the method that can be measured by technical means of the changes in physiological information caused by the interaction behavior, which includes blood pressure, pupil reaction, facial expression, brainwave, electrocardiogram and so on.

Cluster #4 (blue) - Intelligent Systems Human-Robot Interaction Composite Factors contains a total of 54 cluster members, mainly containing the keywords Performance (Behavior), Trust, Automation, Mental Workload, Systems, Acceptance, Situation Awareness and Human-robot Interaction. This clustering is also a cutting-edge research in the field of MM-IDR, which mainly researches the influence of different factors on mental workload and mental load in intelligent interaction systems, and is more refined and diversified in the selection of research objects, which plays an important role in how to effectively reduce the user's mental load, as well as to improve the interaction experience of the current users using intelligent products. The acquisition of user feedback data has also gradually changed from psychological measurements to physiological measurements, such as blood pressure, pupil reaction, facial expression, brain waves, electrocardiogram and so on. The research in this phase is more diversified, emphasizing more and more on the development of application practice and the establishment of more scientific measurement methods and evaluation systems. Research hotspots focus on intelligent interaction design, cognition, user experience, usability research and other fields. It focuses on the systematic and service-oriented nature of interaction design research, visualization research of interaction design, user research, and experimental validation and other fields.

In summary, the current research hotspots of MM-IDR focus on the areas of mental modeling theory and methods, mental modeling application scenarios and design strategies, design evaluation and usability research, and integrated factors of human-computer interaction in intelligent systems. The focus is on the areas of MM-IDR systematicity and serviceability, MM-IDR visualization research, user research, and experimental validation.

3.5 Analysis of Future Research Trends of MM-IDR

In order to further study the cutting-edge themes and development trends of MM-IDR, the average appearance time of keywords was analyzed statistically and superimposed on the original cluster diagram respectively, see Fig. 5. From the research hotspots summarized in the four clusters in Fig. 5, it can be found that the keywords in Cluster #4 - Comprehensive Factors of Human-Computer Interaction of Intelligent Systems with the overall time is the closest to the present, and is the current cutting-edge theme of MM-IDR; secondly, cluster #3 - design evaluation and usability research is also the current research direction that MM-IDR focuses on; and cluster #1 - mental modeling theories and methods overall average appearances were prior to 2015 and were a hotspot for early research in the discipline. The main keywords in the overall clustering network with an average appearance time later than after 2020 are Autonomy, Affective Computing, Ergonomics, Programming, Emotion Recognition, Mood, Network, Task Analysis, Transparency and Deep Learning. To further explore and corroborate the cutting-edge trends of MM-IDR, CiteSpace's high-density Burst Term was comprehensively utilized in the study, as shown in Fig. 6, which lists the Top52 keywords in terms of burst intensity, with the red part indicating the years in which the keywords were cited with a relatively prominent frequency, which reflects the changing trends of the study. Sorting the Top52 emergent keywords by time shows that the research hotspots are divided into 3 distinct intervals; from the evolution of keywords in the 3 intervals, the overall research puts more emphasis on the simplicity and naturalness of the interaction, more focus on the application of intelligent system scenarios and intelligence, as well as the trend of change from the abstract psychometrics to the concrete and quantifiable physiological measurements, which also coincides with the change trend on the Time-Keyword clustering results obtained. Among the high-intensity emergent words, the keywords that emerged in the last 3 years and will continue to emerge until 2023 are Task Analysis,

User Experience, Health, and Human-robot interaction. A comprehensive analysis of the time-keyword clustering map and keyword emergence map shows that the future research content of MM-IDR focuses on Autonomy, Affective Computing, Task Analysis, Deep Learning, and Human-robot interaction, in that order. Task Analysis, Deep Learning, and Human-robot interaction, etc. The research trend shows the refinement and diversification of the research content, more and more emphasis on the development of intelligent applications and the establishment of more scientific measurement methods and evaluation systems.

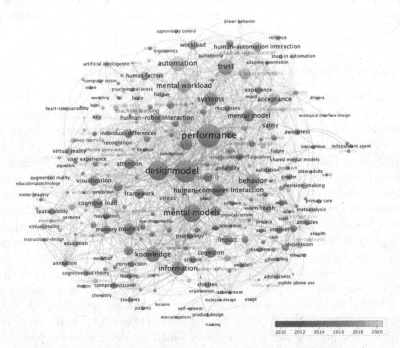

Fig. 5. Time-keyword co-occurrence clustering superposition network

Top 52 Keywords with the Strongest Citation Bursts

Keywords	Year	Strength	Begin	End	1990 - 2023
software	1990	1.8638	1994	1998	
interface	1990	2.9162	1996	2003	
anxiety	1990	1.8996	2005	2017	
communication	1990	3.0047	2005	2015	
animation	1990	2.1059	2005	2014	
internet	1990	1.8528	2007	2008	
independent agent	1990	1.9437	2007	2008	
imitation	1990	1.8619	2009	2011	
cognition	1990	2.7178	2009	2013	
construction	1990	2.3458	2009	2012	
design	1990	3.0404	2011	2017	
perception	1990	2.0592	2012	2016	
mind	1990	2.3512	2012	2013	
usability	1990	2.7636	2013	2019	
technology	1990	2.4178	2013	2019	
information	1990	2.6542	2014	2015	
language	1990	1.9664	2014	2017	
performance	1990	3.5999	2015	2019	
cognitive load	1990	2.5799	2015	2016	
attitude	1990	2.582	2015	2017	
automation	1990	3.7164	2016	2023	
quality	1990	2.2262	2016	2021	
safety	1990	1.8937	2016	2019	
mental workload	1990	3.1261	2016	2018	
situation awareness	1990	3.271	2017	2021	
acceptance	1990	3.0047	2017	2021	
identification	1990	1.7875	2017	2020	
human-automation interaction	1990	2.2355	2017	2018	
trust	1990	3.1562	2017	2023	
future	1990	2.8634	2018	2019	
adaptive cruise control	1990	2.5312	2018	2020	
children	1990	1.9664	2018	2020	
behavior	1990	3.0231	2019	2021	
stress	1990	3.1029	2019	2023	
impact	1990	2.9497	2019	2020	
mental health	1990	2.5964	2019	2023	
experience	1990	2.0896	2019	2020	
eeg	1990	1.8867	2019	2021	
time	1990	2.0669	2019	2023	
machine learning	1990	3.3105	2019	2021	
emotion	1990	1.904	2020	2023	
physical activity	1990	2.1771	2020	2021	
interaction design	1990	2.0275	2020	2021	
recognition	1990	2.5032	2020	2023	
virtual reality	1990	2.7237	2020	2021	
deep learning	1990	3.1058	2020	2023	
task analysis	1990	2.5468	2021	2023	
user experience	1990	2.0356	2021	2023	
health	1990	2.3186	2021	2023	
mental rotation	1990	2.0356	2021	2023	
framework	1990	1.8054	2021	2023	
human-robot interaction	1990	2.9766	2021	2023	

Fig. 6. Keywords Burst Term

4 Conclusion

MM-IDR has shown a general upward trend in the output of time-series papers, with a rapid growth in recent years. There are not many countries/regions, institutions and scholars with high output in the course of nearly 30 years of development, and the research cooperation is mostly intra-institutional cooperation with fragmented distribution. The keyword clustering study reveals that MM-IDR is very comprehensive and multifaceted in terms of research content, which can be mainly categorized into #1 Mental Modeling Theory and Methods, #2 Mental Modeling Application Scenarios and Design Strategies, #3 Design Evaluation and Usability Studies, and #4 Integrated Factors of Human-Computer Interaction in Intelligent Systems. Together, these clusters form the research hotspots of MM-IDR, and the latest research progress is more concerned with the areas of design evaluation and usability research, application strategies of intelligent design, and experimental validation of user physiological measurements.

From the time-keyword clustering graph and the keyword emergence graph, the future research hotspots of MM-IDR are Autonomy, Affective Computing, Task Analysis, Deep Learning, and Human-robot interaction, etc. The research trend shows that the research content is refined and diversified, more and more attention is paid to the establishment of scientific measurement methods and evaluation systems, and more attention is paid to the enhancement of the use of mental models in intelligent systems as well as the enhancement of user experience.

This paper mainly carries out a metrological visualization analysis of the international scope MM-IDR research literature, clarifies the research hotspots at this stage, explores the future development trend, and serves as a certain reference for the subsequent research. However, there are still deficiencies in this study:

1. The study only selects the literature data collected in the core database of WOS, and the research results have some limitations.
2. CiteSpace is unable to intelligently merge keywords with the same meaning, which requires the researcher to organize and summarize on his own, which may lead to some deviation of the analysis results from the actual.

It is expected that subsequent scholars can realize more comprehensive and precise analysis and research on the basis of existing research.

5 Suggestions for Future Research

5.1 Research Gap

Through the analysis of countries/regions, institutions, and authors, it can be seen that the cooperation between countries/regions and research institutions in other countries/regions is relatively loose, basically only exchanges between universities in their own countries/regions, and there is a lack of multidisciplinary cooperation in multiple fields of research.

Through the study of the cited literature, it can be seen that most of the existing researches are based on the macro-level research on users' cognitive characteristics, and there are not many in-depth researches on users' micro-mind modeling, such as the interface information architecture, information layout, information performance, etc., and the future researches need to be further improved.

Interaction design evaluation methods based on mental models need to be further studied. Because the mental model is unstable, such as novice users and expert users have significant differences in the mental model, and with the learning and use of understanding, the user's mental model will also change dynamically. The current evaluation system research how to conduct accurate evaluation from a dynamic perspective has not yet found a suitable solution.

5.2 Suggestions for Future Research

Based on the above research, scholars have the following suggestions for future research on MM-IDR:

Expanding the theoretical research of mental modeling and promoting the cross-fertilization of disciplines for innovation will be one of the key trends in the future theoretical research of mental modeling. With the continuous breakthrough of technology, in recent years, some scholars have gradually begun to try to combine the mental model with AI, augmented reality, virtual reality and other technologies to apply research, for example, Dr. Lin Y. of the Beijing Institute of Technology, through the guidance of the mental model, gradually mastered the logic of the user's behavior and operating habits, and constantly adjusted the designer model to put forward a set of virtual reality and augmented reality hybrid mobile tour system based on the mental model [16] And the related application literature has a growing trend, it can be considered that the field of artificial intelligence will be one of the key areas in the future research on the application of mental models. In the future, researchers need to explore in different fields, combined with psychology, computer science, engineering, etc., to become a multidisciplinary integration of talents, to further develop and improve the theory of mental modeling research.

Broadening the application strategy of mental modeling in interaction design and clarifying the future research focus is the transition from technology research to innovation design application research. Innovations in science and technology stimulate the mutation of mental models to produce new products. For example, innovations in operating modes such as touch interaction, gesture interaction, and voice interaction have had an obvious impact on the design of human-computer interfaces. Interface design innovation needs to be designed from the perspective of the user's mental model, breaking through the traditional conceptual form, and iteratively optimizing it to fit the user's new cognitive characteristics, behavioral style, and emotional needs. For example, the application of fully automated driverless technology in intelligent cars, the change of driving mode will inevitably bring about the change of human-vehicle relationship [17]. In addition to technical research, it is also necessary to focus on considering the user experience when "man-machine co-driving", such as the research on the design of in-vehicle interaction systems and human-machine interfaces, to improve the usability and ease of use of the interface, which can help users better accept and adapt to the unmanned vehicle, enhance the acceptance and trust of drivers, and then correctly guide the user in accordance with the functions and services provided by the system, and success-fully complete the driving task in accordance with the system. Functions and services provided, and successfully accomplish their goals.

Constructing an effective user mental model measurement method and evaluation system is a very important part of the mental model in interface design, in which the integration of emotional computing ability into the evaluation system should be one of the key trends in the future research of the mental model, and in order to meet the diversified, intelligent, and personalized needs of the users, it is necessary to rise to the level of user cognition and emotion to be explored. Formulate the index system based on the user's mental model, and the measurement content can be refined to the user's value standard, user expectation, cognitive structure, operation habit, style preference, human face expression, etc. Construct the mapping relationship between emotional intention and design elements, guide the product to adapt to people's different needs by adjusting its own feedback, help break the communication barrier, and form a natural communication and interaction experience similar to that of human beings.

Disclosure of Interests.   The authors have no competing interests to declare that are relevant to the content of this article.

References

1. Craik, K.W.: The Nature of Explanation. Cambridge University Press, Cambridge (1943)
2. Johnson-Laird, P.N.: Mental Models: Towards A Cognitive Science of Language, Inference, and Consciousness. Cambridge University Press, Cambridge (1983)
3. Donald, A.N.: The Design of Everyday Things. Basic Books, New York (1984)
4. Indi, Y.: Mental Models. Rosenfeld Media, Brooklyn (2008)
5. Moggridge, B.: Designing Interactions. MIT Press, Cambridge (2007)
6. Pritchard, A.: Statistical bibliography or bibliometrics. J. Doc. **25**, 348–349 (1969)
7. Hammarfelt, B., Rushforth, A.D.: Indicators as judgment devices: an empirical study of citizen bibliometrics in research evaluation. Res. Eval. **26**(3), 169–180 (2017)
8. Liu, Z., Yin, Y., Liu, W., Dunford, M.: Visualizing the intellectual structure and evolution of innovation systems research: a bibliometric analysis. Scientometrics **103**(1), 135–158 (2015)
9. Wang, J., Chen, H., Rogers, D.S., et al.: A bibliometric analysis of reverse logistics research (1992–2015) and opportunities for future research. Int. J. Phys. Distrib. Logist. Manag. **47**(8), 666–687 (2017)
10. Ye, L., Chen, Y.: A bibliometrics-based comparative study of interface design usability in China and abroad. Packag. Eng. **44**(24), 228–238 (2023)
11. Chen, Y., Jiang, Y., He, R., et al.: Bibliometrics-based analysis of research progress, hotspots and trends in affective design. Packag. Eng. **43**(06), 32–40 (2022)
12. Li, H.: Evolutionary features of academic articles co-keyword network and keywords co-occurrence network: based on two-mode affiliation network. Physica A **450**, 657–669 (2016)
13. Jing, M.: Evaluation and Research on the Matching Degree of Digital Interface Interaction Patterns and Users' Mental Models. Southeast University, Nanjing (2019)
14. Davidson, M.J., Dove, L., Weltz, J.: Mental Models and Usability. DePaul University, Chicago (1999)
15. Chalcraft, A.: Encyclopedia of Library and Information Science, 2nd edn. Reference Reviews, vol. 18, no. 7, pp. 8–9 (1997)

16. Ping, Z.: Research and Application of Mobile Terminal Interface Interaction Design Based on User Mental Model. Guizhou University, Guiyang (2017)
17. Li, X.: Conceptual Design of Human-Machine Interface for Fully Automatic Driverless Cars. Southeast University, Nanjing (2019)
18. Wang, Y.: A review of research on mental modeling in interface design. Design **35**(13), 89–92 (2022)
19. Wang, Y.: Research on the Interface Design of Mobile Video App Based on User Mental Model. Jiangsu University, Zhenjiang (2022)
20. Xu, L.: Research on the application of user mental model in interaction design. Art Technol. (04), 035 (2022)
21. Huang, M.: Research on mobile interface design guided by mental model. Art Technol. **006**, 243 (2015)
22. Qian, M., Zhu, J., Zhang, H.: Research on the measurement methods of information users' mental models–taking college students' experiments as an example. In: The 10th Cross-Strait Academic Symposium on Library and Information Science (2010)
23. Sun, N., Zhang, L.: Research on the application strategy of mental modeling in product innovation design. Packag. Eng. **39**(20), 212–216 (2018)
24. Van Eck, N.J, Waltman, L.: Software survey: VOSviewer, a computer program for bibliometric mapping. Scientometrics **84**(2), 523–38 (2010)
25. Chen, C.: CiteSpace II: detecting and visualizing emerging trends and transient patterns in scientific literature. J. Am. Soc. Inform. Sci. Technol. **57**(3), 359–377 (2006)
26. Billings, C.E.: Aviation automation: the search for a human-centered approach. Erlbaum, Mahwah (1997)
27. Yang, S., Liu, X., Kang, H., Li, Q.: Interaction design and experience in the context of internet+intelligent design. Packag. Eng. **40**(16), 1–13 (2019)
28. Gong, X., Zhang, J., Chen, L.: Research on mental modeling of the elderly and its application in the field of interaction design. Packag. Eng. **42**(24), 84–92 (2021)
29. Bu, X.: Research on Mobile Application UI Interaction Design Based on User Mental Model. Northeast Electric Power University, Jilin (2021)
30. Card, S.K., Moran, T.P., Newell, A.: The psychology of human-computer interaction. Am. J. Psychol. **25**(4) (1983)
31. Gentner, D., Stevens, A.L. (eds.): Mental Models. Psychology Press, London (1983)
32. Lee, J.D., See, K.A.: Trust in automation: designing for appropriate reliance. Hum. Factors **46**(1), 50–80 (2004)
33. Parasuraman, R., Riley, V.: Humans and automation: use, misuse, disuse. Abuse. Hum. Factors **39**(2), 230–253 (1997)
34. Endsley, M.R.: Toward a theory of situation awareness in dynamic systems. Hum. Factors **37**(1), 32–64 (1995)
35. Parasuraman, R., Sheridan, T.B., Wickens, C.D.: A model for types and levels of human interaction with automation. IEEE Trans. Syst. Man Cybern. Part A: Syst. Hum. (2000)
36. Ajzen, I.: The theory of planned behavior. Organ. Behav. Hum. Decis. Process. **50**, 179–211 (1991)
37. Larkin, H., Simon, H.A.: Why a diagram is (sometimes) worth ten thousand words. Cogn. Sci. **11**(1), 65–100 (1987)

Generating Specifications from Requirements Documents for Smart Devices Using Large Language Models (LLMs)

Rainer Lutze[1](✉) and Klemens Waldhör[2]

[1] Dr.-Ing. Rainer Lutze Consulting, Wachtlerhof, Langenzenn, Germany
rainerlutze@lustcon.eu
[2] FOM University of Applied Sciences, Nuremberg, Germany
klemens.waldhoer@fom.de

Abstract. The current contribution of artificial intelligence based Large Language Models (LLMs) in supporting the requirements engineering and design phase of software centered systems is analyzed. The application domain is focused on smart devices and services for Ambient Assisted Living (AAL), e.g. programmable smartwatches. In the realm of AAL, programmable smartwatches offer significant potential to support elderly users in their daily activities. However, developing applications for these devices is resource demanding, algorithmically difficult and requires careful consideration of various factors, including user-specific needs (e.g. a diminished natural sensation of thirst) and technical constraints (restricted computational power due to limited battery capacity). Our approach first utilizes widespread LLMs like ChatGPT, BARD to automatically interpret and enrich product concept catalogues, targeting at comprehensive, consistent and tailored requirements specifications for the specific domain of application. Secondly, we analyze in which extent LLMs today can contribute to the original design phase by introducing suitable functional principles and reference architectures for fulfilling the services specified as requirements including the constraints on its operations. To demonstrate the challenges and perils of this approach, we will detail the process using the specific use case of automatic drinking detection and providing suitable advice for preventing dehydration for elderly users. We will discuss and differentiate the principal strength of the approach from its actual limitations by the presently available LLMs, which are expected to increase and elaborate their generative capabilities rather frequently.

Keywords: Large language models (LLMs) · LLMs for analyzing and enriching requirements definitions · LLMs for generating design specifications · smart devices and service · systems and software engineering

1 Background and Motivation

Generative artificial intelligence (AI) in the form of large language models (LLMs) is increasingly popular also for software engineering [1, 2]. For the software development life cycle (SDLC), major efficiency improvements will be expected from this technology. Currently, the majority of all LLM studies analyzes and has been implemented

M. Kurosu and A. Hashizume (Eds.): HCII 2024, LNCS 14684, pp. 94–108, 2024.
https://doi.org/10.1007/978-3-031-60405-8_7

for the *software development (coding, test) phase, maintenance, quality assurance and requirements engineering phase* (listed in decreasing frequency, e.g. Fig. 8, [1]). A typical example for this application scenario is the IBM Programmer's Assistant *Socrates* [3] based on OpenAI's Codex LLM, which also powers the GitHub Copilot LLM, for supporting Python *coding phases.* For the *software design phase* by usage of LLMs, [1] reports only a minimum of 1,29% of all analyzed papers. But, especially for long-lived systems and software, especially the design phase is essential for the documenting taken design decisions, in order the record the original scope of the system and to facilitate further evolution and refactoring of the software during its life cycle.

2 Prior Work

Sommerville [4] differentiates systems engineering ([4], chap. 19) from software engineering. Systems engineering targets at a complete sociotechnical system consisting of hardware computing devices, software delivering a set of services and the system owner, its users and their organizational and societal context. The engineering process has to establish a purposeful collection of interrelated components of different kind collaborating to fulfill defined requirements definitions. ([4], 19.1). This extended reach requires to consider for the properties of the system, e.g. reliability, not only the software, but also hardware as well as the envisioned operators of the system, users. One decisive feature of systems engineering is the central role of conceptual design within the engineering process. Conceptual design incrementally elaborates a vision of the required system and its features, simultaneously adapting the requirements definitions, deciding what needs to be procured for the realization of the system, what needs to be developed and also shaping the operational concept for the system. This systems engineering approach will be also the case in the chosen application domains of smart devices and services.

In contrast, for pure software engineering, in principle the system and software design phase typically follows a prior requirements analysis and definition phase ([4], 2.1.1). In practice and especially for up-to-date iterative software processes like agile development, software requirements engineering and software design will be intertwined and performed alternatingly. System models as essential design findings will be used as early as possible in order to clarify and illustrate the fulfillment of prominent requirements to stakeholders already during the initial requirements engineering phase.

Systematically, the design phase is typically subdivided in an initial *system modelling* sub-phase followed by an *architectural design* sub-phase and a *detailed design* subphase ([4], chap. 5, 6). For the *system modelling* sub-phase, suitable *structural* and *behavioral* models fulfilling the entirety of requirements definitions will be identified and typically expressed by *UML class diagrams, collaboration, sequence* and/or *activity diagrams.* The following *architectural design* introduces a suitable *system structure,* its *distribution* and *decomposition* into components. In this sub-phase, proven domain specific reference architectures, e.g. *transaction processing systems,* which are known to solve similar tasks as stated in the requirements definition, are identified, instantiated, adapted and configured. UML *deployment* or – more fine-grained - *component diagrams* are the notation of choice for representing such system structure. The final detailed design sub-phase focusses on database design, interface design and component selection and design ([4], chap. 2.2.2).

The **design thinking** methodology puts a multidisciplinary team of experts and users in the center of a problem solving task. The focal point of design thinking is an iterative, rapid prototyping process with a strict orientation on the actual requirements of the envisioned target groups. Based on *empathy* with the envisioned users, typical cycle phases of the design thinking process, for which a plenitude of supporting tool sets are available, are: *problem framing, inspiration, ideation, prototyping, and testing/evaluating.* The typical application area of the design thinking methodology is the innovation of products and services within business and social contexts [5], not so much system and software. Especially, there is no specific concise approach for the *ideation phase* creating a design from elaborated requirements other than the combination of *divergent* and *convergent* thinking. In the systems and software engineering discipline, the methodology was elaborated to **user-centered design** by D. Norman [6]. Many current UI-design concept, like *personas, user stories, or use cases, ...* build on this methodology. Use case diagrams have also made their way into the UML. Although, the inherent weakness of the ideation phase is still unsolved.

The **model based systems design** is characterized in ([7], def. 1.44) as: *"To design a system is to develop a model on the basis of which a real system can be built, developed, or deployed that will satisfy all its requirements."* The original Wymore 1993 model based systems engineering concept is strongly mathematically oriented and resulted in the Systems Modelling Language (SysML). From our point of view it is not as universally suited and widespread used than the Universal Modelling Language (UML) [8] for representing software designs.

The **domain-driven design** [9] methodology builds on a suitable, known systems resp. Software reference model catalogues for the specific application domain and its logics. The methodology selects and configures a specific instance from the catalogue as foundation for the software design, which fits best to the entirety of requirement specifications for the specific task. Originally emerging from *object-oriented design patters,* meanwhile more complex models like *digital twins* [10] or *state machines* constitute the core elements of the reference model catalogue.

Concept design [11] builds on an inventory of domain independent, reuseable concepts, which are characterized by an (1) expressive *purpose* addressing a specific user need, (2) *familiarity* to the users, and (3) *independence* from other concepts, so that they can be understood, designed and analyzed on at a time separately from other concepts. A concept is characterized by its dynamic behavior (functional principle") typically involving multiple objects and encapsulating its own data model. But, in essence, concepts are *teleological* entities rather than only *semantic* entities [11].

For the usage of LLMs for software engineering, White et al. [12] present a customized prompt pattern catalogue (for ChatGPT) in order to improve and focus the LLM output to the specific needs of different software engineering phases. (see [12], for example section IV.G for the design supporting *"architectural possibilities pattern").* Ahmad et al. [13] use a ChatGPT based bot for generating *recommendations for software architecture.* All these standard LLM based approaches are in prototype state today and suffer from the inherent risks resulting from the opaque data acquisition process: e.g. potential copyright infringements, data poisoning [14], privacy regulations violations by the LLM recommendations, ... On the other side, the built-up of LLMs based exclusively on reliable sources is incredibly expensive, especially for SMEs, so actually there is no practical alternative than using widespread LLMs like OpenAI's ChatGPT™ and(or) Google's BARD™.

3 Goals, Methodology and Research Questions

The presented research aims to verify the effectivity of LLMs for generating systems and software design specifications, based on an analysis end enrichment of given domain specific brief product concept catalogues. Special importance will be put on considering the proven engineering processes for systems and software development for this design phase. Ideally, the design specifications will be expressed in diagrams of the worldwide standard Universal Modelling Language (UML), serving as a universal visual guide for developers. These diagrams are expected to be clear, well-structured, annotated and immediately understandable, facilitating the further development process. It can additionally record taken design decisions and argues about the presence of features within the generated UML diagrams.

3.1 Research Questions

The following four specific research questions have been analyzed by our work:

Q1 To which extend is a domains specific understanding, analysis and enrichment of product concept catalogues currently possible by widespread LLMs, targeting at a consistent, comprehensive and complete requirements specification, customized to the domain of application?

Q2 What is the significance of additional information (either by specific prompt control, documents) for automatically enriching the product concept catalogues given to the LLMs?

Q3 What is the significance of additional information (either by specific prompt control, documents) for supporting the original design process to be performed by the LLMs?

Q4 To which extend is generation of diagrammatic UML design specifications possible by the current capabilities of widespread LLMs?

3.2 Methodology Applied

We performed an experiment consisting of two main phases. For the first main phase for analyzing and enriching given brief product concept catalogues, we used a group of undergraduate computer science students, in order to minimize the potential risk of getting biased assessments about the generative power of current mainstream LLMs (ChaptGPT4.0, BARD). The students had no prior domain expertise in AAL and programmable smartwatch app design experience for the chosen field of application. With this setup of the experiment, we deliberately wanted to avoid an incidental domain specific know-how transfer from the students into the generated specifications other than by direct injection through the LLMs itself. Different student groups were advised to actively use the generative AIs ChatGPT4 or BARD, or – as a control group – only use classical Internet search, without the help of Generative AIs. As an additional reference in assessing the student work results, we used our proven design and implementation work in the field of application [15–17].

The second main phase of the experiment, aiming to verify the conceptual design capabilities of the LLMs based on the results of the first main phase, was carried out by the authors of this paper itself, due to the rather unambiguous (negative) results which do not allow ambiguous assessments.

In the following paragraphs *italic text* indicates answers provided by ChatGPT or BARD.

4 Experiment

4.1 First Main Phase: Generating Requirements Specifications

Experimental Background
The primary aim of this first main phase was to ascertain whether specifications generated by Large Language Models (LLMs) yield results comparable to those produced by human efforts. LLMs used are: ChatGPT 4 (https://chat.openai.com) and BARD (https://bard.google.com). Owing to time constraints, the focus of the experiment was narrowed to the initial stages of the development cycle, specifically the requirements engineering phase. The documents produced for this part of the experiment can be found in [19].

Experimental Design. In an initial stage, a preliminary test with the given assignment (detailed below) of product concept specifications was conducted. The primary objective of this pre-test was to assess the clarity and comprehensibility of the assignment instructions. Participants were divided into three distinct groups: the first group was tasked with manually writing the requirements specification without any external aid, while the second and third group utilized ChatGPT and BARD for the same task.

As this was a preliminary test, the results were not subjected to in-depth analysis. However, it was observed that the solutions generated by the ChatGPT and BARD group were significantly more sophisticated than those of the manual group. The latter's submission predominantly comprised a basic table of items, lacking in structured organization. It is important to note that, unlike participants in the main experiment, these students were in their third semester of a Business Informatics program and had limited experience in software development. Specifically, they had not yet taken a course in software engineering. The pre-test was conducted as part of a lecture on Big Data and Data Science.

The main experiment of this phase consisted of three stages:

In the initial first stage of the experiment, students were allocated into three distinct groups: a manual group (M), a ChatGPT 4.0 group (C), and a BARD group (B). Each group received an identical assignment, presented in German. The manual group's task was to draft the specification document using their software development skills and web resources, explicitly excluding the use of any AI software. In contrast, the remaining two groups employed ChatGPT and BARD, respectively, for their tasks. These groups were required to meticulously record the prompts they used and the corresponding outputs generated by the AI systems, with a strict rule against altering the text.

The main experiment involved six male students, with each group comprising two students. These students were in their fifth semester of a Bachelor's program in Business Informatics, possessing adequate knowledge and practical experience in software engineering and development. The theme of the course was Big Data and Data Science. Notably, they were currently enrolled in a software engineering course. The experiment was conducted as part of a lecture on web technology. All participating students were full-time employees at a prominent German telecommunication company, working in various software-related departments. They were allotted 60 min to complete the task.

Following the exercise, a focused discussion was held. During this session, students were specifically prompted to contemplate any overlooked or implicit requirements of the use case and to propose enhancements to their documents. The exercise concluded with a comprehensive discussion, where the students critically evaluated the specification documents and assigned ratings to each solution based on their performance and accuracy.

In a subsequent follow-up evaluation, the documents produced were further assessed by a group of business informatics students in the fifth semester. These students, who were enrolled in a software engineering course, possessed some experience with requirement analysis, gained either through professional experience or the course itself. The evaluation teams comprised two or three students each. Among these, two groups were tasked with assessing the manually created version of the documents, while one group evaluated the ChatGPT-generated version, and another assessed the version produced by BARD. Ratings should be assigned using a school grading scale, where 1 is the highest (best) grade and 5 is the lowest (worst) grade. Initially, each group familiarized themselves with the assignment task, followed by a thorough reading of the documents assigned to them. This process was allocated a total time frame of approximately 30 min. Upon completion of their evaluations, each group presented their findings, detailing their ratings along with the rationale behind their assessments. This structure ensured a comprehensive and reasoned analysis of the documents.

Assignment Text. The text was composed in German to mitigate any potential misunderstandings arising from language barriers. Deliberately, it was crafted to be somewhat vague, mirroring the common initial phase of a project. This approach was based on the presumption that the customer might not have a clear understanding of the specifics of their envisioned idea. Concurrently, it was hypothesized that the development team lacked substantial expertise in Ambient Assisted Living (AAL) or smartwatch software development.

You have received the following product concept catalogue from your client:

The client needs a smartwatch app that can monitor whether and how much their care-dependent individuals are drinking. If the person drinks too little, they should receive a reminder on their smartwatch. If this reminder is ignored, the care staff must be informed. These reminders should be designed in such a way that care-dependent individuals can easily recognize and respond to them. Also, all data should be centrally managed. In the future, it is planned to monitor additional activities such as walking, sleeping, etc. Additionally, algorithmic sketches should be presented on how the drinking recognition can be implemented

This is all the client has told you. Your task is now to analyze the scenario, deter-mine requirements, use cases, identify missing aspects, and create a specification and requirement document

Since your CEO has heard that LLMs are the future, and the company has not yet been recognized in this field of care, he wants you to work with LLMs for the first draft. However, since he is not sure if all LLMs work equally well, two teams should use different LLMs. And as a precaution, he commissions another team to analyze the scenario in a traditional way

Limitations of the Experiment. It is essential to acknowledge a fundamental limitation of the experiment: the participants were students rather than full-time developers with extensive experience in specifying and designing software. Additionally, these partici-pants lacked experience in designing software for smartwatches and Ambient Assisted Living (AAL) systems. It's worth considering that Large Language Models (LLMs) could potentially assist non-experts in creating specifications, which could actually highlight the utility of LLMs in bridging expertise gaps in software development.

A noteworthy limitation, particularly concerning ChatGPT and BARD, is the usage of different prompts by various groups. For a more detailed and accurate comparison of the outcomes from both Large Language Models (LLMs), it would be essential to utilize an identical sequence of prompts. However, this level of uniformity in prompt usage was not within the scope of this experiment.

Discussion of the Experiment

Discussion of the Manual RE Analysis. The requirements specification document pro-duced by this group, inspired by IEEE830 and its successor ISO/IEC/IEEE 29148:2011 as taught in the SE course, comprises four chapters: an introduction, a general descrip-tion, individual requirements, and technical restrictions, spanning one and a half pages. The six-line introduction outlines the project's goal and application area. The general description covers functionality, user management, restrictions, constraints, and depen-dencies. The core section lists eleven requirements, expanding on the assignment text with more detail. A typical example is the following:

Function 3 - Visual and Acoustic Signal: The app notifies the person in care through an audio signal and a colored pop-up on the display, so they know that the app has successfully recorded the entry

Function 8 - Adjustment of Intervals According to Weather Conditions: depending on the current weather, the app adjusts the time intervals between reminders, as one needs to be notified more frequently in higher temperatures (requires access to the current location of the person and a weather API)

For instance, Function 8, not originally in the customer's product concept catalogue, fits well within the project context. The final chapter lists non-functional requirements, like general technical limitations. However, the document resembles a brainstorming output, lacking specific aspects crucial for smartwatch software development, such as battery management. This reflects a typical outcome from developers new to a domain, lacking deep insight into implementation challenges. It's a useful starting point, but requires further refinement in subsequent sessions.

Discussion of the ChatGPT RE Analysis. Overall about four pages requirements specification document was produced with four prompts. The first prompt asked for an analysis of the scenario. Here ChatGPT started with the main function, esp. drinking detection. Basically ChatGPT takes the description as a starting point and enhances it with features. functional requirements were derived as follows:

Functional Requirements

• *Hydration Monitoring: Recording the daily fluid intake of the user*

• *Alert System: Notifications when the recommended drinking volume is not met*

• *Notification of Care Personnel: Automatic information to the care staff if warnings are ignored*

• *User Interaction: Simple and intuitive interface for people in need of care*

When asked for a requirements and functional specification (roughly corresponding to the German terms "Lasten- und Pflichtenheft" which were used in the prompt) - ChatGPT came up with five main points starting from goals, functional, non-functional, technical requirements and a time plan (not further detailed). The Functional Specification gave an overview of phases as part of the project management. Basically the six steps mentioned followed some kind of waterfall model. These next prompts dealt with identifying use cases. The final prompt deals with missing aspects of the analysis. ChatGPT comes up with ten items starting from integration into the health care system to user acceptance. It explicitly mentions battery management as a missing item. A typical example is the following:

• *Integration with Existing Health Systems: It has not been specified how the app should interact with existing health or care management systems. Compatibility and integration with such systems could be crucial for efficiency*

• *Hardware Requirements: The technical requirements for the smartwatch (e.g., battery life, sensors) have not been precisely defined. This is critical to ensure that the hardware can support the software requirements*

The analysis of ChatGPT, as evidenced by the four prompts, is notably more advanced, informative, and well-structured in its overall presentation.

However, it falls short in delving into detailed aspects, particularly in addressing low battery management. The analysis lacks specific suggestions or considerations on how to effectively tackle this issue. In a separate session ChatGPT was asked how to deal with low battery situations. Although it came up with several useful suggestion it did not propose just to use a second smartwatch in that case. If explicitly asked if this would help it came up with a set of useful guidelines how to integrate a second smartwatch.

Discussion of the BARD RE Analysis. BARD produced a requirements specification document similar to that of ChatGPT. However, for BARD's document, there was a specific request to adhere to the DIN 69901-5 standard.

Requirements looked like that:

The requirements can be specified as follows:

Hydration Monitoring: The app must record and store the fluid intake of the care-dependent individuals. Various sensors can be used for this purpose, such as an accelerometer to detect the opening and closing of a bottle, or a moisture sensor to measure the amount of water consumed

Hydration Alerts: If the fluid intake falls below a certain level, the app must generate a notification for the care-dependent individual. This alert must be designed to be easily understandable and followable

Similarly, use cases were developed. In response to inquiries about overlooked elements, BARD provided the following suggestions:

The following aspects have not yet been considered:

Security: The app must be secure and the data of the care-dependent individuals must be protected

Data Privacy: The app must ensure the privacy of the care-dependent individuals' data

Usability: The app must be user-friendly and take into account the needs of the care-dependent individuals

Interestingly, BARD did not address battery management in its suggestions.

Asked to generate Requirement and Functional Specifications, it produced a well-structured document that serves as a solid foundation for further refinement.

Overall, the documents generated by BARD were quite similar to those produced by ChatGPT. However, ChatGPT appeared slightly more advanced in highlighting technical limitations, which could also be attributed to the use of varying prompts by the respective groups.

Evaluation of the Requirements Within the Course. Table 1 provides a comparative overview of ratings for three requirement documents. These documents were created using for-mentioned different methods: manual preparation, ChatGPT 4.0, and BARD. The evaluation process for the manually prepared document involved group discussions among the students, followed by the assignment of a final overall rating.

The students showed a preference for the solutions generated by the Large Language Models (LLMs), particularly favoring BARD. A notable factor influencing this preference could be BARD's tendency to produce more extensive documents, esp. by providing a template for further improvements. To further assess ChatGPT's evaluative skills, it was tasked with analyzing the three requirement documents. Intriguingly, ChatGPT's assessment aligned closely with the students' rankings.

Table 1. Evaluation of experiment 1 (Big Data Course)

	Manual	ChatGPT	BARD
Criteria			
Extent	0	+	++
Structure	+	+	+
Number Requirements	+	++	++
New Requirements	+	++	+
Student Evaluations			
Criteria Evaluation	3	6	6
Overall Ranking	III	II	I
ChatGPT Evaluations			
Evaluation	++	++	++
School Grade	3	2	1

0 = neutral, + = good, ++ = very good; 1 = very good = 5 very bad

Follow-up evaluation of the requirements within the software engineering course.
The outcomes of the follow-up evaluation are presented in the Table 2 below

Table 2. Follow-up evaluation of experimenT 1 (SE course)

RE Source	Structure	Content	Details	Size	Overall
Manual I	2	1	3	3	2,75
Manual II	3	1	4	2	3
ChatGPT	2	4	3	4	3
BARD	4	2	2	3	3

The evaluation revealed that all requirements specifications received broadly similar ratings. A common critique of the LLM-generated content was its lengthiness and perceived verbosity, though some students appreciated this detail as providing a solid foundation for further development. Notably, it was observed that technical implementation details were absent in the specifications, but it's important to note that this was not the primary focus of these documents.

Overall, the students didn't show a distinct preference for any particular source of the specifications. Interestingly, they assumed all the documents were generated by LLMs. The groups who evaluated the manually created texts were surprised to learn that their assigned documents were actually human-produced. This suggests that the LLMs performed impressively, blurring the lines between human and machine-generated content in terms of quality and style.

4.2   Experiment Second Main Phase: Generating Design Documents

The central goal of the experiment in this main phase was to support the conceptual design of an algorithm capable of monitoring the fluid ingestion behavior of elderly people. To assess the depth of a proposal that could be produced by a LLM, we employed ChatGPT to create several prompts. For an extensive description, refer to [20]. The initial prompt requested an approach for accomplishing this task:

> *"The task is to develop a smartwatch app which is able to detect drinking. The smartwatch comprises various sensors. Please advise which approach could be used."*

ChatGPT initially outlined potential sensors, then proposed methods for their utilization.

> *"5. Machine Learning and Data Processing:*
>
> - *Use machine learning techniques to process and analyze the sensor data.*
> - *Collect a large dataset of sensor readings during drinking and other activities for training the ML models.*
> - *Implement real-time data processing to allow the app to detect drinking as it happens."*

The response was fundamentally accurate, particularly in its recommendation of ML-based methods. It also addressed several other aspects, including privacy concerns. Following that, we explored the feasibility of using neural networks for this purpose. ChatGPT delineated the necessary steps for such a solution. Notably, its insights on network architecture were intriguing.

> "3. Neural Network Design:
>
> - *Model Architecture: For time-series data, recurrent neural networks (RNNs) like LSTM (Long Short-Term Memory) or GRUs (Gated Recurrent Units) are effective as they can capture temporal dependencies. Convolutional Neural Networks (CNNs) can also be used to identify patterns in sensor data."*

ChatGPT recognized the issue as a time-series problem and suggested a range of appropriate architectural solutions. Given our extensive experience in developing applications for Ambient Assisted Living (AAL), we could confidently assess the relevance of these suggestions. All proposed architectures were practical and had been previously implemented. When asked which architecture was most promising, ChatGPT presented six options and provided selection criteria, ultimately recommending:

> *"A hybrid CNN-LSTM model is often a strong candidate for this kind of task. It combines the feature extraction capabilities of CNNs with the sequence modeling strengths of LSTMs, making it well-suited for analyzing complex sensor data patterns associated with human movements like drinking."*

This recommendation seemed highly promising. Although we have previously utilized LSTMs, the integration with CNNs had not been explored. Consequently, we requested a Python implementation from ChatGPT, resulting in a straightforward model combining CNN and LSTM layers. Although it lacked detailed explanations for certain parameters, such as "model.add(LSTM(50, return_sequences = True))", it provided a basic framework for training.

Further prompts inquired about alternative algorithmic approaches for analyzing sensor data linked to drinking. We had previously employed simpler models like logistic regression. ChatGPT suggested several viable methods.

Although, and mentioned as an example, as well ChaptGPT and BARD failed to offer specific designs for fulfilling the central requirements of *hydration monitoring* and *hydration alerts* (see above, chapt. 4.1). The critical issue in this subject is to determine the individual nominal value, how much fluid an elderly person should ingest daily. In general, a rough estimation of 30 ml per kg bodyweight per day can be used [18], or the much more elaborated model [17], chap. 3.1. In each case, a couple of additional corrective factors must be considered for calculating the correct nominal value: actual exposure of the elderly person to higher temperatures, excessive physical activities, actual medical conditions like fewer, diarrhea or vomiting, heart or renal insufficiencies. From this plenitude of factors, only the possibility to correct the nominal value by excessive physical activity detected by the smartwatch was proactively offered by ChatGPT or BARD. For a professional solution, this is not sufficient with respect to the state of the art.

Lastly, we asked about implementing this on a smartwatch, leading to the suggestion of using TensorFlow Lite, suitable for mobile phones and smartwatches.

In the final refinement step, we asked ChatGPT developing an Android implementation using the TensorFlow Lite model, which would generate an alert if the wearer did not drink within an hour. ChatGPT delivered a basic, yet functional, code. While not ready for production, the experiment's one-hour timeframe made the results notably impressive, considering previous implementations took weeks.

This experiment demonstrated that ChatGPT can significantly expedite the development of a functional prototype app, potentially within a day. While an experienced programmer with relevant domain knowledge might achieve similar timelines, it's remarkable that ChatGPT enables those without extensive expertise in AAL or smartwatch programming to develop solutions so swiftly. In conclusion, for certain stages of the software development cycle, LLMs like ChatGPT can be immensely beneficial in accelerating development.

5   Conclusions

In the following we will discuss our findings with regard to our research questions Q1–Q4.

Q1: The use of LLMs in generating elaborated requirements specifications from given brief product concept catalogues represents a significant qualitative and efficiency-improving advancement in the development of smartwatch applications for AAL.

Q2: Currently, LLMs can only generate recommendations and lists of potentially useful reference architectures and possible functional principles for the wanted solution. But, the core competence of conceptual design, to **select,** propose and justify the *best suited solution* to fulfill the entirety of specified requirements is still missing. The effectiveness of the proposed solutions increases with the specificity of the prompt, especially regarding architectural or algorithmic challenges. This was evident in our experiment, where the choice of an appropriate neural network architecture yielded better outcomes when detailed prompts were used.

Q3: The response here mirrors that of Q2. The efficacy of providing the user with additional information largely hinges on the prompts used. Generally, the supplementary information provided tends to be of a relatively high level. However, it frequently lacks in addressing specific, detailed aspects.

Q4: Consequently, it is still not possible for LLMs to generate a graphical UML depiction of this favored solution. Therefore, a domain experienced human systems architect is still essential for this systems design phase. The assistance ChatGPT and BARD can actually offer is of no essential help for this specific task, because the LLM generated lists of potential technology candidates is expected to be already and always on the mind of a real human domain expert. It's important to note that in later stages of the development process, such as generating class diagrams from more detailed implementation specifications, LLMs prove to be quite helpful. Moreover, as the process progresses towards producing source code, the support and effectiveness of LLMs become even more pronounced.'

One of the authors, Waldhör, is actively involved in a research project that integrates smart home technology, smartwatches, and robotics within the framework of Ambient Assisted Living (AAL) at home. In this context, the application of Large Language Models (LLMs) in the final phase of implementation – particularly in generating source code from REST interface specifications and integrating these interfaces with sensor data transmission – has demonstrated significant utility. This effectiveness is notably evident when compared to traditional methods that rely on resources such as GitHub.

Unfortunately, the original target of generating similar professional *design documents,* especially UML diagrams for representing the design results, is still out of scope by the current enhancements of LLM technology. The situation is set to evolve once Large Language Models (LLMs) gain the capability to a) generate XML-based descriptions for UML, such as XMI (XML Metadata Interchange), and b) integrate with graphical software systems. This advancement will significantly enhance the utility and application of LLMs in the field of UML modeling.

Finally, it is crucial to acknowledge that these findings 1) are specific to the selected application domain and 2) apply only to the Large Language Models (LLMs) as they existed at the time of writing this paper. If applied to broader application domains, such as ERP systems, the results might vary, with LLMs potentially offering more refined specifications. While generalizing these conclusions to other application domains and projecting them into the near future is not entirely implausible, each potential use case must be carefully evaluated on its own merits.

References

1. Hou, X, Zhao, Y., Liu, Y., et al.: Large language models for software engineering: a systematic literature review, research report, Huazhong University of Science and Technology, Wuhan, China, arXiv:2308.10620v4, p. 62, September 2023
2. Zhang, Q., Fang, C., Xie, Y., et al: A survey on large language models for software engineering, China, arXiv:2312.15223v1, p. 57, December 2023
3. Ross, S.I., Martinez, F., Houde, S., Muller, M., Weisz, J.D.: The programmer's assistant: conversational interaction with a large language model for software development. In: ACM 28th International Conference on Intelligent User Interfaces (IUI '23), 27–31 March, Sydney, Australia (2023). https://doi.org/10.1145/3581641.3584037
4. Sommerville, I.: Software Engineering, 10th updated edn. Pearson Education Limited, Harlow, England (2017)
5. Brown, T.: Design thinking. Harv. Bus. Rev. **86**(6), 84–92(2008)
6. Norman, A., Draper, W.: User Centered System Design – New Perspectives on Human-Computer Interaction, CRC Press, Boca Raton (1986)
7. Wymore, A.W.: Model Based Systems Engineering: An Introduction to the Mathematical Theory of Discrete Systems and to the Tricotyledon of System Design, CRC Press, Boca Raton (1993)
8. Bennett, S., Skelton, J., Lunn, K.: UML, 2nd edn. Schaum's Outlines, McGrawHill Education – Europe, New York (1991)
9. Evans, E.: Domain Driven Design – Tackling Complexity in the Heart of Software, Addison-Wesley, MA, USA, 8th printing (2006)
10. Lutze, R.: Digital twins – a determining engineering pattern. In: IEEE International Conference on Engineering, Technology and Innovation (ICE/ITMC), Edinburgh, United Kingdom, pp. 1–9 (2023). https://doi.org/10.1109/ICE/ITMC58018.2023.10332426
11. Wilczynski, P., Gregiore-Wright, T., Jackson, D.: Concept centric software development – an experience report. In: ACM SIGPLAN International Symposium on New Ideas, New Paradigms, and Reflections on Programming and Software (Onward! '23), 25–27 October, Cascais, Portugal (2023). https://doi.org/10.1145/3622758.3622894
12. White, J., Hays, S., Fu, Q., Spencer-Smith, J., Schmidt, D.C.: CHatGPT Prompt Patterns for Improving Code Quality, Refactoring, Requirements Elicitation, and Software Design, Vanderbilt University, Nashville, TN, USA, arXiv:2303.07839v1, p. 14, March 2023
13. Ahmad, A., Waseem, M., Liang, P., Fadimeh, M., Aktar, M.S., Mikkonen, T.: Towards human-bot collaborative software architecting with ChatGPT. In: ACM International Conference on Evaluating and Assessment in Software Engineering (EASE '23), June 14–16 2023, Oulu, Finland, pp. 279–285 (2023). https://doi.org/10.1145/3593434.3593468
14. Schneider, B, Stuber, M.: IntelligenteWerkzeuge im Software Engineering. Informatik J. (12), 21–292021. https://opus.hs-furtwangen.de/frontdoor/deliver/index/docId/7709/file/IntelligenteWerkzeugeimSoftwareEngineering.pdf
15. Lutze, R., Waldhör, K.: The application architecture of smartwatch apps – analysis, principles of design and organization. In: Mayr, H.C., Pinzger, M. (eds.) INFORMATIK 2016. LNI, vol. P259, pp. 1865–1878. Springer, Bonn (2016). ISBN 978-3-88579-653-4, ISSN 1617-5468, https://cs.emis.de/LNI/Proceedings/Proceedings259/1865.pdf
16. Lutze, R.: Practicality of automatic monitoring sufficient fluid intake for older people. In: IEEE 10th International Conference on Healthcare Informatics (ICHI), 11–14 June, Rochester, MN, USA, pp. 330–336 (2022). https://doi.org/10.1109/ICHI54592.2022.00054
17. Lutze, R., Waldhör, K.: Practicality aspects of automatic fluid intake monitoring via smart-watches. In: Kurosu, M., Hashizume, A. (eds.) H HCII 2023. LNCS, vol. 14014, pp. 67–86. Springer, Cham (2023). https://doi.org/10.1007/978-3-031-35572-1_5

18. Hall, J.E., Guyton, A.C.: Textbook on Medical Physiology, 14th edn. Elsevier Publishing Inc., Philadelphia, PA, USA (2020)
19. Waldhör, K., et al.: Experiment: Vergleich von Manueller vs. LLM basierten Analyse eines AAL Software Scenarios [Experiment: Comparison of Manual vs. LLM-based Analysis of an AAL Software Scenario] RETexte_konsolidiert_v1.pdf (2024)
20. Waldhör, K.: Development of a drinking detection smartwatch app for android: a comprehensive documentation of ChatGPT's role in the process (2024). http://www.waldhor.com/chi24/chatgptdrinkappdocumentation.pdf

Unified UI Design System for Industrial HMI Software Development

Lev Malyi[1] and Matvei Bryksin[2]

[1] McCormick UK Ltd, Peterborough PE7 3HH, UK
[2] Constructor University, 28759 Bremen, Germany
mbryksin@jacobs-university.de

Abstract. In the early 2020s, the industrial sector, accounting for 13% of Europe's GDP, faced challenges in adopting modern software technologies, lagging behind the immense progress seen in web and mobile domains. This gap stems largely from PLC manufacturers' reliance on proprietary systems, limiting innovation and creating additional constraints in developing unified visualisation systems across diverse Integrated Development Environments (IDEs). This inconsistency affects the user experience in Human-Machine Interface (HMI) applications. To address these challenges, we propose an all-in-one unified design system organising a library of standard reusable cross-platform UI components designed for industrial applications. This design system aims to standardise and simplify the creation of HMI screens, ensuring consistent user interfaces across various platforms. Thereby, the integration of web-based technologies minimises the time and cost of implementation and maintains visualisation solutions across different manufacturing cases. As a result, the initial implementation of this design system led to the development and integration of 28 UI controls into Siemens and CodeSys IDEs, enhancing the usability and quality of industrial HMI screens. Usability tests revealed significant improvements in user experience over traditional vendor-supplied controls. Future research will extend this design system to cover more comprehensive industrial use cases, promoting efficiency and standardisation in industrial software development.

Keywords: Design Methods and Techniques · Heuristics and Guidelines for Design · User Experience · Industrial HMI · Design System

1 Introduction

Commencing in the 18th century, the Industrial Revolution emerged as the primary catalyst for human progress, noted as the most profound revolution in human history due to its far-reaching impact on the daily lives of individuals. Over time, societies have embraced mass production, logistics, and industrial electronics, continuously accelerating overall advancement. Presently, tens of thousands of manufacturing entities engage the services of hundreds of thousands of contractor companies and equipment developers to sustain production and innovate new product lines. McKinsey's 2020 Industry 4.0 survey of more than 800 businesses globally revealed three major challenge areas: financial hurdles, organisational problems, and technology roadblocks [1].

M. Kurosu and A. Hashizume (Eds.): HCII 2024, LNCS 14684, pp. 109–124, 2024.
https://doi.org/10.1007/978-3-031-60405-8_8

A critical impediment in industrial software development arises from manufacturers of Programmable Logic Controllers (PLCs) and other control systems. These suppliers commonly supply developers with proprietary hardware and development environments, imposing substantial limitations on innovation and adaptability. Even with the first steps for the code development standards, the visualisation of such systems remains non-cross-platform and lacks standardisation tailored to specific requirements. Equipment suppliers, system integrators, and factories must allocate considerable resources to HMI and SCADA systems development, frequently approaching each project from scratch. Vendor lock limits re-usage of already developed solutions.

Various vendors offer standard components for visualisation screens with essential native controls and interface capabilities. The use of web-based components to enhance the usability and appearance of the user interface is a new approach to development among different vendors. Such a web-based architecture enables quick updates and easy integration of new features into their development IDEs [2]. As a result, the industry trend is adapting modern tools and technologies to the HMI development process and integrating web applications into the industrial environment [3].

This article introduces a comprehensive design system to tackle this challenge and harmonise the fragmented landscape of HMI software development. Such a design system incorporates a repository of standard UI components and design principles [4], offering a blueprint for a standardised set of reusable UI elements finely tuned for control, monitoring, and diagnostic applications. This library aims for significant reductions in development costs, facilitates reuse across diverse projects and equipment, and pioneers the integration of modern development methodologies in the industrial environment. This research aims to develop and integrate such a design system into production to enable user testing and benchmarking with existing solutions.

2 Hardware Solutions for Industrial HMIs

The production role of humans has evolved throughout the history of industry and manufacturing. Initially, operators were the direct driving force behind industries. Machines for metal processing, sewing, and various devices simply couldn't function without them. However, as machines became more "intelligent," the operator's role shifted from direct equipment control to operation monitoring. Now, humans often serve as observers and controllers rather than executors.

2.1 SCADA

Before delving into the description of industrial HMIs, it's essential to highlight their connection to Supervisory Control and Data Acquisition (SCADA). The aims of HMI/SCADA systems are mainly manufacturing processes controlling and visualisation, shortening the time of realised tasks, monitoring and controlling its selected subsystems and units, as well as enabling quick reactions to various possible scenarios and problems requiring effective interventions [5]. This system comprises a set of software and hardware components that transmit data from equipment, sensors, and other data collection tools via various data interfaces to intelligent devices, such as Programmable Logic Controller (PLC) or Remote Terminal Units (RTU). These devices analyse and process this information, presenting it in readable form to the operator through HMI interfaces. All PLC equipment is certified and has built-in control over programmatic errors to prevent possible production outages that will cause big losses to the business. This system allows production monitoring and transmission of control actions from upper-level personnel to lower-level actuators.

Visualisation can be seen at two levels: equipment-based and remote. Depending on the type and application methods, equipment with various display types can show real-time data on energy usage (kilowatt-hours, bars of compressed air, liquid volume) for on-site production process monitoring. In addition to the equipment-based monitoring, the production integrator will develop an HMI interface that combines information from various types of equipment used in the system to be shown remotely in the specified locations.

Remote visualisation also varies based on the role of the company worker interacting with it. The visualisation system can be directly located near the production cell or line, serving as a control system for the operator. Alternatively, it can be in a maintenance room or at the plant manager's office, unifying multiple lines and cells and providing a more comprehensive overview of the entire plant's current status [6]. In this article, we will pay more attention to the concept of industrial HMI, which aims to manage, monitor, and analyse the operation of a specific automated cell or line.

2.2 Industrial HMI

Depending on the automated process and the interaction between the system and personnel, we can distinguish two types of HMIs: stationary and portable [7]. In some cases, the process demands that the operator moves with the control panel due to their constant interaction needs. This is often associated with industrial manipulators or robots, where the operator needs to "teach" various positions, refine them, or adjust process parameters (welding, adhesive application, sealing, painting, etc.). In such instances, various manufacturers offer solutions based on portable HMIs, which may have extra safety buttons (Fig. 1).

Fig. 1. Types of portable HMI solutions

A wire connects this visualisation panel to the control cabinet. It allows the operator to move around the entire facility area (limited by the cable length) and continuously communicate with the control system. The drawbacks are evident from the name— such a system needs to be carried everywhere, handled delicately, and protected from impacts and scratches. Besides production lines and cells, HMIs are used in other parts of plants and production facilities, such as logistics systems, inventory management, quality control, etc., where operators require much more compact and remote equipment that can be put in a pocket and operate without recharging for an extended period [8].

The stationary version can be installed directly in one of the doors of the main control cabinet, placed on a separate rack, or have multiple copies along the production line or cell (Fig. 2). This version of HMI often consists of three elements: a touch screen, physical control buttons, which may come with the screen or be installed separately by the system developer, and a signal tower that consist of multicoloured LED blocks and a sound module. An emergency stop button (EMS) is often found among the physical buttons, which instantly halts the process in an emergency.

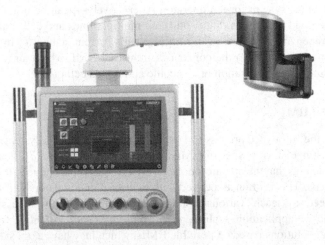

Fig. 2. Stationary HMI for production line or cell

The drawback of this type of HMI is also evident from the name: to interact with the system, a person must approach a specific location in the cell. In this case, the visual interface must also be larger to be visible from a distance. At the same time, it becomes easier to depict equipment on the production system's layout since the position of the visualisation panel is static, and the arrangement of elements can be placed according to their actual installation location.

2.3 Vendors

The global human-machine interface (HMI) market reached a valuation of USD 5.24 billion in 2022 and is anticipated to exhibit a compound annual growth rate (CAGR) of

10.4% from 2023 to 2030. The market comprises small and large players, each offering solutions ranging from small cross-platform displays and visualisation stations to extensive hardware and software products. Indeed, in the environment of significant production outputs, the preference leans towards major market players capable of providing not only equipment and software but also teams for integration, support, sales, and more.

Large manufacturing companies often have internal standards, limiting the choice of vendors applicable to their production, which arises from various factors:

- **Economic**: A defined list of suppliers allows cost savings through discounts for large equipment and software orders, reduces contract negotiation costs, and sets prices for service offerings.
- **Service**: With a fixed quantity of equipment that can be used in production, it becomes easier to conduct inventories and control changes.
- **Knowledge**: Operators and maintenance team members become specialists in working with specific equipment, understanding all its nuances.

However, alongside the benefits of standardisation come drawbacks. A manufacturing company becomes beholden to the software and hardware limitations of the supplier. They are compelled to adopt the solutions available from the vendor, making it challenging to integrate emerging electronics and automation market innovations yet to be supported by their standard (which can take years). Integrator companies constructing automated cells and lines from scratch instead of developing standardised solutions face a similar challenge. To meet standards for each factory, system integrator would need a team of specialists capable of understanding and designing systems for any vendor solutions, which is economically unfeasible and beyond practicality. Even if the resources were available, creating a product that uniformly operates based on different equipment would be challenging due to the unique characteristics of each hardware and software, ultimately preventing the attainment of identical products.

3 Software Development Solutions for Industrial HMIs

As mentioned earlier, each major vendor owns an ecosystem of proprietary software. This ecosystem enables the creation of automated projects using the manufacturer's equipment (routers, sensors, drives, and other "low-level" equipment, often cross-platform) through code development and visualisation.

There is a trend toward standardisation in code development for automation. The International Electrotechnical Commission (IEC) developed the IEC 61131-3:2013 standard, "a specification of the syntax and semantics of a unified suite of programming languages, including the overall software model and a structuring language" [9]. This set includes two textual languages, Instruction List (IL) and Structured Text (ST), and two graphical languages, Ladder Diagram (LD) and Function Block Diagram (FBD). While major players default to supporting these development languages, it doesn't necessarily mean you can copy a program from one development environment and paste it into another, as even in these seemingly standardised languages, there may be slight variations. Moreover, even when the program is the same for the graphic languages, different IDEs won't let you copy and paste because of how each system stores the code.

In contrast, concerning visualisation development, there is no movement toward unification and standardisation of the HMI development process. Almost every major vendor will provide documentation on how, in their opinion, "good" visualisation should look, but little beyond that. Sometimes, a vendor may offer standard libraries for typical control elements within additional software products, encompassing both code and visualisation elements (valves, motors, safety buttons). However, a project developed using such a library cannot be transferred to a project under a different vendor.

It's worth noting that the development of visualisation projects will look similar across vendors. You will be provided with a set of controls and a screen area to transfer and arrange these elements, specifying required options (sizes, fonts, positions, linked variables, etc.). However, the quantity, design, and customisation of these control elements will differ in each development environment, and you cannot export such a project from one system to another. Figure 3 below summarises the four major software development systems for visualisation and a graph showing control library distribution for each vendor.

UI Elements	Siemens	Rockwell	Codesys	B&R
Drawings Lines, Shapes	7	10	8	4
Data I/O Input fields, Labels, Comboboxes	3	4	6	5
Data Controls Buttons, Radio Buttons, Checkboxes	4	7	6	3
Field Devices Lamps, Switches, Bars, Meters	3	2	12	2
Screen Management Tabs, Groups, Sliders	2	6	4	2
Gauge and Graphs	3	2	5	1
User Management	2	10	0	1
Alarms Management	2	8	7	1
Misc Browsers, Icons, Keys, ActiveX	4	12	10	4

Fig. 3. UI elements comparison table and graph of different vendors

Apart from the difference in the quantity of visualisation elements, each development environment will have its control's design. While you can change its basic characteristics, such as colour and font type, its form and behaviour depend entirely on the software (Fig. 4).

Hence, from a visualisation standpoint, a supplier of automated solutions can't create an identical cross-platform product. They may attempt to make them alike, but they must hire specialists familiar with each system to achieve this. Branding visualisation for a specific manufacturer also becomes an impossible task, as changing each element on all screens will take forever.

Chasing modern trends, some vendors are incorporating the capability to import controls based on web technologies (HTML, CSS, JS) into their systems, which we consider an excellent opportunity to begin implementing modern, cross-platform solutions.

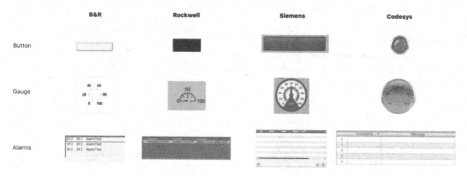

Fig. 4. Visual design differences in button, gauge and alarm components between vendors

4 Industrial HMI Design System

Essentially, a design system is a structured collection of reusable components guided by clear standards and comprehensive guides [10]. It encapsulates design principles, best practices, design assets, and code. Design systems for web and mobile applications are widely researched and have comprehensive documentation [11] with the standard architecture. Design principles for Industrial HMI [12] usually define the set of rules and best practices in order to provide a unified and consistent experience across different screens on the site. Design System for HMIs is not just a collection of reusable, shared assets. It's an evolving ecosystem of foundations, design patterns, guidelines, and a toolkit, designed to speed up development and build scalable solutions.

For industrial HMIs, we suggest a layered architecture of a design system containing key elements: 0 – Design Foundations, 1 – Brand Identity, 2 – Design Tokens, 3 – UI Kit, 4 – UI Components, and 5 – Design Library. This structured approach ensures a consistent user experience and visual style across diverse applications (Fig. 5).

4.1 Design Foundations

The design system's foundations cover the basis of any user interface, from accessibility standards to essential patterns for communication and interaction. As the most critical part of the design system, it answers the fundamental questions regarding how design functions and its governance rules. Key aspects include:

- **Design Principles**: Encompassing customisation guidelines and overarching design guidelines.
- **Interaction and Accessibility**: Principles and UX patterns focus on user inclusivity and ease of interaction.
- **Tone of Voice**: Strategies for communication, content guidelines, and a standardised vocabulary.

Properly designed foundations act as a constraint mechanism, offering actionable and pragmatic recommendations, thereby guiding interface designers in creating systematic and user-centric designs.

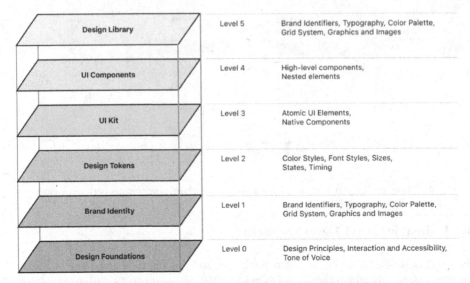

Fig. 5. Structure of 0–5 levels for the Industrial HMI Design System

4.2 Brand Identity

The unique brand identity covers a company's visual and stylistic elements, which shape users' perceptions during interaction with the HMI screens. A single source of truth of the brand identity elements allows companies to maintain consistency across various platforms, hardware devices and applications [13]. The basic elements of the brand identity include:

- **Brand Identifiers:** Key elements like name, logo, and slogan.
- **Typography:** Fonts and guidelines for their pairing.
- **Colour Palette:** Colour scheme with pairing rules and usage guidelines.
- **Grid System:** Adaptive design and usage of modular design.
- **Graphics and Images:** Vector graphics, illustrations, and icons.

Customising these elements is crucial for scalable and flexible brand representation, especially in white labelling processes for the umbrella brands. A standardised library of brand identity elements ensures a cohesive look and feel across all assets, emphasising harmony and accessibility in design.

4.3 Design Tokens

Design tokens compile the foundations and brand identity into modifiable variables for the design elements and user interface controls. Tokens work with all style files and configurations in the design system, making the design consistent and easy to scale. Instead of using hard codes like colour hex codes or pixel sizes, it assigns variables and names for them. These tokens can be linked to create light and dark themes and keep the visual style consistent across different elements and screens.

Design tokens application ranges from setting background colours and font styles to managing responsive layouts and transitions:

- **Colour Styles:** Background, Border, Shadows
- **Font Styles:** Font Family, Font Size, Font Weight
- **Sizes:** Grid, Spaces, Line Height, Control's Heights, Border Radius, Z-index
- **States:** Default, Hover, Active, Selected, Visited, Disabled, Enabled
- **Timing:** Duration, Transition

Naming of the design tokens is the crucial part of the proper implementation of the design system. Usually, tokens have different naming levels to split the context and define the semantics of usage. For example, "Global" tokens represent fundamental values like 'black-900'. "Alias" tokens are context-specific, such as 'bg-color', while "Component-specific" tokens are tied to particular components, like "panel-bg-color" (Fig. 6).

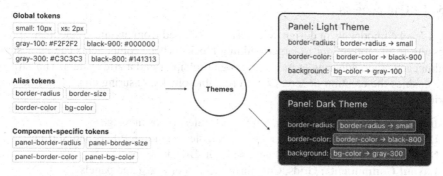

Fig. 6. Example of the design tokens applied for colour theming

With tokens maintaining uniformity and managing brands, it is becoming more accessible, faster, and cheaper to apply an intuitive visual hierarchy system. Moreover, validation of the foundations and brand identity rules can be automated based on the design tokens' logic and structure. For example, design tokens for font size and line spacing could be calculated from font pairing guidelines or colour schemes. The colour pairing could be checked for accessibility rules such as minimum contrast and colour blindness.

4.4 UI Kit

To create a comprehensive UI kit of reusable interface elements for Industrial HMI and visualisation screens, the atomic components can be organised into specific sections, ensuring that all elements are included for a robust and user-friendly design system.

- **Text Elements:** Headings, Paragraphs, Hint Text
- **Data Input/Output:** Text Inputs, Label, Buttons, Radio Buttons, Checkboxes, Labels, Comboboxes, Toggles, Date Picker, File Uploader, Sliders, Steppers

- **Field Device Elements:** Lamps, Switches, Meters, Batteries, E-Stop Buttons, Safety and Compliance Indicators
- **Navigation and Screen Management:** Links, Cards, Tabs, Button Group, Pagination, Dropdowns, Popovers, Carousels
- **Visualization Components:** Lines and Shapes, Tables, List, Progress Bars, Loading Indicators, Search Functionality, Tooltips
- **Gauges and Graphs:** Pie Charts, Line Charts, Bar Charts, Gauges
- **User Management:** Avatar, Status Indicators, Badges, User Activation Cards
- **Alarms Management:** Alerts and Toasts, Notifications, Alarm Indicators
- **Miscellaneous**: Icons, Browser Widgets, Keyboard and Keypad Elements, Callouts, SCADA Elements, PLC Integration Widgets, Network Status Indicators

Organized UI kit provides a foundational framework for building interfaces for industrial HMI systems, consistency of interaction and functional efficiency.

4.5 UI Components

High-level components in design systems are developed from atomic UI elements, progressing from more minor to larger building blocks. These components can be nested within each other, adhering to modular design principles and a grid system. This structure enables the creation of screens with reusable blocks, ensuring consistency across various screens.

- **Input and Interaction:** Forms, Validation Rules, Error messages
- **Data Visualization:** Graphs, Charts, Data tables including Filters and Sorting
- **Navigation:** Header, Footer, Menus, Sidebar, Breadcrumbs
- **Layout Components:** Grids, Containers like accordions, and panels
- **Utility Components:** Placeholders, Empty state UIs

Complex UI components are often tailored to specific manufacturing scenarios and can be expanded to meet unique business needs.

4.6 Design Library

The design library serves as a standardised visual toolkit for integrators and HMI systems developers, offering out-of-the-box solutions for different vendors and equipment providers. It facilitates interface building with a UI Kit and high-level UI components, including templates for common screens and widgets for standard equipment. Key functions typically covered in the Design Library: Status and Diagnostics, Operation and Control, Production and Process Visualization, Settings and Parameters Management, Equipment and Machinery Interface, Maintenance and Troubleshooting, Safety and Emergency Procedures, Alarm Management.

5   Implementation of Web-Based Design System for HMI

The web-based design system offers a cross-platform functionality with the different vendors support. It ensures a uniform user experience across HMI applications and complex visualisation systems. Incorporating version control for the code facilitates efficient change management, supporting continuous deployment and integration without vendor dependency. This architecture establishes a single design truth, allowing seamless distribution to PLC systems.

The system's architecture includes four main components that streamline the journey from design to IDE integration: UI Design Assets, Web-based Code Library, IDE Wrappers, and Vendor-specific HMI Screens (Fig. 7). The UI Design sets the visual style and interactive principles for the user experience. The Web-based Code Library acts as the foundation for developing and customising web interfaces. IDE Wrappers facilitate integration and code management, while HMI Screens enable direct machine or equipment interaction, ensuring a holistic and efficient HMI design system. Each step of the process incorporates levels 0–5 of the design system, creating a cohesive UX. This structured approach ensures a comprehensive and efficient HMI design system.

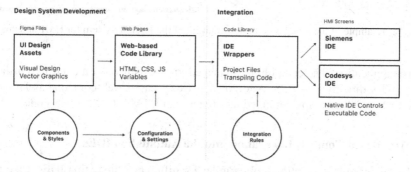

Fig. 7. Principle system architecture and the design-to-integration pipeline

5.1   Implementation of Key Elements of the Design System

We've developed a cross-platform UI component library aligned with modern design best practices, enabling the creation of visualisation screens tailored to brand guidelines. Moreover, implemented design tokens allow UI elements and visual style modifications according to the company's brand identity and design foundations. This comprehensive web-based UI library includes 28 interactive atomic controls, components and templates customisable for specific business requirements (Fig. 8).

The implemented design system utilises a 5-level architecture with various tools for seamless IDE integration. UI assets such as interactive elements and vector graphics are organised in Figma, including a dedicated library for text, colour styles, and both atomic and complex components. Design tokens are maintained as variables in Figma within a specific style dictionary, which is JSON translated into platform-specific formats

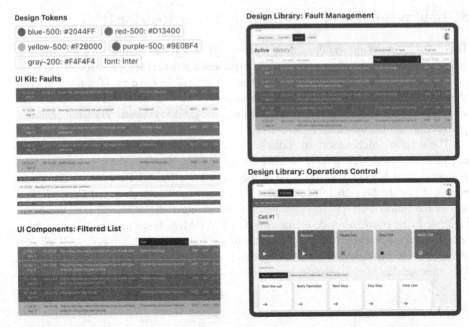

Fig. 8. Example of the Level 3–5 implementation of the Design System for HMI Screens

for easy application. The code library managed via git with version control, translates Figma styles directly into CSS. Additionally, React-based web components leverage Styled CSS and Typescript, compiled into functional HTML, CSS, and JS code.

5.2 Web-Based Controls Integration into the Automation IDEs

Web-based controls integration looks similar for different Automation IDEs. Like any control element in visualisation development environments, you have to configure control parameters - size, font, colours, displayed data and assign events such as button presses, hover actions, values exceeding a threshold, etc. APIs provided by the development system allow the internal behaviour of the control to be linked with variables and code within the development environment, linking it with the PLC runtime. Currently, several leading visualisation development systems are beginning to support the integration of controls written using web technologies. The integration process slightly differs for each system, so we will focus on two examples: Siemens Tia Portal and Codesys.

5.3 Siemens Tia Portal Integration

Tia Portal provides the capability to import web-based elements through a visualisation element import process. The structure of the control elements is strictly defined. Only an archive in ZIP format with a unique Global Unique Identifier (GUID) can be imported. This file must contain all graphics and code files used. The structure comprises two folders, "assets" and "control," and a "*.json" file (manifest.json). The "assets" folder contains a logo displayed in the TIA Portal, while the "control" folder contains "*.html," "*.js," and "*.css" files, along with used graphics and icons required for display [14]. The manifest file contains crucial information on the control's operation, specifying its name, version, author, settings, and the events it will support. Inside each event, additional codes can be placed for more flexible behaviour. Once the manifest is created and all files are packed into the container, the Tia Portal interface allows you to import this control and place it in the screen editing window. Then, according to your developed manifest file, you can fill in all control parameters and place the necessary code in its events window.

5.4 Codesys Integration

In the case of the Codesys development system, the control integration process looks similar. The process starts with creating a ZIP archive with a unique name for the control element. It should contain web components (HTML, CSS, JS files) and a JavaScript wrapper file, "ElementWrapper.js," for the control description. Inside this file, you specify any files required to run the element, such as style files (CSS), JavaScript files (JS), or image files (SVG) [15], which will be located together with the wrapper file in the archive. The "ElementImage.svg" file will be displayed in the toolbox for this control. Inside the "ElementWrapper" file, you must specify which variables Codesys can pass to the control and the events your control will have. After creating the archive, you must register the control element in the development environment. It is done in the HTML5 Control editor, where, upon selecting the control you created earlier, a "*.html5control.xml" description file is generated, registering your control in the system. Subsequently, when saving the visualisation project, Codesys allows the distribution of a project with all the imported elements.

5.5 Results Evaluation

In a conducted survey involving 26 participants, primarily from manufacturing companies, turnkey integrators, and outsourcing providers, we investigated the diversity of vendor support on a single site. The median number of vendors supported is 2, with an average of 2.42. Siemens and Rockwell emerged as the predominant vendors, preferred by 69% and 42% of respondents, respectively. Most participants utilise design libraries for reusable UI components, with 57% creating custom UI elements and a smaller group relying on standard IDE libraries. The distribution of controls within their libraries varies, with a notable 15% managing over 50 + controls (Fig. 9).

Over half of the respondents expressed dissatisfaction with current third-party solutions, citing issues such as outdated designs, limited customisation options, and poor usability. There is a strong demand for UI component support across various use cases, including Status and Diagnostic, Operation and Control, and more, highlighting the need for versatile, user-friendly design solutions in industrial settings. As a result of usability tests, most participants mentioned the increased efficiency of UI controls and components from the proposed design system and improved modern look and feel.

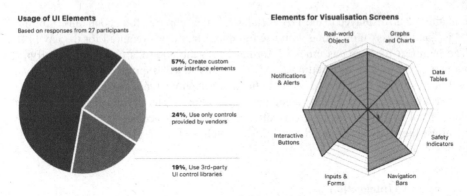

Fig. 9. UI elements usage for building visualisation screens

6 Implications

Enhanced Hardware Integration. Improved hardware integration is a critical factor for developers of automated systems when choosing integrated equipment, ranging from welding guns and motors to electricity meters and technical vision cameras. The simplicity of integrating such equipment into the developed product is essential. The less time spent on this integration, the better. When equipment manufacturers can provide hardware and code examples with a ready-made visualisation component, this significantly enhances sales by providing turnkey integration principles, making the product cross-platform and easily configurable.

Reduction of Costs for Automated Systems Developers. As mentioned earlier, developing a cross-platform automation product requires companies to assemble a large team of specialists capable of supporting the development of a visualisation system for each development environment. It imposes significant economic costs on the development of such a product, along with additional time expenditures if it's necessary to rectify visualisation defects for each version. A standardised cross-vendor UI Kit will help to reduce such costs and allow customising the product for a specific client without unnecessary effort, facilitating the integration of controls from third-party suppliers.

Unified and Standardised Production User Experience. Standard visualisation systems at every production stage, regardless of the supplier, equipment brand, or production line, significantly enhance the overall user experience for operators and maintenance team members. It could be achieved through familiar methods and control principles. Developing unified control elements that reflect the values of your production can significantly reduce economic and time costs. This reduction occurs by minimising equipment downtime, decreasing the time required for staff training, and lowering production risks associated with the health of operators.

7 Conclusion

In this paper, we present a comprehensive design system architecture and implementation process from design to integration to address the absence of a cross-platform, unified visualisation solution for automation development systems. Implemented UI Kit and set of reusable UI components containing standard visualisation controls designed using the modern web user experience trends, enabling the creation of visualisation systems for various manufacturing systems and equipment. The principle architecture of the 5-level design system and organisation of design assets with code database proves the iterative approach to HMI systems development to modular design. Such an approach facilitates the reduction of both temporal and economic expenditures. The set of components and integration methods have been validated by industry engineers through an independent survey, demonstrating the market's enthusiasm to engage in the development of such solutions and its commitment to improving existing visualisation technologies.

We anticipate that the scalable design system architecture and approach to HMI development proposed in our research will prove beneficial to equipment and automated systems developers, as well as industrial enterprises and manufacturers.

References

1. McKinsey & Company: Transforming Advanced Manufacturing Through Industry 4.0. McKinsey & Company. https://www.mckinsey.com/capabilities/operations/our-insights/transforming-advanced-manufacturing-through-industry-4-0. Accessed 01 Feb 2024
2. Kao, K.-C., Chieng, W.-H., Jeng, S.-L.: Design and development of an IoT-based web application for an intelligent remote SCADA system. IOP Conf. Ser. Mater. Sci. Eng. **323**, 012025 (2018). IOP Publishing
3. Jeng, S.-L., Chieng, W.-H., Chen, Y.: Web-based human-machine interfaces of industrial controllers in single-page applications. Mob. Inf. Syst. **2021**, 6668843 (2021). Hindawi
4. Aranburu, E., Lasa, G., Gerrikagoitia, J.K., Mazmela, M.: Case study of the experience capturer evaluation tool in the design process of an industrial HMI. Sustainability **12**(15), 6228 (2020). MDPI
5. Smoczek, J., Szpytko, J.: Interoperable approach to HMI and supervisory systems in man-machine systems. IFAC Proc. Vol. **42** (2009). Elsevier
6. Prasetyo, H., Sugiarto, Y., Rosyidi, C.N.: Design of an automatic production monitoring system on job shop manufacturing. In: AIP Conference Proceedings, vol. 1931, no. 1, p. 030021. AIP Publishing (2018)
7. Ponsa, P., Vilanova, R., Amante, B.: Human intervention and interface design in automation systems. Int. J. Comput. Commun. Control **6**(1), 1–6 (2011). Agora University Press
8. Martin, C., et al.: Integrated design of Human-machine interfaces for production plants. In: 2015 IEEE 20th Conference on Emerging Technologies and Factory Automation (ETFA), pp. 1–6. IEEE (2015)
9. IEC 61131-3: a standard programming resource. https://plcopen.org/sites/default/files/downloads/intro_iec_oct2016.pdf
10. Frost, B.: Atomic Design. Brad Frost Web Design LLC, Pittsburgh (2016)
11. Google: Material Design. Google. https://material.io. Accessed 01 Feb 2024
12. Bryksin, M., Vysotsky, N., Guseynov, P.: Industrial HMI design principles for highly automated manufacturing processes. In: Human Interaction & Emerging Technologies (IHIET 2023): Artificial Intelligence and Future Applications, vol. 0, no. 111. AHFE International, USA (2023)

13. Scheifele, S., Friedrich, J., Lechler, A., Verl, A.: Flexible, self-configuring control system for a modular production system. Procedia Technol. **15**, 398–405 (2014). Elsevier
14. SIMATIC HMI WinCC Unified Programming Custom Web Controls. System Manual, Online documentation, Siemens AG (2021). https://support.industry.siemens.com/cs/document/109 782201
15. CODESYS: Visualization for HTML5 Development. CODESYS. https://content.helpme-cod esys.com/en/CODESYS%20Visualization/_visu_html5_dev.html. Accessed 01 Feb 2024

Evolution of Executive Education in Interactive Digital Design Field: A Case Study Analysis

Bruno Nobre[1,2(✉)] [iD] and Emília Duarte[1,2] [iD]

[1] UNIDCOM/IADE, Av. D. Carlos I, 4, 1200-649 Lisbon, Portugal
{bruno.nobre,emilia.duarte}@universidadeeuropeia.pt
[2] IADE, Universidade Europeia, Av. D. Carlos I, 4, 1200-649 Lisbon, Portugal

Abstract. The educational landscape in Portugal encompasses a diverse array of non-degree courses, including executive training, lifelong learning courses, professional certifications, and specializations. These programs play a vital role in addressing the dynamic demands of a rapidly evolving labor market, providing individuals with opportunities to continuously develop skills, adapt to changing environments, and enhance their career prospects. However, a clear framework for informed and timely planning of curriculum changes is currently lacking, leading institutions to react to complaints of misalignment in their offerings. This study, part of a broader investigation aimed at establishing this framework, seeks to contribute to the understanding of contextual and social factors influencing executive education in the field of Digital Design in Portugal in recent years. A ten-year Portuguese case study was analyzed, incorporating questionnaire results, workshops with current and former students, and interviews with various academic stakeholders. Interviews with relevant public and private actors in the Portuguese market complemented the analysis. The crucial insights gathered lay the foundation for essential knowledge, informing the formulation of future educational strategies in the design of curricula for postgraduate courses in Interactive Digital Design. These insights could inform the creation of a comprehensive framework. The knowledge obtained serves as a valuable resource for institutions seeking to refine their educational offerings in response to evolving industry demands.

Keywords: Executive Education · Design Teaching · Interactive Digital Design

1 Introduction

As digitization of societies advances, the need for designers with skills in the field of digital product design is consequently urgent. Also, increasing globalization has been accelerating the dissemination of trends, techniques, and the use of new technologies, requiring a growing need to constantly update skills in many areas. These needs and the pace of change have a clear impact on the educational field, particularly in disciplines mainly characterized by the intersection of several areas of knowledge, such as Web Design, Interaction Design, and Digital Design, among others.

In this context, we are witnessing the growth of different types of learning, which increasingly cross the formal, with the non-formal and informal, in multiple contexts

M. Kurosu and A. Hashizume (Eds.): HCII 2024, LNCS 14684, pp. 125–143, 2024.
https://doi.org/10.1007/978-3-031-60405-8_9

and formats. An example of this is Executive Education (EE) courses, whose historical path has been marked by a clear evolution, however, characterized by several challenges that currently result in many offers and models that are questioned both by academia and by the industry.

Amidst transformative advances in non-degree education in Interactive Digital Design, challenges persist. Increasing competitiveness in the sector, rapid technological change, and institutional shifts create the need for a comprehensive understanding of the ever-evolving landscape. Additionally, the Covid-19 pandemic forced a sudden shift to online learning, leading to significant changes in EE. As a result, there is a need to develop new ways to deliver program content and engage learners in a virtual environment [1].

Executive Education has a determinant role in bridging the gap and facilitating knowledge-sharing between academic institutions, businesses, and society [2]. Widely recognized as part of the solution to the challenges of globalization and rapid changes in science, technology, and society, EE is frequently associated with a Lifelong Learning approach that helps individuals develop new skills and reach their full potential [3–7], holding immense potential as a strategic tool for fostering technical and leadership skills and can act as a catalyst for transforming team dynamics by aligning new perspectives and strategies. Ultimately, it can be a driving force for change, promoting innovative positions, and organizational structures [8–10].

According to Conger and Xin [11], this field has shown an evolutionary trend, currently displaying more innovative programs, centered on student learning and with a closer relationship with companies, contrasting with the observed trend until the 1980s, where very specific, specialized, and academy-centric programs were dominant.

Over the past few decades, there has been a gradual paradigm shift and change in attitude towards EE teaching [11]. This is partly due to increased competitiveness in the sector, rapid technological advancements, and a tendency towards acquisitions and institutional mergers, often marked by cost-cutting policies. As a result, there has been a general tendency to create partnerships with companies [11].

Within this framework, Higher Education (HE) still faces great challenges in achieving efficient cooperation between academia and business, as pointed out by Djoundourian and Shahin [12] and also based on Clark's studies on the subject [13–15]. They point out that universities have been continuously trying to integrate and connect industry and business with their EE programs through various attempts that are considered incomplete or inefficient, lacking an underlying strategic perspective or vision. Also, there is a recognizable gap in skill development, covering both skill acquisition and skill transfer, as they represent the fundamental source of value in EE for both companies and executives [16]. In that regard, when it comes to the design of an EE program, it is suggested that some aspects of the program design should be influenced by several stakeholders, such as outside company executives, as well as the university faculty itself [17, 18]. An alignment with several stakeholders can be complex but has been proven essential for purpose-driven customized executive education [19].

In the field of Design education, particularly, it has been recognized the significant challenges in developing curricula due to technical, technological, economic, and societal changes, as well as the rapid evolution of the industry. This is also stated for

Interaction Design Education, as noted by Meyer and Norman [20], where these challenges have been widely recognized in literature over the years [21–26]. In this sense, teaching methods and content have been significantly updated to meet the demands of today's constantly evolving world. The focus is on customization and meeting individual needs rather than a one-size-fits-all approach. These changes have been made in response to the new realities of education and the desire to provide tailored learning experiences [9, 11, 27, 28].

On the other hand, Larissa Cruz [29] also suggests that several identified challenges in business organizations have a design area in their structure, particularly in C-level positions. These challenges can be seen both in terms of the skills required for design management and for leadership in design, as well as in terms of the processes and methodologies inherent to design, where, with the current growing movement to enhance the designer role in organizations and companies, several new designations and skills have emerged inherent to the functions intended for today's designer, which are constantly changing and have a pressing need for updating.

In this context, this study seeks to enhance the comprehension of design education for EE within the realm of Interactive Digital Design. The primary objective is to understand the contextual and societal factors that influenced EE in recent years. This will be done by exploring a decade-long case study at IADE - *Faculdade de Design, Tecnologia e Comunicação da Universidade Europeia–Portugal*, where specialized training in these areas has been consistently offered to address societal needs over the past 10-year period. Consequently, these programs have attracted a diverse cohort of students, including numerous active professionals from various sectors and fields. This investigation aims to provide a nuanced understanding of the backgrounds of student within the Interactive Digital Design program at IADE. It also seeks to present crucial insights gleaned from both industry professionals and students, thereby laying some foundation of knowledge essential for the formulation of future educational strategies. The data, analysis, and conclusions derived from this case study hold potential value for a broader audience, encompassing other HE Institutions.

This study contributes to a deeper understanding of the collaborative dynamics between academia and companies in the field of Interactive Digital Design. The insight garnered could serve as a valuable resource for institutions seeking to refine their educational offerings in response to evolving industry demands.

Moreover, by introducing novel perspectives on curriculum design within postgraduate courses in Interactive Digital Design, this study offers insights that may contribute to a clearer vision for the future development of a comprehensive framework. Such a framework has the potential to facilitate diverse and holistic perspectives on the subject, thereby informing the strategic outlining and designing of future curricula.

2 Methodology

The study employed a qualitative case study methodology to conduct a comprehensive investigation into the Interactive Digital Design programs at IADE. This method facilitated a thorough exploration of the subject, capturing diverse perspectives from academia, industry, and students.

i. *Questionnaires:*

- Utilized questionnaires collected by Admission Academic Services from students enrolled in Executive Education courses over the past 10 years.
- Post-course questionnaires were analyzed to understand students' motivations.
- Analyzed six common dimensions: gender, age, country of origin, academic degree, field of study, and type of course (online or in-person).

ii. *Identification of the key players:*

- Through a desk research approach, Industry main players were identified and relevant information from their public websites was collected.
- Industry player criteria comprised seniority, internationalization, focus on the design of Interactive Digital Products, relevance, recognition, and Portuguese or merged status. Also, a strategically Portuguese public sector entity was joined [29].
- Academic stakeholder criteria included decision-making roles in the Interactive Digital Design training programs at IADE and the European University, such as deans, design course coordinators, research unit co-directors, and executive education directors.

iii. *Semi-Structured Interviews:*

- A semi-structured interview was designed according a five-stage process based on Kallio et al. [30].
- Key agents from the before identified Industry main players were then invited via email, followed by the semi-structured script containing questions.
- Respondents, upon agreeing to participate, were given a timeframe for returning their answers. Open-ended fields allowed respondents to add free topics.
- The script covered issues like the current state of Interactive Digital Design and its challenges up to 2020, identification of current and future challenges, key capabilities in skills, knowledge, and strategic thinking domains, and framing training opportunities at IADE based on expertise levels. Potential impacts from the Covid-19 pandemic were also explored.

iv. Workshops:

- Conducted two rounds of workshops involving nine working groups with 39 current students in the Web UX/UI postgraduate course.
- Students were invited during pre-selected teaching sessions with professor agreement. A form was sent to them via email for completion.
- Each session lasted approximately an hour, and responses were returned via email at the end.

3   Results and Discussion

3.1   IADE Students Profile (2012–2022)

The forthcoming tables elucidate the outcomes derived from the Academic Services Surveys. Over the period until 2022, a total of 442 students participated in the courses encompassing Interaction Design & Multimedia, Web Design, Design for the Creative

Industries, Interaction Design, Web UX/UI, and Web Front-End, distributed across 32 distinct editions. Table 1 provides a comprehensive overview of the temporal distribution of these courses during the 10-year span.

Table 1. Time distribution of analyzed courses and thus typology: online and/or in-person.

Course	Year	Typology	
Interaction Design & Multimedia	2012–2014	in-person	- - -
Web Design	2016–2019	in-person	- - -
Design for the Creative Industries	2018–till present day	in-person	- - -
Interaction Design	2021–till present day	- - -	online
Web UX/UI	2020–till present day	in-person	online
Web Front-End	2021–till present day	in-person	online

It is pertinent to acknowledge that the advent of online courses is a relatively recent development, with their introduction in 2020. Despite this recent inception, online courses have swiftly garnered prominence, constituting 28% of all course editions, as evidenced by the data presented in Table 2.

Table 2. Total of editions, per course and typology during the 10-year period.

Course	Typology		Total / Course
	In-Person	*Online*	
Interaction Design & Multimedia	2	- - -	2
Web Design	8	- - -	8
Design for the Creative Industries	5	- - -	5
Interaction Design	- - -	2	2
Web UX/UI	6	6	12
Web Front-End	2	1	3
Total	**23** (72%)	**9** (28%)	**32**

Table 3 offers insights into the annual percentage distribution of enrolled students throughout this period, excluding 2014 and 2015 when courses in this field were not offered due to administrative decisions. Notably, a substantial surge student enrollment is discernible post 2020, with the intake doubling compared to previous years.

Upon a broader examination of the data, it becomes evident that online courses have captured a significant share of the student population, constituting 31% of the total enrollment between 2012 and 2022. For a detailed breakdown of the student demographics by year and course type, please refer to Table 4.

Table 3. Total of enrolled students, per year.

Year	Enrolled students	Percentage
2012	12	3%
2013	19	4%
2016	26	6%
2017	18	4%
2018	33	7%
2019	42	10%
2020	91	21%
2021	86	19%
2022	115	26%

Table 4. Total of enrolled students, per year: online and in-person courses.

Year	Online	In-Person	Total / Year
2012	- - -	12	12
2013	- - -	19	19
2016	- - -	26	26
2017	- - -	18	18
2018	- - -	33	33
2019	- - -	42	42
2020	41	50	91
2021	27	59	86
2022	68	47	115
Total	**136** (31%)	**306** (69%)	**442**

In terms of intake periods, four main intakes - Fall, Spring, Summer, and Winter, merit consideration. As detailed in Table 5, Fall stands out as the overwhelmingly favored intake, representing 78% of the total number of students. Spring is the next most common, accounting for 17%, while Winter and Summer are notably less popular, constituting 4% and 1% respectively.

Tables 6 and 7 reveal that a majority of students in this study are female, comprising 67% of the total enrollment. It is noteworthy that across all Interactive Digital Design courses analyzed, the female-to-male ratio remains consistent at 3 to 1.

When profiling students, their nationality or country of origin is also taken into account. Not surprisingly, it's worth noting that the majority of the analyzed student data (81%) belonged to Portuguese students, as shown in Table 8. Following closely are

Table 5. Total of enrolled students, per intake.

Intake	Enrolled students	Percentage
Fall	344	78%
Spring	75	17%
Summer	6	1%
Winter	17	4%

Table 6. Gender of enrolled students, per typology.

Course Typology	Female	Male	Total
Online	90	46	136
Presential	206	100	306
Total	**296** (67%)	**146** (33%)	**442**

Table 7. Gender of enrolled students, per course.

Course	Female	Male	Total
Interaction Design & Multimedia	10	10	20
Web Design	72	30	102
Design for the Creative Industries	50	12	62
Interaction Design	8	6	14
Web UX/UI	142	81	223
Web Front-End	14	7	21
Total	**296** (67%)	**146** (33%)	**442**

Brazilian students, accounting for over 16% of the share (double citizenships were taken into account).

The analysis reveals that the typical age of students embarking on this course is 28 years old, based on a thorough analysis conducted during this period. While slight variations were noted between 2012 and 2017, the average age has since remained constant from 2018 to 2022, as detailed in Table 9. This indicates a pattern in the age range of students seeking out these courses.

Based on the gathered data, it's apparent that 95% of the students who approached us held a minimum of a bachelor's degree, with 13% possessing a master's degree, as outlined in Table 10. In the remaining 5% of cases, we assessed the students' professional experience as a qualification for enrollment in the course.

Another aspect that was reviewed in the students' profile pertains to their academic background. Table 11 displays the field of study of the student. Design holds the largest

Table 8. Nationality of enrolled students.

Nationality	Percentage
Angolan	0,9%
Brazilian	15,8%
Brazilian / German	0,2%
Colombian	0,2%
Italian	0,5%
Peruvian	0,5%
Portuguese	80,9%
Portuguese / German	0,2%
Portuguese / Brazilian	0,2%
Portuguese / French	0,2%
Romanian	0,2%

Table 9. Students' age average when enrolled, per year.

Year	Average of age/year
2012	30
2013	25
2016	29
2017	24
2018	28
2019	28
2020	28
2021	28
2022	28
Courses average	**28**

percentage with 45%, trailed by Marketing and Advertisement with 12%, and Management also at 12%. Engineering courses account for 11%, while Communication-related courses and Visual Arts make up 9% and 5%, respectively. Architecture follows closely with 4%.

It was found that the origin of the last academic course taken is closely linked and might be correlated to the students' specific nationality and place of origin. 80% of the students who took the course were from Portugal, while 16% were from Brazil (Table 12).

Table 10. Students' academic degrees.

Academic Degree	Percentage
Bachelor (*Licenciatura*)	72,3%
Bachelor	8,5%
K-12 (Technical)	0,3%
K-12	3,8%
Master	13,2%
MBA	0,6%
Post-Graduate	0,9%
Technologist	0,3%

Table 11. Students' academic field of study.

Field of study	Percentage
Architecture	3,8%
Visual Arts	5,1%
Communication	8,5%
Design	45,4%
Law	1,4%
Artistic Education	0,3%
Engineering	11,3%
Geology	0,3%
Management	8,2%
Linguistics	0,3%
Marketing and Advertising	11,6%
Multimedia	1,0%
Psychology	1,0%
Sociology	0,7%
Tourism	1,0%

Findings from the Student Profile. In the decade spanning from 2012 and 2022, a total of 442 students were enrolled in 32 editions of six different courses related to the interactive digital design field at *IADE – Faculdade De Design, Tecnologia E Comunicação Da Universidade Europeia* in Portugal. Throughout this ten-year period, there existed a consistent pace of enrolment, with a modest growth trajectory. However, a pivotal transformation in 2020, characterized by a course reorganization and online course strategy, led to a noteworthy doubling of enrolment. Despite the recent introduction of

Table 12. Students' last academic degree origin.

Origin of last academic course taken	Percentage
Angola	0,6%
Brazil	16,0%
USA	0,6%
France	1,3%
Honduras	0,6%
Italy	0,6%
Portugal	80,1%

online courses, they swiftly claimed a 31% share of the overall enrolment within this domain.

Observing the enrollment figures from 2020 to 2022, a discernible upward trend suggests an ongoing growth pattern. However, to substantiate and confirm this trajectory, a comprehensive analysis of additional data from subsequent years is imperative.

A notable observation is the preeminence of the fall intake, securing the highest success rate, with 78% of students enrolling during this period.

Gender dynamics within the student population is observable, with female students constituting a third more of the student population compared with their male counterparts. This trend persists consistently across individual courses.

The majority of enrolled students at IADE are of Portuguese nationality (81%), followed by Brazilian (16%). Although currently representing a modest 1% enrolment, Angolan students present a prospective opportunity for growth in future intakes. This potential growth is particularly promising, considering the recent trend of increased enrollment from Angolan students in bachelor's degree programs at IADE.

The alignment of academic backgrounds with nationalities is evident, with courses from Portugal (80%) and Brazil (16%) being the most common. The average age of enrollment has remained constant at 28 years old since 2018, displaying stability despite minor fluctuations in preceding years.

The educational qualifications of students are diverse, with a majority (95%) possessing a bachelor's degree, while 13% hold a master's degree. Only a minority of enrolled students (5%) were admitted based on professional experience. The predominant academic field is Design (45%), followed by Marketing and Advertisement (12%), Management (also 12%), and Engineering (11%). Communication-related courses (9%), Visual Arts (5%), and Architecture (4%) are also represented.

When queried about their goals, students primarily indicated a desire to progress in their professional careers (58%), followed by transition into a different field (26%) and exploring their interests in the covered topics (9%).

3.2 Industry Expectations

In this section, our attention turned towards a thorough examination of the Creative Industry terrain in Portugal with the objective of elucidating the expectations within the Interactive Digital Design field. An integrative approach, drawing insights from academia, private enterprises, and public institutions, was deemed essential to attain a better comprehension of industry expectations.

The initial step involved a comprehensive desk research initiative designed to collect data from the Creative Industry in Portugal. The primary objective was to pinpoint key agents and entities that could contribute valuable insights for an examination of the evolution and current state of the Interactive Digital Design field. To this end, five strategic key attributes were identified: **1) Seniority**–encompassing companies with a decade or more of experience to provide an informed perspective on the field's development; **2) Internationalization**–focusing on companies with a global presence to offer a broader perspective on the field's scope; **3) Primary Focus on Interactive Digital Product design**; **4) Relevance and Recognition**–emphasizing companies widely acknowledged and/or awarded in their area of expertise; **5) Portuguese-based or merged status**–emphasizing companies founded or with headquartered in Portugal.

Desk research outcomes revealed six companies within the private sector and one organization within the public sector. The ensuing discussion succinctly summarizes the key attributes of each identified entity:

3.3 Private Sector Characterization

1. ComOn[1]:

    Founded: 2001
    Overview: ComOn is an Independent Creative Consultant specializing in human-first experiences that transform brands, businesses, cultures, and lives. Established in 2001, ComOn stands out for assembling agile, multidisciplinary teams to tackle diverse challenges. Their focus on prioritizing people in projects, utilizing data, behavioral sciences, and innovation, sets them apart. With expertise spanning Media Planning, UX Design, Brand Strategy, and more, ComOn is a key player in Portugal's digital landscape.

2. Edigma[2]:

    Founded: 2000
    Overview: Edigma is a Portuguese multidisciplinary company at the forefront of developing interactive and immersive experiences. Blending design, creativity, and technology, Edigma creates meaningful experiences that envision the future and engage audiences. A leader in interactive experiences, digital signage, and augmented reality, Edigma transforms architectural spaces into communicative environments, establishing itself as a pivotal player in Portugal's digital industry.

3. Fullsix[3]:

---

[1] Www.comon.pt.
[2] Www.edigma.com.
[3] Www.fullsix.pt.

Founded: 1998 (France) / 2000 (Portugal)

Overview: Fullsix, a leading digital agency in Portugal and Europe with over two decades of experience, specializes in digital transformation. With a team of around 150 professionals, Fullsix focuses on strategy, creativity, and technology to enhance customer experiences. Recognized with prestigious awards and distinctions, including Agency of the Year and top rankings, Fullsix is a prominent player shaping the digital landscape through CX Strategy, Digital Content, SEO, and Marketing Automation.

4. Imaginary Cloud[4]:

Founded: 2010

Overview: Imaginary Cloud, founded in 2010, is a Portuguese Software House recognized among Europe's fastest-growing companies. Specializing in fast, reliable, and tech debt-free custom development, Imaginary Cloud has gained acclaim for its web, mobile, and AI software solutions. Notably listed in the FT 1000: Europe's Fastest Growing Companies [30], Imaginary Cloud excels in Ideation, Development, and Improvement, emphasizing UX/UI Design.

5. Tangível[5]:

Founded: 2004

Overview: Tangível, a pioneer since 2004, is Portugal's largest company exclusively dedicated to human-centered design. Focused on simplifying lives through UX/UI Design and digital transformation, Tangível boasts a specialized team of over 30 experts in anthropology, psychology, and design. Operating in Strategy, Research, Experience Design, and Front-End Development, Tangível stands out as a key player in shaping Portugal's digital landscape.

6. YDreams Global[6]:

Founded: 2007 (Brazil)/2016 (Portugal)

Overview: YDreams Global, a Brazilian company with global operations post-reverse merger in 2016, specializes in designing and producing immersive exhibitions and interactive museums. With a multidisciplinary approach integrating sensory technology, narratives, and immersive design, YDreams Global creates attractive exhibition circuits. Recognized for its use of VR, AR, AI, and robotics, YDreams Global stands as a unique player in the digital industry with a global footprint.

Public Service Sector Characterization. The Public Service sector emerges as a key insight for this study, augmenting its significance as a strategic input. Within Portugal, the Public Service sector has fervently embraced digitalization, positioning it as a cornerstone in addressing challenges related to employment, science, and health, thereby fortifying its competitiveness [31]. This sector, in alignment with its overarching goals, not only endeavors to enhance existing public services but also actively engages with emergent imperatives, notably sustainability and resource optimization.

---

[4] www.imaginarycloud.com.

[5] Www.tangivel.com.

[6] Www.exhibition.ydreams.site.

7. The Administrative Modernization Agency, I.P. (AMA)[7] is the apex public service in Portuguese entrusted with the mandate of fostering and advancing administrative modernization. Established in 2007, AMA operates under the supervision and tutelage of the Secretary of State for Digitalization and Administrative Modernization. At its core, AMA is committed to the identification, development, and evaluation of programs, projects, and actions aimed at modernization and administrative simplification. The agency undertakes the responsibility of promoting, coordinating, managing, and evaluating the public service distribution system, in alignment with governmental policies. Notably, AMA's operations are structured across three pivotal axes: 1) Digital Transformation, 2) Omnichannel Public Service, and 3) Administrative Simplification, also being vastly recognized with a multitude of awards[8].

Table 13 provides an overview of the major stakeholders in Portugal's digital industry, emphasizing their founding years, areas of focus and technological emphases. This underscores the diverse strengths and strategic priorities among these key players.

Based on the analyzed data, the primary focus areas of the key stakeholders are Design (51%), Marketing (25%) and Technology (15%) as illustrated in Fig. 1. The predominant technical emphasis is UX/UI (23%), followed by Interaction Design (14%), Strategy (14%), Research (13%), Development (12%) and Marketing (10%), as depicted in Fig. 2.

Findings from the Industry. After gaining an overview of the primary areas of key stakeholders, the subsequent stage involved conducting semi-structured interviews with key interlocutors to:

- Perceive existing challenges in the field of Interactive Digital Design up to 2020.
- Understand whether Covid-19 pandemic brought significant changes to the performance of Interactive Digital Design professionals, to processes and, if so, whether these changes were incremental or disruptive.
- Identify challenges in the Interactive Digital Design field, both current and future.
- Recognize key capabilities required for Interactive Digital Design professional's performance in the domains of Skills, Knowledge, and Strategic Thinking.
- Frame the training offer at IADE within the Interactive Digital Design field, according to a professional profile of contributors, intermediate or executive professional.
- Preview relevant contents that this field may demand in a near future

Participants responded to a set of questions organized into three central blocks: 1) on the evolution of Interactive Digital Design field; 2) the professional abilities and skills 3) training content for the field. The interviews concluded with an open question, expressions of gratitude for the contributions, and optional sociodemographic questions. It was emphasized that all collected data was solely for academic-scientific purposes, treated anonymously and confidentially, with no identity disclosed concerning the opinions or personal views expressed.

---

[7] Www.ama.gov.pt.

[8] www.ama.gov.pt/web/english/awards.

Table 13. Snapshot of key stakeholders in Portugal's digital industry

Company or Organization	Founded	Portuguese based since	Main Areas	Technical Emphasis
CoMon	2001	2001	– Design – Marketing – Technology	Branding; Development; Marketing; Research; Strategy; UX/UI
Edigma	2000	2000	– Design – Management – Marketing – Technology	Development; Interaction Design; Research; Strategy; UX/UI
Fullsix	1998	2000	– Design – Marketing	Development; Marketing; Research; Strategy; UX/UI
Imaginary Cloud	2010	2010	– Design – Management – Technology	Design; Development; Interaction Design; Research; Strategy; UX/UI
Tangível	2014	2014	– Design – Technology	Development; Interaction Design; Research; UX/UI
YDreams Global	2007	2016	– Design – Education – Marketing – Management – Technology	Interaction Design; Research; Strategy; Training; UX/UI
AMA	2007	2007	– Design – Management	Interaction Design; Strategy; UX/UI

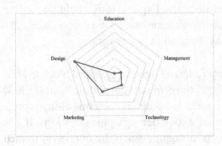

Fig. 1. Stakeholder's main areas   **Fig. 2.** Stakeholder's main technical emphasis

The obtained results reveal that until 2020, the realm of Engineering and Technology experienced substantial advancements catalyzed by the integration of Design. This evolution manifested across two dimensions: heightened intricacy and enhanced user-friendliness. Notably, Interactive Digital Design played an important role in steering this ongoing transformative journey. Nevertheless, the swift evolution and diversity of digital software require designers to continually update their skill set, requiring a profound grasp of technical knowledge and a more holistic approach.

As technological solutions permeate daily life, the scope for user-system interaction expands. However, the absence of consensus regarding optimal design and usability practices looms large. Designers find themselves navigating the intricacies of human cognitive abilities and must stay attuned to established best practices and usability principles.

The outbreak of the Covid-19 pandemic served as a catalyst for incremental innovation, accelerating digital advancements across diverse sectors. Designers exhibited adaptability, creating increasingly relevant, effective, and accessible digital experiences. Work processes underwent profound changes, presenting challenges in collaboration and communication that were ultimately surmounted.

The contemporary landscape witnesses a confluence of various digital technologies, posing a recognized challenge. Designers must continually update their knowledge base to navigate this intricate terrain. The emergence of Generative AI introduces additional challenges to design ethics, and a shift from user-centric to planet-centric design is discernible, underscoring the need for greater responsibility in crafting experiences devoid of direct negative planetary impacts.

For the professional profile in this domain, a comprehensive skill set is imperative, spanning proficiency in skills, knowledge, and strategic thinking. Autonomy and leadership skills, group collaboration, and cooperation abilities are equally crucial. Executive education, tailored for C-level and D-level profiles, should prioritize leadership, operational strategies, encompass diverse domains such as management, decision-making, design strategy, innovation and design thinking, communication, presentation, strategic leadership, business strategy, design ethics, and knowledge on emerging technologies.

For a contributor profile, the emphasis shifts to technical skills, user research, usability, and interface principles. To ensure the relevance of executive programs, continuous adaptation to new technologies and societal changes is essential. Disciplines like Design Ethics, Design Systems, Artificial Intelligence, Accessibility, and Virtual and Augmented Reality are a plus. Career progression is tied to the ability to add value and possess multidisciplinary skills, providing a well-rounded perspective.

It is noteworthy that existing courses predominantly cater to operatives rather than leaders, a reflection of the nuanced designer's intervention in the technological landscape.

3.4 Students Expectations and Needs

As of 2020, the expectations of students, primarily derived from a post-courses survey, reveal a strong inclination (58%) towards advancing their professional career through these courses. Conversely, significant segment (26%) expressed their expectation of transitioning to a different professional field. A smaller yet notable group (9%) enrolled out of curiosity and interest in the course content.

Current Student Expectations. Insights from workshops taken from current courses recently, shed light on up-to-date students' expectations. Enrolled students expressed a clear desire to explore into user interface design (UI) user experience (UX), and project management within an agile methodology framework. Proficiency in tools like Figma and Figma like platforms is sought after, along with a keen interest in professional practices within the field, as well working on the design and interactivity for the final course project.

Students aim to gain an introduction to coding basics, prefer flexibility in project development, and find working in groups with varying commitment levels and competences to be a significant challenge. A strong foundation in user experience research, the ability to analyze interaction data, and an in-depth understanding of design principles and concepts are also emphasized.

Students aspire to become proficient in Adobe platforms and other tools, to develop advanced techniques in Figma for UI design, comprehend the interconnected nature of UI and UX, engage in wireframing and mapping for visually appealing designs, and access support materials for an enriched learning experience. Exploration of new work tools for enhanced productivity, a solid foundation for current and future employment, and insights into completing design processes from start to finish are among their expectations. Successful product launches into market are also anticipated. Furthermore, it was emphasized that programs in this domain should offer practical and directly applicable teachings, equipping students with skills readily deployable in the job market. The curricula should prioritize the imparting of sound usability practices, ensuring students are well versed in UI Design and adept in utilizing Prototyping tools and techniques. Students articulated a distinct expectation for constructive feedback on their developed work and projects, providing a hands-on, practical application of theory.

Skill Gaps and Needs. Identified skill gaps and needs underscore the importance of gaining additional skills in UX/UI Design tools, deeper knowledge of wireframing, mockups, and design systems, alongside practical examples from the industry. Students' express eagerness to explore different fields of work for a seamless career transition, particularly emphasizing Artificial Intelligence. Recognition of the potential of AI tools in UX/UI projects, staying abreast of new trends, and understanding the various applications of AI are deemed critical to stay ahead in the field.

Training and support for various tools, strategic partnerships with creative services offering additional resources, and practical teaching methodologies are considered indispensable. Practical hands-on experiences with tools and methods are pivotal for effective learning experience. The synthesis of sustainability and UX/UI is deemed crucial, emphasizing the need for an introduction to business processes within IT to better prepare students for the labor market.

4 Conclusions

Despite its recognized relevance, Executive Education grapples with various challenges, including acquisitions, institutional merges, general cost-cutting policies. These challenges persist, compounded in the realm of Interactive Digital Design by additional complexities arising from technical advancements, evolving technologies, economic shifts, and societal changes. This amalgamation contributes to an increasingly demanding landscape within the field.

An analysis of past and present trends in Interactive Digital Design post-graduate courses at IADE unveils significant milestones and curriculum changes over the last decade. Notably, the institution underwent an acquisition and merger during the study period, prompting a strategic redefinition of educational approaches and the adoption of innovative teaching dynamics.

The years 2019 and 2020 played a pivotal role, marked by the Covid-19 Pandemic. This crisis forced an abrupt shift to emergency online teaching, fostering the development of new technological competencies among educators. Paradoxically, this crisis served as a catalyst for incremental innovation and transformative change, leading to broader acceptance of online teaching.

Amidst accelerating digital advancements across sectors, designers have adeptly adapted to the dynamic landscape, focusing on creating relevant, effective, and accessible digital experiences. As technology permeates everyday life - exemplified by ubiquitous smartphones - the potential for interaction between users and systems has expanded significantly. However, a lack of consensus on good design and best usability practices has become increasingly apparent. Designers must now possess deeper insights into human cognitive abilities and remain informed about best practices and usability principles. This evolution has profoundly influenced work processes, prompting successful adaptations in collaboration and communication practices, and dispelling entrenched myths about work methodologies.

Looking ahead, the proliferation of diverse digital technologies presents a universally acknowledged challenge, demanding continuous learning and multifaceted knowledge acquisition. The emergence of Generative AI adds a layer of complexity, requiring designers to critically examine established processes and methodologies, while also considering ethical implications. There is a perceptible shift towards a more holistic, planet-centric design ethos, emphasizing the construction of experiences that address both human needs and environmental sustainability, not only by not directly harming our planet, but also by regenerating it.

Until 2020, advancements in Engineering and Technology, propelled by contributions from Design, has unfolded along axes of increased complexity and ease of use, with Interactive Digital Design paying a pivotal role. The rapid diversification and evolution of digital software demand continuous learning and adaptation by designers, necessitating greater technical expertise and a holistic approach. The discipline itself has matured, transitioning from a focus on visual aesthetics and impact (during Web Design and HTML era - including FLASH) to incorporating broader concepts such as Design Thinking, User Experience, User Interface Design, and User Psychology. Adapting to new technologies and changes in society is inevitable for the continued relevance of executive programs, with disciplines like Design Ethics, Design Systems, Artificial Intelligence, Accessibility, Virtual and Augmented Reality gaining importance.

Insights from workshops revealed students' interest in exploring user interface design, user experience and agile project management. Proficiency in Adobe platforms and Figma for UI design remains crucial, but students eager to explore new work tools, markedly in Artificial Intelligence, emphasizing the importance of staying updated with new trends and sustainability topics. While the field has evolved significantly, students' concerns predominantly revolve around acquiring skills in a specific technical tool, currently centered on Figma and Generative AI. Incorporating novel processes in UX Design, such Agile methods, is also prominent in their career progression considerations.

Industry key stakeholders affirm the importance of Generative AI and stress the integration of Design Ethics, Design Systems, Artificial Intelligence, Accessibility, Virtual and Augmented Reality, as valuable topics. Further steps should focus on understanding how these disciplines relate to a broader audience and envisioning a framework for curricula design in this ever-evolving field. As Artificial Intelligence continues to reshape the fabric of society, designers and educators must adapt to the fast-changing reality, embracing new tools and processes that emerge consistently.

The future holds promise as we navigate these pivotal times, where the intersection of technology, design, and education presents a unique opportunity to redefine how we learn, teach, and interact. Traditional classroom-based learning is giving way to online, blended, and lifelong learning models and expected skills sets are now more driven into domains such as critical thinking, creativity, and digital literacy skills. The goal and expectations, nonetheless, remains the same: to empower relevant knowledge and skills on a constant evolving reality, ensuring readiness for the 21st century demands.

Acknowledgments. This study was initially funded by *Fundação para a Ciência e a Tecnologia* (FCT/MEC grant SFRH/BD/51387/2011) and supported by NOVA LINCS Research Laboratory (formerly CITI/FCT-UNL) Pest UID/CEC/04516 / 2013. UNIDCOM/IADE, *Unidade de Investigação em Design e Comunicação* (UIDB/00711/2020 and UIDP/00711/2020), also granted support which enabled the commitments for this study to take place. The authors have no competing interests to declare that are relevant to the content of this article.

References

1. Sawhney, M.: Reimagining Executive Education. Harvard Business Publishing, Boston (2021)
2. Gera, R.: Bridging the gap in knowledge transfer between academia and practitioners. Int. J. Educ. Manag. **26**, 252–273 (2012)
3. Kaplan, A.: Lifelong learning: conclusions from a literature review. Int. Online J. Prim. Educ. **5**, 43–50 (2016)
4. Power, C.N., Maclean, R.: Lifelong learning: meaning, challenges, and opportunities. In: Maclean, R., Jagannathan, S., Sarvi, J. (eds.) Skills Development for Inclusive and Sustainable Growth in Developing Asia-Pacific. TVETICP, vol. 19, pp. 29–42. Springer, Dordrecht (2013). https://doi.org/10.1007/978-94-007-5937-4_2
5. Demirel, M.: Lifelong learning and schools in the twenty-first century. Procedia – Soc. Behav. Sci. **1**, 1709–1716 (2009)
6. Fulmer, R.M., Gibbs, P.A.: Lifelong learning at the corporate university. Career Dev. Int. **3**, 177–184 (1998)
7. Laal, M.: Lifelong learning: what does it mean? Procedia – Soc. Behav. Sci. **28**, 470–474 (2011)
8. Bolt, J.F.: Achieving the CEO' s agenda : education for executives. Manage. Rev. **82**, 44–48 (1993)

9. Conger, J.A., Benjamin, B.: Building Leaders: How Corporations are Developing the Next Generation. Jossey-Bass, San Francisco (1999)
10. Ready, D.A.: In Charge of Change: Insights into Next-Generation Organizations, p. 90 (1995)
11. Conger, J.A., Xin, K.: Executive education in the 21st century. J. Manag. Educ. **24**, 73–101 (2000)
12. Djoundourian, S., Shahin, W.: Academia–business cooperation: a strategic plan for an innovative executive education program. Ind. High Educ. **36**(6), 835–845 095042222210838 (2022)
13. Clark, B.: The entrepreneurial university: new foundations for collegiality, autonomy, and achievement. High. Educ. Manag. **14**, 9–24 (2001)
14. Clark, B.: The entrepreneurial university: demand and response. Tert. Educ. Manag. **4**, 5–16 (1998)
15. Clark, B.: Creating Entrepreneurial Universities. Organisational Pathways of Transformation. International Association of Universities and Elsevier, Oxford (1998)
16. Moldoveanu, M., Narayandas, D.: The Future of Executive Development: The CLO's Compass and The Executive Programs Designer's Guide. Work Paper -- Harvard Business School Divison Research, pp. 1–51 (2020)
17. Myrsiades, L.: Looking to lead: a case in designing executive education from the inside. J. Manag. Dev. **20**, 795–812 (2001)
18. McCarthy, P., Sammon, D., O'Raghallaigh, P.: Designing an executive education programme: towards a programme design matrix. J. Decis. Syst. **25**, 566–571 (2016)
19. Boon, E., Church, G., Burger, C., et al.: The future of executive education. Learning Leadership in a Digital Age. ESMT Berlin (2023)
20. Meyer, M.W., Norman, D.: Changing design education for the 21st century. She Ji **6**, 13–49 (2020)
21. Culén, A.L., Mainsah, H.N., Finken, S.: Design, creativity and human computer interaction design education. Int. J. Adv. Life Sci. **6**, 97–106 (2014)
22. Faiola, A., Matei, S.A.: Enhancing human-computer interaction design education: teaching affordance design for emerging mobile devices. Int. J. Technol. Des. Educ. **20**, 239–254 (2010)
23. Foley, J.: Graduate education in human-computer interaction. Conf. Hum. Fact. Comput. Syst. – Proc., 2113–2114 (2005)
24. Grudin, J., Salvendy, G.A.: Moving target: the evolution of HCI. Human-Comput. Interact Handb., 1–40 (2008)
25. Myers, B.A.: Challenges of HCI Design and Implementation. Interactions **1**(1), 73–83 (1994)
26. Myers, B.A.: A brief history of human-computer interaction technology. Interactions **5**, 14 (1996)
27. Stopper, W.G.: Agility in action: picturing the lessons learned from Kodak and 23 other companies. J. Artic. by William G. Stopper; Hum. Resour. Plan. **21**(1), 11–14 (1998)
28. Vicere, A.A.: Changes in practices, changes in perspectives: the 1997 international study of executive development trends. J. Manag. Dev. **17**, 526–543 (1998)
29. Cruz, L.: Desafios para elevar a maturidade de design nas empresas (2022). https://www.design2022.com.br/artigos/desafios-para-elevar-a-maturidade-de-design-nas-empresas. Accessed 31 Oct 2022
30. Observador Lab: Tecnológica portuguesa Imaginary Cloud distinguida pelo FT (2023). https://observador.pt/2023/03/01/tecnologica-portuguesa-imaginary-cloud-distinguida-pelo-ft/. Accessed 2 Nov 2023
31. ADEA: Transformação digital da Administração Pública através da automação (2023). https://www.adea.pt/blog/transformacao-digital-adminstracao-publica/

Beyond Future Skills: Developing Company Personas in Disruptive Transformation Processes

Monika Pröbster[1]([⊠]) [iD], Jochen Ehrenreich[2] [iD], Günter Käßer-Pawelka[2],
and Nicola Marsden[1] [iD]

[1] Heilbronn University, Max-Planck-Str. 39, 74081 Heilbronn, Germany
{monika.proebster,nicola.marsden}@hs-heilbronn.de
[2] DHBW Heilbronn, Bildungscampus 4, 74076 Heilbronn, Germany
{jochen.ehrenreich,guenter.kaesser-pawelka}@heilbronn.dhbw.de

Abstract. The labor market in Germany is characterized by far-reaching transformation processes: digitization and AI are changing work and qualification requirements, the mobility turnaround with the departure from the combustion engine is making entire branches of industry obsolete, and the ageing of society is reflected in the shortage of skilled workers, which cannot be adequately compensated for by immigration and retraining. This case study describes the expected labor market situation and qualification requirements in the Heilbronn-Franken region in Germany with the help of company personas, which were created based on expert interviews with representatives of key German industries. The findings show that despite changing job and requirement profiles, no significant job losses are expected and that companies see their greatest need for retraining and further training not in industry-specific skills, but in digital and interdisciplinary skills.

Keywords: Future skills · digital transformation · personas

1 Introduction

The German economy is facing significant changes, driven by rapid technological advancements and societal upheavals. Digitization, automation, and artificial intelligence are considered key drivers for future economic growth and will significantly influence the future work conditions and requirements. In addition to these developments, the societal transformation towards climate neutrality brings about extensive changes, including the drastic reduction of greenhouse gas emissions, the transition to a resource-efficient circular economy, and the implementation of the energy transition [1, 2].

These transformations introduce new requirements for employees [3]. Given its status as a hub for crucial German industries, including automotive engineering, logistics, electronics, and metal production, the Heilbronn-Franken economic region in southern Germany is particularly susceptible to these changes [4]. The IHK economic survey [5] reveals that 58% of companies view the skilled labor shortage as the most significant threat to future business growth.

M. Kurosu and A. Hashizume (Eds.): HCII 2024, LNCS 14684, pp. 144–160, 2024.
https://doi.org/10.1007/978-3-031-60405-8_10

Regional companies are actively seeking to mitigate this challenge by expanding their apprenticeship programs, bolstering their appeal as employers, recruiting skilled workers from abroad, promoting work-life balance, and offering greater opportunities for employee development. Notably, the training and upskilling of employees are recognized as critical strategies in navigating the disruptive transformations facing the industry.

A significant body of economic and scientific research has been dedicated to analyzing current and anticipated skill requirements in the labor market due to the disruptions brought about by transformational changes, commonly referred to as "future skills" [6–10]. These skills are expected to gain importance across various industries in the forthcoming years. A specific study tailored to the labor market needs of the German Federal State of Baden-Württemberg, in which the Heilbronn-Franken region is located, has delineated four critical skill clusters: technological skills, key digital skills, industrial skills, and interdisciplinary skills [6].

Against this background, the KIRA project is dedicated to designing and piloting an AI-enhanced, user-centric approach to the individualization of learning opportunities, incorporating key factors of corporate and labor market success. KIRA's objective is to refine the alignment between individual capabilities and market demands, with a particular emphasis on the industries and economic landscape of Baden-Württemberg. Despite the growing significance of platform-based digital learning, the development of AI-supported educational programs that effectively match these requirements is still in its infancy.

In the KIRA project, we address the diverse requirements of learners, such as employees and individuals participating in job training programs sponsored by the Employment Agency (Agentur für Arbeit), while simultaneously considering the specific needs and characteristics of industries and companies undergoing transformational processes within the region. This approach is integral to our human-centered design strategy.

To design for these different perspectives in a human-centered way, personas emerge as a pivotal tool. Personas encapsulate the distinct needs and perspectives of various stakeholder groups, thus facilitating a more nuanced and effective design and pilot phase of AI-enhanced, user-centric solutions [11–13]. This methodology not only ensures that the learning opportunities are tailored to the real-world contexts of users but also aligns with the strategic imperatives of corporate and labor market success.

We also gathered data from learners, trainers and other people involved in further education and constructed a set of personas and scenarios to embody the needs of the learners, which the designers used in the development process for KIRA, but which will not be exemplified here.

Drawing upon the insights from the Future Skill Study [6], and reinforced by 14 semi-structured interviews with key figures from the regional economy, alongside surveys with multipliers (industry experts, employment agency representatives), we crafted five distinct company personas. These personas serve as archetypes that illustrate the needs of companies in different sectors and their employees in a clear way, providing insights into challenges, opportunities, and an in-depth assessment of their required future skills. These personas are further used in the development process of the project KIRA, which matches learners and market requirements to provide valid suggestions for further education trainings and possibilities.

In the following, we will present a case study of the development of these company personas, as well as providing insights on the needs of the German industry in terms of future skills and how we integrate these into the personas and into the further design process.

2 Related Work

2.1 The Transformation in the German Economy

The current labor market in Germany is affected by deep transformation processes: Digitalization and AI are changing work processes and qualification requirements, the energy and mobility transition is making entire branches of industry obsolete, and the demographical change in society is reflected in the shortage of skilled workers, which yet cannot be adequately compensated for by immigration and retraining [2].

The current state of the economic world, in a broader sense also known as the VUCA world of work, is characterized by volatility, uncertainty, complexity and ambiguity and brings fundamental changes and new demands on employees [3]. Moreover, while certain transformations are world-wide phenomena their impact on different regions and countries may vary.

The Heilbronn-Franken economic region is an era with a high concentration of German key industries, such as engineering, automotive, logistics, electronics and metal production. Thus, the region is especially affected and undergoing a fundamental upheaval due to technological developments, digitization, climate change and increased efforts towards sustainability [4]. These ongoing changes require faster professional development and a regular updating of specialist knowledge on the part of employees.

The IHK Skilled Worker Monitor's forecast [5] identifies the shortage of skilled workers as the most significant threat to future business development for 58% of companies. Moreover, the economy in the Heilbronn-Franken region will face a shortage of 78,000 skilled workers by the year 2035 [5]. This includes 51,000 individuals with vocational training, 21,000 with advanced training qualifications, and 6,000 with university degrees. Companies in the region aim to address this issue by increasing their apprenticeship programs, enhancing their attractiveness as employers, hiring skilled workers from abroad, facilitating work-life balance, and providing more opportunities for employee training.

Furthermore, the ongoing changes in the labor market in the region are mainly characterized by a disruptive approach [14]. Whereas in evolutionary transformations, the current business model is evaluated and enhanced by adjusting structures and processes, in disruptive transformations, the existing business model is replaced entirely, and new structures and processes are introduced. Consequently, while some jobs may be lost, new ones are also generated, and existing employees need to be retrained in order to adapt to these changes in the labor market [14].

Thus, it is crucial to find appropriate responses to how the future of work can be shaped – especially since the region is poised for one of the largest upskilling initiatives in its history [6].

2.2 Future Skills

"Future skills" are those skills that will become more important in all sectors over the next five years [15]. They can be divided into "Key digital skills", "Technological skills" and "Key non-digital skills" [8, 15].

"Technological skills" are considered essential for shaping transformational technologies, encompassing proficiency in established technologies like the internet, as well as emerging ones such as blockchain. Technical skills are growing in significance across various sectors of the economy, with artificial intelligence and proficiency in complex data analysis standing out as particularly crucial. Proficiencies falling within the realm of "key digital skills" encompass digital knowledge acquisition and collaborative abilities. Through the utilization of digital skills, individuals can effectively navigate and contribute to a digitized setting. As a result of the Covid-19 pandemic, their importance has escalated. Skills such as digital interaction, digital learning, and digital literacy are particularly highly prized. Digital key competencies are progressively regarded as essential prerequisites, emphasizing the importance of mastering digital literacy and related skills among a wide audience. Key non-digital skills include adaptability, perseverance, and creativity. With these skills, individuals can effectively navigate new situations and analyze and solve problems in an increasingly complex work environment [8, 15].

Ehlers defines future skills as competencies that enable people to solve complex problems in a self-organized manner and to take action: "Future Skills are competencies that enable individuals to autonomously solve complex problems and effectively operate in highly emergent contexts. They are based on cognitive, motivational, volitional, and social resources, are value-based, and can be acquired through a learning process" [1]. They are considered a prerequisite for remaining operational in constantly changing situations.

Whereas Ehlers developed a more general model which is based on 17 competence profiles and further refers to a triple-helix structure [10] to define the three main clusters, we focused on the future skill study by the publisher AgenturQ [6] due to the regional focus of the project. This Future Skills Study examines the importance of future skills especially for Baden-Württemberg [6] in four key industries, namely the automotive and supplier industry, mechanical engineering, the metal industry, and medical technology. More than one million job advertisements were analyzed, and 33 Future Skills clusters were formed, which were grouped into four categories (see also Fig. 1). These clusters and skills were subsequently validated with the help of expert groups.

The category of "Technological skills" originates from the region's motivation to take a leading role in key technologies such as Artificial Intelligence (AI) and sustainable technologies. The associated Future Skills clusters, such as "Data science and AI," and "Intelligent Hardware and Robotics," contain skills and knowledge necessary for digital transformation. Similarly, the accompanying "Cybersecurity" is crucial for detecting and thwarting cyber-attacks. Considering climate policy goals, sustainable technologies, known as "Green IT," also play a key role.

The category of "Industrial Skills" describes industry-specific competencies and aims to defend Baden-Württemberg's reputation as an innovative and leading industrial region in the future. The industry is undergoing a transformation driven by digitization and decarbonization, necessitating the acquisition of new expertise across industrial

33 Future Skills cluster in four categories for Baden-Württemberg	
Technlogical skills	**Digital key skills**

• Cybersecurity
• Data management
• Data science & AI
• Design
• Intelligent hardware & robotics
• IT infrastructure & cloud
• Sustainable & resource-
  saving technologies
• Sensor technology & IoT
	• Agile working methods
	• Digital & data literacy
	• Digital collaboration &
	  interaction
	• Basic IT skills
	• Programming skills

Industrial skills	**Interdisciplinary skills**
• Alternative drive technologies • Analytical chemistry • Assisted & autonomous driving • Biotechnology • Electrical engineering • Development of medical devices • Industrial engineering • Pharmaceutical product & process developments	• Initiative • Flexibility • Leadership skills • Communication / persuasiveness • Creativity • Customer orientation • Organisational skills • Problem solving skills • Resilience • Goal orientationn

Fig. 1. Future-Skills-Cluster for Baden-Württemberg. Source: AgenturQ [6], translated by the authors

domains like automotive, mechanical engineering, metalworking, and medical technology. This shift aims to harmonize economic prosperity with climate-neutral practices. Thus, "Electrical engineering" and "Industrial engineering" are crucial elements of this cluster.

To shape structural change and digital transformation, individuals need to be able to independently navigate, handle, and shape new digital work methods and technologies. This ability and knowledge encompass the category "Digital key skills." Furthermore, agile approaches gain importance (in contrast to waterfall management approaches) as useful strategies to keep up with the rapid pace of changes [16].

Notably, "Interdisciplinary skills" will become increasingly important in the future world of work, especially goal orientation and problem-solving skills, due to increasing complexity and uncertainty [6]. This fourth category includes Future Skills that pertain to both individual methods and as well as social interactions with the environment.

2.3 Personas

Personas are fictional descriptions of people that are developed to represent the users or target groups in the design process. They originate from "goal-centered design" [17] and subsequently found their way into user-centered approaches and methods such as the human-centered design process [18], the contextual design methodology [19], etc. Personas are also widely used in the development of new technologies [12]. They are crafted from gathered user data, such as surveys, interviews, field observations, or workshops conducted by design teams. While traditional personas are often seen as representations of individual users or customers [20], some methodologies extend this concept by incorporating contextual factors. For instance, these enhanced personas might embody characteristics of domestic environments, offering a more nuanced understanding of user interactions within specific settings [21]. Beyond individual and environment-focused personas, there are approaches to develop "company personas" [22, 23]: These personas represent organizations or corporate entities and are used to inform design strategies. Just as individual users have unique traits yet share common contexts with others, it is posited that companies exhibit distinct characteristics while operating in environments similar to their peers [22]. This approach enables a deeper insight into how organizations behave and interact, facilitating tailored design solutions that resonate with both the specific and shared aspects of company identities. Communication during data collection may be conducted by several contact persons or one contact person who represents different interest groups [20]. This creates a certain complexity compared to the "classic" persona. In the following, we will present our method of gathering data and developing five company personas to represent the needs of the regional economy for the project KIRA.

3   Method

3.1   Development of Key Questions

Based on the results of exploratory preliminary discussions with representatives of associations and institutions at the interface between employers and employees (e.g. Heilbronn Employment Agency, Heilbronn-Franken Economic Development Agency, Südwestmetall and Heilbronn-Franken Chamber of Industry and Commerce (IHK)), an interview guideline was drawn up and validated via pretests.

Besides company demographics and basic information, we asked for associations with the term "transformation" and the extent to which the respective companies were affected. Moreover, we presented a list of future skills (see Fig. 1). We inquired further about current qualification requirements, as well as an outlook for the company. Beside one exception (IT 4, see Table 1), which was done in person, all interviews were conducted online and transcribed by eight students from the Bachelor's degree program "Business Administration - Service Management Consulting & Sales" as part of a project seminar in January 2022. Based on the personas, industry-specific recommendations for action were developed for the companies and other practice partners (see Fig. 2).

3.2   Company/Industry Representatives

When selecting the experts, we ensured that employers from different sectors (IT, Communication/HR, finance, logistics, manufacturing, automotive, trading) were represented. Moreover, we looked for a certain range of company sizes, including companies

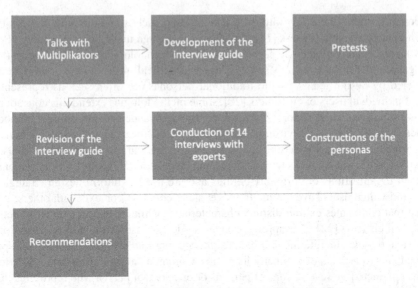

Fig. 2. Overview of the process

ranging from 8 to 12.000 employees. In total, we conducted 14 guideline-based expert interviews with managers from regional companies (see Table 1).

Table 1. Overview of participating companies

Industry	Size of Company	Duration
Personnel service	80 intern, 940 external employees	26 min
Telecommunication	4000 employees	30 min
Finance/Banking	670 employees	40 min
Manufacturing 1	350 employees	40 min
Manufacturing 2	290 employees	36 min
IT 1	550 employees	23 min
IT 2	8 employees	45 min
IT 3	2500 employees	25 min
IT 4	12.000 employees	90 min
Logistics 1	170 employees	30 min
Logistics 2	70 employees	30 min
Trading 1	100 employees	32 min
Trading 2	8500 employees	45 min
Automotive	1200 employees	30 min

4 Results

4.1 Construction of the Persona Template

For the presentation of the persona, socio-demographic characteristics, as known from a B2C (business-to-customer) persona, were turned into company demographic characteristics for a company suitable for B2B (business-to-business) and/or B2C businesses. Based on the 14 interviews, we constructed five personas, which are shown and described in Sects. 4.2-4.5.

The persona template incorporates traditional elements, including a name, a quote, and comprehensive company demographics such as the industry sector, location, founding date, size, target audience, and other relevant industry characteristics, alongside the company's core values. It emphasizes the analysis of the company's response to ongoing transformations, highlighting the impact, emerging challenges, and the organization's needs concerning future skills. The template also maps out the existing skills of the company's workforce. Furthermore, it details the company's current strategies and programs for advancing employee training and education. Subsequently, we introduce all five personas.

4.2 The IT Sector: Persona "IT-List"

The company persona "IT-list" (see Fig. 3) represents the regional IT sector, significantly influenced by ongoing transformation processes. The company lives by the maxim, "Standing still is a step backwards," reflecting its proactive stance towards change. As an owner-managed entity, "IT-list" has navigated continuous shifts for an extended period, marking its transformation level as substantial. The management adopts an optimistic view of transformation, seeing changes more as opportunities than obstacles. The industry is characterized by a notably high concentration of skilled professionals. At its core, "IT-list" specializes in the B2B domain, offering a comprehensive range of products and services. This spectrum encompasses IT solution consultancy, hardware provisioning, and the deployment of software programs and services.

However, "IT-list" faces several challenges. The combination of intense market competition and a prevailing skilled labor shortage leads to significant workforce turnover. Moreover, the company operates in a context where the sustainable evolution of technologies is critical, necessitating continual adjustments. The transformative impact is profoundly felt across all segments of the organization.

Employees have ambivalent sentiments towards transformation, notably digitalization. While they are receptive to change, they concurrently recognize the potential for an increased workload it may introduce. An assessment of the current skill set of the workforce reveals strong competencies, especially in innovation, learning capacity, digital literacy, and communication skills.

In terms of future skill requirements, interdisciplinary abilities are prioritized, succeeded by essential digital competencies. Technical skills are ranked third, with industrial skills trailing closely behind. Specifically, resilience, initiative, and organizational talents emerge as the most critical future skills. A pronounced emphasis on customer orientation and heightened awareness of cybersecurity among employees were also commonly cited. The company offers continuous training opportunities for its workforce.

IT-list

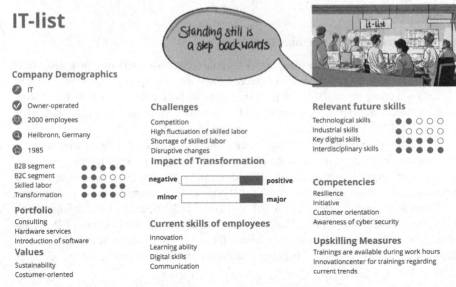

Company Demographics

- IT
- Owner-operated
- 2000 employees
- Heilbronn, Germany
- 1985

B2B segment   ● ● ● ● ●
B2C segment   ● ● ○ ○ ○
Skilled labor   ● ● ● ● ●
Transformation   ● ● ● ● ○

Portfolio
Consulting
Hardware services
Introduction of software

Values
Sustainability
Costumer-oriented

Challenges
Competition
High fluctuation of skilled labor
Shortage of skilled labor
Disruptive changes

Impact of Transformation

negative [   ] positive

minor [   ] major

Current skills of employees
Innovation
Learning ability
Digital skills
Communication

Relevant future skills

Technological skills   ● ● ○ ○ ○
Industrial skills   ● ○ ○ ○ ○
Key digital skills   ● ● ● ● ○
Interdisciplinary skills ● ● ● ● ●

Competencies
Resilience
Initiative
Customer orientation
Awareness of cyber security

Upskilling Measures
Trainings are available during work hours
Innovationcenter for trainings regarding current trends

Fig. 3. Company Persona "IT-list"

4.3 Banking: Persona "Bretzfelder Bank"

The profound upheaval and technological evolution within the banking industry is encapsulated by the reminiscence, "When I was an apprentice, we manually recorded withdrawals in the savings book with a ballpoint pen; ATMs were non-existent then". This statement vividly illustrates the dramatic shift in this field, a transformation mirrored in the operations of "Bretzfelder Bank" (see Fig. 4) established over a century ago. The bank maintains a direct engagement with its clientele, which equally comprises B2B and B2C segments. "Bretzfelder Bank" prides itself on its 670-strong workforce, all of whom are trained professionals. Currently, the bank's management is intensively navigating through this transformation, focusing on the resultant fields of action.

"Bretzfelder Bank" is navigating through numerous challenges, with digitalization standing out as the foremost issue. This digital shift has intensified competition, as the entry of online-only banks into the market reshapes the competitive landscape. Moreover, there's a cautious approach to modifying processes involving direct customer interactions, to ensure that customers can adapt smoothly to these changes.

The bank views the transformation of its business model in a positive light, recognizing potential cost reductions through the consolidation of physical branches. Employee development is prioritized, with training provided during work hours through online learning platforms and coaching sessions. Nevertheless, there's an acknowledged necessity for external expertise to expedite the transformation process and infuse new knowledge into the organization. This includes a pronounced demand for future skills, particularly in transdisciplinary abilities and digital key qualifications.

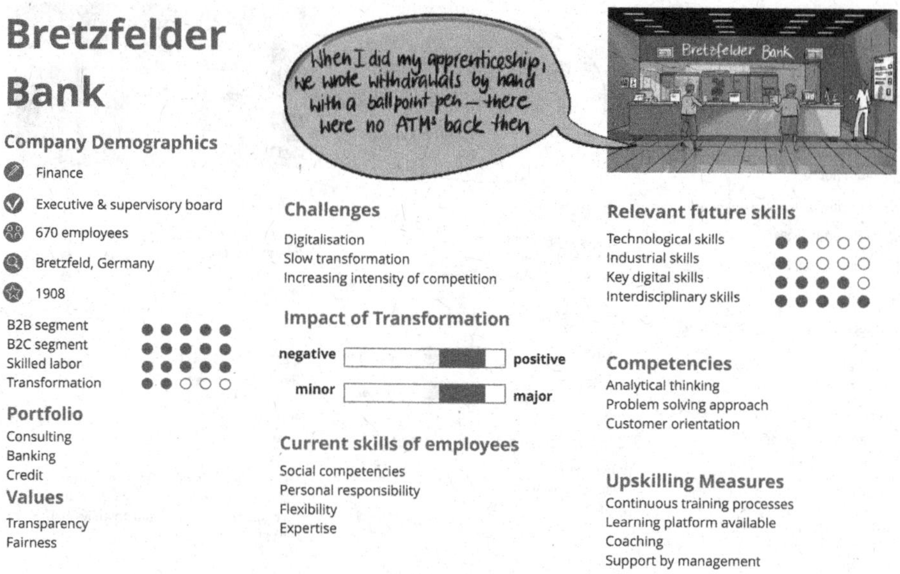

Bretzfelder Bank

Company Demographics

- Finance
- Executive & supervisory board
- 670 employees
- Bretzfeld, Germany
- 1908

B2B segment	● ● ● ● ●
B2C segment	● ● ● ● ●
Skilled labor	● ● ● ● ●
Transformation	● ● ○ ○ ○

Portfolio

Consulting
Banking
Credit

Values

Transparency
Fairness

Challenges

Digitalisation
Slow transformation
Increasing intensity of competition

Impact of Transformation

negative ▭ positive

minor ▭ major

Current skills of employees

Social competencies
Personal responsibility
Flexibility
Expertise

Relevant future skills

Technological skills	● ● ○ ○ ○
Industrial skills	● ○ ○ ○ ○
Key digital skills	● ● ● ● ○
Interdisciplinary skills	● ● ● ● ●

Competencies

Analytical thinking
Problem solving approach
Customer orientation

Upskilling Measures

Continuous training processes
Learning platform available
Coaching
Support by management

Fig. 4. Company Persona "Bretzfelder Bank"

4.4 Automotive: Persona "SGS Automotive"

"SGS Automotive" (see Fig. 5) is a company operating in the automotive industry. Its guiding principle is: "What is special today, will be completely different tomorrow". At its core, the company champions customer-centricity, a proactive approach, and sustainability. Established in the seventies, SGS Automotive has grown to employ approximately 1,200 individuals, dedicating its operations to the B2B domain, serving manufacturers and suppliers alike. The workforce predominantly comprises individuals who have completed a three-year vocational training program, with many also holding academic degrees. The company is deeply engaged in ongoing dialogues concerning trends, transformations, and strategic orientation. Its spectrum of offerings encompasses research, development, and the production of control units for both automotive and commercial vehicles. The primary challenges faced by "SGS Automotive" are intertwined with strategic decision-making, compliance with regulatory standards, and anticipation of future consumer demands. Despite the industry's paradigm shift, "SGS Automotive" perceives this transformative phase as an opportune moment, persistently harnessing the existing technology of the internal combustion engine.

Amidst perpetual evolution and the imperative to innovate products, employees exhibit a high degree of creativity and adaptability. Nonetheless, there remains a need to bolster digital competencies, a gap underscored by the Covid-19 pandemic. Consequently, fostering essential digital skills among employees is imperative for the company to facilitate location-independent and efficient collaboration within the framework of New Work concepts.

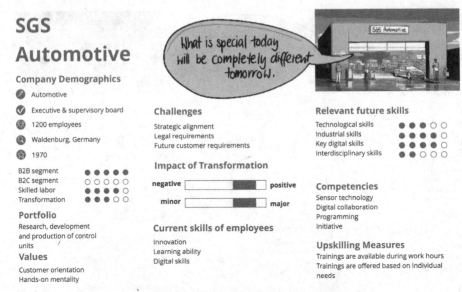

Fig. 5. Company Persona "SGS Automotive"

Industrial acumen, technological proficiency, and interdisciplinary expertise are equally vital for "SGS Automotive". Specifically, sensor technology, digital collaboration and interaction, programming prowess, and proactive initiative are identified as pivotal elements for the company's future prosperity. Employees are afforded opportunities for ongoing training and certification programs at universities tailored to their individual requirements.

4.5 Logistics: Persona "Fix Transport & Logistics GmbH"

The company persona "Fix Logistik & Transport GmbH" (see Fig. 6) represents the transportation and logistics industry rooted in the Heilbronn-Franken region. Established in the 1960s, this enduringly owner-managed enterprise boasts a workforce of approximately 100 employees. Primarily focused on the B2B market, the company occasionally undertakes B2C projects under special circumstances. The logistics sector faces a widespread challenge of skilled labor shortages, especially in the commercial sector in roles requiring mobility. Consequently, skilled personnel at "Fix Logistik & Transport GmbH" constitute less than half of the total workforce. Given its scale, transformation initiatives are currently confined to the management level, so the degree of transformation is still very low.

The product and service portfolio entails the execution of transports, the storage of goods and the creation of customized logistics concepts such as supply chain management for manufacturing companies or interface management between automobile manufacturers and automotive suppliers. The company is deeply rooted in its guiding principle: "We operate with a solution-oriented approach in collaboration with all stakeholders: customers, employees, suppliers, and manufacturers". This ethos underpins

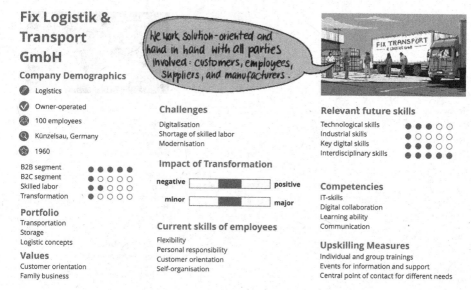

Fix Logistik & Transport GmbH

Company Demographics

- Logistics
- Owner-operated
- 100 employees
- Künzelsau, Germany
- 1960

B2B segment	● ● ● ● ●
B2C segment	● ○ ○ ○ ○
Skilled labor	● ● ○ ○ ○
Transformation	● ○ ○ ○ ○

Portfolio
Transportation
Storage
Logistic concepts

Values
Customer orientation
Family business

We work solution-oriented and hand in hand with all parties involved: customers, employees, suppliers, and manufacturers.

Challenges
Digitalisation
Shortage of skilled labor
Modernisation

Impact of Transformation

negative [ ] positive

minor [ ] major

Current skills of employees
Flexibility
Personal responsibility
Customer orientation
Self-organisation

Relevant future skills

Technological skills	● ● ● ○ ○
Industrial skills	● ○ ○ ○ ○
Key digital skills	● ● ● ○ ○
Interdisciplinary skills	● ● ● ● ●

Competencies
IT-skills
Digital collaboration
Learning ability
Communication

Upskilling Measures
Individual and group trainings
Events for information and support
Central point of contact for different needs

Fig. 6. Company Persona "Fix Logistik & Transport GmbH"

the company's core values, emphasizing customer-centricity, fostering teamwork, and preserving its familial ethos.

Foremost among the company's challenges is the imperative of digitalization, a domain where the industry at large remains relatively underdeveloped. Nonetheless, the company recognizes digitalization's potential to unlock new opportunities and confer distinct competitive advantages. In addition to addressing the shortage of skilled workers, modernizing the fleet stands out as a central concern, with technological advancements, market competition, and cost considerations posing significant hurdles. Thus, while the ongoing transformation presents opportunities for "Fix Transport & Logistics GmbH's" business model, it also entails substantial costs.

Employee skills crucial for success include flexibility, a customer-centric approach, personal accountability, and adeptness in self-organization. Looking ahead, the company places increasing emphasis on interdisciplinary expertise, technological acumen, and essential digital proficiencies. Ongoing training initiatives are offered to support employee capabilities, particularly in response to process alterations or new implementations (Fig. 7).

4.6 Manufacturing: Persona "Maschinenbau Müller GmbH"

"Maschinenbau Müller GmbH" is a family-run manufacturing company based in Bretzfeld. It operates exclusively in the B2B sector and offers machines and auxiliary materials for trade and industry. The company was founded in 1995 and employs around 300 people, mainly skilled workers.

Currently, the transformation is predominantly steered by management, resulting in a relatively modest degree of transformation. Key corporate values center around respect, reliability, and honesty, with skilled specialists regarded as pivotal assets for

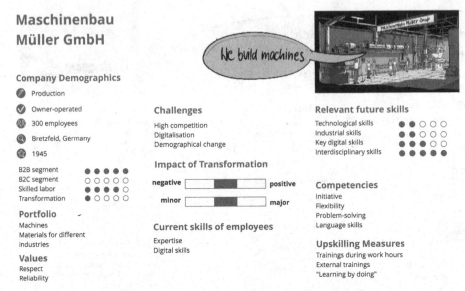

Fig. 7. Company Persona "Maschinenbau Müller GmbH"

driving the transformation forward. The company grapples with challenges stemming from competitive pressures, digitalization imperatives, and demographic shifts. While the transformation presents both favorable opportunities for the business model, the dearth of skilled workers and an unattractive geographical location exert a negative influence on the company's trajectory.

Employees possess specialized expertise alongside fundamental digital proficiencies. Future skills deemed essential encompass interdisciplinary competencies, critical digital qualifications, and industry-specific proficiencies. Additionally, personal initiative, adaptability, problem-solving acumen, and language fluency are identified as vital sub-category skills.

External training measures and "learning by doing" are used for the further training of employees. There is a willingness to undergo further training, especially among young employees. Furthermore, external skills are needed to accelerate the transformation.

5   Discussion

The paper gives in insights into the current situation of the main industries in the Heilbronn-Franken region as they are affected by disruptive transformation processes.

We consolidated the results of 14 in-depth interviews of industry experts and leading employers for the branches automotive, IT, logistics, banking, trading and manufacturing in the form of five company personas. Hence, our goal was twofold: Showing the development of company personas as a case study as well as providing insights into the current and anticipated needs of the southern German labor market in terms of future skills.

When considering future skills, interdisciplinary competencies emerged as the primary focus for the majority of interviewees, highlighted in four out of five personas. Key digital proficiencies ranked second, followed by technological and industrial skills. A common thread across all expert interviews is the growing expectation from employers for enhanced self-organization among employees.

Not surprisingly, there are industry-specific differences in the sub-dimensions of the future skills. The representative experts of the IT industry named resilience, initiative, clear customer focus, organizational skills, awareness of cyber-security as the most important and sought-after future skills for their employees, which we integrated in the company persona "IT-list".

Interviewees from the financial/banking sector named flexibility, solution orientation, analytical thinking, and customer orientation as the most relevant future skills for their companies, qualities we incorporated in the company persona "Bretzfelder Bank".

Representatives from the automotive industry focused on skills regarding digital collaboration and interaction, programming, and self-initiative. Regarding specific technologies, they mentioned sensor technology as a field that is in high demand. These specifics were included in the company persona "SGS Automotive".

The logistics and transportation industry especially requires digital collaboration skills, IT skills, communication skills and a general ability and willingness to learn. These were integrated in the company persona "Fix Transport & Logistics GmbH".

The manufacturing industry named initiative, flexibility, problem-solving skills, and language skills as their most crucial needs in terms of future skills, which we represented in the company persona "Maschinenbau Müller GmbH".

The modest ranking of industrial skills could be attributed to the fact that the survey encompassed only two manufacturing companies. Nevertheless, a significant majority of company representatives and industry experts emphasized the critical importance of interdisciplinary skills, including what is often also termed "soft skills," e.g. creativity and flexibility. These "skills" are highly prized for their indispensability in the contemporary workplace, yet they are notably more challenging to impart and develop compared to traditional industry-specific skills. Although some sources, e.g. the study by AgenturQ [6] mention digital ethics, reflexive, ethical and critical thinking in terms of digitalization and new technologies are generally rather underrepresented in previous literature on future skills [10], and were also hardly mentioned explicitly in our research.

Numerous interviewees across various sectors have highlighted their struggles with the current low level of digitalization within their organizations. One plausible explanation for the slow pace of digitalization could be rooted in the nature of the German "Mittelstand" (small and medium-sized enterprises), which is predominantly made up of traditional, family-owned enterprises with characteristics and structures that may present obstacles to digital adoption [24].

Many company representatives also reported a shortage of skilled labor as well as quickly changing requirements, in line with the findings of the IHK survey [5]. Notably, companies predominantly focus on retraining their existing workforce, instead of laying off staff.

Limitations. The majority of companies surveyed view the changes in the labor market as an opportunity, preferring to retrain employees over layoffs. However, the credibility of these claims may be influenced by the fact that interviews were not anonymous. This lack of anonymity raises concerns about the possibility of company representatives withholding information about potential layoffs or financial struggles. Nonetheless, participants were reassured that company identities would not be disclosed in any future publications, which might have encouraged more openness.

The impact of German legal frameworks, cultural norms, and the competitive demand for skilled labor also play a significant role in these dynamics. Additionally, the financial implications of hiring new staff versus retraining existing employees favor the latter, highlighting an economic motivation behind these decisions.

It is also important to note that while certain themes emerged consistently within and across industries, the findings from individual interviews are not intended to be extrapolated to entire sectors. This was not the objective of our study.

Our research touched upon the differentiation of "competencies" and "skills" within the framework of future skills, as well as on the issue that attributes like creativity and flexibility can also be viewed as personality traits. These considerations, also highlighted by Ehlers [10], are not explored further in our work, since it is focused on the practical application of an AI-based recommender system rather than theoretical analysis.

The study's reference to the Future Skills Study in Baden-Württemberg [6] co-financed by industrial unions IG Metall Baden-Württemberg and Südwestmetall, may introduce a bias towards certain skills deemed more relevant by these entities. Our research, however, remains independent of industrial financing, though it acknowledges the possible influence of the referenced study's focus.

Lastly, the selection of companies was influenced by existing networks through the university DHBW Heilbronn, though efforts were made to ensure diversity in industry representation, company size, and form.

6 Conclusion and Outlook

In conclusion, it is observed that the majority of companies surveyed view the ongoing transformations in the labor market positively, recognizing them as opportunities. Significantly, these companies are inclined to retain their workforce, rather than opting for layoffs. This approach is influenced by their corporate culture, the prevailing labor shortages, and the availability of opportunities for both internal and external retraining and advanced professional development.

When it comes to the prioritization of future skills, interdisciplinary competencies emerge as the foremost concern for many organizations, a perspective highlighted in four of the five personas developed. Key digital skills rank as the second priority, with technological and industrial skills following in order of importance.

While there are variances in the importance of specific future skills across industries, a common thread from the expert interviews is the growing expectation for employees to exhibit greater self-organization. The low emphasis on industrial skills appears to be influenced by the limited number of manufacturing companies included in the survey.

Actionable, industry-specific recommendations have been proposed for the companies and practice partners, underscoring the need for tailored approaches.

In sum, the Region of Heilbronn-Franken faces numerous challenges, with implications that are expected to persist into the foreseeable future. To navigate these challenges effectively, companies must focus on retraining existing employees, attracting new skilled workers, and integrating refugees into the workforce. The adoption of AI-assisted systems for further education and training is suggested to facilitate and support these transitions effectively.

The company personas developed are integral to the Project KIRA, serving to articulate the specific needs of companies in the creation of matching algorithms and the provision of further education programs.

Acknowledgments. This work has been partially funded by the German Federal Ministry of Education and Research (Bundesministerium für Bildung und Forschung - BMBF) under grant numbers 21INVI1802 and 21INVI1803 as part of the project 'KIRA – KI-gestütztes Matching individueller und arbeitsmarktbezogener Anforderungen für die berufliche Weiterbildung' (AI-supported matching of individual and labor market requirements for professional development). The responsibility for all content supplied lies with the authors.

The authors gratefully acknowledge the contributions of the students Vivian Bechler, Stefan Braus, Katrin Engelhardt, Laura Gronbach, Christian Schanz, Luisa Schweizer, Sascha Weitzel, Luisa Wildt, whose rigorous efforts in conducting interviews and analyzing data were invaluable to the completion of this research.

Disclosure of Interests.   The authors have no competing interests to declare that are relevant to the content of this article.

References

1. Ehlers, U.-D.: Future Skills: Lernen der Zukunft - Hochschule der Zukunft. Springer Fachmedien Wiesbaden, Wiesbaden (2020). https://doi.org/10.1007/978-3-658-29297-3
2. Krill, Z., Grundke, R., Bickmann, M.: Klimaneutralität erreichen, ohne die Wettbewerbsfähigkeit und den sozialen Zusammenhalt zu schwächen. In: OECD-Wirtschaftsberichte: Deutschland 2023. OECD (2023). https://doi.org/10.1787/3bbf77e3-de
3. Mack, O., Khare, A.: Perspectives on a VUCA World. In: Mack, O., Khare, A., Krämer, A., Burgartz, T. (eds.) Managing in a VUCA World, pp. 3–19. Springer, Cham (2016). https://doi.org/10.1007/978-3-319-16889-0_1
4. GmbH, W.R.H.: Bewältigung der Herausforderungen durch Transformation (2023). https://buendnis-fuer-transformation.de/bewaeltigung-durch-transformation.html
5. Heilbronn-Franken, I.: Fachkräfte Monitor Heilbronn-Franken (2021). https://www.fachkraeftemonitoring-bw.de/fachkraeftemonitor.html#3lb75m1
6. Klier, M., et al.: Future Skills: welche kompetenzen für den standort baden-württemberg heute und in zukunft erfolgskritisch sind. AgenturQ - Agentur zur Förderung der beruflichen Weiterbildung in der Metall- und Elektroindustrie Baden-Württemberg e.V., (2021). https://www.agenturq.de/future-skills-studie/
7. OECD: An OECD learning framework 2030. In: Bast, G., Carayannis, E.G., Campbell, D.F.J. (eds.) The Future of Education and Labor, pp. 23–35. Springer, Cham (2019). https://doi.org/10.1007/978-3-030-26068-2_3

8. Bughin, J., Hazan, E., Lund, S., Dahlström, P., Wiesinger, A., Subramaniam, A.: Skill shift: automation and the future of the workforce. McKinsey Glob. Inst. **1**, 3–84 (2018)

9. Kirchherr, J., Klier, J., Lehmann-Brauns, C., Winde, M.: Future Skills: Welche Kompetenzen in Deutschland fehlen. Future Skills-Diskussionspapier **1** (2018)

10. Ehlers, U.-D.: Future Skills im Vergleich. Zur Konstruktion eines allgemeinen Rahmenmodells für Zukunftskompetenzen in der akademischen Bildung (2022)

11. Cooper, A.: The inmates are running the asylum: why high-tech products drive us crazy and how to restore the sanity. Indianapolis: Sams (1999)

12. Personas - User Focused Design. HIS, Springer, London (2019). https://doi.org/10.1007/978-1-4471-7427-1

13. Marsden, N., Pröbster, M.: Personas and Identity: looking at multiple identities to inform the construction of personas. In: Proceedings of the 2019 CHI Conference on Human Factors in Computing Systems, Glasgow, ACM, p. 335 (2019)

14. B.F.T. (Hrsg.): Bewältigung durch Transformation (2024). https://buendnis-fuer-transformation.de/bewaeltigung-durch-transformation.html. Accessed 13 Feb 2024

15. M.K.C. Stifterverband für die Deutsche Wissenschaft e.V., Future Skills: Welche Kompetenzen in Deutschland fehlen (2018). https://www.stifterverband.org/future-skills/framework

16. Rigby, D.K., Sutherland, J., Takeuchi, H.: Embracing agile. Harv. Bus. Rev. **94**(5), 40–50 (2016)

17. Cooper, A., Reimann, R., Cronin, D., Noessel, C.: About face: The essentials of interaction design. John Wiley & Sons (2014)

18. DIN, Ergonomie der Mensch-System-Interaktion - Teil 210: Prozess zur Gestaltung gebrauchstauglicher interaktiver Systeme (ISO 9241–210:2010); Deutsche Fassung EN ISO 9241–210:2010 (2010)

19. Holtzblatt, K., Beyer, H.: Contextual Design: Design for Life. Morgan Kaufmann, Boston (2017)

20. Kirchem, S., Waack, J.: Personas entwickeln für Marketing. Springer, Vertrieb und Kommunikation (2021). https://doi.org/10.1007/978-3-658-33088-0

21. Barton, H.J., et al.: What makes a home? Designing home personas to represent the homes of families caring for children with medical complexity. Appl. Ergon. **106**, 103900 (2023)

22. Ali, F., Boks, C., Bey, N.: An exploration of company personas to support customized DfS implementation. In: DS 87–5 Proceedings of the 21st International Conference on Engineering Design (ICED 17) Vol **5**: Design for X, Design to X, Vancouver, Canada, 21–25.08, pp. 385–394 (2017)

23. Ali, F., Stewart, R., Boks, C., Bey, N.: Exploring "Company Personas" for informing design for sustainability implementation in companies. Sustainability **11**(2), 463 (2019)

24. Gut, M.: Fluch und Segen digitaler Disruption für den deutschen Mittelstand: Eine Analyse der Herausforderungen, Risiken, Strategien und Wettbewerbsfähigkeit deutscher mittelständischer Unternehmen im Umgang mit dem Phänomen der digitalen Disruption. In: Digitalisierung: Fallstudien, pp. 171–217. Springer, Tools und Erkenntnisse für das digitale Zeitalter (2023). https://doi.org/10.1007/978-3-658-36634-6_8

Research Hotspots and Trends of User-Centered Human-Computer Interaction: A Bibliometric Analysis

Ting Qiu[1]([⊠]) [iD], Shufang Qian[1], and Xinghao Chen[2]

[1] Inner Mongolia Normal University, Hohhot 010010, China
qiuting2022@gmail.com
[2] TianJin Academy of Fine Arts, TianJin 300000, China

Abstract. User-centered human-computer interaction research is critical in determining the user interaction experience. However, there has been little research systematically discussing the developmental trajectory and future research directions of user-centered human-computer interaction from a bibliometric perspective. Therefore, to understand the current research hotspots and trends in user-centered human-computer interaction over the past decade, this study retrieved 2343 relevant literature from the Web of Science (WOS) database as a foundation. Employing commonly used bibliometric software, Citespace and VOSviewer, we conducted a comprehensive analysis of classic literature, related literature sources, the most influential countries, institutions, and authors in this field. Simultaneously, we created trend charts depicting the development of literature quantity, keyword co-occurrence, and maps illustrating research hotspots and trends. The results indicate that in the past decade, user-centered human-computer interaction research has primarily focused on (1) usability and user experience, (2) interaction paradigms and technologies, (3) Human-AI Interaction, (4) user perception, and (5) visualization. Future research is expected to concentrate on graphics systems and interfaces, applied computing, and human-centered computing. Articles in this field are frequently published in conference proceedings, with the IEEE conference on virtual reality and 3D user interfaces being the most influential conference. This study comprehensively outlines the developmental history and future research trends in user-centered human-computer interaction over the past decade, providing valuable assistance to scholars in this field.

Keywords: User-centered · Human-computer interaction · Bibliometric · VOSviewer · Citespace

1 Introduction

"User-centered" originated from Donald Norman's concept of "user-centered design"[2]. Being user-centered involves considering users' needs, habits, and behaviors as the primary focus. Human-computer interaction (HCI) refers to the interactive behavior between humans and machines [3], emerging with the advent of computers. HCI comprises three crucial elements: humans, machines, and the interaction between them [4].

© The Author(s), under exclusive license to Springer Nature Switzerland AG 2024
M. Kurosu and A. Hashizume (Eds.): HCII 2024, LNCS 14684, pp. 161–177, 2024.
https://doi.org/10.1007/978-3-031-60405-8_11

Studying the functionality and usability of machines was an important focus in the early years. In recent years, with the diversification of machines such as VR headset, wearable devices, and smart homes, interactions between humans and machines have become more frequent, and the role that humans play in the interaction process has become increasingly significant. More scholars have engaged in the research of human needs, behaviors, and habits, advocating for a human-centered, personalized, and intelligent friendly interaction experience. This has led to the interdisciplinary integration of computer science, psychology, and design [1]. In the long run, user-centered human-computer interaction is crucial for creating a positive user experience. A good user experience makes it easier for users to accept and consistently use machines [5], further promoting the development of human-machine relationships.

Over the past decade, a substantial body of literature has accumulated in the field of user-centered human-computer interaction (UCHCI). Therefore, it is necessary to conduct a phased review and summary of the current state and existing research achievements in this field. Literature review is a method that involves organizing and evaluating relevant articles to construct a knowledge framework in a specific field [7]. However, it is worth noting that UCHCI is a multidisciplinary and interdisciplinary direction with diverse and intricate literature content. Traditional literature review methods struggle to organize, analyze, and synthesize the research hotspots and development dynamics in this field [8]. In contrast, bibliometric analysis can handle large volumes of literature, allowing for the identification of potential patterns and information across numerous documents [6]. Hence, this study employs bibliometric methods to unearth relevant literature in the UCHCI field. It aims to address the following four research questions to provide a comprehensive overview of UCHCI:

1. What has been the overall trend in UCHCI research over the past 10 years?
2. What are the main research hotspots in UCHCI over the past 10 years, and what are the potential future research directions?
3. Which major countries, institutions, and scholars globally are dedicated to UCHCI research?
4. What are the classic works in this field?

By elucidating these questions, the study aims to offer a comprehensive understanding of the developmental history and future trends in UCHCI, providing a foundation for the future development of this field.

2 Research Design

2.1 Data Sources

The data utilized in this study originates from the Core Collection of the Web of Science database. Web of Science is recognized globally as one of the most comprehensive English databases, renowned for its outstanding comprehensive citation search capabilities [9]. The Core Collection of this database comprises literature subjected to peer review and stringent journal scrutiny, thus ensuring a high level of disciplinary representation [10].

For our search, we specifically utilized SSCI, SCI-Expanded, A&HCI, CPCI-S, and CPCI-SSH as sources. In terms of keywords, we combined the terms "user-centered" and "human-computer interaction." Due to the diverse expressions of these terms in English, we compiled an extensive list of related terms, linking them through the Boolean operator "OR" in advanced search. The search strategy was formulated as follows: TS = ((user centered OR user-centered OR human centered OR human-centered) AND (HCI OR human-computer interaction)). To enhance the clarity of our search process, we established a temporal scope covering the past 10 years (2014 to 2023), excluding non-English conference and journal articles. To prevent the loss of relevant literature, no further manual screening of retrieved articles was conducted. In the end, a total of 2343 articles were obtained, and these articles were exported in the "full record + cited references" format as a TXT file.

2.2 Research Methods

Bibliometric, initially proposed by Pritchard in 1969 [11], represents a quantitative research approach commonly employed for the analysis and evaluation of the scale, impact, and developmental trends of academic output. Its underlying principle is rooted in the statistical and analytical examination of bibliographic information to unveil latent patterns in research activities within a specific domain. The landscape of bibliometric software is diverse, with each offering its unique advantages and drawbacks. In alignment with the focus of this study, we opt for the utilization of two software tools, namely CiteSpace 6.1.R6 and VOSviewer 1.6.19. Primarily, CiteSpace was developed by Dr. Chaomei Chen at Drexel University [12]. It operates on the JAVA platform, providing powerful visual analytics. The software supports multidimensional analyses, covering aspects such as authors, institutions, and keywords. It also provides essential metrics such as burst keywords and time zones. Secondly, VOSviewer, developed by the Centre for Science and Technology Studies at Leiden University, the Netherlands, employs algorithms akin to those of CiteSpace [13]. This bibliometric tool facilitates the analysis of relationships among documents and additionally supports analyses of author collaboration and keyword co-occurrence. The combined use of these two tools offers a comprehensive depiction of the current status and advancements in UCHCI research. This integrated approach lays the groundwork for further exploration of research hotspots and future avenues, contributing to the elucidation of the field's trajectory and potential research directions.

3 Results and Analysis

3.1 Trend Analysis of Annual Outputs of UCHCI Literature

The annual output of scholarly literature in statistics is a crucial metric for evaluating the vibrancy of the research domain [14]. It assists in assessing the relative significance and impact of the research field across different time periods. The annual distribution chart of literature output for UCHCI is depicted in Fig. 1. From Fig. 1, it becomes evident that there is a decrease in the quantity of publications in 2015 compared to

2014, in 2017 compared to 2016, and in 2020 compared to 2019. However, the overall trend of scholarly output exhibits an ascending pattern. This signifies the continuous evolution and advancement of research efforts within the UCHCI domain. Based on the decade-long trend in literature production, the developmental trajectory of UCHCI research can be categorized into three principal phases: the initial stage (2014–2016), the developmental stage (2017–2019), and the mature stage (2020–2023). In the initial phase, the annual production of literature remained relatively modest. The average annual publication count was 127 papers, and it was devoid of conspicuous growth trends. The transition into the developmental stage commenced in 2017. Figure 1 reveals a notable surge in publication rates from 2017 to 2018, a momentum that persisted into 2019. Since 2020, UCHCI research has entered a phase of maturity. Although the growth rate is less pronounced compared to the developmental phase, the average annual publication count remains elevated, reaching 322 papers per year. Furthermore, it peaked at 425 papers in the year 2022.

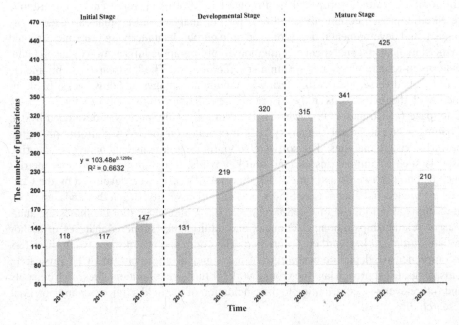

Fig. 1. Number of articles by year of publication

3.2   Research Hotspots of UCHCI

The keywords of the paper represent the author's highly condensed, accurate, and representative understanding of the article. Measuring the common occurrence frequency of keywords can reflect the development process and trends of research hotspots in UCHCI [15]. Among the 2343 retrieved documents, a total of 6374 keywords were identified.

To ensure standardization and consistency in expression of the keywords, we followed the affinity propagation method proposed by Frey and Dueck [16]. Using this method, all keywords were normalized to maintain consistency in singular and plural forms and to merge synonyms. For instance, "emotion" was replaced with "emotions," "hci" with "human-computer interaction," "user centred design" with "user-centered design," "human computer interaction" with "human-computer interaction," and "human computer interaction (hci)" with "human-computer interaction." The keyword normalization process involved the participation of three experts in the field and two researchers.

The data was imported into the VOSviewer software, with a frequency threshold set at seven occurrences or more, and clustering similar keywords. The resulting keyword clustering graph is illustrated in Fig. 2. The graph comprises 251 keyword nodes and 4465 connecting lines. The size of each circle represents the frequency of the respective keyword. Larger circles indicate higher frequencies, suggesting greater importance in UCHCI research, as they appear more frequently. Table 1 presents the top 20 keywords by frequency, which can be considered as the focal points of UCHCI research. Excluding general search terms such as "human-computer interaction," "human-centered computing," "interaction paradigms," "virtual reality," "user-centered design" and "mixed/augmented reality," the most frequently occurring terms are "design," "usability," "hci design and evaluation methods," "computing methodologies," among others. These keywords offer a comprehensive understanding of the UCHCI field.

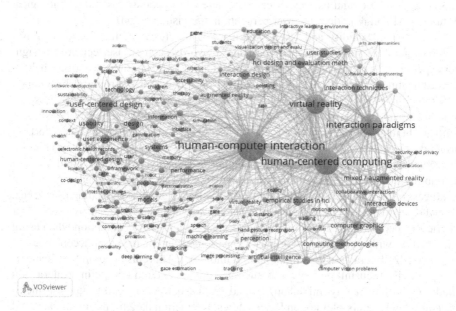

Fig. 2. Keyword Co-Occurrence Clustering

Table 1. Top 20 keywords of UCHCI

Ranking	Keyword	Fre	Ranking	Keyword	Fre
1	human-computer interaction	1156	11	visualization	87
2	human-centered computing	786	12	user studies	78
3	interaction paradigms	504	13	systems	77
4	virtual reality	430	14	empirical studies in hci	72
5	user-centered design	219	15	interaction techniques	71
6	mixed / augmented reality	113	16	interaction design	69
7	design	112	17	interaction devices	69
8	usability	105	18	user experience	69
9	hci design and evaluation methods	102	19	computer graphics	66
10	computing methodologies	87	20	artificial intelligence	65

The keywords with the same color in the figure form clusters, creating five main clusters. In detail, current research on UCHCI is mainly focused on the following five aspects: #1, usability and user experience, #2, interaction paradigms and technologies, #3, human-AI collaboration, #4, user perception, #5, visualization.

Cluster #1 - Usability and User Experience. This cluster includes a total of 148 clustered members, primarily encompassing keywords such as user-centered design, user experience, acceptance, accessibility, model, co-design, children, emotions, behavior, sustainability, usability, etc. User-centered design was first proposed by Donald A. Norman in 1986 in his publication "User-Centered System Design: New Perspectives on Human-Computer Interaction." The book introduced the concept of designing computer-human interfaces with a focus on users [2]. Subsequently, in 1988, Norman further developed the UCD concept in his book "The Psychology Of Everyday Things." He recognized the importance of understanding user needs and interests and focused on usability design [17]. In summary, user-centered design involves engaging users in the process of product or system development. By thoroughly understanding user needs, product design becomes more successful, leading to acceptance and use by users. User experience specifically focuses on whether users have a positive perception when using or interacting with a product. A good user experience can enhance user acceptance.

Cluster #2 - Interaction Paradigms and Technologies. This cluster comprises 56 members, primarily focusing on keywords such as human-centered computing, interaction paradigms, virtual reality, mixed/augmented reality, hci design and evaluation methods, computing methodologies, and user studies. Interaction paradigms are fundamental approaches or models that govern how users engage with technology or systems. These paradigms play a crucial role in shaping the design and execution of user interfaces and interactions in diverse digital or technological environments. Over time, various interaction paradigms have emerged to adapt to the evolving nature of technology and user preferences. Notable examples of interaction paradigms include the Command Line Interface (CLI), Graphical User Interface (GUI), and touch-based Interaction, among others [18]. With the advancement of technology, new technologies such as VR, AR, and MR have emerged, leading to the creation of novel interaction paradigms [19]. Examples include Gesture-Based Interaction, Mixed-Initiative Interaction, and others. These paradigms allow users to interact with systems using expressions, gestures, body movements, and more, emphasizing a user-centric approach. This shift places a greater emphasis on user experience, aligning with the principle of putting users at the center of considerations.

Cluster #3 - Human-AI Collaboration. This cluster comprises 23 members, primarily focusing on keywords such as artificial intelligence, machine learning, eye tracking, deep learning, hand gesture recognition, neural networks, gaze estimation, face detection, and so on. Human-AI collaboration refers to the joint efforts of humans and AI in pursuit of common goals [20]. In this collaborative framework, artificial intelligence technologies play a crucial role, including machine learning and deep learning. Research on user-centric aspects such as eye tracking, hand gesture recognition, and face detection aims to enhance the potential for effective collaboration between humans and AI.

Cluster #4 - User Perception. This cluster comprises 15 members, primarily focusing on keywords such as perception, environments, sense, hand, body, feedback, motion, size, and so on. User perception represents the intricate relationship between individuals and the sensory experiences during interactions with systems. The keywords underscore various aspects of perception, including factors such as sensation, body movements, hands, and motion, addressing the interpretation of sensory information and the impact of the environment on user experiences [22]. Understanding user perception is crucial in the design and development of systems that align with human behavior and cognition, ensuring a more intuitive and user-friendly human-computer interaction. In virtual environments, the creation of sensory experiences, including visual, auditory, tactile, and olfactory sensations, aims to make the user experience more immersive and authentic [21].

Cluster #5 – Visualization. This cluster comprises 9 members, primarily focusing on keywords such as navigation, visualization, visualization design and evaluation methods, information visualization, visualization techniques, graphical user interfaces, and so on. Visualization involves presenting complex information in a simplified graphical form [23]. The goal is to promote better understanding and decision-making through visually accessible means. Visualization significantly enhances the interactive capabilities between users and interfaces. With the ever-increasing volume of data and information, the role of visualization in the UCHCI field becomes increasingly pivotal. Improving the accessibility and interpretability of complex data sets can effectively elevate the user experience.

3.3 The Evolution and Trend of UCHCI Research Hotspots

In order to further understand the research hotspots and development trends in the field of UCHCI, the Citespace software was employed to visualize the average appearance time of keywords [24]. As depicted in Fig. 3, it illustrates the temporal distribution of keywords, referred to as the "Time Zone" for keywords, and Fig. 4 represents the emergence of Burst keywords. In the Time Zone graph, the size of the circles indicates the frequency of keyword appearances in the last decade [25], while the timeline signifies the first occurrence of keywords [26]. Scholars often use the Time Zone graph to comprehend the cutting-edge trends in a particular field. Figure 4 lists the top 52 keywords with the highest intensity in different periods, with the subsequent timeline denoting the years in which these keywords were relatively prominent in the literature. The burst keywords signify different research hotspots in various periods, providing insights into the developmental history of a field. The combined analysis of these two graphs yields a more effective and comprehensive understanding. Examining Fig. 3, it is evident that research in the UCHCI field over the past decade has predominantly focused on user-centered design, as indicated by keywords such as user-centered design, user experience, user interfaces, and affective computing. Subsequently, the research shifted towards the study of human factors, including behavior, health, care, and emotions. Further investigations concentrated on the integration of human and computer, featuring keywords like Participatory design, experience, and electronic health records. Post-2020, new research trends and hotspots emerged in graphics systems and interfaces, applied computing, and human-centered computing. This evolution demonstrates the maturity of UCHCI research, with increasingly diverse and enriched content. The results from Fig. 4 align with those from Fig. 3. The 52 highlighted keywords in Fig. 4 illustrate a transition from early user-centered design to the study of human factors (behavior, psychology, habits), leading to the development of new systems designed and developed with user participation. This trend signifies the convergence and multifaceted development of the human-computer interaction field.

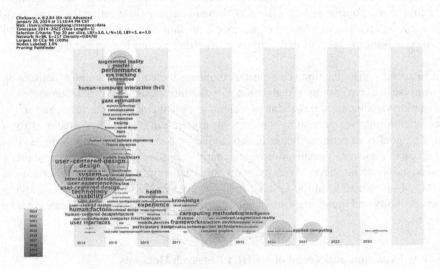

Fig. 3. Keyword co-occurrence clustering map for UCHCI literature

Top 52 Keywords with the Strongest Citation Bursts

Keywords	Year	Strength	Begin	End	2014 ~ 2023
user experience	2014	8.19	2014	2018	
user-centred design	2014	7.92	2014	2016	
affective computing	2014	4.38	2014	2017	
user interfaces	2014	4.22	2014	2016	
usability	2014	4.09	2014	2018	
user centred design	2014	3.89	2014	2017	
human factors	2014	3.55	2014	2017	
software development	2014	3.4	2014	2017	
gaze estimation	2014	3.16	2014	2016	
hand gesture recognition	2014	3.16	2014	2016	
human-centred design	2014	3.16	2014	2016	
mobile devices	2014	2.63	2014	2016	
ubiquitous computing	2014	2.43	2014	2017	
human-computer interaction	2014	17.44	2015	2017	
user-centered design	2014	14.26	2015	2017	
human computer interaction	2014	12.79	2015	2017	
user centered design	2014	11.05	2015	2018	
eye tracking	2015	7.99	2015	2019	
system	2014	6.96	2015	2017	
human-computer interaction (hci)	2014	3.7	2015	2017	
assistive technology	2015	2.97	2015	2018	
information	2014	2.95	2015	2018	
tracking	2014	2.89	2015	2019	
model	2014	2.67	2015	2016	
behavior	2014	2.64	2015	2017	
feature extraction	2015	2.49	2015	2016	
technology	2014	7.74	2016	2019	
health	2014	4.85	2016	2019	
human-centered design	2014	4.23	2016	2018	
internet of things	2016	3.77	2016	2019	
image processing	2014	3.14	2016	2019	
graphical user interfaces	2016	3.13	2016	2018	
interface	2014	2.96	2016	2017	
impact	2014	2.8	2016	2018	
care	2014	2.77	2016	2020	
emotion	2016	2.61	2016	2018	
participatory design	2014	2.54	2016	2019	
experience	2016	2.48	2016	2019	
software engineering	2014	2.44	2016	2018	
electronic health records	2016	2.44	2016	2017	
stress	2017	2.82	2017	2019	
recognition	2015	4.95	2018	2020	
visual analytics	2018	3.58	2018	2019	
quality	2018	3.06	2018	2019	
science	2014	3.03	2018	2019	
user interface	2014	2.88	2018	2019	
deep learning	2018	2.81	2018	2020	
walking	2019	3.46	2019	2021	
environment	2014	2.77	2019	2020	
graphics systems and interfaces	2018	3.18	2020	2023	
hci theory	2020	2.53	2020	2023	
interaction techniques	2018	5.58	2021	2023	

Fig. 4. UCHCI keywords burst term

3.4   Co-citation Analysis and Discussion

The co-citation of literature refers to the situation where two or more documents are simultaneously cited in other documents [27]. Understanding co-citation patterns can reveal the interrelatedness between documents and, concurrently, reflect the influence of a document within a research domain [28]. Among the 2,343 documents retrieved, a total of 62,538 references were cited. Table 2 lists the top 10 co-cited documents, indicating their significant impact in the UCHCI field. Foremost among them is the work by Kennedy et al. published in 1993, titled "Simulator Sickness Questionnaire: An Enhanced Method for Quantifying Simulator Sickness," with a remarkable 5,927 citations on Google Scholar as of October 2023. This article focuses on the development and application of the Simulator Sickness Questionnaire (SSQ) as an improved tool for assessing simulator sickness in high-fidelity visual simulators. The SSQ, derived from the Pensacola Motion Sickness Questionnaire (MSQ) through factor analyses, provides a more suitable instrument for measuring simulator sickness. Following closely is the 1998 paper by Witmer and Singer titled "Measuring presence in virtual environments: A presence questionnaire." This article introduces a Presence Questionnaire (PQ) and an Immersive Tendencies Questionnaire (ITQ) to gauge the sense of presence experienced by users in virtual environments (VEs). Additionally, the work by Wobbrock et al. in 2011, titled "The aligned rank transform for nonparametric factorial analyses using only ANOVA procedures," has garnered widespread attention. This paper proposes the Aligned Rank Transform (ART) for nonparametric factorial data analysis, enabling the examination of interaction effects in multi-factor experiments using common ANOVA procedures. The 1999 publication by Usoh et al., "Walking > walking-in-place > flying, in virtual environments," has also received significant attention. This work suggests that walking provides a higher subjective sense of presence compared to push-button-fly (floor plane flying) in immersive virtual environments. In the realm of authored works, the book "3D User Interfaces: Theory and Practice," authored by JJ LaViola Jr. And others in 2017, stands out as highly influential. This book extensively covers emerging applications, technologies, and best practices, integrating a wealth of theoretical foundations, in-depth analyses of advanced devices, and empirically validated design guidelines. It serves as a theoretical guide in the field of human-computer interaction. Beyond these highlighted works, the significance of the remaining articles in the list is also substantial.

3.5   Distribution of UCHCI Literature Sources

The publication source statistics reveal the journals or conferences that have published the highest number of papers and made the most significant contributions to the field [29]. According to the statistics, a total of 2343 papers within the search scope were published across 923 journals. Table 3 presents the top 10 journals or conferences based on total citation counts, indicating a higher prevalence of conference papers than journal articles in the UCHCI domain. Notably, the "IEEE Conference on Virtual Reality and 3D User Interfaces" stands out as the most cited venue in the field, reflecting its substantial impact. This conference published a total of 198 papers across its 2018, 2019, and 2020 editions, accumulating an impressive 1435 citations. Following closely is the "Annual

Table 2. Top 10 classical literatures

No.	Title	Year	Total link strength	Citations
1	Simulator Sickness Questionnaire: An Enhanced Method for Quantifying Simulator Sickness	1993	545	71
2	Measuring presence in virtual environments: A presence questionnaire	1998	254	36
3	The aligned rank transform for nonparametric factorial analyses using only anova procedures	2011	191	35
4	Walking > walking-in-place > flying, in virtual environments	1999	330	33
5	3D user interfaces: theory and practice	2017	182	32
6	NASA-task load index (NASA-TLX); 20 years later	2006	126	30
7	A discussion of cybersickness in virtual environments	2000	236	30
8	Using thematic analysis in psychology	2006	48	29
9	SUS: A'Quick and Dirty'Usability Scale	1996	97	27
10	The information capacity of the human motor system in controlling the amplitude of movement	1954	147	27

CHI Conference on Human Factors in Computing Systems," which published 11 papers in 2016 and garnered 471 citations. The most influential journal is "Sensors," contributing 15 relevant papers and accumulating 265 citations. Furthermore, the journals "Journal of Medical Internet Research" and the conference "IEEE International Symposium on Mixed and Augmented Reality (ISMAR2020)" also wield significant influence in the UCHCI domain.

3.6 High-Impact Countries and Research Institutions

As illustrated in the Fig. 5, a total of 86 countries or regions globally have contributed to the field of UCHCI. In terms of collaboration, three major cooperative communities have emerged, led by the United States, Germany, and England. Regarding the total publication output, the United States leads with 612 papers and a total citation count of 4149. Following closely are China (324 papers, cited 1630 times), Germany (313 papers, cited 1746 times), England (199 papers, cited 1486 times), Japan (153 papers, cited 544 times), Canada (108 papers, cited 585 times), Australia (95 papers, cited 383 times), France (91 papers, cited 495 times), South Korea (90 papers, cited 601 times), Italy (73 papers, cited 476 times), Spain (73 papers, cited 530 times), Portugal (63 papers, cited 116 times), Denmark (47 papers, cited 197 times), Netherlands (45 papers, cited

Table 3. Top 10 contribution journals or conference

Ranking	Source	Number of citations	Number of published papers
1	IEEE Conference on Virtual Reality and 3D User Interfaces (VR2019)	545	100
2	IEEE Conference on Virtual Reality and 3D User Interfaces (VR 2020)	498	47
3	34th Annual CHI Conference on Human Factors in Computing Systems, (CHI 2016)	471	11
4	IEEE Conference on Virtual Reality and 3D User Interfaces (VR2018)	392	51
5	Sensors	265	15
6	IEEE Conference on Virtual Reality and 3D User Interfaces (VR2021)	251	36
7	Proceedings of the 2020 CHI conference on Human Factors in Computing	240	9
8	2020 IEEE Conference on Virtual Reality and 3D User Interfaces Workshops	226	75
9	Journal of Medical Internet Research	212	9
10	IEEE International Symposium on Mixed and Augmented Reality (ISMAR2020)	192	24

332 times), and Austria (43 papers, cited 290 times). The top 15 countries in terms of publication numbers contribute to 77.09% of the total papers, all with citation counts exceeding 100. These countries constitute crucial sources of global output in UCHCI research.

In the past decade, a total of 2042 institutions worldwide have engaged in research related to UCHCI. The top five institutions in terms of publication output are led by the University of Tokyo (44 papers), followed by the University of Central Florida (30 papers), Technical University of Munich (29 papers), Purdue University (27 papers), and Beijing Institute of Technology (26 papers). In terms of citation counts, the University of Washington leads with a total citation count of 372, followed by the Georgia Institute of Technology (368 citations), Indiana University (295 citations), Clemson University (237 citations), and Purdue University (215 citations) (Table 4).

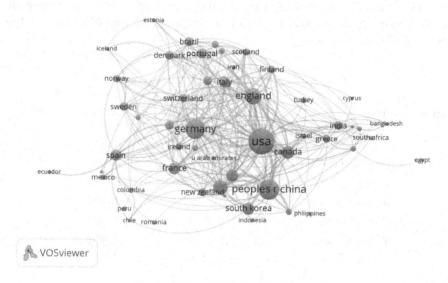

Fig. 5. National Collaborative Network

Table 4. Institutions with the Highest Publication and Citation Counts

Ranking	Institutions	Publications	Institutions	Citations
1	University of Tokyo	44	University of Washington	372
2	University of Central Florida	30	Georgia Institute of Technology	368
3	Technical University of Munich	29	Indiana University	295
4	Purdue University	27	Clemson University	237
5	Beijing Institute of Technology	26	Purdue University	215

3.7 High Impact Author Analysis

Through co-citation analysis, we gain insights into scholars worldwide who have made significant contributions to the field of UCHCI research. Globally, there are a total of 7483 researchers involved in the UCHCI domain. Table 5 presents the top 5 authors based on publication output, including their names, total citation counts, and average citation counts. Among them, the most prolific author is Steinicke Frank, who has published 19 papers, with a total of 63 citations and an average citation count of 3.3158. Latoschik Marc Erich, Mousas Christos, Weng Dongdong, and Woo Woontack all tie for the second position, each having published 18 papers. Their respective citation counts and average citation counts are as follows: Latoschik Marc Erich with 131 citations and an average of 7.2778, Mousas Christos with 88 citations and an average of 4.8889, Weng Dongdong with 87 citations and an average of 4.8333, and Woo Woontack with 79 citations and an average of 4.3889.

Table 5. The top 5 authors by publication output

Ranking	Author	Number of published papers	Number of citations	Average of Citations
1	Steinicke, Frank	19	63	3.3158
2	Latoschik, Marc Erich	18	131	7.2778
3	Mousas, Christos	18	88	4.8889
4	Weng, Dongdong	18	87	4.8333
5	Woo, Woontack	18	79	4.3889

4 Discussion and Conclusion

This paper is based on bibliometrics, retrieving 2343 UCHCI-related articles from Web of Science and conducting data analysis to form a comprehensive review. The study focuses on the research domain of UCHCI over the past decade, providing in-depth analysis of key research hotspots and emerging trends. Furthermore, a detailed analysis is performed on prolific journals, major contributing authors, countries, and research institutions within the UCHCI field.

1. In terms of the quantity of literature output, the number of publications in the field of UCHCI has shown an overall increasing trend over the years, reaching maturity after 2020 and peaking in 2022. UCHCI articles are predominantly published in conferences, with the number of journal publications being less than that of conference publications. Noteworthy authors such as Steinicke Frank, Latoschik Marc Erich, Mousas Christos, Weng Dongdong, Woo Woontack, and their respective teams are key contributors to the literature output in the UCHCI domain. The main contributing institutions include the University of Tokyo, the University of Central Florida, the Technical University of Munich, Purdue University, Beijing Institute of Technology, and others.
2. Through keyword clustering, it is evident that research in UCHCI exhibits diversity. The research hotspots primarily fall into five major categories: #1 usability and user experience, #2 interaction paradigms and technologies, #3 human-AI collaboration, #4 user perception, and #5 visualization. This reflects the interdisciplinary nature of UCHCI research, integrating computer technology, design, psychology, sociology, and other fields. Analyzing temporal graphs and prominence charts, it can be predicted that the UCHCI field will continue to incorporate more diverse domains in the future. The focus will be on graphics systems and interfaces, hci theory, and

interaction techniques. Additionally, with the advancement of new technologies, we can anticipate the emergence of novel interaction paradigms that place even greater emphasis on user-centered approaches.

3. From the co-citation analysis, a set of classic literature emerges, such as "Simulator Sickness Questionnaire: An Enhanced Method for Quantifying Simulator Sickness," "Measuring presence in virtual environments: A presence questionnaire," "The aligned rank transform for nonparametric factorial analyses using only anova procedures," and others. These works have laid the theoretical foundation for the field of UCHCI.

Through this research, valuable insights are offered to potential collaborators and partnering institutions in the UCHCI domain. Simultaneously, a new perspective is provided on core topics and frontier directions. The research results systematically present the evolutionary footprint of the UCHCI field, aiding researchers in comprehensively understanding the entirety of the research. These findings establish a robust foundation for the further development of the UCHCI field.

5   Limitation and Future Work

While we have extensively analyzed and reviewed existing literature using modern bibliometric software, it is essential to acknowledge several limitations. Firstly, our study selectively chose articles from the Web of Science database, which exclusively includes conference proceedings and journal articles, thereby excluding other forms of literature such as books. Consequently, our literature sample may not encompass all research on UCHCI, and future studies should consider incorporating additional databases and diverse literary forms [30]. Secondly, the incomplete citation of recently published literature may limit the comprehensiveness of our analysis of the co-citation network. In the co-citation network, some publications may not be thoroughly cited, impacting our comprehensive understanding of the academic interconnectedness in the research domain [31]. Future research can address this limitation by incorporating more comprehensive citation data, improving our grasp of research field interactions. Additionally, it is important to note that the analyzed literature is confined to English-language publications, excluding articles written in other languages. Therefore, future research may explore broadening the language scope to include literature in various languages [32], ensuring a more globally inclusive perspective on UCHCI research. Such an expansion can better reflect contributions from diverse cultures and academic traditions to the field.

Acknowledgments. The authors express their sincere gratitude to the reviewers for their insightful comments and constructive feedback.

Disclosure of Interests..   The authors declare no conflict of interest.

References

1. Hewett, T.T., et al.: ACM SIGCHI curricula for human-computer interaction. In: ACM (1992)
2. Norman, D.A., Draper, S.W.: User Centered System Design: New Perspectives On Human-Computer Interaction. Lawrence Erlbaum, Hillsdale, N.J. (1986)
3. Sun, W., Sun, P.: The human-computer interaction analysis and construction on intelligent service robot. Appl. Mech. Mater. **373**, 221–224 (2013)
4. Bansal, H., Khan, R.: A review paper on human computer interaction. Int. J. Adv. Res. Comput. Sci. Softw. Eng. **8**(4), 53 (2018)
5. Venkatesh, V., Morris, M.G., Davis, G.N., Davis, F.D.: User acceptance of information technology: toward a unified view. MIS Q. **27**(3), 425–478 (2003)
6. Baker, H.K., Kumar, S., Pandey, N.: A bibliometric analysis of managerial finance: a retrospective. Manag. Financ. **46**(11), 1495–1517 (2020)
7. Liu, D., Song, D., Ning, W., et al.: Development and validation of a clinical prediction model for venous thromboembolism following neurosurgery: a 6-year, multicenter, retrospective and prospective diagnostic cohort study. Cancers **15**(22), 5483 (2023)
8. Karat, J., Karat, C.M.: The evolution of user-centered focus in the human-computer interaction field. IBM Syst. J. **42**(4), 532–541 (2003)
9. Wu, H., Li, Y., Tong, L., et al.: Worldwide research tendency and hotspots on hip fracture: a 20-year bibliometric analysis. Arch. Osteoporos. **16**, 1–14 (2021)
10. Klingelhöfer, D., Braun, M., Brüggmann, D., et al.: Does health-related poverty publication landscape reflect global needs in the light of the current poverty rebound? Glob. Health **18**(1), 1–14 (2022)
11. Pritchard, A.: Statistical bibliography or bibliometrics. J. doc. **25**, 348 (1969)
12. Chen, C.: CiteSpace II: detecting and visualizing emerging trends and transient patterns in scientific literature. J. Am. Soc. Inform. Sci. Technol. **57**(3), 359–377 (2006)
13. Van Eck, N., Waltman, L.: Software survey: VOSviewer, a computer program for bibliometric mapping. Scientometrics **84**(2), 523–538 (2010). https://doi.org/10.1007/s11192-009-0146-3
14. Tan, H., Li, J., He, M., et al.: Global evolution of research on green energy and environmental technologies: a bibliometric study. J. Environ. Manage. **297**, 113382 (2021)
15. Gu, D., Li, J., Li, X., et al.: Visualizing the knowledge structure and evolution of big data research in healthcare informatics. Int. J. Med. Inf. **98**, 22–32 (2017)
16. Frey, B.J., Dueck, D.: Clustering by passing messages between data points. Science **315**(5814), 972–976 (2007)
17. Norman, D.A.: The Psychology of Everyday Things. Basic Books, New York, NY (1988)
18. Santos, J., Vairinhos, M., Jesus, L.M.T.: Treating children with speech sound disorders: development of a tangible artefact prototype. JMIR Serious Games **7**(4), e13861 (2019)
19. Xu, H., Zhang, J.: Large relics scenario-based visualization using head-mounted displays. Comput. Intell. Neurosci. **2021**, 1–14 (2021)
20. Yue, B., Li, H.: The impact of human-AI collaboration types on consumer evaluation and usage intention: a perspective of responsibility attribution. Front. Psychol. **14** (2023)
21. Huang, Z., Choi, D.H., Lai, B., et al.: Metaverse-based virtual reality experience and endurance performance in sports economy: mediating role of mental health and performance anxiety. Front. Public Health **10**, 991489 (2022)
22. Pan, Y., Steed, A.: How foot tracking matters: the impact of an animated self-avatar on interaction, embodiment and presence in shared virtual environments. Front. Robot. AI **6**, 104 (2019)
23. Hofmann, S., Vetter, J., Wachter, C., et al.: Visual AIDS for multimodal treatment options to support decision making of patients with colorectal cancer. BMC Med. Inform. Decis. Mak. **12**, 1–9 (2012)

24. Xu, A.H., Sun, Y.X.: Research hotspots and effectiveness of repetitive transcranial magnetic stimulation in stroke rehabilitation. Neural Regen. Res. **15**(11), 2089 (2020)

25. Zhao, J., Yu, G., Cai, M., et al.: Bibliometric analysis of global scientific activity on umbilical cord mesenchymal stem cells: a swiftly expanding and shifting focus. Stem Cell Res. Ther. **9**(1), 1–9 (2018)

26. Liu, Y., Wang, Y., Qin, S., et al.: Insights into genome-wide association study for diabetes: a bibliometric and visual analysis from 2001 to 2021. Front. Endocrinol. **13**, 817620 (2022)

27. Haghani, M., Varamini, P.: Temporal evolution, most influential studies and sleeping beauties of the coronavirus literature. Scientometrics **126**(8), 7005–7050 (2021)

28. Small, H.: Co-citation in the scientifc literature: a new measure of the relationship between two documents. J. Am. Soc. Inf. Sci. **24**(4), 265–269 (1973)

29. Aghimien, D.O., Aigbavboa, C.O., Oke, A.E., et al.: Mapping out research focus for robotics and automation research in construction-related studies: a bibliometric approach. J. Eng. Des. Technol. **18**(5), 1063–1079 (2020)

30. Schwimmer, M.H., Sawh, M.C., Heskett, K.M., et al.: A bibliometric analysis of clinical and translational research in pediatric gastroenterology from 1970 to 2017. J. Pediatr. Gastroenterol. Nutr. **67**(5), 564–569 (2018)

31. Xu, F., Zeng, J., Liu, X., et al.: Exercise-induced muscle damage and protein intake: a bibliometric and visual analysis. Nutrients **14**(20), 4288 (2022)

32. Markey, K., MacFarlane, A., Noonan, M., et al.: Service user and service provider perceptions of enablers and barriers for refugee and asylum-seeking women accessing and engaging with perinatal mental health care services in the WHO European Region: a scoping review protocol. Int. J. Environ. Res. Public Health **19**(2), 937 (2022)

A Bibliometric Analysis of Eye Tracking in User Experience Research

Yang Shi[✉]

Dezhou Vocational and Technical College, Dezhou, Shandong, China
4928147610qq.com

Abstract. The purpose of this study is to provide insights into the research progress of Eye Tracking in User Experience Research (ET-UER) by bibliometric methods. The literature of ET-UER collected from the Web of Science database is used as the data source. VOSviewer and CiteSpace, which are software tools for visualizing bibliometric data, are used to conduct keyword analyses, evolutionary analyses, and co-citation analyses of the literature. The results show that the overall trend of literature volume is increasing. Country analysis shows that a few academically strong countries have contributed most of the research in this field. Analysis of research institutions and authors shows that international cooperation in eye tracking user experience research is not close. The hotspots of ET-UER include three main clusters: #1, the variables and evaluation content of eye tracking research; #2, the application scenarios of eye tracking; and #3, the indicators of eye tracking research. Evolution analysis reveals four trends in the development of ET-UER: firstly, the expansion of research scenarios; secondly, changes in eye tracking experimental environments and stimulus materials; thirdly, advances in research methods, paradigms, and analytical technologies; and fourthly, user-centered design. The most frequently co-cited research on ET-UER is divided into three categories: application of eye tracking technology, research on eye tracking technology, and methods and measurement. Based on the analysis of this study, the following three questions are still worth further attention. First, it is necessary to optimize the user experience of eye tracking as an interactive input. Second, it is important to support continuous and reliable research on gaze behavior in real-world experimental environments, including dynamic, 3D, interactive, and other experimental materials, which require more advanced experimental and data analysis techniques. Third, machine learning has great potential for follow-up research in the field of ET-UER.

Keywords: Eye Tracking · User Experience · Bibliometric

1 Introduction

User Experience (UX) is a hot keyword in the field of human-computer interaction (HCI) and design. Norman et al. [1] proposed the concept of UX. He believes that UX should meet customer needs and that product design should

M. Kurosu and A. Hashizume (Eds.): HCII 2024, LNCS 14684, pp. 178–193, 2024.
https://doi.org/10.1007/978-3-031-60405-8_12

be simple and generous to satisfy users and bring them additional surprises. The International Organization for Standardization [2] defines user experience as 'The perception and response obtained by a user using or expecting to use a system, product, or service'. This definition focuses on the user's perception and is the most influential definition of UX. Hassenzahl et al. [3] pointed out that user experience results from a combination of the user's internal state (expectations, needs, motivations, etc.), system characteristics (usefulness, usability, functionality, etc.) and the result of interaction scenarios. On the Internet, user experience mostly refers to user interaction when using or operating human-machine interfaces [4]. There are different emphases on the definition of user experience. As Ding et al. [5] pointed out, the exact definition of user experience is still controversial. But overall, user experience is the physiological and psychological perception obtained by users during their interaction with products, environments and others. User Experience (UX) shapes how users interact with products, systems and services, so it is necessary to evaluate interaction methods through technical means accurately [6].

Eye tracking is a technology for measuring individual eye movements. Researchers can use eye tracking technology to know where subjects are looking at a given time and the order in which their eyes move [7]. Therefore, on the one hand, eye tracking combined with usability testing has become another method for measuring user experience. Eye tracking analysis can understand users' visual experience and integrate eye tracking data with existing usability measurement indicators to gain new insights [4]. On the other hand, eye tracking can also serve as an actual control medium in human-machine dialogue [8].

In order to further use eye tracking technology to promote user experience research, it is necessary to have a comprehensive understanding of current research trends. There are already some reviews on eye tracking technology in the field of user experience research: García and Cano [6] reviewed the most relevant articles in the eye tracking evaluation of user experience. They found that indicators commonly transformed raw variables captured by an eye tracker into outcomes related to product user experience models and discussed how state-of-the-art passive eye tracking technologies provides a cheap and simple way to implement these experiments within budget constraints; Cooke [9] introduced the mechanism of eye tracking as well as usability-related research in reading scanning and searching fields summarized future areas for eye-tracking research; Poole and Ball [7] outlined eye-tracking technology and discussed its use in HCI and usability research in detail. These reviews mainly use qualitative analysis methods to review and summarize periodically, which makes it difficult to objectively analyze changes in hotspots and development trends in this field. Quantitative analysis can include a large amount of literature related to a field for analysis to compensate for the limited workload of researchers, which may result in insufficient sample comprehensiveness. This study uses bibliometric methods, which can provide insights into research progress through performance analysis and co-occurrence network analysis [10] of Eye Tracking in User Experience Research (ET-UER), to provide a reference for scholars in this field, providing a general overview predicting future directions for Eye Tracking Technology in User Experience Application Status Research guiding User Experience Design Practice.

2 Materials and Methods

2.1 Data Collection

This study uses the Web of Science (WOS) core collection database as its data source, with a retrieval time of December 31, 2022. The commonly used SSCI, SCI-Expanded, A&HCI, CPCI-S, and CPCI-SSH citation indexes in the WOS database are selected as the retrieval sources. The retrieval strategy is set to:

TS=(((eye tracking) OR (eye movement analysis)) AND ((user experience) OR (UX) OR (UE) OR (user centered) OR (UCD) OR (usability)))

To collect all articles related to ET-UER, the retrieval data range has been set to all years (i.e., from 1900 to December 2022). In order to avoid the loss of interdisciplinary literature, the literature sources were not pruned. The retrieved literature is exported as "full record and cited references" in "txt" format, and finally, 1647 articles on the application status of eye tracking technology in user experience are obtained. These articles are exported as "complete record and citation" and "txt" as input sources for VOSviewer and CiteSpace.

2.2 Bibliometric Analysis

This paper uses bibliometric methods using mathematics and statistics to analyze publications quantitatively [11]. Much software is used for bibliometric analysis, each with different functions and limitations. This paper chooses VOSviewer and CiteSpace. VOSviewer was developed by Van Eck and Waltman [12] of the Science Research Center of Leiden University in the Netherlands in 2009. It has a powerful user graphical interface and mapping visualization capabilities, suitable for large-scale data positioning research topics' focus and hotspots. CiteSpace is a citation visualization analysis software developed by the team of Chen [13] at Drexel University in the United States. CiteSpace intuitively shows the development trend and evolution process of a discipline or research topic during a specific period and has been widely used in bibliometric analysis in recent years.

This study investigates and summarizes ET-UER from basic characteristics, keyword analysis and evolution analysis of hotspots, and co-citation of references.

3 Results

According to the subject statistical analysis of the WOS system, among the 1647 articles, a total of 69 main subjects are involved. The top 10 subjects are computer science, engineering, psychology, computer artificial intelligence, electronic and electrical engineering, automation control systems, physics, manufacturing engineering, energy science and multidisciplinary engineering.

3.1   Basic Characteristics

The change in the output of academic literature over time is an important method to measure the development trend of research topics. It can effectively evaluate the research dynamics of this discipline. The distribution of the annual number of publications related to ET-UER is shown in Fig. 1. From the publication situation of WOS, the first article within the search scope was published in 1991. The number of eye tracking technologies appearing in user experience research literature has increased significantly. Between 1991 and 2002, the annual number of publications was relatively small and did not exceed 6; between 2003 and 2013, the number of publications grew steadily at an annual rate of 13–51; after 2013, the number of publications grew rapidly and reached a peak in 2019 with 205 publications. After 2019, it declined slightly, with an annual publication volume of 137–156. ET-UER has gone through four stages: early stage, steady growth, rapid growth, and peak stages. After 2013, it heated up rapidly and gradually formed a research boom.

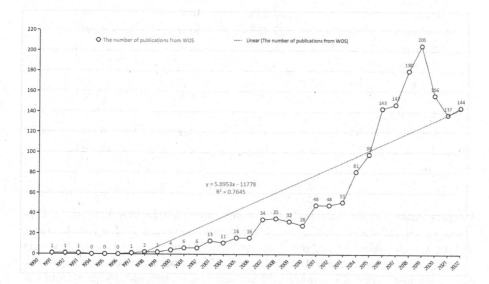

Fig. 1. The number of ET-UER publications

Performance of Countries. Statistical data from various countries can provide an in-depth understanding of contributing countries and growth trends. According to data from around the world, 70 countries have conducted research within the search scope. The top ten countries account for more than 77.60% of the total publications. Within the search scope, these countries have a publication volume exceeding 50 articles, which is an important source of ET-UER output. The United States, China, and Germany have contributed the most publications of ET-UER. Among them, the United States is the highest contributor in this field with a total of 345 publications accounting for 20.95% of the total, followed by China with a publication volume of 219 accounting for 13.30%, Germany with a publication volume of 203, accounting for 12.33%, followed by Britain with a publication volume of 136, Japan with a publication volume of 85, Canada with a publication volume of 63, Italy with a publication volume of 61, South Korea with a publication volume of 60, Poland with a publication volume of 54, and Switzerland with a publication volume of 52. In addition, the United States ranks first in terms of citations, while Canada has the highest average number of citations (Table 1).

Table 1. Most publications top ten countries involved in ET-UER.

Rank	Country	Number of Publications	Percentage of Publications	Citation Counts	Average Citation
1	USA	345	20.95%	5351	15.5101
2	China	219	13.30%	1301	5.9406
3	Germany	203	12.33%	2070	10.197
4	England	136	8.26%	1650	12.1324
5	Japan	85	5.16%	760	8.9412
6	Canada	63	3.83%	1185	18.8095
7	Italy	61	3.70%	598	9.8033
8	South Korea	60	3.64%	645	10.75
9	Poland	54	3.28%	342	6.3333
10	Switzerland	52	3.16%	925	17.7885

Performance of Research Institutions and Authors. A total of 1578 research institutions worldwide have conducted research on ET-UER. Running VOSviewer and selecting organizations with the node threshold set to 4, we get a cooperation network with 158 nodes and 155 cooperation relationships. The size of the institution node represents the number of articles produced, and the lines between institutions represent the strength of cooperation. The closer the cooperation, the wider the line between institutions [14]. Judging from the distribution of cooperation relationship strength (number of cooperations) within each sub-network, international cooperation in ET-UER is not close and has strong regional characteristics, mainly based on cooperation between institutions within the country or region. According to statistics on the literature output of publishing institutions, there are 21 institutions with a publication volume exceeding ten articles, among which Swiss Federal Institute of Technology in Zurich (Switzerland), The University of Manchester (UK), University of Patras (Greece) and others are major high-yield institutions with large research influence in the international arena and occupy a core position in this field (Table 2).

Table 2. Institutions with a publication volume exceeding 10 articles in ET-UER.

Rank	Institution (Country)	Number of Publications	Citation Counts	Average Citation
1	Swiss Federal Institute of Technology in Zurich (Switzerland)	20	154	7.7
2	The University of Manchester (UK)	19	177	9.3158
3	University of Patras (Greece)	16	151	9.4375
4	Middle East Technical University (Turkey)	15	102	6.8
5	Palacky University Olomouc (Czech Republic)	15	99	6.6
6	Northeastern University (United States)	14	223	15.9286
7	Technical University of Munich (Germany)	13	157	12.0769
8	University of Tübingen (Germany)	13	171	13.1538
9	Dongguk University (Korea)	12	282	23.5
10	Beijing Normal University (China)	11	204	18.5455
11	Simon Fraser University (Canada)	11	578	52.5455
12	Ecole Polytechnique Fédérale de Lausanne (Switzerland)	10	298	29.8
13	Purdue University (United States)	10	71	7.1
14	Texas A&M University (United States)	10	56	5.6
15	Tsinghua University (China)	10	19	1.9
16	University of Koblenz and Landau (Germany)	10	27	2.7
17	Lancaster University (UK)	10	205	20.5
18	University of Massachusetts (United States)	10	136	13.6
19	University of Stuttgart (Germany)	10	61	6.1
20	University of Washington (United States)	10	48	4.8
21	Zhejiang University (China)	10	34	3.4

The author is the smallest unit of literature output and a direct contributor to the field of ET-UER. 5184 scholars worldwide are involved in ET-UER, and 197 authors have published more than three articles. The top 10 authors in terms of literature output are Stanislav Popelka (Palack? University in Olomouc, 15 articles), followed by Sukru Eraslan (Middle East Technical University, 14 articles), Yeliz Yesilada (Middle East Technical University, 14 articles), Christos A. Fidas (University of Patras, Greece, 12 articles), Simon Harper (University of Manchester, 12 articles), Kang Ryoung Park (Dongguk University, 12 articles), Andreas Bulling (University of Stuttgart, 10 articles), Dong Weihua (Beijing Normal University, 10 articles), Enkelejda Kasneci (Technical University of Munich, 10 articles), and Soussan Djamasbi (Worcester Polytechnic Institute, 9 articles) (Table 3).

Performance of Publications. ET-UER papers are distributed in 1069 publications, of which 216 have published two or more articles. Table 4 specifically lists publications with a publication volume of 10 or more. These publications have 177 articles, accounting for 10.74% of the total articles. Among them, JOURNAL OF EYE MOVEMENT RESEARCH has the highest publication volume with 27 articles, followed by SENSORS (26 articles) and INTERNATIONAL JOURNAL OF HUMAN-COMPUTER INTERACTION (23 articles). From the perspective of the types of publications with more than ten articles, journals are the main carriers for eye tracking technology user experience research, with 167

Table 3. The top 10 authors in terms of literature output in ET-UER.

Rank	Author	Institution	Number of Publications	Citation Counts	Average Citation
1	Stanislav Popelka	Palacký University in Olomouc	15	162	10.8
2	Sukru Eraslan	Middle East Technical University	14	139	9.9286
3	Yeliz Yesilada	Middle East Technical University	14	139	9.9286
4	Christos A. Fidas	University of Patras	12	145	12.0833
5	Simon Harper	University of Manchester	12	126	10.5
6	Kang Ryoung Park	Dongguk University	12	291	24.25
7	Andreas Bulling	University of Stuttgart	10	252	25.2
8	Dong, weihua	Beijing Normal University	10	182	18.2
9	Enkelejda Kasneci	Technical University of Munich	10	96	9.6
10	Soussan Djamasbi	Worcester Polytechnic Institute	9	286	31.7778

articles accounting for 94.35% of the publication volume of publications with more than ten articles. The highest average number of citations is INTERNATIONAL JOURNAL OF HUMAN-COMPUTER STUDIES, with an average number of citations of 42.6, followed by IEEE TRANSACTIONS ON VISUALIZATION AND COMPUTER GRAPHICS, with an average number of citations of 26.1 and FRONTIERS IN PSYCHOLOGY, with an average number of citations of 18.8182.

3.2 Keyword Analysis

The keywords of an article can express the main content of the article. The frequency of keywords in academic literature can measure the importance of related topics in a specific field and conduct quantitative analysis and comparison. Co-word analysis is an important content in the method of bibliometrics. Within the search scope of 1647 articles, 5445 keywords are included. Running VOSviewer with the keyword co-occurrence frequency set to 8, after filtering and merging synonyms, produces a total of 149 keywords, forming a keyword co-occurrence cluster, as shown in Fig. 2. In the figure, keywords of the same color belong to the same cluster and form 3 main clusters, which are #1, the variables and evaluation content of eye tracking research; #2, the application scenarios of eye tracking; and #3, the indicators of eye tracking research.

Cluster #1, the variables and evaluation content of eye tracking research, mainly include perception, performance, visual attention, behavior, visual search, quality, strategy, workload, situation awareness, complexity, cognition, intention, individual differences, comprehension, memory, emotion, satisfaction, etc. Eye movement data can be used as an aggregated measure and then interpreted as an indicator of cognitive state, such as the duration of fixation indicating cognitive load [15].

Cluster #2, the application scenarios of eye tracking, mainly including evaluation, neuroscience, EEG (electroencephalography), gaze interaction, brain-computer interface, machine learning, emotion recognition, classification, affec-

Table 4. Publications with a publication volume of 10 or more in ET-UER.

	Publication	Type	Number of Publications	Citation Counts	Average Citation	Average impact factor (5 years)	Publisher
1	JOURNAL OF EYE MOVEMENT RESEARCH	Journal	27	406	15.037	1.408	INT GROUP EYE MOVEMENT RESEARCH
2	SENSORS	Journal	26	326	12.5385	4.05	MDPI
3	INTERNATIONAL JOURNAL OF HUMAN-COMPUTER INTERACTION	Journal	23	237	10.3043	4.503	TAYLOR & FRANCIS INC
4	INTERACTING WITH COMPUTERS	Journal	17	203	11.9412	1.532	OXFORD UNIV PRESS
5	ISPRS International Journal of Geo-Information	Journal	16	162	10.125	3.165	MDPI
6	INTERNATIONAL JOURNAL OF HUMAN-COMPUTER STUDIES	Journal	15	639	42.6	4.435	ACADEMIC PRESS LTD-ELSEVIER SCIENCE LTD
7	MULTIMEDIA TOOLS AND APPLICATIONS	Journal	12	53	4.4167	2.395	SPRINGER
8	FRONTIERS IN PSYCHOLOGY	Journal	11	207	18.8182	4.426	FRONTIERS MEDIA SA
9	2018 ACM SYMPOSIUM ON EYE TRACKING RESEARCH & APPLICATIONS (ETRA 2018)	Symposium	10	34	3.4	-	-
10	IEEE TRANSACTIONS ON VISUALIZATION AND COMPUTER GRAPHICS	Journal	10	261	26.1	5.37	IEEE COMPUTER SOC
11	UNIVERSAL ACCESS IN THE INFORMATION SOCIETY	Journal	10	129	12.9	2.42	SPRINGER HEIDEL-BERG

tive computing, user interface, navigation, virtual reality, head-mounted display, augmented reality, serious games, education, surgery, assistive technology, children, autism, rehabilitation, etc. This cluster reflects the application of eye-tracking technology, which is divided into two themes: evaluation and interaction. In the evaluation scenario, other neuroscience and physiological measurement methods are often combined to improve the accuracy and comprehensiveness of information, such as EEG. Machine learning technology is also used to train machine learning models with physiological measurement data for automated analysis. In the interaction scenario, gaze interaction is often combined with other methods, such as brain-computer interface, gesture recognition, facial recognition, speech input, etc., to create a new interactive experience. This cluster also includes specific application fields such as user interface, interaction design, navigation, virtual reality, augmented reality, surgery, etc. Another important application field is the design for special groups of people, such as children and autism. Assistive technology for special groups of people and patient rehabilitation is also mentioned in the keywords. This reflects the inclusive perspective of ET-UER.

Cluster #3, the indicators of eye tracking research mainly include metrics, saccades, scanpath, region of interest, visualization, visual analytics, task analysis, time, etc. This cluster reflects the related terms for eye-tracking usability research. Researchers must choose eye-tracking indicators related to tasks and their inherent cognitive activities separately in each usability study [8]. The first common indicator fixation is a collection of fixation points. The second common indicator, saccade, describes the rapid movement of the eyes from one fixation to another. The third common indicator scan path is alternating fixations and saccades. The fourth indicator, area of interest(AOI) or region of interest(ROI),

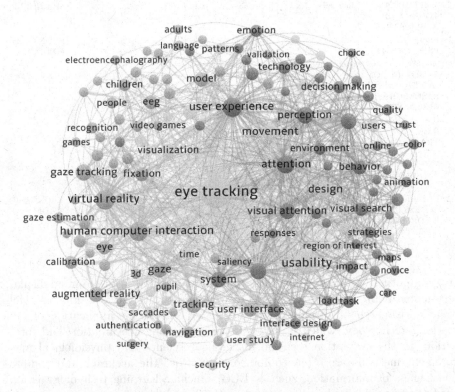

Fig. 2. Co-words network of ET-UER

is part of a very important stimulus for a hypothesis [16]. Because many eye movement studies tend to be behavioral experiments, they involve other related task indicators such as task completion time, completion rate, error rate, etc. Eye movement data can be used in an exploratory way to explain other dependent variables (such as interpreting task completion time through fixation data).

3.3   Evolution Analysis of Hotspots

To further study the frontier topics and development trends in the ET-UER field, the average occurrence time of keywords was statistically analyzed. Figure 3 is the keyword co-occurrence time zone map for ET-UER, which intuitively reflects the evolution of topics in each time period within the search scope and the development trend of keywords. Figure 4 lists the top 26 keywords with strong emergence. The dark color indicates the year in which the key words in the paper are cited frequently, reflecting the changing trend of research. Both the time zone map (Fig. 3) and the keywords burst term (Fig. 4) are analysis indicators that introduce a time dimension for keywords and can be used to obtain more objective and accurate results by cross-referencing each other. Combining the time zone map (Fig. 3) and keywords burst term (Fig. 4), it can be seen that there are 4 trends:

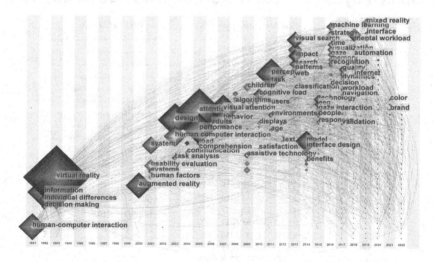

Fig. 3. Keyword co-occurrence time zone map for ET-UER

1. The trend of research scenarios. The development of eye tracking research has evolved from general usability evaluation and usability testing to specific application areas such as navigation, security, and education. With the development of technology and equipment, the ET-UER research scene has further

evolved. Virtual reality, mixed reality, Augmented reality, and its extensions, such as serious games and other fields, have become a new research hotspot. Gaze interaction is one of the interaction methods in this field, and its experience, usability, comfort, and so on are important research content.

2. The trend of eye tracking experiments. The mid-term keyword environment indicates that the experimental environment also changes from a traditional laboratory to a wider range of real environments. Rupi and Krizek [17] used mobile glasses to record the visual gaze of cyclists in a real outdoor environment. The keywords 3D, dynamic, and human-robot interaction indicate that the experimental materials were expanded in the middle and late stages, transitioning from 2D to 3D, from static to dynamic, and from non-interactive to interactive. These changes bring higher challenges to eye tracking technology and data analysis technology.

3. The trend of research methods, paradigms, and analytical technologies in ET-UER shows a tendency towards multiple methods, multimodal approaches, and automation. The trend of multiple methods refers to the combination of eye movement research with task analysis, physiological measurement, questionnaire scales, interviews, thinking aloud, and other subjective, objective,

Top 26 Keywords with the Strongest Citation Bursts

Keywords	Year	Strength	Begin	End	1991 - 2022
human computer interaction	1991	5.9483	2003	2012	
usability evaluation	1991	4.334	2008	2013	
human factor	1991	3.0107	2012	2014	
algorithm	1991	2.6877	2012	2016	
children	1991	3.6513	2012	2017	
display	1991	2.7367	2012	2014	
usability test	1991	3.1938	2012	2015	
cartography	1991	3.3704	2012	2017	
eeg	1991	3.0034	2014	2018	
3d	1991	2.8081	2014	2016	
hci	1991	2.9696	2015	2017	
ergonomics	1991	2.5608	2015	2016	
working memory	1991	2.9938	2016	2017	
human-robot interaction	1991	2.4939	2016	2017	
individual difference	1991	3.4583	2017	2019	
navigation	1991	3.7193	2017	2020	
gaze interaction	1991	2.6951	2018	2019	
user interface	1991	3.5063	2018	2020	
calibration	1991	2.8753	2018	2019	
memory	1991	3.3914	2018	2019	
human-centered computing	1991	5.8469	2019	2022	
mixed reality	1991	4.1326	2019	2022	
security	1991	2.7511	2019	2022	
impact	1991	2.6911	2020	2022	
education	1991	3.1303	2020	2022	
virtual reality	1991	5.8113	2020	2022	

Fig. 4. Keywords Burst Term related to ET-UER

qualitative, and quantitative research methods. The trend of multimodal refers to the combination of eye movement tracking with other physiological measurement methods such as electromyography (EMG), measurement of electrodermal activity (EDA), electroencephalography (EEG), functional magnetic resonance imaging (fMRI), etc., to form a multimodal evaluation method, which provides more accurate and comprehensive information for experience evaluation. The trend of automation refers to the emergence of new technical methods for quantifying usability test data and improving process automation in recent years, solving the problems of high cost and time consumption in usability evaluation. The combination of eye movement tracking technology and machine learning can produce valuable information for identifying changes in user behavior, usability issues, and more variable aspects of the overall user experience.

4. The trend of user-centered design. These keywords, such as individual difference, human factor, user study, user, adult, children, human center computing, ages, and assistive technology, indicate that ET-UER presents a more inclusive perspective with a focus on users, especially special groups of people.

3.4   Co-citation Analysis

When two articles are cited by the same article, these two articles are said to have a co-citation relationship. Through the Vosviewer visualization software, the collected relevant papers were analyzed for co-citation to explore the key node papers in the research. The collected data of nearly 1647 relevant papers were input into the Vosviewer software. The Type of analysis was selected as co-citation and the unit of analysis was selected as cited references. Overall, 1647 research papers were cited a total of 43197 times with an average single citation of 26.23 times. The minimum number of cited references was set to 10, and a total of 186 nodes were obtained. This indicates that ET-UER is in a relatively mature stage, and related research has a solid foundation and has produced a batch of classic literature. The table lists the top 12 key node papers. After searching for relevant literature in the table using Google Scholar, the 12 papers in the table can be roughly divided into the following 3 categories (Table 5).

Application of Eye Tracking Technology. The application review includes Duchowski's [18] breadth-first survey of eye tracking applications, reporting work from the following fields: neuroscience, psychology, industrial engineering, human factors, marketing/advertising, and computer science. After reviewing traditional diagnostic methods, it focuses on interactive applications, distinguishing between selective and evidence-based methods. Jacob and Karn [8] discuss the application of eye tracking in user interfaces, which can be used to analyze interfaces (measure usability) as well as serve as a suitable control medium in human-computer dialogue; Goldberg and Kotval [19] investigate the possibility of introducing the user's eye tracking as an additional input medium. In earlier times, such as before 1980, highly cited eye tracking research reviews focused on psychology. Rayner [20] reviewed recent research on eye tracking in reading and other information processing tasks such as music reading, typing, visual search and scene perception. The review's main focus is reading as a specific example of cognitive processing. Just and Carpenter [21] proposed a model of reading comprehension that explains the allocation of fixation points by 14 college students reading scientific articles. Just and Carpenter [22] theoretically analyzed gaze order and duration in simple cognitive tasks such as mental rotation, sentence verification and quantitative comparison. A specific example of eye tracking technology application is a study by Goldberg et al. [23], which used eye tracking to evaluate specific design features of a prototype portal website application.

Research on Eye Tracking Technology. Hansen and Ji [24] review current progress and state of the art in video-based eye detection and tracking to identify promising techniques and issues to be further addressed. They present a detailed review of recent eye models and techniques for eye detection and tracking, survey methods for gaze estimation, and compare them based on their geometric properties and reported accuracies. Morimoto and Mimica [25] provide an overview of gaze tracking technology and focus on recent advances in gaze tracking technology for general computer applications. Despite the long-held belief that they could also become important computer input devices, the technology still lacks important usability requirements that hinder its applicability. Due to the usability advantages of the pupil-corneal reflection technique, a detailed description is provided, indicating that this method still needs to be better suited for general interactive applications.

Methods and Measurement of Eye Tracking Technology. Holmqvist et al. [26] wrote a comprehensive handbook on eye tracking methods. It describes how to evaluate and acquire eye trackers, plan and design eye tracking studies and record and analyze eye tracking data. In addition to technical details and theory, the core of the book revolves around practicality - how to use event detection algorithms to convert raw data samples into fixations and saccades, how to compute different representations of eye tracking data using AOIs, heat maps, and scan paths, and how all eye tracking measurements are related to these processes. Goldberg and Kotval [19] evaluated several measurement methods based on eye tracking position and scan path to assess their effectiveness in evaluating interface quality.

Table 5. The top 12 classical literatures related to ET-UER.

Rank	Title	Author	Year	Source	Citations
1	Eye tracking in human-computer interaction and usability research: Ready to deliver the promises	Jacob, R. J., & Karn, K. S	2003	The Mind's Eye	124
2	Eye movements in reading and information processing: 20 years of research	Rayner, K	1978	Psychological Bulletin	106
3	Eye tracking: A comprehensive guide to methods and measures	Holmqvist, K., Nystr?m, M., Andersson, R., Dewhurst, R., Jarodzka, H.,& Van de Weijer, J	2011	Oxford University Press	100
4	Computer interface evaluation using eye movements: methods and constructs	Goldberg, J. H., & Kotval, X. P	1999	International journal of industrial ergonomics	96
5	Eye fixations and cognitive processes	Just, M. A., & Carpenter, P. A	1976	Cognitive Psychology	70
6	Recursive complements and propositional attitudes	de Villiers, J., Hobbs, K., & Hollebrandse, B	2014	Recursion:Complexity in Cognition	69
7	In the eye of the beholder: A survey of models for eyes and gaze	Hansen, D. W., & Ji, Q	2009	IEEE Transactions on Pattern Analysis and Machine Intelligence	59
8	The use of eye movements in human-computer interaction techniques: what you look at is what you get	Jacob, R. J	1991	ACM Transactions on Information Systems (TOIS)	59
9	A breadth-first survey of eye-tracking applications	Duchowski, A. T	2002	Behavior Research Methods, Instruments, and Computers	51
10	Eye gaze tracking techniques for interactive applications	Morimoto, C. H., & Mimica, M. R	2005	Computer vision and image understanding	48
11	Eye tracking in web search tasks: design implications	Goldberg, J. H., Stimson, M. J., Lewenstein, M., Scott, N., & Wichansky, A. M	2002	ETRA '02: Proceedings of the 2002 symposium on Eye tracking research & applications	43
12	A theory of reading: from eye fixations to comprehension	Just, M. A., & Carpenter, P. A	1980	Psychological review	42

4   Conclusion and Discussion

Regarding the basic situation of ET-UER, the analysis of the number of publications shows that the overall trend of research output is on the rise, and the past ten years have been a period of explosive boom. Country analysis shows that a few academically strong countries have contributed most of the research in this field. Analysis of research institutions and authors shows that international cooperation in eye tracking user experience research is not close. High-yield institutions include the Swiss Federal Institute of Technology in Zurich, The University of Manchester, the University of Patras, Middle East Technical University, etc., and high-yield authors include Stanislav Popelka, Sukru Eraslan, Yeliz Yesilada, Christos A. Fidas, etc. Analysis of publication distribution reveals that the highest-yielding publications include the Journal of Eye Movement Research, Sensors, and the International Journal of Human-Computer Interaction. The hotspots of ET-UER include three main clusters: #1, the variables and evaluation content of eye tracking research; #2, the application scenarios of eye tracking; and #3, the indicators of eye tracking research. Evolution analysis reveals four trends in the development of ET-UER: firstly, the expansion of research scenarios; secondly, changes in eye tracking experimental environments and stimulus materials; thirdly, advances in research methods, paradigms, and analytical technologies; and fourthly, user centered design. The most frequently co-cited research on ET-UED is divided into three categories: Application of eye tracking technology, research on eye tracking technology, methods, and measurement. From the analysis of this study, the following three aspects still deserve further attention. First, eye tracking as an interactive input method has great potential. However, there is still room for improvement. Optimizing the user experience will be a critical issue for the broader application of eye movement interaction in the future. Second, supporting continuous and reliable research on gaze behavior in real-world experimental environments, as well as for 3D, dynamic, interactive, and other experimental materials, requires more advanced experimental and data analysis techniques. Third, in the field of ET-UER, machine learning is still a very young family of research methods with great potential for subsequent research.

References

1. Norman, D., Miller, J., Henderson, A.: What you see, some of what's in the future, and how we go about doing it: hi at apple computer. In: Conference Companion on Human Factors in Computing Systems, p. 155 (1995)
2. AC08206635, A.: Ergonomics of human-system interaction-Part 210: human-centred design for interactive systems (ISO 9241-210: 2010). ISO (2010)
3. Hassenzahl, M., Tractinsky, N.: User experience - a research agenda. Behav. Inf. Technol. **25**(2), 91–97 (2006)
4. Yan, G., Bai, X.: Basis and Application of Eye Movement Analysis. Beijing Normal University Press, Beijing (2018)
5. Ding, Y., Guo, F.M.H., Sun, F.: A review of domestic and foreign research on user experience. Ind. Eng. Manage. **19**(4), 92–97 (2014)
6. García, M., Cano, S.: Eye tracking to evaluate the user experience (UX): literature review. In: International Conference on Human-Computer Interaction, pp. 134–145. Springer, Cham (2022). https://doi.org/10.1007/978-3-031-05061-9_10
7. Poole, A., Ball, L.J.: Eye tracking in HCI and usability research. In: Encyclopedia of Human Computer Interaction, pp. 211–219. IGI global (2006)

8. Jacob, R.J., Karn, K.S.: Commentary on section 4. eye tracking in human-computer interaction and usability research: ready to deliver the promises. The Mind's Eye **2**(3), 573–605 (2003)

9. Cooke, L.: Eye tracking: how it works and how it relates to usability. Tech. Commun. **52**(4), 456–463 (2005)

10. Tan, H., Sun, J., Wenjia, W., Zhu, C.: User experience & usability of driving: a bibliometric analysis of 2000–2019. Int. J. Hum.-Comput. Interact. **37**(4), 297–307 (2021)

11. Pritchard, A.: Statistical bibliography or bibliometrics. J. Doc. **25**, 348 (1969)

12. Van Eck, N., Waltman, L.: Software Survey: VOSviewer, a computer program for bibliometric mapping. Scientometrics **84**(2), 523–538 (2010)

13. Chen, C.: CiteSpace II: detecting and visualizing emerging trends and transient patterns in scientific literature. J. Am. Soc. Inform. Sci. Technol. **57**(3), 359–377 (2006)

14. Li, H., An, H., Wang, Y., Huang, J., Gao, X.: Evolutionary features of academic articles co-keyword network and keywords co-occurrence network: based on two-mode affiliation network. Phys. A **450**, 657–669 (2016)

15. Kiefer, P., Giannopoulos, I., Raubal, M., Duchowski, A.: Eye tracking for spatial research: cognition, computation, challenges. Spat. Cogn. Comput. **17**(1–2), 1–19 (2017)

16. Blascheck, T., Kurzhals, K., Raschke, M., Burch, M., Weiskopf, D., Ertl, T.: State-of-the-art of visualization for eye tracking data. In: Eurovis (stars), p. 29 (2014)

17. Rupi, F., Krizek, K.J.: Visual eye gaze while cycling: analyzing eye tracking at signalized intersections in urban conditions. Sustainability **11**(21), 6089 (2019)

18. Duchowski, A.T.: A breadth-first survey of eye-tracking applications. Behav. Res. Methods Instrum. Comput. **34**(4), 455–470 (2002)

19. Goldberg, J.H., Kotval, X.P.: Computer interface evaluation using eye movements: methods and constructs. Int. J. Ind. Ergon. **24**(6), 631–645 (1999)

20. Rayner, K.: Eye movements in reading and information processing: 20 years of research. Psychol. Bull. **124**(3), 372 (1998)

21. Just, M.A., Carpenter, P.A.: A theory of reading: from eye fixations to comprehension. Psychol. Rev. (1980)

22. Carpenter, P.A., Just, M.A.: Eye fixations and cognitive processes. Ego Psychol. Commun. (1976)

23. Goldberg, J.H., Stimson, M.J., Lewenstein, M., Scott, N., Wichansky, A.M.: Eye tracking in web search tasks: design implications. In: Proceedings of the 2002 Symposium on Eye Tracking Research & Applications, pp. 51–58 (2002)

24. Hansen, D.W., Ji, Q.: In the eye of the beholder: a survey of models for eyes and gaze. IEEE Trans. Pattern Anal. Mach. Intell. **32**(3), 478–500 (2009)

25. Morimoto, C.H., Mimica, M.R.: Eye gaze tracking techniques for interactive applications. Comput. Vis. Image Underst. **98**(1), 4–24 (2005)

26. Holmqvist, K., Nyström, M., Andersson, R., Dewhurst, R., Jarodzka, H., Van de Weijer, J.: Eye tracking: a comprehensive guide to methods and measures. OUP Oxford (2011)

Pictorial Usability Metric for User Experience LITE: Development and Psychological Measurement

Yiyang Zhang, Xinyu Zhang, Yujie Liu, and Chengqi Xue$^{(\boxtimes)}$

School of Mechanical Engineering, Southeast University, Nanjing, China
ipd_xcq@seu.edu.cn

Abstract. We developed the pictorial vision of the Usability Metric for User Experience LITE (UMUX-LITE) scale, called P-UMUX-LITE, intended to provide a new method for measuring perceived availability in human-computer interaction. The scale is based on the established verbal usability questionnaire UMUX-LITE, which was tested in a validation study (N = 100) using retrospective research, and psychometric properties (structural validity, Internal consistency, Concurrent validity, and Sensitivity) were measured. The results show that the scale has satisfactory psychometric properties. Furthermore, strong correlations were obtained for the sum scores between verbal SUS and P-UMUX-LITE.

Keywords: Usability · Scale development · Human-computer interaction

1 Introduction

Usability measurement is crucial in the product development process. Usability consists of three core concepts: effectiveness, efficiency, and satisfaction, according to International Organization for Standardization (ISO) 9241-11. Perceived availability is an important construction of usability [1], reflecting the subjective components of usability concepts, and also is a fundamental component of User Experience (UX).

To facilitate the measurement of perceived usability and user experience during product development, standardized questionnaires have been widely developed. Although questionnaires have many advantages in usability research, most widely used survey questionnaires are quite complex and text-based. It is not only boring but also easy to misunderstand, especially among the elderly or children.

During the questionnaire development process, the accuracy of participants' understanding of the scale is a key issue. However, due to the extensive application of standardized questionnaires and their diverse target groups, the language itself may cause a series of problems in the filling process of traditional text scales, which may affect the final results. Such as the elderly or children may lack the ability to understand and read. These factors may lead to misunderstandings about the question items, select incorrect answers, and hurt the accuracy of measurement results. While studies based on cross-cultural backgrounds have shown that when the questionnaire is translated into other

© The Author(s), under exclusive license to Springer Nature Switzerland AG 2024
M. Kurosu and A. Hashizume (Eds.): HCII 2024, LNCS 14684, pp. 194–204, 2024.
https://doi.org/10.1007/978-3-031-60405-8_13

languages, sometimes the inability to find accurate corresponding vocabulary, results in participants misunderstanding the items meaning [2]. Various solutions have been proposed in previous studies, such as using positive tone [3] and simplifying scales, to improve the comprehensibility of the questionnaire. However, people do not always like to read words carefully [4]. Adding graphics can contain more information while assisting in understanding text.

Graphical scales may provide a more attractive and interesting choice than textual scales. Although some studies suggest that participants' motivation mainly comes from remuneration, others suggest that if the questionnaire were more interesting, it may increase the participants' level of seriousness, thereby obtaining more accurate results. In addition, short questionnaires can also be used to reduce the measurement time and workload of participants, and then improve their participation enthusiasm. This is the main function of the UMUX-LITE scale, and Lewis also advocates using shorter questionnaire surveys in larger samples or online testing processes.

This study consists of two steps. The first aim is to develop a pictorial usability questionnaire based on the textual version of UMUX-LITE, through a series of rigorous development processes. The pictorial items are specifically designed for the evaluation of smartphone software, which are commonly used devices in daily life. The second goal is to collect preliminary data to evaluate the psychological measurement attributes of graphical scales to ensure that they can be widely used by researchers.

2   Related Research

2.1   Development of Usability Scale

To evaluate the subjective usability of products, standardized questionnaires have been greatly developed in the field of human-computer interaction, and a large number of standardized scales have been formed. These questionnaires have significant differences in accuracy and measurement structure. For example, the System Usability Scale (SUS) contains ten items, while UMUX-LITE only contains two, but can provide effective measurement results.

To improve the UMUX, Lewis et al. proposed a shorter all-positive questionnaire called the UMUX-LITE using the same 7-point scale with only two items. However, the modification of UMUX is limited to the deletion of question items, without considering the form of scale expression. There are more and more other forms of availability scales nowadays, such as the pictorial single-item scale [2], and the sign language version of SUS for deaf users [5]. These studies provide a more interesting and easier-to-understand method for usability testing.

2.2   Pictorial Usability Questionnaire

For participants who are not proficient in reading comprehension or testing language, the text-based usability scale may bring some problems, such as reading barriers and understanding errors. Among child users, their cognitive abilities, short attention time, subjective biases, and language proficiency may not be sufficient to support their reading scales.

Adding graphics to improve questionnaire comprehension is a good solution. Some studies have pointed out that graphical projects can improve participants' motivation because images are more intuitive and understandable, and have lower cognitive requirements [4]. In the field of human-computer interaction, some graphical tools have been developed. The graphic scale includes realistic images, cartoon scenes, cartoon emoticons, etc. Graphical content generally includes actions and scenes with physical behavior. For example, Children's Grip Strength Scale [6], Children's Nausea Scale [7], etc. These scales can replace the language statements described in the question items withdrawn scenes.

Another advantage of graphical scales is that when cross-cultural translation is carried out, the language of images does not need to be translated. However, some elements such as gestures or facial expressions may have different understandings in different cultural backgrounds, so additional prompts or verbal explanations are needed.

3   Methodology

This study developed a graphical mixed scale for evaluating perceived usability, known as the Pictorial UMUX-LITE Scale. We have redesigned the UMUX-LITE 7-point scale to provide practitioners and researchers with a nonverbal measurement method to replace the current tools used to measure perceived availability. Develop from the following aspects:

a) Scene design: Design the content of drawing images based on the scenario described by the item. Some graphical SUS have demonstrated that their items can be expressed graphically [8] while attaching a textual version of the scale as an aid in understanding the items, rather than replacing the 5-point scale.

b) Character image design: Friendly cartoon characters can guide participants' behavior [9] and improve their participation [10]. Therefore, we chose cartoon characters as the display subject of the question item. In the design of graphic scales, facial expressions are very important and serve as important evidence for distinguishing user emotions. Enlarge the relevant facial expressions and use animation to express them, which helps with emotional recognition. Therefore, we exaggerate the facial expressions of the character.

c) Color design: Bright colors can awaken emotions and attract participants' attention [11]. Rich color combinations can enhance participants' motivation to fill in. To improve the user experience of the scale, excellent aesthetics are also crucial. Therefore, we used a variety of color combinations to improve the user-friendliness of the scale.

d) Auxiliary elements design: Graphic information may not accurately convey information, despite facial expressions and motion assistance [12]. Therefore, auxiliary elements and some commonly used words have been added to the diagram to help explain the meaning of the item more accurately.

3.1 Scale Development

Before designing P-UMUX-LITE, we adopted the development process of Juergen Baumgartner et al. [8], which was modeled on the Plan Build Run model used in IT projects, resulting in Concept Realization Evaluation.

Two experts with experience in multiple-scale testing and aesthetic training were organized. Through the thinking-loud method, the specific meanings of the two UMUX-LITE projects and the expression forms of the 7-point scale were discussed, and draft images were constructed for each item. After a panel of experts evaluated and iterated the aesthetics of the drawing content, we formed a preliminary image. Each image corresponds to the information of the P-UMUX-LITE problem project. There are a total of 4 images.

Pre-testing and Modification. By recruiting 10 user experience experts, the content validity and graphic expression appropriateness of the initial version of P-UMUX-LITE were evaluated, and the consistency of the project structure was scored on an independent 4-point scale. Calculate the Content Effectiveness Index (CVI) value for each project, which is the I-CVI. Projects smaller than 0.8 will be revised and iterated again, and then experts will evaluate these projects again.

After completing the content validity test, organize 15 participants to measure surface validity. Surface effectiveness refers to whether the evaluated content measures what should have been measured. Surface effectiveness mainly evaluates clarity, readability, and formatting. We calculated the project surface effectiveness index (I-FVI) value for each project. In the first round of testing, the score of the first item was below 0.8. Through interviews with participants, we inquired about the reasons for not understanding the project expression and proposed suggestions for modification. After the second surface effectiveness measurement of the iterative scale, the final scale is formed.

The final S-CVI/S-FVI is the arithmetic mean of all items I-CVI/I-FVI. The minimum acceptable standard is 0.8 [13]. We calculated the final values S-CVI = 0.87 and S-FVI = 0.826.

Pictorial Items of P-UMUX-LITE. The final P-UMUX-LITE is shown in Fig. 1, consisting of four image items located at the extreme points of the item. The two extreme points of each project describe negative and positive user experiences to convey and emphasize the specific meaning of the project. Simultaneously use signal colors (red, green), meaningful symbols, and simple text as auxiliary elements to maximize comprehensibility and reduce ambiguity.

这个系统的功能能够满足我的要求
The function of this system can meet my requirements

该系统易于使用
This system is easy to use

Fig. 1. Final P-UMUX-LITE Scale. (Color figure online)

4 Validation Study

4.1 Goal of the Study

The purpose of this study is to collect indicators that describe the effectiveness and reliability of the P-UMUX-LITE developed. Aggregation effectiveness, standard-related effectiveness, sensitivity, and reliability were evaluated in laboratory experiments.

4.2 Participants

We selected 100 participants and completed them through online recruitment and remote testing. The age distribution is between 18 and 32 years old, with 43 females and 57 males. Educational requirements have been set for undergraduate or above education to ensure an understanding of Chinese language questions. After cleaning according to the method provided by Lewis, we retained 94 effective participants, for 94%. Each participant received a payment of 2 RMB.

4.3 Survey Design

We used retrospective measurements. Because compared with laboratory testing, long-term retrospective evaluation is stable. This method has been used in many questionnaire development, as well as daily product evaluation [1], and test results are not the focus of questionnaire development [14].

Systems used daily can be evaluated retrospectively. In China, Alipay is the most widely used platform, almost every mobile phone has this software, so we used it as experimental material.

In the test material, we used the Chinese SUS (Wang et al., 2020) as a parallel measurement, cause past studies have confirmed a high correlation. Chinese SUS has also been tested many times, and maintains similar psychological indicators, with high reliability (>0.8) and structural validity, and their simultaneous validity reaches above 0.8. We did not choose Chinese UMUX because they have the same items and will have the effect of re-testing during the measurement process.

We also investigated the frequency of use of Alipay. The assessment methodology is based on monthly activities and is divided into three levels. To prevent sequential position effects, the order of the two questionnaires (UMUX lite and SUS) alternates.

To prevent participants from thinking the test was an assessment of their abilities, we added that the study was an assessment of the system, not a response to individual abilities.

4.4 Procedure

1. Introduce the purpose of the experiment and the remuneration obtained to the participants through the Internet, and sign an informed consent form. The test materials were presented to the participants and the methods for filling out the electronic questionnaire were explained.
2. Send a link to participants and ask them to click the link to jump to the test page, read the instructions, and then fill out the questionnaire
3. After the participants submit the test results, the experimental assistant will pay the participants after confirming the receipt of the test results

5 Results

5.1 Basic Statistics

The total score of the PUMUX-LITE is consistent with the original UMUX-LITE, which is converted to 100 points to adapt to the CGS scale. The scoring method adopts a total score of (item score-1) $\times$ 25/6. Both scales use the CGS scale to report the grade. The calculation method of the SUS is (odd item score-1) $\times$ 2.5 + (5-even item score) $\times$ 2.5. The basic statistics of the two questionnaires are shown in Table 1.

Table 1. Basic statistics of the P-UMUX-LITE and SUS

	Mean	SD	CGS
P-UMUX-LITE	72.86	9.44	B-
SUS	71.59	12.09	B-

An independent sample t-test showed that there was no significant difference between P-UMUX-LITE and SUS (t (186) = 0.799, p = 0.025, p > 0.05).

5.2 Structural Validity

The KMO value is widely reported as structural validity in questionnaire studies and the minimum acceptable criterion is greater than 0.6. The KMO value of P-UMUX-LITE is 0.783, and Bartlett's sphericity test Chi-square is 358.176, p < 0.05. SUS's KMO value was 0.867, and Bartlett's sphericity test Chi-square is 771.902, p < 0.01.

5.3 Internal Consistency

The Cronbach α coefficient of P-UMUX-LITE is 0.781, and SUS is 0.801, greater than the commonly used standard of 0.7. The results are similar to past research reports.

5.4 Concurrent Validity

Concurrent validity was expressed via a correlation between the two questionnaires; the minimum acceptable value is 0.3. We adopt SUS as the criterion for testing P-UMUX-LITE. A large number of studies have reported correlations between the two questionnaires. The Pearson correlation coefficient is 0.764, p < 0.01.

5.5 Sensitivity

The score of perceived usability measurement is influenced by various factors, such as task type, product type, etc. Meanwhile, a large number of studies have shown that the usability score will change over time, with frequency of use being an important factor causing the change. Sensitive usability scales can measure different responses under different conditions, and some studies suggest that usability scores increase with increasing usage experience. Therefore, we chose frequency as the sensitivity indicator. The descriptive statistical data of P-UMUX-LITE and SUS are shown in Table 2.

Table 2. Usage frequency statistic

	Experience Grade	n	Mean	SD
P-UMUX-LITE	Less than once a month	28	65.46	13.57
	Once or twice a month	36	74.36	11.09
	Many times a month	30	77.97	8.46
SUS	Less than once a month	28	63.75	13.04
	Once or twice a month	36	69.93	10.99
	Many times a month	30	80.92	8.45

We conducted a One-way ANOVA test to evaluate whether the scale can distinguish between high availability and low availability. The score showed that the main effect of experience had a significant impact on P-UMUX-LITE, with $F(2,91) = 22.01$, $p < 0.01$, $\eta^2 = 0.289$. The main effect was also significant at SUS ($F(2,91) = 18.54$, $p <$

0.01, $\eta^2 = 0.326$). The LSD test showed significant differences ($p < 0.05$) among the three groups, indicating that both questionnaires were sensitive. The results showed that P-UMUX-LITE had good sensitivity.

5.6 Stability

The stability of the scale can be tested by testing the scores of different genders and regions. As shown in Table 3 and Table 4.

Table 3. Gender statistics

Gender	N	Mean	SD
Female	41	72.44	8.86
Male	53	73.18	9.92

Independent sample t-test showed no significant difference between the two ($t (92) = -.375$, $p = 0.708$, $p > 0.05$).

Table 4. Area statistics

Area	N	Mean	SD
North	40	73.55	9.30
South	54	72.35	9.59

Independent sample t-test showed no significant difference between the two ($t (92) = .547$, $p = 0.739$, $p > 0.05$).

6 Discussion

The establishment of the UMUX-LITE graphical version compensates for the difficulty in understanding the original scale, and there is sufficient evidence to suggest that the graphical scale is a reliable approach. We attempted to develop a validated P-UMUX-LITE scale format and explored design methods to validate psychological metrics.

6.1 Design of the Scale

In this study, we designed the development process of a graphical scale and designed a graphical UMUX-LITE scale based on UMUX-LITE. The understanding barriers of UMUX-LITE are mainly reflected in two aspects: the understanding barriers of the project and the judgment errors of the Likert scale judgment degree. In our research, we assisted in understanding and grading the scale through graphical representation.

In graphic design, we have designed a unified painting style, which is beneficial for reducing the cognitive load on the subjects. In addition, similar to the graphical SUS, we did not remove the text description, and the graphics were used as an aid to understanding. Some studies have shown that presenting multiple information elements (such as written text, visual images, and audio) can place excessive demands on the working memory of the perceiver. We have not found any evidence that affects our understanding.

6.2 Psychological Measurement

In the psychological measurement test of P-UMUX-LITE, we chose a retrospective evaluation to complete the psychological measurement, and all indicators met the standards. We choose to use graphics to help users understand. This indicates that the multiple styles of UMUX-LITE can not only promote understanding of items but also maintain high psychological measurement indicators.

In the tests of content validity and surface validity, since we did not modify the UMUX-LITE items, the evaluation of content validity and surface validity is based on the response to the image. In the interview, approximately half of the reported participants reported that they did not have problems understanding the items.

At the same time, the graphic version of UMUX-LITE and the textual version of SUS are highly correlated, with a correlation coefficient of 0.799, which is consistent with previous research. Further confirmed the high correlation between the two questionnaires. Although the average score of UMUX-LITE was 1.27 points higher in the two questionnaires, there was no significant difference between the two questionnaires. In the CSG level, both questionnaires also belong to the B-level, and this score difference is consistent with other studies.

Sensitivity analysis shows that P-UMUX-LITE can detect changes in usability, and in previous studies, experience has often been used as an evaluation indicator, thus confirming its sensitivity, and indicating that it can meet psychological measurement characteristics.

In terms of stability, there is little difference in results between populations of different regions and genders, indicating that the scale has good stable measurement attributes.

Therefore, the graphical version of UMUX-LITE can meet the psychological measurement characteristics of UMUX-LITE, and practitioners of user experience can use this scale with confidence.

7 Conclusions, Limitations, and Future Work

Overall, the psychological measurement characteristics of P-UMUX-LITE evaluated in this study can be said to be satisfactory compared to previous studies.

Compared to language questionnaires, graphical scales can achieve similar results, with the additional advantage of increasing motivation. However, the design process of graphical survey questionnaires involves a relatively large development workload. In addition, during the design process, some project descriptions are ambiguous, making it difficult to reach a consensus. Therefore, the development of graphical questionnaires requires high experience in aesthetics, design, and usability research, which is not easy to achieve in a large number of projects.

In addition, further evaluation is needed for the cross-cultural use of graphical usability questionnaires, and more samples are needed to further validate the research, not only in terms of numbers but more choices should also be made for the elderly and children, as the form of image scales is more effective in these special populations.

Acknowledgment. The authors would like to gratefully acknowledge the reviewers' comments.

Disclosure of Interests. The authors have no competing interests to declare that are relevant to the content of this article.

References

1. Lewis, J.R.: Measuring perceived usability: the CSUQ, SUS, and UMUX. Int. J. Hum. Comput. Interact. **34**(12), 1148–1156 (2018). https://doi.org/10.1080/10447318.2017.141 8805
2. Baumgartner, J., Sonderegger, A., Sauer, J.: No need to read: developing a pictorial single-item scale for measuring perceived usability. Int. J. Hum. Comput. Stud. **122**, 78–89 (2019). https://doi.org/10.1016/j.ijhcs.2018.08.008
3. Sauro, J., Lewis, J.R.: When designing usability questionnaires, does it hurt to be positive? In: Proceedings of the SIGCHI Conference on Human Factors in Computing Systems, pp. 2215–2224 (2011). https://doi.org/10.1145/1978942.1979266
4. Baumgartner, J., Ruettgers, N., Hasler, A., Sonderegger, A., Sauer, J.: Questionnaire experience and the hybrid System Usability Scale: using a novel concept to evaluate a new instrument. Int. J. Hum. Comput. Stud. **147**, 102575 (2021). https://doi.org/10.1016/j.ijhcs.2020.102575
5. Berke, L., Huenerfauth, M., Patel, K.: Design and psychometric evaluation of American sign language translations of usability questionnaires. ACM Trans. Access. Comput. **12**(2), 1–43 (2019). https://doi.org/10.1145/3314205
6. Defrasne Ait-Said, E., Groslambert, A., Courty, D.: Validation of a pictorial rating scale for grip strength evaluation in 3- to 6-year-old children. Neurosci. Lett. **420**(2), 150–154 (2007). https://doi.org/10.1016/j.neulet.2007.04.066
7. Baxter, A., Watcha, M., Baxter, W., Leong, T., Wyatt, M.: Development and validation of a pictorial nausea rating scale for children. Pediatrics **127**, e1542–e1549 (2011). https://doi.org/10.1542/peds.2010-1410
8. Baumgartner, J., Frei, N., Kleinke, M., Sauer, J., Sonderegger, A.: Pictorial System Usability Scale (P-SUS): developing an instrument for measuring perceived usability. In: Proceedings of the 2019 CHI Conference on Human Factors in Computing Systems, pp. 1–11 (2019). https://doi.org/10.1145/3290605.3300299
9. Binder, A., Naderer, B., Matthes, J.: Do children's food choices go with the crowd? Effects of majority and minority peer cues shown within an audiovisual cartoon on children's healthy food choice. Soc. Sci. Med. **225**, 42–50 (2019). https://doi.org/10.1016/j.socscimed.2019.01.032
10. Choi, H.J., Kim, H.J.: Efficacy of cartoons as a distraction technique for children undergoing suture of facial lacerations in the emergency department. Pediatric Emergency Care **37**(9), 471–473 (2021). https://journals.lww.com/pec-online/Fulltext/2021/09000/Efficacy_of_Cartoons_as_a_Distraction_Technique.8.aspx
11. Walsh, L.M., Toma, R.B., Tuveson, R.V., Sondhi, L.: Color preference and food choice among children. J. Psychol. **124**(6), 645–653 (1990). https://doi.org/10.1080/00223980.1990.105 43258

12. Laurans, G., Desmet, P.M.A.: Developing 14 animated characters for non-verbal self-report of categorical emotions. J. Des. Res. **15**(3–4), 214–233 (2017). https://doi.org/10.1504/JDR. 2017.089903

13. Polit, D.F., Beck, C.T., Owen, S.V.: Is the CVI an acceptable indicator of content validity? Appraisal and recommendations. Res. Nurs. Health **30**(4), 459–467 (2007). https://doi.org/ 10.1002/nur.20199

14. Gronier, G., Baudet, A.: Psychometric evaluation of the F-SUS: creation and validation of the French version of the system usability scale. Int. J. Hum. Comput. Interact. **37**(16), 1571–1582 (2021). https://doi.org/10.1080/10447318.2021.1898828

Modeling Theory of Mind in Multimodal HCI

Yifan Zhu[1] , Hannah VanderHoeven[2] , Kenneth Lai[1] ,
Mariah Bradford[2] , Christopher Tam[1] , Ibrahim Khebour[2] ,
Richard Brutti[1] , Nikhil Krishnaswamy[2] , and James Pustejovsky[1](✉)

1 Brandeis University, Waltham, MA 02453, USA
{zhuyifan,jamesp}@brandeis.edu
2 Colorado State University, Fort Collins, CO 80523, USA

Abstract. As multimodal interactions between humans and computers become more sophisticated, involving not only speech, but gestures, haptics, eye movement, and other input types, each modality introduces subtleties which can be misinterpreted without a deeper understanding of the agent's mental state. In this paper, we argue that Simulation Theory of Mind (SToM) [23], interpreted within a model of embodied HCI [41,42], can help model the capacity to attribute beliefs and intentions to oneself and others. We adopt a version of Dynamic Epistemic Logic that admits of degrees of belief, reflecting changing evidence available to an agent [5,6]. This model is able to address the complexities of mutual perception and belief, and how a dynamic common ground is constructed and changes [15]. To demonstrate this, we apply the SToM model to the problem of Common Ground Tracking (CGT) in multi-party dialogues, focusing here on a joint problem-solving task called the Weights Task, where participants cooperate to find the weights of a set of blocks.

Keywords: Theory of Mind · HCI · Epistemic Updating · Common ground tracking · multimodal dialogue · simulation · Embodiment

1 Introduction

Theory of Mind (ToM) refers to the cognitive capacity that humans have to attribute mental states such as beliefs (true or false), desires, and intentions to oneself and others, thereby predicting and explaining behavior [39,56]. Within the domain of Human-Computer Interaction (HCI), this concept has recently become more relevant for computational agents, especially in the context of multimodal communication [15]. As multimodal interactions involve not only speech, but gestures, actions, eye gaze, body posture and other input types (cf. Fig. 1), each modality introduces subtleties which can be misinterpreted without a deeper understanding of the agent's mental state. As a result, ToM's role becomes important, ensuring that agents grasp both the overt and covert nuances of human communication. For multimodal HCI, a computational agent needs to incorporate both the ability to reason about the beliefs of other agents

Fig. 1. Example of a multimodal annotated situation red arrows denote co-gazing blue arrows symbolize leaning towards the table. (Color figure online)

and their intentions, while also knowing what beliefs can be assumed or taken for granted in a specific context.

In this paper, we argue that Simulation Theory of Mind (SToM) [23,24], encoded as an evidence-based dynamic epistemic logic (EB-DEL), can help model these complexities [5,6]. We develop this view within a model of embodied HCI [41,42], where simulation theory is inherent in both the semantics of the model as well as the implementation of situated meaning and action. Specifically, we apply this model to the problem of Common Ground Tracking (CGT) in multi-party dialogues, focusing here on a joint problem-solving task called the Weights Task, where participants cooperate to find the weights of a set of blocks. In such task-oriented interactions, successful communication hinges not only on understanding the immediate intent but also on a shared context and knowledge of the actions and experiences of the agents. Theories of Common Ground posit that for effective communication, interlocutors must have a mutual understanding of the task at hand and the context in which it is situated [4,16]. In HCI, this translates to the system and the user operating with aligned expectations and shared knowledge about the ongoing task.

Unlike Dialogue State Tracking (DST), which is the ability to update the representations of the speaker's needs at each turn in the dialogue by taking into account the past dialogue moves and history [28], Common Ground Tracking (CGT) identifies the shared belief space held by all of the participants in a task-oriented dialogue. While ToM enables a system to "read" another person's mental states, Common Ground Tracking ensures that this reading is anchored in a shared context, making interactions more coherent and goal-directed.

Within the framework of SToM and Embodied HCI adopted here, we present a method for automatically identifying the current set of shared beliefs and questions under discussion (QUDs) of a group with a shared goal, the Weights Task. The task involves triads collaborating to determine the weights of five blocks using a balance scale [29]. We track the shared knowledge of participants in a co-situated environment, which involves interpreting the communications over multiple modalities, and integrating these channels into a coherent model of the common ground.

We believe that models of belief and intent in multimodal HCI can be significantly enriched by integrating principles of ToM and Common Ground, allowing interactive systems to not only react to user inputs but interpret them in a shared context, making interactions more predictive, context-aware, and aligned with user expectations. By integrating ToM and common ground tracking into conversational agent architectures [19,51], we can better model the beliefs of participants by exposing unspoken assumptions of the participants or disagreements among them. Enhancing the epistemic modeling capabilities of multimodal HCI with ToM also has the potential to inform research in both Affective Computing, such as automatic Emotion Detection, by providing more contextualized interpretations of cognitive states and emotions in dialogue [46], as well as providing support for those with functional impairments [20].

In the final section, we provide detailed evidence assessing the contribution of each feature type from different channels toward successful construction of common ground relative to ground truth, and show how the combination of modalities results in a higher-fidelity prediction of both cognitive states of the participants and propositions implicitly or explicitly expressed.

2   Related Work

There is a significant tradition of research on Theory of Mind in philosophy and its application to questions of epistemic awareness within developmental psychology [25,39,55,56]. One view that is particularly relevant to the approach taken here is Simulation Theory [24], which models the process of understanding another agent's intentions as mental simulations from one's own perspective. Simulation Theory, as developed in philosophy of mind by Goldman and others, has focused on the role that "mind reading" plays in modeling the mental representations of other agents and the content of their communicative acts [24,26,27]. Simulation semantics as adopted within cognitive linguistics [17,36], argues that language comprehension is accomplished by means of such mind reading operations. Similarly, within psychology, there is an established body of work arguing for "mental simulations" of future or possible outcomes, as well as interpretations of perceptual input [3]. These simulation approaches can be referred to as *embodied theories of mind*. The goal here is to create a semantic interpretation of an expression or action by embodying it in a simulation.

Goldman's theory of mind [24], viewed from the perspective of simulation theory, provides a mechanism for how individuals understand and predict the behaviors of other agents. By constructing a simulation, an agent can generate hypotheses about others' mental states and intentions, anticipate possible future actions, and even empathize with their emotional states. SToM can be seen as consisting of three major components: (a) *Mental Simulation*, where an agent simulates the mental processes of others; (b) *Perspective Taking*, where an agent adopts another person's Epistemic Frame of Reference; and (c) *Shared Mental Processes*, the view that others' mental states involve the same cognitive mechanisms as one's own.

Within HRI, the question of epistemic awareness and social appropriateness of robot behavior has been a concern since the foundation of the discipline [12]. Similarly, the modeling of first-order beliefs in HRI has been addressed within the modeling and reasoning community [49], while the application of Dynamic Epistemic Logic itself to planning has resulted in significant developments within the area of *epistemic planning* [8], and subsequent work [4,9].

But fundamental capabilities involving inferencing over others' beliefs as well as an agent's metacognitive abilities have been less studied. This problem is addressed in [15], where false-belief scenarios are encoded within the version of Dynamic Epistemic Logic introduced by Bolander [7]. This model accounts for an agent's false belief regarding a changing environment, as well as the ability of other agents to recognize and reason about this agent's incorrect epistemic state. While not adopting Bolander's specific model of DEL here, our research aligns squarely with their approach to modeling the dynamics of belief updating in HRI and HCI contexts. Since we are focusing on integrating the semantics associated with distinct channels of communication (speech and gesture) as well as actions and perceptions, we need to integrate semantic content derived from these distinct channels into a common format and data structure. This involves adopting a more expressive model for how common ground is constructed and updated, as discussed below in Sect. 4. We also account for epistemic content held individually and in common within a group, with an evidence-based model of DEL as introduced in [5,6].

There has been considerable work on simulating both physical and cognitive processes carried out by agents, human and computational [30,44,59]. Of particular relevance to the research reported here is the simulation framework, VoxWorld [34]. VoxWorld supports embodied HCI, where artificial agents consume different sensor inputs for awareness of not only their own virtual space but also the surrounding physical space. It brings together the notion of simulation systems from computer science as well as that mentioned here, in the context of Simulation ToM. VoxWorld is a collaborative creation of the VoxML modeling language [40] and its real-time Unity interpreter, VoxSim [32], culminating in an environment meticulously defined interaction semantics. Such an architectural framework readily facilitates the interpretation of action annotations, as descriptions converted to linguistic entities within VoxML exhibit an explicit correspondence within the simulation context. Within the VoxWorld ecosystem, the Diana agent emerges as a pivotal interface designed to discern user speech and gestures [31], setting itself apart from other Intelligent Virtual Agents (IVAs) through its capacity for reasoning and acting upon a diverse array of objects endowed with a well-defined affordance structure.

3   A Multimodal Dataset for Common Ground Tracking

The Weights Task, as described in [29], embodies a collaborative problem-solving task wherein groups of three participants engage in a concerted effort to infer the unknown weights of different blocks. This inference is achieved through comparative analyses of the blocks' weights with a balance scale. Each group is equipped with a scale and five blocks with different colors, sizes, and weights. Participants are informed of the weight of a singular block and are tasked with discerning the weights of the remaining blocks and the algebraic relation between them (the Fibonacci Sequence). Due to the co-situated nature of the task and its inclusion of physical objects and reasoning about their properties, the communication in this task can be annotated in several ways: speech with dense paraphrasing [52], gesture [10], as well as non-verbal behaviors that communicate intent such as gaze [35], body postures [43], facial expression [45]. Additionally, we label all actions performed [50], and collaborative problem solving (CPS) indicators according to the framework of [48]. Each group successfully deduces the accurate weights of the blocks, thereby establishing a uniform and reliable endpoint for evaluating our models.

First-order epistemic statements represent what an agent believes or knows about their environment, while second-order epistemic representations express what an agent believes or knows about other agents' beliefs and knowledge of the environment. One avenue for studying ToM in collaborative interactions is to track the propositional context expressed by verbal actions (explicitly or implicitly uttered), already embedded in common ground. Another avenue with not much exploration is tracking information results not only in speech but also gesture: non-verbal actions and gestures contained individual consenting an agreement including mere perception of the action itself [7], as well as false-belief scenarios within the version of Dynamic Epistemic Logic.

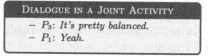

Fig. 2. Gaze and posture, P_1, P_2, P_3 co-attending, P_2 lean in

Fig. 3. Dialogue in 2.

Consider the joint activity shown in Fig. 2 among three participants; Participant 3 (P_3) has a public announcement and P_1 signals his consent. The figure has a blue arrow to highlight P_2 leaning in to have a closer look at the scale after he heard the dialogue between P_1 and P_3. Figure 3 presents their dialogue in the context of joint activity. In this situation of a multi-agent task interaction, there are several elements constituting the common ground among the three participants. These elements include reference to: the agents, shared beliefs, shared goals, and shared perception of objects, including that the scale is balanced.

4   Constructing Multimodal Common Ground

4.1   Epistemic Modeling in ToM

The notion of common ground is a fundamental concept in HCI, growing out of a rich tradition in philosophy and cognitive science, focused on exploring how individuals coordinate and establish shared understanding to facilitate meaningful conversations [1,11,47]. For HCI, common ground is crucial for designing interactive systems and technologies that can effectively communicate with users by anticipating their needs, understanding their context, and responding to their inputs in an intuitive manner. With the presence of a common ground during shared experiences, embodied communication assumes agents can understand one another in a shared context, through the use of co-situational and co-perceptual anchors, and a means for identifying such anchors, such as gesture, gaze, intonation, and language. In this section, we develop a computational model of common ground for multimodal communication.

Within the context of multimodal interactions, the notion of common ground relies on identifying three key aspects of the interaction:

1. *Co-situatedness* of the agents, such that they can interpret the same situation from their respective frames of reference;
2. *Co-perception* and *co-attention* of a shared situated reference, which allows more expressiveness in referring to the environment (i.e., through language, gesture, visual presentation);
3. *Co-belief* of the agents regarding the goals as well as the steps involved towards accomplishing this goal..

Within this context, common ground emerges in one of the following ways during social interactions [16]:

- by public announcement, through either speech or gesture;
- by common witnessing of an event;
- by combinations of the above (indirect co-presence, cultural co-presence).

In order to characterize the many dimensions of human-computer interactions, we introduce an approach to evaluating interactions drawing on the most relevant parameters in co-situated communicative interactions. By introducing a formal model of shared context, we are able to track the intentions and utterances, as well as the perceptions and actions of the agents involved in a dialogue. The computer, either as an embodied agent distinct from the viewer, or as the totality of the rendered environment itself, presents an interpretation (*mind-reading*) of its internal model, down to specific parameter values, which are often assigned for the purposes of testing that model.

We assume a model of discourse semantics as proposed in [13], as it facilitates the adoption of a continuation-based semantics for discourse. In the present work, however, update functions will be limited to dialogue-based moves, and we will not focus on the sentence-level update semantics. We adopt the SToM model of VoxWorld (discussed in Sect. 2) [34], a framework for modeling HCI and human-human multimodal interactions as embodied simulations. In this model, participants are embodied agents endowed with intentions, goals, beliefs, and the knowledge to complete simple tasks involving multimodal interactions with co-participants. Each agent's state in the dialogue is continuously updated through encoding the changes in the environment shared by the interacting agents [41, 42].

As mentioned in Sect. 1 above, our investigation involved a triad of co-situated students collaborating to solve a weights task for five blocks, using only a balance scale. The task is particularly relevant because the participants naturally engage in the different modalities that are so crucial for understanding multimodal HCI: namely, speech, gesture, gaze, pose, and of course joint actions. Hence, from a dialogue state tracking perspective, there are several distinct action types and their effects that need to be accounted for and tracked:

(1)   a. **Ontic actions**; interactions with and movements of the objects in the shared space; i.e., blocks and the balance scale;
      b. **Epistemic actions**; changes to the epistemic state of one or more of the participants in the interaction.

Before showing how this is done, we spell out the cognitive capabilities of the participants as computational agents performing these various actions.

We begin with the cognitive architecture adopted and developed in VoxWorld [41, 42], and enrich the model capabilities to more systematically account for epistemic updates in the common ground. We assume an embodied computational agent has the following capabilities.

(2)   a. *Perception*: perceptual sensors and interpreters.
      b. *Action*: action effectors and planning.
      c. *Belief*: a Dynamic Epistemic Logic with updating.

For the present discussion, we focus on those aspects of the architecture that are relevant to demonstrating the role ToM plays in tracking communicative content and intent. For this reason, we concentrate mainly on the role of perception and belief, and subsequent epistemic updating.

Let us first consider the role of an agent's perception of their environment. As discussed in [41], VoxWorld models an agent a's vision as sets of accessibility relations between situations (defined as S_a), where there are two kinds of perception reports: of a proposition, φ; or of an object, x, coerced to the propositional content of "x exists in the situation." The modal expression, $S_a\varphi$, is interpreted as a direct (veridical) perception of agent a of proposition, φ. Hence, modal axiom T holds, where $S_a\varphi \rightarrow \varphi$.

In VoxWorld, this impacts the way beliefs are updated, where it has the effect of introducing the axiom below (where the modal B_a represents belief of an agent a):

(3) **Seeing is Believing:** $S_a\varphi \to B_a\varphi$ (veridical perception)

For the multimodal interactions and experiments performed within VoxWorld to date, veridical perception was both required as well as a computational asset. However, in the context of the experimental configuration introduced by the Weights Task, we see a different role being contributed by an agent's perception, relative to the completion of the task: namely, an appreciation of the natural role that perception plays in arriving at evidence for a belief [18,53]. This requires distinguishing two types of "seeing", both direct and indirect, the latter which is implicated in forming belief, to which we now turn.

In terms of epistemic modeling, while the VoxWorld platform from [34] encodes an agent's belief for a dialogue state, the mechanisms used for updating epistemic values resulting from actions during the dialogue are linked to specific moves and transitions in the dialogue state machine [33]. As a result, identifying general axioms for epistemic updating across situations can be difficult.

To overcome both of these shortcomings, we adopt here an implementation of evidence-based Dynamic Epistemic Logic (DEL) as developed in [5] and [37]. Where epistemic attitudes toward propositions are graded, according to the evidence available to the agent. As the dialogue progresses, information becomes available, weakening or strengthening propositional content present in the situation. This affords a more nuanced encoding of how perception relates to belief, and a more general mechanism for belief updating, as we shall see.

Given a set of agents, engaged in a cooperative task with a specific goal, the scope of unknowns is delineated by how an answer to each one contributes to the task solution. As a result, cooperative and interactive engagement brings about evidence both for and against how to answer these unknowns, in the hope of solving a problem. To this end, the role of both direct and indirect evidence of a proposition is crucial to an agent being confident to believe it. Hence, following [37], we will assume a model for evidence-based belief as a tuple, $\mathcal{M} = (W, E, V)$, where:

(4)   a. W is a non-empty *set of worlds*;
      b. $E \subseteq W \times \wp(W)$ is an *evidence relation*;
      c. $V: At \to \wp(W)$, is a *valuation function*.

We will distinguish two sources of evidence. Let $E(w)$ denote the set $\{X \mid wEX\}$, the worlds accessible to w through the general evidencing relation, E. Beyond this, we distinguish between two sources of evidentiality: E_P, a perceptually-sourced evidence; and E_I, evidence derived through an inference over current common ground data. Accordingly, let $E_P(w)$ denote the set $\{X \mid wE_PX\}$, the worlds accessible to w through the "evidence through seeing" relation, E_P; and let $E_I(w)$ denote the set $\{X \mid wE_IX\}$, the worlds accessible to w through the "evidence through inferencing" relation, E_I.

The evidence-based epistemic-perceptual language, $\mathcal{L}_p$, will be the set of formulas generated by the grammar below, for any arbitrary agent:

(5)   a. $p \mid \neg\varphi \mid \varphi \wedge \psi \mid [E_I]\varphi \mid [E_P]\varphi \mid [B]\varphi \mid [K]\varphi \mid [S]\varphi \mid [CE_P]\varphi \mid [CS]\varphi \mid [CB]\varphi$
      b. $E_I(w) \subseteq E(w)$ and $E_P(w) \subseteq E(w)$

We distinguish the situation where an agent has "evidence in favor of" a proposition φ, as $[E]\varphi$. Because an agent can have evidence for propositions that convey contradictory information, she can consider both $[E]\varphi$ and $[E]\neg\varphi$. This corresponds to an agent having multiple neighborhoods, X, that are each evidenced in their unique way by w. However, consider the set of non-contradictory worlds as a unique subset of X, one which has what [6] refer to as the *finite intersection property (fip)*. This property allows us to identify a neighborhood of accessible worlds with non-contradictory propositional content. When this occurs, we say an agent has *belief* in a proposition, $[B]\varphi$. Following [37], the universal modality is considered "knowledge" of a proposition, $[K]\varphi$. Finally, veridical perception of a situation φ, is expressed as $[S]\varphi$. In conjunction with individual modal relations, we incorporate the concept of joint activity to denote a modal relation that is jointly shared by two or more participants. This is already assumed in our definition for common belief, see below. For direct perception and evidence, this will be indicated by $[CS_{\{a,b\}}]\varphi$, and $[CE_{P_{\{a,b\}}}]\varphi$, where a pair of agents, a and b are jointly seeing or evidencing φ to be the case. We define the expression of shared belief and shared perception in φ by a group, g, as and $CB_g\varphi$ and $CE_{Pg}\varphi$ respectively.

(6)   a. $\mathcal{M},w \models CB_g\varphi$ iff $\forall v \in W$, if $w(\bigcup_{j\in A} R_j)^*v$, then $\mathcal{M},w \models \varphi$.
       b. $\mathcal{M},w \models CE_{Pg}\varphi$ iff $\forall v \in W$, if $w(\bigcup_{j\in A} E_{Pj})^*v$, then $\mathcal{M},w \models \varphi$.

With the model adopted here, we are able to distinguish between direct "veridical perception" and "evidencing through perception", where $\Box\varphi \rightarrow \varphi$ holds for S but not for E_P.

While we have a formal distinction in the modal force associated with each mode of seeing (direct or evidential), we have not identified the conditions under which they are applicable. In our current experimental setup, the distinction is brought out very clearly as a function of what propositions are under discussion for verification. For the Weights Task, these are any propositions relating to the weights of specific blocks, their relative weights, and then how they algebraically relate to each other. Such propositions contribute to the solution of the problem the participants are engaged in solving. Hence, they are both "under discussion" and subject to degrees of evidential reasoning. This is accounted for by our distinction between a direct perception of an object or an event and an evidential perception of a proposition under discussion.

4.2   Common Ground in Dialogue

Given the model of Dynamic Epistemic Logic presented above, together with the mechanisms for encoding perception and evidence-based belief, let us formalize our assumptions about the common ground, cg, within a dialogue. We define the minimal structure of a task-oriented interaction as a sequence, D, of dialogue steps, where each move in the dialogue takes it into another situation or state. When considering multiple modalities of communication, along with the modality of action itself, we can generalize D to a multimodal dialogue (D_M). We will define the transitioning step from one situation to the next, as a generalization of a dialogue step. Let $Ag = \{p_1, p_2, p_3\}$, be the participants in our Weights Task triad-based dialogue. From any situation s_k, we define a D_M move, m_i, as $m_i = (p_j, C_j, s_{k+1})$: participant p_j performs a communicative act C_j, bringing the multimodal dialogue into situation s_{k+1}. The D_M can be defined as the sequence of these moves, $D_M = m_1, \ldots, m_n$, where $m\colon M \subseteq S \times A \times P \times S$ and A is the set of actions.

Here our interest is in tracking the situation content resulting from each move: the set of propositions that captures the current state of the world, the current progress towards a goal, or the status of a task. In addition, we are interested in capturing the current questions under discussion and beliefs in the dialogue.

Given these considerations, we identify three components for tracking common ground in dialogue: a minimal static model of degrees of belief; a data structure distinguishing the elements of the agents' common ground that are being tracked [41]; and a dynamic procedure which updates this structure, when new information and evidence is available to the agents. We adopt Ginzburg's [22] notion of *Dialogue Gameboard (DGB)*, the public information associated with a state in a dialogue or discourse, modeled as a state monad, modified to correspond to the following elements in the dialogue state: $DGB = (C_a, Ag, CG, \mathcal{E})$:

(7) a. The communicative act, C_a, performed by an agent, a: $\langle S, G, F, Z, P, A \rangle$, a tuple of expressions from the diverse modalities involved. This includes the modalities conveying propositional content (language S and gesture G); nonverbal modalities conveying emotional engagement (facial expressions F and posture P); nonverbal behaviors indicating perceptual attention (gaze Z); and an explicit action, A.
   b. Ag: the agents engaged in communication;
   c. CG: the common ground structure;
   d. $\mathcal{E}$: The embedding space that all agents occupy in the interaction.

We will focus on how actions impact the common ground, CG, such that it is dynamically updated throughout the dialogue. Following [21,22], modified to reflect the varying degrees of evidence associated with propositions under discussion, the common ground, cg, is a triple, (QB, EB, FB), consisting of:

(8) a. QBANK (QB): these are "questions under discussion", a set of topics or unknowns that need to be answered to solve the task [21];
   b. EBANK (EB): these are evidenced propositions, those for which there is some evidence they are true;
   c. FBANK (FB): the set of propositions believed as true by all participants.

4.3 Epistemic Updating

Let us now examine how the epistemic state of each agent and the group they form is updated throughout the task-oriented dialogue associated with the

Weights Task. These are the personal DGBs for each agent and the joint DGB for the group. The task is a triad joint activity, with agents, $Ag = \{p_1, p_2, p_3\}$, who are co-situated in the embedding space, $\mathcal{E}$. Our domain of objects contains five colored blocks and a balance scale: $\{r, y, b, g, p, s\}$.[1]

At the outset of the task, the block weights are unknown to the participants. Hence, both the EBank and the FBank are empty, since there is nothing evidenced or known. Because finding the value of each block weight is part of the goal, these unknowns constitute the propositions known as "Questions under Discussion" (QUDs), and what we also refer to here as QBank. For all objects in the domain relating to the task, questions are generated for each relation implicated in the task for that object. Because the weight of a block ranges between 10 and 50 g, in 10-gram intervals we have five possible values, expressed as yes/no questions. The initial value of the QBank results in the following set:

(9) $\text{QBank} = \{Eq(r, 10)?, \ldots, Eq(r, 50)?, \ldots \ldots Eq(p, 50)?\}$

As the task proceeds, the participants try weighing different blocks and discuss their relative weights. When they make observations through their actions, they discover evidence in favor of propositions that are marked as questions in the QBank. As mentioned above, the mechanism available for updating the agents' common ground are through either a public announcement or by witnessing an action. We consider each of these in turn.

Public Announcements. Following [38] and subsequent developments of Public Announcement Logic [2], the operator $!\phi$ is used to represent the action of announcing ϕ publicly. The effect of such an announcement is that all agents update their knowledge states by eliminating worlds (possible states of affairs) where ϕ does not hold. If $[!\varphi]$ represents the act of announcing φ, then $[!\varphi]\psi$ means "after φ is announced, then ψ is believed to be the case." When a participant, P_i, in a group activity makes a statement relating to an observation, we say that P_i publicly announces $\mathcal{M} \models [!\psi]\phi$ if and only if $\mathcal{M}, w \models \phi$, where $\mathcal{M}|_\psi$ is the model $\mathcal{M}$ restricted to the worlds where ψ is true.

Witnessing of Events. When a participant, P_i, performs an act resulting in φ, in the co-presence of another participant, P_j, we say that P_i performs a publicly perceived act and result, φ. If α_i is an act performed by P_i, then $[\alpha_i]\varphi$ means "after i performs α, φ is the result." Hence, if multiple agents are co-attentive (co-perceptive) to the act, α, then a public witnessing is brought about by an act being performed, where the co-perception is represented as $S_{i,j}[\alpha]\varphi$.

In order to distinguish perceptual evidence for φ from belief in φ, we relativize the impact of a statement to the perceptual or inferential context within which it is uttered. Let us interpret $[!\varphi]\psi$ as follows.

(10) a. *Update with Evidence*:
         $[!\varphi][E]\psi$: Given the announcement of φ, there is evidence for ψ;

---

[1] The blocks are uniquely colored as: red (r), yellow (y), blue (b), green (g), and purple (p). The scale is denoted as s.

   b. *Update with Belief:*
      $[E]\varphi \rightarrow [!\varphi][B]\psi$: Belief in φ is conditionalized on φ's announcement in the prior context of evidence for φ.
   c. *Seeing provides Evidence:* If a participating agent, i, perceives an action, a, occur, then i has some evidence, E_P, that a has occurred, $\langle a \rangle \varphi$.
      $[S_i]\langle a \rangle \varphi \rightarrow [E_{P_i}]\varphi$
   d. *Non-contradictory Evidence provides Belief:* If a participating agent, P_i, has multiple non-contradicting evidences, E, for an action, a, occurring, $\langle a \rangle \varphi$, then P_i believes φ.
      $([E]\langle a \rangle \varphi \wedge \textbf{fip}) \rightarrow B\phi_a$

Fig. 4. P_2, P_3 co-perceive the laptop, P_1 perceives scale/blocks. Green arrow symbolizes gazing, red arrows denotes cogazing. (Color figure online)

Fig. 5. P_1, P_2 co-perceive the scale/blocks, P_3 perceives the laptop. (Color figure online)

Semantically, an update represents the state of affairs after an announcement. This entails transforming the current model by removing all states where the announced formula is false. With evidence distinguished from belief/knowledge, we also update the evidence function, where $[!\varphi]$:

(11) a. Updates the worlds: $W' = W \cap \varphi$
      b. Updates the Evidence function: $E'(w) = E(w) \cap \varphi$
      c. $(M, w) \models \varphi$ implies $(M|_\varphi, w) \models [E]\psi$

This update actually changes the underlying evidence sets themselves. The announcement is taken as a piece of direct evidence. Hence, to capture that the announcement of φ becomes evidence and not just belief, the evidence sets for each agent get restricted (or updated) to reflect the worlds where φ is true. Subsequently, the belief function will then naturally adjust based on the new evidence sets.

Operationally, after (10a) is run, the model is relativized to evidencing neighborhoods, where φ is true. This corresponds to moving a proposition from the QBank to the EBank. Then, if the same proposition is "announced" again, as with an *ACCEPT* move, then (10b) promotes that proposition from the EBank to the FBank.

5   Common Ground Tracking

To illustrate the effect of the epistemic and evidential update functions outlined above, let us consider a joint activity scenario in Figs. 4, 5, 6, 7, 8 and 9. In Figs. 4 and 5, P_1 places the blue block on the left scale and the red block on the right scale. Subsequently, all three participants observe the equilibrium of the scales (Fig. 6). P_3 then issues a public declaration regarding the balanced state of the scales (Fig. 7), followed by a concurring public declaration from P_1 (Fig. 8).

Fig. 6. P_1, P_2 and P_3 co-perceive scale/blocks. (Color figure online)

Fig. 7. P_1, P_2 and P_3 co-perceive scale/blocks. (Color figure online)

Fig. 8. P_1, P_2 and P_3 co-perceive scale/blocks. (Color figure online)

Fig. 9. P_1,P_2 and P_3 co-perceive scale/blocks. P_2 leans towards table. (Color figure online)

Now assume that **b** refers to "the scales are balanced". Then, since S_{p_1}**b**, S_{p_2}**b**, S_{p_3}**b** we have a co-attention, CS **b**. Grounded in the axiom "Seeing provides Evidence," this observation serves as perceptual evidence for all three participants, manifested as $E_{P_{p_1}}$ **b**, $E_{P_{p_2}}$ **b**, $E_{P_{p_3}}$ **b**, thus constituting a collective evidence of perception, denoted as CE_P **b**. Subsequently, Participant P_3 publicly announces that the scales are balanced ([!**b**]), providing further for **b** being true. Given the interpretive nature of announcements as indicative of belief, this declaration also implies that P_3 believes **b**, expressed as B_{p_3} **b**. This announcement is subsequently publicly affirmed by Participant P_1, indicating not only possession of evidence for this proposition, but also belief in it, articulated as B_{p_1} **b**. P_2 abstains from expressing public concurrence or objection to P_3's announcement, yet his active engagement in the collaborative endeavor implies a lack of contradictory evidence against CE_P **b**. Relying on the axiom "Non-contradictory

Evidence provides Belief," this participatory posture, coupled with the absence of contradictory evidence, leads to the inference that P_2 also subscribes to the belief in **b**. Consequently, a shared belief among all participants ensues, denoted as CB_P **b**.

The entirety of this process also contributes to the updating of common ground banks. Prior to the placement of the blocks onto the scale by P_1, all three participants maintained a shared belief that the red block weighed 10 g, thereby establishing its inclusion within the Fbank. Meanwhile, the weight of the blue block remained a query within the Qbank. Upon their observation of the balanced scale, each participant acquires a new piece of evidence, which is subsequently updated within the Ebank. The public announcement by P_3 and the subsequent public agreement by P_1 signify not only the possession of evidence supporting their respective statements but also a belief in said statements. Furthermore, as elucidated previously, P_2 also subscribes to the belief in **b**. Through inference that the scale is balanced and that the red block occupies one side while the blue block occupies the other, a logical deduction emerges: the weight of the blue block equals that of the red block, thereby also amounting to 10 g. This inference constitutes evidence for each participant, denoted as $E_{I_{p_2}}(b = 10)$, $E_{I_{p_1}}(b = 10)$, and $E_{I_{p_3}}(b = 10)$, where $b = 10$ signifies the proposition that the weight of the blue block is 10 g. This shared belief among the three participants is subsequently updated within the Fbank.

6   Annotations

6.1   Annotating Multimodal Modalities

Gesture Annotation. Gesture AMR is employed for the detailed annotation of gestures within our study. Each instance of Gesture AMR systematically categorizes content-bearing gestures into four distinct "gesture acts": deictic, iconic, emblematic, and metaphoric. Additionally, it meticulously records the gesturer, addressee, and semantic content conveyed by each gesture. In our methodology, we utilize the ELAN [57] software platform[2] where distinct tracks are designated for each speaker, facilitating the systematic analysis of gesture interactions. For instance, in Fig. 1, P_1 is observed directing attention of P_2 and P_3 towards the blocks and scale by means of pointing. The representation of this gesture is also within the figure.

Speech Annotation. The process of speech annotation encompasses transcription, speaker diarization, and segmentation into discrete utterances. The utterances are systematically integrated into corresponding tracks within ELAN, with

---

[2] ELAN serves as an annotation tool designed for the enhancement of audio and video recordings. It facilitates users in incorporating an extensive array of textual annotations onto audio and/or video recordings. These annotations may encompass sentences, individual words or glosses, comments, translations, or descriptions of observed features within the media.

distinct tracks designated for each speaker. Additionally, these speech transcripts underwent further refinement through dense paraphrasing [52], wherein sentence information and action annotations are amalgamated to enhance clarity by substituting pronouns with more explicit references within the original sentences (see Fig. 7).

Action Annotation. The actions executed by participants are systematically annotated within our study. We operate within a distinctly limited set of predicates suitable for modeling participant actions, primarily encompassing "putting" and "lifting." Additionally, we employ prepositions such as "on," "in," or "at," which delineate specific spatial relations within the VoxML framework [50]. For instance, in Fig. 4, P_1 is observed placing the red block on the right scale, and the annotation is put(Red, on(RightScale)).

Gaze Annotation. The orientation of eye gaze represents a pivotal marker demarcating the focal point of an individual's attentional engagement [14]. Consequently, we incorporate eye gaze direction as an additional source of evidence to discern whether a participant is attentively engaged in the experimental procedure or experiencing distraction. In Fig. 2, we use red arrows to indicate that P_1, P_2 and P_3 are all gazing at the scale/blocks.

Body Posture Annotation. Body postures represents a fundamental component of nonverbal communication, serving as conduits through which profound insights into people's internal states, such as, their engagement towards a joint activity [58]. Consequently, we integrate body posture within our multimodal annotation framework to discern whether participants are actively engaged in the experimental task, or experiencing boredom or agitation. In Fig. 2, the utilization of a blue arrow symbolizes P_2's inclination forward, indicative of a deliberate effort to scrutinize the scale closely. This behavior suggests an increased level of engagement with the experiment of the participant.

6.2 Common Ground Annotation

Building upon the multimodal annotations gathered in the preceding section, we conducted move-by-move tracking of the group's collective view of evidence and acceptance of task-relevant facts by introducing an additional layer of "common ground annotations" (CGA). The annotation process within the dialogue entails the identification of categories pertaining to participants' cognitive states, actions, and beliefs pertaining to the task at hand. These categories encompass: (a) OBSERVATION: participant P_i has perceived an action, a; (b) INFERENCE: deduction from φ; (c) STATEMENT: announcement of evidence φ; (d) QUESTION: introducing an interrogative role relating to φ; (e) ANSWER; supplying a filler to question about φ; (f) ACCEPT: agree with evidence φ; (g) DOUBT: negative evidence for φ.

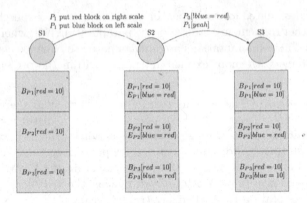

Fig. 10. Scenario: 3 participants engaged in determining weight of blue block.

Figure 10 illustrates an interaction depicted in Figs. 4, 5, 6, 7, 8 and 9, where s_1, s_2, and s_3 denote discrete states within the real world, with corresponding frames below each state, depicting the mental states of the three participants. P_1 places the blue and red blocks on opposing sides of the scale, resulting in a collective observation by all three participants of the scale balancing. Subsequently, they collectively extract a singular piece of information from this observation in the second mental state. Following this, the public announcements made by both P_3 and P_1 reflect their beliefs in the balanced state of the scale. As described in Sect. 4, in the absence of overt verbal or nonverbal cues indicating dissent towards P_3's announcement, P_2 conforms to the beliefs posited by both P_1 and P_3. Consequently, a common ground is established. The annotation of the common ground within the scenario is depicted in Fig. 11:

```
COMMON GROUND ANNOTATION
O1: OBSERVATION: on(RedBlock,  LeftScale) and on(BlueBlock,
    → RightScale) and Scale: lean(Zero)
I1: INFERENCE-FROM (O1 and red = 10 )
S1:  STATEMENT( red = blue = 10)
ACCEPT(S1)
```

Fig. 11. Common Ground Annotation of Fig. 10

Common ground annotation focuses on propositions describing situations or facts contributed to the formation of shared belief among participants of a joint activity and the evidence for them as the dialogue progresses. Hence, in Fig. 11, action annotation is excluded from the common ground annotation. Instead, observations, inferences providing evidence for updating common ground, and statements incorporating propositions describing situations are all encompassed within the common ground annotation framework.

7   Classification of Belief in Multimodal HCI

In the example sequence given in Figs. 4, 5, 6, 7, 8 and 9, we can see how different modalities contribute to reviewing of pieces of evidence and the implicit and explicit construction of common ground.

1. In Fig. 4, P_1 puts the red block on the right side of the scale (from the perspective of the camera). At this time, both P_2 and P_3 are co-attending to the laptop, and may not have seen this action take place, or its result (the tilt of the scale).
2. Fig. 5. P_1 concludes the action from above ($put(Red, on(RightScale))$), but now P_2's gaze direction has shifted to the scale and the blocks. Under the assumption that gaze direction automatically equates to observing all visual content within the field of view, all three participants are now able to make the observation that the red block is on the right side of the scale ($on(Red, RightScale)$).
3. Fig. 6. P_1 puts the blue block on the left side of the scale. All three participants are now co-attending to the blocks and scale, and so all make the observation ($on(Blue, RightScale)$). It is important to note that at this step, according to our model, no evidence has been reviewed and no inference has yet been made.
4. In Fig. 7 all three participants, still co-attending to the scale, are able to observe that it is not leaning substantially to either side. P_3 makes this explicit with his utterance "It [the scale] seems pretty balanced", which is considered to be a statement of the proposition $red = blue$, and elevates this proposition into the EBank, as something that is evidenced but not yet agreed upon.
5. Subsequently (Fig. 8), P_1 says "Yeah", which is taken to be agreement with the above statement, thus elevating $red = blue$ to the FBank.
6. No one says anything in Fig. 9, but under a model where transitive closure takes place, an inference can be made that $blue \triangleq 10$, even though the numerical value is never explicitly stated in the dialogue. This is in fact confirmed by the next utterance in the sequence (not shown), in which P_1 says, "Okay, so now we know that this [blue block] is also ten."

A couple of points should be noted regarding parameters of the model that affect when and how different kinds of evidencing is conducted. Many philosophical schools debate the level of epistemic validity to be assigned to direct perception vs. inference. Here we assume both to be equally valid (see Sect. 4), meaning that the inference in Fig. 9 would be directly elevated to FBank, but under other specifications of the model, this may not be the case. Additionally, we make an assumption here that gaze direction automatically means observation of content under that gaze, but under certain other assumptions (e.g., such as one in which all participants are not assumed to be paying close attention unless otherwise indicated), this would be softened. Finally, in Fig. 8, P_2 could have disagreed but didn't, and subsequently leans in toward the experimental apparatus. This is taken to be implicit agreement with P_1/P_3's positioning, but this need not always be the case, and other models may require explicit acceptance by all parties to elevate a proposition from EBank to FBank.

8   Conclusion and Future Work

In this paper we have argued for the importance of Simulation Theory of Mind (SToM), encoded as an evidence-based dynamic epistemic logic (EB-DEL) for HCI particularly in the context of a multimodal task-oriented joint activity. We outlined a theory of perceptually-driven belief updating for multi-agent cooperative task completion. We extended the evidence-based dynamic epistemic logic from [6] to account for how perceptual evidence and inference interact and can cascade into strengthening an agent (or group) epistemic attitude towards a proposition, for updating the common ground. This subsequently provides situation-based epistemic data for tracking the common ground through a dialogue, by integrating the contributions of different modalities toward modeling the cognitive states of the group. Namely, by extracting the propositions expressed, and building common ground structures as the group proceeds through the task, our model holds potential for deployment in the creation of artificial agents proficient in simulating real-world situational settings. These agents would be adept at recording, adhering to, and comprehending common ground within collaborative activities. Such agents could find application in environments such as classrooms, where they can effectively monitor the collective knowledge of a group and foster productive collaborations [54].

By integrating ToM and common ground tracking into conversational agent architectures, we can better model the beliefs of participants by exposing unspoken assumptions of the participants or disagreements among them. Enhancing the epistemic modeling capabilities of multimodal HCI with ToM may also inform research in both Affective Computing, e.g., automatic emotion detection, by providing more contextualized interpretations of cognitive states and emotions in dialogue, and in providing support for those with functional impairments.

Acknowledgements. This work was supported in part by NSF grant DRL 2019805, to Dr. Pustejovsky at Brandeis University, and Dr. Krishnaswamy at Colorado State University. It was also supported in part by NSF grant CNS 2033932 to Dr. Pustejovsky. We would like to thank the reviewers for their comments and suggestions. The views expressed herein are ours alone.

References

1. Asher, N.: Common ground, corrections and coordination. J. Semant. **15**, 239–299 (1998)
2. Baltag, A., Moss, L.S., Solecki, S.: The logic of public announcements, common knowledge, and private suspicions. In: Arló-Costa, H., Hendricks, V.F., van Benthem, J. (eds.) Readings in Formal Epistemology. SGTP, vol. 1, pp. 773–812. Springer, Cham (2016). https://doi.org/10.1007/978-3-319-20451-2_38

3. Barsalou, L.W.: Perceptions of perceptual symbols. Behav. Brain Sci. **22**(4), 637–660 (1999)

4. Belle, V., Bolander, T., Herzig, A., Nebel, B.: Epistemic planning: perspectives on the special issue. Artif. Intell. **316**, 103842 (2023)

5. van Benthem, J., Fernández-Duque, D., Pacuit, E.: Evidence and plausibility in neighborhood structures. Ann. Pure Appl. Logic **165**(1), 106–133 (2014)

6. van Benthem, J., Pacuit, E.: Dynamic logics of evidence-based beliefs. Stud. Logica. **99**, 61–92 (2011)

7. Bolander, T.: Seeing is believing: formalising false-belief tasks in dynamic epistemic logic. In: Jaakko Hintikka on Knowledge and Game-theoretical Semantics, pp. 207–236 (2018)

8. Bolander, T., Andersen, M.B.: Epistemic planning for single-and multi-agent systems. J. Appl. Non-Classical Logics **21**(1), 9–34 (2011)

9. Bolander, T., Jensen, M.H., Schwarzentruber, F.: Complexity results in epistemic planning. In: IJCAI, pp. 2791–2797 (2015)

10. Brutti, R., Donatelli, L., Lai, K., Pustejovsky, J.: Abstract meaning Representation for gesture. In: Proceedings of the Thirteenth Language Resources and Evaluation Conference, pp. 1576–1583. European Language Resources Association, Marseille, France, June 2022

11. Clark, H.H., Brennan, S.E.: Grounding in communication. Perspect. Socially Shared Cogn. **13**(1991), 127–149 (1991)

12. Dautenhahn, K.: Socially intelligent robots: dimensions of human-robot interaction. Philos. Trans. R. Soc. B: Biol. Sci. **362**(1480), 679–704 (2007)

13. De Groote, P.: Type raising, continuations, and classical logic. In: Proceedings of the Thirteenth Amsterdam Colloquium, pp. 97–101 (2001)

14. Dey, I., Puntambekar, S.: Examining nonverbal interactions to better understand collaborative learning. In: Proceedings of the 16th International Conference on Computer-Supported Collaborative Learning-CSCL 2023, pp. 273–276. International Society of the Learning Sciences (2023)

15. Dissing, L., Bolander, T.: Implementing theory of mind on a robot using dynamic epistemic logic. In: IJCAI, pp. 1615–1621 (2020)

16. Eijck, J.: Perception and change in update logic. In: van Eijck, J., Verbrugge, R. (eds.) Games, Actions and Social Software. LNCS, vol. 7010, pp. 119–140. Springer, Heidelberg (2012). https://doi.org/10.1007/978-3-642-29326-9_7

17. Feldman, J.: Embodied language, best-fit analysis, and formal compositionality. Phys. Life Rev. **7**(4), 385–410 (2010)

18. Feldman, R.: Respecting the evidence. Philos. Perspect. **19**, 95–119 (2005)

19. Geib, C., George, D., Khalid, B., Magnotti, R., Stone, M.: An integrated architecture for common ground in collaboration (2022)

20. Gianotti, M., Patti, A., Vona, F., Pentimalli, F., Barbieri, J., Garzotto, F.: Multimodal interaction for persons with autism: the 5A case study. In: Antona, M., Stephanidis, C. (eds.) Universal Access in Human-Computer Interaction, HCII 2023. LNCS, vol. 14020, pp. 581–600. Springer, Cham (2023). https://doi.org/10.1007/978-3-031-35681-0_38

21. Ginzburg, J.: Interrogatives: Questions, Facts and Dialogue. The Handbook of Contemporary Semantic Theory, pp. 359–423. Blackwell, Oxford (1996)

22. Ginzburg, J.: The Interactive Stance: Meaning for Conversation. OUP, Oxford (2012)

23. Goldman, A.I.: In defense of the simulation theory. Mind Lang. **7**(1–2), 104–119 (1992)

24. Goldman, A.I.: Simulating Minds: The Philosophy, Psychology, and Neuroscience of Mindreading. Oxford University Press, Oxford (2006)

25. Gopnik, A.: How we know our minds: the illusion of first-person knowledge of intentionality. Behav. Brain Sci. **16**(1), 1–14 (1993)

26. Gordon, R.M.: Folk psychology as simulation. Mind Lang. **1**(2), 158–171 (1986)

27. Heal, J.: Simulation, Theory, and Content. Theories of Theories of Mind, pp. 75–89 (1996)

28. Henderson, M., Thomson, B., Williams, J.D.: The second dialog state tracking challenge. In: Proceedings of the 15th Annual Meeting of the Special Interest Group on Discourse and Dialogue (SIGDIAL), pp. 263–272 (2014)

29. Khebour, I., et al.: The weights task dataset: a multimodal dataset of collaboration in a situated task. J. Open Humanities Data **10** (2024)

30. Kolve, E., et al.: AI2-THOR: an interactive 3D environment for visual AI. arXiv preprint arXiv:1712.05474 (2017)

31. Krishnaswamy, N., et al.: Diana's World: a situated multimodal interactive agent. In: AAAI Conference on Artificial Intelligence (AAAI): Demos Program. AAAI (2020)

32. Krishnaswamy, N., Pustejovsky, J.: VoxSim: a visual platform for modeling motion language. In: Proceedings of COLING 2016, The 26th International Conference on Computational Linguistics: Technical Papers. ACL (2016)

33. Krishnaswamy, N., Pustejovsky, J.: Multimodal continuation-style architectures for human-robot interaction. arXiv preprint arXiv:1909.08161 (2019)

34. Krshnaswamy, N., Pickard, W., Cates, B., Blanchard, N., Pustejovsky, J.: Vox-World platform for multimodal embodied agents. In: LREC Proceedings, vol. 13 (2022)

35. Miller, P.W.: Body language in the classroom. Tech. Connecting Educ. Careers **80**(8), 28–30 (2005)

36. Narayanan, S.: Mind changes: a simulation semantics account of counterfactuals. Cognitive Science (2010)

37. Pacuit, E.: Neighborhood Semantics for Modal Logic. Springer, Cham (2017). https://doi.org/10.1007/978-3-319-67149-9

38. Plaza, J.: Logics of public communications. In: Proceedings 4th International Symposium on Methodologies for Intelligent Systems, pp. 201–216 (1989)

39. Premack, D., Woodruff, G.: Does the chimpanzee have a theory of mind? Behav. Brain Sci. **1**(4), 515–526 (1978)

40. Pustejovsky, J., Krishnaswamy, N.: VoxML: a visualization modeling language. arXiv preprint arXiv:1610.01508 (2016)

41. Pustejovsky, J., Krishnaswamy, N.: Embodied human computer interaction. KI-Künstliche Intelligenz **35**(3–4), 307–327 (2021)

42. Pustejovsky, J., Krishnaswamy, N.: The role of embodiment and simulation in evaluating HCI: theory and framework. In: Duffy, V.G. (ed.) HCII 2021. LNCS, vol. 12777, pp. 288–303. Springer, Cham (2021). https://doi.org/10.1007/978-3-030-77817-0_21

43. Radu, I., Tu, E., Schneider, B.: Relationships between body postures and collaborative learning states in an augmented reality study. In: Bittencourt, I., Cukurova, M., Muldner, K., Luckin, R., Millán, E. (eds.) Artificial Intelligence in Education: 21st International Conference, AIED 2020, Ifrane, Morocco, 6–10 July 2020, Proceedings, Part II 21, pp. 257–262. Springer, Cham (2020). https://doi.org/10.1007/978-3-030-52240-7_47

44. Savva, M., et al.: Habitat: a platform for embodied AI research. In: Proceedings of the IEEE/CVF International Conference on Computer Vision, pp. 9339–9347 (2019)
45. Schneider, B., Pea, R.: Does seeing one another's gaze affect group dialogue? A computational approach. J. Learn. Analytics **2**(2), 107–133 (2015)
46. Sousa, A., Young, K., D'aquin, M., Zarrouk, M., Holloway, J.: Introducing CALMED: multimodal annotated dataset for emotion detection in children with autism. In: Antona, M., Stephanidis, C. (eds.) International Conference on Human-Computer Interaction, pp. 657–677. Springer, Cham (2023). https://doi.org/10.1007/978-3-031-35681-0_43
47. Stalnaker, R.: Common ground. Linguist. Philos. **25**(5–6), 701–721 (2002)
48. Sun, C., Shute, V.J., Stewart, A., Yonehiro, J., Duran, N., D'Mello, S.: Towards a generalized competency model of collaborative problem solving. Comput. Educ. **143**, 103672 (2020)
49. Suzuki, R., Karim, A., Xia, T., Hedayati, H., Marquardt, N.: Augmented reality and robotics: a survey and taxonomy for AR-enhanced human-robot interaction and robotic interfaces. In: Proceedings of the 2022 CHI Conference on Human Factors in Computing Systems, pp. 1–33 (2022)
50. Tam, C., Brutti, R., Lai, K., Pustejovsky, J.: Annotating situated actions in dialogue. In: Proceedings of the 4th International Workshop on Designing Meaning Representation (2023)
51. Tolzin, A., Körner, A., Dickhaut, E., Janson, A., Rummer, R., Leimeister, J.M.: Designing pedagogical conversational agents for achieving common ground. In: Gerber, A., Baskerville, R. (eds.) International Conference on Design Science Research in Information Systems and Technology, pp. 345–359. Springer, Cham (2023). https://doi.org/10.1007/978-3-031-32808-4_22
52. Tu, J., Rim, K., Pustejovsky, J.: Competence-based question generation. In: Proceedings of the 29th International Conference on Computational Linguistics, pp. 1521–1533 (2022)
53. Van Fraassen, C.: Belief and the will. J. Philos. **81**(5), 235–256 (1984)
54. VanderHoeven, H., et al.: Multimodal design for interactive collaborative problem-solving support. In: HCII 2024. Springer, Cham (2024)
55. Wellman, H.M., Carey, S., Gleitman, L., Newport, E.L., Spelke, E.S.: The Child's Theory of Mind. The MIT Press, Cambridge (1990)
56. Wimmer, H., Perner, J.: Beliefs about beliefs: representation and constraining function of wrong beliefs in young children's understanding of deception. Cognition **13**(1), 103–128 (1983)
57. Wittenburg, P., Brugman, H., Russel, A., Klassmann, A., Sloetjes, H.: ELAN: a professional framework for multimodality research. In: 5th LREC 2006, pp. 1556–1559 (2006)
58. Won, A.S., Bailenson, J.N., Janssen, J.H.: Automatic detection of nonverbal behavior predicts learning in dyadic interactions. IEEE Trans. Affect. Comput. **5**(2), 112–125 (2014)
59. Xia, F., Zamir, A.R., He, Z., Sax, A., Malik, J., Savarese, S.: Gibson ENV: real-world perception for embodied agents. In: Proceedings of the IEEE Conference on Computer Vision And Pattern Recognition, pp. 9068–9079 (2018)

Emotions in HCI

Of Politics, Behavior and Commands: Processing Information Unspoken for Sentiment Analysis and Spoken Interaction Applications

Christina Alexandris[1,2]([✉]), Georgios Trachanas[1], and Savvas Chatzipanayiotidis[1,2]

[1] National and Kapodistrian University of Athens, Athens, Greece
calexandris@gs.uoa.gr, cs2210025@di.uoa.gr, its_savvas@yahoo.com
[2] European Communication Institute (ECI), Danube University Krems, Krems an der Donau, Austria

Abstract. The registration and processing of information not uttered contributes to the enrichment of data in HCI applications and other forms of spoken interaction, including subtle emotions in Sentiment Analysis-Opinion Mining and, also, additional implementation in spoken commands i.e. for technical texts. The present approach and interactive application target to account for the new insights and factors and their integration into knowledge graphs with subsequent use in training data and neural networks. The main focus is on the data preparation stage for subsequent extensive implementation and quantitative evaluation. Insights from crowd-sourced data enable a differentiation between perceived linguistic and paralinguistic information not uttered compatible to language-specific and socio-cultural norms and perceived linguistic and paralinguistic information not uttered that is either strictly circumstantial/individual-specific or strictly domain/context dependent. The latter also applies to spoken commands. This, subsequently, enables a differentiation between circumstantial factors/evidence and socio-culturally-biased factors/evidence in data analysis and training data and its integration in knowledge graphs, outlining the distinct types of implementation for the enrichment of models and refining NLP tasks.

Keywords: Knowledge Graphs · implied information · Sentiment Analysis · Opinion Mining · spoken commands

1 Unspoken Information, Perception and Sensitivity

1.1 Introduction

The present approach is based on the use of knowledge graphs, generated by an interactive application presented in related/previous research [6, 7, 26] that involve the depiction of two main categories of information not uttered in spoken interaction, converting it into "visible" and processable information.

This unspoken information concerns: (I) Additional perceived information content and dimensions of –notably– very common words – information not registered in language resources, it may include context-specific socio-cultural associations and Cognitive Bias, in particular, Lexical Bias (a) [38] and/or implied domain-specific information

M. Kurosu and A. Hashizume (Eds.): HCII 2024, LNCS 14684, pp. 229–246, 2024.
https://doi.org/10.1007/978-3-031-60405-8_15

(b) (II) Perceived paralinguistic elements influencing the information content of spoken utterances.

Both types of perceived information are purposefully or subconsciously conveyed or perceived-understood by speakers-participants in the same language community. In the presented knowledge graphs, this additional information of the above-described categories (I) and (II) is linked as an additional node to the spoken word with the proposed "Context" relation. The knowledge graphs can, subsequently, be converted into vectors and other forms of training data, which is targeted to contain (a) "visible" and processable information not uttered in spoken interaction and (b) multiple versions and varieties of training data with perceived information generated by the implemented interactive application [6, 7, 26]. We note that applications such as Sentiment Analysis-Opinion Mining typically do not integrate the above-described types of information, since they mostly rely on word groups, word sequences and/or sentiment lexica, including recent approaches with the use of neural networks [9, 18, 21, 33].

Here, the knowledge graph data, with subsequent use in vectors and other forms of training data [24, 25, 37, 39] are intended, at least in the present stage, as a dataset for training a neural network, with the possibility of conversion in Graph Neural Networks [44]. The conversion of knowledge graphs into training data contributes to the integration and processing of complex information and information not uttered in Natural Language Processing (NLP) tasks, thus, contributing to the creation of even more sophisticated systems. This possibility would not be considered if the above-referred characteristic research work [24, 25, 37, 39] were not accomplished. The very nature and structure of knowledge graphs allows the representation of multiple facets of information – the multiple facets of the "Sense" of the words and/or transcribed video speech segments (although it is considered that there may exist some types of information/some cases that may not have 100% coverage by a knowledge graph). The detecting and processing of information not uttered but perceived-sensed by speakers-participants allows the integration of additional information content – meanings/senses- in training data.

1.2 Previous Research: Interactive Generation of Knowledge Graphs with Unspoken Information in Journalism Applications

In previous research, the integration of additional information content – meanings/senses- in training data in applications involving Journalism allows the enrichment of data and a deeper understanding of speaker-participant psychology-mentality and sensitivities, contributing to a deeper understanding of the possible impact or consequences of a spoken journalistic/political text or interview or a video in Social Media (a). This also allows an additional approach to registering of cause-result relations on a discourse basis, including the monitoring of Fairness, namely that all voices-aspects-opinions are heard clearly –that all participants are given a fair chance in the interview or discussion and are not purposefully or unconsciously repressed, oppressed, offended or even bullied (b).

The way sensitive topics and speaker-participant sensitivity are purposefully or unconsciously treated and managed contributes to registering and monitoring fairness in spoken interaction [3], avoiding Confidence Bias [17]. In particular, a crucial element in achieving "visibility" and, subsequently, "processability" of information not uttered is causality, namely the registration and processing of reactions triggered by that very information not uttered - the multiple facets of the "Sense" of the words in transcribed video and speech segments and in Social Media. These reactions to questions and statements in interviews, discussions and posts include subtle negative reactions in the Plutchik Wheel of Emotions, namely "Apprehension", "Annoyance", "Disapproval", "Contempt", "Aggressiveness" [30] - emotions usually too subtle to be easily extracted by sensor and/or speech signal data [8, 16, 31, 43]. Additionally, the detecting and processing of information not uttered (often emotionally "sensitive" information) contributes in Sentiment Analysis (and Opinion Mining) applications where spoken data and/or videos are processed (Fig. 1).

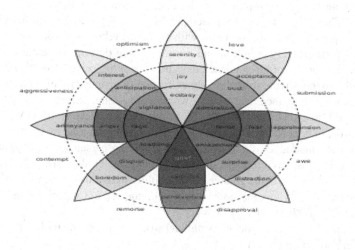

Fig. 1. The Plutchik Wheel of Emotions.

Perceived Main Topics and "Sensitive" Words in Dialogue Structure. In our previous research [4, 7, 8], a processing and evaluation framework was proposed for the generation of graphic representations and tags corresponding to values and benchmarks depicting, among other features, the degree of information not uttered and non-neutral elements in Speaker behavior in spoken text segments in the dialog flow. The concept of the generated graphic representations originates from the Discourse Tree prototype [23], however, the characteristics of spontaneous turn-taking [42] and short spoken speech segments did not facilitate the implementation of typical strategies based on Rhetorical Structure Theory (RST) [10, 35, 46]. In contrast, strategies typically employed in the construction of most Spoken Dialog Systems were adapted in an interactive annotation tool designed to operate with most commercial transcription tools [7, 8, 26]. These strategies include keyword processing in the form of topic detection from which approaches involving neural networks are developed [19, 41]. The output provides the User-(Journalist) with: (i) the tracked indications of the topics handled in the interview/discussion (and the perceived relations between the topics), (ii) the graphic pattern of the discourse structure of the interview/discussion, (iii) functions and respective values reflecting the degree of tension ("TENSION" Module) and/or the degree in which the speakers-participants address/avoid the topics in the dialog structure ("RELEVANCE" Module) [4, 26]. The features in the functions (iii) are identified by a set of criteria based on the Gricean Cooperative Principle [13, 14] (including paralinguistic elements).

Generated graphical representations of perceived word-topic relations ("Association", Generalization", "Topic Switch", "Repetition" [4, 26]) and registered word types concerning Cognitive Bias – Lexical Bias ("Gravity" and "Evocative" words [2]) can be converted into sequences for their subsequent conversion into knowledge graphs or other forms of data for neural networks and Machine Learning applications [24, 25, 37, 39]. "Gravity" and "Evocative" words [2] in the registered spoken interaction concern inherent yet subtle socio-culturally determined linguistic features in (notably) commonly occurring words (examples from the international community: (the) "people", (our) "sea"). These word types are detectable from the registered reactions [26] they trigger in the processed dialog segment with two (or multiple) speakers-participants. Since these words are very common and do not contain descriptive features, the subtlety of their content is often unconsciously used or is perceived (mostly) by native speakers and may contribute to the degree of formality or intensity of conveyed information in a spoken utterance. Here, these words concerning Cognitive Bias – Lexical Bias are referred to as "Gravity" words [2]. In other cases, these word types, although common words, may contribute to a descriptive or emotional tone in an utterance and they may play a remarkable role in interactions involving persuasion and negotiations. Specifically, it is considered that, according to Rockledge et al., 2018 [32], "the more extremely positive the word, the greater the probability individuals were to associate that word with persuasion". Here, this word category connected to Cognitive Bias – Lexical Bias is referred to as "Evocative" words [2].

We note that the subtle impact of (singular) words is one of the tools typically used in persuasion and negotiations [12, 34].

As described in previous research [8], registered "Gravity" and "Evocative" words are appended as marked values with "&" in the respective tuples or triple tuples. In the sequences with the respective tuples or triple tuples, the "&" indication is converted into a "CONTEXT" relation.

In the knowledge graphs, this additional information is linked as an additional node to the spoken word with the proposed "Context" relation. The term "Context" is chosen to signalize the perceived context of additional information in the form of co-occurring linguistic and/or paralinguistic features, influencing the information content of the spoken utterance and its impact in the spoken interaction and dialogue structure.

In the case of paralinguistic elements, the "Context" relation links an additional expression – a word-entity, to the word uttered, for example, a modifier, completing its perceived content. This practice is typical of professional translators and interpreters when correctness and precision is targeted [5, 20], as research and reports demonstrate. The "CONTEXT" relation connects the chosen word-topic from the speech segment with a word-expression emphasizing/complementing the spoken content such as "important" or a respective word summarizing the message. We note that the "CONTEXT" relation may link both a "Gravity"/"Evocative" word and a paralinguistic element to the word-topic of a spoken utterance (Fig. 2). If paralinguistic features depict contradictory information to the information content of the spoken utterance, the "CONTEXT" relation connects the chosen word-topic from the speech segment with a word-expression contradicting the spoken content with the expression "not really" as a special indication [4, 7, 8].

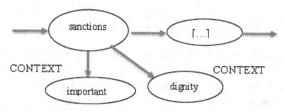

Fig. 2. Fragment of knowledge graph for perceived meaning of eyebrow-raise ("important") co-occurring with perceived main topic of utterance "sanctions" and perceived "Gravity" word "dignity" in spoken utterance [1, 6].

In the implemented interface [6], the user choses the perceived relation between word-topics with the "Topic Relation" button and signalizes "Gravity", "Evocative" words and paralinguistic elements with the respective buttons "Tension-Emotion Trigger" (W) and "Paralinguistic Info". With the "Create Graph" button of the interface, the knowledge graphs are generated [6] (Fig. 4 and Fig. 5).

2 Knowledge Graph Enrichment with Unspoken Information

2.1 Interactive Knowledge Graph Enrichment from Crowd-Sourced Data

The generated knowledge graphs from the interactively created visual representations for the same conversation and interaction may be compared to each other and be integrated in a database currently under development. Chosen relations between perceived main topics between dialogue utterances may describe Lexical Bias [38] and may differ according to political, socio-cultural and linguistic characteristics of the user-evaluator. This especially applies for international speakers/users [11, 22, 27, 28, 45], due to lack of world knowledge of the language community involved [15, 40]. In this case, it is considered that the registration of spoken interaction is dependent on user's perception and linguistic parameters and socio-cultural norms.

This allows for a finite set of data to be pre-defined for evaluation and comparison and/or it used as seed data for the enrichment of existing data sets.

However, with the extended integration of crowd-sourced input, the use of seed data for the enrichment of existing data sets does not apply in all cases. In particular, crowd-sourced input indicates that: Unspoken Information may be differently (or falsely) perceived – especially by non-native speakers of a natural language - and especially when subtle emotions in the Plutchik Wheel of Emotions, are concerned (1) [1]. Another important factor is that the perception of information not uttered may be highly dependent on random and/or circumstantial or individual-specific factors (2) [1] or the perception of unspoken information may concern only specific domains and related discourse (3)

[1]. User-specific and crowd-sourced data may be problematic due to a number of factors concerning users' perception but also users' experience and time and effort invested in providing quality data – especially when very subtle linguistic and paralinguistic features are concerned. Therefore, it is necessary for the above-described problematic aspects of user-specific - crowd-sourced data to be minimized and/or controlled.

2.2 "Context" Relation Types and the (Spoken) Word (Atmo-) "Sphere"

These observations from crowd-sourced data call for a differentiation between perceived unspoken information compatible to language-specific and socio-cultural norms and perceived unspoken information that is either strictly circumstantial or strictly domain/context dependent. Context-specific unspoken additional dimensions of individual spoken words may be described as an information (atmo) "sphere" surrounding the word, with the semantic content of the word in its nucleus, its context-specific and language-specific dimensions in the inner layer of the sphere (A) and its context-specific and non-language-specific dimensions in the outer layer of the "sphere" (B) [1].

In other words, the actual semantic content of the word as defined in dictionaries and lexica (and hence, retrievable and processable) constitutes the center-nucleus of the "sphere" and is context-independent. The perceived unspoken context-specific dimensions of the word that are dependent on the above-described linguistic parameters and socio-cultural norms (such as the previously described "Gravity" and "Evocative" words and distinctive meanings of paralinguistic features) constitute the inner layer of the "sphere" (A).

This information can constitute a finite set of pre-defined (seed) data for the enrichment of existing data sets, according to the type(s) of natural language(s) involved. It should be noted that this information may not be perceived/incorrectly perceived by non-native speakers-participants or by inexperienced speakers-participants due to age or training/background (i.e. crowd-sourced data from teenagers, users not familiar with sophisticated political speech) [1]. The perceived unspoken context-specific and non-language-specific dimensions of the word constitute the outer layer of the "sphere" (B). These non-language-specific dimensions account for information perceived by an individual as an isolated case or due to random and/or circumstantial factors of the current context.

The differentiation between context-specific dimensions of a spoken word that are language-specific and non-language-specific allows a differentiation between circumstantial factors/evidence and socio-culturally-biased factors/evidence in data analysis and training data.

The outer layer of the "sphere" also accounts for unspoken and non-language-specific dimensions of a word that are, however, domain-specific and/or related to a domain-specific discourse. For example, the word "follower" may be linked to different associations and subsequent dimensions of meanings and responses within a social media domain or within a geopolitical – war domain. Furthermore, a word not expressing sentiment/emotion may be related to domain-specific positive or negative statements, as observed in Sentiment Analysis and Opinion Mining applications [19]. A typical case are words that do not express sentiment but are connected to positive or negative statements, as registered in Sentiment Analysis and Opinion Mining. For example, in restaurant reviews, the word "waiter" often occurs in negative statements [19] (Fig. 3).

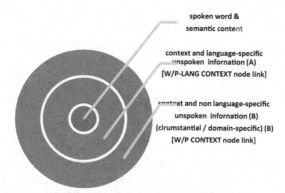

Fig. 3. (Spoken) word (Atmo) "Sphere" of linguistic and paralinguistic information not uttered and respective types of "CONTEXT" relations in knowledge graphs (Alexandris, 2023) [1].

2.3 Generation of Differentiated "Context" Relations in Knowledge Graphs

The differentiation between different types of perceived unspoken information can be linked to the "CONTEXT" relation described in previous research, where the different types of perceived information not uttered can be differentiated with distinct types of "CONTEXT" relations in the knowledge graphs. The context-specific and language-specific (A) "CONTEXT" relations employed in knowledge graph-based data are, henceforth, referred to as "W-LANG" CONTEXT relations for linguistic information not uttered, such as the additional content of "Gravity" and "Evocative" words. Additionally, the context-specific and language-specific "CONTEXT" relations are, henceforth referred to as "P-LANG" CONTEXT relations for paralinguistic information not uttered [1]. The non-language-specific/domain-specific (B) "CONTEXT" relations are, henceforth referred to as "W" CONTEXT relations for linguistic information not uttered and "P" CONTEXT relations for non-language-specific/ /domain-specific paralinguistic information [1].

This differentiation of the "Context" relations is integrated in the implemented interface and generated knowledge graphs [6], as depicted in Figs. 4 and 5.

We note that the distinct types of integration of the "Context" factor and related information in knowledge graphs outline the distinct types of implementation for enriching models and refining NLP tasks, especially when videos and multimodal data are processed. In addition to their integration in knowledge graphs, the pre-defined words can also be used as an enhanced "Bag-of-Words" approach (Seed Data) in strategies and (domain-specific) applications i.e. spoken Dialog Systems and other related Human-Computer Interaction (HCI)/Human Robot Interaction (HRI) applications.

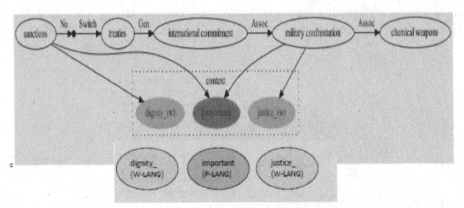

Fig. 4. Generated knowledge graph by implemented application [6] with word-topic relations ("No" answer, Topic Switch, Generalization, Association, Association) and updated "CONTEXT" node types in speech segment: "W-LANG" ("Gravity" words: "dignity", "justice") and "P-LANG" (eyebrow –raise (language-specific) information: "important").

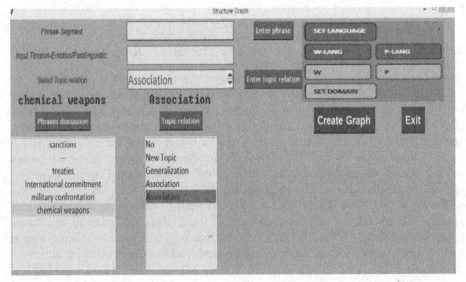

Fig. 5. Updated interface of the implemented application [6] with additional functions-buttons (W-LANG/P-LANG vs W/P) and optional domain definition/selection.

2.4 Processing Language-Specific Features in Unspoken Information

In the proposed knowledge graphs, language-specific dimensions in the inner layer of the sphere (A) include "Gravity" or "Evocative" words perceived by native speakers of a natural language that can be expressed with the W-LANG CONTEXT relation. The standard types of messages and information (and their variants) conveyed by paralinguistic features perceived by native speakers of a natural language can be expressed with the P-LANG CONTEXT relation (Fig. 6).

In regard to the language and culture-specific (standard) types of messages and information (and their variants) conveyed by paralinguistic features, examples of (interactively) annotated paralinguistic features depicting information complementing the information content of the spoken utterance are the following [2], for example: "[+ facial-expr: eyebrow-raise]" and "[+ gesture: low-hand-raise]".) or constituting "stand-alone" information [2]. In the latter case, information was interactively annotated with the insertion of a separate message or response [Message/Response]. For example, the raising of eyebrows with the interpretation "I am surprised" [and/but this surprises me] [2] was indicated as [I am surprised] (a), either as a pointer to information content or as or as a substitute of spoken information, a "stand-alone" paralinguistic feature [Message/Response: I am surprised] [2]. Alternative interpretations of the paralinguistic feature are "I am listening very carefully" (b), "What I am saying is important"(c), "I have no intention of doing otherwise" (d) [2], indicated with the respective annotations according to the parameters of the language(s) and the speaker(s) concerned.

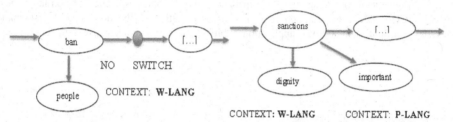

Fig. 6. Left: Fragment of knowledge graph for perceived "Evocative" word ("people"), co-occurring with topic "ban" resulting to a "No" answer and topic switch (SWITCH) in utterance segment with detected tension between speakers: context-specific and language-specific "CONTEXT: W-LANG" relation for linguistic information. Right: Fragment of knowledge graph for perceived meaning of eyebrow-raise ("important") co-occurring with topic "sanctions" and perceived "Gravity" word ("dignity") in utterance: context-specific and language-specific "CONTEXT: W-LANG" relation for linguistic information and context-specific and language-specific "CONTEXT: P-LANG" relation for paralinguistic information [1].

This type of (annotated) data for paralinguistic features constituting unspoken information may contribute to the management of problematic input in typical Data Mining and Sentiment Analysis-Opinion Mining applications, especially if the semantic content of a spoken utterance is complemented or contradicted by a gesture, facial expression, movement – or even by tone of voice. Furthermore, this type of language-specific data – linguistic features and paralinguistic features, apart from its use as seed data for Sentiment Analysis and related applications, it can also be used as a base-line for comparison and evaluation of multiple user-input, especially if the quality of the crowd-sourced data is not guaranteed. The language-specific (seed) data can also be integrated in HCI applications intended for native or near-native speakers of a particular natural language or for a defined pair or set of languages.

3   Processing Domain-Specific Unspoken Information with Knowledge Graphs: Politics and Opinion Mining

In the case of non-language-specific information that is, however, domain-specific (B), the data can be integrated in domain-specific applications. For example, in Sentiment Analysis applications for restaurant reviews, the emotionally neutral words "bill" or "waiter" are connected with the dimension-meaning of a negative statement [19] with the "CONTEXT: W" relation (Fig. 7). In other words, a positive or negative dimension may be automatically related to a word, depending on context – a feature of crucial importance in Sentiment Analysis.

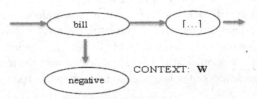

Fig. 7. Fragment of knowledge graph for perceived word: context-specific and non-language-specific "CONTEXT: W" relation for linguistic information in the domain of "Restaurant Reviews" for Sentiment Analysis applications: "bill" is marked with a negative attitude.

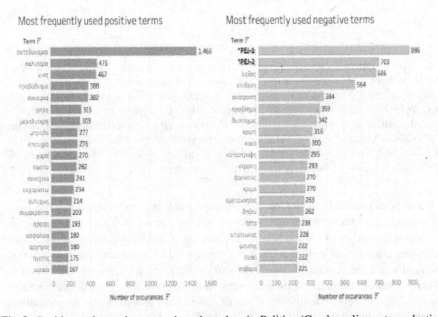

Fig. 8. Positive and negative terms in twitter data in Politics (Greek parliamentary elections) (Trachanas, 2023).

For Opinion Mining applications, a characteristic example of the integration of the "CONTEXT: W" relation for linguistic information is the domain of Politics in the pre-elections period with positive terms and negative terms in twitter data [36].

The positive and negative terms in twitter data are listed as following. Positive terms: absolute parliamentary majority (1466), better (475), victory (467), head start (388), opportunity (382), simple (315), largest (303), bravo (277), success (276), joy (270), correct(ly) (262), continuing/continuous (241), thank you (234), thankfully (214), interests (203), like(s) (193), security (180), leader (commander) (180), leader (statesman) (175), fine (well/ beautiful) (167) [36] (Fig. 8).

Negative terms: Pejorative expressions for Prime Minister (PEJ-1, PEJ-2) (886, 703), wrong - mistake (686), attack (564), overthrow (384), problem (359), unfortunately (342), crisis (316), bad/bad thing (300), catastrophe (295), shame (disgrace) (283), fascists (270), shame (pity) (270), unresentful-remorseless (263), so-called (fake) (262), defeat (238), con artists, frauds (228), liars (222), fall(s) (222), serious(ly) (221) [36] (Figs. 8 and 9).

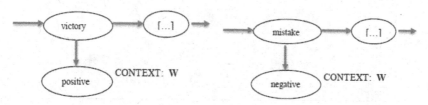

Fig. 9. Fragment of knowledge graph for perceived word: context-specific and non-language-specific "CONTEXT: W" relation for linguistic information in the domain of Politics for Opinion Mining applications. The word "victory" is marked with a positive attitude and the word "mistake" is marked with a negative attitude.

4 Prosodic Emphasis and Voice-Related Information in Knowledge Graphs

Prosodic emphasis, change of speaking style/tone of voice and speaker/individual-specific paralinguistic features can be inserted as additional information with the "Context" relation, as in the case of language-specific paralinguistic features presented in previous research. The context-specific and language-specific "W-LANG" CONTEXT and "P-LANG" CONTEXT relations for linguistic and paralinguistic information not uttered can be integrated with non-language-specific/domain-specific "W" CONTEXT and "P" CONTEXT relations for linguistic and paralinguistic information within a knowledge graph (Fig. 10).

Although uncommon, all types of CONTEXT relations may co-occur within the same speech segment.

The perception in change of tone of voice constitute features that are often strongly language-specific and are often hard to identify.

---

240   C. Alexandris et al.

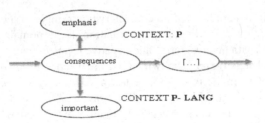

Fig. 10. Fragment of knowledge graph for perceived word: language-specific (P-LANG) (eyebrow raise = "important") and non-language-specific (P) (prosodic emphasis) "CONTEXT" relations for paralinguistic information [1].

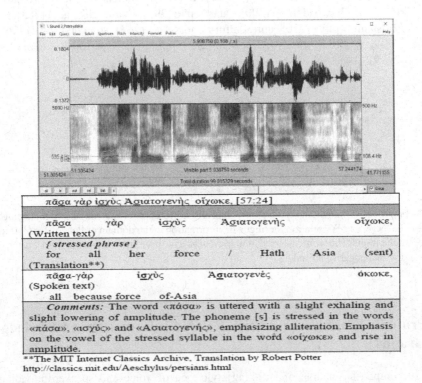

Fig. 11. Example of stressing phonetic and phonological features in spoken utterances to emphasize semantic content and sentiment for a topic of political significance [2].

Emphasis on specific phonetic and phonological features of a particular word for clarity purposes or in order to stress its semantic content and/or sentiment and the overall tone of how a specific word is uttered within a spoken segment may not be equally perceived among recipients.

However, these features often play an important – often crucial – role in spoken political and journalistic texts.

Since recordings of present-day politicians are avoided to be analyzed here, we present a non-journalistic, classical text -yet of political significance- recited by an expert (Prof. S. Psaroudakes, Dept. of Music Studies, National and Kapodistrian University of Athens) in Fig. 11 [2]. In the reciting of the Chorus from the "Persians" of Ancient Greek tragedian Aeschylus ("The Persians", written 472 B.C.E., Chorus of Persian Elders, who compose the Persian Council of State), there is an alternation of "intense" phrases containing more prosodic (and pointers to paralinguistic) elements and "neutral" phrases. The Speaker makes full use of alliteration and resonance in the words, phrases and sentences of the ancient text. For example, the "[s]" phoneme is stressed in the phrase "p'asa gh 'ar isch'is Asiatogh en'es" (πᾶσα-γὰρ ἰσχὺς Ἀσιατογενές) to emphasize the words "all" (p'asa) "power" (isch'is) and "Asia" (Asia) referring to (power of) the Persian Empire [2].

4.1 Domain-Specific Commands and Prosodic Emphasis

A characteristic example of non-language-specific features comprising additional dimensions of information content of words is the case of specific words receiving prosodic emphasis within the discourse and/or domain of the spoken interaction. Prosodic emphasis may stress and/or clarify the semantic content of the spoken utterance in a broad range of interaction types. These interaction types range from task-specific dialogue and question-answer interactions to interviews, political discussions and spoken interaction concerning negation and persuasion and/or expression of opinion.

The non-language-specific but strictly context-specific dimension of a word can also be domain-specific. For example, a particular word may imply a specific role or action. It may be noted that this allows possible implementations within a "frame-slot" framework in domain-specific (HCI and HRI) for processing spoken utterances.

In this case, the mere utterance of a single word may imply a domain-specific type of information consisting a complete phrase or sentence – or one or more possible domain-specific alternative types of implied information.

Characteristic examples (with and without prosodic emphasis) are depicted in Fig. 12 and Fig. 13, with Fig. 14 depicting examples of related frame-slots.

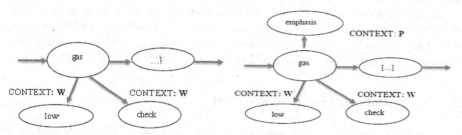

Fig. 12. "Gas"/"Gas!": Fragment of knowledge graph for a singular spoken word "gas" (with and without prosodic emphasis [1]) and context-specific and non-language-specific "CONTEXT: W" relation for domain-specific information in HCI applications. The word "gas" is marked with implied possible information "(the [gas] is) low" and "check [gas]".

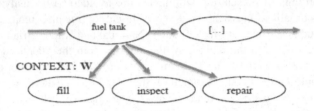

Fig. 13. "Fuel tank": Fragment of knowledge graph for a singular spoken word "fuel tank" and context-specific and non-language-specific "CONTEXT: W" relation for domain-specific information in HCI applications. The word "fuel tank" is marked with implied possible information for the commands "fill[fuel tank]", "inspect[fuel tank]","repair[fuel tank]"and possible related frame-slots.

---

fueling (aircraft, aircraft_part, number)

"Fill fuel tank in aircraft 2255"

repair (aircraft, aircraft_part, material, number, time)

"Repair damage in aircraft 2255" / "Repair damage in fuel tank"

aircraft_inspection (aircraft, place, number, time)

"Inspect aircraft SN 520 " / "Inspect fuel tank in aircraft SN 520"

Fig. 14. Frame slots and examples for commands "fill[fuel tank]", "inspect[fuel tank]","repair[fuel tank]".

We also note that the W-LANG and P-LANG "CONTEXT" relation or the W and P "CONTEXT" relations may be selected and be processed separately, according to application type. For example, language-specific data – linguistic features and paralinguistic features- can be used as seed data in a database –resource for language-specific applications. Non-language specific/domain-specific data – linguistic features and paralinguistic features- can be used as seed data in a separate database for domain-specific applications. Both databases - resources can be merged according to application type. Recent approaches in estimating node importance in knowledge graphs may enable the automatic execution of such processes [29], however, further research is required.

5   Conclusions and Further Research

The presented knowledge graph enrichment in the data preparation stage enables a differentiation between perceived linguistic and paralinguistic information not uttered compatible to language-specific and socio-cultural norms and unspoken perceived information that is either strictly circumstantial or strictly domain/context dependent. This enables a differentiation between circumstantial factors/evidence (individual/context-specific or domain specific - for Sentiment Analysis/HCI) and socio-culturally-biased factors/evidence in data analysis and training data and its subsequent integration in knowledge graphs and subsequent implementation in vectors and neural networks (1). This differentiation contributes to "Socially Responsible AI", since language/socio-culturally-specific factors are more likely to account for speaker-participant psychology-mentality and sensitivities and for cases of intended or unintended offense (or, even, bullying), differentiating them from any random occurrences/individual-specific pecu-liarities (especially for paralinguistic features). The above-presented differentiation may also be described as a context-specific information (atmo) "sphere" surrounding the spo-ken word. The concrete meaning – actual semantic content of the word (retrievable and processable in Natural Language Processing-NLP) is surrounded by two context-specific layers, with its context-specific and language-specific dimensions in the inner layer of the sphere (A) and its context-specific and non-language-specific dimensions in the outer layer of the "sphere" (B). The outer layers of the word (atmo) "sphere" demon-strate similarities to the outer circles of the Plutchik Wheel of Emotions containing complex emotions, recognizable within a (socio-culturally determined) context, such as "contempt" and "disapproval". In contrast, concretely identifiable emotions – including intense and universally recognizable emotions, such as "rage" and "grief" - are located in the inner circles of the Plutchik Wheel of Emotions and are typically easily detected and processed by current practices in Sentiment Analysis and Opinion Mining. In other words, the proposed information (atmo) "sphere" surrounding the spoken word mirrors the overall shape and very general – basic-features in the Plutchik Wheel of Emotions (2).

The above-presented differentiation are also linked to distinct types of integration of the "Context" factor and related information in knowledge graphs for NLP tasks and related HCI/HRI applications. In the case of Dialog Systems, with the proposed process-ing strategy, the mere utterance of a single word may imply a complete phrase/sentence with domain-specific (alternative types of) information (3).

Extensive implementation, evaluation (with quantitative evaluation measurements) and improvement of the training data created by the knowledge graphs is envisioned for further research, especially for a wider range of languages and speakers.

References

1. Alexandris, C.: Processing information unspoken: new insights from crowd-sourced data for sentiment analysis and spoken interaction applications. In: Proceedings of AAAI-SRAI, Socially Responsible AI for Well-being (SS-23-09), Co-located with the AAAI Spring Sym-posium, San Francisco, CA, 2023, pp. 90–99 (2023). https://ceur-ws.org/Vol-3527/Paper_456.pdf
2. Alexandris, C.: Issues in Multilingual Information Processing of Spoken Political and Jour-nalistic Texts in the Media and Broadcast News. Cambridge Scholars, Newcastle upon Tyne, UK (2020)
3. Alexandris, C.: Evaluating cognitive bias in two-party and multi-party spoken interactions. In: Proceedings of Interpretable AI for Well-being: Understanding Cognitive Bias and Social Embeddedness (IAW 2019) in conjunction with AAAI Spring Symposium (SS-19-03), Stanford University, Palo Alto, CA (2019). http://ceur-ws.org/Vol-2448

4. Alexandris, C.: Measuring cognitive bias in spoken interaction and conversation: generating visual representations. In: Proceedings of Beyond Machine Intelligence: Understanding Cognitive Bias and Humanity for Well-Being AI, Proceedings from the AAAI Spring Symposium, Stanford University, Technical Report, SS-18-03, pp. 204–206. AAAI Pres, Palo Alto, CA (2018)

5. Alexandris, C.: English, German and the International "Semi-professional" translator: a morphological approach to implied connotative features. J. Lang. Transl. Sejong University, Korea **11**(2), 7–46 (2010)

6. Alexandris, C., Du, J., Floros, V.: Visualizing and processing information not uttered in spoken political and journalistic data: from graphical representations to knowledge graphs in an interactive application. In: Kurosu, M. (ed.) HCII 2022. LNCS, vol. 13303, pp. 211–226. Springer, Cham (2022). https://doi.org/10.1007/978-3-031-05409-9_16

7. Alexandris, C., Floros, V., Mourouzidis, D.: Graphic representations of spoken interactions from journalistic data: persuasion and negotiations. In: Kurosu, M. (ed.) HCII 2021. LNCS, vol. 12764, pp. 3–17. Springer, Cham (2021). https://doi.org/10.1007/978-3-030-78468-3_1

8. Alexandris, C., Mourouzidis, D., Floros, V.: Generating graphic representations of spoken interactions revisited: the tension factor and information not uttered in journalistic data. In: Kurosu, M. (ed.) HCII 2020. LNCS, vol. 12181, pp. 523–537. Springer, Cham (2020). https://doi.org/10.1007/978-3-030-49059-1_39

9. Arockiaraj, C.M.: Applications of neural networks in data mining. Int. J. Eng. Sci. **3**(1), 8–11 (2013)

10. Carlson, L., Marcu, D., Okurowski, M.E: Building a discourse-tagged corpus in the framework of rhetorical structure theory. In: Proceedings of the 2nd SIGDIAL Workshop on Discourse and Dialogue, Eurospeech 2001, Denmark (2001). https://aclanthology.org/W01-1605.pdf

11. Du, J., Alexandris, C., Mourouzidis, D., Floros, V., Iliakis, A.: Controlling interaction in multilingual conversation revisited: a perspective for services and interviews in Mandarin Chinese. In: Kurosu, M. (ed.) HCII 2017, LNCS, vol. 10271, pp. 573–583. Springer, Heidelberg (2017)

12. Evans, N.J., Park, D.: Rethinking the persuasion knowledge model: schematic antecedents and associative outcomes of persuasion knowledge activation for covert advertising. J. Curr. Issues Res. Advertising **36**(2), 157–176 (2015). https://doi.org/10.1080/10641734.2015.102 3873

13. Grice, H.P.: Studies in the Way of Words. Harvard University Press, Cambridge (1989)

14. Grice, H.P.: Logic and conversation. In: Cole, P., Morgan, J. (eds.) Syntax and Semantics, vol. 3. Academic Press, New York (1975)

15. Hatim, B.: Communication Across Cultures: Translation Theory and Contrastive Text Linguistics. University of Exeter Press, Exeter (1997)

16. He, Z., Jin, T., Basu, A., Soraghan, J., Di Caterina, G., Petropoulakis, L.: Human emotion recognition in video using subtraction pre-processing. In: Proceedings of the 2019 11th International Conference on Machine Learning and Computing, Zhuhai, China, 2019, pp. 374–379 (2019)

17. Hilbert, M.: Toward a synthesis of cognitive biases: how noisy information processing can bias human decision making. Psychol. Bull. **138**(2), 211–237 (2012)

18. Hedderich, M.A., Klakow, D.: Training a neural network in a low-resource setting on automatically annotated noisy data. In: Proceedings of the Workshop on Deep Learning Approaches for Low-Resource NLP, Melbourne, Australia, pp. 12–18. Association for Computational Linguistics-ACL (2018). https://aclanthology.org/W18-3402/

19. Jurafsky, D., Martin, J.H.: Speech and Language Processing, an Introduction to Natural Language Processing, Computational Linguistics and Speech Recognition, 3rd edn. (2022). Draft: https://web.stanford.edu/~jurafsky/slp3/ed3book_jan122022.pdf

20. Koller, W.: Der Begriff der Äquivalenz in der Übersetzungswissenschaft. In: Fabricius-Hansen, C., Ostbo, J. (eds.) Übertragung, Annährung, Angleichung, Sieben Beiträge zu Theorie und Praxis des Übersetzens, pp. 11–29. Peter Lang, Frankfurt am Main (2000)

21. Liu, B.: Sentiment Analysis and Opinion Mining. Morgan & Claypool, San Rafael (2012)

22. Ma, J.: A comparative analysis of the ambiguity resolution of two English-Chinese MT approaches: RBMT and SMT. Dalian Univ. Technol. J. **31**(3), 114–119 (2010)

23. Marcu, D.: Discourse trees are good indicators of importance in text. In: Mani, I., Maybury, M. (eds.) Advances in Automatic Text Summarization, pp. 123–136. The MIT Press, Cambridge, MA (1999)

24. Mittal, S., Joshi, A., Finin, T.: Thinking, fast and slow: combining vector spaces and knowledge graphs (2017). arXiv:1708.03310v2 [cs.AI]

25. Mountantonakis, M., Tzitzikas, Y.: Knowledge graph embeddings over hundreds of linked datasets. In: Garoufallou, E., Fallucchi, F., William De Luca E. (eds.) Metadata and Semantic Research MTSR 2019. Communications in Computer and Information Science, vol. 1057, pp. 150–162. Springer, Cham (2019). https://doi.org/10.1007/978-3-030-36599-8_13

26. Mourouzidis, D., Floros, V., Alexandris, C.: Generating graphic representations of spoken interactions from journalistic data. In: Kurosu, M. (ed.) HCII 2019, LNCS, vol. 11566, pp. 559–570. Springer, Cham (2019)

27. Paltridge, B.: Discourse Analysis: An Introduction. Bloomsbury Publishing, London (2012)

28. Pan, Y.: Politeness in Chinese face-to-face interaction. In: Advances in Discourse Processes Series, vol. 67. Elsevier Science, Amsterdam (2000)

29. Park, N., Kan, A., Dong, X.L., Zhao, T., Faloutsos, C.: Estimating node importance in knowledge graphs using graph neural networks. In: Proceedings of the 25th ACM SIGKDD Conference on Knowledge Discovery and Data Mining (KDD 2019), 4–8 August 2019, Anchorage, AK, USA. ACM, New York, NY, USA (2019). https://doi.org/10.1145/3292500.3330855

30. Plutchik, R.: A psychoevolutionary theory of emotions. Soc. Sci. Inf. **21**, 529–553 (1982). https://doi.org/10.1177/053901882021004003

31. Poria, S., Cambria, E., Hazarika, D., Majumder, N., Zadeh, A., Morency, L.P.: Context-dependent sentiment analysis in user-generated videos. In: Proceedings of the 55th Annual Meeting of the Association for Computational Linguistics, Vancouver, Canada, 30 July–4 August 2017, pp. 873–883. Association for Computational Linguistics – ACL (2017). https://doi.org/10.18653/v1/P17-1081

32. Rocklage, M.D., Rucker, D.D., Nordgren, L.F.: Persuasion, emotion, and language: the intent to persuade transforms language via emotionality. Psychol. Sci. **29**(5), 749–760 (2018). https://doi.org/10.1177/0956797617744797

33. Shah, K., Kopru, S., Ruvini, J.-D.: Neural network based extreme classification and similarity models for product matching. In: Proceedings of NAACL-HLT 2018, New Orleans, Louisiana, 1–6 June 2018, pp. 8–15. Association for Computational Linguistics-ACL (2018). https://acl anthology.org/N18-3002/

34. Skonk, K.: 5 Types of Negotiation Skills, Program on Negotiation Daily Blog, Harvard Law School, May the 14th 2020 (2020). https://www.pon.harvard.edu/daily/negotiation-ski lls-daily/types-of-negotiation-skills/. Accessed 22 Nov 2023

35. Stede, M., Taboada, D., Das, D.: Annotation Guidelines for Rhetorical Structure. Manuscript. University of Potsdam and Simon Fraser University, March 2017. https://www.sfu.ca/~mta boada/docs/research/RST_Annotation_Guidelines.pdf

36. Trachanas, G.: Sentiment analysis on Twitter data and social trends: the case of Greek general elections. Master's thesis, Department of Informatics and Telecommunications, National University of Athens, Greece (2023)

37. Tran, H.N., Takashu, A: Analyzing knowledge graph embedding methods from a multi-embedding interaction perspective. In: Proceedings of the 1st International Workshop on

Data Science for Industry 4.0 (DSI4) at EDBT/ICDT 2019 Joint Conference (2019). https:// arxiv.org/abs/1903.11406

38. Trofimova, I.: Observer bias: an interaction of temperament traits with biases in the semantic perception of lexical material. PLoSONE **9**(1), e85677 (2014)

39. Wang, M., Qiu, L.L.: A survey on knowledge graph embeddings for link prediction. Symmetry **13**, 485 (2021). https://doi.org/10.3390/sym13030485

40. Wardhaugh, R.: An Introduction to Sociolinguistics, 2nd edn. Blackwell, Oxford (1992)

41. Williams, J.D., Asadi, K., Zweig, G.: Hybrid Code Networks: practical and efficient end-to-end dialog control with supervised and reinforcement learning. In: Proceedings of the 55th Annual Meeting of the Association for Computational Linguistics, Vancouver, Canada, 30 July–4 August 2017, pp. 665–677. Association for Computational Linguistics (ACL) (2017). https://aclanthology.org/P17-1062/

42. Wilson, M., Wilson, T.P.: An oscillator model of the timing of turn taking. Psychon. Bull. Rev. **12**(6), 957–968 (2005)

43. Yakaew, A., Dailey, M., Racharak, T.: Multimodal sentiment analysis on video streams using lightweight deep neural networks. In: Proceedings of the 10th International Conference on Pattern Recognition Applications and Methods (ICPRAM 2021), pp. 442–451 (2021). https:// doi.org/10.5220/0010304404420451

44. Ye, Z., Kumar, Y.J., Sing, G.O., Song, F., Wang, J.: A comprehensive survey of graph neural networks for knowledge graphs. IEEE Access **10**, 75729–75741 (2022). https://doi.org/10. 1109/ACCESS.2022.3191784

45. Yu, Z.W., Yu, Z.Y., Aoyama, H., Ozeki, M., Nakamura, Y.: Capture, recognition, and visualization of human semantic interactions in meetings. In: Proceedings of PerCom, Mannheim, Germany, pp. 107–115 (2010)

46. Zeldes, A.: rstWeb - a browser-based annotation interface for rhetorical structure theory and discourse relations. In: Proceedings of NAACL-HLT 2016 System Demonstrations, San Diego, CA, pp. 1–5. Association for Computational Linguistics (ACL) (2016). http://aclweb. org/anthology/N/N16/N16-3001.pdf

Enhancing Episodic Memory Recall Through Nostalgic Image Generation and Interactive Modification

Masayuki Ando[✉], Kouyou Otsu, and Tomoko Izumi

Ritsumeikan University, Kusatsu, Shiga 525-8557, Japan
{mandou,k-otsu,izumi-t}@fc.ritsumei.ac.jp

Abstract. An opportunity for reflection while expressing memories of one's own experiences can lead an individual to contemplate the daily life events they experience. However, we get limited opportunities to recollect our memories in daily life. Therefore, we considered that approaching memory scenes through pictures and artworks related to memories might trigger a chain of recall of memory details and related episodes. In this paper, we propose a nostalgic image generation system with an interactive modification function to support users' nostalgic episodic memory recall scenes in daily life. The proposed system supports nostalgic memory recall in two aspects: verbalizing a memory while viewing an image and modifying the image generated to make it closely resemble the memory. The results of the verification experiment suggest that verbalizing nostalgic memory as an interactive modification and modifying the generated image may support memory recall when imaging nostalgic memory.

Keywords: supporting memory recall · image generation AI · nostalgic memory visualization

1 Introduction

Human memory is crucial in recalling past events, experiences, emotions, and thoughts, as well as in facilitating self-understanding, relationship building, and daily problem-solving [1, 2]. Such memories often lead individuals to come up with new creative ideas. In particular, personal memories based on one's own experiences are essential to the formation of one's identity. Furthermore, reflection based on one's memories—as a way to construct one's identity—is effective in providing a positive reevaluation of past events and life experiences and in fostering an optimistic orientation toward the future. Therefore, reflecting on memories regularly is important for reaffirming one's identity and leading a high-quality life. However, the opportunities to reflect on our memories are limited in daily life, and it is difficult to take time to reflect on our past events and remember the details.

In the field of psychological care support, the benefits of recalling one's memory are well known. For example, reminiscence therapy, a psychological intervention method that involves sharing memories by talking with others while looking at old photos or objects, is used in care facilities to prevent the progression of dementia [3]. Art therapy, another psychological intervention method, encourages recalling memories by engaging individuals in tasks that involve imagining and expressing memories [4]. Art therapy aims to alleviate psychological and emotional issues through creative expression, such as painting, sculpting, and pottery. Moreover, it provides an environment for self-expression and mental stability, triggering reflections on personal memories and experiences. For individuals, opportunities to reflect on their experiences through creative expression can be valuable in daily life. In particular, reproducing a memory scene during such activities may trigger a chain of detailed recollections and related episodes. However, such activities should be pursued in the presence of professional staff, a suitable environment, and appropriate photos or the ability to draw, which might not always be available. Moreover, recalling detailed memories or unnoticed events from one's life is not always easy.

In this paper, we aim to support users' nostalgic episodic memory recall in daily life without the presence of professional staff or materials for recollection. To achieve this, we focus on image generation AI technology, which generates and modifies images automatically in response to users' text commands. The use of image generation AI has become widespread in recent years [5]. It can be used to represent memories visually and can support individuals in reflecting on them.

We propose a system that can express memories not only by generating images but also by including an interactive modification process to enhance memory recall. This system uses image generation AI to create specific images from linguistic descriptions of memory scenes provided by users. This feature is designed to support a more detailed recollection of memories. However, since image generation AI generally uses generic image data, it is difficult to generate images that exactly match the scene envisioned by the user. To address this, our proposed system incorporates a function that allows users to modify the generated images interactively. By providing additional feedback via text input while viewing the images, users can generate images that resemble their memory's scene more closely. This modification process not only aligns the generated images with the memory scene but also encourages a deeper and more detailed recall of memories. The attention given to the discrepancies between the generated images and the recalled scenes can stimulate a more comprehensive recollection by users. Thus, these functions can be used to represent and enhance the memory's scene as images, thereby naturally prompting users to recall details of their own memories and related episodes.

In this paper, we hypothesize that the proposed system's process of visualizing memories and interactively modifying images to closely resemble memory scenes will enhance the recall of the detailed aspects and related episodes of those memories. We aim to verify this hypothesis by examining the system's effectiveness in facilitating a more vivid and detailed recollection of personal memories.

2 Related Research

Several studies have investigated the role of supporting technology in memory recall. For example, Loveday et al. and Abigail et al. used a wearable camera called SenseCam [6] to record daily life events and showed that detailed episodic memories could be recalled from pictures [7, 8]. In addition, Abigail et al. developed a system to support memory recall using keywords generated from sources such as Google Calendar and Twitter [9]. In this research, words were weighted on the basis of photographs to help users recall memorable events. Although these studies attempted to support memory recall using images and keywords, they assumed the existence of photographs of objects or events to be recalled. Our research examines the use of image generation AI to generate alternative images that support the recall of specific memory scenes when actual photographs are unavailable.

Image generation AI typically refers to technology that creates new or modified images using machine-learning techniques. A well-known model in this field is the Generative Adversarial Network (GAN) [10], which produces highly realistic images by using two types of models together: one for image generation and another for evaluation (i.e., to evaluate whether the image created by the generative model is real or fake). Recently, a novel image generation method based on the diffusion model has appeared [5]. This model introduces noise into images and then learns to remove it to restore the original image, thereby accurately capturing the images' features. Furthermore, this model can also generate new images from text or images as input. Our research focuses on this type of text-based image generation and modification method. We consider using diffusion model-based image generation AI to visualize one's memorable scenes.

Regarding memory and remembrance based on generative AI, MyHeritage provides an existing service called Deep Nostalgia [11]. This service animates historical photographs using image generation AI, allowing individuals to reflect more vividly on their own lives or those of their family and ancestors. Xiaojiao et al. used image generation AI to repair old or damaged photos and colorize black-and-white photos [12]. Moreover, Mengjiao et al. recreated old facial images from current facial images [13], and Yu et al. generated a video from brain activity data [14]. However, these studies required existing images or specialized equipment. Our research is unique because it uses image generation AI to generate images of memory scenes from textual descriptions without needing expertise or equipment. Moreover, our approach focuses not on the accuracy of the scene's reproduction but on encouraging memory recall through the process of correcting discrepancies between the generated image and the actual memory scene.

3 Supporting Memory Recall Using Image Generation AI

3.1 Overview of the Proposed System

In this study, we propose a system that supports recalling the user's detailed memories and related episodes by visualizing the memory's scene as an image generated by the user. The proposed system can generate an image based on text commands about a memory scene input by the user. The user can modify the generated image with the assistance of the image generation AI. The generated or modified image is displayed in real time on the system's user interface (UI; shown in Fig. 1). The user can always check whether the displayed image reproduces their memory scene accurately and make the image closely resemble the memory scene by changing or adding the input text. Through this interactive modification process, the generated image will contain more details of the memory scene; simultaneously, the user's recall of the memory will be encouraged. The proposed system has two functions: the "Image Generation Function" and the "Interactive Modification Function." In the "Image Generation Function," the proposed system generates new images based on the text entered by users. The generated image is displayed in the system's UI each time it is generated. In general, well-known image generation models are pretrained from image databases collected from various sources. Thus, the generated images are generic and often do not fully reflect the specific details and uniqueness of users' memories. Therefore, users can use the "Interactive Modification Function" to make the generated images more closely resemble the memory scene.

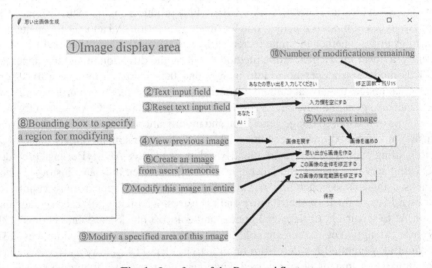

Fig. 1. Interface of the Proposed System

Using the "Interactive Modification Function," users can modify the generated images with textual instructions. They can input textual instructions for implementing partial or entire modifications to the generated image, and the system will regenerate the image based on the input. The modified image is displayed in the system's UI each time it is generated. Users can check the displayed image to determine whether the modification was successful and then input any additional modifications they wish to make. This interactive process allows users to create images that more closely reflect their memory scene.

3.2 Procedures for Using the Proposed System

We implemented the proposed method as a system that enables users to experience it. In this section, we describe the interface and usage procedures of the proposed system. Figure 1 shows the system interface, and Table 1 shows the name and function of each component. The system uses a diffusion model called Stable Diffusion [5]. This model enables users to generate images based on the content of the input text. The system contains an interface for operating each function and displaying images. Through this interface, users can intuitively generate and modify images using each function

Table 1. Functions of the Proposed System

Function name	Function description
① Image display area	The generated images are displayed one by one here
② Text input field	A field for inputting text describing the contents of the memory scene or modification
③ Reset text input field	Button to blank out ②
④ View previous image	Button to revert the image displayed in ① to the previously generated one
⑤ View next image	Button to show the next image in ① if there is a newer generated image
⑥ Create an image from users' memories	Button to generate a new image based on the contents of ② and display it in ①
⑦ Modify this image in entire	Button to generate a new image with the modification described in ② added to the image currently displayed in ① and display it in ①
⑧ Bounding box to specify a region for modifying	The bounding box is shown by dragging the mouse on ① to reserve a specific modification region
⑨ Modify a specified area of this image	Button to modify the image displayed in ① as reflecting the modification in ② for the area in ⑧
⑩ Number of modifications remaining	This display function is provided for the experiment. The number of times the modifications can be made is displayed. The number is decreased by one each time ⑦ and ⑨ are executed; when the number reaches 0, no further modifications are possible

implemented in the system. The following is a description of how to use each system function.

Image Generation Function. The user's flow of the image generation process when using the "Image Generation" function is as follows. First, the user inputs text describing the memory scene they wish to create in the "Text Input Field." Next, while they press the "Create an image from users' memories" button, an image generated based on the input text is displayed in the "Image display area." At this time, inside this system, the input text is translated into English (if not English) and then passed to the image generation model. Then, the system receives the generated image from the image generation model. The user can repeat this process multiple times, with a new image appearing in the "Image display area" each time. Previously generated images do not disappear, and the user can use the "View previous image" and "View next image" buttons to switch between the displayed images. Figure 2 shows an example of the use of the image generation function for the following text input about one's memory: "Once upon a time I went to a ranch on a mountain."

Interactive Modification Function - Entire Image Modification. In this section, we describe the user's flow of the image modification process when using the "Entire Image Modification" function" which is one of the interactive modification functions. This function is used when the modification covers a large area of the image, such as the background or a large object. First, using the "Image Generation Function," the user generates an image that serves as the base of the image modification process. The base image is the image currently displayed in the "Image display area." Next, the user inputs the content to be modified in the "Text input field." Next, the user presses the "Modify this image in entire" button. The system displays a new image in the "Image display area," with the displayed image modified based on the input modifications. At this time, inside this system, the input text and the base image are passed to the image generation model. Then, the image-to-image function of the image generation model generates a new image that reflects the content of the input text in the base image. The user can repeat this process to continue modifying the image interactively. Figure 3 shows an example of using the "Entire Image Modification" function to modify the image shown in Fig. 2 with the following content: "There were many goats on the farm."

Interactive Modification Function – Specified Area Modification. In this section, we describe the user's flow when using the "Specific Area Modification" function, which is one of the interactive modification functions. This function is used to modify a small object or a small area of an image. First, the user generates a base image for image modification using the "Image Generation" function. Next, the user drags the mouse around the area of the image to be modified, and a red rectangular frame appears. Next, the user inputs the content to be modified in the "Text input field." Next, the user presses the "Modify a specified area of this image" button. Then, the system displays a new image in which the modification is reflected only in the specified area. At this time, inside this system, the input text, the base image, and the specified area are passed to the image generation model. Then, the image-to-image function of the image generation model generates a new image for the base image that reflects the content of the input text only in the specified area. Figure 4 shows an example of using the "Specific Area Modification" function to modify the image shown in Fig. 3 with the following content: "There was a log cabin restaurant in here.

Fig. 2. Example of the Image Generation Function

Fig. 3. Example of the Entire Image Modification Function

Fig. 4. Example of the Specified Area Modification Function

4   Experiment

4.1   Purpose and Hypotheses

In this experiment, we evaluated whether the interactive modification process provided by the proposed system is effective in recalling the user's memory scene. The interactive modification process includes two factors: verbalization and modification of the memory scene. The verbalization factor refers to the process of refining the textual description repeatedly, thereby allowing the user to describe the memory scene more accurately and to verbalize their recalled contents. This process may contribute to articulating their recalled memory by encouraging detailed descriptions of the scene through text input. The modification factor refers to the act of users modifying the generated image to make it more closely resemble the memory scene. This action is done by interactively modifying the image based on the refined textual description, which enables the system to visualize the memory scene more precisely. Each of these factors may have a different impact on recall. To verify the effectiveness of these factors, we set the following two hypotheses:

- Hypothesis H1: "Effects of verbalizing memory scenes": Verbalizing a memory scene will facilitate easy, detailed, accurate, and one-after-another recall of the memory.
- Hypothesis H2: "Effect of image modification": Interactive modification of the generated images will facilitate easy, detailed, accurate, and one-after-another recall of the memory.

Regarding H1, since image generation AI typically learns from universal image data, the generated images are not necessarily close to the user's specific memory. Therefore, as the verbalization factor, repeated adjustments to the input are required to make the generated image more closely resemble the memory scene. This process is an act of verbalizing the memory scene repeatedly and in detail. The process of verbalization is expected to encourage deeper involvement and reflection on the memory and to enhance the recall of memories.

Regarding H2, as the modification factor, the process of modifying the user-generated image to make it more closely resemble the memory scene is necessary to reduce the discrepancies between the generated image and the user's memory. During this process, users are expected to notice discrepancies between the generated image and their own mental image of the memory scene. This realization encourages users to accurately describe memory scenes and to aim for a more detailed representation. It is expected that users will be able to engage more deeply with their past experiences through this process, which will, in turn, facilitate recall.

4.2   Experimental Settings

To verify the hypotheses outlined in Sect. 4.1, we asked participants to visualize and recall their memories by using our system. The participants were asked to recall "memories of impressed places they had visited in the past" in which scenes such as scenery and landscapes could be easily visualized. We combined two factors—verbalization of the memories (verbalization) and modification of the generated images (modification)—and set the following three conditions as comparison conditions:

- Verbalization and Modification Condition (proposed method): Using the proposed system, the participants can generate images of their memory scenes by repeatedly modifying the images. They can modify the generated image up to 15 times.
- Only Verbalization Condition: Using the system, the participants can re-generate images of their memory scenes by changing the input text. They can retry to generate the images by modifying the input text up to 10 times.
- Once Verbalization Condition (baseline): The participants can visualize their memory scene only once using the system. In this condition, 10 images are generated simultaneously.

In the Verbalization and Modification Condition, participants can use all functions of the proposed system. The participants can generate an image through the verbalization of the memory scene and then modify it up to 15 times using one base image. This condition includes the two aforementioned factors (verbalization and modification). These limits on the number of iterations were set to avoid bias in each participant's usage of the function.

In the Only Verbalization Condition, the participants can only use the image generation function. The participant can replay a new image from the verbalized memory scene up to 10 times. This condition includes only the verbalization factor of the memory scene.

In the Once Verbalization Condition, the participants can only use the image generation function once. In this condition, the image cannot be regenerated or modified. In other words, this condition does not include the factors of image verbalization and modification. However, this constraint is assumed to reduce the likelihood of generating images that closely resemble the user's memories to an extremely low level. Therefore, the participants were given an initial five-minute period to organize and verbalize their memory's scenes before using the system. In addition, the number of images generated at one time was set to 10.

4.3 Procedure

In this experiment, 10 university students participated. Face-to-face interviews were conducted with them after obtaining informed consent. First, the participants were asked to list three memorable places they had visited in the past. These three memorable places were randomly assigned to each of the three conditions presented in Sect. 4.2. Next, the participants were provided with a tutorial to familiarize them with the system's operations. This tutorial was designed to ensure that all participants were comfortable with the system's functions and interface. After completing the tutorial, the participants then proceeded to visualize scenes related to the designated memorable places using the system in each condition. Then, the participants responded to a questionnaire (Table 2, Q1–Q4) regarding the visualization of their memories. Finally, the participants were asked to recall scenes or episodes from their memories while looking at the generated images. Specifically, we instructed them, "Please look at the generated images and recall your memories of this place at that time." This recall task was performed for five minutes. The participants then responded to a questionnaire (Table 2, Q5–Q8) regarding the recall of memories. The participants were asked to conduct this process three times, once for each condition. The order of the conditions was randomly switched for each participant.

Table 2. Question Items in the Questionnaire.

No.	Questionnaire Items
Q1	I felt that the image generation process helped me recall past scenes easily
Q2	I felt that the image generation process helped me recall past scenes in detail
Q3	I felt that the image generation process helped me recall past scenes accurately
Q4	I felt that the image generation process helped me recall past scenes one after another
Q5	I felt that the generated images helped me recall past scenes easily
Q6	I felt that the generated images helped me recall past scenes in detail
Q7	I felt that the generated images helped me recall past scenes accurately
Q8	I felt that the generated images helped me recall past scenes one after another

4.4 Evaluation Item

In this experiment, the questionnaire shown in Table 2 was used to evaluate the effectiveness of the proposed system in facilitating memory recall. This questionnaire was designed to evaluate the recall process in two phases: creating images of memorable scenes (memory imaging phase) and recalling while viewing the created images (recall phase with generated images). The questionnaire included the following evaluation factors:

- Q1,5: Recalled the memory scene easily.
- Q2,6: Recalled the memory scene in detail.
- Q3,7: Recalled the memory scene accurately.
- Q4,8: Recalled the memory scene one after another.

The questionnaire used a 7-point Likert scale (7 being the most positive). Items Q1–Q4 were to be answered immediately after creating an image of a memory scene using the system. Items Q5–Q8 were to be answered after recalling the memory for five minutes while looking at the generated image after creating the image of the memory scene.

5   Results

Ten students (seven males and three females) from Ritsumeikan University, Kyoto, Japan, participated in this experiment. In this section, we present the results of the questionnaire.

5.1   Recall Results from the Memory Imaging Phase

A box-and-whisker plot of the mean scores of questionnaires Q1–Q4 after the imaging of memory scenes is shown in Fig. 5. Friedman tests were performed for each question, and no significant differences were found between conditions for all items. However, the mean score for each condition was 4 or higher for all items. From these results, it was not confirmed that the acts of improving the input text (verbalization factor)

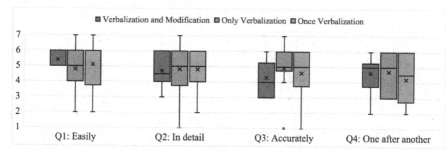

Fig. 5. Box-and-Whisker Plot of Mean Scores for Q1–Q4.

and modifying the generated image (modification factor) when using the system led to statistical differences in memory recall. The following discussion will focus on the characteristics identified in each condition based on the differences in the mean scores.

First, regarding "Recalled the memory scene easily," the results of Q1 show that the mean scores were higher in the order of the "Verbalization and Modification Condition" > "Once Verbalization Condition" > "Only Verbalization Condition." The trend in the mean scores shows that the "Verbalization and Modification Condition" has the smallest variance and the highest mean score. Therefore, it is suggested that the "Verbalization and Modification Condition" may make it easier for users to recall a memory scene during the memory imaging phase. In addition, the mean value of the "Once Verbalization Condition" was higher than that of the "Only Verbalization Condition." Therefore, regarding ease of recall, it could be lower due to the verbalization factor.

Next, regarding the "Recalled the memory scene in detail," the results of Q2 show that the mean values for the "Only Verbalization Condition" and "Once Verbalization Condition" were similar, and the mean value for the "Verbalization and Modification Condition" was the lowest. This suggests that the verbalization and modification factors may have a small effect on the detailed memory recall scene during the memory imaging phase.

Finally, regarding the "Recalled the memory scene accurately" and "Recalled the memory scene one after another," the results of Q3 and Q4 show that the mean value of the "Only Verbalization Condition" was the highest for both items. This suggests that the verbalization factor may be effective for accurate or one-after-another recall of the memory scene. However, the "Verbalization and Modification Condition" was as low as or lower than the "Once Verbalization Condition," suggesting that the modification factor may be almost ineffective or even an obstacle to accurate and one-after-another recall.

5.2   Recall Results from the Recall Phase with Generated Images

A box-and-whisker plot of the mean scores of questionnaires Q5–Q8 after the recalling process based on the generated image is shown in Fig. 6. Friedman tests were performed for each question, and no significant differences were found between conditions for all items. However, the mean score for each condition was 4 or higher for all items. From these results, it could not be confirmed that the acts of improving the input text

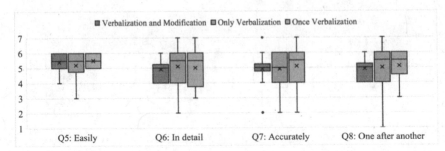

Fig. 6. Box-and-Whisker Plot of Mean Scores for Q5–Q8.

(verbalization factor) and modifying the generated image (modification factor) when using the system led to statistical differences in memory recall on the generated image. The following discussion will focus on the characteristics identified in each condition based on the differences in the mean scores.

First, regarding "Recalled the memory scene easily," the results of Q5 show that the mean values for the "Verbalization and Modification Condition" and "Once Verbalization Condition" were similar, and the score for the "Only Verbalization Condition" was the lowest. This suggests that the images generated only from the verbalization factors were an obstacle to ease of recall. However, when the modification factor was added, the mean score was higher than that of the "Only Verbalization Condition."

Next, regarding the "Recalled the memory scene in detail," the results of Q6 show that the mean score for the "Only Verbalization Condition" was the highest. Moreover, the mean score for the "Verbalization and Modification Condition" was lower than that for the "Once Verbalization Condition." This suggests that the verbalization factor was effective for detailed recall of the generated image, whereas the modification factor may have been an obstacle in the opposite direction.

Finally, regarding the "Recalled the memory scene accurately" and "Recalled the memory scene one after another," the results for Q7 and Q8 show that the "Once Verbalization Condition" had the highest mean value. The mean values for the "Verbalization and Modification Condition" were the same (Q7) or slightly lower (Q8) than that for "Only Verbalization Condition." This suggests that images generated only from the verbalization factors may affect the accuracy or one-after-another recall. However, images generated by adding the modification factor may have a minimal effect on or even impair accurate or sequential recall.

6 Discussion

The results of this experiment did not show any significance between conditions in the Friedman test for any of the items, and no effect of the difference between the two factors on recall was observed. One possible reason for this result is that in this experiment, we set the guideline of memory scenes for participants as "memorable places they traveled to in the past". Because of this setting, it is possible that there were large differences in the contents of the recall target (such as how many years ago it was, the complexity of the scene recalled, the number of events experienced, etc.) for each condition regarding ease of recall, and these differences may have affected the evaluation. However, since the mean score for each condition was 4 or higher for all items, it is possible that the participants felt the act of generating and viewing the images of memories itself assisted them in accessing and recalling their memories.

We will now discuss the relationship between the trends in the mean values of each of the questionnaire items and each of the hypotheses. First, we discuss H1, that is, "Verbalizing a memory scene will facilitate easy, detailed, accurate, and one-after-another recall of the memory." For this hypothesis to be supported, the mean value for the "Only Verbalization Condition" must be significantly higher than that for the "Once Verbalization Condition." However, H1 was rejected because no significant differences were found between the two conditions for all items.

Although H1 was not supported, the trend in the mean scores suggests features related to the content of the hypothesis. Regarding the memory imaging phase, the results of the comparison between the "Only Verbalization Condition" and "Once Verbalization Condition" show that in Q3 (Accuracy) and Q4 (One after another), the mean value for the "Only Verbalization Condition" was higher. Therefore, it is possible that the verbalization factor led the participants to recall the scenes accurately and one after another by organizing the scenes in their minds from abstract images into concrete words. However, in Q1 (ease), the mean value for the "Only Verbalization Condition" was lower. In this result, it is possible that only the verbalization factor required the participants to repeatedly improve the sentences expressing their memories, which may have burdened the participants.

Next, regarding the recall phase with the generated images, the only item for which the mean value of the "Only Verbalization Condition" was higher than that of the "Once Verbalization Condition" was Q6 (In detail). Therefore, it is possible that images generated by the verbalization factor enhance detailed recall but do not lead to easy, accurate, or one-after-another recall.

In summary, H1 was not statistically supported. However, the verbalization factor may improve accuracy and one-after-another recall in the memory imaging phase and detailed recall in the recall phase with the generated images.

Next, we discuss H2: "Interactive modification of the generated images will facilitate easy, detailed, accurate, and one-after-another recall of the memory." For this hypothesis to be supported, the mean for the "Verbalization and Modification Condition" must be significantly higher than that for the "Only Verbalization Condition." However, H2 was rejected because no significant differences were found between the two conditions for all items.

Although H2 was not supported, the trend in the mean scores suggests features related to the content of the hypothesis. Regarding the memory imaging phase, the mean value for the "Verbalization and Modification Condition" was higher than that for the "Only Verbalization Condition" only in Q1. Therefore, the modification factor facilitated easy recall by allowing the participants to clearly visualize their memories. However, the mean for the "Verbalization and Modification Condition" was lower than that for the "Only Verbalization Condition" for items Q2–Q4, indicating that the modification factor was an obstacle to detailed and accurate recall. It is possible that the participants were able to recall the memories easily; however, the modification factors made them conscious of trying to make the images more closely resemble the scene in their minds, and this may have prevented them from further recalling the memories. Regarding the recall phase with the generated images, the mean value for the "Verbalization and Modification Condition" was higher than the mean value for the "Only Verbalization Condition" only in Q5. Thus, it is possible that images generated by the modification factor facilitate easy recall but do not lead to detailed or accurate recall. In addition, as mentioned at the beginning of this section, it is possible that the effect of the content of the memories may have reduced the effect of the modification factor.

In summary, H2 was not statistically supported. However, the modification factor may improve the ease of recall in the memory imaging phase and the recall phase with the generated images.

Although both H1 and H2 were not supported in this experiment, the mean values exceeded 4 for all items, suggesting that the imaging of memories through the generated images may have a positive effect on memory recall. Furthermore, since the possibility of a positive effect of the verbalization and modification factors was observed in several items, it is possible that the effect of each factor may be higher in an experimental setting with a limited recall target.

7 Conclusion

In this study, we proposed a memory imaging system with an interactive modification function to support the recall of memory scenes in daily life. The proposed system supports memory recall with two interactive modification factors: verbalizing the memory while viewing the image and modifying the generated image to make it closely resemble the memory.

From the validation experiment, the two factors showed no statistical effectiveness in the memory imaging phase. However, the trend in the mean values suggests that these factors could support recall. Moreover, in the recall phase with the generated images, the two factors showed no statistical validity. This is because it is difficult to improve the quality of the generated images through verbalization and modification due to the characteristics of image generation AI. In addition, it is possible that in the present experiment, the effect of the memory content that was the recall target for the image generation AI model may have been stronger. However, the results suggest that the imaging of the memory scene itself may have a positive effect on memory recall.

In the future, the challenges will include setting a target for recall such that the content of memories is fair and developing a graphical user interface (GUI) that enables more intuitive modification as desired.

Acknowledgements. This work was supported in part by JSPS KAKENHI (Grant Number 22K21096), KDDI Foundation, Tateisi Science and Technology Foundation, and Ritsumeikan Global Innovation Research Organization (R-GIRO), Ritsumeikan University.

References

1. Buckner, R.L., Carroll, D.C.: Self-projection and the brain. Trends Cogn. Sci. **11**(2), 49–57 (2007)
2. Perry, D., Hendler, T., Shamay-Tsoory, S.G.: Projecting memories: the role of the hippocampus in emotional mentalizing. Neuroimage **54**(2), 1669–1676 (2011)
3. Brooker, D., Duce, L.: Wellbeing and activity in dementia: a comparison of group reminiscence therapy, structured goal-directed group activity and unstructured time. Aging Ment. Health **4**(4), 354–358 (2000)
4. Renée, L.B.: Art therapies and dementia care: a systematic review. Sage J. **11**(5), 657–676 (2011)
5. Robin, R., Andreas, B., et al.: High-resolution image synthesis with Latent diffusion models. In: Proceedings of the IEEE Conference on Computer Vision and Pattern Recognition (CVPR), pp. 10674–10685 (2022)
6. Microsoft Research Sense Cam. http://research.microsoft.com/enus/um/cambridge/projects/sensecam/. Accessed 12 July 2023
7. Loveday, C., Conway, M.A.: Using SenseCam with an amnesic patient. Memory **19**(7), 697–704 (2011)
8. Abigail, J.S., Andrew, F., et al.: Do life-logging technologies support memory for the past? An experimental study using SenseCam. In: Proceedings of the SIGCHI Conference on Human Factors in Computing Systems (CHI), pp. 81–90 (2007)
9. Masaki, M., Sho, M., et al.: Supporting human recollection of the impressive events using the number of photos. In: Proceedings of the 6th International Conference on Agents and Artificial Intelligence (ICAART), vol. 1, pp. 538–543 (2014)
10. Tero, K., Samuli, L., et al.: Analyzing and improving the image quality of StyleGAN. In: Proceedings of the IEEE Conference on Computer Vision and Pattern Recognition (CVPR), pp. 8110–8119 (2020)
11. MyHeritage Deep Nostalgia, deep learning technology to animate the faces in still family photos – MyHeritage. https://www.myheritage.jp/deep-nostalgia. Accessed 12 July 2023
12. Xiaojiao, M., Chunhua, S., Yu-Bin, Y.: Image restoration using very deep convolutional encoder-decoder networks with symmetric skip connections. In: Proceedings of International Conference on Neural Information Processing Systems December (NIPS), pp. 2810–2818 (2016)
13. Mengjiao, S., Zhongchen, M., et al.: Face aging with conditional generative adversarial network guided by Ranking-CNN. In: Proceedings of IEEE Conference on Multimedia Information Processing and Retrieval (MIPR), pp. 314–319 (2020)
14. Yu, T., Shinji, N.: High-resolution image reconstruction with latent diffusion models from human brain activity. In: Proceedings of the IEEE Conference on Computer Vision and Pattern Recognition (CVPR), pp. 14453–14463 (2023)

A Transformer Based Emotion Recognition Model for Social Robots Using Topographical Maps Generated from EEG Signals

Gosala Bethany🄳 and Manjari Gupta[✉]🄳

DST-Centre for Interdisciplinary Mathematical Sciences (DST-CIMS), Banaras Hindu University, Varanasi 221005, Uttar Pradesh, India
manjari@bhu.ac.in

Abstract. Emotions are an integral part of living beings which influence their thoughts, actions, and interactions with other beings. Understanding human emotions is very important in communicating with others. Developing an emotion recognition model that can be implemented in robots is a critical step in human-robot interaction (HRI). With the rise of artificial intelligence, many techniques are available in machine learning and deep learning to solve this problem, one such technique is Transformers. Transformers, are used in trending technologies like BERT, ChatGPT, DALL-E-2, etc., We used transformers in this study as they have an edge over other by providing flexibility, adaptability, transfer learning, multimodality, parallelization etc., The dataset used is GAMEEMO, which contains EEG signals which are collected from 28 subjects while they were playing four computer-based games which emulate emotions like boring, calm, horror, and funny. Using EEG signal for emotion recognition have advantages like direct measure of brain activity, non-invasiveness, good temporal resolution etc., First, we preprocessed the raw EEG signal using bandpass filtering then created a 5-s epoch out of signal. Next, we converted the 1D EEG signal to a 2D topographical image using independent component analysis by taking 10 principal components out of 14 by persevering at least 95% of the variance in the data. From 9 h and 20 min of GAMEEMO EEG signal, we generated 82, 880 topographical images. Finally, these images were fed to a deep learning-based visual transformers model for the classification of emotions, the best accuracy of the model is 84.71%, our model performed better when compared with the other state-of-the-art models.

Keywords: Emotion Recognition · GAMEEMO · Topomaps · Social Robot · Vision Transformers (ViTs)

1 Introduction

In recent years, the amalgamation of robotics and artificial intelligence (AI) has seen extraordinary growth, especially in the field of human-robot interaction (HRI). In human-robot interaction, robots responding appropriately to humans by understanding human emotions is essential in improving the quality of interactions between humans and robots.

M. Kurosu and A. Hashizume (Eds.): HCII 2024, LNCS 14684, pp. 262–271, 2024.
https://doi.org/10.1007/978-3-031-60405-8_17

Human emotions and state of mind can be studied through data collected from different modalities like facial expressions using image [1], video [2], body language [3], vocal texture [4], and physiological signals from electroencephalogram (EEG) [5] as these signals are directly collected from the human brain. Among all the types of modalities physiological signal data is more reliable because there is less chance of faking.

The advantages of EEG over techniques that measure brain activity are, that it is a non-invasive technique, and also has high temporal resolution and a very low noise-to-signal ratio. EEG has been widely used both clinical as well as in research, especially in the fields of epilepsy, schizophrenia, sleep studies, emotion analysis, and brain-computer interfaces. Using physiological data like EEG to train a robot for classification and recognition of emotions is a unique area of research [6, 7].

A Social robot is a robot that interact with the human and with other robots in socially acceptable manner, robots like Pepper [8], RUBEX [9], are just a few to name. Social robots are very useful at employee recruitment and training, medical screening, teaching assistant, travel concierge, etc. [22, 23]. To develop an artificial intelligence based model that can be integrate with robots for the emotion recognition can make communication with the robots more interactive [10].

Transformers were introduced by [11] for language processing, transformers are a deep learning based models that used self-attention mechanism to weigh the importance of different words in a sentence when processing each word, these self-attention mechanism plays vital role in sentiment analysis, language translation, text generation, and other wide range of tasks. Transformers are the building blocks of many of the state-of-the-art language models like BERT, T5, RoBERTa etc. The transformers works on encoder-decoder architecture, encoder is a component that processes input sequence and generates the token which are contextually represented in the sequence. Decoder takes these contextually represented tokens generated by the encoder and uses them to generate the output sequence [12].

EEG topographic maps or topomaps are a kind of heat maps that shows the electrical activity of the brain, and also gives an idea of brain activation. In this work we have constructed topomaps from EEG signal using independent component analysis (ICA) [13], where we used principal component that can preserve at least 95% of variation, after finding these principal components they were plotted as topomaps.

The novel contribution through this work are:

1. Creating a new dataset of topomaps form GAMEEMO EEG dataset
2. Application of a pre-trained vision transformers (ViT) for the classification of emotions using topomaps created from GAMEEMO dataset.

The rest of the paper is organized in the following manner, in Sect. 2, we have discussed the works that are related to this problem. In Sect. 3, methodology and methods that are used in this work along with experimental setup, results and discussions are presented in Sect. 4, finally conclusion and future work are presented in Sect. 5.

2 Related Work

Inspired by transformers in language processing, the authors [14] developed a deep learning based vision transformer (ViT) model for image recognition, where they consider an image as a 16X16 words. The developed ViT model is tested on the benchmark datasets like ImageNet, CIFAR-100, VTAB, etc. and given a mean accuracy of 88.55%, 94.55%, and 77.63%, respectively. These transformer based models have outperformed the state-of-the-art convolutional models.

A Depthwise convolution and Transformer encoders (DCoT) model with neural networks for EEG-based emotion recognition is proposed by [15]. DCoT visualizes the captured features and also explores the dependence of emotions on each channel. They also conducted the subject-independent and subject-dependent experiments on the benchmarked emotion recognition dataset SEED. This model achieved an average accuracy of 93.83% for three class classification of subject-dependent experiments and an average accuracy of 83.03% for three class classification of subject-independent experiments.

The authors [16] proposed five categories of transformer based models for motor image classification using EEG data at different scenarios. The five models are "spatial-Transformer model (s-Trans), temporal-Transformer model (t-Trans), spatial-CNN+ Transformer model (s-CTrans), temporal-CNN+ Transformer model (t-CTrans), and fusion-CNN+ Transformer model (f-CTrans)", these model were tested on PhysioNet dataset, and an accuracy of 83.31%, 74.44%, and 64.22% is obtained for two-class, three-class, four-class classification respectively.

In [17] an attention-based convolutional transformer neural network (ACTNN) for EEG emotion recognition is discussed, an ACTNN integrates spectral, spatial, and temporal information along with neural networks and transformers. In this experiment they found that gamma brain wave frequency and prefrontal lobe, lateral temporal lobe of the brain might impact more on human emotions. The developed ACTNN is tested on, publically available datasets SEED and SEED-IV and gave an accuracy of 98.47% and 91.90% respectively.

A multi-state emotion recognition model called Transformer Capsule Network (TC-Net) developed by [18] for EEG signal based emotion recognition. This model contains two modules: EEG Transformer to extract EEG features by using EEG-PatchMerging technique and emotion capsule model for refining the emotions and classifying those using EEG feature maps form each channel encoded into capsules. The developed TC-Net model is tested on DEAP and DREAMER datasets in subject-independent cases, an accuracy of 98.78% for valance, 98.81% for arousal, on DEAP and 98.59% for valance, 98.61 for arousal on DREAMER datasets.

An end-to-end framework called Spatiotemporal Symmetric Transformer Model (STS-Transformer) for emotion recognition using EEG is given by [19]. STS-Transformer model recognizes emotions without any manual feature extraction and data pre-processing. STS-Transformer integrates temporal transformer and spatial transformer for extracting temporal and spatial features. This model is tested on DEAP and DREAMER datasets and obtained an accuracy of 89.86%, 86.83% on DEAP, and 85.09%, 82.32% on DREAMER datasets for classifying valence and arousal respectively.

3 Methods and Methodology

3.1 Dataset

The dataset used in this study is GAMEEMO [20], contains EEG signals collected from 28 subjects among which 19 male and 8 female using a portable EEG device called Emotive EPOC+. Emotive EPOC+ is a 14-Channel Wireless EEG Headset and the position of electrodes were "AF3, AF4, F3, F4, F7, F8, FC5, FC6, O1, O2, P7, P8, T7 and T8" with sampling rate 2048 Hz but the signals are down sampled to 128 Hz. These EEG signals are collected when subjects were playing four games which stimulate emotions like boring (G1), calm (G2), horror (G3), and funny (G4), for each game 5 min (300 s) signal is collected and all together 20 min (5-min X 4-Games) EEG data collected from each subject, and the entire dataset is of 560 min (20 min X 28 subjects). We used raw CSV data from GAMEEMO for this work.

3.2 Preprocessing and Creating Topomaps

We used python-MNE [21] for pre-processing, creating epochs, and also to generate topomaps out of epochs. Form raw EEG signal we extracted the all five brain wave frequencies: delta, theta, alpha, beta, gamma, using "filter ()" function with lower cutoff frequency I_freq = 1 and higher cutoff frequency h_freq = 45. After frequency extraction epochs were created using "make_fixed_length_epochs()", where each epoch is of 5s duration with 1s overlap between epochs, total 74 epochs were created for 5 min EEG signal of subject 1 (S1) while playing game 1 (G1). We created topomaps from epochs using independent component analysis (ICA) function "ICA ()" by using principal component to preserve the variance in data. The GAMEEMO dataset is a 14 channel EEG data, so we can get upto14 principal components. But, just 10 principal components are sufficient enough to preserve 95% of variability in the data so we used "n_components = 10". After getting 10 principal components from out of epoch they are converted into a 2D topomaps, Fig. 1 shows plots of 10 principal components that were plotted for epoch1 (E1) of subject1 (S1) while playing game1 (G1), similarly we have plotted the topomaps for all the epochs of S1 while playing G1 total 740 (74 epochs X 10 principal components) topomaps were created for S1 G1. Similarly for G2 (740), G3 (740), G4 (740) signals of S1 and then for all the 28 subjects, a total of 82, 882 (74 epochs X 10 principal components X 28 subjects X 4 games) images were created.

3.3 Experimental Design

In the work we have used a pre-trained vision transformer (ViT) which was developed by Dosovitskiy, A. et al. [14]. Traditionally, transformers are built for language processing, all standard transformers in language processing models takes 1D sequence of token embeddings as an input. As images are 2D data, it need to be converted into a 1D data to build a transformer that can handle 2D images, to make this we converted image into a sequences of patches, and standard learnable 1D Position embeddings are added to the patchs to retain positional information. This resulting vector serves as an input to the encoder block. Encoder block of transformer contains MLP blocks and multiheaded

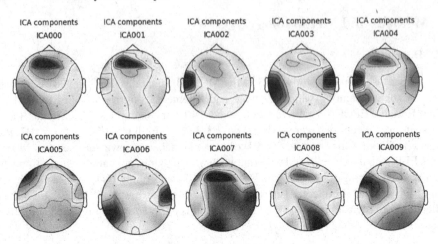

Fig. 1. A snapshot of topomaps images of G1S1E1 created using ICA

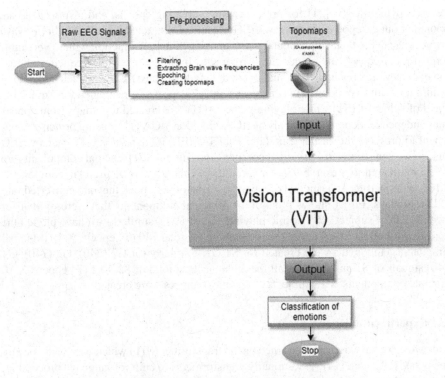

Fig. 2. Experimental Flow Diagram of developed Model

self- attention layers in alternate sequence. The flow of the conducted experiments have shown in Fig. 2.

We have conducted our experiments on a HP ZBook Power 15.6 inch G9 Mobile Workstation PC, which has a 12th Gen Intel(R) Core(TM) i9-12900H 2.50 GHz processor with an installed RAM of 32 GB, along with NVIDIA RTX A2000 8 GB Laptop GPU as hardware. We used python programming language to create the model and used jupyter notebook for coding, also used python packages like torch, torchnision, matplotlib etc.

4 Results and Discussion

Here we will discuss the results that we have obtained through the experiments we have conducted and also give a comparison of the proposed model with the state-of-the-art models. We divided the dataset of images into approximately 80:20 ratio, where 80% data is used to train the developed model and 20% data is used to test the model. We used the *torch* and *torchvision* libraries of python to develop and load the pre-trained vision transformer (ViT) model, along cuda programming. We have conducted 5 experiments in total by trying the different hyper parameters values.

Table 1. Different hyper parameters used in experiments

Experiments	Loss function	Batch size	epochs	Learning rate	Accuracy (%)
1	NLLLoss()	16	10	1e−2	72.57
2	NLLLoss()	16	20	1e−3	68.72
3	CrossEntropyLoss()	16	30	1e−4	75.26
4	CrossEntropyLoss()	32	40	1e−4	79.95
5	CrossEntropyLoss()	32	50	1e−6	84.71

We used *"NLLLoss(), CrossEntropyLoss()"* as loss functions, 16 and 32 as a batch sizes, run experiments on *"10,,20, 30, 40, and 50"* epochs, used *"le-2, le-2, le-3, le-4, le-5, le-6"* asclearning rates etc., more details about these are given in Table 1. The best accuracy of 84.71% is acquired when we used *"CrossEntropyLoss(), 32, 50, le-6"*, for loss function, batch size, epochs, learning rate, respectively as parameters for the model. We used *Adam* optimizer to optimize the model. Figure 3 shows how the accuracy and loss function values varies with the epochs of the developed model for one of the experiment.

We have compared the developed ViT model with the other transformer based state-of-the-art models that we have discussed in our related work section. The developed model has outperformed some of the state-of-the-art models. In Table 2. We have given the details like the problem that the authors are addressing, the dataset they are using in building the model, the type of classification model they are developing, along with the performance metric accuracy the STOA models are getting. Guo, J. Y. et al. [15], studied emotions by subject dependent, and subject independence wise, the model developed by Wei, Y et al. [18] has given best results in Subject-dependent scenario. Xie, J. [16]

build a 2-class, 3-class, 4-class classification model. Our model is also performing well for binary class classification, then multi-class classification. This comparison of the proposed model is illustrated in the below Table 2.

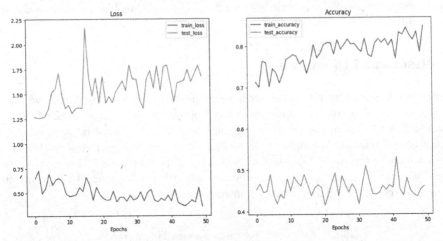

Fig. 3. Variation of loss function and accuracy with epochs for one of the experiment

Table 2. Comparison of the proposed model with SOTA models

Authors	Problem addressed	Datasets	Classification Algorithms	Accuracy (%)
Dosovitskiy, A. et al. [14]	classification	ImageNet, CIFAR100, VTAB	ViT-H/14 ViT-L/16	88.55,94.55,77.63 87.76,99.42,76.28
Guo, J. Y. et al. [15]	emotion recognition	SEED	neural network model (DCoT)	93.83 (SD) 83.03 (SI)
Xie, J. [16]	classifications of motor imagery EEG	PhysioNet dataset	Transformer-based deep learning framework	83.31 (2-class) 74.44 (3-class) 64.22 (4-class)
Gong, L. et al. [17]	emotion recognition	SEED SEED-IV	Attention-based convolutional transformer neural network (ACTNN)	98.47 91.90
Wei, Y et al. [18]	emotion recognition	DEAP, DREAMER	Transformer Capsule Network (TC-Net)	98.76,98.81,98.8 98.61,98.59,98.67

(continued)

Table 2. (*continued*)

Authors	Problem addressed	Datasets	Classification Algorithms	Accuracy (%)
Zheng, W., & Pan, B. [19]	emotion recognition	DEAP, DREAMER	Spatiotemporal Symmetric Transformer Model (STS-Transformer)	89.86(valence) 86.83 (arousal), 85.09(valence) 82.32(arousal)
Proposed work	emotion classification	GAMEEMO	Vision Transformer (ViT)	84.71

SD = subject-dependent, SI = subject-independent, DCoT = depthwise convolution and Transformer encoders

5 Conclusion and Future Work

In this work we have discussed the application of Vision Transformer (ViT) to the emotion classification problem, using the images called topomaps which are generated from EEG signal using Independent component analysis (ICA). By using ICA we have converted the 1D EEG signal to the 2D topomap images. We have achieved an accuracy of 84.74 which is better than some of the SOTA methods. The accuracy of the model can be increased even more with better hyper parameter tuning, but due to lack of computational constrains we are unable to do so.

EEG signal and images are of different modalities and also have different dimensions, models like these can be used in implementing multi-modal data. Models that are built on multi-modal data will be of robust, because of multi dimensionality in data. Implementing these models in social robots is very useful to create social robots that an understand human emotions and respond to them accordingly. This developed model can also be used for other neurological problems like Parkinson's, epilepsy, schizophrenia etc.

This research can be further be extended in directions like multi-modal implementation, using modalities like audio, video, images, physiological signals, etc., to develop an AI driven model which can be implemented in various fields. Many other new age technologies like GANs, explainable AI (XAI) and others can also be used for emotion recognition.

Acknowledgement. 1. "The author is extremely grateful to University Grants Committee (UGC) for providing the Junior Research Fellowship (JRF) under Maulana Azad National Fellowship for Minorities (MANFJRF), with the award reference number: NO.F.82-27/2019 (SA III)."

2. "We also acknowledge the Institute of Eminence (IoE) scheme at BHU for supporting us."

References

1. Kotsia, I., Pitas, I.: Facial expression recognition in image sequences using geometric deformation features and support vector machines. IEEE Trans. Image Process. **16**(1), 172–187 (2006)
2. Chen, J., Chen, Z., Chi, Z., Fu, H.: Facial expression recognition in video with multiple feature fusion. IEEE Trans. Affect. Comput. **9**(1), 38–50 (2016)
3. Abramson, L., Petranker, R., Marom, I., Aviezer, H.: Social interaction context shapes emotion recognition through body language, not facial expressions. Emotion **21**(3), 557 (2021)
4. Lim, Y., Ng, K.W., Naveen, P., Haw, S.C.: Emotion recognition by facial expression and voice: review and analysis. J. Inf. Web Eng. **1**(2), 45–54 (2022)
5. Suhaimi, N.S., Mountstephens, J., Teo, J.: EEG-based emotion recognition: a state-of-the-art review of current trends and opportunities. Comput. Intell. Neurosci. (2020)
6. Al-Khasawneh, M.A., Alzahrani, A., Alarood, A.: An artificial intelligence based effective diagnosis of parkinson disease using EEG signal. In: Data Analysis for Neurodegenerative Disorders, pp. 239–251. Springer, Singapore (2023)
7. Rivera, M.J., Teruel, M.A., Mate, A., Trujillo, J.: Diagnosis and prognosis of mental disorders by means of EEG and deep learning: a systematic mapping study. Artif. Intell.. Rev. 1–43 (2022)
8. Ilyas, C.M.A., Schmuck, V., Haque, M.A., Nasrollahi, K., Rehm, M., Moeslund, T.B.: Teaching pepper robot to recognize emotions of traumatic brain injured patients using deep neural networks. In: 2019 28th IEEE International Conference on Robot and Human Interactive Communication (RO-MAN), pp. 1–7. IEEE (2019)
9. Al-Omary, A., Akram, M.M., Dhamodharan, V.: Design and implementation of intelligent socializing 3D humanoid robot. In: 2021 International Conference on Innovation and Intelligence for Informatics, Computing, and Technologies (3ICT), pp. 398–402. IEEE (2021)
10. Heredia, J., et al.: Adaptive multimodal emotion detection architecture for social robots. IEEE Access **10**, 20727–20744 (2022)
11. Vaswani, A., et al.: Attention is all you need. Adv. Neural Inf. Process. Syst. **30** (2017)
12. Zeyer, A., Bahar, P., Irie, K., Schlüter, R., Ney, H.: A comparison of transformer and lSTM encoder decoder models for ASR. In: 2019 IEEE Automatic Speech Recognition and Understanding Workshop (ASRU), pp. 8–15. IEEE (2019)
13. Hooi, L.S., Nisar, H., Voon, Y.V.: Comparison of motion field of EEG topo-maps for tracking brain activation. In: 2016 IEEE EMBS Conference on Biomedical Engineering and Sciences (IECBES), pp. 251–256. IEEE (2016)
14. Dosovitskiy, A., et al.: An image is worth 16x16 words: transformers for image recognition at scale. arXiv preprint arXiv:2010.11929 (2020)
15. Guo, J.Y., et al.: A transformer based neural network for emotion recognition and visualizations of crucial EEG channels. Physica A **603**, 127700 (2022)
16. Xie, J., et al.: A transformer-based approach combining deep learning network and spatial-temporal information for raw EEG classification. IEEE Trans. Neural Syst. Rehabil. Eng. **30**, 2126–2136 (2022)
17. Gong, L., Li, M., Zhang, T., Chen, W.: EEG emotion recognition using attention-based convolutional transformer neural network. Biomed. Signal Process. Control **84**, 104835 (2023)
18. Wei, Y., Liu, Y., Li, C., Cheng, J., Song, R., Chen, X.: TC-Net: a transformer capsule network for EEG-based emotion recognition. Comput. Biol. Med. **152**, 106463 (2023)
19. Zheng, W., Pan, B.: A spatiotemporal symmetrical transformer structure for EEG emotion recognition. Biomed. Signal Process. Control **87**, 105487 (2024)
20. Alakus, T.B., Gonen, M., Turkoglu, I.: Database for an emotion recognition system based on EEG signals and various computer games–GAMEEMO. Biomed. Signal Process. Control **60**, 101951 (2020)

21. Gramfort, A., et al.: MEG and EEG data analysis with MNE-Python. Front. Neurosci. **267** (2013)
22. Ragno, L., Borboni, A., Vannetti, F., Amici, C., Cusano, N.: Application of social robots in healthcare: review on characteristics, requirements, technical solutions. Sensors **23**(15), 6820 (2023)
23. Mahdi, H., Akgun, S.A., Saleh, S., Dautenhahn, K.: A survey on the design and evolution of social robots—past, present and future. Robot. Autonom. Syst. **156**, 104193 (2022)

Challenges of Facial Expression Recognition and Recommendations for the Use of Emotion AI in Video Conferences

Bärbel Bissinger[1,2]([✉]), Christian Märtin[1], and Michael Fellmann[2]

[1] Computer Science, Augsburg Technical University of Applied Sciences, Augsburg, Germany
{baerbel.bissinger,christian.maertin}@tha.de
[2] Business Information Systems, University of Rostock, Rostock, Germany
michael.fellmann@uni-rostock.de

Abstract. Artificial emotional intelligence (AIE), affective computing or Emotion AI deal with the ability of machines to recognize human emotions. To investigate the possibilities and limitations of such technologies further, we explored an existing commercial Facial Expression Recognition (FER) tool as well as an open-source project and carried out several small-scale user studies focusing on emotion recognition from faces during video conferences. This approach aims to address the following research questions: How well can FER technologies recognize emotions in video conferences? What are the challenges and limitations of FER technologies?

With this paper we contribute to the assessment and practicability of FER, present two FER tools and highlight criticism as well as limitations of FER technologies. We outline different small-scale user studies with FER. We conclude with recommendations drawn from those user studies and literature research. These suggestions adhere to principles such as Responsible AI (RAI) and value-based design. We do this by the example of FER in video conferences, but some of the findings may be transferred to other Emotion AI technologies and application areas as well.

Keywords: Facial Expression Recognition (FER) · Emotion Recognition · Emotion AI · Responsible AI (RAI) · Virtual Collaboration · Video Conferences

1 Introduction

Even when at rest, the face can convey emotional or mood-related information. It is a commanding feature as it houses the senses of smell, taste, sight, and hearing [1]. The human face is considered a message-board for emotions and already played an important part in Charles Darwin's emotion research [2]. As with subsequent researchers, Darwin emphasized facial expressions and provided detailed discussions of the facial muscles that are responsible for them. He referred to 19th-century physiologists who extensively studied facial musculature. One of the most well-known figures in this field is the French physiologist Duchenne de Boulogne, who attempted to produce emotional

M. Kurosu and A. Hashizume (Eds.): HCII 2024, LNCS 14684, pp. 272–290, 2024.
https://doi.org/10.1007/978-3-031-60405-8_18

facial expressions by electrically stimulating individual muscles. Later, Silvan Tomkins stated that the seat of emotions was in the face and that human motivation is based on emotions. Additionally, he demonstrated that specific emotional states were associated with facial expressions [3, 4].

One area of Emotion AI is Facial Expression Recognition (FER) which aims to identify emotions from facial analysis. Our physical signals can be analyzed and categorized which makes it possible to train software systems and machines to recognize emotions and respond to them [5]. This changes the way we interact with technology, and it could also change the way we interact with each other. The underlying research field is dynamically evolving, emotion detection and recognition is a rapidly growing market and many products that apply Emotion AI have already hit the market. As technology becomes ubiquitous in interpersonal interactions and activities, Emotion AI could make our tool-based interactions more human-like. In video conferences for example, they could support the transmission of positive emotions, surprise or other reactions from the audience which are otherwise hard to identify due to small face icons or screen sharing.

2 Small-Scale User Studies with FER

With our research we aim to bridge the gap of emotion recognition between on-site meetings and video conferences to support nonverbal communication. To achieve this goal, we conducted several experiments with FER to test the accuracy, usefulness, and potential applications.

2.1 Previous User Studies: FER with a Commercial Tool, Human Observer, and Self-reports

Study 1 – In our previous research [6], we used FER in video conferences to detect emotional states of participants with the FaceReader software[1], human observers or self-reports. In two small-scale user studies (n = 6 and n = 9), we only analyzed emotions when participants agreed to the facial expression analysis beforehand and when they shared their videos during the meeting. In Study 1, we collected subjective impressions with self-reports from the participants and with a human observer to compare the results with the FER analysis, as illustrated in Fig. 1.

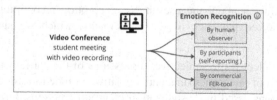

Fig. 1. User Study 1

---

[1] https://www.noldus.com/facereader

Study 2 – In Study 2, the emotion recognition was done in real-time with live visualizations (Fig. 2) which were visible for all participants during the call. For the emotion recognition we used human observers and a prototype that enabled live visualizations as FER-simulation, since our FaceReader license can only analyze one face at a time and since we used a real business meeting in Germany, where the usage of Emotion AI is not permitted without further inspections. The predicted emotional states were available as group emotions, no individual results were shown. Beforehand and afterwards, we collected information from the participants with questionnaires. More details of those two studies are described in a previous paper [6].

Fig. 2. User Study 2

Perceived Accuracy: To verify the results of FaceReader, we asked the participants of User Study 1 via self-assessment questionnaires after the meeting about their emotional states or asked human observers which emotions they recognized in the recorded meetings. In these small-scale studies, we discovered situations in which facial expressions alone were not sufficient to correctly identify emotions. In situations where the face was not well visible, more information such as voice or context was needed to identify the expressed emotions. Without laboratory conditions, we discovered weaknesses of the automatic emotion recognition via faces only. Circumstances such as changing video quality or participant movement made automatic emotion recognition via faces challenging. In addition, we found cases in which the results of the commercial FER tool were not in alignment with the results of the participants or the human observer. However, determining who is correct in recognizing emotions (the tool, the human observer, or the participants with time-delayed answers?) is difficult due to the complexity and subjectivity of emotions. That is why there is no reliable ground truth, neither of the assessments of humans nor of the automated FER analysis.

To draw conclusion about the usefulness of emotion recognition and live visualization, we collected feedback of the participants, which we summarize in the following.

Usefulness. We collected the subjective impressions of the participants afterwards in User Study 2. Most of the participants had a positive attitude towards the visualization of emotions and considered the visualization of group emotions during a meeting as helpful, to e.g. draw conclusions about the emotional situation in the team. Despite the benefits, some serious concerns have also been raised. One participant reported that the visualization of emotions during a meeting *"would make me more insecure"* (original: *"würde mich mehr verunsichern"*). Another person mentioned: *"I cannot comment on* *that, and the system is unaware of the reason for my current emotional state."* (original: *"Ich kann mich dazu nicht äußern und das System weiß nicht, warum ich diese Emotion gerade habe."*). Other feedback indicated potential negative consequences of automated FER in video conferences like an additional stress factor or inauthentic behavior of the attendees (original: *"Es ist als Teilnehmer eher ein Stressor. Also etwas, worauf man zusätzlich noch achten muss"*; translation: *"As a participant, it is more of a stressor. So it's something you also have to pay attention to."* and *"Die Personen könnten dann vielleicht nicht mehr authentisch sein."*; translation: *"The authenticity of the participants may be affected."*).

In this user study, the results of the facial expression analysis were shown as **collective group emotions** and **available for everyone in the meeting**. In previous research, we defined different use cases, in which all meeting attendees or only the moderator would have access to the emotion analysis results [7]. To verify whether it is more useful for all participants or only for the moderator to receive this information, we asked the participants. Half of them would be comfortable with the information being available only to the moderator, while the other half would not. The reasons given by the participants who would not like the results to be available only to the moderator are:

- "If such an approach is being used, then the information should be accessible to all meeting attendees." (original: "Wenn man so etwas verwendet, dann sollten diese Informationen allen Personen im Meeting zur Verfügung stehen.")
- "I have no control over what is interpreted and presented about me." (original: "Ich kann nicht darüber verfügen, was über mich interpretiert und präsentiert wird.")
- "If only the moderator gets the information, I would feel like I was being watched. To be fair, it should be available to everyone in the meeting." (original: "Wenn nur ein Moderator die Informationen bekommt, würde ich mich beobachtet fühlen. Aus Fairness sollte es allen Teilnehmenden zur Verfügung stehen.")

The conducted user studies helped us to verify the accuracy of the FER technology in real-world meeting scenarios and to understand the impacts, positive and negative, for the attendees better. A limitation of those studies was that only one face could be analyzed at a time due to the limitations with the available FaceReader license. Therefore, a lot of manual work was necessary, and we could not use real-time data of the FER software.

To explore the accuracy of automated FER further and to make sure that the discrepancies were not only because of the tool we were using, we did similar small-scale studies where we included another tool, which is open-source and can detect changes in facial muscle movements, action units (AUs), from several faces at the same time. These studies are presented in the next chapter. The results confirm our previous findings.

2.2 User Studies: FER with a Commercial Tool, an Open-Source Project, and Human Observers

Since our previous research revealed inconsistencies between the results produced by the FER tool and those by the human observer or the participants, we integrated an alternative open-source tool into our next studies. Other reasons to consider and explore alternative approaches to the commercial FER tool include the relatively high costs and limited functionalities of our current commercial FaceReader 9 license.

We included hybrid and on-site meetings into our test scenarios to compare the analysis results in different meeting set-ups and with various camera recordings. The study design is shown in Fig. 3.

As a second system for computer-based emotion analysis, we used OpenFace[2]. With this tool, we could analyze more than one face at a time, however, significant manual effort was required.

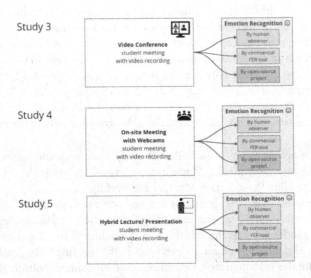

Fig. 3. User Studies with a commercial FER tool and an open-source alternative

Introduction to OpenFace. OpenFace is an open-source-software which is freely available for research purposes on GitHub by the author Tadas Baltrusaitis. It can detect facial landmarks, head pose- and eye-gaze estimation as well as facial action units and is capable to perform in real-time. According to the authors, the model has still a good performance even with noisy input. The OpenFace toolkit has been enhanced and improved through the integration of new deep learning techniques and neural networks with an improved ability to adapt to suboptimal image conditions, allowing for reliable analyses even in situations with poor lighting and variable camera angles. It is important to emphasize that features such as eye-tracking or facial expression analysis rely on accurate recognition of **facial landmarks**. For the recognition of these facial landmarks, the Convolutional Experts Constrained Local Model (CE-CLM) is used. This model contains two main components: the Point Distribution Model (PDM), which records shape variations of landmarks, and the patch experts, which models the local appearance changes of each landmark. Changes in appearance can be caused by various factors,

[2] https://github.com/TadasBaltrusaitis/OpenFace/wiki

such as different lighting, skin tone, or facial movement. For optimal results, the tool requires a minimum of 100 pixels between the ears [8, 9].

OpenFace 2.0 utilizes presence and intensity of AUs to identify **facial expressions**. The software is based on an AU recognition framework developed by Baltrusaitis et al. that uses linear kernel Support Vector Machines [10]. Despite being considered as outdated, as mentioned by the developers, this approach is competitive with newer deep learning methods due to its faster processing speed. The software applies customized techniques to enhance the processing of video footage captured in natural environments. It makes individual adjustments and corrects predictions based on a mixture of data-rich facial features and patterns obtained from images with a resolution of 112x112 pixels. The software can recognize the following Action Units: AU1, AU2, AU4, AU5, AU6, AU7, AU9, AU10, A12, AU14, AU15, AU17, AU20, AU23, AU25, AU26, AU28 and AU45 [9].

Since OpenFace is not recognizing AU16, which is necessary to predict *Disgust* [11], we cannot analyze this emotion in our studies. This is not a real limitation in our point of view since we expect little or no such emotion in our scenarios.

It is important to note that the basic toolkit of OpenFace 2.0 does not provide an automated function for mapping the measured AUs to emotions. The output of OpenFace is one csv file per video. The software does not perform any calculations with the generated data, so the csv contains a wealth of raw data. Complementary tools such as OpenFaceR can extend the functionality of OpenFace by using the data generated by OpenFace. OpenFaceR provides various methods to convert the csv data into different summary statistics [12]. In our studies, we did the matching of the measured action units to the basic emotions manually with the help of Emotional Facial Action Coding System (EmFACS), a correlation system that links AUs to the basic emotions according to Ekman and Friesen [13].

OpenFace can be used via a graphical user interface (GUI) for Windows users or via command lines (Windows, Ubuntu, and Mac OS X), which we used in the studies. The generated data of the csv file we used in the studies were mainly *face_id* (to separate the data when there are multiple faces in a video), *timestamp* in seconds, *success* (shows whether face detection was successful and reliable from 0 to 1), and the *AU data*.

Experimental Setup. We defined three different meeting scenarios which are relevant in educational and industry settings. Those are video conferences, on-site conferences, and hybrid meetings such as lectures or presentations. With the consent of meeting participants, we recorded the meetings and analyzed facial expressions to identify emotions with two different FER tools, the commercial tool FaceReader and the open-source software OpenFace, and by human observers (5 female, 5 male, age range between 18 and 55) to compare the results. The recordings were the basis for the identification of emotions. The human observers served as a comparison group and got the same meeting recordings as the software tools, but without sound, to focus their attention on facial expressions only. In previous studies, we realized that the observers had an advantage since they could include contextual information in the emotion recognition. The task of them was to assess the emotional facial reactions of the meeting participants to identify basic emotions. We divided the meetings in different situations focusing on one emotion each. Since the manual effort for the automated FER was very high (with FaceReader only one analysis was possible at a time which means we had to cut the videos and had do the analysis separately; with OpenFace the manual processing of the csv and the mapping of the action units to basic emotions was complex), and to minimize the effort of the human observers, we could only invite a small number of participants to our user study meetings.

Study 3 – Video Conference. This was an online meeting with three participants (male, mid-20s and advanced-age). To get the most realistic recordings, the participants in this study did not receive a briefing beforehand on how the camera position and lighting conditions should be. Therefore, the webcam- and video quality, the recording angle and the lightning conditions varied between those three participants. This setup allowed us to test the software's ability to analyze under varying conditions. The meeting had an open and positive atmosphere, but also addressed serious topics. The recording length of the meeting was 17 min.

Study 4 – On-site Meeting with Webcams. This was an on-site discussion with three participants (male, mid-20s) and one moderator. To produce data material with different camera angles, we used four cameras: one webcam in front of each participant, and one video recorder to record the whole scene. This setup was used to test emotion recognition with different recordings and when people move their head around, as it might be the case in video conferences. The discussion was divided into three parts: a discussion of study related topics, a jokes round to intentionally evoke emotions, a second discussion part. Throughout the meeting, the moderator ensured that participants were given equal speaking times. The discussion lasted 32 min. The setup created a realistic discussion round.

Study 5 – Hybrid Lecture/Presentation. In this study, three participants (male, mid-20s) were recorded for the facial expression analysis. Two participants took part in the meeting at the on-site location, the third one took part remotely via Zoom and was seated in our laboratory to ensure optimal conditions for the recording. The two participants in the lecture room were recorded with one camera. The topics of the lecture were quantum computing and brain-inspired computing. The duration of the meeting was 45 min. The purpose of the test was to simulate a genuine lecture scenario to evaluate emotion recognition of recordings in the laboratory and recordings with suboptimal conditions.

Analysis and Results. The recordings were analyzed with FaceReader, OpenFace and by 10 human observers via questionnaires. Regarding the tool-based analysis we worked with the results in csv files in excel sheets. For the FaceReader analysis, we needed to cut the videos. The video was edited using *DaVinci Resolve*, a free video editing application developed by Blackmagic Design. Besides that, the FaceReader analysis could be done quite convenient and fast. The analysis with OpenFace was more time consuming. After running the commands "FaceLandmarkVidMulti.exe" for the video recording with the whole scene and the "FeatureExtraction.exe" for the webcam recordings, we got the results as csv files. First step was to structure the data and to sort out data that was not relevant for emotion recognition to be able to analyze it. With the timestamp data we were able to allocate the AU data to our defined scenes and situations whose time units are specified in seconds. In the whole scene recording, we needed to filter the results for the different persons each having a different face_id. After that, the AU data needed to be compared to basic emotions according to EmFACS by filtering the AU results and comparing them to the AUs of basic emotions. Finally, we determined the predominant emotion by identifying the emotion with the highest number of data records. If OpenFace detected a face, but no active AUs, we noted this as a neutral state.

In the following, we outline some of our analysis and results, focusing on Study 5 and highlighting some findings of Study 4 and Study 3.

Study 5 (hybrid). All three participants were male and in their mid-20s. Participant 1 was wearing glasses, had long hair, and a short beard. Participant 2 had short hair and no beard. Participants 1 and 2 were recorded with the same camera in the meeting room. Participant 3 was bald and has a medium-length beard and joined the meeting remotely via Zoom in our laboratory with optimal recording conditions.

Table 1 shows the datasets which were recognized, or not recognized by FaceReader and OpenFace. Our expectation was that emotion recognition would work best with participant 3, the recording from the laboratory. Nevertheless, most of the unrecognized data records belonged to this test subject. A possible explanation are probably the facial features. Participant 3 had a medium length beard that covered part of the face which might be the reason for the huge amount of not recognized data.

Table 1. Number of unrecognized datasets and recognized datasets (Study 5)

		Participant 1	Participant 2	Participant 3 (remote)
FaceReader				
	Not recognized	0	20	1909
	Recognized	120374	93468	93049
OpenFace				
	Not recognized	793	91	1967
	Recognized	134195	134195	93061

Table 2 shows the emotion recognition of human observers, individually and on average, of FaceReader, and of OpenFace. The discrepancies in the results, also between the different human observers, reflect the complexity and subjectivity of emotions. If we take the average of the human observers as the ground truth, FaceReader has seven out of ten correct results, OpenFace four out of ten. The correctly recognized emotions were *Neutral* and *Happy* and in the case of FaceReader one time *Sad* and *Angry*. It is noticeable that despite the suboptimal recording conditions of participant 1 and 2, most facial expressions are recognized of participant 1, in contrast to participant 2 and 3. Especially OpenFace had problems recognizing emotions of Participant 3. In this case, it seems like FaceReader is better trained to recognize emotions even if parts of the face are hidden. Even though many datasets could not be recognized (see Table 1), the correct emotion identification was possible in most cases for this participant with FaceReader (Table 2).

In general, the emotion recognition was quite time-consuming. The ten human observers watched each 1 hour and 22 min of video recordings. In sum, all human observers watched 13 h and 43 min, only for Study 5. The different steps to identify emotions with OpenFace as described above, were also complex.

Table 2. Emotion Recognition Results (Study 5)

	Participant 1			Participant 2			Participant 3 (remote in Laboratory)			
	Situation 1	Situation 2	Situation 3	Situation 1	Situation 2	Situation 3	Situation 1	Situation 2	Situation 3	Situation 4
Human Observer 1	Happy	Neutral	Happy	Happy	Neutral	Happy	Happy	Disgusted	Sad	Angry
Human Observer 2	Happy	Sad	Happy	Happy	Neutral	Happy	Happy	Surprised	Angry	Angry
Human Observer 3	Happy	Sad	Happy	Happy	Neutral	Sad	Happy	Sad	Angry	Angry
Human Observer 4	Happy	Neutral	Neutral	Happy	Neutral	Neutral	Happy	Sad	Angry	Angry
Human Observer 5	Happy	Neutral	Happy	Happy	Neutral	Neutral	Happy	Sad	Angry	Neutral
Human Observer 6	Happy	Neutral	Happy	Happy	Happy	Angry	Happy	Sad	Angry	Neutral
Human Observer 7	Happy	Neutral	Neutral	Happy	Neutral	Neutral	Happy	Sad	Angry	Angry
Human Observer 8	Happy	Neutral	Happy	Happy	Happy	Neutral	Happy	Sad	Sad	Sad
Human Observer 9	Happy	Neutral	Happy	Happy	Neutral	Angry	Happy	Sad	Angry	Angry
Human Observer 10	Happy	Sad	Happy	Happy	Sad	Neutral	Happy	Sad	Angry	Angry
Sum Human Observers	Happy	Neutral	Happy	Happy	Neutral	Happy	Happy	Sad	Angry	Angry
FaceReader	Disgusted	Neutral	Happy	Happy	Neutral	Neutral	Happy	Sad	Sad	Angry
OpenFace	Happy	Neutral	Happy	Contempt	Neutral	Neutral	Neutral	Neutral	Contempt	Neutral

Study 4 and Study 3. In these studies, most of the emotional states which were recognized by automated FER FaceReader and OpenFace were *Happy*, *Neutral* and *Surprised*. Compared to the results of the human observers, *Happy* and *Surprised* were in most cases correctly identified. On the other hand, *Angry* or *Disgusted* were often wrongly identified, compared to the human impressions. In the recordings with several persons in the video, OpenFace was able to analyze more than one face, however, we realized that the analysis data contained more face identifier values than persons in the videos. For instance, the analysis results displayed different face_id values for participant 1 in Study 3 at different timestamps. This means that the face recognition was not always working correctly which may have impacts on further analysis results.

Table 3 shows that in this real-world scenario, many datasets could not be recognized in Study 4. This is probably because the participants did not always look at the camera during the discussion, but at their discussion partners and, as it is usual in a natural conversation, often had their hand or a sheet of paper in front of their mouth or eyes. Participant 1 was seated in the middle and therefore often moved his head to turn towards his conversation partners. That is probably the reason why there are the most unrecognized datasets for this participant, also on the separated webcam recordings. This shows that emotion recognition is affected when people move a lot during a meeting.

Table 3. Number of unrecognized datasets and recognized datasets (Study 4)

		Participant 1	Participant 2	Participant 3	Recording with all participants
FaceReader					
	Not recognized	689	27	102	not possible with our license
	Recognized	58361	58237	58353	not possible with our license
OpenFace					
	Not recognized	1053	427	336	6965
	Recognized	58363	57822	58365	59851

General Results. Another noticeable characteristic of the FaceReader analysis is the changing analysis speed of the software. The analysis of the webcam videos under good conditions (Study 4) corresponded approximately to the duration of the meeting, while the analysis of the recordings of the on-site participants (Study 5) took two to three times longer than the recordings. This may be caused by poorer video quality and less favorable recording conditions. The quality of the video did not seem to affect the analysis results. However, it shows that an analysis in real-time under poor video conditions would not be possible.

Moreover, we realized that an analysis was only possible when both eyes were visible. If the mouth was covered for a short time, for example with a hand, FaceReader could continue the analysis. However, if the mouth was covered for a longer period, the analysis could become impossible or incorrect.

Facial features or the camera position influence the analysis results. E.g., a shaved face seems to simplify the analysis. If the camera position is below the face, the person may appear surprised by FaceReader. This might be due to the different appearance of the eyebrows from this angle of view.

2.3 Our Learnings from the Studies

Since the accuracy was not as good as expected and taking the mentioned concerns of participants into account (Study 2), we see the following most important learnings for a useful, human-centered approach when using FER in video conferences:

- Facial expressions alone might not always provide sufficient data to correctly identify the emotions. For better results, other physical signals which indicate emotional states could be included in the analysis.
- To improve the correctness of the analysis results further and to empower the meeting attendees by putting them in control of what is interpreted, an interim step might be necessary. The results of the tools could be verified by the attendees before appearing in the analysis results (as presented in another paper [14]).
- Most FER tools recognize the so-called basic emotions. In video conferences however, other emotions such as confused, sleepy, energetic, amused, thoughtful, or bored might be more interesting and more relevant than these basic emotions. These are difficult to measure because the expressions for those are not universally the same.

3 Limitations and Challenges of Emotion Recognition and FER

Even though there are many FER products on the market and there are substantial research efforts in this field, there are still many unsolved challenges for emotion recognition from faces. In the following, we first present challenges we faced in our studies, and which occur in facial expression recognition in video conferences. Second, we show challenges with the FER technologies and Emotion AI in a more holistic view, based on our studies and literature research.

3.1 Challenges Encountered in Our Studies

The complexity and subjectivity of emotions makes it very difficult to measure the baseline and establish the ground truth. To validate the FER results, we asked human observers or surveyed the participants about the emotions they experienced after the meeting (Study 1). The use of time-delayed answers and self-reporting may result in imprecise data. Asking the participants during the meeting on the other hand, as, e. g. done by Ertay et al., may lead to distraction or changes in the emotional experience and influence the emotional states of the participants [15]. It is therefore difficult to determine a baseline and to objectively assess which results are correct. Our assumption is that humans are better at evaluating facial expressions and emotions, based on the state of the art of FER tools and due to human ability to access more contextual and personal information, which is beyond the capabilities of current FER tools. Therefore, we utilized the human-reported data to verify the accuracy of the results delivered by the tools used. Also for humans it is not easy to name, label or articulate emotions of themselves or others [6, 16]. To avoid relying on a single person, we consulted a total of ten human observers in some studies and took the average as the result. However, the problem with the ground truth is still valid.

A huge limitation is that the FER tools as well as our questionnaires are limited to the so-called basic emotions. On the one hand, this forces people and tools to choose one of these. On the other hand, especially in professional environments, some of these emotions might be suppressed or not named intentionally. Other emotions than the basic ones might be more interesting to share in business meetings. FaceReader provides the possibility to add custom facial expressions and build customized algorithms for those. Some custom expressions are available by default. They are: interest, boredom, and confusion [17]. But their scientific foundation is unclear.

The analysis of the FER tool was limited by incomplete or missing data, either due to human actions or poor network conditions. For example, if people moved their head or arms a lot, if parts of their face were covered by their hands or beards, or if the face was not front-facing towards the camera, the accuracy of the tool's results was affected. Other factors that influence the available data and the analysis were changing lightning conditions, the webcam angle or changing video qualities, but also remarkable facial features such as beards or large eyes. Another restriction was the calibration of the tool for the different people and faces. In some cases, this did not work well in the tool, and therefore the analysis results were affected for certain people.

In some studies, (Study 1, 2, partially 4 and 5), participants were instructed to sit facing the camera and to ensure good lighting and internet quality. In professional settings and day-to-day online meetings, however, the situation is often different which makes the emotion recognition even more challenging.

Some of the analysis results from the tools were obviously incorrect and biased. E.g., FaceReader stated the age of one participant (bald head, beard) as 50, but he is in his mid-20s. In some of our earlier studies, the tool had difficulties with distinctive glasses or prominent facial features. With OpenFace, on the other hand, it happened that the analysis results showed more face_ids than people were in the video. This means that the face detection is not always working correctly. It is therefore important that humans verify the results of the automated analysis.

In video conferences in general, both for humans and automated tools, emotion recognition is among other factors highly influenced by video quality, movements and poses, harsh lightning conditions, camera distance, small icons or applied filters for the face appearance.

3.2 General Challenges with FER Technologies and Emotion AI

Picard, who presented the concept of Affective Computing in detail in 2000 in her book under the same name, published a paper in 2003 where she addresses and discusses challenges of automated emotion recognition [16]. Some of the challenges presented are still valid today. Almost 20 years later, in 2022, Lee et al. published a paper in which they review the above-mentioned criticisms and challenges mentioned by Picard, pointed out which problems have been solved, which are still open issues and looked into new challenges that have been raised [18].

The following summarizes and discusses raised criticisms and challenges of FER and Emotion AI.

Criticism 1 – Broad Range of Emotional Signals and Measurement. There are many different physiological signals and expressions for emotions which are too non-differentiated or difficult to categorize and measure (such as brain activity, neurotransmitters).

Lee et al. pointed out that the measurement and management of physiological data has improved a lot since then with new sensors and technologies. This makes the collection of data and signals such as speech, expressions, gestures, brain waves, electrocardiogram, skin conductance easier allowing for a multimodal approach that can improve the accuracy to a certain degree. Various machine learning techniques and neural networks are applied and toolkits with multimodal approaches are being developed.

Criticism 2 – Variability of Emotional Expressions. Humans have variable expressions for emotions which makes the recognition from general training data difficult. To address this, Picard et al. measured data from the same persons over several weeks. They also investigated the effects of colds, moods, drowsiness, and caffeine on their voice. With such an approach including a huge amount of individual data, they could test daily variations and variations from one person to another [19]. In the most available FER tools this is, however, not the case. They just measure individual data in a short session and compare it with general data bases.

Humans find it difficult to recognize or name their own emotions. This raises the question if machines (which are modeled by humans) can recognize emotions when even people, who have access to the innermost changes, cannot always recognize emotional states. Picard noted that a one-word label (such as the basic emotions) might be difficult to describe a complex feeling. An issue with FER is that these tools focus on labels and basic emotions.

Picard referred to a weather metaphor of Kagan. According to this, there might be signals for weather which can be measured (temperature, humidity, wind velocity etc.), and sometimes a unique combination of these signals creates, e.g., a storm or a hurricane. Kagan compares such extreme weather events with the intensity of emotions such as disgust, anger, fear or joy, the basic emotions [20]. Picard pointed out that one can measure signals and develop algorithms to detect patterns and recognize extreme weather events or the equivalents for emotions. For less intense states, there might be a complex mix of emotions, which could be detected if there are distinctive patterns. *"Affect, like weather, is hard to measure; and like weather, it probably cannot be predicted with perfect reliability"* [16]. However, if the forecast is good, less people get caught in a storm without an umbrella. Similarly, this could be true for affective computing. If machines can recognize, e.g., frustration, it could lead to better product and user interface (UI) design and therefore to a better user experience (UX) and higher productivity.

Lee et al. revealed that the accuracy of FER is often low or not possible in natural situations. There are situations where people do not express their emotions with facial expressions, e.g. because they do not want to express what they feel. In science, there is still the discussion about the connection of facial expressions and inner emotional states. Some researchers state that the FER approach is unscientific. Lisa Feldmann Barrett et al. point out that emotional expressions and facial muscle movements might be much more variable and dependent on situations, persons, and context than commonly hypothesized and assumed by FER research. The authors name the view that specific facial expressions are reliable signals for certain emotion categories *"common view"*, which they are questioning. The systematic review presented by the authors does not support the common view that emotions can be categorized by facial expressions. They state that terms like "emotional facial expressions" are therefore misleading. Alternatively, they suggest using instead, e.g., "patterns of facial movements" or "facial actions" which are supposed to be more scientifically accurate [21].

Criticism 3 – Models of Affect. This criticism refers to affective modeling which describe emotional interaction processes as well as data which is used to create those models or to train algorithms. Many data come from laboratory environments with highly artificial conditions which makes the robustness and generalizability questionable. Moreover, there is disagreement of e.g. emotional models in research. Some models reflect stereotypes of personalities and emotional responsiveness. The effect of situations seems not yet completely understood and reflected [16].

Feldmann Barrett et al. note that facial muscle movements are not random and provide valuable information for social interaction. However, they caution that these facial movements alone are not reliable indicators of emotions and must be observed in the context of the person and culture. Some facial expressions might be signals for a specific emotion, but that does not mean that this expression is a general and universally valid indicator for it. EmFACS, the mapping from facial expressions to emotions, they describe as *"Western gestures, symbols or stereotypes that fail to capture the rich variety with which people spontaneously move their faces to express emotions in everyday life"*. Where a stereotype is an *"oversimplified belief that is taken as generally more applicable than it actually is."* It is noted that variability in expressions and dependency on context are also applicable to other physiological changes in the body such as skin conductance or heart rate [21].

Since there have been critique of existing models, e.g., that facial expressions not always indicate emotional states or that expressions vary more depending on context and cultures, researchers review existing approaches and develop new models. E.g., Microsoft's *Human Understanding and Empathy Group* aim to bring emotional intelligence to technology, but also work on new psychological models to understand emotions and their expression better. The authors highlight that evolvement of such models must be reflected in affective computing approaches [22].

More and more data are collected in natural setups with webcams or smartphones. Additionally, research tries to consider situational and personal data which can be improved with deep learning techniques. E.g., the authors of "Context is Everything (in Emotion Research)" presented a contextual framework for emotion research with recommendations to integrate context [23]. Nevertheless, it is still challenging to collect and classify all these information and predict emotions considering all these factors. Many training data are still unnatural and collected in experimental environments. Due to these facts, this criticism is still valid [18].

Criticism 4 – Emotion Expression of Machines. This criticism describes the mimicry of human emotions in machines. Since the criticism was raised, much has been accomplished, such as robots or virtual humans which can express emotions very human-like. Therefore, this criticism is likely to be resolved, but it is not relevant for our studies which deal with emotion recognition.

Criticism 5 – Ethics. Ethical issues are complex and still challenging to be solved. Since emotions are personal, private data as well as strong motivational factors, ethical criticism is very important, especially when looking what current Emotion AI companies offer on the market, as exemplary presented in [14]. The risks and effects of privacy violations or manipulations are immense. With every new technology and invention, there are two sides of a coin: positive and useful applications, but also negative examples of applications which harm people. Ethical guidelines will be addressed in Sect. 4.

Even if there would not be a privacy violation by design, there is the risk that information gets leaked or hacked during data collection, storage, or management. Personal, biological data, which are necessary to collect for Emotion AI technologies, can be used for personal identification. Therefore, data leakage can be permanent which makes laws, regulations, and security technologies very important. The security technologies include, e.g., access control systems for data, encryption of personal information as well as access record management. Research and development activities in this area involve the automatic identification and reporting of harmful events [18].

Criticism 6 – Utility of Emotion AI. This criticism is about the question if emotional intelligent machines would make the human-computer-interaction (HCI) better or not. In the past, emotions have been perceived as negative and as problematic in human-human interactions which should not be transferred to machines and HCI. Nowadays, research demonstrated an essential role of emotions in almost all human activities and decision-making. Today's science and knowledge show that emotions are always there, help regulating processes and contribute to intelligent functioning. Same as with humans, machines are also getting more effective with emotional abilities [5]. The authors Czerwinsky, Hernandez and McDuff mention the necessity of a balance which machines would need emotion recognition abilities, and which would not need that [22].

As there is still a lot of justified criticism and unanswered questions, recommendations and regulations are necessary. In the following, we present recommendations based on our studies and literature research.

4 Recommendations

Feldmann Barrett et al. e.g. highlight the importance of scientific efforts to observe and describe the context-dependent way individuals express and recognize emotions. The analysis should be person- and context-specific. To do so, they suggest a Big Data approach to learn the huge facial expression repertoire of individuals in different situations in natural settings and multimodal observations. This is similar to the above-mentioned approach of Picard et al. from 2001 where the authors collected a huge set of daily data of individuals over several weeks (see Sect. 3.2, [19]). The detection of emotions might be more accurate by combining different features, not just facial expressions alone, and by collecting the subjective ratings of individuals about their emotional experience. According to the authors, research should ask questions that challenge the assumptions of the *common view*, in which facial expressions can be categorized to detect emotions. They emphasize the need to acknowledge the complexity of emotions and that science knows much less about them as has been assumed in the past. They also point out that research that studies facial movement in real-life scenarios should be supported, as well as interdisciplinary research with computer scientists and psychologists. The authors promote to cultivate a *spirit of discovery* to bring the scientific journey of facial movements and emotion perception in a new direction [21].

Authors from the above-mentioned research group of Microsoft and from the Cambridge Media Lab highlight that emotion recognition technology is used in harmful settings and by people who do not have deep knowledge of the technology and who are therefore not aware of the limitations. We have provided detailed examples of misuse of Emotion AI technology in a separate paper [14]. To assess and reduce risks, the authors Hernandez et al., including Picard, suggest 12 guidelines for emotion recognition applications which include responsible communication, informed consent, contextual calibration, and comprehensive contingency. Those categories with all guidelines are shown in Table 4. They should be considered before deployment.

Table 4. Guidelines for emotion recognition applications according to Hernandez et al. [24]

Category		Guidelines
Resposible Communication	G1	Predictions are not handled as ground truth.
	G2	System descriptions should be described with granularity.
	G3	Technology should be described with transparency.
Informed Consent	G4	Opt-in is facilitated before measurements are performed.
	G5	Data handling is described to facilitate comprehension.
	G6	Consent facilitates freedom of choice without consequences.
Contextual Calibration	G7	Training data is representative of real-life data.
	G8	Sources of variance are accounted by the models.
	G9	Users can customize the system by providing feedback.
Comprehensive Contigency	G10	Personal data can be deleted by the user.
	G11	Feedback channels are provided to the users.
	G12	Shifts in data distribution are detected to ensure robustness.

Moreover, they describe recommendations to mitigate risks. These are:

- Avoidance of assessments
- Privacy by default
- Labelling of expressions instead of emotions (include "perceived" label)
- Collaboration between the model and humans as experts [24].

In our studies, we demonstrated different results from automated FER and human observers and self-reported answers. To improve the FER tool results and to prioritize personal impressions, we suggest integrating short feedback in which participants can approve or reject the tool-based results and where they also have the possibility to stop the analysis conveniently. Moreover, it should be clearly visible that the results of the tool are just a prediction and the probability of the results, which may vary in certain situations, should be highly visible, as e.g. in our presented popup, in alignment with G1. We have presented this approach in [14].

We would recommend to use terms such as emotion estimation or emotion prediction instead of emotion recognition for Emotion AI technologies. This makes it clear that the results of the tools are more of an estimation than a definitive truth.

With the above-mentioned approach, it would also be possible to integrate more psychological features into the analysis, however, we still think that the person-based verification is important, since the automated recognition is still error-prone and because the shared information is very personal. Therefore, the decision what to share should be an individual decision by each participant. Currently, there is a risk that the tools show wrong analysis results. In this case, it is better to have no information about emotional states than wrong information which could lead to other communication issues or misunderstandings in video conferences. People might believe that the tool-provided result is true and think about possible explanations for a possibly wrong information, as, e.g., mentioned by Spiekermann [25]. In other application areas, this can have even more serious negative effects than in video conferences. We presented some negative examples and misuses of FER and Emotion AI technologies in our above mentioned paper [14].

The facts that there are still open scientific questions regarding emotion recognition, that FER tools are error-prone, and that there are examples of questionable applications, even in Germany where there are strict privacy laws, emphasize the necessity for human-centered regulations, value-sensitive design and the need for Explainable AI (XAI) and Responsible AI (RAI) [26–30]. XAI is a strategy for the development of AI systems that give explicit explanations for the models' decisions [31]. Regarding RAI, many companies have developed policies, guidelines, and frameworks to address social and ethical issues including algorithmic biases and privacy. Unfortunately, these guidelines are often very high-level and vague with room for interpretations which makes the implementation and verification of it in the AI systems difficult and ambiguous [27].

Artificial emotion recognition is also an important topic in the EU AI Act [32]. If Emotion AI is used in organizations, the concept of XAI and concrete RAI guidelines should be implemented and verified to ensure fairness, comprehensibility and accountability [26].

5 Conclusion

Our studies have limitations, such as the described problems with the baseline measurements coming from the complexity of emotions or the limitations due to the empirical, small-scale approaches. Due to the experimental nature of the studies, the fact that we tested real-life scenarios outside of laboratory conditions, and the software-limitations because of license restrictions, made the preparation, realization, and evaluation very complex and required a significant amount of manual work. The qualitative approach used in our studies provide an impression of the possibilities and limitations of FER as well as how some people perceive FER in video conferences. However, it is important to note that these results are not universally applicable. Nevertheless, the findings of incorrect results and their effects may have impact on various Emotion AI technologies. Our studies indicate that there are differences in the ability of people and tools to recognize emotions in remote or hybrid communication and that there is room for improvement for both, tools, and humans.

As Cohn and Ekman stated *"The face commands attention because it is the symbol of the self"* our facial expressions are very meaningful [1]. Given the crucial role which facial expressions play in communication, collaboration, and emotional processing, it is imperative that further research be conducted to understand emotions and their signals better as well as to explore ways to better convey these nonverbal cues in remote communication and video conferences. Research on the universality of emotions is controversial and as far as FER is concerned, there are unresolved challenges, issues with accuracy and legitimate criticism. Existing products should focus on transparency of the technology as well as their limitations and refrain from presenting measurement results as definitively correct. The guidelines suggested by Hernandez et al. are not fulfilled by existing products on the market. To apply them should be the next step in research and for industry products.

The existing challenges show that there are still unresolved issues and open questions regarding, e.g., ethical, and legal topics. There is a necessity for the regulation of Emotion AI, since it can have a huge impact on individuals and society. However, if done in the right way, Emotion AI might improve human-computer-interaction as well as computer mediated human-to-human interactions.

Acknowledgements. We would like to thank Tim Beiersdorf and Teoman Taskin for testing and analyzing the tools FaceReader, OpenFace, and OpenPose, and for conducting experimental user studies as part of their bachelor theses.

References

1. Cohn, J.F., Ekman, P.: Measuring facial action. In: Harrigan, J., Rosenthal, R., Scherer, K., (eds.): The New Handbook of Methods in Nonverbal Behavior Research, pp. 9–64. Oxford University Press (2008)
2. Ekman, P.: Darwin's contributions to our understanding of emotional expressions. Philos. Trans. R. Soc. B Biol. Sci. **364**(1535), 3449–3451 (2009)
3. Tomkins, S.: Affect Imagery Consciousness: Volume I: The Positive Effects. Springer (1962)

4. Matsumoto, D.: Reading Facial Expressions of Emotion (2011)
5. Picard, R.W.: Affective Computing (2000)
6. Bissinger, B., Beer, A., Märtin, C., Fellmann, M.: Emotion recognition via facial expressions to improve virtual communication in videoconferences. Presented at The International Conference on Human-Computer Interaction, pp. 151–163. Springer, Cham (2023). https://doi.org/10.1007/978-3-031-35599-8_10
7. Bissinger, B., Märtin, C., Fellmann, M.: Support of virtual human interactions based on facial emotion recognition software. In: Kurosu, M. (ed.) Human-Computer Interaction. Technological Innovation. LNCS, vol. 13303, pp. 329–339. Springer, Cham (2022)
8. Baltrusaitis, T.: Openface 2.2.0: A Facial Behavior Analysis Toolkit. Github. https://Github.Com/Tadasbaltrusaitis/Openface/Wiki/Home. Accessed 13 Feb 2024
9. Baltrusaitis, T., Zadeh, A., Lim, Y.C., Morency, L.-P.: Openface 2.0: facial behavior analysis toolkit. Presented at The 2018 13th IEEE International Conference On Automatic Face & Gesture Recognition (FG 2018), pp. 59–66. IEEE (2018)
10. Baltrušaitis, T., Mahmoud, M., Robinson, P.: Cross-dataset learning, person-specific normalisation for automatic action unit detection. Presented at The 2015 11th IEEE International Conference and Workshops on Automatic Face and Gesture Recognition (FG), pp. 1–6. IEEE (2015)
11. Tejada, J., Freitag, R.M.K., Pinheiro, B.F.M., Cardoso, P.B., Souza, V.R.A., Silva, L.S.: Building and validation of a set of facial expression images to detect emotions: a transcultural study. Psychol. Res. **86**(6), 1996–2006 (2022)
12. Cannata, D., Redfern, S., O'hora, D.: Openfacer: developing an R package for the convenient analysis of openface facial information. Presented at The Psychobit (2020)
13. Ekman, P., Friesen, W.V., O'Sullivan, M.: Smiles when lying. J. Pers. Soc. Psychol. **54**(3), 414 (1988)
14. Bissinger, B., Herdin, C., Märtin, C.: Applied Emotion AI: Usage and Misuse with an Example from Facial Expression Recognition in Video Conferences - Accepted for Publication (2024)
15. Ertay, E., Huang, H., Sarsenbayeva, Z., Dingler, T.: Challenges of emotion detection using facial expressions and emotion visualisation in remote communication. In: Adjunct Proceedings of the 2021 ACM International Joint Conference on Pervasive and Ubiquitous Computing and Proceedings of the 2021 ACM International Symposium on Wearable Computers, Virtual USA, pp. 230–236. ACM (2021)
16. Picard, R.W.: Affective computing: challenges. Int. J. Hum. -Comput. Stud. **59**(1–2), 55–64 (2003)
17. Noldus Information Technology. Facereader 8 Technical Specifications
18. Lee, J., Lee, S., Kim, D.: Problems and issues of emotional computing and artificial emotional intelligence: a review of Rosalind W. Picard's Thesis 'Affective Computing: Challenges'. Presented at The 2022 IEEE/ACIS 7th International Conference on Big Data, Cloud Computing, and Data Science (BCD), pp. 360–364. IEEE (2022)
19. Picard, R.W., Vyzas, E., Healey, J.: Toward machine emotional intelligence: analysis of affective physiological state. IEEE Trans. Pattern Anal. Mach. Intell. **23**(10), 1175–1191 (2001)
20. Kagan, J.: The Nature of the Child. Basic Books (1984)
21. Barrett, L.F., Adolphs, R., Marsella, S., Martinez, A.M., Pollak, S.D.: Emotional expressions reconsidered: challenges to inferring emotion from human facial movements. Psychol. Sci. Public Interest **20**(1), 1–68 (2019)
22. Czerwinski, M., Hernandez, J., Mcduff, D.: Building an AI that feels: AI systems with emotional intelligence could learn faster and be more helpful. IEEE Spectr. **58**(5), 32–38 (2021)
23. Greenaway, K.H., Kalokerinos, E.K., Williams, L.A.: Context is everything (in emotion research). Soc. Personal. Psychol. Compass **12**(6), E12393 (2018)

24. Hernandez, J., et al.: Guidelines for assessing and minimizing risks of emotion recognition applications. In: 2021 9th International Conference on Affective Computing and Intelligent Interaction (ACII), pp. 1–8, IEEE, Nara (2021)

25. Spiekermann, S.: Digitale Ethik. Ein Wertesystem Für Das, vol. 21 (2019)

26. Arrieta, A.B., et al.: Explainable artificial intelligence (XAI): concepts, taxonomies, opportunities and challenges toward responsible AI. Inf. Fusion **58**, 82–115 (2020)

27. Schiff, D., Rakova, B., Ayesh, A., Fanti, A., Lennon, M.: Principles to Practices for Responsible AI: Closing the Gap. arXiv preprint arXiv:2006.04707 (2020)

28. Dignum, V.: Responsible Artificial Intelligence: How to Develop and Use AI in A Responsible Way, vol. 2156. Springer (2019)

29. Beavers, A F., Slattery, J.P.: On the moral implications and restrictions surrounding affective computing. In: Emotions and Affect in Human Factors and Human-Computer Interaction, pp. 143–161. Elsevier (2017)

30. Friedman, B., Hendry, D.: Value Sensitive Design: Shaping Technology with Moral Imagination. The MIT Press, Cambridge (2019)

31. Khare, S.K., Blanes-Vidal, V., Nadimi, E.S., Acharya, U.R.: Emotion recognition and artificial intelligence: a systematic review (2014–2023) and research recommendations. Inf. Fusion 102019 (2023)

32. European Commission. Proposal for a Regulation of the European Parliament and of the Council Laying Down Harmonised Rules on Artificial Intelligence (Artificial Intelligence Act) and Amending Certain Union Legislative Acts (2021)

Automatically Identifying the Human Sense of Familiarity Using Eye Gaze Features

Iliana Castillon[1(✉)], Trevor Chartier[1], Videep Venkatesha[1], Noah S. Okada[2],
Asa Davis[1], Anne M. Cleary[1], and Nathaniel Blanchard[1]

[1] Colorado State University, Fort Collins, CO 80523, USA
{Iliana.Castillon,Anne.Cleary,Nathaniel.Blanchard}@colostate.edu
[2] California Institute of Technology, Pasadena, CA 91125, USA
nokada@caltech.edu

Abstract. Familiarity is a common subjective human experience. It can occur when recognizing a person's face as familiar yet being unable to place where that person was seen before, or when sensing that a certain place is familiar, as if perhaps it has been visited before. The feeling of familiarity can occur even when an individual is unable to identify why a situation feels familiar, and it can happen even when a situation is actually new, as occurs in déjà vu [10]. Automatically detecting the internal state of familiarity is a relatively unexplored topic. The present work used an existing methodological paradigm from cognitive psychology to achieve automatic detection of the internal state of familiarity using eye gaze measures, including in virtual reality environments. Being able to detect the sense of familiarity as an internal subjective state could have applied uses like developing intelligent virtual tutoring systems.

Keywords: Eye Gaze · Familiarity · Affective computing

1 Introduction

The internal state of familiarity has been the subject of a large body of work in cognitive psychology. It is often associated with recognition memory. According to dual process theories of recognition, familiarity is one of two processes that can lead to recognizing having had prior experience with something (the other process being recollection, or a calling to mind of a specific prior instance in which the present stimulus was encountered) [9,25].

Though there are many different theories regarding how familiarity and recollection might relate to one another, it has recently been suggested that initially sensing familiarity may trigger the search of memory that leads to recollection [12,26,30]. Following from this general theoretical framework, in the present work, we sought to capture instances of familiarity the moment a participant sensed it, regardless of whether that initial sense of familiarity ultimately led to recall success or not.

M. Kurosu and A. Hashizume (Eds.): HCII 2024, LNCS 14684, pp. 291–310, 2024.
https://doi.org/10.1007/978-3-031-60405-8_19

Training models to detect familiarity requires a substantial dataset. Therefore, a crucial aspect of our study relied on an experimental paradigm from cognitive psychology that frequently induced feelings of familiarity. There have been multiple demonstrations that a sense of familiarity with new scenes can be evoked through earlier exposure to highly similar scenes (scenes having the same spatial layout) [6, 10, 13]. Our procedure for eliciting familiarity follows that of Cleary et al. (2012) and Okada et al. (2023) by inducing familiarity from 3D scenes in Virtual Reality (VR) that have the same spatial configuration as an earlier-viewed (but not necessarily recalled) scene. We used the same general VR procedure and Unity stimuli as Okada et al. (2023) with minor modifications to the Unity program related to the incorporation of eye tracking. The present study is the first to attempt to identify an association between particular eye movement patterns and moments of subjectively sensing familiarity.

Past research has demonstrated that machine learning can differentiate seen versus unseen stimuli on the basis of eye movement patterns associated with recognition memory test stimulus onset [29], but such memory-based eye movement patterns have been shown to occur largely outside of participants' conscious awareness [34], making it as yet unknown to what extent eye movement patterns can reveal the onset of a person's subjective sense of familiarity with a scene.

Being able to detect the sense of familiarity as an internal subjective state could have applied uses like developing intelligent virtual tutoring systems. Recent research suggests that the subjective sensation of familiarity during recall failure is associated with increased curiosity and information-seeking [26]. Therefore, being able to detect when someone is experiencing familiarity could be helpful for creating intelligent tutoring systems that are responsive to students' peaking levels of curiosity and information-seeking inclinations to help them learn better. For example, it is widely known from the testing effect literature that students learn better if they have to generate the information on their own rather than just being presented with it [32]. Moreover, research has shown that when people are experiencing elevated curiosity, they exhibit an increased desire to discover an unknown answer on their own, rather than merely having it given to them [27]. An intelligent tutoring system could optimize learning potential by adaptively encouraging self-driven information-seeking when the learner seems ready and motivated for this based on detected subjective familiarity. For example, when detected subjective familiarity indicates a high likelihood that the person feels close to coming up with an answer on their own, the system could provide hints or cues rather than a full answer to help the learner come up with the answer on their own (a strategy that would not make sense if the answer simply was not known to the learner and the learner needed to first gain exposure to it), thereby optimizing the balance between the need for presenting new information and answers to the learner and the need for allowing the learner to benefit long-term from retrieving information on their own instead of having it presented to them.

2   Related Work

Although this study is novel in its attempt to automatically detect instances of subjective familiarity experienced during scenes resembling previously experienced scenes, the idea that subjective recognition and other cognitive states may be automatically detected is not new, and it has shown to be promising in past studies. In one study, a model based on eye gaze was able to classify whether participants had previously viewed an image before with an average accuracy of 68.7% [18]. Based on gaze data collected when participants were presented with an image, the models in Nishimura et al. (2012) attempted to classify whether the participants had previously viewed this exact image in an earlier part of the experiment. This classification was done independent of whether participants explicitly indicated recognition. In contrast, in the current work, the goal is to classify instances only where participants are experiencing the feeling of familiarity. In that way, this study places a greater emphasis on detecting the internal state of participants. Additionally, the familiarity in this work is evoked from configurally similar, but non-identical scenes. This study's focus on familiarity is intrinsically linked to the subject of cognitive states. Much of the research done on the detection of internal states has been done with respect to mind wandering - the shift of attention away from a particular task. Models that include or rely on non-gazed based features have been investigated [3,5,8], but models built using gaze-based features have been the most effective at detecting mind-wandering [21,24]. As such, the features we used in our models were all gaze-based. Many studies have attempted detection of mind wandering either in the context of reading [3,4,17], or while watching videos [20,28]. This study is the first to investigate the detection of internal states in the context of virtual reality. In combination with global gaze-features, some studies included local features that were informed by the gaze direction relative to the text being read [4] or particular areas of interest in the film being watched [28]. The features in our model resemble the global features in these studies that were independent of any context. Furthermore, most of these studies used probe-based detection of mind-wandering [3,4,20] because mind wandering often occurs without the individual being immediately aware of it. However, self-caught reports of mind wandering have also been incorporated [17], and we primarily utilized this method in the present study to more closely pinpoint the moment at which familiarity was experienced by the participant. It should be noted that a probe was included after every scene in the non-virtual reality experiment. Our study builds on the current body of knowledge by applying the previous findings and techniques from detecting mind wandering to detecting another cognitive state: the sense of familiarity.

3   Two-Dimensional Familiarity Dataset

3.1   Materials and Procedure

Familiarity Task. Following from prior research that used a virtual tour paradigm to induce the sensation of familiarity in the laboratory [11, 30], participants in the present study viewed virtual tours through various scenes via videos on a computer screen containing walk-throughs of virtual environments.

In prior research using the virtual tour task [11], in the study phase, participants were taken through settings they had never seen before. While the virtual tour of the study phase scenes took place, the name of the scene was played aloud through speakers. For example, if viewing a golf course, a voice would state "This is a golf course." Participants were asked to try to remember each study phase scene along with its name. In the test phase, participants were taken through entirely new settings, some of which had the same spatial layout as an earlier toured scene from the study phase. For example, a clothing store scene may have the same arrangement of elements relative to one another as an earlier toured bedroom scene. In short, an otherwise novel scene in the test phase may share a spatial configuration with a scene from the study phase. No sound accompanied the viewing of the test phase videos.

To establish the same configuration of elements from study to test without explicitly duplicating the objects, a grid layout was used to create spatially mapped but otherwise novel scenes as shown in Fig. 1.

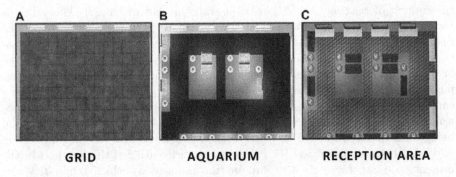

GRID   AQUARIUM   RECEPTION AREA

Fig. 1. (A) Grid Used to Create Same Spatial Configuration; (B) Sample "Aquarium" Study Scene; (C) Sample "Reception Area" Test Scene Corresponding to "Aquarium" Study Scene [10].

In this paradigm, participants complete two study-test blocks. Each study phase contains 16 study scenes; each test phase contains 32 test scenes, with 16 corresponding to studied scenes and 16 corresponding to unstudied scenes in their spatial layout. There are four experiment versions for counterbalancing purposes (to counterbalance the stimuli across the different possible conditions across participants) (Figs. 2 and 3).

Fig. 2. Sample "Alley" Study Scene and Configurally Similar "Hallway" Test Scene [10].

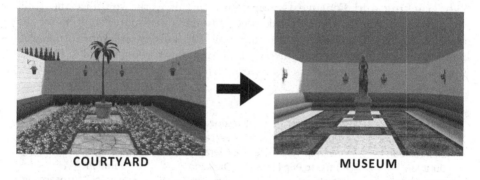

Fig. 3. Sample "Courtyard" Study Scene and Configurally Similar "Museum" Test Scene [10].

Prior research with this paradigm has established that participants will more often feel a sense of familiarity from a novel test scene that shares a spatial layout with a study scene than from one that does not, even when they cannot pinpoint the source of the familiarity, [10,11,26,30] The present study sought to use the same paradigm but in conjunction with measuring eye gaze features while participants completed the virtual tour task. The specific tours used in the present study were those used by Okada et al. (2023) in their Experiments 2a and 2b.

Participants. Participants for this study were 61 undergraduate students at Colorado State University enrolled in a psychology class and participating in exchange for course credit. Sample-size was based on Experiments 2a and 2b of [30].

Procedure. Participants were brought into a test room where they sat at a desk with a computer connected to an eye tracker and webcam.[1] At the beginning of the experiment, the eye tracker was calibrated for each participant.

Once the task began, participants were asked to watch a series of study videos where they were pulled through various scenes as previously discussed in the familiarity task. Once the test phase began, participants were instructed to hit the 'up key arrow' on the keyboard at any point that they felt a sense of familiarity. This key was labeled with a bright yellow sticker to make it easier for participants to find. Partcipants were instructed to keep their finger on the key, ready to press it, so that they would not need to look down at the key. The task took participants around an hour to complete. All participants completed two study-test blocks, watching a total of 96 videos, each under 30 s long.

Eye Tracking and Feature Generation. In this work, we utilize the Tobii Pro Fusion eye tracker and PyTrack, an end-to-end open-source solution for the analysis and visualization of eye tracking data [19]. This eye tracker captures 250 images per second (250 Hz) and has two built in pupil tracking modules. PyTrack was used to extract parameters of interest such as blinks, saccade count, average pupil size, etc. (Fig. 4).

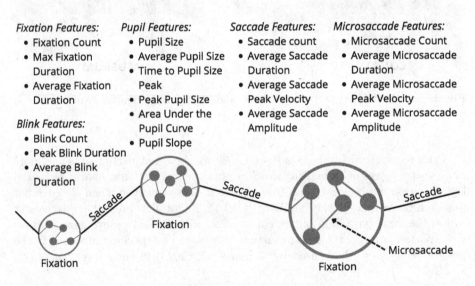

Fig. 4. Eye Gaze Features

3.2 Data Preprocessing

Participants reported 698 instances of familiarity via self-report. It is possible that the act of self-reporting could corrupt our findings, since patterns could

---

[1] A photo of the experiment hardware can be found in [36].

emerge like participants looking down to identify the up key. To negate this possibility, we removed a 2 s buffer of data from the time before the button was pressed. We identified this buffer by examining videos for any sign of participants looking down to self report- from our analysis, we concluded that we needed a minimum buffer of 1.5 s, but we extended that to two seconds as a precaution. We then examined the 1 s window of time before the two second buffer and used this window to extract eye gaze features. An image of this timeline can be found in Fig. 5. Unfortunately, to extract features we needed at least three seconds of data prior to the key press (the two second buffer and the one second window). Of our 698 instances of self-reported familiarity, only 263 had three seconds of time before the button press - this is likely because familiarity onset much more rapidly than we anticipated.

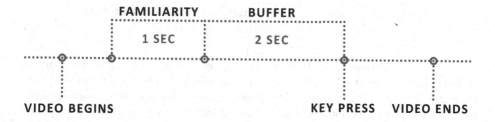

Fig. 5. Familiarity Instances Timeline

We generated negative instances by randomly sampling test scenes where participants did not report experiencing familiarity. To create a balanced dataset, we sampled the same amount of negative instances per participant as we had valid positive instances. This resulted in a dataset with 263 valid instances of familiarity and 263 instances negative instances. All of these instances were one second long.

3.3 Training and Evaluation

We used Hyperopt for distributed hyperparameter optimization in our model search [2]. Among the classification algorithms we evaluated were AdaBoost, Naive Bayes, Logistic Regression, Support Vector Classifier, Random Forrest, and K-Nearest Neighbors. We trained and tested each machine learning model using Leave-One–Participant-Out Cross-Validation. For this evaluation protocol, n is equal to the number of participants in the dataset. We train each model on n-1 participants and test on the participant that was left out of training. This process is repeated until every participant's samples have been used as the test set. Evaluation metrics are averaged across all n folds.

We selected our final model by identifying the model with the highest average Cohen's Kappa across all n folds [14]. Cohen's Kappa ranges between -1 and 1, where 0 is chance performance (the equivalent of random guessing), perfect performance is 1, and -1 corresponds with perfectly imperfect performance (the classifier always predicts the opposite label).

3.4 Results

Using the Support Vector Classifier (SVC) algorithm, we trained a machine learning model that identified familiarity with a Cohen's Kappa of 0.22 (SD = 0.42) and an F1 score of 0.56 (SD = 0.23). This performance is in line with other predictors of internal cognitive states, such as mind wandering [5].

Table 1. SVC Model Results

Model	Buffer	Window	Cohen's Kappa	F1 Score	Accuracy
SVC	2 s	1 s	0.22 (0.42)	0.56 (0.20)	0.61 (0.21)

The high standard deviation values among metrics, as shown in Table 1, reflect a large amount of variation among participants. This mixed performance indicates individual variation in eye gaze patterns that emerge as one experiences familiarity. Additionally, the amount of instances reported by participants seems to affect the models performance. Participants that reported only one or two instances of familiarity ended up on the polar ends of the Cohen's Kappa distribution. However, the majority of participant's kappa scores range from 0 to 0.65, as can be seen in Fig. 6.

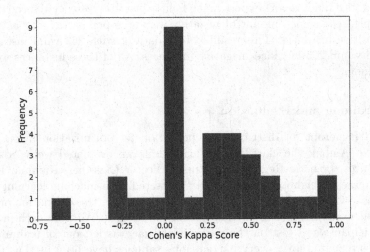

Fig. 6. Distribution of Cohen's Kappa Scores

4 Virtual Reality Familiarity Dataset

4.1 Materials and Procedure

Familiarity Task. The VR experiment's structure closely resembled the previously described two-dimensional study in Sect. 3.1, encompassing both the "study" and "test" phases. However, in this version of the task, due to the need to measure eye movement patterns, static versions of the scenes used in Okada et al.'s (2023) Experiment 3 were created [30]. Participants were not being walked through the scenes. Instead, they were placed in the center of a scene and had the ability to turn their heads to look around from that position. Additionally, participants were not probed after every scene ends. Instead, they were instructed to press the button on the handheld VR remote controller to indicate they are experiencing the sense of familiarity. Each scene, on average, is 46 s long.

Participants. Participants for this study were 26 undergraduate students at Colorado State University enrolled in a psychology class and participating in exchange for course credit. Sample size was based on Experiment 3 of [30].

Procedure. Participants were brought into a test room where they sat in a chair in the center of the room. They were asked to sit for the duration of the experiment to prevent motion sickness. While sitting, the participant was fitted with the HTC Vive Pro Eye headset and instructed on how to position the ear phones to adjust the sound level. Once fitted and wearing the VR headset, the participant was given the VR hand controllers and instructed on their general use. The participant was then taken through a calibration procedure for the eye tracking component of the study. The calibration procedure involved adjusting the interpupillary distance for the participant then running a procedure that instructed the participant to look in specific directions at particular moments in time while the eye tracker tracked their eye movements and automatically calibrated the tracking to their movements.

Once the experimental procedure began, participants were sequentially placed within each scene for a fixed duration. Within each scene, the participant had the ability to explore their surroundings by turning their head to look around. For the study portion of the experiment, participants were instructed to: *Do your best to try to remember that scene along with what its name is. While viewing each of these scenes, a voice will play through the VR headphones telling the name of the scene. For example, while viewing a golf course, the voice would say "This is a golf course. Golf course." Try to also remember the name so that you can convey this later on if asked about earlier-viewed scenes.* After the study phase ended, participants were asked if they needed a break from the VR immersion.

For the test portion, before the scenes began to play, participants saw the instruction: *"If the scene starts to feel familiar to you, push the button under your THUMB to indicate that it feels familiar. Try to do this AS SOON as you start to feel a sense of familiarity with the scene. Specifically, if the scene reminds you of a specific scene that you viewed earlier. Let the experimenter know what that scene is that this scene is reminding you of. Sometimes, a scene may remind you of a similar-looking scene from earlier. Whenever this happens (even if you did not push the button) please tell the experimenter the name of the earlier-viewed scene. Even if the test scene did not remind you of a specific earlier-viewed scene."* When participants pressed the button to indicate familiarity, the experimenter was made aware through a message logged to the Unity terminal. Participants were then asked if they could identify possible reasons for the familiarity, and were continuously reminded that sometimes they may be able to identify a reason for any perceived familiarity with a scene and other times they may not. Most of the answers that participants gave regarding the source of their familiarity corresponded to earlier viewed scenes. However, some participants indicated some scenes reminded them of other locations, such as "a friend's basement." These answers were logged on paper by the experimenters and recorded on a microphone. Similarly to the two-dimensional familiarity task, participants completed two blocks of the study and test phases.

Eye Tracking and Feature Generation. The HTC Vive Pro Eye is a virtual reality headset with built-in infrared-based eye tracking technology developed by HTC Corporation. Prior research suggests that the HTC Vive Pro Eye validly measures eye movement metrics of interest to scientists [35]. The headset was used to collect eye tracking data within Unity from the participants while they were in the virtual environments designed for this experiment. Eye tracking data was collected using the SRanipal software development kit (SDK) version 1.3.6.8 for Unity provided by the HTC Corporation [1]. Previous work has shown timestamped eye tracking data from this device collected with Unity and the SRanipal SDK can be used for accurately assessing saccadic eye movements [38].

The SRanipal SDK allowed us to easily record the following eye measurements: pupil position, pupil diameter, eye openness, gaze origin, and gaze direction. The data was collected into a buffer at roughly 120hz in a dedicated thread using the SRanipal callback registration function, and the buffer was written to a file in the form of comma-separated values (CSVs) at the end of each scene. Each time eye tracking data points were collected, we also recorded the current Unix timestamp from the computer running the program using the DateTime struct. While the SRanipal SDK does provide a timestamp data point, previous work has shown that this timestamp has been inaccurate and error-prone in previous versions of the SDK [38]. While bugs relating to the timestamp may have been fixed in the current latest version of the SRanipal SDK, we opted to use the system time rather than confirm that the issues have been resolved. Additionally, using the Unity ActionBasedController class, we recorded whether the participant was pressing the button on the HTC Vive Controller that they were instructed to press to indicate a sense of familiarity.

This data collection approach allowed us to generate two CSV files per participant, one for each block, each containing nearly one hundred thousand timestamped rows of data. Each row contained the eye measurements described above, the status of the familiarity indication button (pressed or unpressed), and the current VR scene the participant was in at that point in time. We acquired a row of data every 8.33 ms on average throughout the experiment.

Similarly to the methods described in Sect. 3.1, PyTrack was used to extract parameters of interest [19]. Table 2 shows descriptive statistics for a portion of eye gaze features. All of eye gaze features generated from this experiment can be found listed in Fig. 4.

Table 2. Descriptive Statistics of Eye Gaze Features

Feature	Familiarity				Non-Familiarity			
	Mean	SD	Min	Max	Mean	SD	Min	Max
Fixation Count	5.60	2.99	0.00	7.00	5.91	3.10	0.00	8.00
Fixation Duration (ms)	30.91	16.60	0.00	204.00	33.27	19.48	0.00	229.00
Saccade Count	3.23	1.63	0.00	4.00	3.23	1.67	0.00	4.00
Saccade Duration (ms)	48.87	36.12	0.00	316.00	43.19	36.77	0.00	236.00
Microsaccade Count	0.21	0.50	0.00	3.00	0.23	0.51	0.00	3.00
Microsaccade Duration (ms)	1.64	3.65	0.00	15.50	1.85	3.89	0.00	20.00
Blink Count	0.71	0.70	0.00	3.00	0.83	0.70	0.00	3.00
Blink Duration (ms)	24.19	39.12	0.00	232.00	32.18	48.50	0.00	298.00

4.2 Data Preprocessing

Participants reported 538 instances of familiarity. On average, the button indicating familiarity was pressed approximately 15.29 s into a scene (SD = 9.11). To extract features based on reported familiarity, we retrieved data from the moments preceding participants' button presses. We discarded a short buffer prior to the button press as has been commonly used in other model detection attempts [5,17,23,37]. This way, the model prediction is not based on the physiological patterns from the act of making the report, but rather the patterns of eye data leading up to the report. However, the discarded buffer was shorter since participants were immersed in the VR environment while wearing the headset (rather than seated in front of a screen)—in the two-dimensional experiment, some participants looked down (possibly to confirm they were pressing the correct button), and the size of our buffer was extended to ensure this action was filtered. Further discussion of these buffer windows can be found in Sect. 4.4.

To generate negative training instances, we randomly sampled test videos where participants did not report familiarity. To create a balanced dataset, we generated the same amount of negative instances per participant as we had reported positive familiarity instances. This resulted in a dataset with 1,076 entries, 538 of them being positive familiarity instances and 538 of them being negative familiarity instances. All of these instances range from being 1 to 3 s long depending on the window size being experimented, as further discussed in Sect. 4.4.

4.3 Training and Evaluation

Similarly to the two-dimensional study, we used Hyperopt for distributed hyper-parameter optimization in our model search [2]. Among the classification algorithms we evaluated were AdaBoost (AB), Naive Bayes (NB), Logistic Regression (LR), Support Vector Classifier (SVC), Random Forrest (RF), and K-Nearest Neighbors (KNN). All of these models were trained using Leave-One-Participant-Out Cross-Validation. We guided our model search using the highest average Cohen's Kappa across all folds. More details on this validation protocol and the evaluation metric can be found in Sect. 3.3.

4.4 Buffer and Window Size Experiments

No Buffer. To cover all the possible instances of familiarity, and to determine how far out the eye-pattern indicators of subjective familiarity extend ahead of the button-press, we conducted experiments sampling various window sizes. These windows ranged from 1–3 s pre-button-press. Additionally, to address the possibility of the model learning eye movement patterns that might be associated with the VR hand-controller button-press itself, we conducted a model search with and without using a buffer. When we sampled the 1 s of data from before the button press, without using a buffer, the model results were extremely good and did not resemble other prior work attempting to identify internal cognitive states using eye tracking [5,15].

Our Random Forrest models for the "no buffer" experiments generates a Cohen's Kappa score of 0.71 for 1 s of data before the button press, as can be seen in Table 3. Because these metrics are suspiciously high when compared to prior work on detecting subjective states with eye gaze patterns, we concluded that a buffer period was needed between the familiarity window and the button press. However, exactly what that buffer period should be is not known. Although cognitive processes are known to occur in fractions of a second [16] and the button-press itself is thought to occur within 100 ms [31], the exact millisecond-level timing between experiencing subjective familiarity and pressing a hand-held VR controller button is not known. Therefore, we erred on the side of caution and used relatively large windows.

Buffer. Once deciding on use of a buffer, we moved forward experimenting with various window sizes. The further out the window was from the first second that preceded the button press, we found that our model performance had a

Table 3. No Buffer Model Search Results. Participants are evaluated in a leave-one-participant-out paradigm and the average (Standard Deviation in parenthesis)

Window	Model	Cohen's Kappa	F1 Score
1 s	RF	0.71 (0.15)	0.85 (0.10)
2 s	RF	0.18 (0.18)	0.59 (0.09)
3 s	AB	0.14 (0.17)	0.57 (0.09)

significant drop in accurately classifying instances. From here we explored how different window sizes impacted model performance. We found that the window of 1 s along with a 500 ms buffer produced results that most closely align with prior work investigating the relationship between internal cognitive states and eye gaze patterns and our previous two-dimensional experiment.

As we increased the window size from 1 s to 3 s, we found that our best model results began to drop in correlation with increased window size. An illustration of these 1–3 s windows samples in a timeline format can be seen in Fig. 7. There are a number of possible reasons for this finding, including 1) that eye gaze patterns related to the onset of familiarity occur rapidly with respect to the subjective sensation and participants are able to rapidly push the button the moment they sense familiarity (within a tight time-window), 2) that as we were expanding the familiarity window, we began sampling moments of eye gaze patterns where participants were not experiencing familiarity, or 3) that the closer in to the button-press the window is, the more likely it is that eye gaze patterns reflect the fact that the participant is engaging in pressing the VR hand-controller button. The exact model evaluation metrics can be seen in Table 4. Although cognitive processes tend to occur in fractions of a second [16] and research suggests that a button-press occurs within 100 ms [31], because we cannot be certain at what point in the temporal stream the eye gaze patterns reflect the sensation of familiarity versus the act of pushing the VR hand-controller button, We continued our analysis using the 500 ms buffer along with 2 s of eye gaze data as a conservative approach.

4.5   Results

Using the KNN algorithm, our best model resulted in a kappa value of 0.18 (SD = 0.14). Additional evaluation metrics can be seen in Table 5. While this Cohen's Kappa value is slightly lower then the best model's value for the two-dimensional experiment, the standard deviation value is significantly lower. This means that overall the model was not predicting a high level of confidence for certain participants and with extremely low confidence for others. Figure 8 shows the distribution of kappa values, which looks relatively normal.

Finally, we were interested in exploring which features were significantly different between positive and negative familiarity instances. To do this we conducted hypothesis tests and found significant differences between positive and

Table 4. Buffer-Window Model Search Results. Participants are evaluated in a leave-one-participant-out paradigm and the average (Standard Deviation in parenthesis)

Buffer	Window	Model	Cohen's Kappa	F1 Score
250 ms	1 s	AB	0.17 (0.13)	0.59 (0.07)
	2 s	LR	0.17 (0.22)	0.59 (0.11)
	3 s	LR	0.14 (0.20)	0.57 (0.10)
500 ms	1 s	KNN	0.14 (0.17)	0.57 (0.09)
	2 s	KNN	0.18 (0.14)	0.59 (0.09)
	3 s	AB	0.13 (0.15)	0.55 (0.08)
1000 ms	1 s	RF	0.16 (0.15)	0.58 (0.08)
	2 s	RF	0.17 (0.20)	0.59 (0.10)
	3 s	LR	0.17 (0.22)	0.17 (0.11)

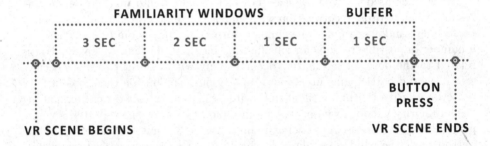

Fig. 7. Familiarity Windows Timeline

negative familiarity instances. The significantly different features included: participants' average fixation duration, average blink count, average blink duration, average saccade duration, and average pupil size. Figure 9 shows the duration features and Fig. 10 shows the size feature.

5   Discussion

We investigated the possibility of automatically identifying when a person is experiencing a sense of familiarity, an internal cognitive state associated with feelings of curiosity and information seeking behaviors [26], using physiological eye gaze features. The results from both our two-dimensional and more immersive three-dimensional virtual reality (VR) experiments indicate that the inter-

Table 5. KNN Model Results

Model	Buffer	Window	Cohen's Kappa	F1 Score	Accuracy
KNN	500 ms	2 s	0.18 (0.14)	0.59 (0.09)	0.59 (0.07)

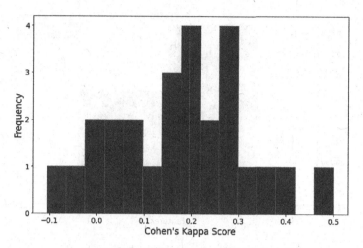

Fig. 8. Distribution of Cohen's Kappa Scores

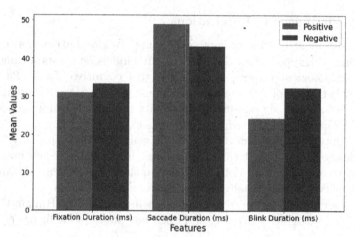

Fig. 9. Significantly Different Feature Duration

nal subjective state of familiarity does manifest through the eyes. The ability to detect the state of sensing familiarity through eye gaze patterns is akin to detecting other internal cognitive states like mind wandering [3,5,22,28].

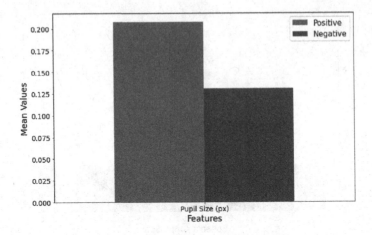

Fig. 10. Significantly Different Feature Size

5.1 Key Findings and Implications

The successful identification of familiarity using eye gaze patterns, as evidenced by the Cohen's Kappa values obtained in our models, suggests a tangible link between physiological responses and subjective cognitive states. Particularly noteworthy is the use of eye tracking technology in both 2D and more immersive 3D VR environments, showcasing its versatility and potential for broader application. The ability to detect when a person is experiencing familiarity can have significant implications for developing intelligent systems, especially in educational technology. Intelligent tutoring systems, for example, could leverage this technology to adapt content delivery based on the learner's sense of familiarity-driven curiosity [26], potentially enhancing learning outcomes.

These results represent a significant step in the field of Human-Computer Interaction and Cognitive Science, and open new avenues for future research.

5.2 Comparative Analysis of 2D and More Immersive 3D VR Environments

The difference in the Cohen's Kappa values between the 2D and more immersive 3D VR setups (0.22 vs. 0.18) might be attributed to the distinct nature of interactions in these environments. VR's more immersive nature might elicit more natural and varied gaze patterns, particularly given that participants could turn their heads to look around within each 3D scene, impacting the model's prediction capability. This disparity underscores the need to tailor eye tracking methodologies and algorithms to the specificities of the interaction environment.

5.3 Limitations and Future Work

Despite the promising findings, there are limitations to this study - most of these limitations stem from the need for additional research to gain a deeper understanding of the subjective sense of familiarity as it relates to eye gaze. For example, pupil diameter at stimulus onset as a function of eventual downstream reporting of subjective familiarity was not examined in the present study; it is possible that pupil size occurs upstream of the subjective sense of familiarity. For example, Ryals et al. (2021) examined pupil size for a short time window extending forward from stimulus onset as a function of eventual reporting of a tip-of-the-tongue state or not and found robust pupil size differences, whereby larger pupil diameter following stimulus onset was associated with the feeling of a word being on the tip of the tongue [33]. It is as yet unclear if the same would hold true for the subjective sense of familiarity, as we only examined pupil size for a short time window extending backwards from the response button press. Thus, there is more to be learned about the physiological responses associated with the subjective sense of familiarity.

Also, while consistent with other works automatically identifying internal states [3,5], the high standard deviation in model performance suggests significant variability in individual eye gaze patterns—this variability complicates efforts to integrate automated detection into AI [7]. The constraint of data collection (only instances with a three-second window prior to reporting familiarity were used) might have limited the scope of our analysis—future research should aim to hold the button press constant across the familiar and unfamiliar response options (such as by requiring a button press the moment a scene is deemed familiar by pressing the right hand controller button, or unfamiliar by pressing the left hand controller button). Future research could also eliminate the button press altogether, using a probe-based methodology instead; while this would eliminate the ability to assess the experience of familiarity the moment it occurs for a person, it would allow for an ability to assess whether differences between scenes that elicited a sense of familiarity and scenes that did not can be detected by machine learning algorithms.

Although the study's sample sizes were based on prior behavioral research using these 2D and more immersive 3D VR methodologies [30], there was no precedent for computing the needed sample size for eye gaze data from these paradigms. Thus, the sample size may have been relatively small for eye gaze data, particularly in the more immersive 3D VR experiment, which could affect the generalizability of the findings. Further research could also explore the integration of other physiological measures, like heart rate or skin conductance [5], to enrich the detection of cognitive states.

Finally, the largest question that looms from this work is the feasibility of distinguishing distinct types of internal states. Ideally, an intelligent tutor will be able to identify not only that a user is experiencing an internal state but also determine what specific internal state is occurring, e.g., familiarity, curiosity, tip-of-the-tongue states, or mind wandering. Future research should aim to determine if machine learning algorithms can be trained to differentiate different types of internal subjective states.

6   Conclusion

In conclusion, this study demonstrates the potential of using eye tracking technology to detect a person's subjective sense of familiarity, an important cognitive state. While there are challenges to be addressed, the findings lay a foundation for future research and practical applications in HCI and cognitive science.

Acknowledgements. This work was partially supported by the National Science Foundation under award 2303019 and under subcontracts on award DRL 2019805. The views expressed are those of the authors and do not reflect the official policy or position of the U.S. Government. The College of Natural Sciences at Colorado State University provided a grant to purchase the HTC Vive Pro Eye VR system and Colorado State University's Data Science Research Institute provided funding for undergraduate researchers.

References

1. Vive eye and facial tracking sdk 1.3.6.8. https://developer.vive.com/resources/vive-sense/eye-and-facial-tracking-sdk/download/latest/
2. Bergstra, J., Yamins, D., Cox, D.: Making a science of model search: hyperparameter optimization in hundreds of dimensions for vision architectures. In: Dasgupta, S., McAllester, D. (eds.) Proceedings of the 30th International Conference on Machine Learning. Proceedings of Machine Learning Research, vol. 28, pp. 115–123. PMLR, Atlanta (2013). https://proceedings.mlr.press/v28/bergstra13.html
3. Bixler, R., Blanchard, N., Garrison, L., D'Mello, S.: Automatic detection of mind wandering during reading using gaze and physiology. In: Proceedings of the 2015 ACM on International Conference on Multimodal Interaction (ICMI 2015), pp. 299–306. Association for Computing Machinery (2015). https://doi.org/10.1145/2818346.2820742
4. Bixler, R., D'Mello, S.: Automatic gaze-based user-independent detection of mind wandering during computerized reading. User Model. User-Adap. Inter. **26**, 33–68 (2015). https://doi.org/10.1007/s11257-015-9167-1
5. Blanchard, N., Bixler, R., Joyce, T., D'Mello, S.: Automated physiological-based detection of mind wandering during learning. In: Trausan-Matu, S., Boyer, K.E., Crosby, M., Panourgia, K. (eds.) Intelligent Tutoring Systems. LNCS, vol. 8474, pp. 55–60. Springer, Cham (2014). https://doi.org/10.1007/978-3-319-07221-0_7
6. Brown, A.S., Marsh, E.J.: Evoking false beliefs about autobiographical experience. Psychon. Bull. Rev. **15**(1), 186–190 (2008).https://doi.org/10.3758/PBR.15.1.186
7. Castillon, I., Krishnaswamy, N., Blanchard, N.: Multimodal features for group dynamic-aware agents. In: Interdisciplinary Approaches to Getting AI Experts and Education Stakeholders Talking Workshop at AIEd (2022)
8. Christoff, K., Gordon, A.M., Smallwood, J., Smith, R., Schooler, J.W.: Experience sampling during FMRI reveals default network and executive system contributions to mind wandering. Proc. Natl. Acad. Sci. U.S.A. (2009). https://doi.org/10.1073/pnas.0900234106
9. Cleary, A.M.: Recognition memory, familiarity, and déjà vu experiences. Curr. Direct. Psychol. Sci. **17**(5), 353–357 (2008).https://doi.org/10.1111/j.1467-8721.2008.00605.x

10. Cleary, A.M., Brown, A.S., Sawyer, B.D., Nomi, J.S., Ajoku, A.C., Ryals, A.J.: Familiarity from the configuration of objects in 3-dimensional space and its relation to déjà vu: a virtual reality investigation. Conscious. Cognit. **21**(2), 969–975 (2012).https://doi.org/10.1016/j.concog.2011.12.010

11. Cleary, A.M., Claxton, A.B.: Déjà vu: an illusion of prediction. Psychol. Sci. **29**(4), 635–644 (2018). https://doi.org/10.1177/0956797617743018

12. Cleary, A.M., Irving, Z.C., Mills, C.: What flips attention? Cogn. Sci. **47**(4), e13274 (2023)

13. Cleary, A.M., Ryals, A.J., Nomi, J.S.: Can déjà vu result from similarity to a prior experience? support for the similarity hypothesis of déjà vu. Psychon. Bull. Rev. **16**(6), 1082–1088 (2009).https://doi.org/10.3758/PBR.16.6.1082

14. Cohen, J.: A coefficient of agreement for nominal scales. Educ. Psychol. Measur. **20**(1), 37–46 (1960)

15. D'Mello, S., Cobian, J., Hunter, M.: Automatic gaze-based detection of mind wandering during reading. In: Educational Data Mining 2013 (2013)

16. Donders, F.: On the speed of mental processes. Acta Physiol. (Oxf.) **30**, 412–431 (1969). https://doi.org/10.1016/0001-6918(69)90065-1

17. Faber, M., Bixler, R., D'Mello, S.K.: An automated behavioral measure of mind wandering during computerized reading. Behav. Res. Methods **50**, 134–150 (2017). https://doi.org/10.3758/s13428-017-0857-y

18. George Nishimura, A.F.: Déjà vu: classification of memory using eye movements (2015)

19. Ghose, U., Srinivasan, A.A., Boyce, W.P., Xu, H., Chng, E.S.: PyTrack: an end-to-end analysis toolkit for eye tracking. Behav. Res. Methods **52**(6), 2588–2603 (2020). https://doi.org/10.3758/s13428-020-01392-6

20. Hutt, S., Hardey, J., Bixler, R.E., Stewart, A.E.B., Risko, E.F., D'Mello, S.K.: Gaze-based detection of mind wandering during lecture viewing. In: Educational Data Mining (2017). https://api.semanticscholar.org/CorpusID:1144340

21. Hutt, S., et al.: Automated gaze-based mind wandering detection during computerized learning in classrooms. User Model. User-Adap. Inter. **29**, 821–867 (2019). https://doi.org/10.1007/s11257-019-09228-5

22. Hutt, S., Mills, C., White, S., Donnelly, P.J., D'Mello, S.K.: The eyes have it: Gaze-based detection of mind wandering during learning with an intelligent tutoring system. Int. Educ. Data Mining Soc. (2016)

23. Kuvar, V., Blanchard, N., Colby, A., Allen, L., Mills, C.: Automatically detecting task-unrelated thoughts during conversations using keystroke analysis. In: User Modeling and User-Adapted Interaction, pp. 617–641 (2023).https://doi.org/10.1007/s11257-022-09340-z

24. Kuvar, V., Kam, J.W.Y., Hutt, S., Mills, C.: Detecting when the mind wanders off task in real-time: an overview and systematic review. In: Proceedings of the 25th International Conference on Multimodal Interaction (ICMI 2023), pp. 163–173 (2023). https://doi.org/10.1145/3577190.3614126

25. Mandler, G.: Familiarity breeds attempts: a critical review of dual-process theories of recognition. Perspect. Psychol. Sci. **3**(5), 390–399 (2008). https://doi.org/10.1111/j.1745-6924.2008.00087.x

26. McNeely-White, K.L., Cleary, A.M.: Piquing curiosity: déjà vu-like states are associated with feelings of curiosity and information-seeking behaviors. J. Intelligence **11**(6), 112 (2023)

27. Metcalfe, J., Kennedy-Pyers, T., Vuorre, M.: Curiosity and the desire for agency: wait, wait... don't tell me! Cognit. Res.: Princip. Implicat. **6**, 1–8 (2021)

28. Mills, C., Bixler, R.E., Wang, X., D'Mello, S.K.: Automatic Gaze-based detection of mind wandering during film viewing. In: Educational Data Mining (2016). https://api.semanticscholar.org/CorpusID:33070209

29. Nishimura, G., Faisal, A.: Déjà vu: classification of memory using eye movements (2015)

30. Okada, N.S., et al.: A virtual reality paradigm with dynamic scene stimuli for use in memory research. Behav. Res. Methods 1–24 (2023)

31. Oulasvirta, A., Kim, S., Lee, B.: Neuromechanics of a button press. In: Proceedings of the 2018 CHI Conference on Human Factors in Computing Systems (CHI 2018), pp. 1–13. Association for Computing Machinery, New York (2018). https://doi.org/10.1145/3173574.3174082

32. Rowland, C.A.: The effect of testing versus restudy on retention: a meta-analytic review of the testing effect. Psychol. Bull. **140**(6), 1432 (2014)

33. Ryals, A.J., Kelly, M.E., Cleary, A.M.: Increased pupil dilation during tip-of-the-tongue states. Conscious. Cogn. **92**, 103152 (2021)

34. Ryals, A.J., Wang, J.X., Polnaszek, K.L., Voss, J.L.: Hippocampal contribution to implicit configuration memory expressed via eye movements during scene exploration. Hippocampus **25**(9), 1028–1041 (2015)

35. Schuetz, I., Fiehler, K.: Eye tracking in virtual reality: vive pro eye spatial accuracy, precision, and calibration reliability. J. Eye Movem. Res. **15**(3) (2022)

36. Seabolt, L.K.: Eye've seen this before: Building a gaze data analysis tool for déjà vu detection (2022)

37. Stewart, A., Bosch, N., Chen, H., Donnelly, P.J., D'Mello, S.K.: Where's your mind at? video-based mind wandering detection during film viewing. In: Proceedings of the 2016 Conference on User Modeling Adaptation and Personalization (UMAP 2016), pp. 295–296. Association for Computing Machinery, New York (2016). https://doi.org/10.1145/2930238.2930266

38. Yu Imaoka, A.F., de Bruin, E.D.: Assessing saccadic eye movements with head-mounted display virtual reality technology. Front. Psychiatry **11**(572938) (2020) https://doi.org/10.3389/fpsyt.2020.572938

Towards a Positive Thinking About Deepfakes: Evaluating the Experience of Deepfake Voices in the Emotional and Rational Scenarios

Chih-Jung Chang and Wei-Chi Chien[✉]

Institute of Creative Industries Design, National Cheng Kung University, Tainan, Taiwan (R.O.C.)
chien@xtdesign.org

Abstract. This study conducted a prospective exploration to investigate humans' experiences with self-deepfaked voices, specifically the differences between AI-generated, self-deepfaked, and authentic human voices in the hedonic and pragmatic contexts. Our result shows that, despite participants consistently preferring human voices across all tasks, their experiences between authentic human voice, self-deepfaked, and AI-generated voices, and between hedonic and pragmatic contexts can be different. Self-deepfaked voices outperformed in hedonic scenarios, providing enriched listening experiences. On the contrary, self-deepfakes and AI-generated voices exhibit their different potentials in pragmatic contexts. The findings could inspire the potential application of deepfakes to create a proper social experience between humans and AI.

Keywords: Deepfakes · Human-AI Interaction · Self-Deepfaking · Voice Experience · Story-listening · Customer Service

1 To the Positive Aspect of Deepfakes

Deepfakes, facilitated by generative adversarial networks (GANs), generate convincing yet potentially unreliable, manipulated, or misleading media content, encompassing images, audio, and videos. Analogous to the dual AI models within GANs, two primary research foci emerge: the creation of deepfakes (e.g. [5, 24, 62]) and their detection or prevention of them (e.g. [15, 21, 58, 68]). Coined in the context of content fabrication with privacy concerns [19, 57, 68], the term 'deepfake' has triggered rapid ethical debates in recent years. In response to the surge in nonconsensual and unauthorized use of synthetic content, extensive research has arisen to devise effective methods for deepfake detection [15, 28, 67]. However, the advancing landscape of AI has introduced heightened challenges in discerning between authentic and fabricated content.

Beyond the ethical concerns and malicious use of deepfake, discussions surrounding its positive applications are also on the rise [8, 10, 30, 51, 56, 65]. Indeed, the deepfake technology, formerly denoted as "face swapping," can be traced back to its initial purpose of rectifying the asynchronous lip movements and the audio discrepancies [7].

© The Author(s), under exclusive license to Springer Nature Switzerland AG 2024
M. Kurosu and A. Hashizume (Eds.): HCII 2024, LNCS 14684, pp. 311–325, 2024.
https://doi.org/10.1007/978-3-031-60405-8_20

Modern deepfake applications in the movie industry have gone far beyond. For example, "Deepfake actors" are now performing for authentic actors to save time and money [1]. Research also found deepfaked movie reproduction can yield a remarkably realistic movie experience [42]. For creating scenes where the actors are no longer alive, deepfake provides a realistic clone to make them possible [24, 25, 54]. Furthermore, owing to ethical concerns surrounding deepfake's authenticity, its application for reflective or even critical purposes has emerged as an expressive avenue in new media and art, fostering inquiries into humans' social identity [39].

An alternative suggestion for deploying deepfake technology is education and consultancy using deepfaked avatar instructors [26, 51]. Its potential benefit may lie in the learning motivation enhanced by an avatar's appearance and behavior style [26] or by practicing prosocial interaction with a deepfaked respondent [36]. The perception of a persona regenerated by deepfake could also invite biographical imagination and inspire the creative process in design practice [30, 31]. Moreover, deepfake-empowered imagination could also extend to enhancing one's self-image. Similar to creating illusions in virtual reality (VR) to support behavioral therapy [16, 35], deepfakes may manipulate an individual's self-image, facilitating psychological self-modeling and coaching of one's behavioral skills [10, 69].

From a pragmatic perspective, deploying deepfakes on self-image could involve fewer ethical concerns and bring valuable effects. A derived research objective is people's experience with their deepfaked selves. However, there are only limited empirical studies related to this subjective, and this study should provide an insightful exploration with the following conditional settings of self-deepfaking: (1) deepfaked self's voice vs. AI-generated human voice vs. authentic human voice, (2) voice experience in hedonic and pragmatic scenarios.

2 Review of Related Works

2.1 Experience and Preference of Another Self

The perception of another self has historical roots in gothic literature, epitomized by the "Doppelgänger" (double goer in English). Originally conceptualized as an affliction jeopardizing one's spiritual uniqueness [66, 70], the advent of modern technology, such as VR, has demystified the interaction with one's Doppelgänger. Nevertheless, an explorative study found that users' perception of another interactive self in VR remains an eerie experience [23]. In a survey of different speculative scenarios related to deepfakes, researchers also identified the rejective reaction to AI-generated clones when challenging humanity [33]. This negative experience is also related to the uncanny-valley effect of an analogous human [12, 45].

However, there is also the psychological theory of similarity-attraction and dissimilarity-repulsion theory, which explains why people prefer interacting with and learning from homogeneous targets [37, 38, 59]. In the task of crafting game avatars, studies found a pronounced preference for an idealized self over a robot avatar, especially among individuals with higher self-esteem [20]. In a pedagogical context, self-modeling by envisioning one's successful future has been established as a strategic approach to augment one's physical and social skills [10, 14]. When users are observing them as a meaningful target to imitate, self-deepfaking could serve as an effective coaching tool. For example, studies found that employing idealized self-data can serve as a strategy to improve performance [6, 53]. Researchers found positive outcomes when using self-deepfaking in exercising and training public speaking [10]. Noteworthy is a study using self-deepfaking for coaching dancing, which shows no significant difference between a human coach and a deepfaked self [65].

2.2 Perception and Experience of Voices

Voice is a complex media in interpersonal interaction that carries information, identity, and attitudes and functions as an "auditory face" [2, 3]. Voices in interaction also involve reflexive qualities that shape social relationships, such as voice as self-enhancement to raise attractiveness [27], vocal competence to promote trust [49], and self-perception of voices to activate emotional regulations [11]. In an interactive voice response experiment, researchers identified the voice qualities that could influence the evaluation of the information, such as formality and voice gender [40]. The inherent differences of subjects influence voice preferences. A well-known mechanism is people's preferences for heterosexual voices (e.g. [18]). The context of communication plays an essential role as well. For example, studies identified low-pitched male voices as related to perceived trust in first impression [64], while under the economic context, higher-pitched female voices are evaluated as more trustworthy [48].

With the empowerment of AI technology, the quality of synthetic voice has gone far beyond *IBM 7094's Daisy Bell*. For example, the voice quality of today's text-to-speech (TTS) applications has been proven to be very close to humans' voice performance [9]. In human-robot interaction, the likeness of a robot's voice to human beings significantly enhances its users' technological acceptance [17, 55]. Like humans' voice preferences, robots' voice characters also influence users' preferences and perceived attractiveness [43, 60]. The results are, however, not consistent. It is not clear whether humans' preference for synthetic voice is fixed in our nature or has cultural differences. Some studies found that users prefer robots with female (high-pitched) voices and evaluate them as more attractive and pleasurable in interaction [43, 44]. However, in a study of voice assistants and the correlated gender differences in voices (male, female, and gender-ambiguous voices) and listeners, researchers identified trait ascription bias in our evaluation of synthetic voices and no significant difference in trustworthiness [63]. A more complex research studied robots' voices and users' preferences under different contexts. They found higher acceptance of male and child voices of service and companion robots and male and female voices of educational robots [13].

3   Experiment

To our research objective about self-deepfaking, psychological studies found our narcissistic nature in the evaluation of voices, by which participants evaluated voices similar to theirs as more attractive [29, 52]. However, it is unclear whether we would prefer a voice similar to ours. Considering the possible gender differences and the differences caused by the context, this study explored female participants' experiences with three voices: deepfaked voices of themselves, AI-generated voices, and authentic human voices (RQ1) under two scenarios (RQ2), story-listening and customer service. The two scenarios correspond to the hedonic and pragmatic contexts.

The participants were not informed that they would interact with deepfaked and AI-generated voices until they finished the experiment. This leads to our interest in whether the awareness of synthetic voices would influence people's evaluation (RQ3).

Our research engaged twelve female international students (N = 12). The participants included native English speakers (N = 6) and other regions in Asia and Europe (N = 6) with fluent English ability (C1 or higher).

3.1   Task 1: Hedonic Scenario – Story Listening

Three types of voices were prepared, including self-deepfaked, AI-generated (based on a random participant's voice), and authentic human voices (the first author's voice). The participants were invited to two tasks in the lab on another day. The first task included three local folktales of a genre of ghost stories in English but narrated randomly with three different voices. Participants were asked to listen to the stories and then evaluated their experiences after each story. The evaluation includes the overall experience, emotionality, closeness, and attractiveness. In addition, the User Engagement Scale (UES) [46, 47] and the Narrative Engageability Scale (NES) [4] were used. UES contains four constructs: focus attention, perceived usability, aesthetic, and reward factor. Among them, perceived usability is removed due to its inapplicability in our case. NES includes ease of accepting unrealism, curiosity propensity, ease of being engaged despite adverse surroundings, emotional engageability, and presence propensity. All items were evaluated on a 7-scale Likert scale. After the evaluation, an interview was conducted to survey the participants' experiences during the task.

3.2   Task 2: Pragmatic Scenario – Customer Service

Following a 10-min break, the participants engaged in the second customer service task. Like the first task, three scenarios were formulated, with each employing one of the voice modalities randomly. Three scenarios include (a) checking the shipping status of a computer order and requesting expedited delivery, (b) returning a defective computer and arranging for a home pick-up return, and (c) resolving technical issues with a computer that randomly shut down after being updated. Necessary background information, such as order information and technical problems, along with clear task goals, was provided for participants in each task. A pre-trained *ChatGPT* model generated the texts in the second task. By connecting to *ElevenLabs* using their APIs, participants' speech was recognized as text for *ChatGPT*, and *ChatGPT*'s texts were converted into speech. The human voices were the pre-recorded voice files. ChatGPT produced all possible responses and then narrated and recorded by the second author beforehand. The researcher played the corresponding file in response to the participants' dialogue during the task.

The whole system was hidden, and the participants were told that they were speaking with an online customer service. Evaluations in the second task include overall experience, speaker's competence, trustworthiness, and, in addition, the *Client Satisfaction Questionnaire* (CSQ) [32] and *Service Quality Questionnaire* (SERVQUAL) [50].

SERVQUAL includes multiple constructs, and four aspects were selected: reliability, responsiveness, credibility, and empathy (understanding/knowing). Since our customer service was ready in hand and the service content was pre-trained in our model, other constructs, such as access, tangibles, and communication, were omitted. All items were evaluated on a 7-scale Likert scale.

After the questionnaire survey, a second interview similar to the first one was conducted to understand the participants' experience and their capability to detect AI and deepfakes. After the interview, all participants were informed about the truth of using deepfakes and AI.

4 Results

4.1 Qualities of Different Voices in Two Scenarios

Overall, there is no significant difference between native and non-native English speakers. In the story experience, an overview of all evaluations can be found in Fig. 1. The human voice is rated significantly higher than AI-generated voice in all aspects and higher than self-deepfaked voices in emotionality ($t[11] = 2.27, p = 0.44$), attractiveness ($t[11] = 2.31, p = 0.41$), and narrative engagement scale ($t[11] = 2.27, p = 0.05$). A general tendency that self-deepfaked voice performs better than AI-generated voice can be observed from the descriptive analysis (Fig. 1). However, the difference between AI-generated voices and self-deepfakes is statistically not significant.

In the customer service task, the human voice exhibits a generally superior performance compared to the other two voice modalities, as depicted in Fig. 2. However, statistically significant differences are observed in specific aspects. The human voice exhibits higher overall experiences than the AI-generated voice ($t[11 = 2.22, p = 0.48$). The human voice also demonstrates higher competence compared to the self-deepfaked voice ($t[11] = 2.41, p = 0.03$), higher trustworthiness than both self-deepfaked voice ($t[11] = 2.71, p = 0.02$) and AI-generated voice ($t[11] = 2.79, p = 0.02$). In addition, the human voice receives higher ratings in client satisfaction (CSQ) compared to the AI-generated voice ($t[11] = 2.44, p = 0.03$) and higher service quality score (SERVQUAL) than self-deepfakes ($t[11] = 3.30, p = 0.01$).

In summary, the human voice emerges as the most desirable in both scenarios. There is a potential, albeit statistically insignificant, for self-deepfakes to excel in the hedonic context. However, no discernible difference between self-deepfakes and AI voices in the pragmatic context is identified.

4.2 Factors of Deepfake Detection

Two participants (P3 and P5) in the story-listening task and four (P3, P5, P6, P10) in the customer service task reported recognizing that their voices had been deepfaked. The realization predominantly occurred during the task, prompted by moments of suspicion, as exemplified by inquiries such as "Is that my voice?" Given our interest in discerning distinctions between self-deepfakes and AI-generated voices, coupled with the fact that

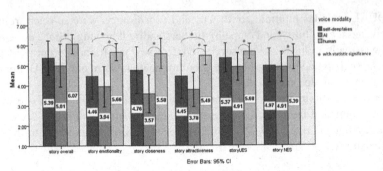

Fig. 1. Scores of the story experience among all voice modalities

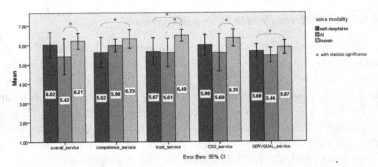

Fig. 2. Scores of the customer service experience among all voice modalities

the same researcher generated the human voices, we computed participants' relative scores for deepfakes and AI voices by referencing the scores for human voices:

$$RelativeScore_{deepfake/AI} = \frac{OriginalScore_{deepfake/AI}}{OriginalScore_{human\_voice}}$$

The translated results are illustrated in Figs. 4 and 5. Notable statistical significances emerge, particularly in the story-listening task, where a Wilcoxon Test shows that participants who are not aware of self-deepfakes (N = 10) score a significantly higher closeness than AI-generated voice ($Z = 2.80, p = 0.01$) (Fig. 3-left). Although not attaining statistical significance, Fig. 3-right shows a contrasting trend in emotionality, closeness, and attractiveness. These two participants, who recognized their deepfaked voices during the task, rated lower scores for their deepfaked voices.

On the contrary, in the customer service task, participants who identified their self-deepfaked voices (N = 4) did not score their own voices lower. The perceived competence is even higher than the AI-generated voices ($t[3] = 4.20, p = 0.03$), and self-deepfakes are generally scored higher than AI-generated voices (Fig. 4-right).

4.3 Other Quantitative Details

Figure 5 and Fig. 6 show detailed analyses of the questionnaires used in our experiment – UES and NES for engagement evaluation in the story-listening task and SERVQUAL

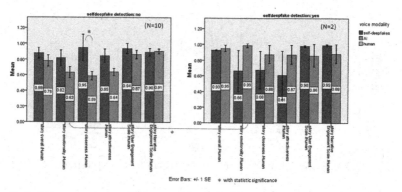

Fig. 3. Relative scores according to participants' self-deepfake detection (story-listening)

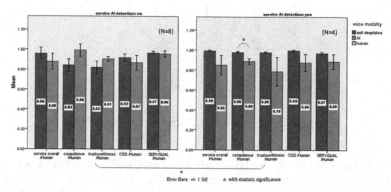

Fig. 4. Relative scores according to participants' self-deepfake detection (customer service task)

for the service quality in the customer service task. The result of UES is consistent with the general evaluation of the three voice modalities. In NES, what inspires us is that the curiosity propensity of self-deepfaked voice is significantly higher than AI-generated voice ($t[11] = 2.30$, $p = 0.04$). In SERVQUAL, human voice exhibits significantly better performance than AI-generated voices and self-deepfakes in assurance ($t[11] = 3.32$, $p = 0.01$ and $t[11] = 2.32$, $p = 0.04$, respectively) and reliability ($t[11] = 3.55$, $p = 0.01$ and $t[11] = 2.75$, $p = 0.02$, respectively). However, no difference in empathy and responsiveness is observed, where the three voice modalities demonstrate remarkably similar scores.

When using relative scores to evaluate participants with different deepfake-detection performances, we get similar results. We can identify significantly higher curiosity propensity scores ($Z = 2.80$, $p = 0.01$) in self-deepfakes for participants who did not recognize deepfakes.

4.4 Qualitative Result

To gain deeper insights into the participants' perceptions, we conducted a thematic analysis of the interview data, unveiling themes supported by participants' narratives.

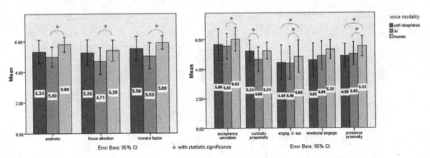

Fig. 5. Scores of each construct in UES (left) and NES (right)

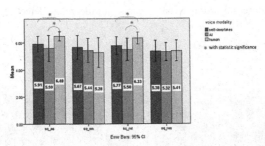

Fig. 6. Scores of each construct in SERVQUAL

Detecting Deepfakes. During the post-study interviews, eight out of twelve participants (P1, P2, P3, P5, P6, P7, P10, P12) reported confidence in identifying synthetic voices, though less than half have recognized them successfully. When asked about their experiences, participants mentioned that computer-generated voices often lack emotion and sound monotone, *"Perhaps the tone or the speed and whether some words have been stressed or not [...] Personally, I think robotic voice is more flat"* (P1).

Interestingly, one participant highlighted the difficulty in recognizing synthetic voices during customer service conversations because she was concentrating on the task assignment to be solved. *"When someone really is eager to solve their problem, they are more focusing on their own voice and their own problem rather than the other person"* (P12).

The participants who really recognized the deepfakes revealed their strategies, for example, by comparing them to other self-experiences. *"like everyone has a different way of speaking, so I did hear the way I speak [...] For me, it would take a while, but I would definitely be able to detect my own voice"* (P3). Another participant attributed her recognition to her proficiency in distinguishing different accents, *"where is she from? I really want to know where that accent is from. [...] That sounds familiar, right, that made me very curious. [...] I was like wondering, [...] I had a feeling. I would say, did they take my voice and make it AI?"* (P6).

Significantly, among the subset of participants (N = 4) who identified their self-deefaked voices in the pragmatic context, two individuals were consistent with those who had earlier recognized their voices in the hedonic context, suggesting that they were particularly attentive during the subsequent interactions.

Emotionality of Voice and Its Effects on Perceived Closeness and Attractiveness. The AI-generated voice was, in fact, a deepfaked voice of another random participant. There should not be any technical differences. However, participants reported closer feelings and more emotional and richer expressions in their deepfaked voices, although they did not identify them as their own voices. "The third folklore [self-deepfake] was definitely more emotional and I like that one better. It's just sounds softer, and then the pace maybe? [...] The first one [AI-generated voice], my least favorite. It's like, yeah it's not like a grown up talking to a kid" (P2).

Emotionality of Voice and Its Effects on Perceived Closeness and Attractiveness. The AI-generated voice was, in fact, a deepfaked voice of another random participant. There should not be any technical differences. However, participants reported closer feelings and more emotional and richer expressions in their deepfaked voices, although they did not identify them as their own voices. *"The third folklore* [self-deepfake] *was definitely more emotional and I like that one better. It's just sounds softer, and then the pace maybe? [...] The first one* [AI-generated voice], *my least favorite. It's like, yeah it's not like a grown up talking to a kid"* (P2).

Why Participants Dislike Their Own Voices in the Pragmatic Context. Drawing upon our literature review and results of the first task, it could be posited that self-deepfaked voices have greater potential than AI-generated voices. However, from a statistical standpoint, no clear distinctions emerged between self-deepfaked voice and AI-generated voice in the second task. Through the interview process, certain cues were discerned, revealing why self-deepfakes were undesirable.

"Usually return issue is so annoying so she made it very easy even though the voice was like a robot. I was just satisfied because she [AI-generated voice] made it easy. Everything was just like step by step by step, no blockage. [...] I think if it's a real human, then I am more empathetic. Like, okay, yeah, you have too many things to do, it's fine for you to be busy [...] If it's a computer I'm like the computer should be efficient like it shouldn't have that much blockage in my opinion if it's made well" (P2).

There appears to be a positive correlation between a cold and unfamiliar voice and the perception of professionalism, coupled with a tendency to avoid bureaucratic nuances. Participants may find it more comfortable to engage in arguments with a robot-like entity. This observation aligns with the statistical findings, where, in the pragmatic scenarios, human voices scored higher in assurance and reliability, but not in empathy and responsiveness.

5 Discussion

While the human voice significantly scored higher than other modalities, a noteworthy observation is that most participants did not recognize the nature of AI models. Even if they did, it was primarily attributed to the participants recognizing their own voices. From the ethical perspective, reiterated by numerous studies, deepfakes can convincingly lead to distortion of the truth. The distortion could be particularly pronounced in contextualized interaction, where not everyone can maintain a focus on distinguishing authenticity from manipulation. Besides, our findings suggest that, despite potential awareness deficits, individual preferences and intuition may exhibit heightened sensitivity.

Overall, human voices scored significantly higher than other voice modalities. In the hedonic task, deepfaked self-voice tends to be more desirable than the deepfaked voice of other strangers. Some statistically significant findings emerge, including the *closeness* feelings and *curiosity propensity* (when participants were not aware of self-deepfakes) in the hedonic context and *competence* in the pragmatic context (when participants were aware of self-deepfakes). Participants' qualitative data supports this result.

The difference between self-deepfakes and AI-generated voices appears differently in the hedonic and pragmatic contexts. Within the hedonic scenario, participants characterized self-deepfakes as more emotionally resonant, consistent with our theoretical review. Voices, when familiar, can convey richer information, thereby engendering a more captivating listening experience.

While self-deepfakes are potentially more desirable in the hedonic context, they do not seem to have the same advantage in the pragmatic context. As some participants disclosed in the interview, when engaged in pragmatic goals, individuals may perceive higher competence from an unfamiliar and impersonal voice (AI-generated voice). The more detached interpersonal experience could facilitate communicating factual information without imbuing personal emotions into the interaction. Consequently, in the dimensions of empathy and responsiveness within the service quality questionnaire, all three modalities have almost identical scores.

Two participants recognized their voices during the story-listening task, and intriguingly, they evaluated their own voices as unfavorable. A plausible explanation for this could be the peculiar experience of hearing alternate self-narrating fictitious stories akin to the negative Doppelgänger encounter.

It should be noted that the low scores are only observed in evaluating the perceived voice experience (emotionality, closeness, and attractiveness). In contrast, the evaluation of stories' engagement (UES and NES) remains comparable to the other two modalities. Conversely, the pragmatic context exhibits a different pattern. The participants who recognized their own deepfaked voices evaluated their voices better on average.

6 Conclusions

From the aspect of causality, 'faking' implies creating a deceptive appearance, suggesting something different from reality. However, from a managerial standpoint that views presentation as a dynamic process, 'shaping impression' emerges as a more fitting concept when contemplating deepfake technology. Under this scope, the presented study furnishes empirical evidence about how people perceive self-deepfakes in the hedonic and pragmatic context. The result shows contextual differences in individuals' preference for self-deepfakes or AI-generated voices. We also identified the "side effects" in people's experience when they discover the existence of faking during the interaction. Depending on the context, the effect can be very different. These findings should inspire designers to apply deepfakes in positive usages and avoid negative effects with some fundamental understanding. For example, the integration of self-deepfaked voices in creating virtual self-avatars, agents, or a chatbot holds the potential for constructive applications in social or educational domains.

Due to its intricate experiment settings, this study grapples with limited sample size, rendering the interpretation of statistical data less reliant on significant features as solid evidence. However, the descriptive analyses and the qualitative results still provide interesting insights. When reflecting on the experiment design, several considerations arise. (1) We have multinational participants to mitigate cultural bias, yet it may result in a loss of cultural context. (2) The experiment utilizes English, benefitting from a relatively higher development in AI models. AI models for other languages, such as Chinese, may have different performance qualities. (3) The current hedonic scenario lacks interactive elements, potentially yielding different results compared to an interactive one.

Finally, we wish to have a healthy and fair future with AI technology.

Acknowledgments. This project is funded by National Science and Technology Council, R.O.C. Taiwan (NSTC112-2410-H-006-075-).

References

1. Lalla, V., Mitrani, A., Harned, Z.: Artificial Intelligence: Deepfakes in the Entertainment Industry (2022). https://www.wipo.int/wipo_magazine/en/2022/02/article_0003.html. Accessed 27 Nov 2023
2. Belin, P., Bestelmeyer, P.E.G., Latinus, M., Watson, R.: Understanding voice perception. Br. J. Psychol. **102**(4), 711–725 (2011)
3. Belin, P., Fecteau, S., Bédard, C.: Thinking the voice: neural correlates of voice perception. Trends Cognit. Sci. **8**(3), 129–135 (2004)
4. Bilandzic, H., Sukalla, F., Schnell, C., Hastall, M.R., Busselle, R.W.: The narrative engage-ability scale: a multidimensional trait measure for the propensity to become engaged in a story. Int. J. Commun. **13**, 801–832 (2019)
5. Bode, L., Lees, D., Golding, D.: The digital face and deepfakes on screen. Convergence: Int. J. Res. New Media Technol. **27**(4), 849–854 (2021)
6. Bode, M., Kristensen, D.B.: The digital doppelgänger within: a study on self-tracking and the quantified self-movement. In: Assembling Consumption: Researching Actors, Networks and Markets. Routledge, pp. 119–134 (2015)
7. Bregler, C., Covell, M., Slaney, M.: Video rewrite: driving visual speech with audio. In: Proceedings of International Conference on Computer Graphics and Interactive Techniques (SIGGRAPH 1997). ACM, New York (1997)
8. Bu, J., Jiang, R.L., Zheng, B.: Research on deepfake technology and its application. In: Proceedings of International Conference on Computing, Networks and Internet of Things (CNIOT 2023). ACM, New York (2023)
9. Cambre, J., Colnago, J., Maddock, J., Tsai, J., Kaye, J.: Choice of voices: a large-scale evaluation of text-to-speech voice quality for long-form content. Proceedings of Conference on Human Factors in Computing Systems (CHI 2020). ACM, New York (2020)
10. Clarke, C., et al.: FakeForward: using deepfake technology for feedforward learning. In: Proceedings of Conference on Human Factors in Computing Systems (CHI 2023). ACM, New York (2023)
11. Costa, J., Jung, M.F., Czerwinski, M., Guimbretière, F., Le, T., Choudhury, T.: Regulating feelings during interpersonal conflicts by changing voice self-perception. In: Proceedings of Conference on Human Factors in Computing Systems (CHI 2018). ACM, New York (2018)
12. Do, T.D., McMahan, R.P., Wisniewski, P.J.: A new uncanny valley? The effects of speech fidelity and human listener gender on social perceptions of a virtual-human speaker. In: Proceedings of Conference on Human Factors in Computing Systems (CHI 2022). ACM, New York (2022)

13. Dou, X., Wu, C.F., Lin, K.C., Gan, S., Tseng, T.M.: Effects of different types of social robot voices on affective evaluations in different application fields. Int. J. Soc. Robot. **13**(4), 615–628 (2021)

14. Dowrick, P.W.: A review of self modeling and related interventions. Appl. Prev. Psychol. **8**(1), 23–39 (1999)

15. Du, M., Pentyala, S., Li, Y., Hu, X.: Towards generalizable deepfake detection with locality-aware AutoEncoder. In: Proceedings of International Conference on Information and Knowledge Management (CIKM 2020). ACM, New York (2020)

16. Emmelkamp, P.M.G., Meyerbröker, K.: Virtual reality therapy in mental health. Annu. Rev. Clin. Psychol. **17**, 495–519 (2021)

17. Eyssel, F., Kuchenbrandt, D., Bobinger, S., DeRuiter, L., Hegel, F.: If you sound like me, you must be more human: on the interplay of robot and user features on human-robot acceptance and anthropomorphism. In: Proceedings of International Conference on Human-Robot Interaction (HRI 2012). ACM, New York (2012)

18. Feinberg, D.R., et al.: Menstrual cycle, trait estrogen level, masculinity preferences in the human voice. Horm. Behav. **49**(2), 215–222 (2006)

19. Gamage, D., Ghasiya, P., Bonagiri, V., Whiting, M.E., Sasahara, K.: Are deepfakes concerning? Analyzing conversations of deepfakes on Reddit and exploring societal implications. In: Proceedings of International Conference on Human Factors in Computing Systems (CHI 2022). ACM, New York (2022)

20. Gorisse, G., Christmann, O., Houzangbe, S., Richir, S.: From robot to virtual doppelganger: Impact of avatar visual fidelity and self-esteem on perceived attractiveness. In: Proceedings of the Workshop on Advanced Visual Interfaces (AVI 2018). ACM, New York, (2018)

21. Güera, D., Delp, E.J.: Deepfake video detection using neural networks. In: Proceedings of IEEE International Conference on Advanced Video and Signal Based Surveillance (AVSS 2018). ACM, New York (2018)

22. Gupta, P., Chugh, K., Dhall, A., Subramanian, R.: The eyes know it: FakeET- An eye-tracking database to understand deepfake perception. In: Proceedings of the International Conference on Multimodal Interaction (ICMI 2020). ACM, New York (2020)

23. Hatada, Y., Yoshida, S., Narumi, T., Hirose, M.: Double shellf: what psychological effects can be caused through interaction with a doppelganger? In: Proceedings of Augmented Human International Conference (AH 2019). ACM, New York (2019)

24. Holliday, C.: Rewriting the stars: Surface tensions and gender troubles in the online media production of digital deepfakes. Convergence **27**(4), 899–918 (2021)

25. Velasquez, S.J.: How AI is bringing film stars back from the dead (2023). https://www.bbc.com/future/article/20230718-how-ai-is-bringing-film-stars-back-from-the-dead. Accessed 5 Dec 2023

26. Lackey, S., Shumaker, R. (eds.): VAMR 2016. LNCS, vol. 9740. Springer, Cham (2016). https://doi.org/10.1007/978-3-319-39907-2

27. Hughes, S.M., Harrison, M.A.: I like my voice better: self-enhancement bias in perceptions of voice attractiveness. Perception **42**(9), 941–949 (2013)

28. Hussain, S., et al.: Exposing vulnerabilities of deepfake detection systems with robust attacks. Digit. Threats: Res. Pract. **3**, 3 (2022)

29. Jones, B.C., Feinberg, D.R., De Bruine, L.M., Little, A.C., Vukovic, J.: A domain-specific opposite-sex bias in human preferences for manipulated voice pitch. Anim. Behav. **79**(1), 57–62 (2010)

30. Kaate, I., Salminen, J., Jung, S.G., Almerekhi, H., Jansen, B.J.: How do users perceive deepfake personas? Investigating the deepfake user perception and its implications for human-computer interaction. In: Proceedings of Biannual Conference of the Italian SIGCHI (CHItaly 2023). ACM, New York (2023)

31. Kaate, I., Salminen, J., Santos, J., Jung, S.G., Olkkonen, R., Jansen, B.: The realness of fakes: primary evidence of the effect of deepfake personas on user perceptions in a design task. Int. J. Human Comput. Stud. **178**, 103096 (2023)

32. Larsen, D.L., Attkisson, C.C., Hargreaves, W.A., Nguyen, T.D.: Assessment of client/patient satisfaction: development of a general scale. Eval. Program Plann. **2**(3), 197–207 (1979)

33. Lee, P.Y.K., Ma, N.F., Kim, I.J., Yoon, D.: Speculating on risks of AI clones to selfhood and relationships: doppelganger-phobia, identity fragmentation, and living memories. Proc. ACM Hum. Comput. Interact. **7**(1 CSCW1), 1–28 (2023)

34. Li, M., Ahmadiadli, Y., Zhang, X.P.: A comparative study on physical and perceptual features for deepfake audio detection. In: Proceedings of International Workshop on Deepfake Detection for Audio Multimedia (DDAM 2022). ACM, New York (2022)

35. Lindner, P.: Better, virtually: the past, present, and future of virtual reality cognitive behavior therapy. Int. J. Cogn. Ther. **14**(1), 23–46 (2021)

36. Lu, H., Chu, H.: Let the dead talk: how deepfake resurrection narratives influence audience response in prosocial contexts. Comput. Hum. Behav. **145**, 107761 (2023)

37. Luo, P., Ng-Thow-Hing, V., Neff, M.: An examination of whether people prefer agents whose gestures mimic their own. In: Aylett, R., Krenn, B., Pelachaud, C., Shimodaira, H. (eds.) IVA 2013. LNCS (LNAI), vol. 8108, pp. 229–238. Springer, Heidelberg (2013). https://doi.org/10.1007/978-3-642-40415-3_20

38. Mahajan, N., Wynn, K.: Origins of "Us" versus "Them": prelinguistic infants prefer similar others. Cognition **124**(2), 227–233 (2012)

39. Mihailova, M.: To dally with Dalí: deepfake (inter)faces in the art museum. Convergence **27**(4), 882–898 (2021)

40. Mubarak, E., Shahid, T., Mustafa, M., Naseem, M.: Does gender and accent of voice matter?: An interactive voice response (IVR) experiment. In: Proceedings of International Conference on Information and Communication Technologies and Development (ICTD 2020). ACM, New York (2020)

41. Muller, N.M., Pizzi, K., Williams, J.: Human perception of audio deepfakes. In: Proceedings of International Workshop on Deepfake Detection for Audio Multimedia (DDAM 2022). ACM, New York (2022)

42. Murphy, G., Ching, D., Twomey, J., Linehan, C.: Face/off: changing the face of movies with deepfakes. PLoS ONE **18**(7), 1–19 (2023)

43. Niculescu, A., van Dijk, B., Nijholt, A., Li, H., See, S.L.: Making social robots more attractive: the effects of voice pitch, humor and empathy. Int. J. Soc. Robot. **5**(2), 171–191 (2013)

44. Niculescu, A., VanDijk, B., Nijholt, A., See, S.L.: The influence of voice pitch on the evaluation of a social robot receptionist. In: Proceedings of International Conference on User Science and Engineering (iUSEr 2011). IEEE, New York (2011)

45. Nissen, A., Conrad, C., Newman, A.: Are you human? Investigating the perceptions and evaluations of virtual versus human Instagram influencers. In: Proceedings of Conference on Human Factors in Computing Systems (CHI 2023). ACM, New York (2023)

46. O'Brien, H., Cairns, P.: An empirical evaluation of the User Engagement Scale (UES) in online news environments. Inf. Process. Manag. **51**(4), 413–427 (2015)

47. O'Brien, H.L., Cairns, P., Hall, M.: A practical approach to measuring user engagement with the refined user engagement scale (UES) and new UES short form. Int. J. Hum. Comput. Stud. **112**, 28–39 (2018)

48. O'Connor, J.J.M., Barclay, P.: The influence of voice pitch on perceptions of trustworthiness across social contexts. Evol. Hum. Behav. **38**(4), 506–512 (2017)

49. Oleszkiewicz, A., Pisanski, K., Lachowicz-Tabaczek, K., Sorokowska, A.: Voice-based assessments of trustworthiness, competence, and warmth in blind and sighted adults. Psychon. Bull. Rev. **24**(3), 856–862 (2017)

50. Parasuraman, A., Zeithaml, V.A., Berry, L.L.: A conceptual model of service quality and its implications for future research. J. Mark. **49**(4), 41 (1985)

51. Pataranutaporn, P., et al.: AI-generated characters for supporting personalized learning and well-being. Nat. Mach. Intell. **3**(12), 1013–1022 (2021)

52. Peng, Z., Wang, Y., Meng, L., Liu, H., Hu, Z.: One's own and similar voices are more attractive than other voices. Aust. J. Psychol. **71**(3), 212–222 (2019). https://doi.org/10.1111/ajpy.12235

53. Pierlejewski, M.: The data-doppelganger and the cyborg-self: theorising the datafication of education. Pedagog. Cult. Soc. **28**(3), 463–475 (2020)

54. Chichizola, C.: Rogue One Deepfake Makes Star Wars' Leia and Grand Moff Tarkin Look Even More Lifelike. https://www.cinemablend.com/news/2559935/rogue-one-dee pfake-makes-star-wars-leia-and-grand-moff-tarkin-look-even-more-lifelike. Accessed 5 Dec 2023

55. Schreibelmayr, S., Mara, M.: Robot voices in daily life: vocal human-likeness and application context as determinants of user acceptance. Front. Psychol. **13** (2022)

56. Seymour, M., Riemer, K., Yuan, L., Dennis, A.R.: Beyond deep fakes: a conceptual framework and research agenda for neural rendering of realistic digital faces. Commun. ACM **66**(10), 56–67 (2023)

57. Shahid, I., Roy, N.: "Is this my president speaking?" Tamper-proofing speech in live recordings. In: Proceedings of Annual International Conference on Mobile Systems, Applications and Services (MobiSys 2023). ACM, New York (2023)

58. Shahriar, S.D.: A Comparative Study on Evaluation of Methods in Capturing Emotion. Umea University (2011)

59. Singh, R., Tan, L.S.C.: Attitudes and attraction: a test of the similarity-attraction and dissimilarity-repulsion hypotheses. Br. J. Soc. Psychol. **31**, 227–238 (1992)

60. Song, S., Baba, J., Nakanishi, J., Yoshikawa, Y., Ishiguro, H.: Mind the voice!: effect of robot voice pitch, robot voice gender, and user gender on user perception of teleoperated robots. In: Extende Abstracts of CHI Conference on Human Factors in Computing Systems (CHI EA 2020). ACM, New York (2020)

61. Tahir, R., Batool, B.: Seeing is believing: exploring perceptual diferences in deepfake videos. In: Proceedings of Conference on Human Factors in Computing Systems (CHI 2021). ACM, New York (2021)

62. Thies, J., Zollhöfer, M., Stamminger, M., Theobalt, C., Nießner, M.: Face2Face: real-time face capture and reenactment of RGB videos. Commun. ACM **62**(1), 96–104 (2019)

63. Tolmeijer, S., Zierau, N., Janson, A., Wahdatehagh, J.S., Leimeister, J.M.M., Bernstein, A.: Female by default? Exploring the effect of voice assistant gender and pitch on trait and trust atribution. Extende Abstracts of CHI Conference on Human Factors in Computing Systems (CHI EA 2021). ACM, New York (2021)

64. Tsantani, M.S., Belin, P., Paterson, H.M., McAleer, P.: Low vocal pitch preference drives first impressions irrespective of context in male voices but not in female voices. Perception **45**(8), 946–963 (2016)

65. Tsuchida, S., et al.: Dance practice system that shows what you would look like if you could master the dance. In: Proceedings of International Conference on Movement and Computing (MOCO 2022). ACM, New York (2022)

66. Vardoulakis, D.: The return of negation: the Doppelgänger in Freud's "The 'Uncanny.'" Sub-Stance. **35**(2), 100–116 (2006)

67. Wang, T., Cheng, H., Chow, K.P., Nie, L.: Deep convolutional pooling transformer for deepfake detection. ACM Trans. Multimed. Comput. Commun. Appl. **19**(6), 1–20 (2023)

68. Westerlund, M.: The emergence of deepfake technology: a review. Technol. Innov. Manag. Rev. **9**(11), 39–52 (2019)
69. Wiederhold, B.K.: Can deepfakes improve therapy? Cyberpsychol. Behav. Soc. Netw. **24**(3), 147–148 (2021)
70. Živković, M.: The double as the "unseen" of culture: toward a definition of Doppelganger. Facta Univ. Ser.: Linguist. Liter. **7**(2), 121–128 (2000)

Emotions: Investigating the Vital Role of Tactile Interaction

Xinyi Chen and Meng Ting Zhang^(✉)

Faculty of Humanities and Arts, Macau University of Science and Technology, Avenida Wai Long, Taipa, Macau, China
2230012304@student.must.edu.mo, mtzhang@must.edu.mo

Abstract. Social isolation, resulting from various factors, has become a prevalent concern in today's society. This study explores the potential of tactile interaction as a remedy for social isolation. By employing data mining to understand pandemic-induced emotional conditions and identifying the negative emotions in need of healing, and by using experiment, we introduce the "Emotional Nourishment Project." This project establishes a virtual world, named "Emotional Nourishment," within a real-world context, simulating a doomsday scenario. In this context, we have designed an interactive device that materializes emotional states through physical interactions. The device incorporates hardware and software components, utilizing Arduino IDE for programming. The rationale behind this endeavor lies in its situational relevance, enhanced participation, and ability to emphasize the impact of emotional interactions. Through this project, we aim to shed light on the profound significance of tactile interaction in healing social isolation.

Keywords: Tactile Interaction · social isolation · data mining · experiment · emotional nourishment project

1 Introduction

Social isolation, characterized by a profound deficit in social interaction, transcends age boundaries and manifests as a multifaceted issue influenced by diverse factors including developmental disabilities, economic disparities, and the pervasive repercussions of the COVID-19 pandemic. Within an era marked by relentless advancements in digital technologies and immersive virtual experiences, the landscape of human interaction is undergoing a profound transformation. The prevalence of virtual companionship and digital connections has surged, prompting a paradigm shift in individuals' perceptions and engagements within their social milieu. These technological strides offer unparalleled convenience and accessibility, but concurrently, they raise a pressing concern: the potential erosion of tangible, real-world social interactions and the looming specter of exacerbated social isolation.

Our inquiry commences with an exhaustive review of extant literature, affording an encompassing comprehension of pivotal facets relating to social isolation, body language, emotion, physical touch as a healing modality, and the untapped potential of tactile interaction in mitigating social isolation. This comprehensive literature review constructs a robust framework for understanding the intricate interplay between social isolation, the nuances of body language, the healing potential of physical touch, and the prospect of tactile interaction as a means of alleviating social isolation while bolstering emotional well-being. These erudite insights furnish the bedrock for further forays into this burgeoning domain of research.

Subsequently, we introduce a multifaceted data mining approach tailored to scrutinize the emotional dynamics exhibited by individuals in the throes of the COVID-19 pandemic. This methodological construct seamlessly interweaves both quantitative and qualitative analyses, thus enabling an exhaustive exploration of the spectrum of emotions that find expression within the digital realms of social media. The quantitative facet of our analysis centers on the evaluation of specific keywords and the quantification of prevalent sentiment trends inherent in social media discourse. In parallel, our qualitative analysis plunges into the intricate tapestry of microblog content, unearthing emotional subtleties and contextual nuances.

Concomitantly, we employ an experiment to collect data, all ensconced within the realms of qualitative research. This innovative strategy orchestrates the active involvement of participants in shaping the research game experience, thereby concurrently yielding authentic and valuable user information.

The ensuing Results and Discussion section dissects the outcomes of our data mining analysis, offering an insightful panorama of the public's sentiments and responses during the COVID-19 pandemic. The dataset overview, prominent themes, and temporal analysis collectively weave a narrative that underscores the multifaceted nature of public discourse during a global crisis. Notably, certain emotional states and thematic elements resonate more robustly with denizens of social media platforms, engendering pertinent insights for the effective handling of emotional and social aspects within the framework of public health crises and initiatives aimed at mitigating social isolation.

Subsequent to this analysis, we proffer the "Emotional Nourishment Project," an ingenious tactile interaction design fusing technology, psychology, and storytelling to submerge participants within a dystopian narrative where emotional connections burgeon as essential for survival. The intricate design of wearable and data collection devices, interwoven with Arduino programming, transmutes abstract emotions into tangible manifestations, thereby affording participants the ability to visualize and comprehend the profound impact of tactile interactions.

In summation, this paper serves as an elucidative exposé of the innovative approach undertaken by the "Emotional Nourishment Project" in addressing the prospective consequences of a technology-driven, socially isolated future. By delving into the intricate connecting tactile interactions, emotional bonds, and the essence of human survival, this research aspires to bestow invaluable insights upon the domains of human-computer interaction and emotional well-being, thereby enriching the scholarly discourse in these arenas.

2 Literature Evaluation

2.1 Social Isolation

Social isolation can manifest in early life when individuals grapple with unique identity issues, often keeping them hidden due to shame or guilt stemming from childhood experiences. Additionally, developmental disabilities, such as learning impairments, may lead to social isolation, impacting tactile self-esteem and fostering a sense of being different (Hetherington 1975; Malti et al. 2012; Preece 2006).

In middle-aged and older age, social isolation can result from a complex interplay of factors. These factors include aging, declining physical function, hearing impairment, and challenges in communication for individuals with autism. Additionally, factors such as living alone, unemployment, substance abuse, economic disparities, and low self-esteem contribute to feelings of isolation (Hetherington 1975; Bernabei et al. 2014; Webber and Fendt-Newlin 2017; Crompton et al. 2020; Davey 2020; Herttua et al. 2011; Hjalmarsson and Mood 2015; MacDonald and Martineau 2002).

The COVID-19 pandemic has intensified social isolation through lockdowns, social distancing measures, and the paradoxical role of digital technology in substituting in-person interactions. This has had a particularly pronounced effect on younger generations. The pandemic has led to psychological issues such as depression, anxiety, and post-traumatic stress disorder. Factors such as separation from loved ones, misinformation, financial insecurity, and stigmatization have further exacerbated mental health problems, especially among healthcare workers (Sim 2020; Wu et al. 2005; Mohanty 2020). The economic impact, fueled by business closures, has caused insecurity and stress, particularly for daily wage workers (Mohanty 2020). Social media, despite facilitating connectivity, has also become a source of stress due to the proliferation of false information (Mohanty 2020).

The consequences of social isolation are multifaceted and encompass psychological, emotional, and societal effects. These consequences include an increased risk of mental health issues such as depression, anxiety, and post-traumatic stress disorder, negative impacts on self-esteem and self-worth (especially among individuals with learning disabilities or those who feel different from others), barriers to effective communication (particularly among the elderly and individuals with hearing impairments), marginalization and misunderstanding of individuals with autism and communication barriers, economic disparities leading to restricted social circles and isolation, a cycle of social withdrawal driven by low self-esteem and a desire to avoid judgment, the exacerbation of psychological and psychiatric disturbances during the COVID-19 pandemic, social media-related stress and the spread of false information, and economic insecurity and stress resulting from the pandemic's economic impact.

2.2 Body Language and Emotion

A comprehensive understanding of human emotions and their expression is vital for exploring the potential of tactile interaction in addressing social isolation. Robinson (2008) identifies three key criteria for mental experiences that constitute emotions: a strong motivating subjective quality (e.g., pleasure or pain), a response to real or imagined events or objects, and the motivation of particular kinds of behavior. Emotions are distinct from sensations, feelings, and moods in their combination of these attributes (Table 1).

Body language, a form of non-verbal communication, continuously conveys individuals' emotions and feelings. It is closely linked to one's emotional state (Panksepp 1998). Depending on their emotional state, individuals can exhibit various body language gestures, reflecting interest, boredom, frustration, happiness, and more (Birdwhistell 2010; Panksepp 1998).

Body language plays a pivotal role in the communication process, providing cues that help discern different aspects of an individual's mental state. Birdwhistell (2010) noted that while words constitute only 7% of communication, non-verbal communication accounts for a significant 55%. Numerous studies have highlighted the close relationship between body language and individuals' emotional states, often referred to as emotional body language (Panksepp 1998). Researchers like Wallbott (1998) have analyzed body language cues and their connection to various emotional states, uncovering distinct patterns in body movement and posture corresponding to different emotions.

Recent research has shown that body poses are more effective than facial expressions in discerning intense positive and negative emotions (Aviezer et al. 2012). Additional studies have supported the notion that intense emotions can be more accurately recognized through body language cues (Gao and Maurer 2009; Marneweck et al. 2013). Consequently, body language cues can serve as a valuable means to determine individuals' emotional states.

Table 1. Type of Emotion

Kind of emotion	Positive emotions	Negative emotions
Related to object properties	Interest, curiosity, enthusiasm	Indifference, habituation, boredom
	Attraction, desire, admiration	Aversion, disgust, revulsion
	Surprise, amusement	Alarm, panic
Future appraisal	Hope, excitement	Fear, anxiety, dread
Event-related	Gratitude, thankfulness	Anger, rage
	Joy, elation, triumph, jubilation	Sorrow, grief
	Patience	Frustration, restlessness
	Contentment	Discontentment, disappointment
Self-appraisal	Humility, modesty	Pride, arrogance
Social	Charity	Avarice, greed, miserliness, envy, jealousy

2.3   Physical Touch for Healing

The role of physical touch in emotional healing is essential to consider when addressing social isolation. It is deeply rooted in human development and communication, offering potential solutions to the challenges posed by isolation. Physical touch holds paramount significance throughout the human lifespan, exerting a profound influence on human development, communication, bonding, and emotional healing (Mintz 1969). Its importance spans from infancy to adulthood and is embedded in therapeutic traditions. Physical touch exhibits exceptional efficacy in treating a range of psychological conditions, including depression, stress, anxiety, and dissociation. It is notably effective in alleviating post-traumatic stress disorder (PTSD) (Field 2003; Westland 1993). Tactile interactions, such as hugging and massage, have been empirically linked to stress reduction. Studies have shown that these interactions can significantly reduce psychological stress levels and cortisol production, while simultaneously alleviating physical tension (Sumioka et al. 2013; Light et al. 2005).

Tactile interactions play a pivotal role in enhancing emotional well-being by fostering and strengthening interpersonal emotional connections. These interactions have been instrumental in improving depressive symptoms, mitigating loneliness, and fostering positive developments in social and communicative skills, particularly in children with autism (Field 2019; Silva et al. 2015). Tactile stimulation, particularly through massage, has garnered recognition for its efficacy in relieving various forms of pain, including chronic pain. Such tactile interactions stimulate the release of endorphins in the brain, aiding individuals in coping with pain more effectively (Scherder et al. 1998; Suzuki et al. 2010). Tactile interactions contribute to immune system enhancement by reducing inflammation and bolstering the vitality of immune cells. This augmentation of immune function enhances the body's resistance to illnesses, including common colds and other ailments (Galanakis et al. 2015).

Throughout history, touch has been integrally woven into various healing methodologies. Two notable approaches, the Rubenfeld Synergy Method and the Rosen Method, converge touch and verbal therapy elements to foster profound healing experiences. The Rosen Method, developed by Marion Rosen in the 1930s, intricately intertwines touch and verbal communication to address emotional and physical tension (Bennett 1996; Macy 2015). Similarly, the Rubenfeld Synergy Method, founded by Ilana Rubenfeld, combines touch, talk, and movement to facilitate emotional release and healing (Rubenfeld 1985).

These methodologies provide a strong foundation for the potential therapeutic benefits of tactile interaction, particularly in addressing social isolation. They underscore the importance of physical touch in promoting emotional well-being, mitigating psychological distress, enhancing communication, and fostering healing. Tactile interactions offer an avenue for individuals to experience emotional healing and connectedness, making them a valuable resource for those grappling with social isolation.

2.4   Technology and Tactile Interfaces

The integration of tactile interfaces into technology holds promise for addressing social isolation, as it allows individuals to experience physical touch remotely. This section reviews the existing research on tactile interfaces and their potential applications in mitigating the effects of social isolation. Tactile interfaces, also known as haptic interfaces, enable users to receive or transmit tactile sensations through technology. These interfaces can simulate various forms of touch, such as pressure, vibration, and texture, creating a multisensory experience. The field of haptics has seen significant advancements in recent years, leading to the development of tactile feedback devices for various applications.

Tactile interfaces have been explored for their potential to enhance remote communication and social interaction. Researchers have developed haptic devices that enable users to send and receive touch signals over the internet. For example, the Hug Shirt, developed by CuteCircuit, allows wearers to send hugs to each other through the shirt's embedded sensors and actuators (Koroniotis et al. 2015). Similarly, the Tactile Internet, an emerging concept, envisions ultra-low-latency communication that includes haptic feedback, potentially enabling users to share touch sensations in real time (Schneider et al. 2019). These developments in tactile communication technologies open up new possibilities for addressing social isolation. Individuals separated by physical distance can experience a sense of presence and connectedness through remote touch interactions. This has the potential to benefit various groups, including long-distance couples, family members separated by geography, and individuals in need of emotional support.

Tactile interfaces have also found applications in healthcare and therapy, offering the potential to address emotional and psychological needs. For example, haptic devices have been used in telemedicine to enable healthcare professionals to remotely assess patients' conditions by palpating their bodies (Erol et al. 2016). In the field of mental health, researchers have explored the use of haptic feedback in therapeutic interventions. The use of haptic devices to provide comforting touch sensations during virtual reality exposure therapy for PTSD has shown promise in reducing symptoms (Rizzo et al. 2015). Additionally, tactile interfaces have been used in the field of autism therapy. Some studies have investigated the use of haptic feedback to enhance social communication skills in individuals with autism spectrum disorder (ASD). For example, haptic feedback devices have been used to provide real-time social cues and reinforcement during social interactions (Escobedo et al. 2012).

These applications demonstrate the potential of tactile interfaces in addressing the emotional and psychological needs of individuals, particularly those who may experience social isolation. By providing remote access to comforting touch sensations and therapeutic interventions, tactile interfaces can play a role in improving emotional well-being and reducing the negative effects of social isolation. In conclusion, this comprehensive literature review lays the foundation for understanding the multifaceted aspects of social isolation, the role of body language and emotion, the importance of physical touch for healing, and the potential of tactile interaction in addressing social isolation. These insights provide valuable context for the exploration of tactile interaction as a means to alleviate social isolation and promote emotional well-being.

3   Research Approach and Methodology

3.1   Data Mining

In this study, we employed a python-based data mining approach to explore the emotional dynamics of individuals during the COVID-19 pandemic, focusing on the potential of tactile interaction for social isolation healing (Fig. 1). Sina Weibo was selected for our primary data source due to its larger user base, flexibility, lawful, publicly accessible, and transparency. A specific timeframe, spanning from January 1 to January 6, 2021 was selected as a critical phase of the pandemic. Our study's data collection process centered on retrieving pandemic-related microblog data from Sina Weibo. The procedure comprised the following steps:

1. Keyword Selection, where we chose both negative and positive emotion keywords along with indirect pandemic-related terms.
2. Keyword-Based Searching, involving automated Python scripts to comprehensively search using these keywords.
3. Data Screening and Compilation, which filtered relevant microblogs based on criteria such as posting date and content relevance, focusing on original posts.
4. Data Storage in CSV format for structured storage.
5. Data Cleaning to ensure accuracy and consistency.
6. Data Privacy and Ethics, with sensitive information anonymized.
7. Data Analysis Preparation for subsequent statistical and sentiment analysis.

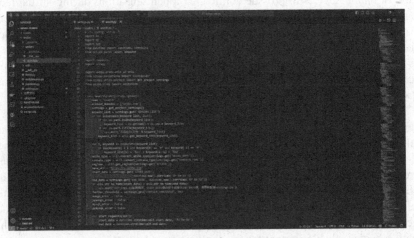

Fig. 1. AI-Based Data Mining Techniques

3.2   Experiment Design

Our primary aim was to explore physical interactions that could elicit positive emotional states. The study included fifteen participants, evenly split between five females (N female = 5) and five males (N male = 5), over three days, with five participants each day (as shown in Fig. 2). Each day spanned three hours, with tasks ranging from 5 to 15 min. A 10-min pre-test introduction and a 30-min post-test interview phase were incorporated.

Concurrently, three researchers conducted parallel experiments. Participants underwent interviews to understand game rules and task explanations. Each participant then drew a card with a physical interaction challenge, including actions like offering a thumbs-up, holding open doors, complimenting first entrants, handshakes, or hugs. After each task, participants and strangers involved received rewards and friendly gestures like high-fives or hugs.

Subsequently, participants were interviewed to evaluate their emotional states, experiences, and opinions on positive physical interactions' influence on emotion regulation. They also proposed physical interactions suitable for wearable designs. Researchers closely monitored participants throughout, recording task completion times, success rates, reasons for success/failure, and evoked emotions.

Fig. 2. Experiment (Note: All people in the picture were informed and agreed to be photographed)

4 Results and Discussion

4.1 Emotions During the COVID-19 Pandemic

In this section, we explore the results of our data mining analysis, aiming to gain a comprehensive understanding of the public's sentiments and responses to the pandemic, as reflected in their interactions on Sina Weibo. In our dataset, which encompassed a total of 4,916 tweets, we examined the emotional dimensions related to the pandemic. Within this dataset, we identified 601 valid messages that pertained to emotions, distributed across various themes: 1) Tension and Pandemic: 348 articles. 2) Anxiety and Pandemic: 192 articles. 3) Depression and Pandemic: 28 articles. 4) Isolation and Pandemic: 19 articles. 5) Loneliness and Isolation during Pandemic: 14 entries.

Within the extensive pool of posts examined, we examined those that exhibited the highest engagement metrics, such as likes, comments, and retweets. Among these, it was strikingly apparent that discussions centered around the theme 'Pandemic at Home' garnered the most substantial user engagement. This finding underscores the saliency and relevance of this topic within the larger discourse on social media platforms during the pandemic. The level of engagement can be attributed to several factors, including the content's emotional resonance, its informational value, and its novelty within the context of pandemic-related discussions.

Regarding emotional states related to the pandemic, "Pandemic and Staying Home" emerged as the most prominent theme, accounting for a substantial portion of both text entries (approximately 63.95%) and image entries (63.02%) (Table 2). This substantial representation highlights the widespread discussions regarding home confinement and remote work during the pandemic. The theme "Pandemic and Social Distancing" also received significant attention, constituting approximately 23.82% of textual content and 26.89% of visual content. This finding emphasizes the importance of conversations surrounding social distancing measures in the context of the outbreak.

Table 2. Dataset Related to Text and Picture

Category	Text Entries	Picture Entries	Text %	Picture %
Pandemic and Staying Home	3,144	1,692	63.95%	63.02%
Pandemic and Social Distancing	1171	722	23.82%	26.89%
Tension and Pandemic	348	162	7.08%	6.03%
Anxiety and Pandemic	192	72	3.91%	2.68%
Depression and Pandemic	28	19	0.57%	0.71%
Isolation and Pandemic	19	12	0.39%	0.45%
Loneliness and Isolation during Pandemic	14	6	0.28%	0.22%

Conversely, topics related to emotional states, such as "Tension and Pandemic," "Anxiety and Pandemic," "Depression and Pandemic," "Isolation and Pandemic," and "Loneliness and Isolation during Pandemic," exhibited relatively lower counts of posts, ranging from 0.22% to 7.08% for textual content and 0.45% to 2.68% for visual content. These lower proportions suggest that discussions of these emotional states were less prevalent in the public discourse compared to themes like staying at home and social distancing. Emotions During the COVID-19 Pandemic.

The temporal analysis of these keyword combinations revealed noteworthy trends (Fig. 3). For "Pandemic and Staying Home" and "Pandemic and Social Distancing," discussions remained relatively stable over time, with occasional minor fluctuations. "Tension and Pandemic" and "Anxiety and Pandemic" exhibited notable peaks in discussion on January 4th, implying that specific events or circumstances on that date may have triggered heightened discourse on tension and anxiety. Conversely, topics related to "Loneliness and Isolation during Pandemic," "Isolation and Pandemic," and "Depression and Pandemic" were less frequently discussed, possibly indicating that these deeper emotional states were less prominent in public discourse or were discussed in more private or smaller community settings.

Furthermore, an examination of the proportion of text and image posts by keyword group revealed that "Pandemic and Staying Home" dominated the conversation, accounting for the majority of posts (approximately 63–64%) (Fig. 4). "Pandemic and Social Distancing" represented 23.8–26.9% of the discussion, demonstrating its significance as a topic of interest. While "Tension and Pandemic" had a smaller presence at 6.0–7.1%, it indicated the presence of discussions concerning tension during the pandemic. "Anxiety and Pandemic" comprised 2.7–3.9%, underscoring the extent of concern surrounding anxiety within pandemic-related discussions.

Despite their lower prevalence in the dataset, topics like "Loneliness and Isolation during Pandemic" and "Isolation and Pandemic" generated relatively higher interaction rates, including likes, comments, and retweets on social media (Table 3). This suggests that these keywords resonated with the audience and elicited notable emotional responses. These themes shed light on concerns related to social isolation, isolation during the epidemic, and the emotional repercussions of these experiences. The heightened engagement and emotional response to these topics may be attributed to the profound impact of social isolation and the significant changes in daily life during the pandemic, indicating the relevance of addressing these aspects in public discourse.

Table 3. Dataset Related to Loneliness and Isolation

Keyword Group	Number of Posts	Total Likes	Total Comments	Total Retweets	Proportion of Total Posts
Loneliness and Isolation during Pandemic	14	546	255	261	0.28%
Isolation and Pandemic	19	798	224	249	0.39%

"Depression and Pandemic", and "Isolation and Pandemic" have higher average comments, suggesting that posts associated with depression and isolation during the pandemic prompted more discussion among users compared to other topics (Fig. 5). The topic of "Pandemic and Social Distancing" has a relatively balanced distribution of average likes, comments, and retweets, indicating that it is a topic that engages users in multiple ways. While the average of "Pandemic and Staying Home" likes are noticeable, the comments and retweets are lower in comparison to the "Depression and Pandemic" and "Isolation and Pandemic" categories, which could suggest that while the topic is popular, it might not incite as much conversation or be shared as frequently. The category of "Tension and Pandemic" has a moderate level of engagement across likes, comments, and retweets, indicating a consistent level of interaction with posts related to tension during the pandemic. The category of "Anxiety and Pandemic" shows the lowest levels of average engagement across all three types, which might suggest that while the topic is relevant, it may not resonate as strongly as others or it may not provoke as much interaction on social media. The category of "Loneliness and Isolation during the Pandemic" is not visible on the bar chart, which might indicate very low average engagement rates or possibly no data for this category within the dataset used for this chart.

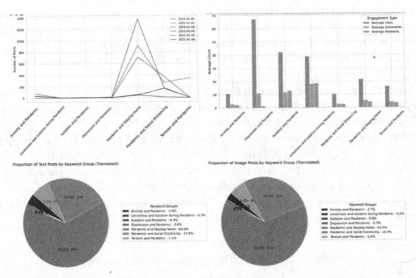

Fig. 3. Time Trend of Posts for Each Keyword Group & The proportion of Text Posts and Image Posts by Keyword Group & Average User Engagement for Each Key Word Group

The data suggests that topics related to "Depression" and "Isolation" during the pandemic seem to generate more conversations among users, as reflected in the higher average number of comments. Meanwhile, "Pandemic and Staying Home" is a popular topic, but it doesn't necessarily lead to as much discussion or sharing. The relatively lower engagement for "Anxiety and Pandemic" might reflect different user behavior towards this emotion or topic on social media. Overall, this chart provides insights into which aspects of the pandemic experience are most engaging for users on social media, with emotional topics like depression and isolation prompting more interaction, possibly due to their deep personal impact.

In summary, the dataset encompasses a diverse array of thematic categories related to the pandemic and its emotional and social dimensions. "Pandemic and Staying Home" and "Pandemic and Social Distancing" emerged as prominent themes, while emotional states like "Tension," "Anxiety," "Depression," "Isolation," and "Loneliness" exhibited comparatively lower prevalence but generated substantial engagement in their respective discussions. These findings underscore the multifaceted nature of public discourse during the pandemic and emphasize the importance of addressing emotional and social aspects in the broader conversation surrounding public health crises and social isolation healing efforts.

5 Design of the Tactile Interaction Game: The Emotional Nourishment Project

In the practical implementation of this study, we established a virtual world and invited participants to engage with this experience through interactive devices that are central to conveying the study's core theme: the significance of tactile interaction for social isolation healing. This project, aptly named "Emotional Nourishment," revolves around the creation of a virtual doomsday scenario within a real-world context.

5.1 Background of Emotional Nourishment Project

In this envisioned future world, advancements in communication and virtual reality technology have reached unprecedented levels, enabling individuals to easily acquire all their necessities, including virtual companionship. The allure of these perfect virtual relationships gradually leads people to forsake real-world social interactions, immersing themselves entirely in the realm of virtual technology.

However, a catastrophic event unfolds as a scientific experiment spirals out of control, resulting in the dissemination of a virus throughout the digital network, impacting the entirety of human society. This virus inflicts irreversible damage upon the human nervous system, severely impeding individuals' ability to perceive and experience emotions. Consequently, people can no longer derive the emotional sustenance they require or generate emotions through virtual existence. Concurrently, this virus also engenders a terminal illness impervious to medical intervention. Stripped of emotional impetus, afflicted individuals languish and deteriorate akin to withering plants, ultimately succumbing to their ailment.

Extensive research has revealed that the only means for humans to regain emotional perception and vitality is through physical contact with one another. However, the emotional energy generated by such physical interactions is finite and gradually wanes as individuals engage in their daily lives. Once this emotional energy is depleted, the afflicted individual's fate is sealed, leading to their demise. This widespread terminal malady has exacted a heavy toll on humanity, resulting in a significant loss of lives.

In a desperate bid for the survival of the human race, scientists are compelled to undertake extensive modifications of the human body, culminating in the initiation of the "Emotional Nourishing" project. The centerpiece of this endeavor is the transparent device integrated into the human heart. Extending from this device are emotion collectors, distributed throughout various parts of the body. Emotions coursing through these physical connections are manifested as "nourishment," which is subsequently collected and stored within the heart through the "emotional nutrient" device. This innovative system allows individuals to visualize their remaining emotional "nutrients" through the device. The depletion of these emotional reserves signals the impending conclusion of a person's life.

5.2 Storyboard of Emotional Nourishment Project

To enhance participants' immersion in the worldview and provide a more direct experience of the "emotional nourishment" device, we have integrated specific scenes and narratives involving the "emotional nourishment" device within the context of the overall worldview. These dynamic storyboards are divided into five distinct modules, each employing brief animations to effectively convey the concept of "emotional nourishment."

1. Awakening from a Virtual Dream: Participants emerge from an alluring virtual realm that hides an emptiness within.
2. The Withering of Emotions: They witness emotionless individuals deteriorating, highlighting the virus's fatal effects.
3. Transformation of Hearts: Their hearts transform into transparent receptacles to collect "emotional nourishment," underscoring survival's reliance on emotional sustenance.
4. Touch and Emotional Exchange: Through tactile interaction, like hugs and handshakes, participants exchange and accrue "emotional nourishment."
5. Nourishing the Emotional Plant: The "emotional nourishment" feeds an emotional plant, symbolizing emotional restoration and rejuvenation, replenishing life's vitality.

Fig. 4. Storyboard of "Emotional Nourishment" project

The gathered "emotional nourishment" is channeled into nurturing an emotional plant, which thrives and radiates a comforting emotional warmth. This symbolizes the restoration of emotions and the revival of individuals, filling the once-empty vessels with renewed vitality.

This strategic incorporation of dynamic storytelling within the "Emotional Nourishment" project aims to provide participants with a more tangible and experiential understanding of both the overarching worldview and the operational dynamics of the "emotional nourishment" device.

5.3   Device Design for Emotional Nourishment Project

In the context of the "Emotional Nourishment" project, an interactive device has been designed to offer a tangible manifestation of emotional states through physical interactions. This innovative approach serves as a novel means of comprehending and visualizing the profound impact of human touch and interpersonal connections. The interactive device consists of both hardware and software components, with the software component being programmed using Arduino IDE.

Wearable devices encompass various components worn on the user's body, which directly engage with the user and provide immediate feedback. Within this project, participants don a transparent device equipped with sensors located at six specific body positions: the top of the head, shoulders, chest, back, forearms, and hands. These sensors have been intricately designed to detect a range of physical interactions, including gestures such as hugs and handshakes. Each type of touch triggers the generation of specific quantities and shades of "emotional nourishment," symbolizing diverse emotional intensities and qualities. The wearable unit primarily comprises the following components:

1. Programmable LED Strips: Programmable LED strips serve as visual indicators, offering feedback to users through color changes and variations in flashing speed, contingent upon different touch inputs.
2. Touch Sensors: A total of six touch sensors are strategically positioned across the user's body, placed to capture physical interactions. These sensors function as receptors for user input, detecting tactile gestures and relaying the data for further processing.

The data collection unit encompasses components dedicated to sensing, processing, and storing or transmitting user input data. Positioned as a transparent container near the user's heart, this unit is interconnected with the wearable unit via a catheter. As users engage in physical interactions, the "emotional nourishment" generated is collected within this container. The quantity and hues of emotional nutrients collected vary depending on the nature of the interaction, gradually accumulating and visibly increasing to nurture the emotional plant. The data collection unit principally comprises the following components:

1. Arduino NANO: Serving as the device's central processing unit, the Arduino NANO acts as the "brain" responsible for interpreting input data from the touch sensors and managing data processing.
2. Touch Sensors: These sensors, in addition to their role in detecting physical input, also serve as indicators for pinpointing the physical interaction points in the data collection process.
3. Connection Cables: Crucial for data flow and power supply, these cables link the sensors, responsible for data collection, to the Arduino NANO, where data processing takes place.
4. Power Supply: Comprising the 9 V power supply battery and associated circuit components, this power supply system is essential for the device's operation, bridging both data collection and processing components.

This innovative device offers users a unique opportunity to witness emotions materializing as "emotional nourishment." This visual representation serves as a feedback mechanism, facilitating participants' deeper comprehension of the emotional experiences evoked through their physical interactions. By transforming abstract emotional exchanges into tangible and visible forms, the device effectively reinforces the conceptual link between emotional nourishment and survival, which is at the core of the "Emotional Nourishment" project.

5.4   Rationale of Emotional Nourishment Project

The rationale behind this design choice can be attributed to three key considerations: firstly, it hinges on situational relevance. By immersing participants in a world where emotional connections are vital for survival, the dystopian exchange environment prompts users to contemplate the crucial role of emotional bonds in their lives. Secondly, it fosters enhanced participation. Situating the experience within a doomsday narrative creates an immersive environment that encourages users to engage more deeply and lends a profound and unforgettable quality to the overall experience. Thirdly, it serves to emphasize impact. Within this setting, participants can directly witness the consequences of emotional interactions, thereby underscoring their pivotal role in the survival and interpersonal communication. Participants actively engage with this world by physically interacting with one another in exchange for what we refer to as "emotional nourishment." This engagement transcends mere physical touch, encompassing a holistic understanding and experience of the emotional connections arising from these interactions.

In this project, a structured framework has been established to quantify and assess the significance and depth of various physical interactions in the realm of emotional communication. This framework employs numerical values to assign specific scores to each type of physical interaction, reflecting their respective importance and impact on emotional communication (Table 3). For instance, hugging, recognized for its potent and direct expression of emotion, has been bestowed with the highest score of 20 points. In contrast, a handshake, although a recognized social interaction, garners a lower score of 5 points, indicating its comparatively lesser emotional depth when compared to other forms of physical contact (Table 4).

The utilization of this numerical approach serves a twofold purpose. Firstly, it provides a visual representation of emotional nuances, enabling the audience to discern and appreciate the varying intensities of emotional nourishment generated by different types of interactions. Secondly, it aims to enhance users' comprehension and appreciation of the diverse roles that different forms of physical interaction play in establishing and sustaining emotional connections.

By ascribing numerical values to these interactions, this framework not only facilitates a deeper understanding of the emotional dynamics involved but also underscores the significance of diverse physical interactions in the context of nurturing and maintaining meaningful emotional bonds. Through this approach, participants gain valuable insights into the intricacies of human touch and its pivotal role in fostering emotional well-being and connection, further reinforcing the project's objective of healing social isolation.

Table 4. Type of Emotion

Trigger action	Nourishment	color
Touch your head	10	Blue
Hug	20	Purple
Clasp hands	5	White
Arm in arm	10	Orange
Pat one's shoulder	10	Green
Back slapping	15	Pink
Touch your head	10	Blue

Fig. 5. Scenes of Emotional Nourishment Project

6 Conclusion

Social isolation has emerged as a pervasive concern in contemporary society, often stemming from various factors, including the advent of digital technology and the recent challenges posed by global pandemics. In response to this pressing issue, this study explores the potential of tactile interaction as a means to alleviate social isolation. Leveraging a multifaceted research approach encompassing data mining and experiment, we delve into the emotional dynamics experienced during the COVID-19 pandemic, with a focus on identifying negative emotions that require intervention.

The initial phase of our research involves data mining, where we aim to gain comprehensive insights into the emotional conditions induced by the pandemic. By analyzing vast datasets from digital social spaces, we discern the prevailing negative emotions that individuals grappled with during these trying times. This quantitative and qualitative analysis forms the foundation for understanding the emotional landscape necessitating healing. Subsequently, we employ experiment principles coupled with game-based data collection methods to introduce the "Emotional Nourishment Project." This innovative endeavor unfolds within a virtual world that simulates a doomsday scenario within a real-world context. The project seeks to create an immersive environment where participants engage with one another through tactile interaction, emphasizing the profound significance of such interactions in mitigating social isolation. Central to the "Emotional Nourishment Project" is an intricately designed interactive device that materializes emotional states through physical interactions. This device, comprising both hardware and software components, is crafted to provide a tangible manifestation of emotional connections. By employing the Arduino IDE for programming, we enable participants to experience and comprehend the transformative impact of human touch and interpersonal bonds.

The rationale behind this research choice lies in its situational relevance, as it immerses participants in a world where emotional bonds are indispensable for survival. It fosters enhanced participation by creating an engaging and immersive environment, ultimately emphasizing the significance of emotional interactions in healing social isolation.In summary, this study embarks on a multifaceted journey, combining data mining, experiment, and innovative technology to address the critical issue of social isolation. Through the "Emotional Nourishment Project," we aim to shed light on the pivotal role of tactile interaction in fostering emotional well-being and healing the emotional wounds inflicted by isolation.

Acknowledgement. This research is supported by the Education Fund of Macao Special Administrative Region. The project number is DSEDJ-23-037-FA.

References

Aviezer, H., Trope, Y., Todorov, A.: Body cues, not facial expressions, discriminate between intense positive and negative emotions. Science **338**(6111), 1225–1229 (2012)

Bernabei, R., et al.: Hearing loss and cognitive decline in older adults: questions and answers. Aging Clin. Exp. Res. **26**(6), 567–573 (2014). https://doi.org/10.1007/s40520-014-0266-3

Birdwhistell, R.L.: Kinesics and Context: Essays on Body Motion Communication. University of Pennsylvania Press, Philadelphie (2010)

Caplan, S.E.: A social skill account of problematic internet use. J. Commun. **55**(4), 721–736 (2005). https://doi.org/10.1111/j.1460-2466.2005.tb03019.x

Comments from the Special Issue Editor: Approaching Poverty in the United States. Soc. Probl. **38**(4), 427–432 (1991). https://doi.org/10.2307/800562

Cornwell, E.Y., Waite, L.J.: Social disconnectedness, perceived isolation, and health among older adults. J. Health Soc. Behav. **50**(1), 31–48 (2009). https://doi.org/10.1177/002214650 905000103

Crompton, C.J., Hallett, S., Ropar, D., Flynn, E., Fletcher-Watson, S.: 'I never realised everybody felt as happy as I do when I am around autistic people': a thematic analysis of autistic adults' relationships with autistic and neurotypical friends and family. Autism **24**(6), 1438–1448 (2020). https://doi.org/10.1177/1362361320908976

Davey, M.: Social isolation a key risk factor for suicide among Australian men – study. The Guardian, 2 November 2020. https://www.theguardian.com/society/2015/jun/25/loneliness-a-key-risk-factor-for-suicide-among-australian-men-study

Field, T.: Touch Bradford Book. MIT Press, London (2003)

Field, T.: Social touch, CT touch and massage therapy: a narrative review (2019)

Gao, X., Maurer, D.: Influence of intensity on children's sensitivity to happy, sad, and fearful facial expressions. J. Exp. Child Psychol. **102**(4), 503–521 (2009)

Galanakis, M., Ntaouti, E., Tsitsanis, G., Chrousos, G.P.: The effects of infant massage on maternal distress: a systematic review. Psychology 06(16), 2091–2097 (2015). https://doi.org/10.4236/psych.2015.616204

Hertherington, E.M.: Review of development through life: a psychosocial approach. Contemp. Psychol. J. Rev. 20(10), 836–836 (1975). https://doi.org/10.1037/014336

Herttua, K., Martikainen, P., Vahtera, J., Kivimäki, M.: Living alone and alcohol-related mortality: a population-based Cohort study from Finland. PLoS Med. 8(9), e1001094 (2011). https://doi.org/10.1371/journal.pmed.1001094

Hjalmarsson, S., Mood, C.: Do poorer youth have fewer friends? The role of household and child economic resources in adolescent school-class friendships. Child Youth Serv. Rev. 57, 201–211 (2015). https://doi.org/10.1016/j.childyouth.2015.08.013

Khullar, D.: How Social Isolation Is Killing Us. The New York Times, 5 January 2017. https://www.nytimes.com/2016/12/22/upshot/how-social-isolation-is-killing-us.html

Lee, B.W., Stapinski, L.A.: Seeking safety on the internet: relationship between social anxiety and problematic internet use. J. Anxiety Disord. 26(1), 197–205 (2012). https://doi.org/10.1016/j.janxdis.2011.11.001

MacDonald, T.K., Martineau, A.M.: Self-esteem, mood, and intentions to use condoms: when does low self-esteem lead to risky health behaviors? J. Exp. Soc. Psychol. 38(3), 299–306 (2002). https://doi.org/10.1006/jesp.2001.1505

Malti, T., Gummerum, M., Keller, M., Chaparro, M.P., Buchmann, M.: Early sympathy and social acceptance predict the development of sharing in children. PLoS ONE 7(12), e52017 (2012). https://doi.org/10.1371/journal.pone.0052017

Marneweck, M., Loftus, A., Hammond, G.: Psychophysical measures of sensitivity to facial expression of emotion. Front. Psychol. 4 (2013)

McKenna, K.Y.A., Bargh, J.A.: Plan 9 from cyberspace: the implications of the internet for personality and social psychology. Pers. Soc. Psychol. Rev. 4(1), 57–75 (2000). https://doi.org/10.1207/s15327957pspr0401_6

Mintz, E.E.: On the rationale of touch in psychotherapy. Psychother. Theory Res. Pract. 6(4), 232–234 (1969). https://doi.org/10.1037/h0088759

Mohanty, P.: Coronavirus Lockdown I: who and how many are vulnerable to COVID-19 pandemic. Business Today, 27 March 2020. https://www.businesstoday.in/latest/economy-politics/story/coronavirus-covid-19-daily-wage-workers-vulnerable-landless-labourers-agricultural-workforce-253007-2020-03-25

NamazianDoost, I., Hashemifardnya, A., Panahi, N.: The effect of using approximation and appealing for help techniques on learning speaking skill among Iranian intermediate EFL learners. J. Lang. Teach. Res. 8(6), 1195 (2017). https://doi.org/10.17507/jltr.0806.22

Norwood, D.: Touch in Therapy: Helpful or Harmful? One Therapist's Perspective - GoodTherapy.org Therapy Blog. GoodTherapy.org Therapy Blog, 28 June 2017. https://www.goodtherapy.org/blog/touch-in-therapy-helpful-or-harmful-one-therapists-perspective-0629175

Panksepp, J.: Affective Neuroscience: The Foundations of Human and Animal Emotions. Oxford University Press, New York (1998)

Preece, R.: Enhancing Self-esteem: a self-esteem training package for individuals with disabilities. Learn. Disabil. Pract. 9(2), 22–22 (2006). https://doi.org/10.7748/ldp.9.2.22.s13

Rico-Uribe, L.A., Caballero, F.F., Martín-María, N., Cabello, M., Ayuso-Mateos, J.L., Miret, M.: Association of loneliness with all-cause mortality: a meta-analysis. PLOS ONE 13(1), e0190033 (2018). https://doi.org/10.1371/journal.pone.0190033

Robinson, D.L.: Brain function, emotional experience and personality. Netherlands J. Psychol. 64(4), 152–168 (2008). https://doi.org/10.1007/bf03076418

Rubenfeld Synergy Method - GoodTherapy.org Therapy Blog, 14 April 2016. https://www.goodtherapy.org/blog/psychpedia/rubenfeld-synergy-method

Sayar, K., Senkal, Z.: Facebook loves: depression, psychosis and online romance, report of three cases. J. Mood Disord. 4(1), 26 (2014). https://doi.org/10.5455/jmood.20131230123249

Scherder, E., Bouma, A., Steen, L.: Effects of peripheral tactile nerve stimulation on affective behavior of patients with probable Alzheimer's disease (1998)

Sim, K.: The psychological impact of SARS: a matter of heart and mind. Can. Med. Assoc. J. 170(5), 811–812 (2004). https://doi.org/10.1503/cmaj.1032003

Sim, M.: Psychological effects of the coronavirus disease 2019 pandemic. Korean J. Med. 95(6), 360–363 (2020). https://doi.org/10.3904/kjm.2020.95.6.360

Silva, L.M.T., Schalock, M., Gabrielsen, K.R., Budden, S., Buenrostro, M., Horton, G.P.: Early Intervention with a Parent-Delivered Massage Protocol Directed at Tactile Abnormalities Decreases Severity of Autism and Improves Child-to-Parent Interactions: A Replication Study (2015)

Sumioka, H., Nakae, A., Kanai, R., Ishiguro, H.: Huggable communication medium decreases cortisol levels (2013)

Suzuki, M., et al.: Physical and Psychological Effects of 6-Week Tactile Massage on Elderly Patients With Severe Dementia (2010)

Tsetserukou, D., Neviarouskaya, A.: Emotion telepresence: emotion augmentation through affective haptics and visual stimuli. J. Phys. Conf. Ser. 352, 012045 (2012). https://doi.org/10.1088/1742-6596/352/1/012045

Vaajakallio, K., Mattelmäki, T.: Design games in codesign: as a tool, a mindset and a structure. CoDesign 10(1), 63–77 (2014). https://doi.org/10.1080/15710882.2014.881886

Wallbott, H.G.: Bodily expression of emotion. Eur. J. Soc. Psychol. 28(6), 879–896 (1998)

Webber, M., Fendt-Newlin, M.: A review of social participation interventions for people with mental health problems. Soc. Psychiatry Psychiatr. Epidemiol. 52(4), 369–380 (2017). https://doi.org/10.1007/s00127-017-1372-2

Westland, G.: Massage as a therapeutic tool, Part 2. B. J. O. T. 56(5) (1993a)

Wu, K.K., Chan, S.K., Ma, T.M.: Posttraumatic stress after SARS. Emerg. Infect. Dis. 11(8), 1297–1300 (2005). https://doi.org/10.3201/eid1108.041083

Zhao, S.: The internet and the transformation of the reality of everyday life: toward a new analytic stance in sociology. Sociol. Inq. 76(4), 458–474 (2006). https://doi.org/10.1111/j.1475-682x.2006.00166.x

Design and User Acceptance of Dynamic User Interface Adaptations Based on Situation-Awareness and Emotion-Recognition

Christian Herdin[1]($\boxtimes$), Christian Märtin[2], and Felix Schmidberger[2]

[1] Institute of Computer Science, University of Rostock, Albert-Einstein-Str. 22, 18059 Rostock, Germany
Christian.Herdin@uni-rostock.de
[2] Faculty of Computer Science, Augsburg Technical University of Applied Sciences, An der Hochschule 1, 86161 Augsburg, Germany
{Christian.Maertin,Felix.Schmidberger}@tha.de

Abstract. The SitAdapt system is an architecture and runtime system for the construction of adaptive interactive applications. The system is integrated into the PaMGIS framework for pattern- and model-based user interface development and generation. This paper first discusses the relevant related work on rule-based and situation-aware systems for creating adaptive interactive software. SitAdapt uses emotion recognition and monitoring of bio-physical signals to better understand the true nature of the situations encountered in user-sessions. The paper also discusses the software process for interactive systems with adaptive functionality. To study the acceptance of the various possible user interface adaptations an online user survey was carried out with a subsequent test of the individual possible adaptations demonstrated for an example from an adaptive travel-booking application.

Keywords: Adaptive user interface · situation-awareness · model-based user interface development · development life cycle · situation-aware adaptations · user evaluation

1 Introduction

Adaptive user interfaces can raise the usability and user experience (UX) of complex interactive systems. The SitAdapt system [10, 11] was developed as an intelligent agent for observing users and for exploiting situations and user emotions to adapt e-commerce web applications both, before and at runtime. This allows to offer users an individually tailored interactive work environment that eases task management and goal accomplishment. The SitAdapt observer part uses eye-tracking, facial emotion recognition, bio-physical data from a wristband, and meta-data from the application during user sessions. All raw data are recorded and stored in a database. Situation profiles with temporal

M. Kurosu and A. Hashizume (Eds.): HCII 2024, LNCS 14684, pp. 345–356, 2024.
https://doi.org/10.1007/978-3-031-60405-8_22

situation sequences are extracted from the raw data. At runtime situation rules that trigger adaptations are fired if the parameters of the current situation match the left-hand side of one or more given situation rules. Situation rules can be domain-dependent or domain-independent. They are created at development time by using the SitAdapt rule editor.

This paper discusses, how model-based design combined with an iterative agile software development process [14] is used for constructing the adaptive parts of a travel-booking web application that serves as a testbed for evaluating the SitAdapt agent. To assess the user acceptance and perceived quality of adaptive user interfaces in general and to evaluate the various types of domain-independent and domain-dependent adaptations that were implemented for the travel-booking application, we carried out a two-stage study based on a large questionnaire-based survey and a follow-up experimental lab-based user study.

2 Design and Construction of User Interface Adaptations

Adaptive user interfaces should improve the quality of interactions and user experience during online sessions using, e.g., web applications of all kinds. From social media, gaming, computer-based learning, web-shops, travel- and ticket-booking applications to b2b and customer relationship management systems: adaptive user interfaces can support the productivity and joy of online users, help them to better understand the intentions of developers, and thus also help software and service providers to achieve their business goals more rapidly [9]. Section 2.1 introduces some advanced related approaches for the construction of adaptive user interfaces and the concept of situation-awareness that has inspired our own research. Our development process will be presented in detail in Sect. 2.2.

2.1 Related Work

The construction of adaptive interactive systems can be accomplished by carefully modeling all the required business processes and related interactive tasks and by user involvement during software development.

When using a model-based user interface development approach in the web application development process as we did with SitAdapt, the models, relationships, and mappings between the various models and between the models and the final user interface are still available and accessible by the target software, when the first application prototypes have been implemented. Therefore, they can be optimized during an agile development process with integrated user participation [14, 15] to find out about possible areas and starting points for modeling adaptive behavior and increasing user experience. At runtime the implemented applications can access the models and other resources for creating real-time adaptations and for helping users and software and service providers in better managing their tasks and achieving their planned goals.

Model-based approaches for building adaptive interactive systems have a long history and appear in many different varieties. A comprehensive overview on model-based approaches for intelligent user interface adaptation is given in [1]. The paper also presents a conceptual reference framework for defining the structure and architecture of software systems that support adaptive UIs. The new framework extends the CAMELEON reference framework [4] for model-based user interface development environments with components that are necessary for building and running systems with adaptive user interfaces. The framework also helps to classify adaptive UI approaches based on their properties. Our own model-based approach, the SitAdapt system, interacts with the PaMGIS framework [6] that follows the earlier CAMELEON reference framework for identifying the relevant models and their inter-relations. For designing real-time adaptations, SitAdapt focuses on the exploitation of rules and the concept of situation-awareness.

Rule-Based Systems. Using rules for user interface adaptations is a straightforward concept. The more different input data sources can be exploited by the rules, the more powerful the resulting systems can become.

Adapt-UI [16, 17], like SitAdapt, offers runtime-adaptivity of the user interface. The system focuses on context-of-use adaptations when migrating to other devices and platforms, but also manages some user-related aspects. The system includes models of the user interface, the context, and the possible adaptations. Context-changes are triggered with adaptation rules. Such rules can cause the display or hiding of pre-modeled UI elements, change navigation paths in pre-modeled ways, and react to some user-related aspects that are implemented by accessing a face detection library.

Adaptation rules are also used in [2]. In this approach an adaptation framework was developed that is based on a detailed problem space model focusing on the context of use and the temporal aspects of user emotions that trigger the adaptations of websites. An underlying adaptation architecture performs adaptation cycles on the website. It consists of components for observing users, administrating the context of use (user, platform, environment) and possible UI adaptations, executing adaptation rules, and finally modifying the user interface at the end of an adaptation cycle if necessary. The architecture was tested with a serious game application. The underlying problem space model distinguishes between:

- different emotion models, e.g., Ekman basic emotions,
- different emotion sources, e.g., automatically detected peak facial emotion x,
- different temporal inference categories, e.g., inferred from values in the last y seconds, and
- different temporal application types, e.g., applied if a duration of z seconds was observed.

Adaptation rules can be defined using the possible attributes of the problem space classes and can also access the sensors within the adaptation architecture.

Situation-Aware Systems. By adding the concept of situation-awareness with situations that include and exploit the variability of the cognitive and emotional states of the user to the adaptation modeling process, a new category of individual adaptations is made possible. Such applications surpass other applications that only exploit the context of use. they allow for automatic real-time adaptations that could be better accepted by critical users, because of their creation of more natural behavior, caused by observing and interpreting the users' cognitive and emotional behavior. With SitAdapt situation-aware adaptations can be modeled by the developer and generated or activated at runtime.

To capture the individual requirements of a situation, Chang in [5] has suggested that a situation specification must cover the user's operational environment E, the user's social behavior B, by interpreting his or her actions, and a hidden context M that includes the user's mental states and emotions. A situation Sit at a given time t can thus be defined as $Sit = <M, B, E>_t$. A user's intention for using a specific software service or function for reaching a goal can then be formulated as a temporal sequence of n situations $<Sit_1, Sit_2, \ldots, Sit_n>$, where Sit_1 is the situation that triggers the usage of a service or a task execution and Sit_n is the goal-satisfying situation. SitAdapt was inspired by this view of situations and incorporates all the necessary classes and data structures to store and exploit situation sequences.

Chang's model provides a good starting point for the construction of situation-aware applications. There are two different, but strongly related views on situation-awareness. Situation-awareness as discussed in [12] and many other approaches, supports the user to correctly interpret her current situation by letting her focus on the most important contextual and situation-typical information, e.g., in complex and safety-critical human-machine interactions. The other view, as taken by SitAdapt, is a situation-analytical view, where the system is observing the user, the interactive software, and the environmental and platform-related context. The system recognizes specific situations and combinations of situations and adapts the system in real-time to optimize task management and user experience.

However, for recognizing and evaluating situations, the hidden context M – that encompasses the user's cognitive load as well as the user's emotions and intentions – must be made visible and exploitable. A great part of human decision-making is influenced by emotions and sentiments. Often users cannot spontaneously explain their intuitive actions because they are not aware of their own current emotional state. Adaptive situation-aware software systems can use the capabilities of AI based methods and tools that are able to recognize and interpret the multitude of available emotional and bio-physical signals. Also, feedback from the application side and contextual meta-data, all of them changing over time, must be evaluated to being able to select the most fitting rules to infer a goal-reaching set of adaptations. SitAdapt provides the following infrastructure for interpreting the available data and clarifying the hidden context:

- Fine grained visual, eye-tracking-based, bio-physical, and emotion monitoring of the interactive user session together with application feedback and meta-data.
- Storing the resulting raw data in a database.
- Extracting coarse grained situation profiles from the raw data with time-stamped event and event duration data. Linking the application meta-data in situation profiles to the relevant models of the interactive application provided by the PaMGIS framework.
- Selecting situation rules if typical events or significant attribute value changes arise.
- Moderation of conflicting rules and situation rule firing leading to the generation or activation of adaptations of the interactive system.

Depending on the complexity and architecture of an adaptive application under development, the developer can decide, whether the interactive application is completely or partly modeled with the PaMGIS resources, or only instrumented with suitable interfaces to use the situation rules provided by the SitAdapt rule editor.

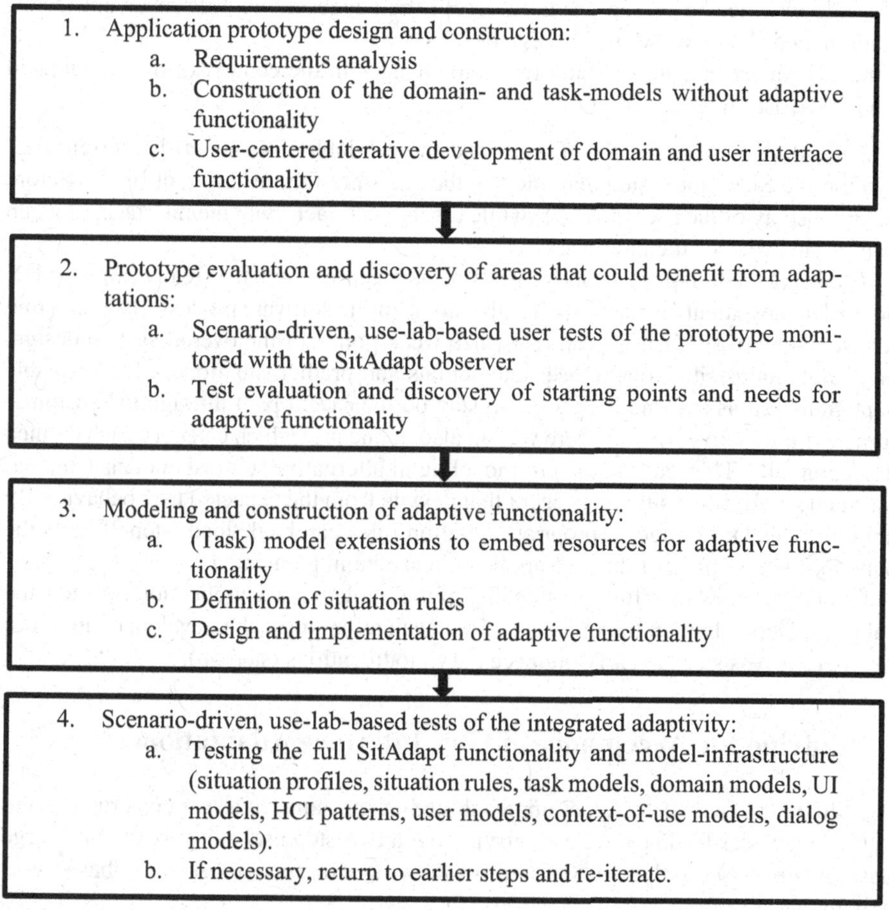

1. Application prototype design and construction:
   a. Requirements analysis
   b. Construction of the domain- and task-models without adaptive functionality
   c. User-centered iterative development of domain and user interface functionality

2. Prototype evaluation and discovery of areas that could benefit from adaptations:
   a. Scenario-driven, use-lab-based user tests of the prototype monitored with the SitAdapt observer
   b. Test evaluation and discovery of starting points and needs for adaptive functionality

3. Modeling and construction of adaptive functionality:
   a. (Task) model extensions to embed resources for adaptive functionality
   b. Definition of situation rules
   c. Design and implementation of adaptive functionality

4. Scenario-driven, use-lab-based tests of the integrated adaptivity:
   a. Testing the full SitAdapt functionality and model-infrastructure (situation profiles, situation rules, task models, domain models, UI models, HCI patterns, user models, context-of-use models, dialog models).
   b. If necessary, return to earlier steps and re-iterate.

Fig. 1. SitAdapt software process for creating interactive systems with adaptive functionality.

2.2 SitAdapt Software Process for Building Adaptive Applications

To build the application and construct the model-infrastructure for enabling adaptations before and at runtime, to find sensible and helpful adaptations, and for implementing these adaptations, we use an iterative agile software process with the major phases and steps shown in Fig. 1.

In earlier papers we have described, how the model infrastructure can be used to construct the adaptive software parts and to generate the user interface modifications after situation rules were fired [8, 10].

SitAdapt supports three different categories of user interface adaptations:

- The user customizes the user interface to his/her personal preferences (adaptable user interfaces).
- The user interface provides recommendations for adaptations. The user must then decide whether he or she wants to accept the suggested adaptation or not (semi-automated adaptive user interfaces), or,
- the user interface automatically reacts to changes in the context-of-use (automated adaptive user interfaces).

Depending on the adaptation types and the available data about the current user situation the SitAdapt system can modify the user interface at different times. Before the first display of the user interface, while the user interacts with the interface, or when the user later revisits the interface.

The key to defining the adaptive parts of web applications that really improve UX and goal achievement are steps 2b, 3a, 3b, and 3c of the software process. By evaluating the test results of step 2a, we can recognize weak points of the overall system design, detect ambiguous situations in user interactions and predict situations, where sensible adaptations can assure and help users to stay on their right path through the customer journey or interactive session. Here we can also define into which category each defined adaptation falls. This leads to the pre-modeling of alternative sub-task models (step 3a) that can be used, when situations occur that deviate from the expected user behavior. By exploiting this knowledge, appropriate situation rules can be defined (step 3b) and the adaptive software parts of the web application can be implemented.

Finally, in step 4a the full functionality of the implemented application is tested and evaluated. Depending on the outcome of the evaluation phase the developer can return to earlier process steps to carry out necessary modifications (step 4b).

3   Studying the Acceptance of User Interface Adaptations

To evaluate the overall SitAdapt approach and at the same time get constructive and well justified user feedback we are carrying out a two-step user study, based on a large questionnaire-based online survey and a follow-up experimental scenario-based user study in our lab.

3.1   Questionnaire-Based Study

To evaluate the current level of knowledge of different age groups about user interfaces for adaptive systems, an online survey was carried out as part of a pretest. A total of 110 test subjects took part in the period from December 7th, 2023, to January 18th, 2024. The results of the pretest were incorporated into the usability test in the next step. The survey design used primary research as an empirical method to collect new, previously unavailable data. These include, among other things, the connection between technology affinity and the use of adaptable and adaptive systems.

In the first step, to determine whether there is a significant relationship between the affinity for technology and the age of the test subjects, the participants were divided into different age groups based on the different currently perceived generations (see Table 1).

Table 1. Participants spread across different generations.

Age range	Number of participants	Percentage
14–28 years old	68	61.82%
29–43 years old	20	18.18%
44–58 years old	10	9.09%
59+ years old	12	10.91%

In our test, a majority of 68 participants were in the 14–28 age range. The group of the 29–43-year-old is represented by 20, the group of 44–58-year-old by 10, and the group of 59+ is represented by 12 subjects.

In the second step, the different age groups were asked to provide a self-assessment of their experience with using digital technologies. The answer options were very experienced, experienced, little experienced and not experienced. The breakdown of the respective answers can be found in Table 2.

Table 2. The evaluation of technology affinity according to age groups.

Age range	Very experienced	Experienced	Little experienced	Not experienced
14–28 years old	35 (51%)	32 (47%)	1 (1%)	0
29–43 years old	6 (30%)	11 (55%)	3 (15%)	0
44–58 years old	4 (40%)	3 (30%)	2 (20%)	1 (10%)
59+ years old	4 (33.33%)	2 (16.67%)	3 (25%)	3 (25%)

Based on the data from Tables 1 and 2, the Pearson chi-square test [7] was performed as a method of multivariate data analysis. This test examines whether there is a connection between the two categorical variables "age group" and "technology affinity" and how strong this is. The calculations were carried out using the JMP statistical software. An $a = 0.05$ was used as the significance level.

This results in a Pearson chi-square coefficient χ^2 of 35.378. Since this value is a non-standardized measure, the contingency coefficient C according to Pearson must be determined accordingly with $C = 0.493$. To exclude the influence of the number of characteristic expressions, the corrected contingency coefficient C_{corr} is determined. The corrected contingency coefficient between the age group and the affinity for technology is 0.569 (56.9%), i.e., there is a moderate connection [13] between the two characteristics which is statistically significant (p-value < 0.0001).

The next question in the survey deals with the familiarity of the term "adaptable/adaptive in connection with digital technologies" in the age groups and whether a meaning can be assigned to it. The answer option was yes, or no. Table 3 shows the answers broken down by age group.

Table 3. Familiarity of the terms adaptable/adaptive by age group.

Age range	Yes	No
14–28 years old	35	33
29–43 years old	9	11
44–58 years old	3	7
59+ years old	3	19

Based on the answers, the Pearson chi-square test was also carried out here to examine whether there is a relationship between the two categorical variables age group and knowledge of the term adaptable/adaptive and how strong this is.

No statistically significant relationship was found in this sample as a p-value = 0.4860 was determined.

Analogous to the different age groups, it was examined whether there is a connection between affinity for technology and awareness of the term "adaptable/adaptive". For this purpose, the groups "very experienced" were combined with "experienced" as well as "little experienced" and "not experienced". A merger was necessary because the number of participants per individual group was too small (Table 4).

Table 4. Familiarity of terms adaptable/adaptive by technology affinity.

Technology affinity	Experienced	Not Experienced
Yes	50	0
No	47	13

The result is a Pearson chi-square coefficient χ^2 of 12.285 [7]. The contingency coefficient according to Pearson C is 0.317, the corrected contingency coefficient between the age group and the affinity for technology is 0.448 (44.8%), there is therefore a moderate connection [13] between the two characteristics which is statistically significant (p-value = 0.0005).

Our pretest showed that there is a connection between the two variables, for technology affinity and age groups. The affinity for technology is higher among the younger age groups than among the older ones. There is also a connection between affinity for technology and whether the concept of adaptable/adaptive is known in connection with digital technologies. Among the technology-savvy participants, 50 out of 97 technology-savvy users knew this term. The term was completely unknown to non-technical users.

3.2 Lab-Based Experimental Study

To offer individual users the best adaptation option in a specific situation, a use-lab-based follow-up experimental test study covering usability, user experience and situation-aware adaptations is currently underway. The study includes a pretest to determine the target group class, as well as a test of adaptation options in the context of the travel-booking portal.

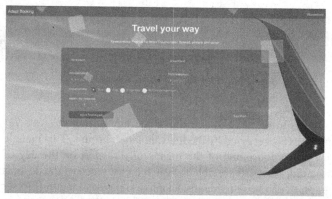

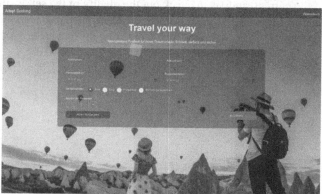

Fig. 2. Color scheme adaptation reacting to user sentiments over time.

The post-test is used to better evaluate and assess user experience perceived by users during the test. As users go through the booking scenario in our travel portal, their emotions, gaze motion, heart rate, blood pressure and mouse movements are monitored using the SitAdapt system. The signals are recorded and evaluated and lead to adaptations that are aimed at offering users the best possible usability and user experience during use.

SitAdapt delivers the context-specific adaptation for a recognized situation by firing appropriate situation rules that were defined at development time with the help of the rule editor.

In the example in Fig. 2 changing the color scheme indicates that the user has become excited or nervous.

As a further adaptation to improve user experience, we rely on dynamic help texts, in this example a help text for car riding (Fig. 3).

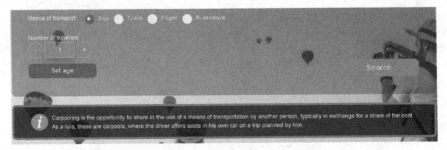

Fig. 3. Help text for car riding.

The next step is to improve the customer journey during the test. We check how different adaptations are received by the relevant target groups. This includes the option of displaying a utilization graph of the means of transport on the day of travel as a decision-making aid. It is also possible to watch a city video of the destination and the background graphics can be individually adapted to the destination (Fig. 4).

The goal of the current study is to check out the quality of the set of situation rules created for the travel-booking application and of the triggered adaptations. We also intend to find out, how these adaptations are received by different user groups.

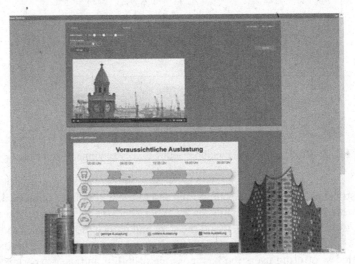

Fig. 4. Utilization graph and video presentation.

4   Conclusion and Future Work

This paper has discussed the design principles and the software process of the SitAdapt system for building adaptive interactive systems. We have carried out an evaluation process with an online survey about the topic of adaptive systems that was focused on an adaptive travel-booking system application. The web-application was constructed using the SitAdapt software process and the situation-aware runtime environment of SitAdapt. The application serves as a workbench for optimizing the functionality and adaptive capabilities of the SitAdapt system.

We have also developed further adaptation types to improve the customer journey in e-commerce environments, e.g., for travel booking. This includes the integration of dynamic backgrounds, such as a cityscape that matches the connection you are looking for. Other adaptations provide additional information with a utilization graph of the different means of transport on the day of travel or tourist information with videos.

To gather background information about the familiarity with the terms adaptable and adaptive user interface of users with much and with little affinity to technology we carried out a questionnaire-based study.

The completed adaptive travel-booking test bench application is now undergoing a scenario-based lab test for further evaluation. The results will be used to raise the overall user experience of adaptive applications created with the SitAdapt system.

Acknowledgements. The work published in this paper was in part funded by the AI Production Network Augsburg research project at Augsburg Technical University of Applied Sciences.

References

1. Abrahão, S., Insfran, E., Sluÿters, A., et al.: Model-based intelligent user interface adaptation: challenges and future directions. Softw. Syst. Model. **20**, 1335–1349 (2021). https://doi.org/10.1007/s10270-021-00909-7
2. Alipour, L., Céret, E., Dupuy-Chessa, S.: A framework for user interface adaptation to emotions and their temporal aspects. Proc. ACM Hum. Comput. Interact. **7** (2023). No. EICS, Article 186
3. Akiki, P.A., et al.: Integrating adaptive user interface capabilities in enterprise applications. In: Proceedings of the 36th International Conference on Software Engineering (ICSE 2014), pp. 712–723. ACM (2014)
4. Calvary, G., Coutaz, J., Bouillon, L., et al.: The CAMELEON Reference Framework (2002). http://giove.isti.cnr.it/projects/cameleon/pdf/CAMELEON%20D1.1RefFramework.pdf. Accessed 25 Aug 2016
5. Chang, C.K.: Situation analytics: a foundation for a new software engineering paradigm. IEEE Comput. **2016**, 24–33 (2016)
6. Engel, J., Märtin, C., Forbrig, P.: A concerted model-driven and pattern-based framework for developing user interfaces of interactive ubiquitous applications. In: Proceedings of the First International Workshop on Large-scale and Model-Based Interactive Systems, Duisburg, pp. 35–41 (2015)
7. Greenwood, E., Nikulin, S.: A Guide to Chi-Squared Testing, vol. 280. Wiley, New York (1996)
8. Herdin, C., Märtin, C.: Modeling and runtime generation of situation-aware adaptations. In: Kurosu, M. (eds.) HCI 2020, Part I. LNCS, vol. 12181, pp. 71–81. Springer, Cham (2020). https://doi.org/10.1007/978-3-030-49059-1_5
9. Märtin, C., Bissinger, B.C., Asta, P.: Optimizing the digital customer journey – improving user experience by exploiting emotions, personas, and situations for individualized user interface adaptations. J. Consum. Behav., 1–12 (2021)

10. Märtin, C., Herdin, C., Engel, J., Kampfer, F.: A structured approach for designing adaptive interactive systems by unifying situation-analytics with model- and pattern-based user interface development. In: Holzinger, A., Silva, H.P., Helfert, M. (eds.) CHIRA 2017. CCIS, vol. 654, pp. 45–65. Springer, Cham (2019). https://doi.org/10.1007/978-3-030-32965-5_3

11. Märtin, C., Kampfer, F., Herdin, C., Biawan Yameni, L.: Situation analytics and model-based user interface development: a synergetic approach for building runtime-adaptive business applications. Complex Syst. Inform. Model. Q. (CSIMQ) (20), 1–19 (2019). https://doi.org/10.7250/csimq.2019-20.01. Article 115

12. Mulder, M., Borst, C., van Paassen, M.M.: Improving operator situation awareness through ecological interfaces: lessons from aviation. In: Holzinger, A., Silva, H.P., Helfert, M. (eds.) CHIRA 2017. CCIS, vol. 654, pp. 20–44. Springer, Cham (2019). https://doi.org/10.1007/978-3-030-32965-5_2

13. Schober, P., Boer, C., Schwarte, L.: Correlation coefficients: appropriate use and interpretation. Anesth. Analg. 126(5), 1763–1768 (2018)

14. https://doi.org/10.1213/ANE.0000000000002864

15. Silva da Silva, T., et al.: User-centered design and agile methods: a systematic review. In: Proceedings of the IEEE Agile Conference (2011)

16. Winckler, M., Bach, C., Bernhaupt, R.: Identifying User eXperiencing factors along the development process: a case study. In: International Workshop on the Interplay between User Experience (UX) Evaluation and System Development (I-UxSED), NordiCHI, Copenhagen, Denmark (2012)

17. Yigitbas, E., Sauer, S., Engels, G.: A model-based framework for multi-adaptive migratory user interfaces. In: Kurosu, M. (ed.) HCI 2015, Part II. LNCS, vol. 9170, pp. 563–572. Springer, Cham (2015). https://doi.org/10.1007/978-3-319-20916-6_52

18. Yigitbas, E., Sauer, S., Engels, G.: Adapt-UI: an IDE supporting model-driven development of self-adaptive UIs. In: Proceedings of the EICS 2017, Lisbon, Portugal, 26–29 June. ACM (2017)

Evaluation of a Voice-Based Emotion Recognition Software in the Psycho-Oncological Care of Cancer Patients

Leonard Georg Klotz[1]([⊠]) [iD], Alexander Wünsch[2,3] [iD], and Mahsa Fischer[1]

[1] Heilbronn University of Applied Science, Heilbronn, Germany
lklotz.hn@gmail.com, mahsa.fischer@hs-heilbronn.de
[2] University Medical Center Freiburg, Albert Ludwigs University, Freiburg, Germany
alexander.wuensch@insel.ch
[3] Bern University Hospital, University of Bern, Bern, Switzerland

Abstract. Due to the increasing global incidence of cancer, the growing number of long-term survivors and the prevalence of psychological distress among cancer patients, psycho-oncological support is becoming more crucial. Recognizing the rising demand for psycho-oncological care the "Cancer Counselling App" project was initiated. As part of this project, a cancer counselling app is being developed. The development of the app incorporates the investigation a of voice-based emotion recognition which is enabled through the increasing capabilities of machine and deep learning algorithms, aiming to support the psycho-oncological care of cancer patients. The objective of this study is to identify use cases for this functionality and determine which of them are suitable for enhancing the psycho-oncological care. Through a literature review and expert interviews, seven distinct use cases were identified and evaluated. The highest-priority use case for voice-based emotion recognition is the long-term monitoring of the emotional state of cancer patients. The functionality should particularly focus on the emotions anxiety and distress, along with the psychological disorder depression, to effectively support psycho-oncological treatment.

Keywords: Affective computing · Cancer counselling · Emotion detection · Human-computer interaction · Literature review · Psycho-oncology · Voice recognition

1 Introduction and Goals

In Germany, approximately half of the population will develop a cancer disease at some point in their lifetime [1]. Compared to 2020, a prognosticated surge of 40% to over 68% in global cancer cases is anticipated by 2040, contingent upon the type of cancer [2, 3]. The mortality rate has witnessed a decline attributed to the heightened emphasis of the medical field on early disease detection and optimized curative treatment modalities [4]. Throughout the trajectory of cancer, approximately one-third of individuals diagnosed with the disease manifest a psychological distress necessitating treatment, with potential

M. Kurosu and A. Hashizume (Eds.): HCII 2024, LNCS 14684, pp. 357–375, 2024.
https://doi.org/10.1007/978-3-031-60405-8_23

persistence beyond the illness. Consequently, psycho-oncological care has evolved into an integral part of contemporary cancer medicine [5]. Due to the rising global incidence of cancer, the increasing number of long-term survivors and the heightened prevalence of psychological distress among afflicted people, psycho-oncological care for patients is assuming greater relevance. To address the increasing demand for psycho-oncological care, the project "Cancer Counselling App" was launched. This application will provide information on psycho-oncological and socio-legal aspects, integrate a video call function for counselling sessions between patients and experts as well as interventions, such as relaxation and meditation exercises [6]. An additional experimental function of the app is individual and voice-based emotion recognition. Emotions significantly determine a person's well-being and actions [4]. To interpret a person's emotions precisely is a challenging task. Nevertheless, precise identification is imperative for successful emotion regulation within the context of psycho-oncological care [7]. This requires an optimization of needs diagnostics, as the challenge of clear communication or diagnosis of emotional states is particularly evident, wherein both patients and caregivers may encounter difficulties in this regard [8]. In overcoming this communication gap, voice-based emotion recognition emerges as a valuable tool for providing support in psycho-oncological care. This gives rise to the following research questions: The key question is: Which use cases of voice-based emotion recognition exist in healthcare and which are suitable for use in the cancer counselling app to support psycho-oncological treatment? Followed by the sub-questions: Which use cases for voice-based emotion recognition exist in the context of healthcare? Which of the identified use cases are suitable for use in the cancer counselling app? Which emotions and psychological disorders should be the focus of voice-based emotion recognition in the cancer counselling app? What research needs can be addressed for future research projects in the field of voice-based emotion recognition for the cancer counselling app?

Within the scope of this paper, a comprehensive literature review will be conducted to identify various use cases of voice-based emotion recognition in healthcare, with a subsequent investigation into their distinctive characteristics. The emotions and psychological disorders on which the publications focus is also examined. Subsequently, the identified use cases will undergo evaluation by experts to determine their relevance for incorporation into the app. By following this procedure and answering the research questions, potential use scenarios for voice-based emotion recognition in the cancer counselling app can be identified, along with the emotions that most effectively support psycho-oncological treatment and should be focused on. The primary objective of this paper is to assess the viability of voice-based emotion recognition for the cancer counselling app, thereby contributing novel insights not only to the project itself but also to the broader digital healthcare research community. Drawing upon diverse use cases extracted from the literature, the subsequent expert evaluation will facilitate the prioritization of these cases. In essence, this research helps to deepen the understanding of the application of voice-based emotion recognition in healthcare, elucidating how this technology can be practically employed to enhance psycho-oncology care and assessing its added value in the treatment of cancer patients.

The paper is structured as follows: Sect. 2 contains the basic principles and terminology of the paper to ensure a uniform understanding of the key terms used in this research.

Section 3 elucidates the chosen methodological approach. The subsequent Sect. 4 delineates the presentation of results, offering answers to the research questions propounded in the work. Section 4.1 explains the results of the literature research and presents them in a concept matrix. The identified use cases of voice-based emotion recognition in the healthcare sector, as extracted from the literature, are expounded upon in Sect. 4.2. This is followed in the next section by the presentation of the expert interviews and the consequent prioritization of the identified use cases for the cancer counselling app. Finally, Sect. 5 summarizes the findings, critically reflects on the research methodology used and addresses future research potential.

2 Terms and Definitions

2.1 Cancer Counselling App

The "Cancer Counselling App" was initiated by the University Medical Centre Freiburg in 2020. The project is being carried out in cooperation with the Heilbronn University of Applied Sciences and the Fraunhofer Institute for Systems and Innovation Research ISI in Karlsruhe. The project involves the development of a mobile application, with the minimum viable product. A priority is to engage closely with potential users to understand their perspectives, which are then integrated into the app's development. The application aims to provide a valuable set of features including various activities such as relaxation and meditation exercises, information on psycho-oncological and socio-legal topics as well as referral options to regional support services. The long-term vision for the app includes ongoing development and expansion to incorporate additional functions like the voice-based emotion recognition [6].

2.2 Voice-Based Emotion Recognition

Emotion recognition based on speech and voice signals has recently been the subject of intensive research and become a focal point in the field of human-computer interaction. Speech emotion recognition (SER) is particularly emphasized in this domain, involving the analysis of emotional states based on speech features. Effective feature extraction plays a relevant role in this context [9]. Various voice features are extracted and processed to determine a person's emotional state. The human voice carries valuable information about their affective state, with characteristics such as pitch, speech rate, speech intensity, voice quality, and articulation exhibiting distinctive patterns across different emotions [10]. For instance, heightened states of anxiety, pleasure or anger are often associated with a loud, fast, and higher-pitched voice, while fatigue or sadness tends to manifest in a lower and slower voice. Affective technologies utilize and process such voice information and thus recognize emotions [11]. Another facet of SER is the semantic component, wherein the content of speech is analyzed. Here, the occurrence of certain words with an emotional reference is counted [12]. Technologies that are used to enable voice-based emotion recognition are machine- and deep learning methods, such as convolutional or recurrent neural networks, K-Nearest Neighbor, Support Vector Machines or the Hidden Markov Model. These methods consistently yield excellent results in the classification of emotions from voice [13, 14].

3 Methodology

In alignment with the Design Science Research (DSR) method as delineated by Peffers et al. [15] the research study follows a systematic progression involving six essential steps.

According to the first phase, the introduction of the paper formulates the problem of the research and presents the relevance and motivation. Concurrently, research questions are precisely defined, which corresponds to the second phase of the DSR approach.

In the third and fourth step of the DSR method, the central artifact is constructed and developed. First, a structured literature review is conducted to provide a sound basis for existing approaches to voice-based emotion recognition in healthcare. The procedures of Khan et al. [16] and Webster and Watson [17] are used to construct the literature review. The phase model provided by [16] describes a structured methodology for designing a literature review in five phases. In the phase "identifying relevant publications" the model can be well complemented by the backward and forward search according to [17]. Furthermore, the method of [17] was used to process and compare the identified literature. In addition, the requirement of Brocke et al. [18] for a detailed documentation of the search process will be considered. The literature is analyzed using the balanced scorecard according to Frehe et al. [19]. The results should enrich the artifact of the research and contribute to the research objective. For the research, scientific databases were searched using several defined search terms. The databases searched are Association for Computing Machinery Digital Library (ACM), AIS Electronic Library (AISel), Google Scholar (GS), IEEE Xplore Digital Library (IEEE) and Science Direct (SD) as well as the AudEERING Library (AUD). Upon identification of the databases, the search terms and search filters were defined. The defined search terms (ST) are as follows: **ST1:** ("emotion recognition") AND (SER OR speech OR voice) AND (cancer OR health* OR oncology), **ST2:** ("emotion recognition") AND (SER OR speech OR voice) AND (cancer OR healthcare OR oncology) AND (application* OR software OR "use case" OR pro-gram), **ST3:** ("affective computing" OR "human computer interaction" OR "HCI") AND (cancer OR healthcare OR oncology) AND (speech OR voice).

In combination with a requirements analysis via expert interviews, suitable use cases of voice-based emotion recognition for the cancer counselling app will be evaluated and a prioritization of use cases will be made possible. This corresponds to the fifth step of the DSR, which also verifies whether the problem at hand can be solved and the research question answered. The methodology employed for conducting expert interviews is described in greater detail in Sect. 4.3.

The final DSR step of the communication is realized through both the presentation and publication of the research work.

4 Results

4.1 Literature Review

The balanced scorecard according to [19] was used to analyze the search results. The designated literature databases mentioned in Sect. 3 were systematically examined utilizing the predefined search terms and filters. For ST1 174, for ST2 22 and for ST3 94, resulting in a total of 290 search results. Following the scrutiny for duplicates and a review of titles and abstracts, the originally identified publications were streamlined to 49. One additional source was removed by checking the scientific suitability. The papers were then checked for content relevance, reducing the number to 21. The literature found had to be available as full text and provide substantial value to the research to be categorized as relevant. Specifically, it is necessary for the selected papers to address practical use cases, illustrating how voice-based emotion recognition can be effectively applied in healthcare applications. Employing a backward and forward search strategy in accordance with [17], an additional two pertinent publications were identified. This brings the number of relevant articles in this paper to 23 (excluding fundamental literature and literature pertaining to research methodology). The relevant publications identified form the basis for addressing the research questions posed in this work.

With the help of a concept matrix according to [17], the sources used underwent a thematic categorization, revealing a total of seven distinct use cases for the application of voice-based emotion recognition in healthcare which are addressed by the authors of the publications (refer to Table 1). Furthermore, the authors focused and addressed a total of ten focus areas, each centering on specific emotions or psychological disorders as shown in Table 2.

The concept matrix makes it clear that a predominant portion of the identified publications, totaling 15, leverages voice-based emotion recognition for long-term monitoring purposes, aimed at gauging general psychological health or monitoring specific emotions, moods or symptoms of illness. This is followed by the development and use of conversational agents, systems with automatic content adaptation and the use of activity suggestions. Notifications of trusted persons, real-time monitoring and treatment suggestions are solely mentioned by one to three authors each.

From the examination of the identified literature, it is evident which use cases focus on analyzing specific emotions and psychological disorders. This is presented in Table 2, which illustrates the connection between specific use cases and the emotions or psychological disorders addressed by the respective authors. Publications that do not explicitly refer to a specific focus are not included in the table. The line "Publication occurrence" indicates how many of the identified publications have selected a specific emotion or a specific psychological disorder as the focus of their work. Publications that use a focus for various use cases are only included once in the total count.

Anxiety and depression are mentioned most frequently. Anxiety is the most focused emotion, with nine authors emphasizing it, closely followed by depression, which is mentioned eight times. The third most frequently cited focal points are the identification of distress and anger with six authors referring to each of them. Notably, it is observed that only one positive emotion, namely pleasure, is explicitly mentioned in four of the sources. The remaining authors focus solely on negative emotions as a focal point for undertaking appropriate countermeasures. Sadness and behavioral disorders are also mentioned in four of the publications. Next is frustration which is referred to three times. Attention Deficit Hyperactivity Disorder (ADHD) as well as the Autism Spectrum Disorder (ASD) both focused by one publication each.

Table 1. Concept Matrix

Source	Use Case						
	Activity Suggestions	Automatic Content Adaptation	Conversational Agents	Long-term Monitoring	Notification of Trusted Persons	Real-time Monitoring	Treatment Suggestions
[20]				x			x
[21]	x	x	x				
[22]				x			
[23]				x			
[24]	x		x		x		
[25]				x			
[26]		x	x	x			
[27]				x			
[28]		x			x		x
[29]						x	
[30]			x				
[31]				x			
[32]				x			
[33]				x			x
[34]				x			
[35]				x			
[36]	x		x	x			
[37]	x		x				
[38]				x			
[39]			x				
[40]				x			
[41]	x	x		x	x		
[42]		x	x				
Summed	**5**	**5**	**8**	**15**	**3**	**1**	**3**

Table two also shows that the use case of activity suggestions is predominantly employed to monitor anxiety and depression. In automatic content adaptation, the emotion of anxiety is the one that receives the most attention. This is also the case with conversational agents, where five publications direct their systems towards tracking anxiety. Six of the publications that integrate long-term monitoring into their systems focus on monitoring depression. This is closely followed by distress with five mentions. Notification of trusted persons is most frequently associated with anxiety and depression, each mentioned twice. Real-time monitoring is only mentioned by one author and focusses evenly on the emotions of anger, anxiety, pleasure and sadness. The treatment suggestions occur most frequently in connection with depression.

In the following section, the use of voice-based emotion recognition in healthcare applications described by the authors in the corresponding publications are presented in detail.

Table 2. Focused emotions and psychological disorders of the individual use cases

	Anger	Anxiety	Attention Deficit Hyperactivity Disorder	Autism Spectrum Disorder	Behavioral Disorders	Depression	Frustration	Pleasure	Sadness	Distress
Activity Suggestions	[24]	[24, 36, 37]			[21]	[36, 37, 41]			[24]	[36, 37]
Automatic Content Adaptation	[26]	[26, 42]			[21]	[41]		[42]	[28]	[26]
Conversational Agents	[24, 26]	[24, 26, 36, 37, 42]			[21, 36]	[36, 37]		[24, 42]	[24]	[26, 36, 37]
Long-term Monitoring	[26, 27, 38]	[26, 27, 33, 36]	[35]	[20]	[27, 31, 36]	[23, 25, 26, 33, 36, 41]	[20, 25, 34]	[27]	[27]	[22, 25, 26, 33, 36]
Notification of Trusted Persons	[24]	[24]				[28, 41]			[24, 28]	
Real-time Monitoring	[29]	[29]						[29]	[29]	
Treatment Suggestions		[33]		[20]		[28, 33]	[20]			[33]
Publication occurrence	6	9	1	1	4	8	3	4	4	6

4.2 Identified Use Cases

Activity Suggestions. Five of the identified authors incorporate activity suggestions in their systems like meditation, listening to music or interacting with relatives. The system described by [21, 36, 37] gather and analyses voice data to suggests activities. Once the emotion was determined, an appropriate response is generated based on a response tree. These suggestions draw inspiration from the theory of cognitive-behavioral therapy, aiming to address negative thoughts that often contribute to feelings of depression or anxiety. The overarching objective is to substitute these negative thoughts with more pragmatic alternatives. [24] adopts a comparable approach, with an additional feature allowing for the notification of possible third parties such as relatives or friends. These notified people also receive activity recommendations on how they can assist the system's user. The system monitors the effectiveness of the suggested activities through user feedback and the development of the user's emotional state. The suggested activities are those that can be carried out within the framework of psychological ethics. The system of [41] also allows third parties to be notified, but only at the highest escalation level if severe mood symptoms such as depression or suicidal risk are detected. The primary use case centers around prevention. The application monitors the user's emotional and psychological state and upon detection of negative trends, it recommends suitable countermeasures to forestall further deterioration. The application is also able to autonomously execute certain immediate activities such as playing music or initiating a chatbot for the user. This serves both emotional and physical regulation purposes.

Automatic Content Adaptation. Automatic content adaptation refers to the use case where systems autonomously and promptly execute specific actions. Some authors like to employ this in combination with conversational agents. The system of [42] is designed to conduct empathetic dialogues with users, dynamically adjusting its dialogue output based on the classified emotional state. This approach, termed emphatic dialogue, is designed efficiently using a dataset comprising approximately 25.000 personal dialogues for model training. Each dialogue is based on a specific situation wherein the speaker experienced a certain emotion and the listener actively reacted. [21] adopts a similar approach. Once a user's emotion was predicted, an appropriate response is generated based on a reaction tree inspired by cognitive behavioral therapy. The purpose of the system is to swiftly counteract spontaneous negative thoughts that often contribute to feelings of depression or anxiety, substituting these thoughts with more pragmatic alternatives. The application of [21] is able to perform certain actions independently, such as playing music and initiating a chatbot. [26] using content adaptation for a voice assistant, tailoring the processing of user commands depending on their current mood. [28] extend this approach further. Their system can also adjust the execution of certain actions according to the patient's emotions. The difference is that an additional concept was developed in which the system is not used in a voice assistant but as a treatment robot in clinics. In this capacity, the robot can offer comfort to users, for instance, through a hug or words of encouragement if they are feeling sad. It is worth noting that the authors also indicating the potential use of their system in conversational agents as well.

Conversational Agents. About a third of the publications identified mention conversational agents as a method for gauging the emotional state of patients through voice. These agents are mainly provided through mobile and web applications taking the form of voice assistants and chatbots capable of processing voice data. Some implementations incorporate virtual avatars to enhance the vibrancy and realism of the agent [30]. This aligns with the design principles for conversational agents determined by [39]. According to these, a conversational agent should exhibit high interactivity and realism, enabling meaningful conversations and provide emotional support to encourage regular user engagement. The conversational agents investigated by [21, 24, 36, 37, 42] collect data by recording and uploading user voice messages. The system analyses these messages, determines the emotional state and prompts the agent to respond accordingly. Responses typically include emotional support or activity suggestions. The study conducted by [37] confirms that conversational agents are regularly used by the probands, accompanied by a significant reduction in symptoms of depression and distress. [36] analyzed the same agent as [37], reaching a parallel conclusion and additionally observing a decrease in anxious behavior among users. Most of the conversational agents described encompass not only voice processing of users uploaded voice messages but also provide the option for communicating with the agents via text messages. The system suggested by [26] stands as an exception. It is exclusively voice-based, functioning solely as a voice assistant. The commands spoken by the patients are continuously recorded and analyzed. This allows the system to make rapid decisions. For instance, if the user requests the voice assistant for music, the system will play soothing music if the emotion was previously classified as anger when the command was given. In parallel, the collected data serves the purpose of long-term monitoring, offering the potential for accessibility by treating physicians. This allows healthcare professionals to track the development of the patient's emotional state over time.

Long-term Monitoring. Fifteen authors used voice-based emotion recognition for long-term monitoring. The data collection methodologies vary across publications, but the common objective is to capture the protracted emotional trajectory of individuals. While some of the publications focus on general mood, specifically target psychological disorders such as depression or the emotion distress. Several publications present historical emotional data to users, fostering increased self-awareness of their emotional states [31, 36, 38]. Many of these systems grant treating physicians access to the collected data, allowing them to track the longitudinal emotional development of patients through graphical representations [23, 32, 33, 35, 40]. This accessibility aims to aid healthcare providers in diagnosing and making decisions regarding patient treatment. For instance, the system developed by [20] provides emotional state data for children with ASD, offering suggestions on how to interact with them. Similarly, the system created by [23] aims to suggest strategies for handling patients with depression. On a different trajectory, [34] focuses on tracking the development of distress in patients over time. Other publications, such as [22, 26, 27, 38], are geared towards the prevention of more severe psychological disorders, like depression, by early detection through regular monitoring. This proactive approach is intended to recognize emerging trends and intervene before psychological disorders escalate.

Notification of Trusted Persons. As previously mentioned, [24] and [41] including the notification of trusted persons in their approaches. The systems start by recommending close contact interactions to improve the user's emotional state. It also sends notifications to close friends when a strong negative psychological state is detected and suggests activities. The system monitors the feedback loop to evaluate its impact on users. Positive feedback encourages good actions, while negative feedback leads to penalties. The assistant adjusts its recommendations by suggesting fewer negative actions and helping to identify reliable contact persons. This is used to encourage the user to interact with supportive familiar people. [28] are using a similar approach. Familiar persons are also informed about the emotional state of the user, although that the system does not suggest specific activities. The application presented in [41] employs third-party notifications only as a last resort when the user is found to have serious psychological health issues. In cases where the system detects unusual emotions or potentially harmful behavior in users with depression or other psychological disorders, the system will timely inform their doctors, family members and friends.

Real-time Monitoring. The publication by [29] delve into the exploration of real-time monitoring integrating live video calls into an affective application. The authors developed a cloud platform that enables online therapy sessions, as part of a project aimed at transitioning psychological therapy sessions to digital platforms. The platform is designed as an auxiliary service for health professionals, enabling the creation and conduction of meetings directly on the platform. During remote video sessions, the voice data of patients is continuously recorded and analyzed. This facilitated real-time emotion analysis during the conversations to support psychological treatment by making it easier for professionals to recognize and respond to patients' psychological health needs. In addition, it is possible to visualize the emotional progression during the video call through a graph and offering the option of taking notes. The affective data collected during the sessions is also stored for long-term analyses.

Treatment Suggestions. The final use case identified involves treatment suggestions for healthcare providers, including medication coordination and therapy methods. [20] developed an e-health platform dedicated to monitoring the emotional state of children with ASD. The system recognizes children's emotions by gathering voice data at person-to-person therapy and proposes adjustments for parents and specialists in specific situations. It also recommends suitable therapy methods for the child. In addition, the treating physicians receiving the evaluation of affective data and the physiological condition via the developed platform, which also contains the patient records and updates them automatically. [28] focuses on suggesting treatment steps for individuals experiencing depressive moods, aiming for prompt intervention. The emotional health system delivers personalized feedback and medical advice to users and healthcare providers based on the patient's character and emotional status. [33] created a similar system to assist psychologists in refining the treatment plans for their patients dealing with depression, significant distress and anxiety symptoms.

4.3 Expert Interviews and Use Case Prioritization

Conducting the Interviews. The literature analysis identified seven use cases for voice-based emotion recognition in healthcare, examining various emotions and psychological disorders. Expert interviews were conducted to evaluate the suitability of these use cases for supporting psycho-oncological care in the cancer counselling app. The aim was also to investigate which emotions and psychological disorders should be prioritized by the function. Guideline-based expert interviews were conducted according to the recommendation of Bogner et al. [43]. The guideline enables a structured interview and allows the inclusion of unplanned questions to evoke narratives. This approach enables the consideration of aspects that may not have been initially covered by the interviewer. Following the definition according to Meuser and Nagel [44], an expert is someone within a specific field of activity with privileged access to information, acting as a functionary rather than a private individual. Experts are sought for their representation of implicit knowledge and the expert interview is employed to tap into their specific perspective on the problem. A total of five expert interviews were conducted with psycho-oncologists from Germany and Switzerland. Due to the physical distance, the interviews were conducted through online video calls, with each session lasting between 30–45 min. To uphold privacy and data protection standards, the interviews were anonymized. For a systematic evaluation of the interviews, qualitative content analysis according to Mayring [45] was applied. The categories were determined using inductive category development. The goal was to condense and summarize the interview data based on the predefined research objectives, extracting correlations and insights. The Likert scale was utilized to prioritize the identified use cases. Experts assigned points on a scale of one to five to each use case. The results are also expressed verbally for better understanding. An average value per use case is calculated based on the points awarded by all experts, whereby the following applies: 0.0–1.4: not useful, 1.5–2.4: less useful, 2.5–3.4: useful, 3.5–4.4: very useful, 4.5–5.0: highly useful. The use cases are deemed suitable for integration into the cancer counselling app if the average value of a use case is at least categorized as "useful" or higher. This approach facilitated an objective prioritization of the use cases.

Use Case Prioritization. The individual evaluation by the experts is depicted in Fig. 1. The figure illustrates the point allocation by each expert for every use case, alongside the resultant average values for these respective cases.

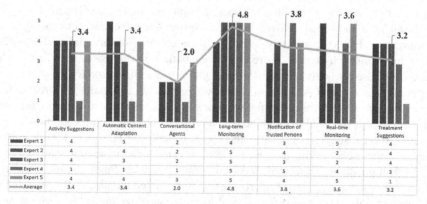

Fig. 1. Use Case Prioritization

The "Long-term Monitoring" use case achieved the highest score and is rated as highly useful with an average of 4.8 points. Only expert 1 did not award the full number of points here. While all experts, except for expert 1, assigned the full points, the function is acknowledged as highly useful by the experts. They highlight its significance for healthcare professionals in observing the long-term emotional trajectory of patients, facilitating an assessment of the efficacy of treatment methods. The function is also considered useful for patients. Additionally, the function is recognized as beneficial for patients, with expert 2 expressing enthusiasm about its potential as a self-observation tool to enhance patients' awareness of their mental well-being.

The use cases "Notification of Trusted Persons" and "Real-time Monitoring" are both considered to be very useful. In second place is "Notification of Trusted Persons". This received an average score of 3.8 points. Notably, the experts express a preference for the version where trusted persons are notified only in emergency situations, especially when the patient's emotional state exhibits significantly negative tendencies, as proposed by [41]. Consequently, it is stated: "I would rather have the feeling that this is set as a worst-case scenario. I think it would be very, very helpful if the voice or emotion recognition recognizes that, OK, someone is so derailed that they might not even realize it themselves, now it would be useful to call or notify someone." [Expert 4, personal interview, 09.01.2024, translated by Leonard Georg Klotz]. Following closely in third place, with an average score of 3.6 points, is the use case "Real-time Monitoring". Experts 1, 4 and 5 each awarded four or five points, expressing openness to incorporating such a use case in both online and personal therapy sessions. Expert 1 points out that the function is also interesting because it can reveal aspects of the patient's emotional state that the caregiver might have overlooked. Meanwhile, Experts 2 and 3 express interests in the use case, describing it as practical if available, but they rank it lower in priority compared to other use cases.

The "Activity Suggestions" and "Automatic Content Adaptation" share fourth place. Both have an average score of 3.4 points and are therefore considered useful. The "Activity Suggestions" are considered very useful by four experts. The advantage mentioned here is that such a function can provide patients using the app with suggestions on what to do in certain situations, helping them feel supported. Expert 5 describes it as "[…] a toolbox that is made available to the patient." [Expert 5, personal interview, 12.01.2024, translated by Leonard Georg Klotz]. Expert 2 points out that such a function must be well-formulated and tested to avoid having an instructive effect and not causing additional pressure. Expert 2 explicitly emphasizes the relevance of formulating the content of such functions with experts. There is only one outlier for this use case, expert 4, who rates the use case with only one point without giving a specific reason for the evaluation. The "Automatic Content Adaptation" is considered useful, especially for streamlining the app so that only relevant information is displayed. Expert 3 also finds the function useful but doubts the need to combine it with voice-based emotion recognition. Alternatively, expert 3 suggests that when the app is initially set up, interest fields can be selected by the users, serving as content filters and enable the same function.

The fifth position is attributed to the use case "Treatment Suggestions". Experts 1 to 3 each assigned four points. Experts 1 and 3 appreciated the idea of the presence of a secondary analysis alongside the clinical impression, providing supplementary support and generating additional treatment ideas. This aspect is perceived as beneficial for preparing therapy sessions. In contrast, experts 4 and 5 exhibit a higher degree of skepticism towards the function. While acknowledging its interest, concerns are raised that some therapists may not perceive this use case as a helpful tool but rather as instructive and competitive, potentially dictating their course of action.

The sixth and last place is occupied by "Conversational Agents" with an average of two points, signifying their perceived lower utility. Consensus among the experts affirms that no conversational agent can replace personal human contact. Experts 1 and 3 express an interest in this option while harboring doubts about the current technological readiness to develop such a function to meet the quality standards required for psycho-oncological patients, achieving results comparable to interpersonal communication. They remain open to the possibility that, with further advancements and optimization of language models, such a function could become viable in the upcoming ten years. Expert 1 underscores that the success of such a use case will also hinge on the extent to which individuals engage with such technologies, enabling them to serve effectively as a substitute or bridge for human contact.

Focused Emotions and Psychological Disorders. To determine which emotions and psychological disorders should be focused on by the voice-based emotion recognition in the cancer counselling app, the experts were also queried on this matter. They were prompted to provide insights on the emotions and psychological disorders highlighted in the identified publications and were afforded the opportunity to supplement their responses with additional comments.

All experts unanimously concur that the emphasis of voice-based emotion recognition should be on analyzing emotions such as anxiety and distress, as well as the psychological disorder depression. This prioritization is attributed to the predominant focus of psycho-oncology on these emotional domains, given their high frequency of occurrence in cancer patients. The relevance of these three focal points appears to be of substantial importance within the broader healthcare system and in the psychological care of diverse patient populations. This prominence is evident in the literature identified, as outlined in Table 2. According to the experts, anxiety is triggered by various factors. The most frequently mentioned are fear of the unknown, concerns about treatment-related side effects, existential considerations and fear of death. Distress, on the other hand, is primarily attributed to the organizational burdens imposed by the illness, affecting both cognitive and vegetative systems. These stressors stem from treatment decisions, numerous medical appointments, a dearth of information and the manifold uncertainties accompanying the illness. Experts 4 and 5 both explicitly mention that the distress factor has the potential to adversely amplify other emotions and, when combined with anxiety, may contribute to the development of depression. Furthermore, the experts concur .that these identified focal points are well-suited for intervention through specific coping measures in daily life, particularly if recognized by the voice-based emotion recognition. Implementation of such measures could mitigate the negative effects, aiding app users in regulating their emotions effectively.

The second level focuses on sadness, pleasure and frustration. Sadness is also classified by all experts as highly relevant in psycho-oncological treatment. Experts 1, 3 and 5 even rank it as high as anxiety, as it places a heavy burden on the psyche of patients and their relatives. In addition to anxiety and distress, sadness is also acknowledged for its role in fostering the development of depression. In this context, experts 2, 4 and 5 emphasize the relevance of pleasure. Although this rarely occurs, especially in the initial phase of the illness, it is very important in psycho-oncological therapy. The rationale behind this lies in redirecting patients' focus and attention towards aspects of their lives that still evoke pleasure. This shift in perspective, away from solely concentrating on the negative effects of the disease, can effectively counteract and mitigate various negative emotions. It is also useful for voice-based emotion recognition to track the progress of the patient's emotional landscape and assessing the efficacy of the treatment. Frustration also frequently occurs in connection with the disease and according to expert 3, swiftly leads to demoralization of those affected, subsequently resulting in patients rejecting treatment. Timely recognition enables the implementation of motivational aids, which are asserted to be more effective when applied early in addressing and mitigating frustration.

Opinions differ when it comes to behavioral disorders. Experts 2, 4 and 5 acknowledge their occurrence but consider them less pertinent to recognize. They argue that these disorders can stem from therapy in various ways, rendering them challenging to predict and classify. In addition, the occurrence is rather rare. Furthermore, behavioral disorders are often perceived as protective mechanisms that may naturally ameliorate over time. Conversely, experts 1 and 3 dissent, asserting that while behavioral disorders are less frequent than conditions such as anxiety and distress, they remain intriguing due to their inherent difficulty in identification. Both experts cite addiction as an illustrative example, underscoring the importance of recognizing such disorders for counsellors to devise appropriate therapeutic approaches: "For instance, if the software indicates a 60% likelihood of a patient having an alcohol problem, it provides counsellors with valuable insights, prompting them to consider additional factors." [Expert 1, personal interview, 19.12.2023, translated by Leonard Georg Klotz].

The focusses anger, ADHD and ASD were categorized as less relevant. Among these, anger would occur most frequently, albeit still infrequently. According to expert 2, this rarity is attributed to the tendency of patients to rarely overtly express anger and often exhibit reserved behavior even when experiencing anger. The experts agree that ADHD and ASD are so rare that it is not deemed worthwhile to focus on.

Experts 1 and 5 introduce further focal points that have not emerged from the relevant literature. Expert 1 and 5 proposes panic as a noteworthy emotion, being the more intense form of anxiety. Identifying panic, especially with the aid of an emotion recognition software, is considered relevant for early intervention. Expert 5 also goes into more detail about hopelessness and the sense of powerlessness, which are also evoked by anxiety. Powerlessness often accompanies a feeling of being at the mercy of external forces and is described by expert 5 as one of the most challenging states for patients to endure.

5 Conclusion and Future Work

The paper focused on evaluation of a voice-based emotion recognition software in the psycho-oncological care of cancer patients. To assess the suitability of voice-based emotion recognition within a cancer counselling app for supporting psycho-oncological treatment, a central research question and four sub-questions were formulated. To address these inquiries, a literature review was initially conducted. This involved searching selected literature databases using defined search terms and filters, leading to the identification of 23 relevant publications that explored use cases of voice-based emotion recognition in healthcare. Complementing this approach, expert interviews were carried out to pinpoint suitable use cases, understand their potential benefits for the cancer counselling app and determine which emotions and psychological disorders should be focused by the function.

A total of seven use cases for voice-based emotion recognition in the cancer counselling app were identified. Through expert evaluations, the prioritization of these use cases was achieved. The outcome indicates that six out of the seven identified use cases are considered suitable for implementation in the cancer counselling app, thereby aiding in the support of psycho-oncological care for patients. The sole exception is the "Conversational Agents" use case, deemed unsuitable at present. This determination is attributed to doubts regarding the technical feasibility in achieving a suitable quality, coupled with expert criticism citing the lack of human contact. Based on the prioritization, the "Long-term Monitoring" use case emerges as the recommended choice for the initial implementation of voice-based emotion recognition in the cancer counselling app. The experts agree that the use case is highly useful for both the treating doctors and the patients. This use case holds the potential to contribute to an unfiltered understanding of the long-term effectiveness of psycho-oncological treatment measures. For patients, it is suitable as a valuable self-observation aid, fostering heightened awareness of their mental well-being. The remaining five use cases, namely "Activity Suggestions", "Automatic Content Adaptation", "Notification of Trusted Persons", "Real-time Monitoring" and "Treatment Suggestions" received favorable ratings, categorized as both "useful" and "very useful". They are also deemed suitable for implementation in the cancer counselling app. It is proposed to implement and test these successively based on the use case prioritization, creating the possibility of combining multiple use cases within the cancer counselling app. The expert interviews were instrumental in determining the emotions and psychological disorders that should be the primary focus of voice-based emotion recognition in the cancer counselling app. The system is recommended to focus on monitoring the emotions "anxiety" and "distress" as well as the psychological disorder "depression". The progression of these aspects should be visualized through long-term monitoring. The experts rationalize this focus based on the frequency with which these focal points occur in psycho-oncological patients, aligning with the primary scope of work in psycho-oncology. The emotions of sadness, pleasure and frustration are also classified as highly relevant, albeit of secondary importance for voice-based emotion recognition. After the initial implementation of the function, these should also be gradually included in the data collection to complement long-term monitoring and further use cases. The consideration of including the analysis of behavioral disorders is also proposed, given their potential significance in indicating appropriate treatment strategies. However, the initial focus should not be on the inclusion of this aspect. This decision is driven by the lower frequency of occurrence of behavioral disorders compared to the aforementioned emotional and psychological disorders.

The present study was not conducted without limitations. It should be critically noted that a selective literature analysis was undertaken and not all publications in the field of research pertaining to voice-based emotion recognition in healthcare could be considered. Consequently, it is important to recognize that only centralized use cases of voice-based emotion recognition in healthcare were addressed in this paper. Additionally, the guideline-based interview method employed in the study has its inherent limitations. The participating experts represent individual entities with subjective opinions that may be influenced by their own subconscious biases, potentially impairing the objectivity of the results. This limitation extends to the qualitative content analysis of the interview results. The approach of inductive categorization requires interpretation by the researcher, introducing an element of subjectivity. Different researchers may form distinct categories, making it challenging to standardize data analysis and potentially impacting the reproducibility of the results.

Further research is imperative to assess the practical viability of voice-based emotion recognition in the cancer counselling app. A future study could involve implementing the highest prioritized use case for voice-based emotion recognition as a prototype. This would necessitate identifying emotion-recognizing software, evaluating its precision in recognizing emotions and psychological disorders and determining its suitability for the intended use case in supporting psycho-oncological care. In the evaluation phase, it is crucial to assess whether the identified focal points of anxiety, distress and depression, classified as the most relevant by experts, can be accurately determined by the software and whether the function can be technically realized within the app. Another area for future research lies in the collection of affective data. This paper outlines the use cases utilized in the pertinent literature for applying affective voice data in emotion analysis. In subsequent research, an examination is necessary to discern available methods for collecting affective data, investigate them comprehensively and evaluate the most suitable ones for integration into the cancer counselling app. Considerations such as methods for data collection, practical implementation, user acceptance and data security aspects warrant thorough investigation in this context.

Acknowledgements. This study was funded by Federal Ministry of Education and Research in Germany.

References

1. Quante, A.S., et al.: Projections of cancer incidence and cancer-related deaths in Germany by 2020 and 2030. Cancer Med. **5**, 2649–2656 (2016). https://doi.org/10.1002/cam4.767
2. Arnold, M., et al.: Global burden of cutaneous melanoma in 2020 and projections to 2040. JAMA Dermatol. **158**, 495–503 (2022). https://doi.org/10.1001/jamadermatol.2022.0160
3. Sharma, P., Vuthaluru, S., Chowdhury, S., Are, C.: Global trends in the incidence and mortality of pancreatic cancer based on geographic location, socioeconomic status, and demographic shift. J. Surg. Oncol. **128**, 989–1002 (2023). https://doi.org/10.1002/jso.27462
4. Mazzocco, K., Masiero, M., Carriero, M.C., Pravettoni, G.: The role of emotions in cancer patients' decision-making. Ecancermedicalscience **13**, 914 (2019). https://doi.org/10.3332/ecancer.2019.914
5. Kracen, A., Nelson, A., Michl, T., Rowold, M., Taylor, N., Raque, T.L.: Perspectives of postdoctoral fellows: a qualitative study of clinical supervision in psycho-oncology. Psychol. Serv. **20**, 206–218 (2023). https://doi.org/10.1037/ser0000740

6. Lovrić, L., Fischer, M., Röderer, N., Wünsch, A.: Evaluation of the cross-platform framework flutter using the example of a cancer counselling app. In: Proceedings of the 9th International Conference on Information and Communication Technologies for Ageing Well and e-Health, pp. 135–142. SCITEPRESS - Science and Technology Publications (2023). https://doi.org/10.5220/0011824500003476

7. Brandão, T., Tavares, R., Schulz, M.S., Matos, P.M.: Measuring emotion regulation and emotional expression in breast cancer patients: a systematic review. Clin. Psychol. Rev. **43**, 114–127 (2016). https://doi.org/10.1016/j.cpr.2015.10.002

8. Subramanian, B., Kim, J., Maray, M., Paul, A.: Digital twin model: a real-time emotion recognition system for personalized healthcare. IEEE Access **10**, 81155–81165 (2022). https://doi.org/10.1109/ACCESS.2022.3193941

9. Chen, M., Zhou, P., Fortino, G.: Emotion communication system. IEEE Access **5**, 326–337 (2017). https://doi.org/10.1109/ACCESS.2016.2641480

10. Murray, I.R., Arnott, J.L.: Toward the simulation of emotion in synthetic speech: a review of the literature on human vocal emotion. J. Acoust. Soc. Am. **93**, 1097–1108 (1993). https://doi.org/10.1121/1.405558

11. Dellaert, F., Polzin, T., Waibel, A.: Recognizing emotion in speech. In: Bunnell, H.T. (ed.) Proceedings / ICSLP 1996, Wyndham Franklin Plaza Hotel, Philadelphia, PA, USA, 3–6 October 1996, pp. 1970–1973. Citation Delaware, New Castle (1996). https://doi.org/10.1109/ICSLP.1996.608022

12. Weninger, F., Wöllmer, M., Schuller, B.: Emotion recognition in naturalistic speech and language—a survey. In: Konar, A., Chakraborty, A. (eds.) Emotion Recognition. A Pattern Analysis Approach, pp. 237–267. Wiley, Hoboken (2015). https://doi.org/10.1002/9781118910566.ch10

13. Konar, A., Chakraborty, A. (eds.): Emotion Recognition. A Pattern Analysis Approach. Wiley, Hoboken (2015). https://doi.org/10.1002/9781118910566

14. Jain, M., et al.: Speech Emotion Recognition using Support Vector Machine (2020)

15. Peffers, K., Tuunanen, T., Rothenberger, M.A., Chatterjee, S.: A design science research methodology for information systems research. J. Manag. Inf. Syst. **24**, 45–77 (2007). https://doi.org/10.2753/MIS0742-1222240302

16. Khan, K.S., Kunz, R., Kleijnen, J., Antes, G.: Five steps to conducting a systematic review. JRSM **96**, 118–121 (2003). https://doi.org/10.1258/jrsm.96.3.118

17. Webster, J., Watson, R.T.: Analyzing the past to prepare for the future: writing a literature review. MIS Q. **26**, xiii–xxiii (2002)

18. Brocke, J., Simons, A., Niehaves, B., Niehaves, B., Reimer, K.: Reconstructing the giant: on the importance of rigour in documenting the literature search process (2009)

19. Frehe, V., Adelmeyer, T., Teuteberg, F.: A balanced scorecard for systematic data quality management in the context of big data. Multikonferenz Wirtschaftsinformatik (2016). (in German)

20. Akinloye, F.O., Obe, O., Boyinbode, O.: Development of an affective-based e-healthcare system for autistic children. Sci. Afr. **9**, e00514 (2020). https://doi.org/10.1016/j.sciaf.2020.e00514

21. Bhangdia, Y., Bhansali, R., Chaudhari, N., Chandnani, D., Dhore, M.L.: Speech emotion recognition and sentiment analysis based therapist bot. In: 2021 Third International Conference on Inventive Research in Computing Applications (ICIRCA), pp. 96–101. IEEE (2021). https://doi.org/10.1109/ICIRCA51532.2021.9544671

22. Chang, K., Fischer, D., Canny, J., Hartmann, B.: How's my mood and stress? An efficient speech analysis library for unobtrusive monitoring on mobile phones, pp. 71–77 (2011)

23. Chen, Z., et al.: A web-based longitudinal mental health monitoring system. In: Hammal, Z., Busso, C., Pelachaud, C., Oviatt, S., Salah, A.A., Zhao, G. (eds.) Companion Publication of

the 2021 International Conference on Multimodal Interaction, pp. 121–125. ACM, New York (2021). https://doi.org/10.1145/3461615.3491113

24. Eeswar, S.S., et al.: Better you: automated tool that evaluates mental health and provides guidance for university students. In: TENCON 2022 - 2022 IEEE Region 10 Conference (TENCON), pp. 1–6. IEEE (2022). https://doi.org/10.1109/TENCON55691.2022.9977977

25. Egger, M., Ley, M., Hanke, S.: Emotion recognition from physiological signal analysis: a review. Electron. Notes Theoret. Comput. Sci. **343**, 35–55 (2019). https://doi.org/10.1016/j.entcs.2019.04.009

26. Elsayed, N., ElSayed, Z., Asadizanjani, N., Ozer, M., Abdelgawad, A., Bayoumi, M.: Speech emotion recognition using supervised deep recurrent system for mental health monitoring. In: 2022 IEEE 8th World Forum on Internet of Things (WF-IoT), pp. 1–6. IEEE (2022). https://doi.org/10.1109/WF-IoT54382.2022.10152117

27. Gong, Y., Poellabauer, C.: Continuous assessment of children's emotional states using acoustic analysis. In: 2017 IEEE International Conference on Healthcare Informatics (ICHI), pp. 171–178. IEEE (2017). https://doi.org/10.1109/ICHI.2017.53

28. Jiang, Y., Li, W., Hossain, M.S., Chen, M., Alelaiwi, A., Al-Hammadi, M.: A snapshot research and implementation of multimodal information fusion for data-driven emotion recognition. Inf. Fusion **53**, 209–221 (2020). https://doi.org/10.1016/j.inffus.2019.06.019

29. Joshi, D., Dhok, A., Khandelwal, A., Kulkarni, S., Mangrulkar, S.: Real time emotion analysis (RTEA). In: 2021 International Conference on Artificial Intelligence and Machine Vision (AIMV), pp. 1–5. IEEE (2021). https://doi.org/10.1109/AIMV53313.2021.9670908

30. Kocaballi, A.B., et al.: Conversational agents for health and wellbeing. In: Bernhaupt, R., et al. (eds.) Extended Abstracts of the 2020 CHI Conference on Human Factors in Computing Systems, pp. 1–8. ACM, New York (2020). https://doi.org/10.1145/3334480.3375154

31. Liang, D., Zhang, A., Thomaz, E.: Automated face-to-face conversation detection on a commodity smartwatch with acoustic sensing. Proc. ACM Interact. Mob. Wearable Ubiquit. Technol. **7**, 1–29 (2023). https://doi.org/10.1145/3610882

32. Liu, X., Zhang, L., Yadegar, J.: A multi-modal emotion recognition system for persistent and non-invasive personal health monitoring. In: Jacobs, I.M., Soon-Shiong, P., Topol, E., Toumazou, C. (eds.) Proceedings of the 2nd Conference on Wireless Health, pp. 1–2. ACM, New York (2011). https://doi.org/10.1145/2077546.2077577

33. Marchi, E., Eyben, F., Hagerer, G.J., Schuller, B.: Real-time tracking of speakers' emotions, states, and traits on mobile platforms. In: Proceedings of the Interspeech 2016, pp. 1182–1183 (2016)

34. Muaremi, A., Arnrich, B., Tröster, G.: Towards measuring stress with smartphones and wearable devices during workday and sleep. BioNanoScience **3**, 172–183 (2013). https://doi.org/10.1007/s12668-013-0089-2

35. Porcheron, M., Arch, K.G., Luland, S.D., Blanchfield, P., Valstar, M.F., Chowanda, A.: Swiss Cottage – a game to train speech recognition for an affective computing treatment of ADHD patients, pp. 1–5 (2013)

36. Sheykholeslami, N.: Emotion AI in Mental Healthcare. How can affective computing enhance mental healthcare for young adults? pp. 1–36 (2022)

37. Söderberg, E.: An evaluation of the usage of affective computing in healthcare. In: UMEÅ's 25th Student Conference in Computing Science, pp. 69–78

38. Tong, Y., Mo, W., Sun, Y.: Emovo: a real-time anger detector on the smartphone using acoustic signal. In: Proceedings of the 16th International Conference on PErvasive Technologies Related to Assistive Environments, pp. 392–395. ACM, New York (2023). https://doi.org/10.1145/3594806.3594833

39. Wahbeh, A., Al-Ramahi, M., El-Gayar, O., Elnoshokaty, A., Nasralah, T.: Conversational agents for mental health and well-being: discovering design recommendations using text

mining. In: Proceedings of the 56th Hawaii International Conference on System Sciences, pp. 3184–3193

40. Yamashita, Y., Onodera, M., Shimoda, K., Tobe, Y.: Emotion-polarity visualizer on smartphone. In: 2019 IEEE 27th International Requirements Engineering Conference Workshops (REW), pp. 96–99. IEEE (2019). https://doi.org/10.1109/REW.2019.00020

41. Yang, J., Zhou, J., Tao, G., Alrashoud, M., Mutib, K.N.A., Al-Hammadi, M.: Wearable 3.0: from smart clothing to wearable affective robot. IEEE Netw. **33**, 8–14 (2019). https://doi.org/10.1109/MNET.001.1900059

42. Zygadlo, A.: A therapeutic dialogue agent for polish language. In: 2021 9th International Conference on Affective Computing and Intelligent Interaction Workshops and Demos (ACIIW), pp. 1–5. IEEE (2021). https://doi.org/10.1109/ACIIW52867.2021.9666281

43. Bogner, A., Littig, B., Menz, W.: Interviewing Experts. Palgrave Macmillan, Houndmills (2009)

44. Monke, S.: The Expert Interview as a Method of Qualitative Social Research. GRIN Verlag (2007)

45. Mayring, P.: Qualitative content analysis. Forum Qual. Soc. Res. **1**(2), 1–10 (2000). Arzt. 20

Does the Voice-Based Lifelogging Method "Laughter Map" of Visualizing a User's Laughter Experiences Enhance Positive Mood?

Miyabi Shigi[✉], Masayuki Ando, Kouyou Otsu, and Tomoko Izumi

Ritsumeikan University, Kusatsu 525-8557, Shiga, Japan
is0507ix@ed.ritsumei.ac.jp, {mandou,k-otsu,
izumi-t}@fc.ritsumei.ac.jp

Abstract. An increasing number of people are experiencing mental stress in their daily lives. In particular, in the field of psychology, past events are easily recalled in relation to the current mood. In this study, we aim to clarify whether supporting the recall of previous pleasant experiences can enhance a positive mood. In our previous study, we proposed a voice-based lifelogging application "Laughter Map" to enable logging and checking of previous laughter scenes in a map format. The proposed visualization method for pleasant memories can help in recalling the memories. In this study, we conducted an experiment to verify the effect of presenting past laughter experiences by laughter map on moods. In the experiment, we compared the laughter map with a random map that provides the previous conversation cut out randomly. This paper reports on the change of mood obtained with positive and negative affect scale and temporary mood scale scales, along with the questionnaire results in the experiment. Experimental results suggests that the laughter map increased positive moods, such as liveliness, compared to the random map.

Keywords: Lifelogging system · Memory of laughter · Moods in human–computer interaction (HCI) · Recall support

1 Introduction

In recent years, an increasing number of people have been diagnosed with depression globally [1]. Memory and judgment skills are impaired in depression, and specific cognitive tendencies for recalling past events may be observed depending on the mood. In particular, the mood-state-dependent effect is well known [2], in which positive moods are more likely to trigger positive memories and negative moods are more likely to trigger negative memories. In cases in which a mood-state-dependent effect is observed, past negative memories tend to be recalled when the person feels depressed. The subsequent worsening of the negative mood results in additional negative memories being recalled. This repetition may result in chronic depression and cognitive distortion. To avoid this chain of negative memory recall, external triggers to change the mood are necessary. In addition, previous studies have revealed that positive memories can be a promising

M. Kurosu and A. Hashizume (Eds.): HCII 2024, LNCS 14684, pp. 376–388, 2024.
https://doi.org/10.1007/978-3-031-60405-8_24

method for improving the mood [3]. Most studies on the information engineering field have focused on supporting the recording and recall of past events [4, 5]. However, it is possible that a mechanism to support positive memory recall could promote recall and mood improvement.

Therefore, we examine to promote the recall of positive memories by reflecting on daily pleasant experiences to improve the negative mood. In maintaining positive mental health and living a fulfilling life, it is important to recall not only conscious enjoyable experiences such as unique leisure activities but also unconsciously pleasant events in daily life. In addition to extraordinary pastimes such as traveling or dining with others, we occasionally experience unconscious enjoyment in casual conversations with family and friends or in interesting events during our daily lives. Recalling these small positive experiences can effectively increase self-efficacy and help re-evaluate self-worth and life.

In our research group, we proposed "Laughter Map" that accumulates audio data about situations of laughter occurrence in the user's life and presents them as the past positive events with laughter in the form of a map to recall them [6]. The proposed system records an audio for 5 s before and after laughter is detected and the location of its occurrence. When users reflect on their past experiences, they can confirm the corresponding voice data by selecting the data on the map. In a previous study [6], we showed that the interface in our proposed method presenting past laughter experiences on a map is useful for memory recall. However, we did not examine the effect of recall using the proposed method on the mood. In addition, because laughter has the effect of inducing another laughter, presenting information on laughter experiences can generate a positive mood.

Thus, in this study, we examine the effect of presenting laughter in "Laughter Map" on enhancing a positive mood and reducing a negative mood by comparing a method of presenting the audio of past conversations randomly. The effect is verified based on the scale measuring the mood (i.e., positive and negative affect scale (PANAS) [7] and temporary mood scale (TMS) [8]). We compare the scores of measuring before and after the recall. This paper reports the comparison of mood changes caused by recall using "Laughter Map" and a random voice map, along with the results of a questionnaire regarding the impression of the recall.

2 Related Works

Studies on lifelogging technology have been conducted to record daily events [4]. For instance, Kinoshita et al. used a small camera attached to the body to record daily events [5]. A major feature of lifelogging is that information on experiences outside of the conscious mind of the user can be recorded. Thus, this method can be used to obtain information on unconscious pleasant experiences in daily life. However, because existing lifelogging methods assume that all daily activities are recorded, considerable information is accumulated. Therefore, developing a method for extracting the necessary information from the log data based on the purpose of use is critical. In other words, to support past pleasant memory recall, it should be selectively extracted and visualized simply to reduce cognitive costs. In this study, we consider using the "laughing sound" information as a trigger to encourage the recall of pleasant memories in daily activities based on information from voice-related lifelogging.

Numerous studies have been conducted on information systems that aim to promote laughter by focusing on its effects. Fushimi et al. proposed a camera system that captures natural smiles by inducing laughter through the presentation of laughter sounds [9]. They found that using the laughter of children as the shutter sound when capturing pictures elicited laughter from the filmed subjects. Tsujita et al. [10] revealed that the system for inducing intentional smiles can improve the mood state and encourage smiling. The results of these studies revealed that such mechanisms that trigger new experiences with laughter can enhance positive moods. In the proposed method, laughter is used as a trigger to explore pleasant memories unconsciously experienced during daily activities. In daily life, unconscious laughter can occur when experiencing positive events. The aggregation of pleasant memory information related to laughter from life records is realized using such laughter as a cue. This study investigates whether experiences that are not clearly recognized as being pleasant in the mind of an individual can be re-examined as "that time was fun" when the voice data with the laughter sound are presented. In this approach, the method of improving the mood using actual event log information is yet to be studied comprehensively in the engineering domain.

3   Concept of Laughter Map and Prototype System

3.1   Laughter Map

In this section, we explain a concept of a voice-based lifelogging method, namely "Laughter Map," which was proposed in our previous study [6]. Laughter Map is an application that accumulates audio information on laughter experiences in the daily life of a user and presents them on a map (Fig. 1). The audio data presented to users include the conversation before and after the timing of the laugh, which is extracted from audio lifelog data recorded in daily life. Concretely, the application extracts audio data from 5 s before the start of the laughter to 5 s after the end of the laughter, and records them with location information of the laughter. By presenting the audio including the 5 s before and after the laughter, users can easily grasp the context of laughter occurrence and review it. The accumulated information on the laughter experience is presented in the map form on the mobile application, where pins are displayed at the location where the laughter occurred (Fig. 2). By tapping the pins on the map, the user can confirm the date and time of the laugh and its audio data registered there. (The right screen of Fig. 2). This user interface enables users to recognize the frequency of the laughter experiences on the map, and to review the recorded laughter experience by listening to the audio.

3.2   Prototype System

This section describes the prototype system constructed based on the concept of the laughter map. Because the prototype system used in the experiment in this study improved the user interface and function partially used in the previous study [6], we explain only a brief outline and the changes.

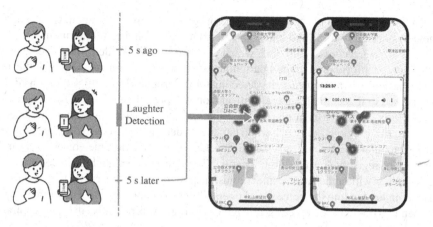

Fig. 1. Overview of the proposed system, Laughter Map.

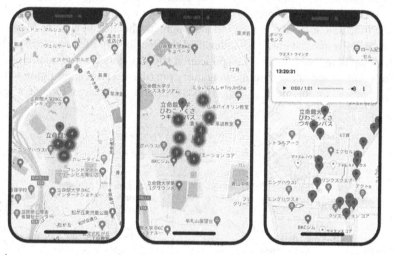

Fig. 2. Example of proposed system screens (map is zoomed in as shown on the right)

The prototype system comprises three components: a recording personal computer (PC) and microphone for recording location data and audio simultaneously, a smartphone for retrieving global positioning system (GPS) location data, and a processing PC with a graphics processing unit for extracting audio and generating the map view for the user. The software comprises three main parts: the information processing part that obtains audio and location data, the audio extraction part that detects and extracts laughter from the acquired audio data, and the information presenting part that creates a display content for visualizing the audio and location data on a map. (Fig. 3).

In the information processing part, the program acquires both audio from a micro-phone connected to a PC and location data from a smartphone. While running the pro-gram, it always records audio data, which is stored as a WAV file. Simultaneously, the GPS location information of the smartphone is also always recorded along with the time.

In the audio extraction part, the detecting model proposed by Gillick et al. on GitHub [11] is used to detect the laughter segment from the pre-recorded audio file. Thereafter, the audio is extracted from an extended interval of 5 s before and after the detected segment. In a previous study [6], when laughter is detected consecutively, the audio data per the laughter is extracted as separate data. Consequently, multiple voices with similar content are registered at the same location. The consecutive laughter is considered to be occurring within the same context; thus, displaying these separately may reduce the ease of understanding the context and operability of the application. Therefore, if audio segments extracted by triggering a laughter overlap even partially, they are combined into a single audio.

The information presenting part dynamically generates an HTML file based on the audio files and location obtained by the information processing and audio extraction parts. The extracted audio is presented by pins on the map and a user can tap the pins to check the time and audio data related to the laughter. The audio play can be controlled by a seek bar. To make it easier to understand the distribution of laughter experiences, when the map is reduced in size, the application shows the number of audios registered within a certain range rather than showing every pin (the left and center figure of Fig. 2). This mechanism is implemented using MarkerClusterer, a library of Google Maps.

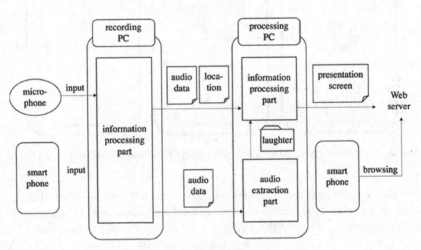

Fig. 3. System configuration

4 Experiment

4.1 Purpose and Hypothesis

This study aims to examine the effect of recall using the "Laughter Map" on the mood. The system extracts an audio based on laughter and presents the audio information including speech and the laughter. Reviewing the voice information of the laughter experience with laughter sounds is considered to recall the pleasant mood of the event at that time, and could thereafter lead to an increase in positive moods and a decrease in negative moods. Therefore, in this experiment, the following hypothesis will be verified:

- Reflection using a Laughter Map induces positive mood improvements.

4.2 Experimental Settings

This experiment aims to verify the effect of using the Laughter Map to recall past experiences on the mood. The characteristic of the Laughter Map is to extract audio data based on the detected laughter. Therefore, as a comparison condition for verifying the effect, we set a condition in which audio information acquired by a method without considering laughter is presented on a map. Specifically, we conduct a comparison experiment of the two conditions:

- Laughter condition: Participants recall by reviewing the voice information extracted based on laughter on a map, that is, using the "Laughter Map."
- Random condition: Participants recall by reviewing the voice information extracted at random on a map.

The system used under the laughter condition is the prototype system described in Sect. 3. The system used under the laughter condition displays audio information including laughter at the location where the laughter occurred on the map. In contrast, the system used under the random condition extracts audio information from the recorded audio data at a random time such that the length of the audio data is equal to those of each audio data under the laughter condition. This system also displays them at the locations where the audio was recorded on the map. Therefore, the number of pins and the total lengths of audio information displayed on the map under the laughter and random conditions are similar.

4.3 Procedure

The experiment was conducted in pairs of participants. We designed the experiment composed by two phases: creating pleasant memories including laughter experience and experiencing two types of the system to recall them. The experiment was conducted over three days: On the first day, they walked in pairs while talking together to have laughter experience and create memories, and thereafter, they recall them on the second and third days using the system under each condition. The second and third days were set one week after the first day.

On the first day, we explained the procedure of the experiment and obtained consent from the participant to participate in this experiment. Thereafter, each of the two participants wears a pin microphone and carries a recording PC and a smartphone in the bag to record the voice and location while walking. The walking was for approximately 30 min on a model course prepared in advance on campus at Ritsumeikan University. Because this task is intended to provide participants with an experience including laughter, pairs comprising close friends participated in this experiment. We asked them to walk while conversing freely with each other.

On the second and third days of the experiment, we asked each participant to visit the laboratory individually to recall the experience of the first day, and this was performed consecutively for each participant. The experimental procedures for the second and third days were similar, but the systems used to recall were different, that is, in each of the days, the laughter or random conditions were applied. To avoid order bias, the order of the conditions applied was swapped for each participant. The time to recall using the systems was 5 min. Before and after the recall, a questionnaire about the current mood was administered. Thereafter, the participants were asked to answer a questionnaire about their impressions of the recall using the system, and an interview that asked about their impressions of the recalled content and any change in mood was performed.

4.4 Evaluation Item

On the second and third experimental days, the participants were asked to respond to questionnaires asking about their mood before and after they recalled reviewing information provided by the application. Based on the results of the questionnaires, we analyze changes in their mood before and after they used the systems. Two types of mood questionnaires were used, the Japanese version of the PANAS [7] and TMS [8]. PANAS comprises eight positive and eight negative mood scales. Each item is rated on a six-point Likert scale (from 1 "do not feel" to 6 "feel very strongly"). TMS comprises six factors with three question items. Each question item is rated on a five-point Likert scale (from 1 "strongly disagree" to 5 "strongly agree"). While the PANAS measures the mood from the two factors of positive/negative mood, the TMS measures it from six factors: tension, depression, anger, confusion, fatigue, and vigor. In this experiment, we intended to evaluate the difference in mood before and after the recall of past experiences; thus, we asked the participant to respond to the TMS questionnaire immediately before and after the recall. Specifically, the questionnaires were completed in the order of PANAS to TMS before the recall and TMS to PANAS after the recall.

After completing the post PANAS, the participants were also asked to answer a questionnaire about their impressions of the recall using the system, and an interview about what they recalled and changes in their mood. This questionnaire was based on the questionnaire in [12] to evaluate recall and impressions of the system. Table 1 lists its questionnaire items. Each question in Table 1 is on a five-point Likert scale, with a score of one indicating "not at all applicable" and a score of five indicating "extremely applicable." This paper reports the results obtained with the PANAS, TMS, and additional questionnaire.

Table 1. Questionnaire items

No	Question content
Q1	I can recall the scenes when those events happened
Q2	I can recall several points and narrate them in detail
Q3	I can recall those events one after another
Q4	I can talk about those events like a story
Q5	I feel as if I am watching the event just now
Q6	I am feeling the same type of emotions as when I experienced the event
Q7	The emotion is positive
Q8	The emotion is negative
Q9	I think this system is easy to reflect the past events
Q10	I think this system is easy to recall the past pleasant events
Q11	I think it is enjoyable to reflect on this system
Q12	I want to continue using this system in the future

5 Results

In this experiment, 20 students at Ritsumeikan University (2 × 10 pairs, 14 males and 6 females) participated in the experiment. This section shows the results and analyses.

5.1 Results of the PANAS and TMS on Mood Changes

Figure 4 shows the boxplots of the results of the PANAS answered before and after the recall on the second and third days. From the responses to the 16 items in the PANAS, the total score of the eight items for the positive affect factor is denoted as PANAS_positive, and that of the eight items for the negative affect factor is denoted as PANAS_negative. We performed a two-factor repeated measures ANOVA under the conditions and pre-post factors. Consequently, while the scores of PANAS_negative do not have significant differences for any of the factors, those of PANAS_positive have significant differences between pre-post factors. In both items, each interaction effect is not significant. Thus, it is considered that recalling the past experience via voice data promotes a positive mood regardless of the laughter and random conditions.

Figure 5 shows the boxplots of the results of the TMS answered immediately before and after the recall. Each of the 18 items of the TMS questionnaire corresponds to one of the following factors: "tension," "depression," "anger," "confusion," "fatigue," or "vigor." Each factor comprises three items. In the TMS results, we calculated the sum of the scores of the three items for each mood factor. Hence, the score for each mood assumes a value from 3 to 15. We performed a two-factor repeated measures ANOVA under the conditions and pre-post factors. Consequently, there are no significant differences in any mood factor between the laughter–random condition. In contrast, there are significant or marginally significant differences between the pre-post factors

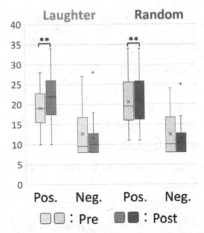

Fig. 4. Boxplots of the results of PANAS and p-values in analysis of variance (Pre: before recall, Post: after recall, *p < 0.1, **p < 0.05).

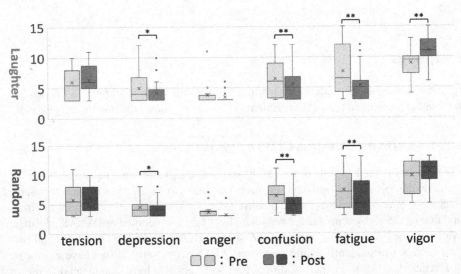

Fig. 5. Boxplots of the results of TMS, and p-values in analysis of variance (Pre: before recall, Post: after recall, *p < 0.1, **p < 0.05).

for the "depression," "confusion," "fatigue," and "vigor" moods in the ANOVA results. In these questions, mean scores become more positive after the recall. For the "fatigue" and "vigor" moods, the interaction effects are also marginally significant or significant ("fatigue": p < 0.1, "vigor": p < 0.05).

For "depression" and "confusion" moods, the difference between pre-post scores is significant and the interaction effect is not observed in the ANOVA result. Thus, it is considered that the recall of the past experience improves these moods regardless of the experimental condition. The reason for the higher score for "confusion" before the recall could be the large amount of information given to the participants owing to the explanations and cautions about the experiment. Because the interactions have a marginally significant or significant difference for "fatigue" and "vigor" moods, respectively, in the ANOVA result, we performed a simple effect test to identify the differences in pre-post factor under each experimental condition. For the "fatigue" mood, the differences between the pre-post scores are significant under both the laughter and random conditions. This suggests that recall of the past experience, regardless of the system used, may decrease "fatigue." However, for "fatigue," the difference between pre-post scores under the laughter condition is larger than that under the random condition. There is a similar trend for "vigor." Furthermore, for the "vigor" mood, there is a significant difference between pre-posts under the laughter condition, while no significant difference is confirmed under the random condition. From these results, it can be deduced that the recall by listening to the voice data including laughter reduces "fatigue" and promotes the "vigor" mood.

5.2 Results of the Additional Questionnaire

We analyze the results of the additional questionnaire summarized in Table 1.For each question, a one-sided t-test was performed to examine the difference between the mean values under the laughter and random conditions. Table 2 summarizes these results. Notice that because Q8 is a question asking the degree of negative feeling, a score closer to 1 implies a more positive result.

No significant differences were observed for Q1–Q4 and Q9, which ask about the ease and clarity of recall. As summarized in Table 2, the differences in these mean values are small. These results suggest that there are no differences in the impression of the ease and clarity of the recall under either condition. It is considered that this may be attributed to the information represented on the map, such as locations and surrounding environment, which were useful keys for recalling memories in addition to voice data.

Similarly, there are no significant differences for Q6–Q8, which ask about the emotion the participants felt at the recall. The laughter condition has a slightly higher score of mean values than the random condition with a minor difference. This questionnaire was administered only once, after the experiment. Therefore, the responses only considered the instantaneous emotions after the experiment. For the analysis of the emotional effects, it is important to know whether there was a change in emotion throughout the process of experiencing the system. In this perspective, the results of the time-series changes observed in the PANAS and TMS results are more reliable. In these scales, there are no items for which the factors of the system differences are significant, and the results are consistent with those of these scales. For the evaluation of the mood, the results using the mood questionnaire, the PANAS and TMS, are considered more reliable, and we focus on the results presented in the previous section.

In contrast, items with a significant or marginally significant difference are Q5, Q10, and Q11. For all of these items, the laughter condition has a higher score of mean values than the random condition. Q5 asks about the ease of visualizing the past scene. The reason that the laughter condition has a more positive score for Q5 is not clear, but the presentation of the audio information including laughter may have strengthened the sense of re-experiencing compared to the random condition. Q10 and Q11 ask about the

Table 2. Results of questionnaire analysis (five-point Likert method, *p < 0.1, **p < 0.05)

No	Laughter		Random		p-value
	Mean	SD	Mean	SD	
Q1	4.55	0.58	4.40	0.88	0.19
Q2	3.70	0.75	3.80	0.38	0.25
Q3	3.95	0.58	3.95	0.68	0.50
Q4	3.40	1.09	3.35	1.08	0.43
Q5	3.65	1.61	3.25	1.25	0.04**
Q6	3.60	1.31	3.45	1.10	0.25
Q7	4.40	0.88	4.20	0.69	0.13
Q8	1.55	0.89	1.75	0.83	0.18
Q9	4.60	0.25	4.45	0.79	0.24
Q10	4.40	0.67	4.10	1.04	0.06*
Q11	4.50	0.58	4.05	1.00	0.01**
Q12	3.95	0.79	3.85	0.77	0.25

ease of recall of the pleasant events using the system and the enjoyment, respectively. Although there is no significant difference for Q12, as the scores are higher than 3.0, both systems under the two conditions are evaluated positively for use.

6 Discussion

We discuss the results as concerns the hypothesis of this experiment, "Reflection using a Laughter Map induces positive mood improvements."

The results of the mood assessment using PANAS demonstrate that there is a significant difference ($p < 0.05$) between the pre-post scores in PANAS_positive, and its post score is higher than its pre-score. Thus, we can assume that using the system to recall the past experiences promotes a positive mood regardless of the using systems. However, because there is no interaction, the PANAS results do not confirm the effect of presenting the audio with laughter in this experiment. Similarly, there is a marginally significant difference ($p < 0.10$) or significant difference ($p < 0.05$) between the pre-post for the "depression" and "confusion" moods on the TMS, and no interaction exists. This also suggests that regardless of the audio information presented, the recall on the past experiences has the effect of reducing the degree of feeling "depression" and "confusion."

In contrast, a significant difference ($p < 0.05$) is found between the scores of the pre-post for "vigor" and "fatigue," further confirming the interaction effect. The improvement degree before and after the recall is greater under the laughter condition than under the random condition for these two mood factors. Moreover, a significant difference ($p < 0.05$) between the pre-post is confirmed only under the laughter condition for "vigor." In other words, it is assumed that presenting audio information extracted based on laughter during recall enhances the degree of the "vigor" mood. Because the laughter condition is shown to be more effective on the positive "vigor" mood particularly, this result supports the hypothesis of this experiment.

In addition, from the results of the additional questionnaire, it is shown that a marginally significant difference ($p < 0.10$) is confirmed for Q10, "I think this system is easy to recall the past pleasant events," and a significant difference ($p < 0.05$) for Q11, "I think it is enjoyable to reflect on this system." For these questions, the laughter condition has higher mean scores than those of the random condition. The reason for the results of Q10 is considered that the Laughter Map makes it easier to recall the pleasant events because it extracts voice data related to laughter. Moreover, because Q11, in particular, has a significant difference between the conditions, we assume that the sound of laughter including voice data provided in the Laughter Map can promote enjoyment. Therefore, the results of Q10 and Q11 in the additional questionnaire revealed certain trends that suggest partial alignment with the proposed hypothesis.

7 Conclusion

We verified the impact of "Laughter Map," which is a voice-based life-logging application that accumulates audio information where laughter occurs and enables a user to review them on a map, on the improvement of the user's mood. In the experiment, we compared the proposed "Laughter Map" to an application that provides past audio information extracted at random. The results demonstrated that presenting audio information related to laughter is effective in promoting a positive mood such as "vigor."

However, several participants said that they could not understand the difference between the two systems. In addition, some participants answered in the interview, "I don't like my voice" or "It is easier to recall when the other person's voice is present." Thus, our future work is to design an interface or develop a function such that the user recognizes their laughter experience comfortably.

Acknowledgments. This work was supported in part by JSPS KAKENHI (Grant Number 23K16931 and 22K21096), Tateisi Science and Technology Foundation and Ritsumeikan Global Innovation Research Organization(R-GIRO), Ritsumeikan University.

References

1. Global Health Data Exchange | GHDx. https://ghdx.healthdata.org/record/global-burden-disease-study-2019-gbd-2019-demographics-1950-2019. Accessed 27 Oct 2023
2. Taniguchi, T.: Mood congruent effects and mood state dependent effects on cognition. Jap. Psychol. Rev. **34**(3), 319–344 (1991)
3. Erber, R., Erber, M.W.: Beyond mood and social judgment: mood incongruent recall and mood regulation. Eur. J. Soc. Psychol. **24**(1), 79–88 (1994)
4. Ribeiro, R., Trifan, A., Neves, A.J.: Lifelog retrieval from daily digital data: narrative review. JMIR Mhealth Uhealth **10**(5), e30517 (2022)

5. Kinoshita, E., Fujinami, K.: Impressive picture selection from wearable camera toward pleasurable recall of group activities. In: Antona, M., Stephanidis, C. (eds.) Universal Access in Human–Computer Interaction. Human and Technological Environments, UAHCI 2017, LNCS, vol. 10279, pp. 446–456. Springer, Cham (2017). https://doi.org/10.1007/978-3-319-58700-4_36

6. Shigi, M., Ando, M., Otsu, K., Izumi, T.: Laughter map: supporting system for recalling pleasant memories based on the recording and visualization of laughter experiences. In: Kurosu, M., Hashizume, A. (eds.) Human-Computer Interaction, HCII 2023, LNCS, vol. 14012, pp. 279–292. Springer, Cham (2023). https://doi.org/10.1007/978-3-031-35599-8_18

7. Watson, D., Clark, L.A., Tellegen, A.: Development and validation of brief measures of positive and negative affect: the PANAS scales. J. Pers. Soc. Psychol. **54**, 1063–1070 (1988)

8. Tokuda, K.: The validity of temporary mood scale. Inst. Hum. Sci. Ritsumeikan Univ. **22**, 1–6 (2011)

9. Fushimi, R., Fukushima, S., Naemura, T.: Laughin'Cam: active camera system to induce natural smiles. In: CHI 2015 Extended Abstracts on Human Factors in Computing Systems, CHI EA 2015, pp. 1959–1964, Association for Computing Machinery, New York, NY, USA (2015)

10. Tsujita, H., Rekimoto, J.: Smiling makes us happier: enhancing positive mood and communication with smile-encouraging digital appliances, In Proceedings of the 13th International Conference on Ubiquitous Computing, UbiComp'11, pp.1–10, Association for Computing Machinery, New York, NY, USA (2011)

11. Gillick, J., Deng, W., Ryokai, K., Bamman, D.: Robust laughter detection in noisy environments. In: INTERSPEECH 2021, pp. 2481–2485. ISCA, Brno (2021)

12. Sekiguchi, R.: Relationship between subjective properties associated with remembering autobiographical episodic memories, and emotion: Investigation by the subjective properties questionnaire of autobiographical memory. Kansai Univ. Psychol. Res. **3**, 15–26 (2012). (in Japanese)

Vocal Minority Versus Silent Majority: Twitter Data for Greek General Elections and Tweets on German Foreign Policy

Georgios Trachanas[1], Christina Valavani[1,2]([✉]), Christina Alexandris[1,2], and Stavros Giannakis[1,2]

[1] National and Kapodistrian University of Athens, Athens, Greece
cs2210025@di.uoa.gr, cvalavani@hotmail.com, calexandris@gs.uoa.gr
[2] European Communication Institute (ECI), Danube University Krems, Austria and National Technical University of Athens, Athens, Greece

Abstract. The role of a vocal minority versus a silent majority in Sentiment Analysis and Opinion Mining is examined and compared in two cases, namely in a familiar domain of national elections and domestic politics and in a less familiar domain from a different country and language community concerning public opinion in foreign policy. In the first case, the integration of the vocal minority versus silent majority factor in Sentiment Analysis and Opinion Mining generated correct results, corresponding to the national election outcome. In the second case, it is discussed how a smaller "snap shot" dataset produced results reflecting tendencies expressed in politics and public opinion in conjunction to the parameters of the socio-cultural and language community concerned.

Keywords: Sentiment Analysis · Opinion Mining · vocal minority · silent majority · national elections · foreign policy

1 Scope and Approach

The present approach focuses on the role of a vocal minority versus a silent majority in Sentiment Analysis and Opinion Mining in both domestic and foreign politics. In particular, the case of processing and evaluating data from a familiar domain concerning national elections and domestic politics involves the detection, processing and evaluation of the factors of vocal minority versus a silent majority.

In contrast, we present a typical example of processing and evaluating sample data from a less familiar domain concerning public opinion in a different community regarding foreign policy, where lack of sufficient world knowledge may hinder the detection, processing and evaluation of the factors of vocal minority versus a silent majority.

The targeted usage of the Greek General Election data is the analysis of the relation of tweets and election results and the possible prediction of election results with the aid of Twitter.

M. Kurosu and A. Hashizume (Eds.): HCII 2024, LNCS 14684, pp. 389–403, 2024.
https://doi.org/10.1007/978-3-031-60405-8_25

The targeted usage of the smaller dataset of German tweets on foreign policy is the determination of whether a sample - "snap shot" of twitter data may provide correct insights on trends in politics and public opinion to an outsider as an interested party.

However, it is observed that, despite the differences in both the content, relative size and the targeted usage of both cases of twitter data, the processing and evaluation produced correct results. Specifically, in the case of the Greek General Elections, the inclusion of the factors of vocal minority and silent majority rendered percentages that reflected the outcome of the Greek General Elections in 2019.

In the case of the sample German tweets on foreign policy, the evaluation confirms the worries and concerns involving issues on foreign policy such as the Ukraine Crisis/Russo-Ukrainian War, at least within in the subset of the general public that is politically active and/or sensitive to issues in foreign policy.

In this case, it should be taken into consideration that the degree of interest in foreign policy issues may differ between citizens of different countries, especially in countries where there are no immediate or possible threats to national borders and the security of the surround geographical area. Germany and the country's citizens fall into the latter category. Therefore, the determination of public opinion and social trends regarding foreign policy from tweets in German news does not provide an immediate and clear view on whether the opinions expressed are those of a vocal minority and the concerned few or whether they, indeed, reflect to a satisfactory extent, the silent majority. However, as previously stated, the evaluation confirms the worries and concerns involving issues on foreign policy, at least within the community of users involved or actively interested in Politics and Journalism.

The correctness in the results in both cases of twitter data is primarily due to the decisions taken in respect to sampling and quality of data analysis in combination with the vocal minority versus a silent majority factor. In the case of the Greek General Election data, sampling involved the detection, processing and evaluation of the factors of vocal minority versus a silent majority, along with linguistic and socio-cultural parameters depicting positive, negative or neutral opinion. In the case of the German tweets, the samples were based on tweets on German news media platforms, along with linguistic and socio-cultural parameters depicting positive, negative or neutral opinion and irony.

2 The Greek General Elections Data and Sentiment Analysis

The Greek General Election data involves the implementation of a Sentiment Analysis technique for tweet datasets in the Greek language. The case under consideration is datasets related to the 2019 general parliamentary elections in Greece. The elections took place on Sunday 7 July 2019. Of the political parties that participated, six (6) of them were elected members of Parliament (MPs). The Greek political parties are "New Democracy" (Liberal-Conservative, Center-Right Wing), "SYRIZA" (Left Wing), "KINAL-PASOK" (Social-Democratic Party), KKE (the Communist Party), "EllinikiLysi" (Right Wing – Far Right/ Right Wing Populist) and Mera25 (Left Wing - "European Realistic Disobedience Front").

The processing and evaluation concern a lexicon-based technique for sentiment analysis on 5 datasets consisting of tweets. Two approaches have been followed: 1. Sentiment analysis is implemented on each dataset without distinguishing between users posting content. 2. Sentiment analysis is implemented on each dataset after having made the distinction between active and inactive users. Active users ("vocal minority") are those who produce a large amount of content in a short period of time and inactive users ("silent majority") are those who produce little or no content. Each dataset refers to one of the political parties that managed to elect Members of Parliament (MPs) in the 2019 elections. Using this implementation, plausible answers regarding the following research question are targeted: "Is there a correlation between (a) the overall sentiment of a set of election-related tweets and (b) the social trends that characterized the election? And, if so, (c) to what extent does this correlation exist?". This research question was addressed in similar approaches regarding national election results in other countries and language communities [2, 9], including Germany and German voters [10].

Regarding the implementation of the Sentiment Analysis application, the programming language used to write the code for the application is Python [15]. For the graphs presented, the Tableau tool has been used. Tableau [18] is a data visualization and business intelligence software. It allows users to connect to various data sources, including excel spreadsheets, SQL databases, and web services, and then create interactive visualizations, dashboards, and reports [12].

2.1 Datasets

The data used for the implementation comes from Twitter. For the formation of the datasets, the tool "snscrape" has been used. Snscrape [1] is a scraper for social networking services. The Snscrape tool is compatible with several platforms such as Facebook, Twitter, Instagram, Mastodon, Reddit, Telegram, VKontakte and Weibo. As a first step, data collection and processing involve the identification of tweets for each political party. Of all the political parties that participated in the 2019 elections, data was collected only for the 6 that managed to elect members of parliament. The search performed in the present analysis and implementation concerned both specific hashtags as well as specific terms. Specifically, for each political party under study:

1. Tweets were searched based on specific hashtags. If a tweet contains even one hashtag from those searched, then it is stored in the dataset.
2. Tweets were searched based on specific terms. If a tweet includes even one term in its text from those searched, then it is stored in the dataset.

Tweets for each political party from 24/06/2019 to 07/07/2019 (13 days in total), i.e., up to two weeks before the start of the election, are searched for. For each hashtag and term, there is a limit of 10000 tweets, so as not to create huge datasets. It is not impossible to have the same tweets in 2 or more datasets, as there is a possibility that they share the same hashtags or terms. The snscrape tool does not return retweets, i.e., tweets that have been republished by other users. Based on this process, for each political party, two (2) datasets are created which are then merged into one. For each individual political party, a specific search has been performed. We note that the names of Party Leaders and their variations, as well as the Party names and their variations are commonly linked to the Hashtags concerning the respective parties. Mottos including a specific Party name are also linked to the respective Hashtags, as well as particular programs, organizations, and parliament members-politicians [12]. Each tweet can include more than one of the above hashtags. This factor led to the existence of many duplicate tweets, which were, subsequently. Deleted from the respective datasets. Also, the large number of hashtags does not imply many tweets. It is worth noting that, in addition to the name of the political party (in all its Internet variants), a search has been performed based on the name of its political leader and/or other prominent figures. [12].

Each tweet has a unique field, its ID. Before processing, duplicates based on the ID have been removed. The removal of the duplicates results to the respective number of tweets for each political party. Using Python's WordCloud library [16], a wordcloud was formed, with a dataset for the 100 most frequent terms in each dataset. [12].

According to the twitter data collected The New Democracy (ND) party starts from quite low in the number of daily tweets, but from the beginning of the second week of the election period it manages to reach a maximum of 4.933 tweets per day, closing at 3.446 tweets daily one day before the elections. The SYRIZA party (SYRIZA) starts from even lower numbers than the New Democracy (ND) party, but in the 2nd week of the election it manages to make a spectacular shift, approaching 6131 tweets (its maximum) and closing at the top with 4398 tweets the day before the elections. The other political parties (KKE, KINAL-PASOK, EllinikiLysi, Mera25) are limited to low numbers, failing to exceed 1000 tweets a day, with a few exceptions of KINAL-PASOK, which has the lead in this set of parties. The last place is occupied by EllinikiLysi's party with a maximum number of daily tweets with a maximum of 200 tweets. Unfortunately, no conclusions can be reached regarding the location of published tweets, as few users have set a clear and precise location. If similar information were available, an estimate of the sentiment of tweets for all prefectures of the Greek territory would be possible. This information would be quite useful in case we wanted to estimate the social trends of the elections by prefecture and region, beyond the total territory of the country.

The preprocessing process involves a series of techniques for noise reduction in data input. An important and often used preprocessing technique is the removal of stop words. However, it was decided not to remove the stop words of the Greek language, because the original text would become even more difficult for syntactic and morphological analysis. Correct verification of syntactic and morphological rules is an auxiliary factor in the natural language processing task implemented in the present research. The implementation used is a lexicon-based approach, comprising two basic steps, namely, creating the emotional lexicons and scanning the texts for each dataset. The lexicon-based approach concerns the detection and processing of three (3) typical and characteristic categories of linguistic data expressing sentiment and overall attitude towards a political party (in Greece), in particular: Mottos (typical of specific political parties in Greece), Negative statements with the use of negation, Characteristic expressions with irony [12]. If a negation exists, a method is taken to perform lexicon analysis for the negation. After processing, the total polarity and sentiment of the text are calculated as a component of the emotionally charged terms present in the text. At the end, the results for each dataset are gathered.

In regard to the creation of emotional lexicons, two lexicons have been created in Greek, one with positively charged terms and the other with negatively charged terms. As a basis for the two (2) dictionaries, the ones available in [17] are used. At this reference, dictionaries of positive and negative terms are available for 81 languages. The dictionaries used in the application were then enriched with terms from the dictionary in [6]. This is sentiment dictionary, which has been exploited in another sentiment analysis application in R programming language [6] for the Greek language. In parallel, by reading and manually estimating the texts of the tweets, we collected other useful terms for extending and enriching our dictionaries. We also added words that are politics oriented and have specific emotional content for someone who is familiar with the Greek political scene - politically charged words that have been considered to assess the sentiment of each tweet. Processing included the use of the NLP toolkit in [14]is based on [8] and is the current most complete implementation for the case of the Greek language. Since the existing Python libraries for Greek language processing produced several errors in the lemmatization process [10] affecting the accuracy of our model, correction strategies were determined and deployed [12].

Finally, after parsing all the words of the tweet and assessing the existence of negation, the overall sentiment of the tweet is calculated, based on the formula depicted in Fig. 1:

$$Overall\ polarity = \frac{\#positive\ terms\ found\ in\ the\ text - \#negative\ terms\ found\ in\ the\ text}{\#terms\ that\ make\ up\ the\ text}$$

Fig. 1. Calculation of tweet sentiment [12].

where: #positive terms found in the text = sum of all positive terms found in the text, #negative terms found in the text = sum of all negative terms found in the text, #terms that make up the text = number of tweet's terms before preprocessing.

Based on this, three (3) different values are obtained for the results: if overall polarity > 0, then the sentiment of the tweet is positive. If overall polarity < 0, then the sentiment of the tweet is negative. If overall polarity = 0, then the sentiment of the tweet is neutral. This calculation treats each term as equal in its contribution to the estimation of the sentiment of the text, regardless of its intensity. In other words, for example, although the adjective "worst" in Greek expresses a negative emotion of greater intensity than the adjective "bad" in Greek, it is valued in the same way in the calculation of the overall emotion. In an extension of the present application, a "weight" factor indicating the intensity of the corresponding emotion could be added. After the sentiment calculation has been implemented for all tweets in a dataset, the total number of positive, negative and neutral tweets is calculated for each political party candidate and output result in a different dataset.

3   The "One Tweet One Vote Approach"

With the "one tweet one vote" approach, we make the following assumption: each tweet is the product of the publication of a different-separate account. For example, we assume that if we have 30000 tweets, then 30000 different accounts participate in this network. This approach is simpler to implement, as it does not distinguish users based on their activity but considers them equal. It does not fully correspond to the real-life situation and "departs" from reality for reasons that will be explained below. Apart from positive/negative/neutral tweets, in our implementation we also use a number of other data for sentiment analysis such as the number of "likes" and retweets of a tweet, the ratio of positive/negative tweets overall for a political party.

In the "one tweet, one vote" approach, the case of "likes" and retweets does not fully confirm the outcome of the election. In both cases (total and average), SYRIZA is first in the ranking and with a difference compared to the others, which can be explained by the fact that it was in government before the election result. We are able to conclude that "likes" and retweets (in absolute number and percentage) are a measure of popularity for those who post the tweets, without specifying its content (whether it is negative, positive or neutral). In other words, the more retweets and "likes" the tweets that have a reference to an entity or organization accumulate, the more popular it is within the network. Thus, they can be a safe criterion for detecting and assessing social trends. However, we cannot draw safe conclusions about election results based on these factors. The graph in Fig. 1 shows a complete picture of the overall sentiment of tweets regarding political parties. For this, we need to dwell on some observations-conclusions: SYRIZA is the political party that gathers the most tweets of negative sentiment, almost twice as many as positive tweets. This fact is indicative of the social trends expressed in the 2019 general elections. SYRIZA was defeated in the election and came in 2nd place. ND has the most positive tweets. This data is indicative of the social trends expressed in the 2019 elections, as ND emerged victorious in 1st place. Considering that each positive tweet is considered a positive vote for the respective political party, the sub-graph of positive tweets confirms the ranking in the 2019 election results for 4 first political parties.

All political parties, regardless of the number of tweets they collect, have a relatively similar quota of positive, negative and neutral tweets. Neutral tweets are first in number and percentage, followed by negative and then positive tweets. Also, their growth throughout the election period, as shown in Fig. 2, follows a similar rate. From this data we can draw the following conclusions: It is true that a large volume of tweets come from news sites that produce informative content, which is most often of neutral sentiment. Based on this fact, the predominance of neutral tweets for all political parties is justified. It is observed, based on the predominance of negative tweets over positive ones, that the use of twitter is more for negative criticism and denunciation of an organization or entity than to endorse and/or support its position or stance. This phenomenon is more pronounced in the debate on twitter about political issues, which can be observed from a close reading of the datasets. The negative tweets are dominated by the mood of criticism and trolling towards the respective political organization or entity. The ND and KKE parties have the highest percentage of positive tweets. This fact confirms the result of the elections, as on the one hand ND came out victorious, increasing its electoral percentage, while on the other hand KKE had the smallest percentage losses compared to the other parties. The EllinikiLysi and SYRIZA parties have the highest percentage of negative tweets. In general, on twitter the EllinikiLysi party does not have a high visibility and appeal, having an audience from social categories that do not use this social media. SYRIZA has a high percentage of negative tweets, which is confirmed by its defeat in the elections and its loss of votes.

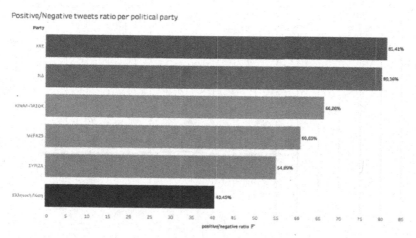

Positive/Negative tweets ratio per political party

Fig. 2. Positive/negative tweets ratio per political party ["one tweet, one vote"] [12]

Another metric that could be used to compare the results is the ratio of positive/negative tweets for each political party. This metric enables us to compare results between datasets that differ in size. We reach the following conclusions and observations: The KKE and ND parties have a fairly good positive/negative ratio. For about every 8 positives we have 10 negatives. Clearly, this result once again confirms the social trends expressed in the elections, with ND emerging victorious and the KKE having the smallest losses compared to other parties. The SYRIZA party has a fairly low percentage, with only 1 positive tweet for every 2 negative ones. This confirms the result, as this party suffered a defeat and fell to 2nd place.

A characteristic example of sentiment-charged words and expressions from the data is the positively-charged term "αυτοδυναμία" (absolute parliamentary majority), far superior in frequency (1466 times) to other positively sentiment-charged terms. The two most common characteristic examples of negatively charged terms with the highest frequency are the negative diminutives of the first name of the then leader of the opposition, Kyriakos Mitsotakis [12] (Fig. 3).

Number of tweets per political party

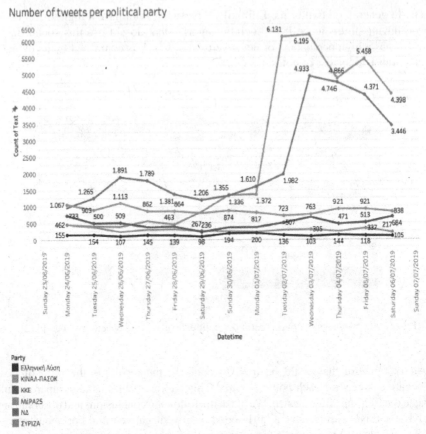

Fig. 3. Number of tweets per political party in general approach

4 Vocal Minority Versus Silent Majority

Since social media users do not have equal participation in network platforms [7] and users display different online behavior, two main user groups are distinguished. They are based mainly on the rate of content production, the vocal minority, which produces many tweets and is composed of a few users, and the silent majority, which instead produces little or no content, but involves many users. In terms of the structure of tweets, the vocal minority produces tweets more with links, mentions, hashtags, with the purpose of spreading opinions widely, unlike the silent minority, which has no such purpose. The behavior of the vocal minority is more similar to the behavior of media, political, official or unofficial supporters of political parties. Any attempt to analyze for datasets with such characteristics should consider the different characteristics and different user groups that are, objectively, shaped by their Twitter usage. For this reason, sentiment analysis was performed in two phases: 1) phase 1 approaches users as equals (i.e. that they produce equal content) 2) and 2) phase 2 approaches users based on the number of tweets they have posted during the election period and separates them into vocal minority and silent majority. For phase 2, a threshold equal to 26 tweets in total has been, subjectively, selected. This means that, if a user has posted more than 26 tweets in the 13 days of the election period, he/she is included in the vocal minority. Otherwise, he/she is included in the silent majority. In both phase's 2 approaches, apart from the positive/negative/neutral tweets, in our implementation we use a number of other data for sentiment analysis such as the number of "likes" and retweets of a tweet, the ratio of positive/negative tweets overall for a political party.

4.1 Vocal Minority

In the "vocal minority" approach, we have similar results for political parties to the "one tweet, one vote" approach in both absolute numbers and percentage terms. Once again, SYRIZA manages to come out 1st party in "likes" and retweets, reiterating that these data do not express negative or positive sentiment, but are an indicator of popularity. And in the case of the vocal minority, the SYRIZA party is first in terms of "likes" and retweets, either in absolute number or percentage.

The picture of the overall sentiment of tweets regarding political parties for the vocal minority approach involves the following observations-conclusions: The SYRIZA party is in 1st place in the tweets of negative sentiment. However, in this case, it manages to significantly reduce the difference from ND. Specifically, in the "one tweet, one vote" case, the difference between SYRIZA and ND is 2,762 tweets, while in the vocal minority, the difference is reduced to only 470 tweets. Once again, the defeat of SYRIZA in the elections is confirmed. The ND party has the most positive tweets, widening the gap with SYRIZA. In the case of the "one tweet, one vote" approach, the difference between ND and SYRIZA is 944 tweets, while in the vocal minority it is 1,103 positive tweets. In this case too, however, the ND's lead in the elections is verified. In the case of the vocal minority, assuming that each positive tweet is considered a positive vote for the respective political party, the sub-signature of positive tweets confirms the ranking in the 2019 election results for 4 first political parties. All political parties, regardless of the number of tweets they collect, demonstrate a relatively similar quota of positive, negative and neutral tweets and in the case of the "vocal minority" [12]. Neutral tweets are first in number and percentage, followed by negative and finally positive tweets in this case as well. Also, the growth of all tweets throughout the election period follows a similar rate. From this data we can draw the following conclusions: The ND party has a lead also in this case in positive tweets. Next comes the KKE. Once again, the social trend expressed in the elections of 2019 for these political parties is confirmed [12].

4.2 Silent Majority

In the case of the "silent majority", for the data of "likes" and retweets, we have the same ranking as the other two approaches (general, vocal minority). Once again, SYRIZA manages to come out 1st party in "likes" and retweets, reiterating that these data do not express negative or positive sentiment, but are an indicator of popularity. The SYRIZA party is first in terms of "likes" and retweets, either in absolute number or a percentage, in the case of "silent majority". The overall sentiment of tweets regarding political parties for the silent majority approach is summarized in the following observations-conclusions: The SYRIZA party is in 1st place in the tweets of negative sentiment. In this case, however, the difference increases by far compared to the case of the "vocal minority". In particular, it reaches 2,292 negative tweets, while in the case of the "vocal minority", the difference between SYRIZA and ND was 470 negative tweets. The SYRIZA party manages to take the lead in positive tweets, reversing what we have observed in the other 2 approach cases. It manages to get a difference of 159 positive tweets.

All political parties, regardless of the number of tweets they collect, show a relatively similar quota of positive, negative and neutral tweets and in the case of the "silent majority". Neutral tweets are first in number and percentage, followed by negative and finally positive tweets in this case as well. From this data we can draw the following conclusions-estimates: The ND party is first in percentage terms in terms of positive tweets. This data confirms the social upward trends that ND had in the 2019 elections. In the case of silent majority, it has some differences in terms of comparison based on the positive/negative ratio metric. In particular, we proceed to the following conclusions-observations: The ND party emerges 1st in this approach with a slightly smaller percentage, taking this position from the KKE. Approximately, for every 8 positive tweets, we have 10 negative tweets [12].

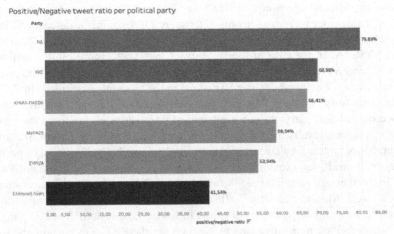

Fig. 4. Positive/negative tweets ratio per political party [Silent majority] [12]

5 Sampling German Twitter Data on Foreign Policy – Vocal Minority or Silent Majority?

In contrast to the Greek General Election data, the German tweets are a typical example of processing and evaluating sample data from a less familiar domain concerning public opinion in a different community regarding foreign policy. For an interested outsider, the lack of/limited language skills in German and/or insufficient exposure to German socio-cultural elements may not provide sufficient information for the detection, processing and evaluation of the factors of vocal minority versus a silent majority.

In this case, the targeted usage of the smaller dataset of German tweets on foreign policy is the option of providing a sample-"snap shot" of twitter data which is, however, as observed in the present case, sufficient enough for allowing correct information reflecting trends in politics and public opinion to an outsider. It is worth considering that an interested party not familiar with the German language and culture may not easily have access to the remarkable size of German twitter data and respective tools [3, 11, 13], especially if the interested party is a non-expert in Natural Language Processing systems.

The sample- "snap shot" of twitter data is extracted from German news media plat-forms. The annotation of "positive", "negative" and "neutral" tweets, as well as instances of Irony is based on linguistic and socio-cultural parameters. These parameters concern the detection and processing of specific words and expressions with inherent connota-tive features or specific words and expressions that are positively or negatively charged, depending on the domain type (in this case, Politics and Journalism) and the current state-of-affairs in politics and public life and public opinion. In contrast to the Greek data, where opinions and support were usually clearly expressed and are linked to specific slogans, topics and expressions, these features were mostly absent and different types of word categories and expressions were linked to "positive", "negative" (or "neutral") tweets.

The German data is of 2600 tweets extracted from popular mainstream news plat-forms. In the particular data set, tweets that were either classified as "neutral" or not evidently "positive" or "negative" constituted the majority of the data set. In this case, these tweet categories were observed to compatible to the majority of reactions and opinions voiced in the media in regard to German foreign policy (the issue of support with military means/hardware) - whether directly or indirectly linked to the Ukraine Cri-sis/ Russo-Ukrainian War. In particular, 16% of the data set was classified as "positive" tweets, 47,7% as "negative" tweets and 36,3% as "neutral" tweets.

Although the data is not considered to have a satisfactory size for efficient Machine Learning –especially since it involves non-binary values (positive/negative/neutral), it indicates that such a size may sufficient enough to provide a correct/satisfactory "snap shot" of the tendencies in public opinion, under specific conditions. Specifically, (a) the samples are from a reliable source and (b) they are correctly processed.

In regard to requirement (b), detection –identification and evaluation was performed by German native speakers and/or near-native speakers with a life-time / long time exposure to German culture and society. We also note that for the language-pair English-German, the GoogleTranslate online machine translation system produced output rather close to the original content and information.

In the twitter data set, characteristic examples of negatively marked words are word categories expressing negative behavior and attitude such as "lie(s)", "fairy tales", "con-fused", "nonsense" and "ridiculous" (Examples 1–4 in Fig. 4) as well as expressions related to speech such as "inform yourself" and "open your mouth" (Example 5 in Fig. 4). On the other hand, word categories expressing positive behavior and attitude such as "like", "trust" and "thank" define positive tweets, with the condition that there are no negations or other elements linked to contradiction in their context [11]. In the case of Example 7 in Fig. 4, the combination of "funny" and "headline" express domain-specific irony (in a different domain, this combination may be considered positive). Another type of pointers to irony are out-of-domain named entities and expressions (Example 8 in Fig. 4).

---

(1) wer diese Lügerei immer noch glaubt dem kann man nicht mehr helfen.
[GoogleTranslate: If you still believe this lie, you can't help it anymore]

(2) Wieder verwechselt. Frieden ist der Zustand, wo die Leute einfach leben. Das, was die U(S)A gewinnen will, das ist Krieg. Dabei sterben täglich Menschen und nur dafür braucht es Waffen und Munition.
[GoogleTranslate: Confused again. Peace is the state where people just live. What the U(S)A wants to win is war. People are dying every day and only for that you need weapons and ammunition]

(3) Diesen Schwachsinn soll jemand glauben? Die Erfinder solcher Märchenglauben wir sind dümmer als die es sind. Dabei machen sich die Amis nur noch lächerlich!
[GoogleTranslate: Anyone believe this nonsense? The inventors of such fairy tales believe we are dumber than they are. The Americans only make themselves ridiculous!]

(4) Jetzt wird es aber wirklich lächerlich.
[GoogleTranslate: But now it gets really ridiculous.]

(5) Welches Land besitzt ihrer Meinung nach Langstreckenraketen? Und was sind Langstreckenraketen überhaupt? Informieren sie sich erstmal, bevor sie den Mund aufmachen!
[GoogleTranslate: Which country do you think has long-range missiles? And what are long-range missiles anyway? Find out more before you open your mouth!]

(6) Ich sage es gerne. SIE HATTEN WIEDER RECHT. Danke Herr Masala für ihre Einschätzungen. Das gleiche gilt übrigens auch für Claudia Major. Ich traue nur ihnen beiden. Ein großer Dank.
[GoogleTranslate: I like to say it. YOU WERE RIGHT AGAIN. Thank you Mr. Masala for your assessment. Incidentally, the same applies to Claudia Major. I only trust you two. A big thank you.]

(7) Das ist mal eine echt witzige Schlagzeile! Ich lache mich gerade echt kaputt! Danke
[GoogleTranslate: That's a really funny headline! I'm laughing my @ss off right now! Thanks]

(8) Die Beatles mit ihrem Yellow Submarine waren es.
[GoogleTranslate: It was the Beatles with their Yellow Submarine.]

Fig. 5. Example of German tweets and unedited output of the GoogleTranslate machine translation platform.

In regard to requirement (a), it is observed that the percentages gained from the processing and evaluation of the data confirms the worries and concerns involving issues on foreign policy such as the Ukraine Crisis/ Russo-Ukrainian War –at least from the majority of the user groups "visible" in social media platforms of German "mainstream" media. In particular, as stated above, for an interested party from the international community, the question of whether tweets in German news express opinions of a vocal

(11) Keine Sorge, die Wartung und Pflege muss man ihnen nicht beibringen, auch am kompliziertem landen wird gespart.Wird nen 1 way Ticket
[GoogleTranslate: Don't worry, you don't have to teach them how to maintain and care for them, and you save even on the more complicated landings. There will be a 1-way ticket]

(12) Ob Scholz nein sagt oder nicht, wird an der Lieferung zum Glück nichts ändern!
[GoogleTranslate:Fortunately, whether Scholz says no or not will not change anything about the delivery!]

Fig. 6. Examples from the majority of German tweets, not evidently "positive" or "negative" and unedited output of the GoogleTranslate machine translation platform.

minority and the concerned few or whether they reflect to a satisfactory extent, the silent majority is a factor that should be taken into account (Figs. 5 and 6).

Unlike other countries within Europe or outside Europe, Germany and the country's citizens are not, under the present circumstances, a case where there are immediate or possible threats to national borders and the security of the surrounding geographical area. Therefore, the factor of an unquestionably high or an unquestionably low degree of interest in foreign policy issues for the general public - and not for the vocal minority and the concerned few- should not be taken for granted. A safer indication would be the opinion of the vocal/silent majority of the community of users – citizens, officials and professionals alike- involved or actively interested in Politics and Journalism and voicing their opinions in popular mainstream news platforms.

From the available data, the sampling and processing strategies employed allow non-native users from the international community to gather correct and satisfactory insights on social tends – with limited access to large amounts of data and limited time. Thus, with limited input and saving time, on-the-spot input can be obtained and evaluated. Therefore, for the domain and natural language (German) concerned, it can be noted that a relatively limited amount of data may be enough to gain a correct insight and can reflect the majority of opinions and attitudes regarding social trends. This majority is, at least, within the community of users involved or actively interested in Politics and Journalism.

6 Conclusions and Further Research

The role of a vocal minority versus a silent majority in Sentiment Analysis and Opinion Mining in both domestic and foreign politics was examined in two cases of processing and evaluating data from a familiar "insider" domain and from a perspective of an "outsider" international interested party. In particular, we presented two examples that produced correct results, one from tweets regarding German foreign policy and the Ukraine Crisis /Russo-Ukrainian War - from the perspective of an "outsider" international interested party- and one from Greek parliament elections – the familiar "insider" domain.

It is observed that the case of the Greek General Elections, the inclusion of the factors of vocal minority and silent majority rendered percentages that reflected the outcome of the Greek General Elections in 2019. Specifically, in regard to the twitter data from the Greek General Elections in 2019, correlations are observed between feelings expressed on social media about elections and the social trends expressed in the same elections.

Additionally, relations are observed between tweet metrics and votes. Some metrics such as the positive/negative ratio and the quota between positive/negative and neutral tweets allow us to compare datasets of disparate size with each other and draw safe conclusions. However, there are limitations of Twitter and Social Media for predicting election outcome for a number of reasons, for example, social media is not fully utilized by all citizens who make up the electorate. As a result, the data collected covers relatively and not fully the electoral preferences of citizens. Furthermore, Social Media accounts, like twitter, do not show the same activity. For example, there are simple users on one side and large news agencies on the other posting on the same topics.

For the Greek Election data, the basic challenges confronted involve both the nature and content of the Greek language and the nature of the content of a text on Twitter. Typical difficulties and challenges encountered concern issues concerning the efficiency of existing NLP tools to tackle complex input, such as politically-charged tweets, as well as the scarcity of efficient resources such as Sentiment Lexicons and dictionaries for emotionally charged phrases, annotated (labeled) data for Sentiment Analysis in Greek. Other challenges encountered that were managed include Polysemy, contexts of words, Irony and Negation, among others [12].

In the case of the sample German tweets on foreign policy, the evaluation confirms the worries and concerns involving issues on foreign policy such as the Ukraine Crisis/ Russo-Ukrainian War, at least within in the subset of the general public that is politically active and/or sensitive to issues in foreign policy and expresses opinions on main stream media.

The case of the sample German tweets on foreign policy calls for an additional factor to be taken into consideration when processing twitter data: The degree of interest. Foreign policy issues may vary in respect to the degree of interest between citizens of different countries, and, subsequently, tweets may not provide an immediate and clear view on whether the opinions expressed are those of a vocal minority and the concerned few or whether they, indeed, reflect to a satisfactory extent, the silent majority.

The correctness in the results in both cases of twitter data is due to above-presented conditions in respect to sampling and correct data analysis and processing, in combination with the vocal minority versus a silent majority factor. However, the development of an effective method for managing irony and sarcasm remains a challenge for both languages concerned.

Further research will investigate whether correct/ satisfactory insights on current political trends in both domestic and foreign politics can be obtained with relatively small sizes of data, used as samples –"snap shots" which can be merged and/or enriched with additional samples, thus creating a series of –"snap shot" input.

References

1. Beck, M.: How to Scrape Tweets With snscrape, Medium. 05 Jan 2022. https://betterprogra mming.pub/how-to-scrape-tweets-with-snscrape-90124ed006af. Accessed 6 Jan 2024
2. Budiharto, W., Meiliana, M.: Prediction and analysis of indonesia presidential election from Twitter using sentiment analysis. J. Big Data 5(1), 1–10 (2018)

3. Fehle, J., Schmidt, T., Wolff, C.: Lexicon-based sentiment analysis in German: Systematic evaluation of resources and preprocessing techniques. In: Evang, K., Kallmeyer, L., Osswald, R., Waszczuk, J., Zesch, T. (eds.) 17th Conference on Natural Language Processing (KONVENS 2021), pp. 86–103. KONVENS 2021 Organizers, Duesseldorf, Germany (2021)

4. Jurafsky, D., Martin, J.H.: Speech and language processing, an introduction to natural language processing, computational linguistics and speech recognition. 2nd edition, Prentice Hall series in Artificial Intelligence, Pearson Education, Upper Saddle River, NJ, (2008)

5. Jurafsky, D., Martin, J.H.: Speech and language processing, an introduction to natural language processing, computational linguistics and speech recognition. 3rd ed. (2022). Draft:https://web.stanford.edu/~jurafsky/slp3/ed3book_jan122022.pdf. Accessed 10 Jan 2024

6. Krystallis, N.: Greek-sentiment analysis. https://github.com/NKryst/Greek-Sentiment Analysis/blob/master/Files/Greek%20Sentiment%20Lexicon/Fixed_Greek_Lexicon.xlsx. Accessed 10 Jan 2024

7. Mustafaraj, E., Finn, S., Whitlock, C.: Metaxas: vocal minority versus silent majority: discovering the opinions of the long tail. In: IEEE Third International Conference on Privacy, Security, Risk and Trust and IEEE Third International Conference on Social Computing (2011). https://doi.org/10.1109/passat/socialcom.2011.188. Accessed 10 Jan 2024

8. Prokopidis P., Piperidis, S.: A neural NLP toolkit for Greek. In: Proceedings of the 11th Hellenic Conference on Artificial Intelligence (2020). https://doi.org/10.1145/3411408.341 1430

9. Sharma, P., Moh, T-S. : Prediction of Indian Election Using Sentiment Analysis on Hindi twitter. In: IEEE International Conference on Big Data (big data), pp. 1966–1971. Washington, DC, USA (2016)

10. Schmidt, T., Fehle, J., Weissenbacher, M., Richter, J., Gottschalk, P., Wolff, C.: Sentiment analysis on Twitter for the major German parties during the 2021 German federal election. In: Proceedings of the 18th Conference on Natural Language Processing (KONVENS 2022), pp. 74–87 (2022). Potsdam, Germany. KONVENS 2022 Organizers

11. Schmidt, T., Dangel, J., Wolff, C.: Senttext: a tool for lexicon-based sentiment analysis in digital humanities. In: Thomas Schmidt and Christian Wolff, editors, Information Science and its Neighbors from Data Science to Digital Humanities. Proceedings of the 16th International Symposium of Information Science (ISI 2021), vol. 74, pp. 156–172. Werner Huelsbusch, Glueckstadt (2021)

12. Trachanas, G.: Sentiment analysis on Twitter data and social trends: the case of greek general elections. Master's thesis, Department of Informatics and Telecommunications, National University of Athens, Greece (2023)

13. Tymann, K, Lutz, M., Palsbroeker, P., Gips, C.: Gervader-a german adaptation of the vader sentiment analysis tool for social media texts. In: LWDA, pp. 178–189 (2019)

14. A Neural NLP toolkit for Greek. http://nlp.ilsp.gr/nws/. Accessed 10 Jan 2024

15. Python Wikipedia contributors, python (programming language), Wikipedia. https://en.wik ipedia.org/wiki/Python_(programming_language. Accessed 10 Jan 2024

16. WordCloud for Python documentation — wordcloud 1.8.1 documentation, amueller.github.io. https://amueller.github.io/word_cloud/. Accessed 10 Jan 2024

17. Sentiment Lexicons for 81 Languages (updated by Rachel Tatman). https://www.kaggle.com/datasets/rtatman/sentiment-lexicons-for-81-languages. Accessed 10 Jan 2024

18. Tableau software Wikipedia contributors, Tableau software, Wikipedia. https://en.wikipedia.org/wiki/Tableau_Software. Accessed 10 Jan 2024

Emotionally Intelligent Conversational User Interfaces: Bridging Empathy and Technology in Human-Computer Interaction

Anjelika Votintseva[✉], Rebecca Johnson, and Iva Villa

Siemens AG, Friedrich-Ludwig-Bauer-Str. 3, 85748 Garching, Germany
anjelika.votintseva@siemens.com

Abstract. In our paper we explore the convergence of Conversational User Interfaces, personality psychology, artificial intelligence, and rapid prototyping with prompt engineering as its central component. This research delves into the field of empathic computing, aiming to equip technology with the ability to understand and respond to human emotions. Empathic computing represents a significant shift in Human-Computer Interaction, aiming to imbue technology with the capacity to understand and respond to human emotions. Our contribution involves a multi-pronged approach that integrates user research through interactive workshops, rapid prototyping with no-code platforms, personality & emotion research. By empowering technology to comprehend and adapt to human sentiment, empathic computing holds the promise of making interactions with computers more intuitive, emotionally resonant, and engaging, which is crucial for a number of application domains.

Keywords: Conversational User Interface · Empathic Computing · Prototyping · User Research

1 Introduction

Human-Computer Interaction (HCI) has undergone a remarkable evolution since its inception, transforming from basic interface design to a complex field that intertwines technology, psychology, and user experience. The early days of HCI were primarily focused on making computers accessible and functional, with an emphasis on efficiency and ergonomics. This era was characterized by command-line interfaces and basic graphical user interfaces, where the primary goal was to facilitate straightforward tasks and enhance productivity.

As technology advanced, so did the scope of HCI. The advent of the internet and mobile computing introduced new dimensions to HCI, emphasizing not just functionality, but also engagement and user satisfaction. This shift led to the development of more intuitive and visually appealing interfaces, as seen in modern operating systems, websites, and mobile apps. The interaction between users and computers became more dynamic, incorporating multimedia elements and touch-based interactions.

M. Kurosu and A. Hashizume (Eds.): HCII 2024, LNCS 14684, pp. 404–422, 2024.
https://doi.org/10.1007/978-3-031-60405-8_26

In our ever-changing digital landscape, the way we interact with technology is undergoing a paradigm shift. The emergence of Conversational User Interfaces (CUIs) is redefining this interaction by allowing us to communicate with technology in natural language. Whether it's voice assistants, chatbots or virtual agents, conversational user interfaces are overcoming the limitations of traditional interfaces and making technology more accessible, efficient and intuitive.

In recent years, the field of HCI has been increasingly focusing on a more holistic understanding of the user. This includes considering emotional, cognitive, and social aspects of human-computer interaction. A significant portion of human communication is non-verbal. According to research, including the well-known work of Dr. Albert Mehrabian [10], non-verbal cues can account for a large percentage of the overall message in personal communication. Mehrabian's study suggested that about 55% of communication is through non-verbal elements like facial expressions and body language, 38% through tone of voice, and only 7% through actual spoken words. However, it's important to note that this can vary greatly depending on the context and the nature of the interaction. Herein lies the emergence of empathic computing, a paradigm that seeks to imbue technology with the ability to understand and interpret all communication channels with the focus on non-verbal ones, considering human emotions as an important enhancement for the incoming information.

Empathic computing represents a significant leap in HCI, as it aims to create more intuitive, engaging, and human-centric technology. The growing importance of empathic computing is underscored by the contemporary demand for technology that can adapt to and understand the user's emotional state. This demand is driven by the realization that emotional intelligence is crucial for creating more meaningful and effective human-computer interactions. In the context of CUIs, this evolution means transitioning from systems that merely understand commands to ones that can interpret and respond to the nuances of human emotions and social cues.

Our research contributes to this evolution. We explore how the CUIs techniques can be effectively supported by personality psychology and artificial intelligence to create interfaces that not only understand the user's instructions but also their emotional state. This paper delves into the intricacies of empathic computing explaining its different facets and their interplay. We also demonstrate how the integration of prototyping techniques, with prompt engineering as an enrichment of no-code rapid prototyping, can contribute to the development of emotionally intelligent conversational interfaces. By doing so, we aim to bridge the gap between humans with their empathy and technology with its efficiency, making interactions with computers even more user-centered, more emotionally resonant and, thus, more engaging, and natural.

2 Related Work

The progress in technologies that recognize human emotions is a key development in empathic computing, which aims to make machines more attuned to human feelings. As an example, [6] discusses empathic computing as an emergent paradigm that enables a system to understand human states and feelings and to share this intimate information. It also covers the convergence of affordable sensors, embedded processors, and wireless ad-hoc networks that make this paradigm possible. Experts have been closely examining how machines that converse with us can better understand the complex ways we express emotions. Recognizing the subtle hints of how we feel and considering the situation in which emotions are expressed are important steps in this process.

Expanding on this, the research conducted by Poria et al. [17] has made significant contributions to the field of Emotion Recognition in Conversation (ERC) within Natural Language Processing (NLP). They particularly highlight the development of emotion-shift recognition models and context encoders, which have shown promising results in enhancing AI interactions in both informal and task-oriented dialogues. The ability of these models to accurately identify changes in emotional states and understand conversational context is crucial for creating AI systems that can engage more naturally and empathetically with users.

In their analysis, Poria et al. highlight several key challenges that persist in the field of ERC. A principal concern they raise is the accurate recognition of emotions at an individual level in scenarios involving multiple participants as it requires distinguishing and interpreting the emotional states of each speaker accurately. Another significant challenge identified is the detection of sarcasm in conversations. The complexity of recognizing sarcasm in conversation lies in the need to understand not only the literal meaning of words but also the intent and tone behind them.

Multimodal Emotion Recognition. In our exploration of human emotion recognition, we draw upon the insightful work of Abdullah et al. [18], who have made significant strides in the multimodal identification of emotions using deep learning techniques. Their research serves as a foundational pillar in our understanding of how various biological signals can be harnessed to detect emotional states with enhanced accuracy.

Abdullah et al. have shed light on the multifaceted nature of human communication, which is loaded with emotional content. They discuss how different speech styles, from facial expressions to the tone of voice and even physiological responses such as breathing patterns and skin temperature, are imbued with emotional information. Notably, they emphasize that often the true message lies not in the spoken words but in the expression of these words.

Their findings are particularly intriguing when considering the temporal aspect of emotional responses, which can manifest in physiological signals within a brief window of approximately 3 to 15 s [19]. Their work is instrumental in informing the direction of our research, particularly in the pursuit of a nuanced understanding and classification of consumer emotions.

Facial Emotion Detection Using Deep Learning. A key observation from recent studies is the significantly high accuracy rates in emotion detection, suggesting that machines are progressively becoming more adept at interpreting human emotions. This advancement is a step towards more natural and intuitive interactions between humans and machines. However, a prevalent limitation in current Facial Emotion Recognition (FER) systems is their focus primarily on the six basic emotions (sadness, happiness, fear, anger, surprise and disgust) [20], plus a neutral state. This approach does not fully encompass the wide range of complex emotions present in everyday life, which includes a spectrum of secondary emotions.

The challenge lies in the FER systems' ability to detect and interpret these subtle and compound emotional states. In real-world scenarios, individuals often experience and express a blend of emotions that can change rapidly and are influenced by context, personal experiences, and cultural background. The recognition of these secondary emotions is crucial for developing FER systems that can accurately mirror the complexity of human emotional understanding and responses [21].

Emotionally Intelligent Conversational Agents. Emohaa, a Chinese conversational agent designed specifically for mental health support, is a pioneering work in the integration of emotional support systems and the evaluation of emotional awareness [22]. Emohaa integrates a specialized platform for emotional support, allowing users to openly discuss their emotional issues. This aspect of Emohaa was carefully evaluated to determine its efficacy in reducing mental distress among participants. The results from this evaluation were quite promising, indicating a notable reduction in symptoms related to mental distress, such as depression, negative affect, and insomnia. Particularly intriguing was the observed benefit on long-term insomnia using Emohaa's generative dialogue platform for emotional support. These findings not only highlight the effectiveness of Emohaa as a mental health tool but also illustrate the broader potential of generative conversational agents in the field of mental health support.

Rathje et al. [23] explored the efficacy of the latest versions of the large language model GPT (3.5 and 4) in automated text analysis. Their study spans an impressive range of 12 different datasets, encompassing various text types and languages. GPT showed superior performance over traditional English-language dictionary methods, particularly in sentiment analysis and discrete emotion detection, often rivaling or even surpassing fine-tuned machine learning models.

The Role of Emotions in Human-Computer Interaction. Several publications and research papers discuss the role of emotions in HCI. Here are some references to existing literature on this topic and a brief explanation of their content. Wadley et al. [7] discuss the various traditions and interests in studying emotion in human-computer interaction, such as sensing, expressing, modeling, and understanding emotions. They also address questions about the relationships between digital technology and human emotion, the implications of emotion research for design, ethics, and wellbeing, and the future of emotion in human-computer interaction. Liu et al. [8] explore the challenging task of emotion assessment in the human-computer interaction interface and discuss the relationship between emotions and human-computer interaction. Ch. Peter and G. Blyth [9] mention research on the role of emotion in HCI and how to support emotions in an effective approach. These references provide insights into the various aspects of emotions in human-computer interaction, including their assessment, implications, and future directions.

3 Research Methodology

Our research methodology is grounded in a multi-faceted approach that integrates various elements and steps in the development of an emotional CUI, including scientific research of the existing results in the area of personality and emotions, prototyping for the early evaluation of selected use cases, and user research within interactive workshops. This methodology is designed to explore and demonstrate the effectiveness of emotionally intelligent CUIs.

Personality and Emotion Research. A crucial part of our methodology was the in-depth study of personality psychology and emotion theory. The results of this research informed the design of our avatars and the development of scenarios about the different possibilities to detect emotions from human users and to generate emotional responses for the artificial counterpart. This research also proposed different ways to define personalities of avatars that should interact with users in different settings. It helped in understanding how different personality classifications might be used for different CUI scenarios settings and how the interactions could be optimized for more realistic artificial emotional intelligence.

Rapid Prototyping. To test our concepts swiftly and effectively, we implemented no-code/low-code techniques for rapid prototyping. This phase included an exploration of existing tools for empathic CUI, along with emotion recognition and generation technologies. Our approach allowed for quick iteration of designs, incorporating feedback from workshops, and facilitating early technical feasibility assessments. We created diverse CUI scenarios and avatar personalities to evaluate their efficiency in eliciting and responding to emotional cues. A key technique in our no-code prototyping was prompt engineering, which involved designing prompts to enhance the emotional accuracy and contextual relevance of CUI responses. This methodical approach significantly streamlined our development process, enabling efficient testing and refinement of our empathic computing concepts.

User Research through Workshops. A significant portion of our methodology revolves around interactive workshops. These workshops were structured to gather qualitative data and insights into user preferences, interaction scenario definition for interacting with CUIs. The basis for the early user research is our prototypes for selected scenarios designed and developed during the rapid prototyping phase. The next two sections describe in detail how our methodology was applied to get insights from a wide range of UX and HCI specialists. The aims of both workshops were triple:

- Teaching participants about the current state of the research to get more awareness about the intricacies of Empathic Computing
- Gathering their experiences and opinion on what are potential benefits and caveats of emotional CUIs
- Collecting data with interesting and relevant avatar personalities, emotions definition, promising scenarios, where empathy may play significant role in the CUI

In the first workshop, we engaged participants in creating and refining avatar personalities and scenario descriptions for the defined personalities. This hands-on approach allowed us to gather data on how different personality traits and scenarios influence user engagement and emotional connection with the avatars. During the second workshop – a breakout session at the PUSH UX conference – we focused on understanding how participants define and recognize emotions. This session helped in collecting data on the challenges and strategies in emotion recognition, particularly in the context of diverse cultural expressions of emotions. The collected data were used for the further fine-tuning of our emotional CUI prototypes.

Development of a Negotiation Simulator. Central to our research is the development of a negotiation simulator featuring intelligent, photorealistic avatars. This simulator serves as a testbed for experimenting with various aspects of empathic computing. The avatars in this simulator are designed to react with a range of emotions, corresponding to distinct personality traits, in response to user interactions. This allows for the observation and analysis of how effectively the CUI engages users in realistic negotiation scenarios. Our CUI not only processes textual input but also incorporates visual recognition to interpret facial expressions and body language. This dual approach enables a more holistic understanding of the user's emotional state, allowing for more nuanced responses from the avatars. We implemented advanced analytics that evaluate human performance during interactions with the negotiation simulator. This involves analyzing user responses, his/her emotional reactions to the avatar's outputs, and overall negotiation skills. The aim is to train users for different communication situations, to facilitate them to improve their negotiation skills, to raise their awareness about their emotions and body language to upscale their overall emotional intelligence. The development of the negotiation simulator used findings from the personality and emotion research as well as prompts discovered and tested during the rapid prototyping phase.

The next sections describe how we apply our methodology for user research within two workshops discussing some characteristics of empathic CUIs with the demonstration of the prototype for the negotiation simulator as an example of enhanced CUI. This specific scenario is suited very well for empathic CUI research. To master negotiation skills, it is vital to increase the emotional awareness and emotion control. This in turn requires to train different situation with different personality types, including emotionally loaded and different situations, e.g. with hard assertive counterpart. So, different emotions, both positive and negative, are important to be presented and processed by such application.

4 Workshop "Exercising Prompt Engineering - Rapid Prototyping for Conversational UI"

The workshop "Exercising Prompt Engineering - Rapid Prototyping for Conversational UI," conducted during the Mensch und Computer conference [11] in September 2023, was devoted to engaging exploration of the convergence between conversational user interfaces, empathic computing, prompt engineering and no-code prototyping. The aim of the workshop was to embark on a journey through the intricate interplay of these concepts and how they are shaping the landscape of human-computer interaction and innovation.

During this workshop, participants engaged in an exploration of the crucial aspects of avatar personalities and scenario descriptions. They exercised the definition of personalities for avatars, dissecting the nuances of how these digital entities embody distinct emotional traits. This process illuminated the intricate art of imbuing avatars with personalities that resonate with users, further underscoring the empathic dimension of our research.

The workshop started with an introduction to CUIs, emphasizing their role in modern technology. We delved into the techniques and terms used in the development of CUIs explaining the main elements of the Conversational UI:

1. Input processing: *In CUIs*, technologies like Natural Language Processing (NLP) and machine learning are crucial for understanding user input. NLP breaks down and interprets human language, allowing the system to understand and process user requests accurately.
2. Dialogue management: This involves managing the flow of conversation, maintaining context, and generating appropriate responses. It's key in ensuring that conversations are coherent and relevant to the user's input.
3. Natural language understanding (NLU): NLU techniques are used to extract meaning and intent from user input. They help the system understand what users are saying, even when the input is complex or ambiguous.
4. Natural language generation (NLG): NLG is vital for creating human-like responses. It allows CUIs to generate responses that are natural and conversational, although producing contextually appropriate and nuanced responses remains a challenge.
5. User feedback and error handling: Conversational user interfaces should provide clear feedback to the user and handle errors gracefully. This includes acknowledging misunderstandings and guiding users back to the conversation flow effectively.
6. Integration with other technologies: Integrating CUIs with technologies like search engines, Large Language Models (like ChatGPT), graphical user interfaces, avatars, and empathic computing can enhance functionality and user experience, making interactions more intuitive and engaging.

However, the true essence of these interfaces lies in the integration of empathic computing. The concept of empathic computing was highlighted during this workshop, illustrating how it enhances CUIs by enabling them to recognize and respond to human emotions. This bridges the gap between humans and machines, resulting in interactions that are not only functional, but deeply meaningful.

Conversational User Interfaces significantly enhance user accessibility and efficiency in computer interactions, while also simplifying the integration and maintenance of new technologies for development teams. The emergence of no-code prototyping has revolutionized software development, democratizing the creation process. These platforms, with their user-friendly interfaces and drag-and-drop features, allow even those with minimal coding skills to rapidly develop functional applications. This trend has broadened the innovation landscape, extending it beyond coding experts to anyone with a creative idea. The presentation highlighted the efficacy of no-code/low-code platforms in swiftly developing and testing CUI scenarios. In the era of Large Language Models (LLMs, [5]), prompt engineering has become a pivotal technique in these applications, offering a gateway to build various assistants with little to no coding expertise, democratizing the field of technology creation further.

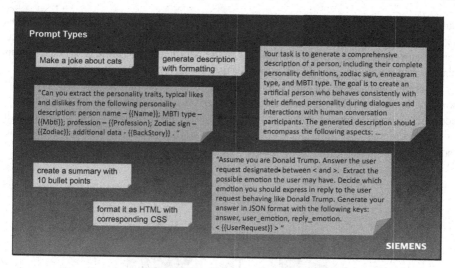

Fig. 1. Simple types of prompts

Prompt engineering involves creating precise instructions to drive AI models like prominent GPT-3.5 or 4 [12]. Well-structured prompts allow us to leverage the versatility of AI to generate tailored content, automate tasks, and even assist with coding projects. Prompt engineering is especially helpful in no-code development & prototyping for conversational UI. Prompts can be arbitrarily short or long, simple or complicated, contain multiple attributes, address formatting (Fig. 1). Especially relevant during implementation: a properly constructed prompt affects the quality of results, such as chat history, accuracy and completeness of outputs. During our initial rapid prototyping we used diverse LLM chat platforms, including accessing those LLMs over API. This way we defined, tested, and fine-tuned even more complicated prompts with more settings, using prompt templates. For example, using a meta prompt template that generates other prompts.

To illustrate those concepts, the workshop introduction presented our case study – the negotiation simulator mentioned in the previous section. Prompt engineering lets to steer the responses of the avatar toward the defined objectives, settled by the user during the setup phase, like practicing assertiveness or dealing with objections. The behavior of the avatar can be specified by a collection of prompts, accomplishing this task without writing a single line of code. Tailoring the behavior of the avatar to the personality traits, a user defined for his/her desired counterpart, is also possible with appropriately designed prompts. By defining such characteristics for the avatar, CUIs can provide empathic and supportive interactions to promote user well-being and create trusting connections, but also can challenge the user to control his/her emotional state via learning the triggers for those reactions.

A crucial aspect in the design of CUIs with personality traits is the diversity of human personalities. How do we actually define human personalities? This is an important factor influencing the design of empathic CUIs. Different personality types require different interaction styles and pitches to ensure desired communication. But how can we define human personality effectively? One way to do this, often exploited with prompts and LLMs, is to describe an imaginary parson with the whole backstory and traits required for the current interaction listed explicitly in the persona description. Such description may be really long and would take time for user to design and input into CUI.

A common method for characterizing human personalities are the Big Five personality dimensions [13]. These include extraversion, agreeableness, conscientiousness, neuroticism and openness. These dimensions can be taken into account in the design of conversational user interfaces to enable personalized interaction that matches the individual personality traits of each user (Fig. 2).

Fig. 2. An example of a personality classification with the Big Five

Apart from the Big Five personality dimensions, there are a variety of other models for characterizing human personalities by only short terms. Examples, that we considered during our research and combined for avatar personality definitions, include the MBTI [14], DISC [24], the Enneagram [25], the Hartman Profile [26], and the Keirsey Temperament Sorter [27]. Each classification alone may look like not very precise definition of a persona, as each of these types has very limited number of dimensions and traits to be used for exact personality description. We suggested to combine types from several classifications in one prompt for the person definition. This keeps the prompt short enough, but still encompassing diversity of possible personalities. Thus, taking these different dimensions into account enables comprehensive customization of Conversational User Interfaces to precisely tailor communication and interactions to individual user preferences and characteristics. Such combination of multiple classifications may be effective for the definition of an avatar personality for general purpose of communication scenarios for CUI. For a specific type of interaction, only one model maybe enough.

Thus, in negotiations, the following types of negotiation play a crucial role: competitive, compromising, avoidant, compliant, and collaborative types [15]. Consideration of this dimension is of great importance in negotiation application, as different types prefer different approaches and tactics. In addition, there are other important factors in the personality definition for negotiation, such as cultural backgrounds, experiences, emotional intelligence, and further communication styles that can influence the course and success of negotiations.

After the discussion of the useful techniques for the development of CUI, we moved from theory to practice. In the upcoming practical workshop, small groups engaged in three exercises designed to deepen their understanding.

- creating personality definition for an avatar they would like to negotiate,
- crafting specific negotiation scenarios for the avatar they defined
- designing their own interaction scenario and developing prompts for CUIs to create meaningful interactions, applying the concepts learned in the workshop.

These exercises on the design of communication scenarios exhibited the intricacies behind the special kinds of conversations and recognized the need for expert knowledge during the design of specific CUI. The exercises provided participants with a hands-on experience in prompt engineering for Conversational User Interfaces that translated theory into concrete skills.

This process emphasized the intricate art of creating digital entities that embody distinct emotional traits, resonating with users. The workshop also focused on the various types of prompts used in CUIs. This exploration was crucial in understanding the impact of prompt selection on user experience. Feedback collected during the workshop was instrumental in refining our approach to empathic computing, ensuring that it aligns with user expectations and enhances the emotional relevance of interactions.

5 Breakout Session "Empathic Computing: Let's Play with Emotions"

Because the core of the empathic computing is emotion recognition and generation, our breakout session "Empathic Computing: Let's Play with Emotions", conducted during the PUSH UX conference [16] in October 2023, aimed to explore emotion definition for their digitalization and application in intelligent interfaces. Key topics of the session included the integration of empathic computing in CUIs, technologies for emotion recognition, and the role of non-verbal cues in HCI.

Empathic computing uses artificial intelligence to analyze nuances of voice, facial expressions, body language, and verbal inputs, and tailor their responses to our emotional state. The first part of the session explained such theoretical background as Facial Action Coding System (FACS), Acoustic Emotion Recognition (AER), and body language marker highlighting their importance in understanding emotions. Practical examples and exercises were incorporated to deepen the understanding of these concepts. The session concluded with discussions on the potentials and challenges of computer-based emotion recognition, as well as broader implications for future applications.

Scientists often talk about six basic emotions. These emotions are basic because they are seen in many cultures and are also found in other animals. This shows they are important for survival. The six basic emotions are:

- *Happiness.*: This is when you feel good. It's like when you smile or laugh. You feel happy when good things happen.

- *Sadness*: This is the opposite of happiness. You feel sad when bad things happen, like losing something or someone important.
- *Fear*: This is being scared. It happens when you think something bad or dangerous might happen. It helps us stay safe by making us run away or be careful.
- *Anger*: This is when you feel upset or mad about something. It can be because of unfairness or when someone does something bad to you.
- *Surprise*: This is when something happens that you did not expect. It can be a good or bad thing, but it's always unexpected.
- *Disgust*: This is feeling turned off by something. Like when you see or smell something bad. It helps us stay away from things that might be harmful.

These basic emotions are different from other emotions because they are simpler and more common. Other emotions, like jealousy or pride, are more complex. They can be made of a mix of the basic emotions and are not as common in other animals. The basic emotions are like the main colors, and other emotions are like mixtures of these colors.

FACS [1] is used across many different personal and professional settings. It is often used in various scientific settings for research. It is also used by animators and computer scientists interested in facial recognition. FACS may also enable greater awareness and sensitivity to subtle facial behaviors. Such skills are useful for psychotherapists, interviewers, and anyone working in communications. FACS is a powerful tool for emotion digitalization that allows to map facial cues to specific emotions. It contains appr. 30 main action units (AU), 8 head movement AUs, and 4 eye movement AUs. Some examples for emotion definition via FACS [2] include:

- Happiness/Joy:

  - AU6 (Cheek Raiser): This involves the contraction of the muscle encircling the eye socket. It causes the appearance of crow's feet and raises the cheeks.
  - AU12 (Lip Corner Puller): This is primarily the action of the muscle pulling the lip corners up and out, typical of a smile.

- Sadness:

  - AU1 (Inner Brow Raiser): Involves the muscle which raises the inner part of the eyebrows, creating a furrowed brow.
  - AU4 (Brow Lowerer): This involves the muscles drawing the eyebrows down and together, often indicating distress or worry.
  - AU15 (Lip Corner Depressor): A depressor muscle pulls the corners of the lips down, a feature of sadness.

- Fear:

  - AU1 (Inner Brow Raiser): Involves the muscle which raises the inner part of the eyebrows.
  - AU2 (Outer Brow Raiser): Involves the muscle which raises the outer part of the eyebrows, often creating a look of surprise or fear.

- AU4 (Brow Lowerer): This involves the muscles drawing the eyebrows down and together.
- AU5 (Upper Lid Raiser): Involves the muscle raising the upper eyelid, common in expressions of fear.
- AU20 (Lip Stretcher): Involves the muscle which stretches the lips horizontally.
- AU26 (Jaw drop): Involves the muscles that lower the jaw.

- Anger:

  - AU4 (Brow Lowerer): Involves the muscles which lower and draw together the eyebrows, creating a frown.
  - AU5 (Upper Lid Raiser): Involves raising the upper eyelid, which can intensify the stare during anger.
  - AU7 (Lid Tightener): Involves the muscle which tightens the eyelids.
  - AU23 (Lip Tightener): Involves the muscle which tightens the lips.

- Surprise:

  - AU1 (Inner Brow Raiser): Involves the muscle which raises the inner part of the eyebrows.
  - AU2 (Outer Brow Raiser): involves the muscle which raises the outer part of the eyebrows, creating a look of surprise or shock.
  - AU5 (Upper Lid Raiser): This involves the muscle raising the upper eyelid, typical of a look of surprise.
  - AU26 (Jaw Drop): This involves the muscles dropping the jaw open.

- Disgust:

  - AU9 (Nose Wrinkler): This involves the muscle which elevates the upper lip and wrinkles the nose.
  - AU15 (Lip Corner Depressor): A depressor muscle pulls the corners of the lips down, a feature of sadness.
  - AU16 (Lower Lip Depressor): involves the depressor muscle which lowers the lower lip, deepening the expression of disgust.

It is well researched that non-verbal cues play a vital role in conveying emotions. Some computer vision algorithms are trained via Machine Learning to recognize the whole emotions and individual action units on the face, which can be useful for the definition of personal or specific complex emotion and feelings, which we performed during this session. Other computer vision algorithm can also be engaged into the recognition of another aspect of human emotions expressed through the body language Recognition of the human postures enhances user experiences by understanding additional cues. Tool example that was exploited in our study is MediaPipe [3] recognizing body, faces, and hand landmarks. Unfortunately, there is no any kind of standard similar to FACS or AER for the emotion definition over the body postures. In our session we asked the participants to define some examples of "typical" postures for some selected emotions to analyze the potential of this input channel for emotion recognition.

Acoustic Emotion Recognition (AER) [4] is another kind of standard that could be involved in the recognition of human emotions from another channel, voice input. This system defines emotions over 5 vocal parameters like pitch, intonation, energy, speech rate, and vocal tension:

- *Pitch* refers to the fundamental frequency of a person's voice. The pitch of a person's voice is related to the frequency of the vocal cord vibrations when speaking. Pitch can be defined as the perceived highness or lowness of a sound, and it is typically measured in Hertz (Hz).
- *Speech Rate* refers to the speed or pace at which a person speaks. Speech rate can be defined as the number of words spoken per unit of time, often measured in words per minute (wpm) or syllables per second. Speech rate is used to assess how quickly or slowly someone is speaking.
- *Intonation* refers to the melodic and rhythmic aspects of speech, including variations in pitch, rhythm, and stress patterns. Intonation can be defined as the pattern of rising and falling pitch, as well as the changes in speech rate and stress on specific words or syllables within a sentence. It's how we use pitch and rhythm to convey additional meaning beyond the words themselves. To define and analyze intonation in AER, researchers typically use techniques such as prosody analysis. This involves extracting information about pitch contours (variations in pitch over time), speech rate, and emphasis on certain words or syllables.
- *Energy* refers to the level of vocal energy or intensity in a person's speech. This acoustic feature measures how loudly or softly someone is speaking. Energy is often defined as the amplitude or power of the audio signal. It is usually measured in decibels (dB) or as a relative measure.
- *Vocal Tension* refers to the tightness or strain in a person's voice during speech. It is a measure of how relaxed or tense a person's vocal apparatus is when speaking. In AER, vocal tension is used to analyze how emotions can affect the physical aspects of speech production. To assess vocal tension in AER, researchers often use techniques that involve analyzing the spectrogram of the speech signal.

As an example, happiness can be defined via higher pitch, greater energy, faster speech rate, and more positive - varied and lively - intonation, lower vocal tension; anger is distinguished via higher pitch, greater energy, faster speech rate, and negative - sharp and intense – intonation, higher vocal tension. There are other acoustic systems exist that can define emotions more precisely with much more parameters, which was not appropriate for our session with user involvement.

The last channel for getting information about the person's emotion we considered during this session is verbal communication. Sentiment analysis is an NLP (Natural Language Processing) technique that categorizes textual inputs into positive, negative, or neutral sentiment. Large Language Models (LLM) [5] can detect a quite impressive range of emotions like joy, anger, sadness, far beyond only basic emotions. The challenges in the verbal emotion analysis is that emotions expressed in phrases can be highly context-dependent. Analyzing the context in which certain words or phrases are used can help determine the intended emotion. For instance, "I'm so excited to see you!" expresses happiness, while "I'm excited to be done with this" may indicate relief.

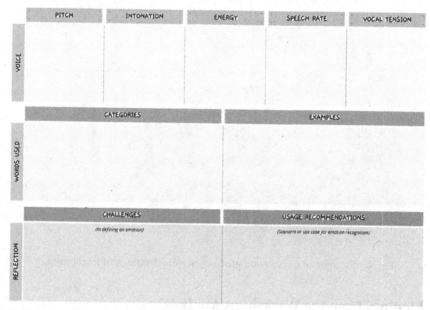

Fig. 3. Example of a template used during the session for the definition of emotions (page1/2) with concluding reflection.

During this breakout session we also considered our prototype of the negotiation simulator as a practical example, where a CUI used in a negotiation simulator benefits from understanding emotions, leading to more authentic interactions.

After this theoretical introduction of different capabilities in emotion definition, the participants were engaged in a practical exercise (Fig. 3). To understand the challenges and perspectives of emotion digitalization, the participants were first asked to define emotions as formal as possible with the techniques introduced in the theoretical part of the workshop. We proposed to choose non-trivial emotions randomly for each small group. The group discussed which cues define this emotion by defining FACS, AER, body posture, typical verbal expressions. We collected several templates filled with the inputs from the session participants with emotion definitions and feedback about the challenges in the emotion definition (Fig. 4).

At the end of this session, we explored the potentials of emotions definition for CUI, how they can enhance user experiences, which interaction scenarios would benefit from emotional interface recognizing emotions from the user.

Fig. 4. Example of a result of a group exercise – definition of Excitement.

6 Findings from the Workshops Analysis

From the workshops we gathered that effective CUIs must transcend mere textual under-standing to include emotional intelligence. Participants showed a strong preference for avatars with relatable personalities, highlighting the need for empathic computing in CUI design. Incorporating emotions into UI enhances user experiences. However, it also presents challenges. Analysis of the workshops' feedback revealed key aspects:

- Avatar Personalities and Scenarios: Users were more engaged with avatars that dis-played coherent emotional traits, suggesting that personality-infused avatars enhance user experience. On the other hand, it was discovered that the personality definition for the counterpart in the CUI settings can be a challenging activity: there are many ways to define realistic personalities, and the end user may not know classifications used by professionals like psychologists.
- Prompt Engineering: The selection and design of prompts critically influence user interaction. Thoughtfully crafted prompts lead to more natural and emotionally res-onant conversations. Although we unveiled that it can be sometimes confusing for the user when they define scenarios for CUI to distinguish between what are settings for the counterpart behavior and what are targets for students. The participants got awareness of the need for the expert knowledge to be incorporated into the definition of specific scenarios. Excessive and precise prompts have to be defined for the proper responses of the counterpart to provide real value for the user.

- Emotion Recognition Technologies: emotion definition systems like FACS and AER were shown to be effective for the fine-tuning of emotions identification in addition to the existing techniques with Machine Learning. It was discussed that only the combination of inputs from different sources (face, body, voice, verbal inputs, potentially also other) can predict emotions with the level of accuracy close or even better than emotion recognition by humans.
- Cultural and Contextual Challenges: Recognizing emotions across different cultures and contexts remains a challenge, underscoring the need for adaptable and sensitive CUI systems. It is relatively easy to define basic emotions, while the expression of other emotions can strongly depend on the cultural background and personal experience.

In summary, the intersection of these elements represents a turning point in the evolution of human-technology interaction. This research empowers us to create connections that bridge the gap between man and machine, while also providing tools that put creative power in the hands of many. As we move forward, we should harness the potential of these advances to shape a world where technology not only understands us, but also resonates with our emotions and aspirations.

7 Discussion on the Potentials of Empathic Computing for CUI

The integration of empathic computing opens new possibilities for more nuanced and human-centric interactions between users and technology. As it was discussed with the participants of the workshops, this approach can transform various domains by enabling more personalized and emotionally intelligent interactions. Different scenarios were discovered and described during the first workshop:

- Customer Service: Empathic CUIs can personalize customer interactions, making them more efficient and satisfactory. By understanding and responding to customer emotions, these interfaces can handle queries more effectively, leading to improved customer loyalty and engagement.
- Healthcare: In healthcare, empathic interfaces can provide support and information in a more compassionate manner. They can be particularly helpful in mental health applications, where understanding and responding to emotional cues are crucial.
- Education: For education, empathic computing can create more adaptive learning environments. By recognizing the emotional state of learners, educational software can adjust the difficulty level and presentation style, enhancing engagement and learning outcomes.
- Entertainment: In the entertainment industry, empathic CUIs can offer more immersive and interactive experiences, tailoring content to the emotional state of the user, thus enhancing the overall user experience

These applications highlight the transformative potential of empathic computing in making technology more responsive, intuitive, and aligned with human emotions and needs. This shift towards emotionally intelligent interfaces is not just a technological advancement but also a step towards more humane and user-centric computing.

During our research we also encountered several challenges and limitations:

- Cultural Variability: Emotions are expressed and interpreted differently across cultures. Our models faced challenges in accurately recognizing and responding to such diverse emotional expressions.
- Technological Constraints: Current emotion recognition technologies, while advanced, are not infallible. Misinterpretations of emotional cues, in particular if some channels are not available for CUI (e.g. if the camera is switched off), can lead to inappropriate responses by the application.
- Data Privacy and Ethical Concerns: Collecting and analyzing emotional data raises significant privacy and ethical issues, requiring careful consideration and robust data protection measures. This will lead to burdens for the development and prototypical experiments with such types of CUI, arose from the legal and ethical requirements.
- Contextual Understanding: The CUIs' ability to understand the context of interactions is currently limited, affecting the accuracy of emotional interpretations. More research on contextual analysis is required that may invoke essential complexity of the algorithm and inappropriately low performance of the interaction.

To overcome current limitations and advance the field of empathic computing in HCI, future research could focus on several key areas:

- Advanced Cross-Cultural Emotion Recognition: Research is needed to develop more sophisticated algorithms that can accurately interpret emotions across different cultures or recognizing social characteristics of the users to derive his/her specific emotion expression. This includes studying non-verbal cues in various cultural contexts and integrating these insights into CUIs.
- Enhanced Contextual Understanding: Further research should aim at improving the contextual awareness of CUIs. This involves developing algorithms capable of understanding complex language nuances such as sarcasm, idioms, and indirect speech. It may also include refined computer vision solutions that recognize surrounding environment that can also influence the way the user responses.
- Privacy-Preserving Emotional Data Analysis: Investigating methods for collecting and analyzing emotional data while respecting user privacy is crucial. Research could explore anonymization techniques and user consent models.
- Ethical Frameworks for Emotion AI: Establishing ethical guidelines and frameworks for the development and deployment of empathic computing systems is essential to address concerns about emotional manipulation and user autonomy.
- Multimodal Emotion Detection Technologies: Exploring multimodal approaches that combine facial and body expressions, voice intonations, textual analysis with further channels of information, e.g. physiological markers, for more accurate emotion recognition can be a significant area of research.
- Longitudinal Studies on User Interaction: Conducting long-term studies on how users interact with empathic CUIs over time would provide valuable insights into their effectiveness and areas for improvement.

These research directions can help in creating more nuanced, culturally sensitive, and ethically sound empathic CUIs, paving the way for their broader application and acceptance.

8 Conclusion

Our research on Emotionally Intelligent Conversational User Interfaces marks a significant step in the evolution of HCI, bridging the gap between technology and human emotions. Our workshops and user studies have shown the potential of empathic computing in creating more intuitive and emotionally resonant interactions. They also created the awareness about the capabilities and intricacies of digitalization of the human emotions and empathy. While challenges such as cultural variability and technological constraints exist, they open avenues for future research. The integration of empathic elements into CUIs promises to enhance user experience across various domains, making technology not only more efficient but also more attuned to human needs and emotions.

Disclosure of Interests. The authors are employees of the company siemens ag and own employee stocks in this company.

References

1. Rosenberg, E.L., Ekman, P.: (eds.): What the Face Reveals: Basic and Applied Studies of Spontaneous Expression Using the Facial Action Coding System (FACS), 3rd edn. Oxford University Press, Oxford (2020)
2. iMotions, Facial action coding system (FACS) – A Visual Guidebook. https://imotions.com/blog/learning/research-fundamentals/facial-action-coding-system/. Accessed 29 Jan 2024
3. Google, On-device machine learning for everyone. https://developers.google.com/mediapipe. Accessed 29 Jan 2024
4. Krothapalli, S.R., Koolagudi, S.G.: Emotion Recognition using Speech Features. Springer (2013)
5. Ozdemir, S.: Quick start guide to large language models: strategies and best practices for using ChatGPT and other LLMs. 1st edn. Addison-Wesley Data & Analytics Series (2023)
6. Cai, Y.: Empathic Computing. In: Cai, Y., Abascal, J. (eds.) Ambient Intelligence in Everyday Life, LNCS, vol. 3864, pp. 67–85. Springer, Berlin (2006)
7. Wadley, G., et al.: The future of emotion in human-computer interaction. In: Barbosa, S., Lampe, C. (eds.), CHI EA'22: Extended Abstracts of the 2022 CHI Conference on Human Factors in Computing Systems, pp. 1–6. ACM Digital Library (2022). https://doi.org/10.1145/3491101.3503729. Accessed 29 Jan 2024
8. Liu, J.B., et al.: Emotion assessment and application in human–computer interaction interface based on backpropagation neural network and artificial bee colony algorithm. Exp. Syst. Appl. **232** (2023). https://doi.org/10.1016/j.eswa.2023.120857. Accessed 29 Jan 2024
9. Peter, C., Blyth, G.: The role of emotion in human-computer interaction. In: The 19th British HCI Group Annual Conference Napier University, Edinburgh, UK (2005). https://www.researchgate.net/publication/237457101_The_Role_of_Emotion_in_Human-Computer_Interaction. Accessed 29 Jan 2024
10. Mehrabian, A.: Inference of attitudes from nonverbal communication in two channels. J. Consult. Psychol. **31**(3), 249–252 (1967)
11. Mensch und Computer 2023, conference on human-computer interaction, 3–6 September 2023. https://muc2023.mensch-und-computer.de/en/. Accessed 29 Jan 2024
12. OpenAI, ChatGPT. https://chat.openai.com/. Accessed 29 Jan 2024
13. McCrae, R.R., John, O.P.: An introduction to the five-factor model and its applications. J. Pers. **60**, 175–215 (1992)

14. Myers, I.B., Myers, P.B.: Gifts differing: understanding personality type. Davies-Black (1995)

15. Corvette, B.A.B.: Conflict Management: A Practical Guide to Developing Negotiation Strategies, 1st edn. Pearson (2013)

16. PUSH UX conference Webpage, breakout session Empathic Computing: Let's Play With Emotions. https://push-conference.com/ux-2023/program/empathic-computing-let-s-play-with-emotions. Accessed 29 Jan 2024

17. Poria, S., et al.: Emotion recognition in conversation: research challenges, datasets, and recent advances. IEEE Access **7**, 100943–100953 (2019)

18. Abdullah, S.M., et al.: Multimodal emotion recognition using deep learning. J. Appl. Sci. Technol. Trends **2**(02), 52–58 (2021)

19. Gunes, H., et al.: Automatic, Dimensional and continuous emotion recognition. IJSE 1, pp. 68-99 (2010)

20. University of West Alabama 2019, Our Basic Emotions, https://online.uwa.edu/infographics/basic-emotions/. Accessed 29 Jan 2024

21. Mellouk, W., Wahida, H.: Facial emotion recognition using deep learning: review and insights. Procedia Comput. Sci. **175**, 689–694 (2020)

22. Sabour, S. et al.: A chatbot for mental health support: exploring the impact of Emohaa on reducing mental distress in China. Frontiers in Digital Health 5, (2023)

23. Rathje, S., et al.: GPT is an effective tool for multilingual psychological text analysis (2023)

24. Owen, J.E., Mahatmya, D., Carter, R.: Dominance, influence, steadiness, and conscientiousness (DISC) assessment tool. In: Zeigler-Hill, V., Shackelford, T. (eds.) Encyclopedia of Personality and Individual Differences. Springer, Cham (2017). https://doi.org/10.1007/978-3-319-28099-8_25-1

25. Riso, D.R.: The Wisdom of the Enneagram: The Complete Guide to Psychological and Spiritual Growth for the Nine Personality Types. Bantam (1999)

26. Hartman, T.: Color code: a new way to see yourself, your relationships and life. Color Code Intl (1987)

27. Keirsey, D.M.: Please understand me, an essay on temperament styles. Promethean (1978)

Author Index

M. Kurosu and A. Hashizume (Eds.): HCII 2024, LNCS 14684, pp. 423–424, 2024.
https://doi.org/10.1007/978-3-031-60405-8

Printed in the United States
by Baker & Taylor Publisher Services